The Twentieth-Century World

The Twentieth-Century World
An International History

Second Edition

WILLIAM R. KEYLOR

New York   Oxford
OXFORD UNIVERSITY PRESS
1992

To Daniel and Justine
From a Loving Father

Oxford University Press

Oxford New York Toronto
Delhi Bombay Calcutta Madras Karachi
Petaling Jaya Singapore Hong Kong Tokyo
Nairobi Dar es Salaam Cape Town
Melbourne Auckland

and associated companies in
Berlin Ibadan

Published by Oxford University Press, Inc.,
200 Madison Avenue, New York, New York 10016

Library of Congress Cataloging-in-Publication Data
Keylor, William R., 1944–
The twentieth-century world : an international history / William
R. Keylor. — 2nd ed.
p. cm. Includes bibliographical references and index.
ISBN 0–19–506803–3. — ISBN 0–19–506804–1 (pbk.)
1. World politics—20th century. 2. International relations.
I. Title.
D443.K399 1992
327′.09′04—dc20 91–15509

9 8 7 6 5 4 3 2 1

Printed in the United States of America
on acid-free paper

Preface to the Second Edition

In the course of revising *The Twentieth-Century World* for this second edition, I took the opportunity to correct a number of typographical mistakes, stylistic infelicities, and factual errors that had somehow crept into the first edition. I also found it necessary to rewrite and expand the sections in Part Four dealing with Latin America and the Far East in order to take into account new factual information and scholarly interpretations; to include a new section on Africa's role in international politics since decolonization, which had received insufficient treatment in the first edition; and to add an epilogue extending the narrative to the year 1991. The Bibliographical Essay has been lengthened to reflect the appearance of new scholarship in the history of international relations since the publication of the first edition. Finally, I have added a glossary of nuclear weapons terminology and expanded the glossary of international economics terminology.

The world of 1991 is a very different place from the world of 1984. The extraordinary events that transpired between the first and second editions of this book have constituted nothing less than the total transformation of the international order. Anyone in 1984 who had predicted the following developments would surely have been dismissed as mentally incompetent: The disintegration of the Soviet East European empire and the emergence of multiparty political systems and market-oriented economies in a large part of what used to be called "the Communist world"; the dissolution of the Warsaw Pact and the transformation of NATO into a something resembling a political association more than a military alliance; the withdrawal of Soviet military forces from Afghanistan and Vietnamese troops from Cambodia; the replacement of the Sandinista regime in Nicaragua by the United States-backed right-wing opposition through a free election; the rapid movement toward full economic integration by the member states of the European community; the reunification of Germany; and the creation of a U.S.-dominated multinational military force (including such an unlikely ally as Syria), which, with the support of the Soviet Union, attacked and de-

feated Iraq in the name of the United Nations. And yet, all of these spectacular and totally unanticipated developments occurred within the brief
seven-year period between the two editions of this book. The Epilogue is
designed both to supply a succinct narrative summary of these and other
significant international developments since the mid-1980s and to advance a
tentative interpretation of their significance for the evolving international
order.

My friend and colleague, James McCann, earned my gratitude by agreeing to read and provide helpful comments on the new chapter on Africa's
role in international politics after independence. I should also like to take
this opportunity to express my gratitude to Nancy Lane, my editor at Oxford
University Press, who supervised the publication of both editions of this
book with her customary wisdom, efficiency, and enthusiasm.

Newton, Mass.   W. R. K.
June 1991

Preface to the First Edition

This study was conceived to meet a need that had been acutely felt by its author throughout a decade of teaching college-level courses dealing with the history of international relations in the modern period. There is no dearth of serviceable textbooks treating the foreign relations of a particular nation or region during the twentieth century. These were evidently composed to accommodate traditional survey courses, such as "The History of American Foreign Relations," "European Diplomatic History," "The Middle East and World Politics," and the like. But an increasing number of historians of international relations have recently expressed dissatisfaction with the limitations inherent in an exclusively national or regional approach to their subject. They have begun to insist that the sovereign political units or regional subsystems of the modern world are all so closely linked, so profoundly interdependent, as to require a global or international perspective on the part of those who study the external relations of states. Evidence of this new attitude is pervasive: Courses entitled "World History" or "International History" have proliferated in undergraduate curricula; professional organizations and scholarly journals have sprouted to promote research in the history of international relations from this broader perspective; perhaps most important of all, there has appeared a vast and growing body of specialized scholarship, built up in the course of the past decade or so, that has transcended the narrowly national or regional approach to the study of the relations between and among states over time. Profiting from the declassification of previously inaccessible government archives in a number of countries, the authors of these recent monographs and partial syntheses have profoundly affected our understanding of the international developments of the twentieth century, overturning or revising judgments of earlier works once deemed definitive. Yet, to my knowledge, there exists no college-level textbook that incorporates the findings of these recent specialized studies in a format that is genuinely global or international in scope. This I have attempted to do in the following pages, signaling the persistence of sharp scholarly controversies where appropriate and offering personal assessments when confidence in my own firsthand knowledge of the subject seemed to warrant them.

The absence of such a textbook is scarcely surprising. One is hard put to imagine a more forbidding enterprise. The writer so presumptuous as to undertake a survey of the entire world of the twentieth century in 400-odd pages promptly acquires the virtue of humility as he confronts the immense corpus of secondary literature on specialized topics far removed from his own particular field of expertise. He learns how utterly dependent he is on the original research of others who have devoted entire careers to the explication of historical developments of which he was either wholly ignorant or only dimly aware.* As he patiently excavates this largely unfamiliar terrain, he must keep in mind an organizational principle under which to subsume the disparate facts and interpretations gleaned from the secondary sources in order to supply the coherence and intelligibility that a textbook for undergraduates ought to have.

Simply put, my purpose has been to provide a narrative account within an analytical framework of the struggle among the major nations of the world for power, prosperity, and prestige in this century. The major advantage of such a guiding principle is its exclusivity. It permits the author to discount or ignore several categories of topics that often occupy prominent places in history textbooks in order to concentrate on those events and processes that relate to the underlying theme. Thus, for example, little attention is devoted to the internal social, political, or cultural history of individual states. Such domestic developments are addressed only when they acquire significance for the interplay of forces in the international arena. On the other hand, topics that usually pass unnoticed or receive only cursory mention in most "diplomatic history" texts are dealt with at length herein. For instance, I have given substantial coverage to international economic relations, with particular emphasis on trade patterns, capital flows, and competition for raw materials, as well as on the larger connection between these economic forces and the international contest for political and strategic advantage.†

A brief explanation is due the reader with respect to my reliance on the customary device of using names of nations or their capital cities to designate the foreign policy-making apparatus of governments. Phrases such as "Great Britain tolerated Japan's expansionist aspirations north of the Yangtze" or "Bonn's search for an accommodation with Warsaw" employ a semantic shorthand for the sake of convenience. It would be tedious to

---

* I have attempted to record my immense debt to other scholars in the bibliographical essay that appears at the end of this work.
† Recognizing that certain technical terms of international economics may be unfamiliar to the student, I have included a glossary which should be consulted when such terms are encountered in the text.

repeat each time what is denoted by these handy labels: the political, economic, and military elites that shape the foreign policies of a state.

The final version of this book reflects the advice and criticism of several friends and colleagues in the Departments of History and Political Science and the Center for International Relations at Boston University. Norman Naimark gave the manuscript a careful reading and rescued it from factual errors and untenable interpretations, especially with respect to Russia and Eastern Europe. Hermann Frederick Eilts also read the entire piece and drew upon his extensive practical as well as scholarly knowledge of the Middle East to enhance my own understanding of that complex region. Dietrich Orlow reviewed the sections dealing with Europe in the interwar period and offered particularly helpful suggestions for improving the treatment of German foreign policy. Roy Glasgow cheerfully shared with me his expertise in the largely unfamiliar subject of Latin American history, calling to my attention several important secondary sources in that field and correcting some of my misconceptions about America's relations with its neighbors to the south. Saul Engelbourg gave careful scrutiny to the subchapters on international economics and offered several suggestions for revision that greatly improved those sections. William Newman helped to guide me toward a firmer grasp of the balance of power in Europe after the Great War. John G. Gagliardo and Arnold A. Offner left their mark on this work in two important ways: first, by serving as models of serious scholarship and dedicated teaching, and second, by engaging me in a decade-long dialogue about many of the issues treated in the following pages. To all of these friends and associates I am grateful.

My affiliation with organizations outside my own institution has enabled me to keep in touch with the work of other scholars of international relations in its formative stages. Professor Jean-Baptiste Duroselle kindly invited me to attend his graduate seminar on the history of international relations at the University of Paris during the 1978–79 academic year, where I learned a great deal from the presentations of several of his students on a variety of topics. I have also benefited from ongoing access to Stanley Hoffman's Center for European Studies at Harvard University, which has long been an indispensable forum for the presentation of work in progress by advanced graduate students and established scholars alike.

I am indebted to Laura Cabot, Stephen Chapman, James T. Dutton, John Pearson, and Jewel Ubben for their prompt and expert work in the typing of the manuscript and to the Graduate School of Boston University for helping to defray the costs of its preparation. My wife, Dr. Rheta Grenoble Keylor, displayed throughout the entire period of this book's composition her customary patience, forbearance, and good sense when various deadlines (both internally and externally imposed) temporarily upset carefully established schedules of parenting and housework.

Newton, Mass.   W. R. K.
April 1983

Contents

The Twentieth-Century World

The Global Context of International Relations at the Beginning of the Twentieth Century

The Europeanization of the World

The most salient feature of international relations at the beginning of this century was the extent to which most of the world had come under the direct or indirect domination of a handful of states all located in the same geographical region: that western extension of the Eurasian land mass bounded by the Atlantic Ocean and the Ural Mountains that we call Europe. The expansion of European power and influence in the world had begun in the sixteenth century, when improvements in the technology of oceanic transportation enabled seafaring adventurers from Portugal, Spain, Holland, England, and France to establish contact with and lay claim to territory on distant continents recently discovered or rediscovered—North and South America, Africa, and Asia. European settlements were subsequently established on the coasts of these exotic lands to facilitate the exploitation of their valuable economic resources, such as the precious metals, sugar, and animal furs of the Americas, the spices of the Far East, and the slave labor of Africa.

By the middle of the nineteenth century the European settler populations in the American hemisphere, their numbers greatly increased by the temptations of a temperate climate and an abundance of arable land, had obtained political independence from their transatlantic colonial masters and were busily engaged in promoting the national unification and economic development of the territory they had inherited or to which they laid claim. The American successor states remained thoroughly Europeanized in the sense that their political institutions, economic practices, religious beliefs, and cultural traditions had been transplanted by the immigrants from Europe who constituted the ruling elites of this region. During the same period the Slavic peoples of European Russia migrated eastward by land into Asiatic Siberia to Europeanize that desolate domain. Finally, during the second half of the nineteenth century and the first decade of the twentieth, the power of the principal states of Western Europe was projected into the Afro-Asian portion of the southern hemisphere that had previously remained beyond the reach of European power. The consequence of this long process of expansion in all directions was the creation, for the first time in history, of a genuinely interlinked and interdependent world with Europe as its focal point. It was at the beginning of our own century that statesmen, diplomats, and military leaders began for the first time to speak of international relations in the global sense to which we have been accustomed ever since.

The explanation for the sudden resurgence of imperial expansion during the second half of the nineteenth century has been hotly debated by historians of the subject. Some have emphasized the role of Western* economic interests in seeking overseas markets for industrial production and investment capital as well as raw materials that were in short supply at home. Others have focused on the activities of Christian missionaries who penetrated the interior of the colonial world in search of souls to save, only to require military protection from their home governments when the indigenous nonbelievers violently resisted conversion. Others have seen the prospect of strategic advantage—in the form both of military manpower recruitable from the native population and of bases of operation abroad—as the principal motivating factor for this expansion abroad. Still others stress the role of national pride and the search for national prestige. But whatever the source of the imperialist impulse, its consequence was unmistakable: the extension of European power and influence throughout the southern half of the globe that we today call the "Third World."

The first two nations to achieve in this way the position of "world power" were Great Britain and France. Both had established coastal footholds along the non-European land masses of the world during the first wave of European imperial expansion: England had disposed of its surplus population during its industrial revolution in the eighteenth and nineteenth centuries by sending large numbers of its nationals to the inhabitable coastlands of North America, Australia, New Zealand, and southern Africa. To the motley collection of islands and coastal enclaves in Latin America, Africa, and the Pacific that had been acquired by England during this earlier era was added the subcontinent of India, which had come under effective British control by the middle of the nineteenth century. France had added the north African territory of Algeria to the remnants of her seventeenth century empire by the same period.

But it was only after the opening of the Suez Canal (built by the French between 1859 and 1869, brought under joint Anglo-French financial control in 1875) that authorities in London and Paris began in earnest to promote the cause of imperial expansion. Henceforth, the sea route running through the Mediterranean, the Suez Canal, and the Red Sea into the In-

---

* The term "Western" shall be employed in this study to designate that portion of the Northern Hemisphere inhabited primarily by Europeans or immigrants of Europe n stock.

dian Ocean—a much more economical and less dangerous route than the passage around the Cape of Good Hope on the southern tip of Africa—came to be regarded by Britain's governing class as a "lifeline" to its possessions in Asia. It was indeed a lifeline in one very real sense: Since her transformation from an agricultural to an industrial economy at the beginning of the nineteenth century, Great Britain customarily produced no more than 30 percent of the food consumed by her population and an even smaller proportion of the raw materials required by her industries; since a considerable portion of her imported foodstuffs and industrial raw materials came from her Asian and Pacific possessions (India, Australia, and New Zealand), Britain's very survival seemed to depend on her ability to keep open the sea lanes over which these vital supplies were transported. Moreover, in order to pay for these enormous imports of food and raw materials, Britain's manufactured products had to be assured unimpeded access to their export markets overseas. For both these reasons, it was deemed essential by the ruling elite of Victorian England that control of the sea lanes to the Far East be firmly in British hands. This implied both the preservation of naval domination of the Mediterranean–Suez–Red Sea–Indian Ocean route as well as the establishment of strategically located bases and refueling stations along the way.

By the end of the nineteenth century, this national obsession with protecting the passage to India, East Asia, and Australia had resulted in the acquisition of a long string of islands, coastal enclaves, and their hinterlands along the southern rim of Asia and the east coast of Africa as well as control of the Egyptian land bridge connecting the two continents and its canal linking the seas. These strategically situated outposts of British imperialism—Gibraltar, Malta, Cyprus, and Suez in the Mediterranean; Aden and Somaliland on opposite shores of the Red Sea; Kenya, India, Burma, Malaya, and Singapore along the Indian Ocean basin—enabled this small island nation to obtain and preserve effective control of the largest empire in the history of the world.

A third motivating factor for British imperialism—in addition to the quests for (1) supplies of foodstuffs and raw materials and markets for industrial production and (2) the naval bases and refueling stations to facilitate control of the sea lanes over which these products moved—was the search for undeveloped areas for investment that could absorb the huge amounts of capital that had accumulated in Britain in the form of profits from industrial enterprise. The regions of Africa and Asia that had recently been opened to European penetration were in dire need of investment capital to build the transportation and communication systems that were a prerequisite of economic modernization. In short order the major financial institutions of London began to invest heavily in railroad and road construction, the improvement of ports and harbors, and other ventures undertaken by British firms as part of the preliminary process of colonial development. In this way thousands of British investors were led to believe that their financial well-being depended on guaranteed markets for capital investment in the empire.

All manner of ideological justifications for the spectacular expansion of British power were advanced by the morally upright Victorians. There was much talk of the solemn responsibility to provide the uncivilized, backward peoples of the colonial world with the fruits of Britain's superior culture, in particular the spiritual inspiration of Christianity and the political benefits of enlightened administration. Altruistic missionaries and idealistic civil servants seem genuinely to have conceived of their role as that of rescuing the indigenous populations of the non-European world from the superstitions of their primitive religions and the barbarity of their native customs. But the self-justifying invocations of the "White Man's Burden" barely concealed the underlying motivation for British colonial expansion, which was primarily economic in nature. Despite the rhetoric of religious conversion and political reform, British colonial policy was designed to leave the preexisting social and cultural arrangements untouched and intact. All that mattered to the government in London was that that imperial system contribute to the efficient operation of the worldwide network of trade and investment upon which (it was thought) Great Britain depended for her economic prosperity if not her national survival.

The reasons for France's acquisition of a colonial empire in the latter part of the nineteenth century are less evident. Self-sufficient in food and far behind Great Britain in industrial development, France was much less dependent on foreign trade for her economic well-being. She had no demonstrable commercial incentive to seek guaranteed markets overseas for manufactured goods she could not produce in sufficient quantity or sources of foodstuffs she did not require. Nor did the French financial community seek colonial outlets for accumulated capital in the manner of the large London banking houses. By and large, that portion of French domestic savings that was invested abroad between 1871 and 1914 went not to distant regions of the Southern Hemisphere but rather to the state treasuries of Southern and Eastern Europe. This was so for two reasons. First, these established governments were presumed, wrongly as it turned out, to afford greater security for investment than more speculative ventures in far-off lands in various stages of political disorganization. More important, the flow of private capital to the developing regions of Eastern Europe was actively promoted by the French government, which, to a far greater degree than its British counterpart, regarded foreign investment as an instrument of diplomacy. If there was no good economic reason for France to covet a colonial empire in the closing decades of the nineteenth century, there was a persuasive diplomatic reason for her to direct her financial resources eastward rather than southward. France's vulnerable position in a Europe dominated by the powerful German Empire that had been formed at her own expense after the Franco-Prussian War (1870–71) dictated a perpetual preoccupation with continental affairs. By encouraging private investment in the Russian, Austro-Hungarian, and Turkish empires, as well as in the fledgling states of the Balkan peninsula, the French government endeavored to surround its only antagonist in Europe, Germany, with a ring of states dependent on France's financial support and therefore presumably amenable to her diplomatic influence.

Yet, in spite of this preoccupation with the German menace in Europe, France simultaneously embarked on a campaign of colonial expansion that left it in possession of the world's second largest empire by the end of the nineteenth century. Historians of French imperialism have sought to explain this paradox by emphasizing a motivating factor that does not lend itself to statistical confirmation in the manner of trade patterns or capital flows. This is the intangible phenomenon of the search for prestige. Abruptly displaced by Germany in 1871 as the dominant power on the European continent, France (according to this analysis) sought the psychological compensation of territorial conquest in distant regions of the non-European world where local authorities lacked the political organization and military power to offer effective resistance. By "France," in this instance, is meant not the government in Paris (which appears to have endorsed this colonial policy belatedly and somewhat reluctantly) but rather the military commanders and merchants on the spot who pursued their own particular interests. One observer went so far as to describe the French empire as having been built by "bored army officers looking for excitement." He might have added: "and by railroad builders and traders in search of quick profits."

In any event, by the end of the nineteenth century approximately a third of the continent of Africa, a large section of Southeast Asia (consolidated politically as "French Indochina"), and a few island chains in the South Pacific had been brought under French control. While Imperial Germany was busy consolidating its dominant position on the continent of Europe, France joined Great Britain in a scramble for control of much of the rest of the non-European world. It is not surprising that French imperialism had received the amiable encouragement of German Chancellor Otto von Bismarck, the architect of his country's continental hegemony. It served to divert French attention from European concerns, particularly the unhealed wound to French national pride represented by the loss of the provinces of Alsace and Lorraine to Germany after the Franco-Prussian War. It also increased the likelihood of tension between France and England in regard to overlapping colonial claims and therefore reduced the possibility of those two nations joining forces to oppose Germany in Europe.

Toward the end of the nineteenth century, however, Britain and France were joined in this massive land grab by two other European states that sought to carve out for themselves a share of the remaining unclaimed territory of the non-Western world. The first of these was Germany itself. In the years following Bismarck's retirement in 1890, the impetuous young German Emperor, William II, grew increasingly dissatisfied with his erst-

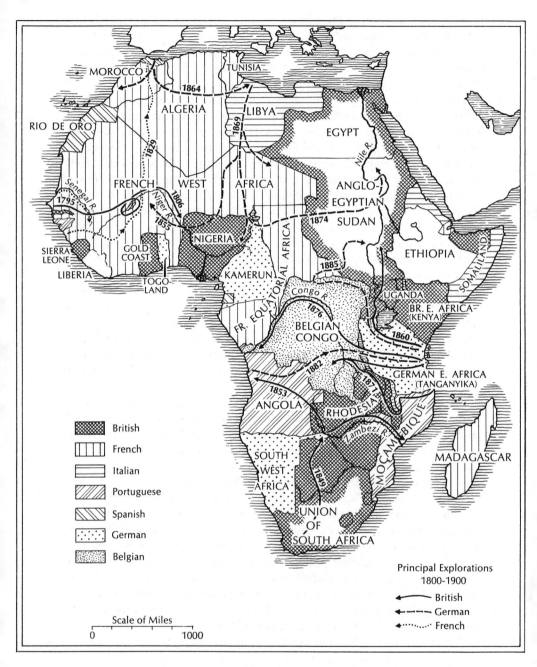

MOROCCO

TUNISIA

1864

ALGERIA

LIBYA

RIO DE ORO

1829

EGYPT

Nile R.

FRENCH WEST AFRICA

1869

ANGLO-EGYPTIAN

1806

Senegal R.

1795

Niger R.

1855

1874

SUDAN

ETHIOPIA

SIERRA LEONE

NIGERIA

GOLD COAST

LIBERIA

TOGO-LAND

KAMERUN

1885

SOMALILAND

FR. EQUATORIAL AFRICA

Congo R.

1876

UGANDA

BR. E. AFRICA (KENYA)

BELGIAN CONGO

1860

1882

1853

1871

GERMAN E. AFRICA (TANGANYIKA)

ANGOLA

RHODESIA

MOÇAMBIQUE

Zambezi R.

MADAGASCAR

SOUTH WEST AFRICA

1849

UNION OF SOUTH AFRICA

British

French

Italian

Portuguese

Spanish

German

Belgian

Principal Explorations
1800-1900

British

German

French

Scale of Miles

0   1000

European Penetration of Africa to 1914

while chancellor's "continental policy." The strategy that had effectively preserved German dominance in Europe began to appear outdated in the age of imperialism. Britain and France were rapidly bringing under their control vast colonial domains containing millions of people and unknown quantities of valuable resources. In 1897 the German Kaiser caused a sensation by announcing that his nation would no longer be content with its exclusively European role. Henceforth it would conduct a *Weltpolitik,* a "world policy," that was designed to project Germany's military, economic, and political power into the worldwide competition for empire. In response to London publicists' boastful characterization of Britain's colonial domain as "the Empire on which the sun never sets," William II asserted Imperial Germany's claim to "a place in the sun." Within a few months this bold declaration of Germany's new global policy was translated into action. Plans were drawn up for the construction of a German navy that would contest British domination of the high seas. The Chinese port of Kiao-Chow on the Yellow Sea was seized as a potential refueling station for a future German Far Eastern fleet. The German Empire, which since its inception in 1871 had operated as the arbiter of European affairs, abruptly put the other great powers on notice that it intended to play an active role on the world stage.

Each subsequent reassertion of Germany's international ambitions increased the sense of insecurity in London and Paris. In 1898 the Kaiser took the occasion of a much-publicized visit to the Ottoman Empire to declare himself "protector" of the 300 million Moslem inhabitants of the earth. This benevolent announcement represented a direct challenge to British and French positions in North Africa and the Middle East. A year later a German firm acquired from the Ottoman Sultan a concession for the construction of a railroad extending from European Turkey to the Persian Gulf. German economic penetration of the Turkish Empire was interpreted by the British and the French as a first step toward German expansion southward into the Mediterranean and that portion of the non-European world that they had reserved for themselves.

The prospect of the dominant land power in Europe challenging Anglo-French imperial interests in Africa and Asia had precisely the effect that Bismarck had feared it would. The Kaiser's *Weltpolitik* prompted the leaders of the two imperial nations to resolve their own conflicting claims to colonial territory in the interests of opposing Germany's bid for a global role. France was above all else interested in securing British cooperation in resisting the expansion of German power on the continent. Britain sought French support against Germany's newly acquired naval and colonial ambitions. All that stood in the way of such a mutually beneficial understanding was Anglo-French antagonism along the southern shore of the Mediterranean that had developed during the period of imperial expansion. British control of the two approaches to that body of water (by means of naval bases at Gibraltar at the western end and Alexandria at the eastern) conflicted with France's new imperial interests in Morocco and old ones in Egypt dating from the Napoleonic era. The two powers finally reached an amicable resolution of their North African rivalry in April 1904. France recognized the British occupation of Egypt (with guarantees of French access to the Suez Canal) in exchange for Britain's endorsement of French designs on Morocco (with guarantees of French disinterest in a buffer zone adjacent to Gibraltar that was eventually transferred to innocuous Spain). In March 1906, at a conference of the great powers that had been convened to adjudicate Germany's challenge to France's claim of priority in Morocco, the British government solidly supported the French and the Germans were forced to back down. Two months earlier the British foreign secretary, Sir Edward Grey, had taken the extraordinary step of authorizing conversations between the British and French general staffs for the purpose of coordinating strategic plans in preparation for a possible war on the continent. Though London was careful to remind Paris that the Anglo-French entente was not an alliance implying any obligation on Britain's part to defend France, the two nations cooperated closely in an effort to check the expansion of German power in Europe as well as in the colonial world.

The other great power of Europe to conduct a policy of imperial expansion during the second half of the nineteenth century was Russia. While the seafaring nations of Western Europe projected their power across the oceans of the world, the Slavs of Russia had expanded from their home base west of the Ural Mountains into the great empty spaces of Asia. This territorial aggrandizement brought under the control of the European Russians a vast collection of foreign peoples with different religions, languages, and traditions who submitted to Russian rule because they lacked the military power to resist it, just as the indigenous inhabitants of North America proved incapable of blocking the relentless expansion of the American frontier from the Atlantic seaboard to the shores of the Pacific. But as the Russian Empire's expanding frontier began to approach the open seas that lay beyond the Eurasian land mass—the Mediterranean, the Persian Gulf, the Indian Ocean, the Pacific—it began to press against the competing interests of other expansionist states. Great Britain, in particular, was intent on protecting the sea communications to its empire in Asia, and therefore strove to prevent Russia from securing a position of power along that route. The result of this British policy, often pursued in partnership with France, was that Russia was condemned to endure one of the most debilitating geographical handicaps imaginable for a state with ambitions of becoming a world power: During the winter months, when ice froze most of her major ports on the Baltic Sea, the North Pacific, and the Arctic Ocean, Russia lacked harbors to accommodate its navy and merchant marine.

The principal year-round ice-free ports that Russia did possess were located on the Black Sea. But the narrow body of water connecting these ports to the Mediterranean—the Bosporus, the Sea of Marmara, and the Dardanelles, collectively designated in diplomatic parlance as "the Straits"—could be closed at will by whatever power occupied its two shores. For centuries, that had been the empire of Ottoman Turkey. Turkish sovereignty over the Straits as well as over the adjacent Balkan peninsula in Southern Europe thus deprived Russia of a secure outlet for her foreign trade and naval power in the Mediterranean. It was in order to break out of this geographical straitjacket that the Russian tsars pursued during the second half of the nineteenth century an active policy in the southwestern corner of their empire, striving to extend Russian influence in the Balkans and to compel the Turkish government to open the Straits to Russian warships and close them to those of other powers.

The geographical attraction that the Balkan peninsula and the Turkish Straits had for Russia was reinforced by an ideological attraction as well: The largest nationality group inhabiting the European possessions of the Ottoman Empire was of Slavic stock and felt a sense of ethnic identity with the politically dominant Slavic population of Russia. This somewhat vague sentiment of ethnic kinship between the Balkan and Russian Slavs had gradually developed in the course of the nineteenth century into a program for political unification. Dating from the first conference of Slavic peoples held in Moscow in 1867, Russian proponents of the ideology of Pan-Slavism envisioned the creation of a vast Slavic empire united under the scepter of the Russian tsar. The tsars themselves cared little about the tribulations of the Slavic peoples beyond their borders and were scarcely sympathetic to the romantic reveries of the Pan-Slavist movement at home. But they promoted and patronized its campaign, partly to divert attention from domestic difficulties, partly to undermine Ottoman authority in the Slavic regions of Southern Europe. Turkish maltreatment of the Balkan Slavs periodically elicited harshly worded protests from Saint Petersburg together with fervent appeals from Pan-Slavist ideologues and ambitious individuals at the Russian court for their liberation from Ottoman oppression. Added to this sentiment of ethnic resentment—and the Russian court's willingness to exploit it for its own ends—was an ancient religious grievance harbored by the Russian clergy against the Turkish regime: For four centuries the city of Constantinople, spiritual capital of the Eastern Orthodox religion (the official faith of the Russian Empire) had remained under the control of the hated Turk. The liberation of the holy city from the clutches of the Moslem infidel had long been a popular cause in Russian clerical circles. Each new report of Turkish misbehavior helped to revive this long dormant issue. The tsar, though considerably more insulated from popular pressures than were the leaders of the other great powers, could ill afford to ignore these ethnic and religious sentiments, particularly when they coincidentally reinforced Russia's strategic and economic interest in challenging Turkey's position in Southern Europe.

The result of these internal pressures and external temptations was a

Russian drive toward the Mediterranean that produced what was called in the diplomatic lexicon of the day "the eastern question." Twice in the second half of the nineteenth century Russia attempted to expand southward at Turkey's expense. Twice she was prevented from doing so by the intervention of the great powers, militarily in the Crimean War (1854–56) and diplomatically at the Congress of Berlin (1878) following the Russo-Turkish War. In the course of the following two decades, the Ottoman Empire lived up to its reputation as the "sick man of Europe" by relinquishing political authority over the Slavic peoples of the Balkans. The independence of Serbia, Romania, Bulgaria, and Montenegro was confirmed, while the remainder of the peninsula seethed with insurrectionary sentiment against Turkish rule.

Into this political vacuum moved the Germanic empire of Austria-Hungary from the north. Though beset by the same kind of nationality problems that confronted the Ottoman state whose disintegrating European domains it coveted, the Habsburg Empire enjoyed the decisive advantage of almost unconditional support from the most powerful nation on the continent. By virtue of the Dual Alliance of 1879 (which was extended to a Triple Alliance including Italy three years later), Imperial Germany had committed itself to the preservation of Habsburg power in Southern Europe. In the face of this joint Germanic opposition to Russian expansion toward the Mediterranean, the Russian government was eventually obliged to postpone its Balkan ambitions. In May 1897 an agreement was struck between Vienna and Saint Petersburg (with the benevolent approval of the other great powers) to preserve the political status quo in the Balkans. The "eastern question" was put on ice, at least for a time.

Frustrated in its ambition to obtain predominance in the Balkan peninsula and control of the Turkish Straits, the Russian regime redirected its expansionist drive further to the east. Claims to disputed territory in southern Asia that had lain dormant for decades were revived at the turn of the century. The nominally independent but politically weak state of Persia blocked Russian access to the Persian Gulf just as Ottoman Turkey guarded the entrance to the Mediterranean. Russian economic penetration of Persia in the early years of the twentieth century, which included the issuance of loans secured by Persian customs revenues, plans to construct a railroad from the Russian frontier to the Persian Gulf, and the acquisition of favorable tariff treatment for Russian exports to Persia, resulted in an acute rivalry with Great Britain. London viewed the prospect of Russian economic hegemony in Persia as a prelude to political predominance there and therefore a grave menace to the security of the British sea lanes to the Far East. Even more threatening to British interests were the progressive Russian commercial encroachments in Afghanistan, the traditional buffer between Russia and British India. As a consequence, Russian expansionism in southern Asia met with British opposition at every turn. British diplomatic pressure in Teheran counteracted Russian efforts to gain financial and commercial ascendency there. In 1901 a New Zealander named William K. d'Arcy secured a sixty-year concession to explore for oil throughout Persia, a privilege that was to give the Anglo-Iranian Oil Company exclusive control of the rich oil fields that were discovered there in 1908. The increasing British financial presence in Persia, supported by British naval squadrons patrolling the Persian Gulf and military garrisons in India, effectively frustrated the ambitions of the "Persian group" at the Russian court.

A far more promising outlet for Russian expansionist energies lay in the Far East. Just as American pioneers moved westward toward the Pacific Ocean at the expense of the indigenous Amerinds and the weak government of Mexico, Russian settlers drove eastward across the sparsely populated wasteland of Siberia toward the opposite shore of that same ocean, subduing the native tribes and wresting territory from the impotent Manchu empire of China. In 1860 Russia acquired from China the Ussuri region on the Sea of Japan and founded the port city of Vladivostok. But this new acquisition did not afford Russia her coveted outlet to the open seas, for Vladivostok's harbor was icebound for most of the winter. Advocates of Russian expansion again turned their attention southward. As with Turkey and Persia, Russian entrée to a year-round harbor was blocked by a politically unstable, economically backward, militarily impotent state. But unlike the situation at the Turkish Straits and Persian Gulf, no European power possessed the capability of propping up the Chinese "sick man of Asia." Great Britain, which had traditionally served as the patron of the Manchu dynasty (in order to dominate it economically by controlling its principal seaports), was helpless to prevent the penetration of China by land. "Sea power had saved Constantinople," observed one historian. "It could not protect Peking." In 1891 the Russian government had begun the construction of a Trans-Siberian Railroad with the assistance of French loans that had begun to flow into the tsar's treasury as part of France's campaign to woo Russia into an alliance directed against Germany. Upon the completion of that railway, military forces could be transported from the heart of European Russia to a frontier that no other great power (and certainly not the Chinese) could defend.

The parts of China that appeared most attractive and most susceptible to Russian exploitation were the two peninsulas that extend from the northeastern Chinese province of Manchuria into the Yellow Sea and afford access to the Pacific. The first of these, the Liaotung Peninsula, included at its furthest extremity the coveted prize of Port Arthur, the year-round ice-free Pacific port of Russian dreams. The second, the peninsula of Korea, represented the key to Russia's control of the Yellow Sea and therefore command of the approaches to its prospective East Asian port.

Fortified with these acquisitions, Russia would be well positioned to participate in the China trade that had begun to exert a strong attraction on the maritime states of the world.

In anticipation of the arrival of Russian military power on the northern frontier of China to fill the vacuum produced by the collapse of Manchu authority, the great powers of Europe moved in to partition the decaying Asian empire into spheres of interest. The German seizure of the port of Kiao-Chow in 1897 set in motion a scramble for economic concessions that rapidly revealed the fictitious nature of Chinese sovereignty. Profiting from China's internal disarray, the Russian government extracted from Beijing in 1898 a long-term lease on the southern portion of the Liaotung Peninsula (including Port Arthur) together with the right to construct a railroad linking the port to the railway network then under construction in Siberia. The territory in between, the province of Manchuria, also became the object of Russian ambition: Control of it would provide a secure land route to Port Arthur and the warm water sea together with privileged access to the vast mineral deposits it was believed to contain. In 1900, following the Russian army's participation in the multinational military force that had suppressed the antiforeign Boxer Rebellion in Beijing, a Russian contingent of a hundred thousand men remained on occupation duty in Manchuria to protect Russian interests there. Demands for far-reaching commercial concessions and the economic penetration of northern Korea soon followed. By the turn of the century Russian domination of the Chinese Empire appeared imminent, pending the completion of the Trans-Siberian Railroad, because the great powers of far-off Europe were incapable of projecting sufficient military force into the region in order to prevent it.

But as Russia pursued its campaign of expansion in East Asia, it was soon to discover that the world beyond the outer reaches of European power did not present the boundless opportunity for exploitation that had been supposed. This was particularly true along the western shore of the Pacific basin, where a non-European power that had adopted European techniques of economic, political, and military organization brusquely asserted its right to participate in the division of the colonial spoils in its own geographical sphere. Whereas the continent of Africa and the southern rim of Asia lay within range of British, French, and German power, the western shore of the Pacific became, at the turn of the century, the object of the imperial ambitions of Japan.

The Rise of Japanese Power in East Asia

Japan is a collection of four main islands and several minor ones off the coast of China. For centuries it had been ruled by a decentralized feudal oligarchy consisting of territorial lords (daimyō) and an aristocratic caste of warriors (samurai). Hampered by the absence of natural resources and a mountainous terrain that left only 20 percent of its land suitable for cultivation, Japan lacked all of the customary prerequisites for economic development. Isolated from the rest of the world by a complex language with no close relatives and an intense consciousness of cultural uniqueness, the Japanese people remained inward looking and resistant to foreign influences well into the second half of the nineteenth century. For all of these reasons Japan seemed destined to remain politically immature, economically backward, and militarily impotent. Yet in spite of these handicaps, this hermit nation was to become the first non-Western state to achieve the position of a modern industrial and imperial power by the beginning of the twentieth century.

Japan's rapid rise to world power began in January 1868, when a political revolution swept aside the authority of the feudal oligarchy and restored the position of the Meiji Emperor as the symbol of national unity and centralized authority. Real political power lay in the hands of a dynamic new ruling elite that was committed to the transformation of Japan from a primitive feudal society into a modern world power. The phenomenal success of the so-called Meiji Restoration was due to the willingness of the new leadership to abandon the isolationist prejudices of the past in favor of Western methods of political, economic, and military organization. The Meiji political class recognized that since the global power of the European nations was the result of their economic modernization, political centralization, and military organization, the best hope of resisting European domination lay in adopting the very practices that had made it possible elsewhere in the world.

The result of this willingness to innovate by imitation was the rapid Westernization of Japan during the closing decades of the nineteenth century. Samurai were required to remove the knot of hair worn on the head and to wear their hair in the Western style; European clothing was given official sanction; the Gregorian calendar was adopted in 1873, changing holidays and festivals. Japanese observers were dispatched to England to study financial, commercial, and naval affairs; to Germany to learn the principles of military organization, strategy, and tactics; and to France for training in law and government. The entire structure of Japanese society was thenceforth reorganized on the basis of these European models. The political and economic power of the daimyō aristocracy was transferred to the central government organized as a European-style cabinet system with a prime minister and a bicameral parliament. The military authority that had previously been the jealously guarded privilege of the samurai warrior class was assumed by the Japanese Imperial Army, which adopted the Prussian institution of universal military service. The development of a nationwide system of banking and currency, transportation, and communication set the stage for Japan's spectacular economic growth during this period. The modernization of the Japanese economy began, as it had in England a century before, in the production of textiles. The silk industry captured a large share of the world market; Japan's silk exports surpassed those of China in 1910, a remarkable feat in view of the relative size of the two countries. In the meantime, the mechanization of cotton spinning and weaving proceeded at a fast pace. By the end of the century, a Japanese shipbuilding and munitions industry had been established. The value of Japanese foreign trade increased from virtually nothing in 1850 to roughly $200 million by 1900.

But the prospects for continued Japanese economic growth were limited by several constraints imposed by the accidents of geography. In addition to the shortage of industrial raw materials and agricultural resources cited earlier, Japan found herself in the midst of a demographic crisis of major proportions as she entered the period of her economic "takeoff." With a land area smaller than the state of Texas and a rapidly expanding population which (at the turn of the century) was almost half that of the United States, the pressure of excess population on land and food supply had become a considerable handicap. In the last decade of the nineteenth century the Japanese ruling class concluded that the only hope for surmounting these geographical and demographic impediments to economic growth lay in colonial expansion. Once again, the European experience furnished the instructive precedent. Just as Great Britain had relieved its population pressures and enhanced its economic productivity by acquiring overseas lands for settlement, investment, and trade, Japan could obtain much needed sources of industrial and agricultural raw materials, markets for its manufactured products, and areas of colonization for its excess population in the hitherto unclaimed territory in the adjacent regions of East Asia.

Less than a hundred miles to the west of the Japanese islands, on the mainland of Asia, the Korean peninsula and its Manchurian hinterland presented an irresistible temptation to Japanese imperialist sentiment. In 1894–95 Japanese forces swept across Korea into Manchuria, destroyed the Chinese army and navy, and laid the groundwork for imperial expansion on the mainland by securing the independence (under Japanese economic domination) of Korea and annexing the offshore island of Taiwan (Formosa). It was this expansion to the mainland that first brought the parvenu power of Asia into conflict with Russia, whose economic penetration of Manchuria and northern Korea had begun in the same period. The inevitable collision came in 1904–05, in the first war between great powers since 1870. The Japanese navy quickly bottled up the small Russian fleet based at Port Arthur while the Japanese army defeated the Russian army stationed in Manchuria. When the thirty-two vessels of the Russian Baltic Fleet arrived at the Tsushima Strait between Japan and Korea after a nine-month voyage from Europe they were engaged by the Japanese fleet and annihilated. As a reward for its spectacular victory, Japan obtained the Russian lease of Port Arthur and the Liaotung Peninsula, a privileged position in Manchuria, and a protectorate over Korea (which it annexed outright in 1910).

The Russo-Japanese War was a watershed in modern history for a number of reasons. It was the first instance in the modern era of a non-Western nation defeating a great power of Europe. As such it provided much encouragement to the emerging leaders of the nonwhite peoples of the world that were intent on liberating themselves from European domination. The Japanese had demonstrated that such resistance was possible provided that it was backed by Western-type technology and military organization. Inspired to a certain extent by the Japanese example, nationalist revolutions erupted in Persia (1905), Turkey (1908), and China (1911). The leaders of these insurrections advocated the introduction of economic, political, and military reforms of the Western type in order to strengthen their peoples in the struggle against Western domination. In a very real sense, the Japanese victory of 1905 marked the beginning of Asia's half-century-long war of liberation against European colonial control. The humiliation of the great Russian Empire by tiny Japan also had the effect of undermining the political authority of the Romanov dynasty. A political revolution that swept Russia in the aftermath of the military defeat of 1905 compelled the Tsar to grant a constitution, convoke a representative parliament, and guarantee fundamental civil liberties for the first time. Though these concessions were diluted by all manner of restrictions on popular sovereignty and democratic rights, the social unrest that had prompted them set in motion a wave of clandestine revolutionary activity that was to culminate in the overthrow of the imperial regime twelve years later.

From the perspective of the shifting balance of power in the world, the most important consequence of Russia's defeat in the Far East was the gradual rapprochement between the Tsarist regime and its other traditional rival, Great Britain. Its expansionist ambitions in East Asia blocked by Japan, the Russian government began to contemplate reviving its long dormant claims to territory and influence at the other end of its empire on the Balkan peninsula of Southern Europe. But before renewing its forward policy in the Balkans, Russia took the precautionary step of seeking a resolution of its long-standing disputes with Great Britain in southern Asia; the focal points of this antagonism were Persia and Afghanistan, the two buffer states between Russian and British power in that region. As it happened, the British government was also anxious to reach an accord with Russia in southern Asia in order to ensure the security of India at a time when Britain felt increasingly menaced by the expansion of German military and naval power in Europe. The destruction of Russian seapower in the Far East had removed one of the principal sources of British hostility to Russia and left Germany as the only potential threat to Britain's mastery of the seas. In short, these two historic rivals in Asia had both come to regard German power in Europe as the foremost obstacle to the pursuit of their respective national interests as they were redefined in the context of the changing international balance of power.

The reconciliation between Russia and Britain after 1905 was actively promoted by the one power that enjoyed cordial relations with both and which had the most to gain from an Anglo-Russian rapprochement: France. After more than a year of intensive negotiations, an Anglo-Russian agreement was concluded on August 31, 1907, which settled all of the important disputes between these two imperial powers in southern Asia. Russia recognized Afghanistan as a British sphere of influence, thereby according India the security on her northeast frontier that London had long sought. Persia, which had been a flashpoint of Anglo-Russian rivalry for over a decade, was partitioned into three zones: the northern zone, adjacent to the Caucasus and including the capital, Teheran, was to be Russia's sphere; the southern zone, adjacent to India and guarding the entrance to the Gulf, became the British sphere; and the territory in between, including the Gulf itself, was neutralized as a buffer zone. Both nations agreed to cooperate in blocking German efforts to obtain a foothold in Persia. Though the Anglo-Russian agreement of 1907 applied only to those two powers' bilateral rivalries in southern Asia, it paved the way for increasingly intimate diplomatic cooperation among Britain, Russia, and France. Observers began to speak of a "Triple Entente" that had emerged as a diplomatic counterpart to the Triple Alliance of Germany, Austria-Hungary, and Italy. Fortified by its amicable settlement with Great Britain in southern Asia, emboldened by the diplomatic support and financial assistance from its ally France, Russia "returned to Europe" after its disastrous adventure in the Far East. The revival of Russian aspirations in the Balkans, undertaken partly to divert public attention from the domestic troubles sketched above, partly in pursuit of long-standing interests in the region, was destined to bring the tsarist empire into conflict with Austria-Hungary and its powerful protector in Berlin.

While Japan was emerging as the dominant power in East Asia, across the Pacific another non-European state that had adopted European ways began to assert its claim to imperial status in the new global order. The geographical condition of the Japanese empire and the American republic could hardly have been more dissimilar. Japan suffered from a shortage of arable land and natural resources and lacked a large internal market for its industrial output. The United States possessed all three in unparalleled abundance as a consequence of its westward territorial expansion in the course of the nineteenth century. Whereas Japan's curse of overpopulation impelled her to seek external outlets for emigration, the United States' opposite problem of underpopulation required the importation of millions of immigrants from Europe to operate its farms and factories. But the striking similarities amid the contrasts between these two nations explain why they simultaneously joined the ranks of the imperial powers at the beginning of the twentieth century. Both were relatively free from the menace of foreign invasion because of the great distances separating them from the centers of military power in Europe. Both were located in the vicinity of politically disorganized and militarily impotent states whose abundant natural resources made them tempting targets for economic exploitation and military domination. This propitious combination of isolation from great power interference and proximity to economically valuable, strategically vulnerable regions propelled the United States into a policy of imperial expansion in its own region during the very period that Japan began its expansion on the mainland of Asia.

The simultaneous emergence of these two powers on the opposite shores of the Pacific inevitably raised the possibility that their aggressive ambitions would overlap in that ocean. Indeed, both societies contained advocates of trans-Pacific expansion. In Japan there was much talk of relieving the pressure of overpopulation by mass immigration to the sparsely settled Pacific islands and the west coast of the United States. Toward the end of the century eastward migration had produced a Japanese majority in the Hawaiian islands. In the meantime, increasing numbers of Japanese nationals had begun to settle in the American coastal state of California, engendering friction with the resident population of European stock that gave rise to demands for exclusionary legislation. During the same period various constituencies in the United States pressed for expansion across the Pacific in the opposite direction. Commercial interests eagerly eyed the "China market" for American agricultural surpluses and industrial products. Christian missionary societies dreamed of converting the heathens on the Chinese mainland to the true faith. American banking houses sought participation in the financial reorganization of the Chinese railroad network in Manchuria that was being prepared by a consortium of European banks. Naval leaders coveted the natural harbors in Samoa, Hawaii, and the Philippines as potential bases for a powerful American Pacific fleet. The subsequent acquisition of these three island groups by the United States at the end of the nineteenth century posed a potential challenge to Japan's imperial aspirations in the western Pacific.

As it turned out, however, the Pacific ambitions of Japan and the United States were prudently postponed by the governments of both countries and subordinated to expansionist activities in regions closer to home. In spite of Washington's determined efforts to establish the principle of the "Open Door" to China through a series of declarations by Secretary of State John Hay at the turn of the century, the two new Pacific powers worked out a vague *modus vivendi* that removed the principal sources of conflict between them: The United States tacitly tolerated Japanese economic penetration of Korea and Manchuria, while the Tokyo government swallowed its pride and accepted stringent American restrictions on Japanese immigration to United States territory. While Japanese imperial energies were thus diverted from the Pacific to the Asian mainland, American ambitions were similarly diverted from the Pacific to the Caribbean.

The Rise of American Power in the Western Hemisphere

The central characteristic of the Western Hemisphere that has decisively influenced the economic and political relations of its constituent states is the enormous disparity in national power between the United States of North America and the disunited states of Latin America.* This "imbalance of power," as one historian has labelled it, was a direct result of the divergent historical experience of the settler populations that inhabited the successor states of the British and Iberian empires in the new world after they achieved their political independence from Europe.

By the middle of the 1860s the English-speaking heirs to the British Empire of North America had definitively partitioned that vast, resource-rich continent into two sovereign political units which rapidly underwent a process of economic modernization based on the model of the industrial revolution of the metropole. The United States had extended its political frontier westward from the Atlantic seaboard to the Pacific between 1783 and the mid-1850s by the alternate means of military conquest and diplomacy, expropriating the tribal lands of the indigenous inhabitants or annexing territory previously claimed by Spain, France, England, and the newly independent state of Mexico. By copying European methods of economic organization and political integration, the American pioneers who pushed westward with the active encouragement of the federal government and the protection of its military forces welded that continental territory into a single political and economic unit. After the failure of the southern states' bid for secession between 1861 and 1865, this politically unified, economically integrated system combined its extraordinary God-given advantages—an abundant supply of natural resources, fertile, well-watered soil, and an excellent system of navigable rivers and lakes that afforded access to both land and markets—with the influx of skilled labor and capital investment from Europe to become the world's most prosperous nation by the end of the century. To the north, the unconnected provinces of Canada, long the object of American annexationist ambition, united as a self-governing federation in 1867.† The withdrawal of British authority over Canadian affairs removed the major obstacle to Canadian-American cooperation. Thereafter the two sovereign political entities of North America developed intimate economic and political relations that complemented their close linguistic and cultural ties. By the end of the century Canada

* By "Latin America" we mean the politically independent states of Central America, South America, and the West Indies where Spanish, Portuguese, or French are the official languages.

† The four original provinces of Canada united under the British North America Act of 1867 (Quebec, Ontario, Nova Scotia, and New Brunswick) were subsequently joined by six others to form the present federation.

had become the principal market for American industrial exports and a major supplier of raw materials and mineral resources to the United States. The Canadian-American border became, and remains to this day, the longest undefended frontier in the world.

South of the Rio Grande, on the other hand, the collapse of Spanish and Portuguese authority between 1808 and 1822 resulted in the political distintegration of the Latin American mainland into what eventually became twenty independent republics.* Despite the dreams of revolutionary leaders such as Simon Bolívar of creating a political federation of Latin America, the new nations tenaciously clung to their newly achieved national identities. Even economic integration, traditionally the preliminary step to political unification, proved an unattainable goal. As a result of tariffs, import quotas, and other impediments to regional economic interchange established by the nationalistically-inclined ruling elites, only a small proportion of the foreign trade of each individual state was conducted within the region. Moreover, instead of following the North American path of economic modernization (which emphasized industrialization and the development of an internal market for domestically produced manufactured goods), the Latin republics preserved and intensified the neo-colonial nature of their economic systems. That is, they produced raw materials and tropical foodstuffs for export and served as markets for finished manufactured products and capital investment from the already developed industrial economies of Western Europe. To make matters worse, whereas feudal practices had been abolished early in England and therefore were not transplanted to British North America, the new Latin American states inherited from Spain and Portugal a feudal land tenure system and a rigidly stratified social structure that remained largely intact after independence.

The failure of the Iberian successor states in Latin America to achieve political and economic integration as a prelude to economic modernization is paradoxical in light of the existence of several conditions that ought to have been conducive to such a development. The Latin Republics had won their political independence early in the nineteenth century. Many of them possessed an ample resource base for economic development in the form of extensive deposits of subsoil minerals and fertile agricultural land. Collectively they possessed a common religion, cultural heritage, and (with the exception of Brazil) language, advantages that had traditionally facilitated regional communication and cooperation. Instead, the perpetuation of the political division and economic backwardness of Latin America for the remainder of the nineteenth century produced an enormous power vacuum in the southern portion of the Western Hemisphere that was to be filled by the newly developed economic and military power of the United States.

* Excluding British, French, and Dutch Guiana (which remained European colonies) and British Honduras (which became a British colony in 1862).

It has long been fashionable, but entirely incorrect, to believe that the establishment of United States hegemony in Latin America at the expense of the great powers of Europe was a consequence of the Monroe Doctrine. President James Monroe's message to Congress on December 2, 1823, had originally been intended as a warning to the European powers (especially France, which was then suspected of harboring designs on the newly independent republics of Latin America) that any attempt to reestablish European colonial power in the new world would be unacceptable to the United States. In fact the Monroe Doctrine was a dead letter from its promulgation to the end of the nineteenth century, for the United States during that period had developed neither the naval power nor the diplomatic influence to enforce such a presumptuous admonition. It was only by the sufferance of Great Britain that the Latin American republics were permitted to enjoy immunity from political interference and military intimidation by the great powers of the old world. By extracting from France a promise of nonintervention, and by maintaining undisputed naval supremacy in the Atlantic and Caribbean, Britain ensured that no European nation would increase its power position on the continent of Europe by acquiring territory in the Western Hemisphere. But the doctrine of nonintervention was scarcely absolute. It was violated with impunity whenever London saw fit for whatever reason to suspend its application. Britain itself intervened militarily in Latin America on four separate occasions after the declaration of the Monroe Doctrine: She conducted joint naval operations with France against the Rio de la Plata (the future state of Argentina) in 1845 and with France and Spain against Mexico in 1861; and she occupied the Falkland Islands off Argentina in 1833 and British Honduras in Central America in 1862. France, in addition to her naval collaboration with England and Spain, overthrew the Mexican government and installed a French client state in 1863 which remained in power for four years. Even Spain was able to reannex the Dominican Republic for a four-year period beginning in 1861. Apart from these overt military operations in direct violation of the Monroe Doctrine, British, French, and German economic penetration of Latin America in the last half of the nineteenth century subordinated the economies of the region to the commercial and financial interests of Europe.

It was not until the decade of the 1890s that the United States, having become an industrial power of the first rank and consolidated political control of the territory on its own continent, acquired the economic and military capability to project its power to the southern half of its hemisphere. The pursuit of American strategic and economic interests in the Caribbean region in particular and in Latin America in general was justified, as has so often been the case in American foreign policy, by a high-sounding moral principle. Just as the westward continental expansion of the nineteenth century was touted as the "manifest destiny" of a chosen people on the march, the subsequent extension of American hegemony over Latin America at the expense of European powers was couched in two moralistic phrases: "hemispheric solidarity" and the more commonly used "Pan-Americanism."

The ideology of Pan-Americanism was rooted in two myths about the geographical and political conditions of the Western Hemisphere. The first was the widespread misconception that the two continents of the new world formed a single geographic unit that stood apart from the other continents of the earth. In reality the continents of North and South America, though connected by a narrow strip of land, achieved their normal communication by sea in the nineteenth century and by air later in the twentieth. By sea, Rio de Janiero is considerably closer to the west coast of Africa than to any port in the United States. By air, Washington is closer to Moscow than to Buenos Aires. The myth of political affinity derived from the use of the term "republic" as a label for the governmental systems of the Latin American nations. As "sister republics," the United States and the countries to the south came to be regarded as joint custodians of a common legacy of democratic government that distinguished them from the monarchical tradition of the old world. The perpetual tendency of the various "republics" of Latin America to lapse into various forms of dictatorship while the nations of Western Europe moved toward democratic rule belied such sentimental invocations of a hemispheric partnership of republicanism.

Nevertheless, beginning with the first International Conference of American States in 1889, the ideology of Pan-Americanism persisted as the moral justification for what rapidly developed into a neocolonial relationship between the North American giant and the weak states to its south. The Commercial Bureau of the International Union of the American Republics, headquartered in Washington under the supervision of the American secretary of state, promoted inter-American economic and political cooperation. Subsequently renamed the Pan-American Union, this organization of free and independent states in the hemisphere became the vehicle for the exercise of American diplomatic influence over the member governments. Though the hopes entertained by some United States officials of establishing a customs union integrating the economies of the sovereign nations of the Western Hemisphere foundered on the shoals of Latin American opposition at the conference, the groundwork was laid for a hemispheric political system dominated by the United States and emancipated from the overbearing influence of the European powers.

But the projection of American power into Latin America required a direct challenge to Great Britain's hitherto uncontested authority in the region. Such a challenge was effectively mounted in the last decade of the nineteenth century, at a time when Britain's imperial energies were engaged elsewhere by disputes that affected her vital national interests much more directly. The precipitating episode in this transformation of the balance of power in the Western Hemisphere was a seemingly trivial boundary dispute between Venezuela and British Guiana. Within the disputed zone lay the mouth of the Orinoco River, the key trade route in the northern portion of the South American continent. Venezuelan appeals to the United States for support, combined with American anxiety about the possible extension of British economic influence along the southern shore of the Caribbean, prompted a spectacular diplomatic initiative from Washington. On July 20, 1895, Secretary of State Richard Olney demanded that Britain agree to submit the issue to arbitration, threatened American intervention on the basis of the Monroe Doctrine if she refused to do so, and issued the following historic declaration: "Today the United States is practically sovereign on this continent, and its fiat is law upon the subjects to which it confines its interposition." He proceeded to observe that America's "infinite resources combined with its isolated position render it master of the situation and practically invulnerable against any or all other powers." The boundary dispute rapidly receded in significance—the arbitration award given four years later actually supported the British position on most points—amid the broad international implications of the Olney Declaration. The United States had unilaterally arrogated to itself the right and responsibility to protect the interests of its neighbors to the south by virtue of its position of superiority within its hemisphere. Great Britain, on account of its preoccupation with the deteriorating political situation in southern Africa and the German government's willingness to exploit it at Britain's expense, chose not to become embroiled in a dispute with the United States and therefore acquiesced in this unilateral declaration of American hegemony in Latin America.

In the year 1898, British imperial authority in the Eastern Hemisphere appeared endangered at every turn by the actions of the other European powers. In March the passage of Germany's first naval law and Russia's acquisition of a naval base at Port Arthur in Manchuria heralded the entry of two new contestants in the scramble for colonies and concessions in Asia. In the autumn Britain and France edged to the brink of war over conflicting territorial claims along the Nile, while tension continued to mount between Britain and the Boer Republics in southern Africa. Consequently, the United States was able to wrest from Spain the Caribbean remnants of her once great empire in the New World (the islands of Cuba and Puerto Rico) after the Spanish-American War without provoking the opposition of a Britain thus elsewhere engaged. By the end of the century the United States had embarked on a naval construction program worthy of its newly acquired status as an imperial power. The advantages enjoyed by the United States over Britain in naval power in the Western Hemisphere became readily apparent. The replacement of the wind-powered warship by the steam-propelled warship, while increasing the fighting strength of the world's battle fleets, had reduced their radius of action by imposing the requirement of an assured source of fuel (coal, until 1912 when the British fleet changed over to oil) on naval task forces operating far from home waters. In 1902 Britain began to transfer the bulk of its Caribbean naval squadron to the North Atlantic in order to offset the growth of German naval power there, in effect conceding American domination of its own hemisphere and recognizing Latin America as an American sphere of interest. In the same year Britain had concluded an alliance with Japan in recognition of that nation's value as a counterweight to Russian power in the Far East, thereby liberating more British battleships for redeployment in home waters. By these two gestures the former "mistress of the seas" accorded the United States and Japan the right to control the sea approaches to their own imperial domains in order to concentrate on protecting the security of the British Isles from the prospective menace of German sea power.

The United States rapidly developed extensive strategic and economic interests in the former Spanish islands in the Caribbean and the independent mainland nations on its shores. Naval strategists, concerned about the growing naval strength of Japan across the Pacific, considered the Isthmus of Panama an ideal site for a canal linking the Atlantic and the Pacific that would permit the concentration of naval forces in either ocean on short notice. American domination of the Caribbean region came to be regarded in American naval circles as necessary for the security of the two coasts of the country as well as for the protection of the eastern approaches of the projected Panamanian canal, just as Britain's control of the North Sea and Japan's control of the China Sea were considered essential by the naval strategists of those two powers.

As "big navy" enthusiasts pressed for the transformation of the Caribbean into an "American lake," American economic interests began to compete with European firms for control of the natural resources of Latin America in general and the Caribbean basin in particular. American penetration of the economies of Latin America characteristically took the form of direct acquisition by United States firms of the agricultural and subsoil mineral resources of the region. Sugar-producing interests obtained a virtual monopoly on the Cuban sugar cane crop. The United Fruit Company of Boston established a huge "banana empire" in Central America, purchasing enormous tracts of land and constructing roads, railroads, and ports to convey the products of its plantations to foreign markets. The petroleum resources of Mexico and Venezuela, Chilean copper, Bolivian tin, and several other industrial raw materials that were in comparatively short supply in the United States came under the direct control of American firms.

By 1901 the last remaining obstacle to American mastery of the Caribbean region was removed. By means of the Hay-Pauncefort Treaty, Great Britain renounced an earlier agreement stipulating joint Anglo-American construction and operation of a Central American canal. Two years later a revolution in Colombia's northwestern province on the Isthmus of Panama received the active support of the American government, which promptly recognized Panama as an independent republic. In February 1904 the new nation signed a treaty authorizing the United States to construct a fifty-mile-long canal across the isthmus in a zone leased and fortified by the government in Washington. In the meantime, steps had been taken to ensure the right of the United States to protect its strategic and economic interests in the Caribbean. The newly created client states of Cuba and Panama were forced to include clauses in their constitutions stipulating the right of the United States to intervene to protect their independence and preserve social order, and both were induced to authorize the construction of American bases on their territory. In 1904 President Theodore Roosevelt imperiously extended the prerogative of intervention to embrace the entire hemisphere: "Chronic wrongdoing, or an impotence which results in a general loosening of the ties of civilized societies," he announced, "may in America, as elsewhere, ultimately require intervention by some civilized nation, and in the Western Hemisphere the adherence of the United States to the Monroe Doctrine may force the United States, however reluctantly, in flagrant cases of such wrongdoing or impotence, to the exercise of an international police power." With his famous corollary to the Monroe Doctrine, Roosevelt in effect redefined the original prohibition against European interference in Latin America as a unilateral assertion of the United States' prerogative to police the region.

America's self-proclaimed right to manage the internal affairs of the Caribbean nations was frequently exercised in the years following the promulgation of the Roosevelt Corollary. In 1905 the United States assumed control of customs collection in the insolvent Dominican Republic and established a system of financial supervision that was to remain in force for thirty-six years. In 1909 American agents fomented a successful insurrection against the nationalistically inclined government of Nicaragua. Three years later American marines were landed to protect the compliant successor regime, whose transfer of authority over its customs service to the United States had produced widespread internal discontent. Though nominally independent, Nicaragua remained under American financial supervision from 1911 to 1924.

But it was the adjacent state of Mexico that became the major victim of American economic penetration. During the last two decades of the nineteenth century and the first decade of the twentieth, Mexican dictator Porfirio Diaz had welcomed American investment in his country's petroleum industry, transportation system, and agricultural resources. At the time of his overthrow by the Mexican Revolution of 1911, American companies had acquired control of 50 percent of the Mexican oil industry and American citizens held title to over 40 percent of Mexican land. Subsequent outbursts of anti-American sentiment in postrevolutionary Mexico, as we shall see, prompted punitive American naval and military interventions that further inflamed patriotic opinion south of the Rio Grande.

By the advent of the First World War the United States had established its undisputed mastery of the Caribbean region, a circumstance dramatically symbolized by the opening of the Panama Canal in August 1914, the very month that the armies of Europe hurled themselves against one another on that distant continent. The subsequent construction of American naval bases at Roosevelt Roads in Puerto Rico and Guantánamo Bay in Cuba was to afford the United States command of the eastern approaches to the canal and therefore a position of strategic invulnerability in its hemisphere. In the meantime, the economy of the Caribbean region had been tightly linked to the superior economic system of what resentful Latin Americans had begun to call "the Colossus of the North." Direct American investment in electric utilities, railways, sugar, oil, bananas, and extractive industries generated substantial profits which were repatriated to fuel the phenomenal economic expansion in the United States. American control of the banking system and customs administration of the Caribbean nations served the dual function of ensuring the repayment of debts to American investors and precluding European interventions on behalf of aggrieved debtors. The prerogative of American military intervention to restore social order or protect foreign economic interests remained in the background as an inducement to good behavior and was exercised as needed. Apart from British, French, and Dutch Guiana on the mainland of South America, British Honduras in Central America, and a few European-controlled islands in the Caribbean, the colonial presence of the Old World powers had been removed from the New World. Though European economic mastery of the South American continent below the American-dominated Caribbean basin persisted well into the twentieth century, that last remnant of European power in the Western Hemisphere was soon to disappear as well, a casualty of the Great War and its aftermath.

A Shrinking Earth and the Geopolitical World View

The projection of Western power all around the world in the closing decades of the nineteenth century was made possible by two technological innovations that revolutionized the way in which people and materials are moved across space. The first of these was the application of steam power to oceanic transport. Though the first steamship was constructed in 1802, it was not until the 1850s that the sailing ship disappeared from the merchant fleets and navies of the sea powers. Liberated from dependence on the vagaries of the wind and capable of previously unimaginable velocities, the steamship powered by coal enabled the industrial nations of Europe to extend their economic activity and project their military power to the previously inaccessible regions of the earth. The initial beneficiary of this technological revolution in oceanic transport was Great Britain, which by midcentury still possessed the most highly organized machine industry and the best supplies of anthracite coal. The problem of keeping the fleets supplied with fuel, which represented a potential constraint on Britain's ability to preserve its mastery of the seas, was solved by the acquisition of coaling bases across the globe. As will be presently seen, the search for refueling stations to accommodate battle fleets and merchant marines played its part in prompting the imperialist expansion of the late nineteenth century, when other aspirants to world power joined the naval race. The result was the transformation of previously formidable oceanic barriers into pathways for intercontinental relations. Warships steamed from base to base displaying the flag as a warning to recalcitrant natives or potential enemies, giving rise to the slogan of the age: gunboat diplomacy. Merchant vessels arrived at far-off ports laden with manufactured products and departed with tropical foodstuffs or raw materials for the return voyage.

The second such revolutionary innovation was the application of steam power to transportation on land. The invention of the railroad locomotive enabled the two gigantic continental nations, the United States and, later, the Russian Empire, to acquire effective political and economic control of the vast wildernesses to which they laid claim. It permitted the previously unified nations of Western Europe, especially Britain and France, to penetrate the interior of Africa from the coastal enclaves they had obtained in earlier centuries. The subjugation of the indigenous populations, the projection of political authority into interior regions, and the exploitation and extraction of economic resources therein, were all facilitated by the establishment of railway communication inland from the coasts.

Accompanying these innovations that revolutionized the manner in which men carried themselves, the products of their labor, and the fruits of the earth across land and sea was the invention of a device to permit the rapid transmission of the human voice across the airwaves above. With the telegraph and, later, the radio, came the ability to convey instructions and requests for information to and from the far-flung outposts of empire throughout the world. Foreign offices and their embassies, general staffs and their overseas commands, and private firms and their foreign branches acquired the capacity to maintain continuous communication with one another. This revolution in communications technology permitted a degree of centralized direction unheard of in the days when envoys, military commanders, and merchants on the spot were required to make extemporaneous policy decisions that often determined the outcome of diplomatic negotiations, wars, or contests for economic advantage.

The consequences of this technological "shrinkage of the earth" became dramatically apparent during the military operations conducted at the turn of the century. The railroad and the steamship rendered military forces more massive and more mobile. Gone were the long marches and risky sea voyages that depleted the strength of fighting men long before they reached the field of battle. Between 1899 and 1902, in an unprecedented projection of military power across the ocean, Great Britain maintained a quarter of a million soldiers at a distance of six thousand miles on the southern tip of Africa to subdue the army of the Boer Republic. In 1904, though with a less happy outcome, Russia conveyed an army of comparable size four thousand miles across the forbidding wastes of Siberia by rail to engage the Japanese forces in Manchuria. Such prodigious feats of strategic transport erased the traditional barriers of space and time that had preserved the isolation of the world's land masses from one another. The entire globe at the beginning of the twentieth century had become a single theater of strategic and economic interaction, knit together by the network of transportation and communication represented by the railroad, the steamship, and the telegraph.

In an effort to advance mankind's comprehension of this new global context of international relations, a new branch of the social sciences called "geopolitics" was established in the centers of higher learning in the Western world. To the extent that it represented a "scientific" (that is, objective) intellectual enterprise, the discipline of geopolitics combined the principles of geography and political science for the purpose of studying the distribution of political power across the surface of the globe. But, as has been the case with many social sciences, geopolitics forfeited its claim to scientific objectivity as its most reputable practitioners employed its teachings to form an ideological apologia for their own nations' right to expand and subjugate. To the geopoliticians, the entire earth represented an arena of acute rivalry in which the great powers struggled for control of economically valuable resources, territory, and populations. No square inch of land, no tiny island in the sea, no river, lake, or ocean was exempt from the operation of the iron law of geopolitics; given the uneven distribution of fertility, natural resources, and strategic opportunity in the world, the handful of nation-states capable of projecting their power beyond their own frontiers were locked in a worldwide contest for control of the unclaimed or indefensible regions of the earth.

It is no surprise that Imperial Germany produced the most detailed and comprehensive doctrine of geopolitics at the turn of the century, when that country's emerging interest in sea power combined with the traditional Prussian preoccupation with land power. In the writings of the German geopoliticians, the entire land mass of Eurasia from Spain to Siberia, from the northern Arctic wastes to the tip of the Indian subcontinent, constituted a vast terrain of land, raw materials, and population the control of which would determine the outcome of what they saw as the forthcoming contest for domination of the world. In light of Germany's superiority in terms of industrial organization and military power, and of Russia's advantage in terms of territory, population, and natural resources, it was understandable that these scholars confidently expected this approaching contest for world domination to take the form of an epic struggle between "Teuton" and "Slav" in the borderlands of Central and Eastern Europe, where Germanic and Slavic populations had intermingled over the centuries. To the underlying principle of German geopolitics—the definition of Eurasia as a geographical space to be filled by the political authority and military power of the strongest nation—was added the Malthusian doctrine of population pressure against food supply and the Social Darwinist concept of the competition of racial groups for survival in the uncongenial natural environment.

This witches' brew of geopolitics, demography, and pseudobiological determinism supplied the requisite intellectual justification for the expansion of German power eastward at the expense of Russia. Germany was an industrialized nation with a rapidly expanding population of racially superior stock cursed with an inadequate supply of foodstuffs and natural resources within its political frontiers. It therefore required additional space for internal migration as well as agricultural land and raw materials for the comfort, nourishment, and prosperity of its people. This space and this soil was ripe for the taking in the fertile plains to the east, which were populated by racially inferior peoples, mainly Slavs, who were deemed incapable of exploiting the potentially productive territory they occupied or of defending it from foreign invasion. Had such theories been confined to the lecture halls and scholarly journals of German universities, they might have represented little more than academic curiosities. But the fact that influential members of the political, economic, and military elite of Imperial Germany began to study them with interest between the turn of the century and the beginning of the First World War transformed them into prescriptions for a German drive for the domination of Eurasia.

The most formidable obstacle to this German geopolitical design was Great Britain, with its string of colonial holdings along the southern rimland of Eurasia and its naval domination of the adjacent seas. It was therefore appropriate that the seafaring people of this island produced the other great geopolitical tradition of the period. Halford Mackinder, in a seminal paper presented to the Royal Geographical Society in 1904, reflected the influence of German geopolitical thinkers such as Friedrich Rätzel while adding a few novel conceptions of his own. Entitled "The Geographical Pivot of History," this presentation extended the scope of geopolitical analysis to encompass the entire globe. The earth, according to Mackinder, was divisible into two regions: The "world island," comprising the interlinked continents of Europe, Asia, and Africa, was the largest, most populous, and richest of all possible land combinations. Arrayed along its periphery were the large insular groups—the Americas, Australia, Japan, and the British Isles. At the center of the world island lay what Mackinder designated as the "heartland," stretching from the Volga to the Yangtze and from the Himalayas to the Arctic. Protected from the menace of sea power by ice-floes to the north and rugged mountains and arid deserts to the south, this vast land surface was vulnerable to foreign invasion only on its western periphery, along the lengthy stretch of lowland connecting Western Europe to Russia. Effective political domination of this space by a single power had been precluded in times past because of the limitations of transportation: The periodic invasions from east to west and vice versa by horse-riding marauders, from the ferocious forays of Attila the Hun to Bonaparte's ill-fated march on Moscow, had failed to establish permanent control of this European gateway to the heartland because of the inability to assure continual supply of men and materiel.

But the invulnerability of the heartland of Eurasia to domination by a single power had been abolished, Mackinder believed, by the revolution in transportation cited earlier in this chapter. Now that Eurasia was about to be covered by a network of railways, he declared, a powerful continental nation stood an excellent chance of extending its political control over the Eastern European gateway as a prelude to its bid for mastery first of the Eurasian land mass and then of the entire globe: "Who rules east Europe commands the Heartland; who rules the Heartland commands the world-island; who rules the world-island commands the world." With this pithy dictum, Mackinder identified the geopolitical nightmare that was to haunt the world's two major sea powers during the first half of the new century—Great Britain and, subsequently, the United States. This nightmare was the prospect that the conquest of Eastern Europe by Germany or Russia would lead to the domination of the Eurasian land mass by a single great power as a prelude to its mastery of the world.

At the heart of Mackinder's doctrine were two axioms that underwent extensive criticism in subsequent years in light of later developments. The first of these was the assumption that, by virtue of the railroad, land power had definitively replaced sea power as the primary mechanism of world domination. The second was the assumption of the preeminent strategic importance of the Eastern Hemisphere (the world island) in the calculations of global power. Both assumptions discounted the potential role of the United States as a participant in the global struggle for empire that he envisioned. Mackinder had formulated his doctrine at a time when America was just beginning to emerge as a world power of the first rank after its victory in the Spanish-American War and its acquisition of the Spanish spoils in the Caribbean and the Pacific. For the first hundred years of its history as an independent nation, the United States was able to abstain from active involvement in the power struggles that transpired across the Atlantic. The advantages of geographical isolation from Europe, Great Britain's policy of using its naval control of the Atlantic to prevent the extension of great power rivalry to the Western Hemisphere, and the presence of weak states on its northern and southern frontiers enabled the American nation to direct its expansionist energies westward toward the Pacific. It is hardly surprising that this expansionist urge did not dissipate once the West was won. As we have seen, the hunger for land and resources that had inspired the conquest of a continent developed naturally toward the end of the century into an aspiration for empire in the Pacific and the Caribbean. In part this imperialist sentiment of the turn of the century was defensive in nature. The shrinkage of the world by the transportation revolution removed the geographical basis for isolation from world affairs just as the protective shield of British naval predominance began to disappear. As distant nations achieved the capability of projecting military power across the oceans in the form of heavily armed, coal-fired battle fleets, they were able to pose a grave menace to the United States, with its long, vulnerable coastlines. The necessity to divide its second-rank naval forces between two oceans and the difficulty of concentrating the two fleets in times of national emergency engendered a sense of vulnerability to attack by sea which stood in glaring contrast to the invincible power of the American nation on its own continent.

This sense of vulnerability to invasion by sea, along with the growing belief in the economic benefits of empire, indicated the need for a powerful American navy and a network of overseas bases and refueling stations to accommodate it. During the great age of imperialism, when Great Britain, France, and Germany acquired possessions abroad, the United States had seemed paralyzed in the posture of a passive observer while the great powers of Europe divided up the unclaimed spaces of the world and competed for control of its waterways.

The consequences of American inactivity during the age of imperialism were first drawn by the American naval strategist Alfred Thayer Mahan, whose book *The Influence of Sea Power Upon History*, published in 1890, supplied the inspiration for America's rise to world power. Writing before the advent of German, Japanese, and American naval power, when Britannia still ruled the waves, Mahan predicted that the new century would usher in developments that would revolutionize the naval balance of power. Huge naval armadas, supported by global networks of bases and refueling stations, would enable the industrialized nations to wage a pitiless struggle for world domination. Any nation caught without sufficient naval power and the capacity to project and sustain it across the seas would at best be consigned to second-rank status and at worst be exposed to foreign invasion. Mahan warned that his own nation was in just such a position and faced just such a risk. The American navy throughout the nineteenth century had been designed for defense of the American coast. The American navy of the future must represent, as the royal navy had for Great Britain, an instrument of policy to enhance the nation's power and prestige in the world.

The influence of Mahan's writings on his own country, either directly or through the mediation of his friends Theodore Roosevelt and Henry Cabot Lodge, is confirmed by the policies that signaled America's rise to the front rank of world powers: the acquisition of naval bases in the Pacific and the Caribbean, the construction of the Panama Canal, and the decision to build a battle fleet capable of operating on the high seas. But as important as Mahan's teachings may have been in promoting American imperialism and navalism at the turn of the century, they had an equally profound impact abroad, particularly in Germany. The Kaiser and his chief naval strategist, Admiral Alfred von Tirpitz, learned from Mahan not only the general truth that sea power was a prerequisite to national security and prosperity in the modern world but also that Great Britain's undisputed naval primacy was about to vanish. The rise of Japanese and American naval power in the 1890s confirmed this prediction by challenging British naval dominance in the Far East and the Western Hemisphere. Only by strengthening its overseas squadrons could Britain reverse this trend and regain its preeminent position abroad. But it was precisely at this moment that the advent of the German naval construction program threatened Britain's security in her home waters. This forced the Admiralty to deplete rather than augment its overseas naval strength in order to preserve control of the sea approaches to the British Isles.

From the subsequent testimony of its architects, we learn that Germany's turn toward navalism was intended to frighten Great Britain into entering into an alliance with Germany that would nullify the threat posed by the alliance concluded between France and Russia in 1894. Instead, it drove the British into the waiting arms of the French, who, as we have seen, renounced their old claims to Egypt in return for British cooperation against Germany in Europe. Thus, the new navalism at the turn of the century had the unintended effect of restoring, at least for the short term, the centrality of the European balance of power to the forefront of British strategic concerns. The simultaneous naval challenge of the United States and Japan was accepted with equanimity in London and resulted in the relatively painless depletion of British naval strength overseas. But the combination of Germany's existing military power on the continent and its potential naval power in European waters reminded British policymakers that the greatest menace to the security of their island lay across the North Sea.

The geopolitical conception of international relations, to which the governing elites of all the major nations subscribed by the beginning of the twentieth century, presupposed a global struggle for power that inevitably ran the risk of degenerating into a general war. The great powers were thus confronted with the challenge of devising a political mechanism for the peaceful resolution of the conflicts that were bound to arise in such an unstable international environment. The avoidance of a world war until the collapse of the international order in 1914 was to a large degree attributable to the universal desire to manage international conflict by diplomatic negotiation. The Berlin Conference of 1884–85 represented an instructive precedent for channeling of expansionist pressures in directions that would reduce the changes of great power confrontation. This gathering of representatives of the principal colonial powers succeeded in devising mutually acceptable ground rules for the European conquest of Africa that permitted each power to obtain its share so as to prevent the development of competing claims that might provoke war. Subsequently, as we have seen, bilateral arrangements were reached between France and England regarding territorial disputes in North Africa, and between England and Russia in southern Asia.

When diplomacy failed, multilateral intervention by third parties succeeded in limiting the geopolitical consequences of armed conflict. The Russo-Turkish War of 1877–78, the Sino-Japanese War of 1894–95, and the Russo-Japanese War of 1904–05 were all terminated before the victor could achieve its major objectives because of the diplomatic intervention of uninvolved powers. The traditional policy of international cooperation to preserve the balance of power in Europe was extended to the entire world in the era of imperial expansion. It reflected the powerful conviction among the ruling groups of the great powers that the prevention or at least the containment of war was essential to the preservation of the domestic and international order from which they derived their positions of power. This tacit agreement to avoid recourse to violence in the pursuit of national objectives in Europe remained in force until the summer of 1914. It dissolved at that time, as will be seen, because two of the European powers—Austria-Hungary and Russia—had come to consider the region of southern Europe where their ambitions collided—the Balkan peninsula—so vital to their national interests as to justify the risk of a general war, and because their two powerful allies—Germany and France, respectively—had developed powerful reasons of their own to favor a military showdown.

The Development of an International Economy

As the great powers sought to reduce the frictions caused by unorganized imperial expansion, a related challenge was posed by the growth of an international economic system which also demanded a high degree of cooperation among the major trading nations of the world. Throughout the first half of the nineteenth century, almost all economic activity was conducted either at the local level or (in those few countries such as Great Britain and France that had succeeded in abolishing internal impediments to economic exchange) on a nationwide scale. Where international trade did exist it was largely confined to distinct commercial regions defined by physical proximity (such as Western and Central Europe, Russia and the Baltic, and the North Atlantic) in which complementary economic systems permitted the direct exchange of products on a bilateral basis. Economic activity could not expand beyond this limited regional context until the two productive factors of economic development, labor and capital, were free to migrate to regions of the earth blessed with abundant natural resources, and until the goods produced by this combination of productive factors were afforded easy access to the markets of the world.

The end of the Napoleonic Wars in 1815 enabled Great Britain to concentrate its national energies on resuming the phenomenal industrial expansion that had begun in the last quarter of the eighteenth century. The restoration of peacetime conditions also promoted the growth of industrialization on the European continent as the governing elites of various states recognized the advantages of economic modernization and sought to emulate the successful British example. During the second half of the nineteenth century, the industrializing countries of Europe had begun to produce a surplus of labor and capital. In the meantime, certain undeveloped regions abroad, notably the continents of North and South America, the Pacific islands of Australia and New Zealand, and the temperate zone of southern Africa, combined the advantages of a rich endowment of natural resources with the disadvantages of an insufficient supply of labor and investment capital to exploit them. The elementary economic law of supply and demand dictated that European workers unable to obtain employment on their overpopulated continent should migrate to those underpopulated spaces with plentiful resources, cheap land, and high wages caused by domestic labor shortages. Similarly, European banks and private individuals whose accumulated savings could no longer command high interest rates at home because of the oversupply of domestic capital should have been enticed to invest abroad to obtain higher returns from the resource-rich, capital-poor areas cited above.

But attempts to expand commercial and financial activities in this economically rational way were frustrated by a combination of politically imposed constraints and technological deficiencies in transportation inherited from the preindustrial era. Tariffs, import quotas, subsidies for domestic industries, and restrictive shipping regulations inhibited the free exchange of products across national frontiers. The absence of a smoothly functioning international monetary system discouraged short-term financing of trade and long-term investment in productive enterprises abroad. The unavailability of cheap, reliable methods of transportation limited international migration of labor in search of employment.

These impediments to the free movement of labor seeking jobs, savings seeking high returns, and exports seeking markets gradually disappeared during the second half of the century. The advent of steamship and railway transportation around midcentury inaugurated a mass intercontinental and transcontinental migration unequaled before or since. Between 1861 and 1920 over forty-five million people left the grinding poverty of overpopulated Europe for the sparsely settled spaces across the seas. The United States received over half of this number, with the remainder going to other underpopulated areas of abundant natural resources and temperate climate such as Canada, Argentina, Brazil, Australia, New Zealand, and South Africa. Joining earlier emigrants who had pioneered the settlement of these virgin lands, successive generations of white Europeans transplanted the economic practices, social customs, and political traditions of the old world to the new. The indigenous inhabitants of the recently settled regions—the Indians and Eskimos of the Western Hemisphere, the aborigines of Australia, the Bushmen of South Africa—were geographically segregated and reduced to economic insignificance and political impotence.

Accompanying this migration of skilled and semiskilled European labor to resource-rich, underpopulated areas abroad during the second half of the nineteenth century was the infusion of European capital to the undercapitalized economies of these lands of recent European settlement. France joined Great Britain as a major source of foreign investment in the 1860s. The newly unified state of Germany entered the ranks of international creditors in the 1880s as its rapidly expanding economy began to generate profits in excess of domestic demand. On the whole, these long-term foreign investments in productive enterprises were concentrated either in the industrializing nations of Southern and Eastern Europe or in the overseas regions of abundant resources and white settlement enumerated above. The United States, originally the primary recipient of European capital investment during the early phase of its industrial revolution, began itself to export capital in the 1890s to developing economies within its own region. By 1914 roughly 40 percent of the total of American foreign investment was in Mexico and almost 30 percent in Canada, with most of the remainder distributed among Latin American countries along the shores of the Caribbean. Though the major proportion of these investments took the form of purchases of foreign government securities to finance the budget deficits of the recipient states, an increasing proportion supplied capital to construct what economists call the "infrastructure." By this is meant public facilities which developing economies require before modern industrial and agricultural systems can function effectively: roads, railroads, ports, power plants, telegraph and telephone systems, and the like. In this way European (and, later, American) investors furnished the capital and European immigrants supplied the skilled or semiskilled labor for the productive development of overseas regions with abundant but previously untapped natural resources.

As the obstacles to immigration and foreign investment began to disappear, so too did the politically inspired impediments to international trade. Here, as in all other areas of economic development in the nineteenth century, Great Britain led the way. The drastic reduction of protective duties on agricultural imports to England (the so-called Corn Laws) in 1846 was followed in 1860 by even more substantial tariff reform which eventually opened the British market to imports without restriction. In short order France, Belgium, Holland, and, later, Germany, reciprocally moderated their duties on imports. The result of this evolution toward free trade was twofold. First of all, it produced an extraordinary increase in the total volume of international commerce which far exceeded the record of any comparable period in history. Secondly, it stimulated the development of product specialization which in turn promoted the growth of world trade. The case of Great Britain provides a striking example of the increasing importance of specialization and the free international exchange of products.

Britain first learned the lesson that a nation could benefit from specializing in the production of those goods that were best suited to its domestic factor endowment, that is, by conserving its scarce (hence expensive) factors and drawing heavily on its abundant (hence cheap) ones. Instead of employing its surplus population and savings to grow high-cost wheat on its insufficient arable land, Britain took advantage of its abundant supply of labor and capital to produce manufactured goods which it sold to other countries with sufficient farmland in exchange for the food it required. Britain's exports and imports tripled in value during the second half of the nineteenth century. She began (after the introduction of refrigeration in the 1870s) to receive beef from Argentina, mutton and wool from Australia, dairy products from New Zealand, as well as a host of other raw materials—iron ore, tin, copper, lead, nickel, cotton, and the like—from abroad. In return, she shipped finished manufactured products, principally textiles, which accounted for half of her total exports in the year 1880. Though the performance of other industrialized nations was less spectacular, their increasing dependence on foreign trade for their prosperity became the central fact of economic life in the modern world.

The explosive growth of world trade and foreign investment in the second half of the nineteenth century was facilitated by the perfection of a mechanism of international financial exchange centered in London. Importers and exporters found it difficult to conduct their operations in the new environment of rapidly expanding international commerce on the basis of cash on delivery. In order to finance their worldwide commercial activities they increasingly resorted to the convenience of short-term borrowing from an emerging network of commercial banks, discount houses, and dealers in bills of exchange. This procedure permitted the exchange of products to transpire without large amounts of gold or currency having to move in either direction, since most transactions could simply be cleared against one another on the books of these London financial institutions. Meanwhile, the accumulation of huge reserves of capital in the major British banks soon impelled them, as we have seen, to branch out into the business of long-term lending to foreign governments and firms. The sale of treasury bonds, railroad stocks, and other foreign securities on the London money market effectively channeled the savings of the British and other European middle classes into the developing economies of the rest of the world.

But the greatest contribution of Great Britain to the smooth functioning of the international network of trade and investment was its effective solution to the problem of foreign exchange. Since each sovereign nation of the world printed its own currency, exporters who sold products abroad accumulated reserves of foreign money that obviously were of no use in discharging debts incurred at home. These exporters therefore required means whereby they could exchange the foreign currencies thus accumulated for an equivalent amount of their own. Conversely, importers had to find a way of paying for the products they purchased in the currency of the exporting country.

Throughout history, up to our own day, the major trading nations of the world have been frustrated in their attempts to establish an orderly relationship among their respective currencies in order to permit the easy exchange of goods across national frontiers. This persistent problem was effectively solved toward the end of the nineteenth century when the British pound sterling became a sort of world currency which all of the major trading nations used to settle their international accounts. Britain's preeminent position in world trade and finance inspired universal confidence in the strength and stability of sterling. It became in the eyes of importers and exporters of goods and capital as "good as gold." Furthermore, it was as "good as gold" in a very real sense. Between 1821 and 1914 the British government faithfully kept its promise to exchange quantities of that precious metal for its national currency at a fixed price. The convenience of dealing in a paper currency that was fully convertible into gold on demand at a predetermined price enticed exporters and importers of all nations to conduct their foreign transactions in sterling. By the early 1870s all of the major nations of Europe, the United States, and several Latin American countries had in turn adopted the gold standard by linking their own currencies to gold at a fixed price. The central banks of these nations were ready to sell all the gold demanded at that price and to buy up all the gold offered at that price. The result was a system among the major world currencies of fixed exchange rates that could not fluctuate because of their relationship to a metal in limited supply whose intrinsic value was universally recognized. Never before or since has the world enjoyed such an effective mechanism for the adjustment of international accounts. The twin evils of exchange instability and inflation, which were later to plague the modern world after the collapse of the gold standard, were nonexistent in this benign era.

Thus, toward the end of the nineteenth century, the international economic system had been tightly integrated by means of a complex network of foreign trade and investment centered in London. The universal adoption of the gold standard permitted the adjustment of temporary disturbances in the international balance of payments. British banks financed international trade and supplied investment capital to developing regions. The British merchant fleet transported more than three-quarters of the total volume of world trade. British insurance companies such as Lloyds of London removed the risk of oceanic transport. The consequent expansion of world trade and investment and the effective functioning of the international monetary system was destined to continue so long as Great Britain was able to retain its preeminent commercial and financial position in world markets. But once that virtual monopoly by a single power was contested, cracks in this seemingly perfect system began to appear. Though they did not fundamentally disturb the effective functioning of the system, they foreshadowed its demise. The first of these ominous developments was the simultaneous emergence of Germany and the United States as productive economic powers of the first rank.

In the middle of the nineteenth century Great Britain was the only industrial power of any importance. By 1914 Germany had surpassed Britain in the production of pig iron and approached her output of coal. The United States, which counted for little before the 1880s, experienced the most spectacular growth of all in the ensuing thirty years. By 1914 she was the world's leading producer of coal, and her pig iron production surpassed that of Great Britain and Germany combined. The destructive effects on Britain's loss of industrial preeminence were not immediately apparent for a number of reasons. First of all, America's enormous internal market absorbed most of its domestically produced manufactured goods. Moreover, that country's impressive agricultural productivity relieved it of the necessity to export finished products to pay for imports of food. As a consequence, America's export trade represented a paltry 8 percent of its gross national product in 1913. Those American goods that were produced in excess of domestic demand came largely from the fertile farmland of the Middle West that was afforded access to foreign markets by the railroad construction of the decade after the Civil War. In 1910 fully 75 percent of American exports fell under the category of agricultural produce or semifinished manufactures, and therefore were complementary to rather than competitive with British exports.

Germany, on the other hand, lacked both the huge internal free trade zone and the advantageous condition of self-sufficiency in foodstuffs enjoyed by the United States. She therefore was driven to seek foreign outlets for trade that threatened to produce an acute commercial rivalry with Great Britain. Moreover, by concentrating on the production of finished steel products, cotton textiles, coal, and chemicals, she competed directly with the products of British industrialism. But that competition was mitigated by a mutually beneficial division of world markets. Germany directed the bulk of its export trade to Eastern and Southern Europe, a region of minimal interest to British merchants, who were content to continue profiting from their lucrative commercial relationships with the Empire and with Latin America.

Even when Britain's exports of finished manufactured products failed to keep pace with her enormous imports of foodstuffs and raw materials, the resulting deficit in the balance of trade was easily covered by her "invisible exports." By this is meant income derived from investments overseas as well as from various services performed for foreign governments, corporations, or individuals, such as banking, insurance, and shipping. In short, Britain's virtual monopoly on the financial and service sectors of the modern world economy afforded her sufficient annual income to balance her international accounts and even reexport a surplus in the form of additional investment in foreign enterprises. But this dependence on invisible exports to preserve her balance-of-payments surplus concealed the ominous threat to Britain's preeminence in world trade posed by the burgeoning industrial systems of Germany and the United States. A nation whose share of the world's industrial production had dropped from 25 percent in 1860 to less than 10 percent in 1913 was unmistakably on the decline in relative terms. It was clearly only a matter of time before the internal market of the United States would become saturated with the products and profits of American industrialism and before aggressive German exporters of merchandise and capital would seek overseas markets in regions previously dominated by British commercial and financial interests. German and American commercial expansion was already in evidence by the turn of the century in Latin America, a traditional British preserve. To make matters worse, Russia and Japan had entered their industrial "takeoff" period in the 1890s and were expected to enter the world market in the not-so-distant future.

These threats to Britain's commercial supremacy were accompanied by the reappearance of political obstacles to international trade throughout the world. Germany had ended its brief experiment with free trade in 1879 by imposing duties on a variety of industrial and agricultural products. France followed suit in 1892. The United States raised its tariff in 1890 and again in 1897. Other European nations quickly fell in line, so that by the turn of the century only Great Britain and Holland remained committed to free trade amid this rising tide of protectionism. The resurgence of economic nationalism was a result of pressure exerted on their respective governments by domestic producers anxious to insulate their own economies from foreign competition in what was widely anticipated to be a forthcoming global contest for markets by the half dozen nations that had undergone the process of industrialization. It marked the first significant departure from the system of free exchange of productive factors upon which the new international economy of the nineteenth century depended for its survival. It foreshadowed the total collapse of the interlocked network of free trade, international finance, and intercontinental immigration, a collapse caused by the First World War.

PART ONE

The Thirty Years' War (1914–1945)

CHAPTER 1

Germany's Bid for European Dominance (1914–1918)

The period from 1914 to 1945 has often been designated as the Thirty Years' War of the twentieth century. No other period of comparable duration has seen so many people killed, so much property destroyed, and so much national wealth squandered for economically unproductive purposes. Though the land combat in the two world wars of this era was confined to the Eastern Hemisphere (principally on the land mass of Eurasia but also, on a reduced scale, in Africa), most of the nations of the Western Hemisphere were at some point drawn into the contest for mastery of the eastern half of the world. The so-called interwar period of the twenties and thirties can scarcely be regarded as an era of peace. It was instead, as the French military commander Ferdinand Foch presciently predicted at the end of the First World War, a "twenty-year truce" that was punctuated by explosions of national animosities, sporadic outbreaks of violence, and great power rivalries that paved the way for the Second World War. The central participant in this thirty-year struggle was the economically advanced, militarily powerful state of Germany. The two world wars were to a large extent the result of that nation's aspiration to achieve domination of the geographical region in which it was located and the determination of other great powers in coalition to prevent it from succeeding, by diplomatic pressure during peacetime and by military force in times of war.

In the course of the 1920s it became fashionable in certain intellectual circles to deny that the German Empire bore any responsibility for the outbreak of what at the time was universally known as the "Great War." Evidence from recently published diplomatic records was marshalled by scholars and publicists (not all of them German by any means) to demonstrate that French vindictiveness, or Russian imperialism, or British duplicity, or a combination of all three, had been responsible for dragging Germany into the contest for European hegemony that began in the summer of 1914. The image of the bloodthirsty Hun in spiked helmet and jackboots rampaging across a prostrate continent, so graphically portrayed by the wartime propaganda agencies of the Allied governments, gradually disappeared from the scene after the end of the war and the advent of the German republic in November 1918. In its place arose the contrary image of the peace-loving German who had sought nothing more than the defense of his legitimate national interests in the face of predatory powers from east and west.

It was not until the post–World War II period that this revisionist conception of Imperial Germany as victim was directly challenged by a school of historians that focused attention on the grandiose and expansionist war aims of the Imperial German government and its domestic supporters. The leader of this school was a distinguished German historian, Professor Fritz Fischer, who was able to demonstrate by exhaustive research and elegant argument that the political, military, and economic elite of the Second Reich had deliberately planned and relentlessly pursued an ambitious scheme to acquire direct or indirect control of the European continent as well as parts of the Middle East and central Africa. That the other principal belligerents, France, Great Britain, Russia, and Italy, also developed imperial ambitions of their own in the course of the war Fischer did not dispute. But what emerged from his study was a massive body of evidence of an aggressive program of economic expansion and territorial acquisition meticulously planned and actively promoted by influential members of the German ruling class from the late 1890s through the final year of the First World War. Though Fischer's work has undergone extensive criticism in recent years, its overall assessment of Germany's expansionist ambitions has (at least in the eyes of this historian) stood the test of time. Since the sources of this aggressive foreign policy are to be found in the interplay of domestic forces, a brief review of the political, economic, and military context of Imperial Germany's power position in the prewar years is in order.

The political structure of the German Reich, as defined by the federal constitution of 1871, may best be described as a facade of a parliamentary monarchy superimposed upon the edifice of an authoritarian state dominated by the reactionary, militarist, landowning aristocracy of Prussia. The hereditary position of German emperor was vested in the king of Prussia, who enjoyed the exclusive power to appoint and dismiss the head of government (the chancellor), to conduct foreign relations, to command the armed forces in time of war, to convoke and adjourn the bicameral parliament, and, through the chancellor, to initiate all domestic legislation. Prussian control of the upper house of the parliament (the Bundesrat) was preserved through a complex system of indirect and weighted representation together with the constitutional stipulation of a Prussian veto on legislation concerning military affairs. Even the lower house of the imperial legislature (the Reichstag), though elected by direct representation on the basis of universal male suffrage, was prevented from exercising the type of legislative authority associated with genuine parliamentary systems such as those of Great Britain and France. The head of government (the chancellor) was responsible to the emperor, while his cabinet ministers were responsible only to him. This meant that a government was free to remain in office without a legislative majority so long as it retained the confidence of the hereditary ruler.

The only significant power enjoyed by the democratically elected lower house was a negative one: It could deny the chancellor the funds required for the operation of the state. The periodic debates over requests for military appropriations, an issue dear to the heart of the Prussian landed elite which monopolized the senior positions in the armed forces, afforded the Reichstag its only opportunity to circumvent the elaborate constitutional limitations on the free expressions of the popular will. But the legislative record in the years before the First World War shows that the policies of successive German governments received the active or tacit support of the principal political parties of the nation. This was true not only of the Conservative Party, political mouthpiece of the Prussian landowning class (the Junkers) upon which the regime was based, but also of parties representing constituencies whose interests and ideology clashed with those of the Protestant, agrarian, military caste. The Center Party, vigilant defender of the rights of the Catholic minority located principally in the southern part of the country, had good reason to mount a campaign of resistance against the Protestant-dominated political apparatus in Berlin. So did the National Liberal Party, which represented the industrial and commercial bourgeoisie concentrated in the western part of the nation, whose commitment to political liberalism and economic modernization seemed antithetical to the reactionary, agrarian ideology of the Junkers. The Social Democratic Party, spearhead of social revolution on behalf of the industrial working class and opponent of militarism, constituted a potential source of violent opposition to the Prussian-dominated state. Yet none of these political parties mounted a sustained campaign against the authoritarian domestic structure and aggressive foreign policy of the Empire. The Center Party became a compliant servant of the imperial system once assured that the anticlerical campaign launched by Bismarck in the 1870s would not be revived and that the Catholics of the south would be free to practice their faith unhindered. The National Liberals sacrificed their democratic principles on the altar of class interest, accepting the undemocratic political institutions of the imperial state and supporting its expansionist foreign policy for economic reasons to be sketched below. The Social Democratic Party, which by 1912 had become the largest political faction in the Reichstag, represented the most numerous and best organized industrial working class in Europe. But the German workers had been transformed into loyal subjects of the Empire as a result of the progressive system of social insurance inaugurated by Bismarck in the 1880s. Its unprecedented provisions for medical insurance and old age pensions, followed in the 1890s by health and safety regulations in factories, afforded the German proletariat more economic benefits and better working conditions than those enjoyed by its counterparts in other industrial nations. It is therefore no surprise that the German Social Democratic Party ceased to take seriously the rhetoric of class conflict and evolved into a party of the loyal opposition, signaling its tacit acceptance of the undemocratic political system from which its working class constituency derived such extensive economic advantages.

The authoritarian political structure of Imperial Germany was reinforced by two striking features of the German economic system that sharply distinguished it from the economic systems of other industrialized nations. The first was the remarkable degree of cooperation between the agricultural interests centered in East Prussia and the industrial, commercial, and financial interests in the west. Whereas industrialization had been achieved in other countries (such as England) at the expense of the landowning class, the German industrial revolution was marked by a marriage of convenience between large-scale agriculture and heavy industry that promoted the expansion of the latter without threatening the socioeconomic position of the former. Both sectors of the German economic system campaigned for and benefited from the protectionist commercial policies inaugurated by the government in 1879. The agricultural estates of East Prussia were shielded from competition from Russian and American grain, while the heavy industry centered in the Rhineland-Westphalia region of the west secured the privilege of dominating the domestic market for manufactured products. This alliance of "rye and steel" saved the Prussian Junkers from the fate of the landed gentry in England, which had earlier been faced with the alternative of socioeconomic decline or accession to the industrial class through intermarriage or business partnership.

The second striking feature of the German economy at the turn of the century was the extent of its concentration and centralization. The key sectors of heavy industry (iron, steel, coal, armaments, chemicals, and electrical products) were dominated by a handful of gigantic firms that had acquired a degree of control over production and distribution unmatched in the industrial world of that time. The cartelization of heavy industry was actively promoted by the Imperial government through a wide range of public subsidies and protective legislation. At the same time, the German financial system was undergoing a similar process of concentration. By 1913 the four largest banking houses controlled 65 percent of the capital reserves of the nation and were closely linked to the oligopolistic industrial firms of the Rhineland-Westphalia complex through a system of interlocking directorates.

This formidable concentration of economic power, which united heavy industry, big agriculture, and high finance in a close partnership with the government, produced a spectacular spurt of economic growth in the quarter century before the First World War. A comparison with other industrial nations, as shown in Tables I and II, reveals that Germany had far

TABLE I   Pig Iron Production of the European Powers, 1870–1914
(In million tons)

	1870	*1880*	*1890*	*1900*	*1910*	*1914*
Germany	1.3	2.5	4.1	7.5	9.5	14.7
Austria-Hungary	0.4	0.5	0.7	1.5	2.0	2.0
France	1.2	1.7	2.0	2.7	4.0	4.6
Great Britain	6.0	7.8	8.0	9.0	10.0	11.0
Russia	0.4	0.4	0.9	2.9	3.0	3.6

TABLE II   Steel Production of the European Powers, 1870–1914
(In million tons)

	1870	*1880*	*1890*	*1900*	*1910*	*1914*
Germany	0.3	0.7	2.3	6.7	13.8	14.0
Austria-Hungary	—	—	0.5	1.2	2.2	2.7
France	0.3	0.4	0.7	1.6	3.4	3.5
Great Britain	0.7	1.3	3.6	5.0	5.9	6.5
Russia	—	—	0.4	1.5	3.5	4.1

Source for Tables I and II: A. J. P. Taylor, *The Struggle for Mastery in Europe, 1848–1918* (London: Oxford University Press, 1954), pp. xxix–xxx. Copyright 1954 Oxford University Press. Reprinted by permission.

outdistanced its continental rivals and had overtaken Great Britain as the most productive economic power in Europe. But the future of this economic dynamism seemed threatened by an ominous statistic: Between 1887 and 1912, while the value of German exports increased 185.4 percent per year, the value of German imports rose 243.8 percent. This dramatic surge in imports, which far surpassed that of any other industrial country, signified to the industrial magnates and their government patrons that German prosperity was becoming critically dependent on foreign sources of industrial raw materials and foodstuffs. Equally as disconcerting was the shift in the direction of Germany's foreign trade away from Europe and toward distant markets and sources of supply in the Southern Hemisphere.

These circumstances were not in themselves sufficient cause for alarm. After all, Great Britain had managed to prosper amid an even more pronounced dependence on imports from far-off lands by exporting her manufactured surpluses in exchange. Theoretically, Germany needed only to expand her exports of finished industrial products to cover her mounting trade deficit. But therein lay what many German industrialists feared was the insuperable limit to future economic growth. The markets of the world were being penetrated, dominated, and increasingly monopolized by the three global world powers: the United States in Latin America, Great Britain in East and South Africa and South Asia, and France in West Africa, the Balkans, and Russia. Soon the Russian and Japanese Empires could be expected to enter the competition for economic advantage in the Far East. Where could Germany turn for new sources of raw materials and foodstuffs as well as the markets for her manufactured products with which to pay for them?

Virtually every attempt to expand Germany's economic power beyond its traditional sphere of activity met with disappointment after the turn of the century. Efforts to penetrate the economies of North Africa, the Balkan states, and the Ottoman Empire encountered stiff competition from British and French firms that had previously obtained footholds there. In the two decades before 1914, France had become the principal source of capital investment for the fledgling nations of the Balkan peninsula as well as for the Russian Empire as it entered the first stage of industrialization. These financial relationships began to incite German fears of economic encircle-ment by Slavic states to the east and south bankrolled by the traditional Gallic enemy to the west. Even the Ottoman Empire, a prime object of German economic ambition since the turn of the century, had begun to re-ceive massive infusions of British and French capital, in the form of both government loans and direct investments in the oil fields of Mesopotamia. The fear of economic encirclement in Europe and the Middle East was heightened by ominous indications that the remainder of the world was being informally partitioned into spheres of economic interest by Great Britain, France, the United States, and Japan.

This concern about the limits to German economic growth coincided with the mounting apprehension in military circles about the undeniable fact that the German Empire was losing its margin of strategic superiority in Europe over the combined armed forces of France and Russia. The Franco-Russian alliance of 1894 had imposed upon German strategic plan-ners the heavy burden that Bismarck's diplomacy had successfully avoided, namely, that of having to contemplate the possibility of a war on two fronts. With France and Russia committed to defend each other against a German military attack, the necessity to divide Germany's forces between east and west seemed to preclude the type of rapid breakthrough that had been achieved against France in 1870. Count Alfred von Schlieffen, chief of the imperial general staff from 1892 to 1906, had devised a war plan that purported to overcome the strategic disadvantage caused by the Franco-Russian alliance. It envisioned the concentration of German mili-tary power in the west in the expectation that the numerically inferior French army could be defeated within a six-week period, after which the bulk of the German forces could be transferred to the eastern front to meet the Russian army before it could penetrate Germany's denuded east-ern defenses. The Schlieffen Plan rested on two critical assumptions. The first was the preservation of overwhelming German numerical superiority against France. The second was the inability of the Russian Empire, with its primitive system of land transportation, to deploy its numerically supe-rior army along the German frontier before the knockout blow in the west.

To the consternation of German military strategists, both of these assumptions were undermined by developments in the years before 1914. In 1913 France extended the period of national military service from two to three years. This meant that, despite its stationary population, France would be able to field a front-line army equal to the size of the German army by 1915 or 1916. In the meantime, the Russian government had launched, with French financial assistance, an ambitious program of strategic railway construction linking central Russia with the western frontier. Since the peacetime size of the Russian army exceeded that of the German and Austro-Hungarian armies combined, the possibility that at some future date this mass military force could be rapidly transported to the German border undermined the strategic assumptions of the Schlieffen Plan and caused considerable anxiety among military circles in Berlin.

It was but a short step from this apprehension of economic encirclement and military vulnerability to the advocacy of preventive war. The temptation of a quick, surgical strike against France in the manner of 1870 was reinforced by the conviction that a delay of two or three years might prove fatal to Germany's preeminent position in Europe. With France and Russia removed as counterweights to Germany on the continent, she could proceed to rearrange the balance of power to suit her military and economic requirements. The cause of economic expansion and preemptive war received strong support from numerous pressure groups in German society that represented a wide range of socioeconomic and professional interests. The officers' corps of the army, in conjunction with expansionist-minded civilians in the Pan-German League, pressed for territorial annexations that would simultaneously remove the strategic menace of France and Russia. The upper echelons of the navy, supported by the propagandistic activities of the Navy League, advocated the construction of a fleet equal to Great Britain's and the acquisition of bases and coaling stations abroad. The interlocked interests of heavy industry and high finance encouraged the government to obtain, by diplomatic pressure if possible or military means if necessary, privileged access to the resources and markets of the continent that the German economy required to sustain its dynamic growth.

Amid this atmosphere of fear mingled with ambition, the long-simmering dispute between Germany's ally Austria-Hungary and the independent Balkan kingdom of Serbia boiled over in the summer of 1914 in such a way as to furnish the Reich with its most promising opportunity for a preventive war against France and Russia. On June 28 the heir to the Habsburg throne, Archduke Franz Ferdinand, was assassinated while attending military maneuvers in the city of Sarajevo, the capital of one of the two former Turkish provinces in the Balkans that had been occupied militarily by Austria-Hungary in 1878 and then annexed outright in 1908. The absorption of this region by the Germanic empire to the north had incited the violent opposition not only of its Slavic inhabitants but also of their ethnic kin across the frontier who dreamed of a Greater Serbia that would include the two annexed provinces. The precise details of the conspiracy that led to the death of the Archduke and his wife, including the complicity of the chief of Serbian military intelligence and the foreknowledge of the Prime Minister in Belgrade, were not revealed until long after the event and therefore had no bearing on the decisions that were promptly taken by the Austro-Hungarian government in response to it. All that was known for certain at the time was that the assassins were ethnic Serbs and that they had committed their crime in the hotbed of Pan-Slavist sentiment within the Habsburg Empire. The immediate significance of the episode was that it afforded the authorities in Vienna a convenient pretext for suppressing once and for all this menace to the cohesion of that empire by striking at the adjacent state that assisted and promoted it.

It was well known to the German government that an Austro-Hungarian military operation against Serbia was almost certain to provoke the intervention of Russia on behalf of its Slavic protégé in Southern Europe. Russia had already suffered a major blow to its power and prestige in the Balkans by acquiescing in the Austrian annexation in 1908 of the two former Turkish provinces that had been earmarked by Pan-Serb enthusiasts for inclusion in a large south Slav state ruled from Belgrade. No one expected a repetition of such inaction on Russia's part while the Habsburg Empire consolidated its control of the Balkans by annihilating the only pro-Russian Slavic state in the region. It was likewise probable that a war between Austria-Hungary and Russia would set in motion the provisions of the competing alliance systems to which those two empires belonged and therefore bring the entire continent to the brink of armed conflict. With full appreciation of these likely consequences, Berlin deliberately encouraged Vienna to issue a humiliating ultimatum to Belgrade on July 23 concerning the investigation of the assassination that the Serbian government could not accept in its entirety without sacrificing its sovereign status. Moreover, the German government assured the Austrian government of its unqualified support in the event of hostilities, and then proceeded to sabotage the efforts of the British government to mediate this bilateral, regional dispute. The expiration of the ultimatum led to an Austrian declaration of war against Serbia on July 28, which in turn provoked the expected decision in Saint Petersburg for a partial Russian mobilization against Austria the following day. But the Tsar and his political entourage soon learned that the Russian general staff had no operational plan for a limited mobilization against Austria alone, believing as it did that a war with one of the Germanic empires would inevitably involve the other. Hence, the Tsar was induced to authorize a full mobilization on July 30 as a precautionary step to protect Russia's frontier with Germany during the forthcoming showdown with Austria. Here was the first instance of military planning and preparation constraining the decision-making authority of the civilian leadership during the crisis. The second was to come when the German high command reminded the government in Berlin that a war against Russia alone was precluded by the German war plan, which dictated an offensive against France to remove it from the war prior to the concentration of German forces in the east against Russia. Hence, an ultimatum was issued from Berlin to Paris which, like the earlier one from Vienna to Belgrade, was designed by its blatantly unacceptable provisions to serve as the pretext for war: France was required to affirm its absolute neutrality in the forthcoming Russo-German war and to transfer to Germany's temporary custody the border fortresses of Toul and Verdun as proof of good faith. In short, as the Balkan dispute degenerated into a war involving most of Europe at the end of July 1914, officials in Berlin did what they could to ensure that this opportunity for a preventive showdown with France and Russia would not be lost. Germany stood an excellent chance of defeating the combined forces of its two adversaries at the opposite ends of Europe in its present state of military superiority. In two or three years, that advantage might very well be lost.

The possibility of British intervention on the side of France and Russia in the impending war on the continent was discounted in Berlin. Some German officials entertained the naive hope that if the Tsar could be induced to mobilize his army first (as indeed he did), British public opinion would refuse to assist what could be made to appear as a Russian war of aggression. More realistic observers knew that the German war plan in the west, which presupposed the invasion of France through the rolling hills of Belgium, would precipitate Britain's entry in the war. This assessment was not based on Britain's commitment to the preservation of Belgian neutrality codified in a treaty of 1839. Such obligations could be conveniently renounced in the name of national interest, as Germany, also a guarantor of Belgian neutrality, promptly proved. Britain's intervention was foreordained because of its long-standing policy of refusing to permit any hostile power to obtain control of the opposite coast of the English Channel as a potential springboard for an invasion of the British Isles. The likelihood of British intervention was accepted with equanimity by Germany because of the universal expectation of a war of brief duration, as in 1870. Britain's naval superiority was useless to prevent the German military conquest of France in the six-week campaign projected by the Schlieffen Plan. The small British professional army of 150,000 counted for nothing against the 1.5 million German conscripts that were to be hurled against France. After the lightning victory against France and the removal of British forces from the continent, Germany would be free to concentrate on destroying Russian military power in Eastern Europe. Britain, with whom Germany had no serious quarrel, could then be offered a separate peace that would confirm German dominance of the continent.

As all of the great powers of Europe except Italy* entered the war in

---

* Italy renounced her treaty obligations to Germany and Austria-Hungary under the Triple Alliance on the grounds that the two Germanic empires had become engaged in an offensive rather than a defensive war.

ICELAND

NORWAY

SWEDEN

FINLAND

GREAT
BRITAIN

DENMARK

NETHER-
LANDS

IRELAND

RUSSIA

ATLANTIC

OCEAN

BELG.

GERMANY

FRANCE

SWITZ.

AUSTRIA-
HUNGARY

ROMANIA

Black Sea

SERBIA

BULGARIA

ALBANIA

ITALY

PORTUGAL

SPAIN

OTTOMAN   EMPIRE

GREECE

Mediterranean   Sea

Anti-German
Coalition
Germany
and its Allies

Italy, though a member of the German Alliance System,
remained neutral at the beginning of the war and
joined the Anti-German Coalition in 1915.

Europe in the First World War

the first few days of August, the governments of the belligerent states began to develop and articulate their respective war aims. The first government to define in considerable detail the concrete objectives it expected to achieve by military victory was that of Germany. Chancellor Theobold von Bethmann-Hollweg strove to mobilize a broadly based domestic consensus in support of the war effort by establishing a persuasive justification for his government's decision to resort to force. This was particularly necessary in the context of the German political situation in 1914. As noted earlier, the Social Democratic Party, led by persistent critics of military expenditures and advocates of international cooperation, had become the strongest party in the Reichstag by 1912; the Socialist trade unions constituted the largest mass political organization in Imperial Germany. In order to forestall left-wing parliamentary opposition to military appropriations and labor agitation against the mobilization decrees, the government was confronted with the necessity of converting the Social Democrats and the union organizations they represented to the cause of war. It was widely known that the German Left was prepared to oppose any attempt to transform the forthcoming conflict into a war of conquest. Thus the Socialist leaders were persuaded to support the war effort as a "defensive" operation against the imperialist aggression of Tsarist Russia. On August 4 the Social Democrats joined the other political parties in declaring a "party truce" in the Reichstag. Unity on the home front was thus ensured at the very beginning of the war.

Once the support of all political parties for the German war effort was secured, the government's public references to a "defensive war" to prevent "encirclement" receded into the background; in their place appeared talk about the necessity to obtain "guarantees" against future military aggression and economic competition on the continent. In this way the defensive rhetoric, intended to allay the suspicions of the German Left and neutralize domestic opposition, rapidly evolved into an ambitious project for continental domination. The German government's war aims were first specified in a statement by Chancellor Bethmann-Hollweg on September 9, 1914. In spite of several temporary deviations and modifications in the course of the war, this "September Program" remained the basis of German military objectives until the Bolshevik revolution and the subsequent withdrawal of Russia from the war. Thenceforth it was extended to embrace an even more grandiose scheme of German military and economic expansion that had been devised by German economic interests at the beginning of the war.

The September Program of the German government sketched the nation's military and economic war aims during the period of great optimism, as the German army seemed on the verge of overwhelming the Anglo-French defenses in the west. The military plan called for the permanent destruction of French military power through the annexation of the territory containing France's principal fortresses along the German frontier, the occupation of France's major ports on the English Channel, and imposition of a crushing financial indemnity that would prevent the reconstruction of France's armed forces in the foreseeable future. Belgium would be compelled to cede her strategic fortresses and permit the establishment of German bases on the Flanders coast (which, in conjunction with the French Channel ports, would constitute a formidable barrier to the reintroduction of British military power on the continent). Once such a punitive peace was imposed upon France and Belgium, Russia was to be systematically "thrust back as far as possible from Germany's eastern frontier and her domination over the non-Russian peoples broken." The removal of France from the ranks of the great powers, the exclusion of Great Britain from continental affairs, and the thrusting back of Russia would definitively establish Imperial Germany as the hegemonic power of Europe. France was then to be offered a pact of mutual cooperation; Great Britain would be given the choice of withdrawing from the war or enduring air attacks launched from ports on the French and Belgian coast.

Closely linked to this military plan for German hegemony in Europe was a project for continental economic domination developed by a group of German bankers and industrialists headed by Walther Rathenau (a leading figure in the electrical industry cartel) and Arthur von Gwinner (director of the Deutsche Bank). These spokesmen for German heavy industry and high finance were motivated by the fear that their country was destined to suffer economic decline unless it obtained control of the resources and markets of the entire continent of Europe to match the gigantic economic blocs of the United States (with Latin America), the British Empire, and the Russian colossus to the east. The recommended method for forging a German-controlled continental bloc was the establishment of "Mitteleuropa." This loosely defined term denoted a total customs union between Germany and the Austro-Hungarian Empire, the annexation of the French iron fields in the Longwy-Briey region of Lorraine, the economic absorption of Belgium and Luxemburg, and the eventual establishment of a European common market through customs treaties linking the German–Austro-Hungarian bloc to France, Italy, Belgium, Holland, Denmark, and such other independent European states as would wish to adhere.

The principal objective of these spokesmen for German heavy industry was the rectification of the potentially serious economic problem of insufficient supplies of industrial raw materials, particularly those required for the production of steel. Though blessed with sufficient quantities of high-grade coking coal located in the Ruhr and Upper Silesia, Germany's prewar steel industry had become heavily dependent on the iron ore of French Lorraine directly across the border. Had the German armies failed to seize and operate the Lorraine iron fields during the war it is likely that the German war machine would have ground to a halt for lack of adequate supplies of armaments and munitions. In 1914 German iron ore reserves totaled 2,300 million tons compared to France's 8,200 million tons (of which 2,755 million were located to the adjacent sector of French Lorraine). Thus, the annexation of the French ore fields would have doubled Germany's iron reserves, according her self-sufficiency while severely weakening the French iron and steel industry as a potential competitor in the postwar period.

Other regions offered tempting targets as well. The representatives of German heavy industry advocated the acquisition of the ore fields of Belgium and control of the coal, iron, manganese, oil, and grain of Poland and southern Russia. The economic value of Belgium and a reconstituted Poland coincided with their strategic value as barriers to Anglo-French military power in the west and Russian military power in the east. Plans for the disposition of Belgium varied from outright annexation to military occupation of strategic fortresses and ports, control of the transportation system, customs and currency union with Germany, and administrative partition into Dutch-speaking Flanders and French-speaking Wallonia. The plan to resurrect Poland as a German client state in the east was complicated, however, by the existence of a substantial Polish population in the German territories of Posen and West Prussia that would be potentially susceptible to the attraction of a reconstituted Polish state. In the eyes of some planners, that problem could best be resolved by deporting the Poles (including the Polish Jews) from the German to the Russian sector and replacing them with German colonists who would establish a "frontier strip" to secure Germany's eastern barrier against the Slavs.

With the failure of the German war plan in the autumn of 1914 came the realization that these ambitious military and economic objectives were unlikely to be achieved by force of arms alone in the foreseeable future. The intervention of Britain and the successful defense of Paris, together with the unexpectedly rapid mobilization of the Russian army in the east, produced a stationary front and the prospect of a long, drawn-out war of attrition. The unprecedented firepower supplied by the machine gun and the heavy artillery piece totally transformed the nature of warfare. The belligerents were compelled to forsake whatever expectations of speedy victory that they had entertained. The infantry forces were issued the only mechanism with which they could escape the murderous barrage of firepower: the trenching spade. By Christmas, 1914, the wasteland of northern France and Belgium was honeycombed with an interlocking network of underground trenches stretching from the Swiss border to the English Channel. Though the war in the east was marked by greater mobility and more frequent exchanges of territory, it too bogged down into a stalemate by the onset of the winter snows.

The Domestic Consequences of Total War

The truism that "generals tend to fight the last war" applies equally to their civilian superiors, and should come as no surprise in the case of those in authority during the Great War. The generation of military and political leaders who supervised their respective nations' war effort in 1914 had reached maturity during a half-century of European peace. The wars of recent memory were those fought in conjunction with the political unification of Italy and Germany between 1859 and 1871. These had been brief, mobile engagements with limited political objectives whose outcome had been determined by such short-term, technical factors as tactical finesse and the efficiency of mobilization and troop transport. These conflicts had lasted for no more than a few months and required only minimal disruption of civilian life behind the lines. Under the sway of this historical experience, none of the leadership groups of the belligerent states in the First World War had thought it necessary to devise plans for sustaining a conflict of long duration. But the establishment of the stationary fronts in the autumn of 1914 had produced an entirely novel type of warfare. The clash of armies in the field was rapidly overshadowed by an epic confrontation of whole peoples. It became the first total war in history, when events at the battlefront were directly experienced by the civilian population, giving rise to the term "home front." The challenge of mobilizing the human and material resources of entire societies caused a revolutionary transformation in the domestic institutions of the belligerent nations.

The most fundamental domestic transformation wrought by the advent of total war was the centralization and regimentation of economic activity. It had rapidly dawned on the ruling elites of Europe that the successful prosecution of a war of indefinite duration would require the production and distribution of war-related materials on an unprecedented scale. All of the combatant nations experienced a severe shortage of munitions and the inability to produce sufficient quantities of artillery shells to meet the demand. The conscription of farmers and agricultural laborers caused a serious decline in food production. The imposition of the British naval blockade disrupted the Central Powers' access to foreign sources of foodstuffs and raw materials. The German occupation of France's most productive industrial region deprived that nation of vital resources and factories. The closing of the Dardanelles by Germany's ally, Turkey, curtailed Russia's ability to import essential materials from foreign suppliers. When the private sector of the economy proved incapable of resolving the impending supply crisis, governments proceeded to acquire extensive control over all branches of production and distribution related to the war effort. Requisitioning of vital resources and transport facilities, the passage of laws forbidding the production of luxury items, the promotion of substitutes and synthetics, the rationing of food and fuel, and the control of foreign trade all constituted unprecedented intrusions of state power in industrial, agricultural, and commercial affairs. The prospect of labor shortages and social unrest prompted the passage of legislation severely restricting labor union activity and authorizing longer working hours and the employment of women and unskilled workers in the war plants.

With the mobilization of domestic production and manpower came the mobilization of capital. Stringent controls of foreign exchange transactions were imposed to stem the flow of domestic capital abroad. Increased taxation and the domestic sale of treasury securities failed to meet the ever-expanding capital requirements of the wartime economies. The growing dependence on foreign sources of raw materials and foodstuffs impelled the governments of France and Britain to borrow the securities of foreign governments and private corporations held by their citizens. They then re-sold these securities on the open market and used the proceeds to purchase essential products in neutral countries such as the United States, Switzerland, and Scandinavian and Latin American nations.

Such regimentation abruptly removed the relatively liberal conditions of economic intercourse that had governed the prewar era. No longer did individual citizens enjoy the freedom to sell their labor and services to the highest bidder or to invest their savings how and where they pleased. No longer could businesses import or export products according to their commercial requirements. The wartime needs of the state replaced the marketplace as the mechanism for the allocation of scarce resources, labor, and capital. The prospect of a seemingly interminable war fought by mechanized forces placed a premium on economic organization: Ultimate victory would come to those nations capable of mobilizing and deploying the greatest amount of human and material resources in the most efficient manner.

The periodic attempts to achieve a decisive breakthrough in the land war merely confirmed the futility of hurling unarmored human flesh against the devastating firepower of the machine gun and heavy artillery. The casualty figures of the abortive offensives reached almost suicidal proportions: In the battle of the Somme from July 1 to November 18, 1916, the Germans and British lost 400,000 each and the French 200,000. The reward for the combined Anglo-French casualties of over 600,000 was a maximum advance of about seven miles. In the same year the Germans conducted a ten-month siege of the French fortress at Verdun at a cost of 336,000 men while the French army's successful defense was paid for with 350,000 lives. At Passchendaele in 1917 over 370,000 British soldiers perished in order to gain forty-five square miles of mud and shell holes.

To meet the challenge to offensive warfare posed by the machine gun, both sides sought technological breakthroughs to restore mobility to firepower. The airplane, successfully tested in the United States ten years earlier and first employed in warfare by the Italians against the Turks in 1911, was originally limited to observation use. Neither side interfered with the reconnaissance flights of the other until it became evident that the information thus obtained was of considerable use to the armies facing each other below. Thereafter machine guns were mounted in the observer's cockpit to enable each side to destroy the planes used by the other. When the Dutch aerial engineer Anthony Fokker designed for the Germans an interrupter gear, which synchronized machine gun fire with the propeller so that bullets could avoid the blades, airplanes became deadly gun platforms and the fighter plane was born. But aside from adding a dash of heroism and glamour to the dreary, slogging land war, the aerial duels had no effect on the outcome of the struggle. Even the German bombing raids of Great Britain, which resulted in 1,300 deaths and 3,000 injuries as well as considerable material damage, paled in comparison to the damage wrought to men and property by the guns on land. The smallness of the planes and the inaccuracy of the bombs prevented aerial warfare from breaking the stalemate.

The technological instrument that finally restored the advantage to the offensive by challenging the supremacy of the stationary machine gun was masterminded by a British colonel named Ernest Swinton. His idea for ensuring the mobility of the machine gun in difficult terrain and the protection of its operator against enemy fire consisted of mounting it on caterpillar tractors that had been used to tow heavy artillery behind the lines and armoring them for offensive action. Once adopted and put into use by the British army, the tank (as the strange-looking contraption was called) revolutionized land warfare and gave the Western allies the wherewithal to penetrate the stationary lines of the enemy. But in spite of great success in the first major use of tanks by the British during the Battle of Cambrai in November 1917, lack of imagination kept the allies from fully exploiting their new weapon to the fullest extent possible. It was only at the time of the dying gasp of the final German offensive in August 1918 that the efficacy of the tank was demonstrated beyond all doubt, as the British Fourth Army used 450 of the new machines to pierce the German defenses near Amiens as part of the Allied counteroffensive that brought the war to an end.

The senseless carnage on the battlefield, together with the economic hardship endured by the civilian populations, severely tested the morale of the belligerent nations. With the prospect of victory fading further into the future, the wartime governments were obliged to devise means of persuading their own citizens that the sacrifice was worthwhile and those in the enemy camp that it was not. The maintenance of morale at home necessitated the suppression of domestic political criticism of the war effort. Accordingly, the Russian Tsar suspended the Duma for the duration of the war in September 1915. In Germany the Political Bureau of the General Staff established a virtual military dictatorship. By 1917 Prime Minister David Lloyd George in England and Premier Georges Clemenceau in France had acquired emergency powers unprecedented in parliamentary regimes, governing through war cabinets in utmost secrecy. The limitation on legislative checks on executive authority was accompanied by measures to forestall opposition from press and people. Censorship of newspapers and periodicals prevented the expression of antiwar sentiment and the publication of accurate casualty figures. People suspected of being

enemy sympathizers as well as those refusing military conscription on con-
scientious grounds were interned or otherwise subjected to limitations on
their civil liberties.

The conduct of political warfare behind enemy lines began early in the
war as a deliberate policy of the German government. The presence of
large numbers of discontented ethnic, religious, and social groups within
the British, French, and Russian empires seemed to offer a tempting target
for German propaganda. The principal objects of this strategy were the
Islamic populations of North Africa, Egypt, India, and southern Russia.
The German emperor's Damascus speech in 1898 had established his credentials as the "protector" of the 300 million Moslems of the earth. The
military alliance between Germany and Turkey signed on August 2, 1914,
resulted in the proclamation by the Ottoman sultan (in his capacity of ca-
liph, or Moslem religious leader) of a jihad, or holy war, which enjoined
the followers of Mohammed to rise up in rebellion against their Christian
European masters. German financial subsidies flowed into the coffers of
Islamic nationalist movements opposed to the rule of London, Paris, and
Petrograd. Similar campaigns were mounted by the German government
to foment insurrection among the non-Russian Christian peoples of the
tsarist empire. Emigrés from Russian Poland, Finland, the Ukraine, Georgia, and Armenia received subsidies and encouragement from German officials for their movements of "national liberation" against Russian oppression. At the same time, the German government established contact
with and supplied funds to various revolutionary Russian emigré groups in
Switzerland and Scandinavia. Foremost among these was the Russian Social Democratic party, which alone among the major working class parties
of Europe had actively opposed its government's war effort from the start
and continued to press for social revolution at home.

The object of the German government's multifaceted propaganda campaign was twofold: to pin down British, French, and Russian military
forces in counterinsurgency operations behind the lines, and to acquire a
reputation (both in neutral countries such as the United States and among
progressive forces in the enemy camp) as the protector of "oppressed
peoples" and the champion of the right of national and political self-
determination. Throughout the first three years of the war, these German
efforts to incite domestic insurrection in the empires of the Entente powers were uniformly unsuccessful. The abortive "Easter Rebellion" in Ireland of 1916, in which a conspirator financed and transported to that island by German agents played a major role, was the closest Berlin came to
success in its campaign of political warfare.

Germany's dual strategy of forming a continental economic-military
bloc controlled from Berlin while promoting the disintegration of the British, French, and Russian empires provoked a series of similar countermeasures from the governments of the Triple Entente. Indeed, it is important
to note, as many critics of the Fischer thesis concerning Germany's war

aims cited at the beginning of this chapter have reminded us, that the member states of the anti-German coalition promptly developed war aims of their own that equaled Germany's in their grandiosity and aggressiveness. In the realm of foreign economic policy, the Allied governments formulated plans for the continuation of inter-Allied economic cooperation after the war in order to shatter the economic foundations of the Central Powers. Just as this economic strategy represented a competitive response to the German Mitteleuropa project, the political strategy of the Entente constituted the reverse side of the German campaign on behalf of revolution behind enemy lines. Great Britain concentrated on inciting an Arab-Moslem revolution within the Turkish Empire; France directed her political warfare campaign at the national groups languishing under Austro-Hungarian rule (principally the Czechs, the Poles, and the southern Slavs of the Balkan peninsula); even Russia paid lip service to the cause of national self-determination by offering independence to Poland under Russian protection in an effort to win the sympathy of the Polish populations of Austrian Galicia and German Posen and West Prussia.

The Entente project for economic warfare against the Central Powers was broached at the Paris Economic Conference held in June 1916. Representatives of Britain, France, Italy, Russia, Belgium, Portugal, and Japan met to discuss ways of giving permanent form to the measures of inter-Allied economic cooperation that had been adopted during the war. The French and British delegations pressed for the creation of an inter-Allied economic bloc linked by preferential tariffs, the pooling of raw materials and shipping, and joint management of financial and currency affairs. Though the resolutions adopted at the Paris Conference fell considerably short of Anglo-French expectations on account of the hesitations of Italy and Russia, they elicited sharp reactions in enemy and neutral countries. The Paris Accords seemed to signify the definitive end of the era of free trade and the beginning of an effort by the anti-German coalition to subdivide most of the world into politically organized regional markets and zones of raw materials. An economic bloc linking the British, French, Russian, Italian, Belgian, Portuguese, and Japanese empires would have sealed off virtually the entirety of Africa and Asia as well as most of Europe from economic competition from the Central Powers and neutral countries such as the United States. Germany would thereupon encounter a form of economic strangulation far worse than the "encirclement" that had allegedly threatened her before 1914.

Linked to this Entente objective of economic warfare against the Central Powers and their allies was the political strategy of inciting nationalist revolution within the states of the German coalition. The first victim of this policy was the Ottoman Empire, whose contribution to the German war effort had been much more valuable than anticipated: The closing of the Turkish Straits had sealed off Russia from her European allies; the Anglo-French effort to force Turkey out of the war in the Dardenelles expedition of 1915 was a costly failure. Turkish pressure on Egypt diverted British forces that might have been deployed elsewhere. But the sultan's appeal for an Islamic holy war against the European nations had failed to rouse his Arab subjects, for whom hatred of Turkish overlordship surpassed in intensity the historic grievance against the Christian West. The Arabs' reluctance to join their Turkish coreligionists afforded the British a promising opportunity to solicit their support for the Allied cause. Negotiations were opened with Hussein, Grand Sharif of Mecca, the most obvious candidate to contest the Ottoman sultan's authority in the Arab world. The results of these discussions were incorporated in correspondence between the Sharif Hussein and the British High Commissioner in Egypt, Sir Henry McMahon, between July 1915 and February 1916. The British government pledged its support for the independence of most of the Arab provinces of the Ottoman Empire in exchange for the declaration of an Arab revolt against Turkish rule. On June 10, 1916, Hussein raised the Arabs in rebellion and was soon joined by various chieftains on the Arabian peninsula. The Arab insurrection pinned down some 30,000 Turkish troops and helped to keep the Red Sea open to Allied shipping. The British military advance from Egypt to Palestine and Syria in 1917–1918 was greatly assisted by guerilla operations against the Turks mounted by Arab contingents in contact with British officers such as the legendary T. E. Lawrence. As will be seen, British support of Arab nationalism was compromised by agreements concluded with rival claimants to Turkish territory. But for the remainder of the war the strategy was effective in curtailing the Ottoman Empire's capacity to fulfill its obligations to its Germanic allies.

In the meantime the Western powers also used their weapons of political warfare to promote nationalist rebellion within the Austro-Hungarian Empire. This policy was initially developed in response to the invitation of the American president, Woodrow Wilson, on December 20, 1916, for the belligerents to specify their war aims. The Germans refused, but the Entente replied on January 10, 1917, with the first public enunciation of the goals that its member states were ostensibly fighting to attain. In addition to the obvious demand for the evacuation of Belgian, French, Russian, Serbian, and Romanian territory under German military occupation, the Allied governments explicitly formulated for the first time their commitment to the "principle of national self-determination." This referred to the liberation of the Italian, Romanian, southern Slav, Czechoslovak, and Polish subject nationalities of the Habsburg Empire, which unmistakably meant the disintegration of that multinational state into its constituent ethnic regions. Such a pronouncement had the dual advantage of arousing American sympathy for the Entente's war effort while appealing to the subject nationalities of Germany's principal ally to cast off the yoke of their German-speaking masters in Vienna. Instances of mutiny and desertion in the Austro-Hungarian army had already appeared before the

Entente's call to arms. They increased thereafter, particularly as exile groups representing the various ethnic factions established headquarters in Paris and fanned the flames of nationalist rebellion behind the enemy lines.

These Allied expressions of sympathy for the cause of national liberation within the two multinational empires in the enemy camp were no less fraudulent than Germany's hypocritical pose as the champion of the Moslems and other subject nationalities of the British, French, and Russian empires. The British government's promise of support for the independence of Turkey's Arab provinces was flatly contradicted by a series of agreements concluded with its allies in the course of the war, which provided for the partition of the non-Turkish portion of the Ottoman Empire into "spheres of interest" among England, France, Italy, and Russia. To complicate further the postwar situation in the Ottoman domains, an official declaration by Britain's foreign secretary, Arthur Balfour, in November 1917 endorsed the proposal advanced by the European devotees of Zionism* for the establishment of a Jewish homeland in Palestine, a Turkish-controlled territory on the Eastern Mediterranean, which at the time contained roughly 60,000 Jewish settlers out of a total population of 750,000 who were mainly Arabs.

In a similar way the commitment to the subject peoples of the Austro-Hungarian Empire was critically compromised in February–March, 1917, when France authorized Russia "to fix her western frontiers as she wished" (a euphemistic phrase that had the effect of sacrificing the independence of Poland). This concession was tendered in return for Russian support for France's acquisition of Alsace-Lorraine and the coal mines of the Saar basin as well as the establishment of an independent state in the Rhineland under French military protection. In April 1915 Italy had been promised territory along the Adriatic coast in direct violation of the principle of national self-determination as it pertained to the southern Slavs who inhabited the region. These instances of great power maneuvering did not prove embarrassing to the Allied cause because they were concluded in utmost secrecy. But there was embarrassment enough in the political institutions and practices of the Russian autocracy, whose very presence in the anti-German coalition mocked the democratic principles that it was ostensibly fighting to defend.

The Significance of the Russian Withdrawal

The Russian Revolution of March 1917, which replaced the Romanov dynasty with a parliamentary provisional government dominated by the parties of the moderate left, together with the intervention of the United

---

* Zionism is a political movement founded in the 1890s by the Austrian journalist Theodore Herzl, which advocated the establishment of a Jewish national state as a haven for the Jewish populations of Europe and Russia that confronted a resurgence of anti-Semitism toward the end of the century.

States in the war against Germany a month later, supplied the ideological consistency that the Entente coalition had previously lacked. The new progressive government in Petrograd was promptly recognized by the Entente powers and announced its intention to honor the military and diplomatic engagements of the old regime. In the meantime, the Wilson administration's ideological crusade against the autocracy of the Central Powers had acquired a momentum of its own. Even before the United States could contribute significant numbers of fighting men to the Entente war effort—which, owing to America's lack of military preparedness, did not take place until the summer of 1918—the American president had furnished the war-weary peoples of Western Europe with the one thing that they had never had—a moral justification for the seemingly pointless slaughter at the front. "The war to make the world safe for democracy," and the struggle for "the right of national self-determination" no longer sounded like hollow slogans. Progressive Russia and Young America, allied with the democratic powers of Western Europe, were now fighting arm in arm for the extinction of tyranny and the liberation of oppressed peoples.

But the euphoria induced by the American intervention was tempered by the overthrow of the Russian provisional government by the Bolshevik movement on November 7, 1917. This event was widely viewed in Allied countries as the first successful application of the German policy of instigating insurrection behind the lines of the Entente. The evidence of a putative German-Bolshevik conspiracy gathered by Allied intelligence agencies was persuasive, though only circumstantial in nature. German government funds had subsidized Russian revolutionary groups in exile. The Bolshevik leader V. I. Lenin had been granted safe transit by railway across German territory from his haven in neutral Switzerland to the Russian capital. Lenin's publicly announced program included the immediate cessation of the war, if necessary by a separate peace with the Central Powers. Allied suspicions seemed to receive further confirmation after the Bolshevik victory. The new Russian government repudiated the tsarist regime's debts to foreign lenders, thereby wiping out roughly a quarter of France's foreign investment portfolio. It published the secret agreements concluded among the Entente powers concerning the postwar redistribution of enemy territory, causing considerable embarrassment to Britain, France, and Italy. Most serious of all, the new Russian government, after inviting all belligerents to make peace on the basis of no annexations and no indemnities and receiving no reply, opened separate peace negotiations with the Central Powers in the city of Brest-Litovsk on December 3, 1917.

The decisive causes of the Bolshevik Revolution in Russia, of course, were traceable to the deteriorating economic conditions of the country itself. Severe food shortages, the maldistribution of arable land, and the mounting casualty rate at the front collectively represented a sufficient incentive for large sections of the Russian population to respond favorably to Lenin's enticing slogan of "bread, land, and peace." But if the causes of the Bolshevik Revolution were largely internal in nature, its consequences were felt throughout all of wartime Europe. After exactly three months of bitter wrangling (December 3, 1917, to March 3, 1918), the Russian and German emissaries at Brest-Litovsk signed a peace treaty that removed Russia from the war. In line with the new German government policy, adopted after the intervention of the United States, the treaty of Brest-Litovsk did not result in the direct annexation of Russian territory. Instead, it represented the new policy of "association." According to the treaty (and supplementary agreements concluded subsequently) the Bolshevik regime was forced to cede virtually the entirety of its non-Russian territories in Europe: Poland, Lithuania, Latvia, Estonia, and Finland in the north, the Ukraine and the provinces of Transcaucasia (Georgia, Armenia, and Azerbaijan) in the south. In all of these regions independence movements had sprouted after the collapse of the tsarist regime, and many of them appealed to Germany for economic and military support. The German government was only too happy to oblige. By supplying "military protection" to these fledgling nations that had been carved out of the decaying carcass of the Russian Empire, the German Reich hoped to achieve by indirect means two of the principal goals of its original war aims program, namely, the removal of Russian power from Europe and the extension of German economic domination to the non-Russian border zone.

As German troops advanced into the power vacuum created by the unilateral Russian withdrawal from the war, the balance of power in Eastern Europe was radically transformed. Russia was virtually cut off from the Baltic by the establishment of the independent states of Finland, Latvia, Lithuania, and Estonia under German military protection. The creation of German client states in the Ukraine, the Crimea, Georgia, and Armenia, coupled with Turkish control of the Moslem state of Azerbaijan, blocked Russian access to the Black Sea and the mineral-rich region of the Caucasus. In the center of Europe, a Polish state was resurrected to serve as a transit zone for the extension of German hegemony in the former Russian territory along the Black and Baltic seas. Russia's retreat from Eastern Europe was further confirmed by the peace treaty between Romania and the Central Powers on May 7, whereby the Romanian annexation of the former Imperial Russian province of Bessarabia was recognized by Germany and Austria.

Notwithstanding the long-term strategic implications of Russia's withdrawal from its European borderlands before the onslaught of German power, the immediate military consequences of the Russian collapse were less than spectacular. The much-discussed redeployment of German military forces from the eastern to the western front in preparation for the great offensive planned for the spring of 1918 did not take place on the scale anticipated. In fact, large numbers of German troops were retained in the eastern theater to preserve Germany's hold on the enormous territory ceded by Russia. The immediate goal of the German government was economic in nature: the application of the program, developed early in the war, to obtain control of the foodstuffs and vital minerals in Eastern Europe and the Russian borderlands. The overall objective was the acquisition of self-sufficiency in food and industrial raw materials, not only on a short-term basis to replace resources denied to the Central Powers by the British naval blockade, but also for the postwar period, when overseas sources of supply were expected to fall within the control of the United States and the British Empire regardless of the outcome of the contest for hegemony on the continent.

The territory under German military domination by the spring of 1918 contained virtually all of the resources required by Germany to terminate its dependence on foreign sources of supply and forge the autarkic economic system first envisioned in the September Program. The oil fields of Romania, the Caucasus, and Turkish-controlled Mesopotamia (Iraq) would assure the Germans self-sufficiency in this vital source of energy. The coal fields of the Don basin in Russia would supplement the rich deposits of the Ruhr, the Saar, Silesia and occupied Belgium in the west. The iron mines of the Ukraine would be added to those of French Lorraine. The manganese of the Caucasus and the Ukraine (which accounted for 50 percent of the world production in 1914 and supplied Germany with three-quarters of its prewar requirements) would now be open to direct German exploitation. The cotton and wool of the Caucasus region offered essential raw materials to the German textile industry. And, most important, the fertile grain-producing plains of the Ukraine, combined with those of the German vassal states in the Balkans, would enable the Reich to break Britain's "hunger blockade" and end its prewar dependence on the United States and Latin America for its food requirements.

Thus, by the spring of 1918 the original objectives of the German war plan had been attained in the east. The establishment of German strategic predominance in the Russian borderlands had tipped the continental balance in favor of the Central Powers. Groundwork had been laid for German economic domination of the region that had been evacuated by the Russian armies. The Austro-Hungarian and Turkish empires, junior partners in the continental coalition ruled from Berlin, opened the path for German expansion overland toward the Arabian peninsula and the Persian Gulf. This land route to the Middle East and southern Asia, which was to be improved by the construction of a railway system financed by German capital, potentially represented a much more secure line of communications to this economically valuable region than did Britain's vulnerable lifeline on the sea. Here was the beginning of the dream come true of the German industrial and financial oligarchy: a vast Mitteleuropa bounded by compliant satellites and subservient allies chained to Germany by military and economic agreements. To complete this grandiose scheme for German control of Mitteleuropa and the Middle East, the expansionists in

Berlin added the project of Mittelafrika: a central African empire, enlarged by the attachment of Belgian, French, and British colonial territory to Germany's existing possessions in Africa and protected by German naval bases on the eastern and western coasts of that continent.

All that stood in the way of the full realization of this plan for German domination of the three interconnected continents of Europe, Asia, and Africa was the Allied military force on the western front. As the American Expeditionary Force began to arrive in large numbers in the spring of 1918, the German high command was confronted with a critical choice: The spectacular military and economic gains in the east might be preserved and even extended by a negotiated settlement of the war in France. Peace feelers had been extended sporadically from London, Paris, Washington, and Berlin during 1917 and early 1918. The German quartermaster general, Erich Ludendorff, had toyed with the idea of exploiting the Western powers' ideological fear of Bolshevism ever since the Allies had begun supporting the counterrevolutionary forces in Russia that had taken up arms against the new Communist government. But a separate peace in the west, with Germany posing as the defender of Western civilization against the Bolshevik peril, would require that Germany renounce its expansionist ambitions in Belgium and eastern France. And this it could not do. A militarily powerful and economically viable France, together with an independent Belgium serving as a vehicle for British interference in continental affairs, would hamper the operation of the Mitteleuropa project. Hence preparations were resumed for a final offensive on the western front. On March 21, 1918, sixty-two divisions of German military forces launched what was expected to be the long-awaited breakthrough that would drive France out of the war and Anglo-American forces out of the continent.

It is noteworthy that all of the major political organizations in Germany had fully supported the program of German military and economic expansion up to the period of this last great offensive. The Reichstag ratified the Treaty of Brest-Litovsk by a large majority, with even the Social Democrats choosing to abstain rather than to oppose what the Russian government, signing under protest, justifiably denounced as a "dictated peace." The Center and Progressive parties defended the treaty as consistent with the principle of "no annexations, no indemnities" (the formula adopted by a majority in the German Reichstag on July 19, 1917), because it did not involve the formal annexation of Russian territory. The Conservative and National Liberal parties criticized the treaty as too weak. On July 13, 1918, just before the failure of the final German offensive in France, the Reichstag once again registered its approval of the high command's offensive in France by passing the twelfth military appropriation law of the war.

The German offensive ground to a halt on July 15, and three days later the Allied armies mounted a counteroffensive that by August 8 began to take on the characteristics of a rout. With the German armies retreating along a broad front during the remainder of August and September, the military leaders recognized for the first time that victory in the west was an impossibility. Ludendorff and his associates thereupon dusted off the alternative strategy that had been under consideration ever since the conclusion of the Treaty of Brest-Litovsk: the exploitation of the Bolshevik peril as a means of securing a moderate settlement with the Allies. Ironically, this new policy of retrenchment in the west received the enthusiastic endorsement of the very spokesmen for German heavy industry who had previously pressed for extensive annexations in Belgium and eastern France. In September 1918 German industrialists such as Hugo Stinnes, Albert Ballin, and Gustav Krupp, in league with National Liberal leader Gustav Stresemann (also a former annexationist), urged the government to preserve Germany's economic and military gains in the east by renouncing its ambitious aims in the west. They also called for the introduction of domestic political reforms that would appeal to public opinion in the Allied camp by removing the stigma of autocracy from the German political system. The internal democratization of Germany would satisfy Wilsonian opinion abroad and progressive critics at home. A Germany serving as the bulwark of Western civilization against the menace of Bolshevism could expect to receive considerable sympathy in France, with its enormous investments in Russia threatened by the Communist revolution, and in Great Britain, with its millions of colonial subjects susceptible to infection by the revolutionary ideas circulating in Moscow and Petrograd.

The continuing deterioration of the German military position in France in the autumn of 1918 caused the high command to adopt parts of this strategy in one final effort to salvage the gains in the east. On October 4, less than a week after Ludendorff had informed the emperor of the need for an armistice as soon as possible, a "parliamentary government" headed by the liberal Prince Max of Baden was formed with the support of the parties of the center and left. On the same day, the German government appealed to President Wilson for an armistice of moderation on the basis of the principles enunciated in his famous "fourteen points." When Wilson replied that he would negotiate only with a genuinely democratic government, the military and political elite in Berlin realized that the cause was lost. Ludendorff resigned on October 27, the Kaiser abdicated on November 9, and on the same day the Social Democratic leader Phillip Scheidemann proclaimed a German democratic republic. On November 11 the German delegates who had been negotiating with Allied military representatives in a forest north of Paris signed an armistice. It provided for the immediate evacuation of all French and Belgian territory as well as all German territory west of the Rhine River. It also stipulated, as a final blow to the hopes of the anti-Bolshevik faction in Berlin, that Germany renounce the treaties of Brest-Litovsk and Bucharest and withdraw all of her military forces from Russia, Romania, Austria-Hungary, and Turkey.

Like the "revolution" that had created a united German Empire in

1871, the "revolution" that established the German Republic in 1918 was accomplished from above, without the participation of the mass of citizens. The part of the German kings and princes in the coronation of William I at Versailles was played by former supporters of the Empire such as Erzberger and Stresemann and moderate leaders of the Social Democrats such as Scheidemann and Ebert. The military leadership did not lift a finger in defense of the repudiated Hohenzollern monarch, who slipped ignominiously across the Dutch border into exile on November 10. The German Republic was not forged by a revolutionary movement fired by democratic enthusiasm and hatred for the authoritarian regime that had brought the nation to defeat. It was created by political leaders who had either supported or acquiesced in the expansionist policies of the empire to the very end. It was tolerated by a military class that was pleased to see the civilian representatives of the democratic parties take responsibility for accepting the humiliating armistice terms dictated by the French generalissimo in the railroad car at Compiègne after defeat in the war of conquest that the German high command had planned, waged, and lost.

The Significance of the American Intervention

At the outbreak of the war in Europe, the United States government had declared its intention to pursue a policy of strict neutrality. No American interests were directly threatened by the fighting across the Atlantic, and no American commitments, even of an informal nature, had been made to any of the belligerents. In the early stages of the war, considerable sympathy for both sides was expressed by various groups within the United States. There was widespread sentimental support for Great Britain for reasons of linguistic and cultural identification. French publicists effectively revived the fading memory of the great debt Americans owed France for its assistance in the War of Independence. On the other hand, this pro-Entente attitude was balanced by the pro-German or anti-British sentiment of the two largest ethnic groups in the United States, the German-Americans and the Irish-Americans. But as the war in Europe developed into a stalemate, the naval and economic policies of the belligerents caused a gradual modification of the American commitment to absolute neutrality in the direction of more active support for the Entente. By the spring of 1915 the British navy, profiting from its superiority in surface shipping, had succeeded in driving German warships and merchantmen from the high seas. Except for one inconclusive engagement in May 1916 off the Jutland peninsula of Denmark, the German High Seas Fleet was to cling to its home bases for fear of facing total destruction at the hands of the British Grand Fleet. Left unprotected by armed warships, the German merchant fleet remained confined to port for the remainder of the war. This forced Germany into total reliance on neutral shipping for its foreign trade. But Great Britain proceeded to impose a blockade on Germany that effectively severed its access to neutral sources of supply and precluded its use of neutral means of transport.

The generally accepted custom of blockade in wartime prescribed the stationing of warships near the ports of the enemy country just outside the three-mile territorial limit. The blockading power was entitled to intercept and inspect the cargoes of merchant vessels seeking admission to the enemy port. Those ships found to be carrying articles of contraband, narrowly defined as weapons, ammunition, and other articles of war, could be denied entry to the port until they disposed of the objectionable cargo. But the British navy violated these regulations in three important respects. First, the blockade flotillas took up their stations on the high seas, invoking as justification for this unorthodox behavior the exceptional menace posed by long-range harbor artillery. This "loose blockade" enabled them to intercept neutral ships headed for neutral countries contiguous to Germany (such as Denmark and Holland) and to confiscate contraband on the pretext that it could easily find its way into enemy hands. Secondly, the British government declared the entire North Sea a "military area" in November 1914 and proceeded to mine it so thoroughly that neutral merchantmen were compelled to stop at British ports for navigational directions. Such instructions were systematically withheld if their cargoes included articles of contraband. Thirdly, claiming that in total war practically every important product, including foodstuffs and textiles for clothing, was of potential value to the enemy, the British extended the definition of contraband to include virtually every item that Germany was required to import.

As a consequence of this calculated policy of economic strangulation, Germany's foreign trade with neutral countries such as the United States slowed to a trickle, while the nations in the anti-German coalition took up the slack by importing huge quantities of munitions, food, and other necessities from Germany's traditional foreign suppliers. In the absence of surface shipping to contest British naval supremacy, Germany was driven to rely on the use of submarines, which could not be easily detected beneath the surface of the sea, to harass British merchant shipping in retaliation against the blockade. The international rules of naval warfare required submarines to surface and issue a warning to a vessel flying the enemy flag in order to afford passengers and crew the opportunity to abandon ship before the torpedo was released. But many of the British merchant ships were armed and their captains were under instructions to open fire on or ram German submarines that complied with this custom. After several incidents of armed resistance and ramming by British merchant ships, the German government issued on February 4, 1915, the definition of a "war zone" around the British Isles, within which all enemy ships would be liable to destruction without warning. Neutral merchant ships were advised to stay out of the zone to avoid cases of mistaken identity (a distinct possibility in view of British merchant ships' practice of hoisting neutral flags to confound enemy submarine commanders). Between February and May 1915, ninety ships went to the bottom in this newly defined zone. On May 7 the British passenger liner *Lusitania,* laden with ammunition and other contraband material purchased in the United States, was sunk by a German submarine off the coast of Ireland. The death of 128 American citizens in this incident prompted such vigorous protests from Washington that Berlin was induced to moderate its policy of unrestricted submarine warfare. Thereafter submarine commanders were instructed to issue warnings to enemy passenger liners before mounting an attack. In May 1916 this modification was extended to merchant ships as well, on the tacit understanding that the American government would persuade Britain to relax its "starvation blockade" of Germany.

The United States, which possessed the third largest navy in the world in 1914, could easily have convoyed its own merchant ships across the Atlantic and compelled Britain to halt its flagrant violations of established naval practices. That it chose not to do so, while continuing to protest German transgressions of the rules of submarine warfare, reflected two considerations that predisposed the Wilson administration to favor the Entente cause. The first of these was the strong sense of kinship with British traditions and institutions felt by key members of the American government, beginning with the president himself. The American ambassador to the Court of Saint James, Walter Hines Page; Secretary of State Robert Lansing (who had replaced the pacifist William Jennings Bryan in 1915); and President Wilson's intimate adviser, Colonel Edward House, all privately championed the Entente cause and opposed efforts to treat British and German violations of international law on an equal basis. The second and more important consideration was that since the British blockade had diverted the American export trade from Germany and adjacent neutral countries to Britain and France and their allies, American economic prosperity and corporate profits had become increasingly dependent on orders from Germany's enemies for munitions, machinery, textiles, grain, oil, copper, steel, and other products. (See Tables III and IV for the importance to the United States of this export trade.)

TABLE III   American Exports to Belligerent and Neutral Countries During the Period of American Neutrality in the First World War (in percentages)

First Trimester

	1914	1915	1916	1917
Allied nations or nations that severed diplomatic relations with Germany	64.62	74.17	87.34	88.67
Neutral countries	16.15	23.55	12.26	10.38
Germany, its allies, and occupied countries	19.23	2.28	.40	.95

Source: Yves-Henri Nouailhat, *La France et les Etats-Unis,* août 1914–avril 1917 (Lille, 1977), p. 627.

TABLE IV   Prices of Selected American Industrial Securities During the
Period of American Neutrality in the First World War

Company	Stock Price on July 24, 1914	Stock Price on Jan. 21, 1916	Gain (%)
American Beet & Sugar	22¾	66¾	193
American Hide & Leather	4	10⅞	171
American Linseed	8¾	22½	157
American Locomotive	28	64½	130
American Woolen	15½	48½	212
Anaconda Copper	30¼	87	187
Bethlehem Steel	39¼	477	1,115
Corning Products Refining	8¼	22½	175
International Mercantile Marine	2	20½	820
Republic Iron & Steel	20	51	155

Source: Nouailhat, p. 507.

Once the nations of the anti-German coalition had exhausted their supply of dollar credits in the United States by liquidating their holdings of American securities, the only means of financing future imports was to obtain loans from the American banking community. Since trade with the Allies had become a critical element in America's recovery from the cyclical recession of 1913–14, the Wilson administration authorized the opening of the Wall Street capital market to the Allied governments. The investment banking firm of J. P. Morgan & Company became the official commercial agent in the United States for the British and French treasuries, coordinating Allied purchasing from American suppliers and organizing banking consortia to furnish the credits required to finance these operations. By the time of the American intervention in the war, private American financial institutions had advanced approximately $2.3 billion in loans and credits to the Allied states compared to only $27 million to the Central Powers. The House of Morgan had placed over $3 billion worth of contracts with American export firms on behalf of the British and French governments. In this way the trading partnership between American exporters and Anglo-French importers, reinforced by the financial relationship between Wall Street investment banking concerns and the state treasuries of Paris and London, gave American economic interests an important stake in the successful prosecution of the Allied war effort.

It was this inequality of economic treatment, together with the American government's failure to exert diplomatic pressure on London to relax its illegal "loose" blockade of Germany, that prompted the Berlin government to announce the resumption of unrestricted submarine warfare on January 31, 1917. Concluding that the United States could hardly be more helpful to the Anglo-French cause as a cobelligerent than it was as a neutral supplier of munitions and food paid for with American credits,

German political and naval authorities chose to risk provoking American intervention. They confidently assumed that the disruption of Britain's transatlantic supply line would force that country out of the war within six months, before an American expeditionary force could be mobilized, trained, and transported through submarine-infested waters to Europe. The Wilson administration responded to the resumption of unrestricted submarine warfare by severing diplomatic relations with Germany and arming American merchant vessels. Hesistant to resume their perilous trade with the Allies, most American shipping firms kept their vessels in port, causing widespread fear of economic depression as products intended for export began to pile up on the wharves of east coast harbors. Many of those that risked the Atlantic crossing were sent to the bottom by German U-boats as they entered the war zone. This disruption of the American export trade supplied Wilson with a sufficient pretext for requesting a congressional declaration of war against Germany, which was granted on April 6, 1917.

During the first year of the American state of belligerency the United States army played no role in the Allied war effort. In April 1917 the American regular army of 130,000 officers and men was smaller than the Belgian army and poorly trained. It was only in the early summer of 1918, after the introduction of conscription and the advent of a military training program, that the American military and naval forces (which by the end of war had swollen to 4,800,000 persons) began to make a critical contribution to the Anglo-French effort on the western front. In the meantime, however, financial assistance from Washington enabled the Allied governments to expand their purchases of American supplies. Upon the American declaration of war, the financing operations of the New York banks were taken over by the Treasury Department. A large proportion of the proceeds from the war bonds that were sold to patriotic American investors were advanced to the Allied governments to finance their purchases in the American market. The German navy's hope of halting the transport of American supplies to France was dashed by British success in convoying merchant ships across the Atlantic.

The years 1914–1918 witnessed a massive international transfer of wealth from the eastern to the western shore of the Atlantic. The liquidation of British and French investments in the United States in the first year of the war erased the debt owed by Americans to European lenders. The subsequent borrowing by Allied governments in the American money market transformed the United States from a debtor to a creditor of the European powers that had depleted their financial resources to pay for a war that seemed as though it would never end (see Table V). Accompanying this shift of financial power from Europe to the United States was a revolutionary transformation in the system of world trade. While Germany was prevented from pursuing its commercial interests abroad by the British blockade, Britain and France were forced to divert their industrial

TABLE V   The International Investment Position of the United States Before and After the First World War (in billions of dollars)

| | *U.S. Private Investments Abroad* | | | | *Foreign Investments in U.S.* | | | |
| | Long-Term | | | | Long-Term | | | |
	Total	*Direct*	*Portfolio*	*Short-Term*	*Total*	*Direct*	*Portfolio*	*Short-Term*
1914								
(June)	3.5	2.7	.08	n.a.	7.2	1.3	5.4	.5
1919	7.0	3.9	2.6	.05	3.3	.9	1.6	.8

Note: n.a. = not available.

Source: U.S. Department of Commerce, Bureau of the Census, *Historical Statistics of the United States* (Washington, 1960), p. 565.

production and their merchant shipping to wartime purposes. In the meantime, the United States expanded its export trade to capture many of the markets previously dominated by European firms. The American economic penetration of Latin America, which had begun at the turn of the century, accelerated during the First World War. Similarly, the Japanese empire, which occupied Germany's possessions in the Far East, expanded economically in that region at the expense of all three of the principal European belligerents. From an economic point of view, the First World War was won by the United States and Japan, both of which avoided territorial destruction and loss of life on a large scale while acquiring economic predominance within their respective geographic regions.

But the long-term implications of this fundamental shift in global economic power away from Europe passed largely unnoticed amid the emotionally charged atmosphere of the months following the armistice. Trade patterns and capital flows meant nothing to a European population that was preoccupied with the more immediate concerns of postwar security and recovery. The choice of the capital city of victorious France as the site of the peace conference that would formally terminate the war reinforced the illusion that Europe, despite its commercial and financial decline during the war years, remained the center of the world.

CHAPTER 2

The Peace of Paris and
the New International Order

The Paris Peace Conference, which was convened on January 12, 1919, at the French Foreign Ministry, constituted the largest and most important diplomatic gathering since the Congress of Vienna of 1814–15. Seventy delegates representing the twenty-seven victorious nations, accompanied by hundreds of advisers, clerks, and journalists, descended on the French capital to participate in the process of peacemaking that customarily follows the conclusion of great wars. The enormity of the human and material devastation recently witnessed hung like a cloud over the deliberations: Ten million lives had been lost during the previous four years. Another twenty million people had sustained war-related injuries. The total direct cost of the war was estimated at $180 billion and the indirect cost at over $150 billion. The four great empires that had exercised authority over hundreds of millions of people in the old world—Hohenzollern Germany, Habsburg Austria-Hungary, Romanov Russia, and Ottoman Turkey—had either disappeared or, in the case of the latter, were soon to expire. From their ashes arose politically unstable, economically backward states whose viability remained problematical. The agenda of the conference was twofold: to repair the political and economic fabric of half the world, and to prevent a recurrence of the type of organized violence that had recently been brought to an end.

The president of the United States, Woodrow Wilson, astonished his compatriots by deciding to attend the peace conference in person, becoming the first American chief executive to travel abroad while in office. All the more shocking, and infuriating to his critics at home, was his insistence on remaining in Europe (except for a brief return journey) for six consecutive months while subordinates in Washington were left to contend with the pressing domestic problems of postwar readjustment. Wilson had arrived in Europe in mid-December 1918 armed with more moral authority than any other national leader in history. His periodic exhortations on behalf of a new world order that would forever banish the scourge of war represented an entirely novel approach to the conduct of international relations, or so it seemed to the millions of war-weary European citizens who greeted him with unrestrained enthusiasm. In those intoxicating weeks before the opening of the conference, it appeared as though an exhausted continent, bled white by the most destructive war yet endured by mankind, had received a savior from across the sea untarnished by the discredited practices of traditional statecraft that had brought Europe to its present plight.

Insofar as one could judge from his public pronouncements on the subject, the American president believed that war in general, and the recent war in particular, was traceable to three principal causes. The first was the practice of secret diplomacy, whereby political leaders surreptitiously concluded military alliances and diplomatic engagements to further their own nation's ambitions. The second was the tendency of politically dominant nationality groups to oppress the ethnic minorities under their control. The third was the political system of autocracy, which enabled a privileged elite to monopolize political power at the expense of the population at large. Remove these impediments to the unfettered expression of the public will, Wilson seemed to be saying, and you will have abolished forever the causes of war. Secret diplomacy would give way to free and open discussion of international issues, a process certain to maximize the beneficent influence of public opinion and minimize the role of secretive intrigues by imperialistically inclined national leaders. The map of Europe was to be redrawn according to the principle of national self-determination so as to liberate the long-suppressed aspirations of nationality groups whose struggle for independence had caused most of the wars of recent memory. And finally, the internal political institutions of Europe would be democratized so as to remove the autocratic constraints on public opinion that had permitted the ruling elites of the Central Powers to wage their war of aggression. Crowning this new achievement of internal and international democratization would be a world organization of free and independent nations empowered to resolve international disputes by negotiation and compromise, just as parliaments in democratic societies adjudicated the conflicting claims of their citizens.

It is easy to appreciate the appeal that this Wilsonian program exercised on the "generation of the trenches" in Europe. It engendered almost limitless hopes and expectations in the minds of a traumatized population craving for assurances that peace would endure. The two slogans most often associated with Wilson's name, "the war to end all wars" and "the war to make the world safe for democracy," both symbolized the widespread anticipation that the recent bloodbath had not been fought entirely in vain: People hoped that eternal peace and universal liberty would become its two unintended legacies.

The disappointment of these optimistic expectations represented one of the most tragic episodes in modern world history. So high were the hopes, so bitter was the disillusionment, that the genuine accomplishments of the

Paris Peace Conference (which, as we shall see, were considerable, in view of the complexity of the problems that it confronted) have receded far into the background of historical memory. What is recalled instead is the enormous gap between intention and achievement. Because the American leader chose to express his foreign policy in the moralistic language of humanitarian idealism, he raised expectations that could not fail to be disappointed. The vague prescriptions for peace and liberty that filled Wilson's speeches crashed on the shoals of political reality in Paris, where fallible human beings assembled to undertake the momentous task of redrawing of the political map of Europe and organizing the economic recovery of the world.

The contrast between Wilsonian theory and practice came to light in the opening sessions of the peace conference, when the heads of government endeavored to establish effective procedures for peacemaking. The principle of equality among sovereign nations, born of the pervasive distrust of great-power diplomacy, dissolved in the decision-making process of these organizational meetings. The two ranking delegates of the five great powers—the United States, Great Britain, France, Italy, and Japan—preempted for themselves the right to adjudicate the important issues before the conference as the "Supreme Council." The leaders of the other twenty-two states in attendance were reduced to pleading their case, either in writing or in person, before these ten plenipotentiaries. When even this truncated decision-making apparatus subsequently proved too unwieldy, the leaders of the four great powers (minus Japan) began to meet in Wilson's quarters to decide among themselves the fate of the world.

The preeminent position of the great powers at the Peace Conference was subsequently extended to the Covenant of the League of Nations, Wilson's cherished scheme for a world organization that was unveiled before the delegates on April 28. While each member state was to be represented by one vote in the General Assembly of the new organization, the principal decision-making body, called the Council, included permanent seats for delegates of the five great powers. A requirement of unanimity assured that each permanent member could veto any proposal that threatened to impinge upon its national interests. Other features of the League Covenant effectively preserved the inequality of power among the member nations. The British and French colonial empires were treated as single political units (except for Britain's self-governing Dominions, which obtained separate representation); at the behest of the American delegation, the Monroe Doctrine was specifically excluded from the purview of the League Covenant (thereby preserving the exclusive prerogative of the United States to maintain the peace in its hemisphere). The right to national self-determination, which was to be applied to the successor states of the German, Austro-Hungarian, and Russian empires in Europe, went unrecognized insofar as the non-European populations of the colonial world were concerned. Attempts by Latin American delegates to invoke the League's protection against interference by the United States in their internal affairs fell on deaf ears, as did efforts by spokesmen for the oppressed nationalities of the British and French empires in Asia to obtain recognition of their right to self-government. The application of Wilsonian principles was evidently to be restricted to the white nations of the Western world, and among those favored states the four great powers of the victorious coalition were to preserve their preeminent position.

The much-heralded Wilsonian principle of open diplomacy was likewise an early casualty of the peacemaking process. It rapidly became evident that the American president's lofty promise of "open convenants openly arrived at" implied merely that the final texts of diplomatic agreements should be published (unlike those "secret treaties" that had codified the various alliances of the great powers before and during the war). What it definitely did *not* mean, as revealed by Wilson's behavior in Paris, was that diplomacy ought to be subject to the influence of public opinion as expressed by press or parliament. The Supreme Council, and later the Big Four, conducted their deliberations in the utmost secrecy, at first even without taking minutes. When the British delegation finally insisted that a written record of the proceedings be preserved, secretaries were admitted on the condition that their notes be withheld from public scrutiny. The press, denied direct access to the decision makers, was compelled to rely on sanitized summaries of the daily deliberations. Most of what we know about the negotiations behind these closed doors comes from the notes taken by the interpreter attached to the French delegation, which were published long after the end of the conference.

If the press had minimal access to and influence on the decision-making process in Paris, the elected legislative representatives of the four great powers had even less. Wilson in particular took little account of public opinion in his own country as recorded in the midterm elections of November 1918, which had returned Republican majorities in both houses of Congress. Instead of selecting a peace delegation that reflected this new shift in public sentiment, he chose men who either shared his own views on world affairs or lacked the authority to speak for the new Republican majority in the Senate (whose votes were required for legislative consent to the agreements reached at the conference). In his relations with the other Allied representatives he relied heavily on his hand-picked associate, Colonel Edward House, a behind-the-scenes political operator who reported directly to his old friend in the White House. Public expressions of legislative opposition to Wilson's policies in Paris, such as the famous "round robin" resolution signed by a sufficient number of senators or senators-elect to deny congressional consent to the treaty, had no apparent effect on the president.

The other Allied leaders were similarly insulated from the influence of domestic public opinion. The French premier, Georges Clemenceau, imposed a rigid censorship on the Parisian press and denied the Chamber of Deputies any role in the peacemaking process. Like Wilson, he ignored the advice of his foreign minister (and of any other elected member of his government), preferring to consult his loyal personal assistant, André Tardieu, on most crucial matters. British Prime Minister David Lloyd George, though more sensitive to political pressures at home, often took positions in the privacy of the conference room that directly contradicted his public utterances. Not only were the covenants not "openly arrived at," they were fashioned amid an atmosphere of duplicity and secrecy reminiscent of the diplomatic practice of the prewar years that had supposedly been repudiated.

These deviations from the high standards of Wilsonianism were prompted not merely by the demands of procedural efficiency: If the complexity and sensitivity of the problems confronting the peace conference required that decision-making authority be centralized in a group of four men meeting in private, then its membership might have been chosen by lot from among the twenty-seven delegations. That it was these particular four men who successfully arrogated unto themselves the function of composing the peace treaties with the defeated enemies reflected the political realities of the postwar world. No amount of lip service to the principle of the equality of nations could conceal the glaring inequality of power relationships among the sovereign states whose leaders deliberated in Paris. The United States, Great Britain, France, and, to a lesser extent, Italy and Japan (the latter's representatives participated only when issues relating to East Asia were on the agenda) dominated the peace conference because they dominated the world after the defeat of Germany and the collapse of Russia. It was these nations that had raised armies of millions of men, mobilized their considerable economic resources, and imposed military defeat on the Central Powers. It was these nations that collectively exercised economic and political dominion over most of the land surface of the globe and naval control over its waterways. It was inconceivable to expect them to relinquish their prerogative to preside over the realignment of international power relationships that necessarily follows major wars. It was equally unrealistic to assume that their policies at the peace conference would reflect anything other than their own governments' conception of what their respective national interests required.

This intrusion of national interest into the decision-making procedures became particularly apparent during the deliberations concerning the redistribution of the territory, resources, and populations of the regions previously under the political control of the defeated powers. For reasons presently to be discussed, the victorious Allies held sharply conflicting views regarding the appropriate means of accomplishing the ultimate objective that they all shared, namely, the reestablishment of peace and security in Europe and economic prosperity in the world. This conflict over means eventually destroyed the spirit of unity that had cemented the victorious wartime coalition. The Paris Peace Conference, which had opened with such high hopes, ended amid an atmosphere of inter-Allied acrimony that was to hamstring efforts to enforce the provisions of the peace treaties that it produced.

The two essential goals of the French delegation at the peace conference were the definitive removal of the menace of German military aggression in Europe and the acquisition of financial assistance to defray the costs of restoring the territory in northeastern France that had been destroyed by the German army during the war. All of the other French objectives at the conference were negotiable. These two were not.

France's preoccupation with obtaining ironclad guarantees against a revival of German military power derived from its vulnerable geographical and demographic situation at the end of the Great War. The long frontier with Germany, unprotected in its northern sector by natural impediments to military aggression such as wide rivers or high mountains, remained a source of grave concern to French military strategists. This sense of vulnerability was heightened by the loss of Russia as an eastern counterweight to German power. Equally alarming were the comparative statistics of population and natality in the two countries. There were 39 million Frenchmen facing 63 million Germans, even with the addition of the nearly 2 million citizens of Alsace-Lorraine. The decline of the French birthrate that had begun long before the war was accentuated by the death of 1.4 million potential fathers on the battlefield. Soon the Germans would be increasing in number at twice the rate of the French. The mid-1930s, when Germany could be expected to renew its bid for continental hegemony, would mark the beginning of a drastic reduction in the pool of French manpower available for military service.

How security against a German military revival could best be obtained became a matter of intense debate within the French government as well as in the country at large. Strident spokesmen for the nationalist Right demanded a return to the policies of Richelieu and Mazarin in the seventeenth century, which had kept France strong and secure by keeping Germany weak and divided. Such a policy implied the forcible partition of the German Reich into the pre-Bismarckian hodgepodge of some two dozen independent political units. The spontaneous emergence of separatist movements in the predominantly Catholic regions of southern and western Germany, which pressed for liberation from Protestant, Prussian domination, represented sufficient temptation for the French government to tender surreptitious support to these centrifugal forces within the enemy's frontiers. But the traditional French maxim that German unity was incompatible with French security was a relic of the "old diplomacy" and its balance-of-power doctrine. It was altogether inappropriate to the "new diplomacy" associated with the Wilsonian program, which valued the right to national self-determination (even when invoked by a former enemy) higher than the claims of continental security. Correctly anticipating vigorous opposition from the American delegation, French Premier Clemenceau presented a scaled-down version of this punitive scheme at the peace conference.

The focus of Clemenceau's strategy for ensuring French security was the region of western Germany sandwiched between the French frontier and the Rhine River, popularly known as the Rhineland. Geographers and military strategists on all sides agreed that control of this buffer zone strategically situated between the two ancient adversaries in Western Europe would determine the future power relationship between them. A German military force ensconced in the Rhineland would find no geographical obstacles between itself and France's major industrial sector in the northeast (including the iron-producing region of Lorraine that had been the prime object of German expansionist ambition during the war) and the center of French administrative authority in Paris. A French military contingent stationed in the Rhineland and on the bridgeheads on the opposite side of the river would be within striking distance of the industrial heartland of Germany located in the adjacent Ruhr Valley. So decisive was the strategic position of the Rhineland that military occupation of it by one of these two powers would almost certainly deter the other from risking an aggressive foreign policy on the continent.

In recognition of this geopolitical imperative, Clemenceau proposed at the peace conference that the Rhineland be severed from Germany and reconstituted as an independent sovereign state under French military protection. Fortunately for the French, the separatist group that had sprouted in this region after the armistice was the most ambitious and vocal of the "anti-Prussian" liberation movements in the predominantly Catholic portions of Germany. Unfortunately, it had failed to secure the support of the majority of the Rhenish population, which remained loyal to the national state with which it shared a common language and heritage. The forcible separation of the Rhineland from Germany would not only violate the principle of national self-determination (since a plebiscite in the region would certainly have resulted in the rejection of independence); it would also, particularly in the eyes of British Prime Minister Lloyd George, have created another Alsace-Lorraine, that is, a perpetual source of friction between Germany and the victorious powers responsible for depriving her of her "lost province."

In the face of intense Anglo-American pressure, which at one point included a veiled threat by President Wilson to abandon the peace conference in midsession, the French premier acquiesced in a compromise arrangement on the Rhine. In return for France's acceptance of German political sovereignty over the Rhineland, the American and British leaders consented to the following set of protective guarantees: the prohibition in perpetuity against the deployment of German military forces or the construction of fortifications on the territory west of the Rhine as well as on a strip fifty kilometers wide on the east bank of the river; the inter-Allied military occupation of the Rhineland for a fifteen-year period (at the end of which, it was presumed, the militaristic spirit of the old Germany would have been snuffed out by the forces of German democracy that had recently come to power); and, just in case, the permanent reduction of the German army to a token force of 100,000 men, the prohibition of the manufacture of military aircraft, tanks, and other offensive weapons by Germany, and an unprecedented commitment by the United States and Great Britain to defend France by force of arms in the event of unprovoked German aggression. These measures satisfied Clemenceau as minimally acceptable guarantees against a future German military threat.

No less important than this search for security was France's economic objective of postwar reconstruction. It was a cruel irony that defeated Germany emerged from the Great War with its national territory virtually untouched by the ravages of combat while the most productive region of victorious France lay in ruins. The ten northern and eastern *départements* of France that had served as the battleground on the western front had been devasted during the four years of combat. To add insult to injury, the retreating German army had deliberately laid waste to the territory they were forced to evacuate; this was done not only to deny its resources to the advancing Allied armies but also to accord German economic interests a competitive advantage over their French counterparts after the war by crippling France's capacity for economic recovery. Coal mines flooded, railways and telegraph lines destroyed, farmland pockmarked with shell holes and honeycombed with trenches, livestock slaughtered, homes put to the torch—such was the somber scene that greeted the Allied armies as they liberated the war zone in the autumn of 1918. This destruction of industrial plant, agricultural acreage, and communication and transportation facilities in the northeastern region, together with the severe labor shortages caused by the wartime casualties, had gravely undermined France's productive capacity. To make matters worse, the liquidation of the major portion of France's foreign investment portfolio to finance the war effort, the incurring of massive foreign indebtedness, and the loss of the extensive prewar investments in Russia, Austria-Hungary, and Turkey had strained the country's financial resources almost to the breaking point. The necessity to reconstruct the devastated regions, to accommodate the needs of the millions of refugees, widows, orphans, and disabled veterans, and to service the enormous foreign debt incurred during the war required an immense effort of national economic recovery that clearly could not be sustained by the nation's depleted financial resources. It was evident that a massive infusion of working capital from abroad was needed to defray the costs of France's postwar economic rehabilitation.

Historians of the Paris Peace Conference have almost invariably portrayed French authorities as united in the expectation that the costs of French economic recovery could and should be borne by Germany. But recent research has revealed that key officials in the Clemenceau government entertained the hope that national reconstruction would be financed not by the defeated enemy but rather by France's two English-speaking associates that had been spared the trauma of military occupation and material destruction. What led France's economic planners to anticipate such assistance from the wartime partners across the Channel and the Atlantic was the development of a remarkable degree of economic cooperation among the Allied nations during the last year of the war. A number of inter-Allied organizations had been established in London to pool and allocate available cargo space on ships, raw materials, and munitions essential for the prosecution of the war. In this way France received from the United States and the British Empire deliveries of coal, oil, wheat, and dozens of other commodities that she was unable to produce domestically in sufficient quantities. The French minister of commerce, Etienne Clémentel, inspired by his enterprising young representative in London, Jean Monnet, mounted a vigorous campaign during the winter of 1918–19 to persuade American and British officials to extend this system of wartime economic cooperation to the postwar period. In Clémentel's scheme, France's economic reconstruction would be treated as an inter-Allied responsibility to be borne jointly by the governments of the victorious coalition on the basis of their financial capacity.

To a certain degree this program of postwar economic cooperation incorporated the spirit of the proposals tentatively adopted by the European Allies at the Paris Economic Conference of 1916. In the course of the intervening two years it had become unmistakably evident that the United States alone possessed sufficient financial resources to underwrite such an ambitious undertaking. At the time of the armistice, therefore, the Clémentel plan revived the idea of a permanent economic bloc of the victorious Allies originally envisioned by the Paris program of 1916, with the critical difference that the United States was to be included within rather than excluded from the proposed system. Furthermore, after the economic revitalization of France and Belgium was completed, Germany would be gradually integrated into what might have been called the new Atlantic economic order after it had been severed from the Central European economic bloc that had begun to take shape after the signing of the Treaty of Brest-Litovsk. In this respect the French plan represented a modified version of Germany's wartime scheme for Mitteleuropa, with the roles reversed. There was originally little serious talk in French government circles about compelling Germany to foot the bill for France's economic recovery, for reasons presently to be sketched. Germany would be expected to contribute its share to the rebuilding of the territory that its armies had devastated, but only as part of a "world reparation fund" to be financed in large part by the United States.

The expectation that the American government would commit substantial public funds to the reconstruction of war-ravaged Europe was ill founded. Throughout the period of America's participation in the war, President Wilson had scrupulously insisted on his nation's separate and distinct status as an "associate" of the European Allies. The United States government had only reluctantly and belatedly associated itself with the inter-Allied economic machinery in the last year of the war, and then mainly for the purpose of limiting and coordinating the European Allies' requests for American aid. Once the victory over Germany had been assured, the United States government saw the area of economic interest that it had in common with its European partners as having narrowed considerably.

The first overt indication of this trans-Atlantic parting of ways appeared on the eve of the armistice, when the American government formally rejected the French proposals for an inter-Allied pooling of economic resources on the basis of need during the period of postwar reconstruction. Even the shrewd attempt by French officials to identify this scheme of international economic cooperation with Wilson's pet project for international political cooperation, the League of Nations, failed to sway American policymakers. The Wilson administration made it clear that it expected the European nations to rely on their own resources to finance their economic recovery; any additional funds required would have to be sought through private investment channels in the American money market. In December 1918, President Wilson dismantled the War Industries Board, thereby removing government controls on raw materials and industrial production in the United States, and within a month he had begun to reduce American participation in the inter-Allied economic committees. In the spring of 1919 the secretary of the treasury announced his intention to terminate all American government loans to the wartime partners. In the future, the European states would be expected to seek the loans and credits they required on Wall Street instead of in Washington. Thus the French scheme for inter-Allied sharing of economic and financial resources was torpedoed by the American government's insistence on the return to the peacetime conditions of the free market. It was to be American investors and American exporters, not American taxpayers, who would supply Europe with the investment capital, raw materials, and products it required, and at the going price. There would be no Marshall Plan for European recovery after the First World War, as Clémentel, Monnet, and other French officials had hoped.

In the face of this abrupt return to economic nationalism by the United States, France was driven to seek relief from its economic distress in the form of "reparation" payments from Germany. As expressed in the meetings of the Reparations Commission of the peace conference, France's claims upon German resources were essentially of two types. The first was deliveries in kind of certain vital raw materials which Germany possessed in abundance but which France lacked, most notably high-grade coal. The second was a relatively moderate debt of cash payments that could be readily "mobilized" (that is, tranformed into negotiable securities available for purchase by foreign investors, presumably Americans, in the secondary bond market) so as to turn the long-term German debt to France into immediately usable American credits. A high reparation bill was consistently opposed by most French financial experts on the grounds that it would have an adverse effect on French commercial interests. It could be paid only from the surplus of German exports over German imports, which would require an expansion of Germany's foreign trade at the expense of France's own exporters who were eager to recapture foreign markets lost during the war. Moreover, France was willing to receive as payment in kind on reparation account only those German goods (such as coal and timber) that did not compete with the products of French industry. To receive manufactured articles from Germany would be to grant German industrialists an inroad in the French market to the detriment of their French competitors.

The French government was therefore perfectly willing to abide by the relatively moderate prescriptions of President Wilson's Fourteen Points, which confined Germany's obligation to the reparation of civilian damages. Such a formula would have resulted in a total German payment of only 19 billion gold marks, of which France would have received 70 percent based on the extent of the damage to its national territory. The fixing of a specific, moderate sum would have greatly increased the chances of German acceptance of the obligation to defray the costs of French reconstruction, which could have been discharged without a drastic reduction in the German standard of living.

But such a moderate settlement of reparation claims was foreclosed by the intransigence of the British delegation at the Paris Peace Conference. Since the damage to civilian property in Great Britain* had been minimal, Lloyd George persuaded Wilson and Clemenceau to include the cost of veterans' pensions and separation allowances in the total bill to be submitted to Germany in order to maximize Britain's share of reparation payments. Although this modification affected only the distribution of receipts among the various recipient countries and did not increase Germany's total liability, it left a lasting impression of Allied greed and unfairness. To make matters worse, the peacemakers decided to postpone the establishment of a total figure for the German liability until May 1921, with the provision that Germany make a down payment of $5 billion in the interim. The ostensible reason for this delay was the necessity to verify the extent of civilian damages by onsite inspection. The real reason was the fear that public opinion in the Allied nations, which had been led to expect fantastic payments from Germany by the electoral rhetoric of the political leaders, would reject any figure as insufficient and take political revenge on any government foolish enough to accept it.

This failure to fix a precise sum of reparation payments produced widespread economic uncertainty and political resentment in Germany. For-

* Caused by bombs dropped by Zeppelin airships and Gotha bombers in cross-channel raids.

eign and domestic investors were understandably reluctant to commit their savings to an economic system that was saddled with an uncertain, and potentially enormous, claim on its productive resources. Public opinion within Germany fulminated against the "blank check" that the Allies had issued on that country's capacity to resume its prewar prosperity. But the greatest source of German resentment against the reparations settlement was purely symbolic, suggesting that symbols are often more important than substance in the formation of public attitudes. The legal justification for the indemnity was enshrined in article 231 of the peace treaty, which established Germany's liability for the damage to civilian property, a responsibility the German government had freely and explicitly acknowledged during the prearmistice negotiations. Inserted at the behest of an American attorney on the Reparation Commission, John Foster Dulles, this article was designed to *protect* Germany against any Allied claims for reimbursement of the total costs of the war: Germany was to be held *morally* responsible for the war and its consequences, but *legally* liable only for the narrowly defined damages specified in the treaty. Somehow this article was taken to imply the establishment of the principle of Germany's unilateral "war guilt." Such an interpretation was entirely baseless. The word "guilt" does not appear in the article. Nor was there any evidence of a "unilateral" indictment of Germany: Almost identical language was incorporated in the treaties subsequently signed with Germany's allies, Austria, Hungary, Bulgaria, and Turkey. Yet the myth of the "war-guilt clause," repeated by successive German governments in the 1920s and later used to good effect by Hitler, was to become as great a source of resentment in Germany as were the actual financial exactions.

It may seem ironic, in view of the British delegation's role in forestalling a moderate and definitive settlement of the reparation issue at the peace conference, that Lloyd George returned from Paris with the reputation as the most vigorous advocate of a peace of moderation. In fact, this reputation was based largely on British opposition to the harsh territorial (as opposed to economic) penalties for Germany that had been sought by France. We have already noted Lloyd George's role in blocking French efforts to establish an independent client state in the Rhineland on the grounds that such a territorial amputation would supply grist for the mill of German revisionism. For the same reason Britain clashed with France in regard to the issue of the territorial settlement along Germany's eastern frontier. In the unsettled borderland of Eastern Europe, with its hundred million people precariously lodged between Germany and Russia, France's policy was to promote a degree of regional security and stability that would enable the newly created or enlarged successor states of the Habsburg and Romanov empires to preserve their independence from their two temporarily weakened but potentially powerful neighbors. The chain of small and medium-sized states stretching from the Baltic to the Balkans were thought by French officials to hold the key to the future balance of power on the continent. The geographical barrier that they collectively formed between Germany and Russia seemed to represent the most effective means of preventing a rapprochement between those two dissatisfied powers at the expense of the victorious Allies. The new nations of Poland, Czechoslovakia, and Yugoslavia, together with the newly enlarged state of Romania, proudly asserted their right to national identity. But the mere declaration of national independence proved much simpler than the task of delimiting national frontiers in a region where the intermingling of populations throughout multinational empires during centuries of migration precluded the formation of ethnically homogeneous states. To complicate matters even further, economic and strategic considerations dictated several egregious violations of the principle of ethnic nationalism. Thus, a million German-speaking citizens of Posen and West Prussia were incorporated into the new state of Poland in order to satisfy that fledgling nation's need for access to a seaport on the Baltic. In order to provide Czechoslovakia with secure defenses, 3.25 million German inhabitants of the borderlands of Bohemia were included in that new state. The German-speaking citizens of the rump state of Austria were expressly forbidden to join Germany proper, because the unification of the Germanic states was deemed an intolerable menace to the security of the new Czechoslovak Republic and therefore to the balance of power in Central Europe. As in the case of the Rhineland, but this time with no success, Britain opposed these violations of German nationality claims on the grounds that they were likely to incite perpetual German dissatisfaction with the peace settlement.

The principal motivation for this conciliatory policy toward Germany in territorial matters may be traced directly to the British government's conception of its nation's vital interests. British policy at the peace conference was dictated by the overriding objective of assuring that Germany would never again threaten the sea lanes of the empire and the sources of supply in the Western Hemisphere. Such a guarantee was obtained through the reduction of the German navy to a token force of six warships and a corresponding number of auxiliary craft, the prohibition of submarines, and the redistribution of the German colonial empire in Africa and the Pacific among the victorious Allies as mandates under the auspices of the League of Nations. This naval and colonial settlement terminated the *Weltpolitik* inaugurated by the ill-fated William II. Thus restored to the continental position that she had occupied under Bismarck, Germany ceased to pose a menace to British imperial and maritime interests. Accordingly, Great Britain reverted to its traditional policy of promoting continental equilibrium in order to free her to play a global role. Specifically, this implied a moderate territorial settlement in Europe that would preserve Germany as a counterweight to French power on the continent. The reestablishment of such a balance between the former ally and the former foe became all the more necessary in British eyes as France began to court the new successor states of the Habsburg Empire in Eastern Europe. The prospect of a French-dominated coalition on the continent was hardly less distasteful to British officials than had been that of a Europe under the German yoke.

Because of the divergent national interests of the British and the French, the wartime coalition did not survive the advent of peace. Soon after the signing of the peace treaty with Germany at the royal palace in the Parisian suburb of Versailles on June 28, 1919, the fissures in the Anglo-French Entente became a matter of public record. As successive French governments struggled to enforce strict adherence to the peace treaty, successive British governments chose to interpret its provisions in the broadest and most lenient sense. The most notable cause of Anglo-French friction over the application of the Versailles Treaty concerned the reparations section. While Lloyd George had forcefully advocated the imposition of a heavy indemnity on Germany at the peace conference, British financial officials were apprehensive about the consequences of such a punitive reparation settlement for their country's economic interests. Inspired by the writings of John Maynard Keynes, an influential treasury official attached to the British delegation in Paris, these economic experts had concluded that a prosperous Germany was essential to the resumption of Britain's prewar trading patterns with Europe. Various arguments were advanced in London to justify drastic reductions in Germany's reparations bill even before it was definitively fixed in May 1921. The first of these centered on Germany's prewar position as a major market for British manufactured products. Large reparation payments to France would inevitably reduce Germany's capacity to import and thereby deprive British industry of a potentially valuable customer on the continent. The second related issue revolved around the so-called transfer problem that had confounded the financial authorities at the peace conference: Germany could transfer her real wealth to France only by generating a foreign trade surplus at the expense of British and other Allied commerce. Britain's export trade, on which she depended so desperately for her economic well-being, would be severely damaged if Germany were permitted to capture foreign markets in order to earn sufficient foreign exchange to discharge its reparation debt to France. During the first half of the 1920s when the British economy entered a prolonged crisis of industrial stagnation and high unemployment, this manner of thinking inspired the reparations policy of the British government, to the continual consternation of the financially hard-pressed French. The reparations imbroglio, aggravated by Anglo-French policy differences concerning Eastern Europe, the Rhineland occupation, and the Middle East,* effectively dissipated the wartime spirit of cooperation.

---

* France and Britain pursued divergent policies during the Greco-Turkish conflict of 1920–22, Paris supporting the Turks, London backing the Greeks. In addition, France suspected Britain of undermining French authority in Syria, which it acquired in 1920 as a mandate under the League of Nations.

This Anglo-French wrangling transpired in the absence of the only power that possessed the economic resources and political influence to ease the world's transition to peacetime conditions. The explanation of America's abrupt withdrawal from world affairs after the close of the Paris Peace Conference is beyond the scope of this book. Suffice it to say that one group of historians emphasizes the shortsightedness and narrowmindedness of the Republican majority in the Senate, which emasculated President Wilson's program of peace in order to avoid the unprecedented global commitments that it entailed; others blame the president's own unbending intransigence in the face of domestic political realities. Whatever the cause, the refusal of the United States Senate to accord its constitutionally prescribed consent to the three pacts signed by President Wilson at Paris—the peace treaty with Germany, the bilateral security treaty with France, and the covenant of the League of Nations—resulted in the termination of America's participation in the peacekeeping machinery. (The only exception to this across-the-board American retrenchment was the maintenance of American military forces in the inter-Allied occupation army in the Rhineland, and even that token commitment was prematurely withdrawn in 1923.) America's return to diplomatic isolation left its wartime associates with the entire responsibility for supervising the peace settlement that Wilson had played such a prominent role in fashioning. With the reduction of Britain's commitments on the continent and the temporary disappearance of Russia from the European scene, that responsibility devolved by default upon France, in association with such small states in Eastern Europe as she could enlist in a coalition committed to the preservation of the political status quo.

But the American extrication from European peacekeeping operations did not signify the disappearance of American power and influence in the world. It merely marked a change in the way that that power and influence was exercised. The United States had entered the Great War with no war aims and came to the peace conference with no demands. It coveted neither territory nor financial indemnities, and received none. All it had hoped to achieve, beyond the vague philosophical goals propounded by Wilson, was the restoration of economic stability in the world. It was under just such normal peacetime conditions that the United States had become the strongest economic power on earth by the beginning of the twentieth century. It was widely assumed in American government and business circles that the resumption of normal patterns of international trade and investment would stimulate a resurgence of economic growth in the postwar era. The removal of American support for the new political order in Europe coincided with a spectacular expansion of American economic power in the world that will be treated in subsequent chapters. As will become evident, what policymakers in Washington failed to realize during the 1920s was the extent to which the very conditions of international economic stability from which the United States was bound to profit depended on an effective solution to the simmering national antagonisms on the continent of Europe.

America's withdrawal from the new international order forged at the end of the First World War had been preceded by the disappearance of Russia as an active participant in world affairs. The fledgling Bolshevik regime that seized power in November 1917 had been forced to pay a high price for the separate peace it concluded with Germany four months later: The Baltic states, Finland, Russian Poland, part of White Russia, the Ukraine, Bessarabia, and part of Transcaucasia were detached from Russia and surrendered to German influence or control. This amounted to a quarter of Russia's territory and over a third of her population. It meant the loss of her most fertile food producing region and her most productive industrial areas. This extraordinary sacrifice was defended by Lenin against the anguished protests of many of his comrades on the grounds that it would provide a breathing spell for the new regime as it consolidated its power. He was also supremely confident that the revolutionary forces that had been unleashed in Russia would spread westward like wildfire across war-torn Europe, inciting the oppressed populations of all countries to overthrow their capitalist masters and establish Soviet republics on the model of the one recently formed in Petrograd. The free, independent, socialist states that would emerge from the ashes of the old empires of Europe would thereupon establish fraternal relations with the Russian regime from which they had gained their inspiration.

In the meantime, however, Lenin's authority over the shrunken remnant of the tsarist empire was forcefully contested by armed groups of counterrevolutionaries that had spontaneously sprouted all along the periphery of Bolshevik-controlled territory. Tsarist officers raised southern Russia in revolt against the Bolsheviks while simultaneously trying to expel the Germans from the Ukraine. In Siberia several anti-Bolshevik "governments" sprang up under the protection of a 50,000-man legion of Czechoslovak prisoners-of-war and defectors who had served in the tsarist army against Austria before Russia's withdrawal from the war. In September 1918 a "provisional all-Russian government" uniting the various anti-Bolshevik factions in Siberia was formed and eventually came under the control of Admiral Alexander Kolchak, the commander of the tsar's Black Sea Fleet. Kolchak assumed the title of "Supreme Ruler" of Russia and obtained the allegiance of most of the leaders of the other White armies operating in the region. In the north, an anti-Bolshevik regime was established in the Arctic port of Murmansk. The tsarist General N. N. Yudenich assembled a counterrevolutionary army in Estonia to mount an assault on nearby Petrograd (from which Lenin had prudently withdrawn in March 1918 to set up his capital in Moscow).

The outbreak of the Russian civil war presented the Allied governments with the opportunity to exploit the situation in the interests of prosecuting their war against the Central Powers. The Americans and British feared that the military supplies they had sent to the previous Russian regime, which were stacked up on the wharves of Russian seaports on the Arctic and the Pacific, might find their way into German hands. To prevent this from happening, a small British force was landed at Murmansk in March 1918; British, American, and French troops occupied Archangel in August for the same purpose; Japanese troops that had been landed at Vladivostok in April were soon joined by a much smaller American contingent. These Allied military forces cooperated closely with the anti-Bolshevik governments that had been formed in the hinterlands of the port cities that they occupied. The Americans and the British confined their activities to protecting the army stores and were reluctant to become embroiled in the civil war between Reds and Whites. But the French government had much more ambitious plans. It hoped that the various groups that had taken up arms against Lenin's regime could unite to form a strong, stable Russian government willing and able to overthrow the Bolsheviks, resume the war against Germany, and relieve the pressure against the Allies caused by Ludendorff's spring offensive. As it turned out, the anti-Bolshevik factions were never able to unite on a common program for Russia's future because they spanned the entire political spectrum, from tsarist reactionaries on the right to Mensheviks and Social Revolutionaries on the left. Hobbled by internecine ideological conflicts and clashes of personalities, the Whites gradually surrendered all the territory they had gained. By the end of 1920 the Russian civil war had come to an end with the Red Army having defeated its counterrevolutionary enemies on all fronts.

The purely military rationale for the Allied intervention in the Russian civil war disappeared with Germany's capitulation in November 1918. But Allied troops remained in the northern Arctic ports until the autumn of 1919 and the Japanese did not evacuate Siberia until the end of 1922. By the latter year the Bolsheviks had freed Russia of all foreign troops and recovered the frontiers of the former tsarist empire on all sides except in the west. There they faced the unrelenting hostility not only of the great powers that had defeated Germany, but also of a string of small independent states that had been carved out of former Russian territory lost at Brest-Litovsk: Finland, Latvia, Lithuania, and Estonia retained their independence under the protection of British warships operating in the Baltic. The greatly enlarged Kingdom of Romania preserved control of the former Russian province of Bessarabia that it had seized during the revolution. And, most ominous of all, a proud, assertive, strongly anti-Communist state of Poland had been reconstituted at Russia's gateway to Europe, with an eastern frontier extending far into former Russian territory.

Lenin's original plans for a Europe-wide Communist revolution that would liberate the masses from their oppressors and remove the threat of aggression against the Soviet state from the west went up in smoke during the first few months after the armistice. The few attempts that had been made by indigenous revolutionary movements in Central Europe to establish Communist regimes on the Russian model were ruthlessly crushed by the forces of counterrevolution with the sympathetic approval of the victorious allies. In January 1919 an insurrection in Berlin sponsored by the Sparticist League, a group of left-wing socialists inspired by the Bolshevik success in Russia, was quelled by the German government with the assistance of the army. A Soviet Republic established in Bavaria in April was forcibly overthrown. The Hungarian Communist Republic set up in Budapest by Béla Kun (a wily veteran of the Bolshevik Revolution in Russia) succumbed to a bloody counterrevolution supported by the invading army of Romania. In short, the Bolsheviks' triumph in Russia proved to be an isolated event rather than the beginning of the worldwide socialist revolution that its architects had confidently anticipated. The ideological hostility of the victorious Allies, coupled with the energetic opposition of the anti-Communist elites that assumed control of the successor states of the defunct empires of Central and Eastern Europe, succeeded in halting the spread of communism. The Allied statesmen meeting in Paris to make peace as the revolutions in Central Europe collapsed in the winter and spring of 1919 could take heart from the fact that, though the triumph of Lenin's movement seemed imminent within Russia in spite of counterrevolution and allied intervention, the "bacillus" of Bolshevism was being quarantined at the western border of the new Soviet state.

It is tempting for the historian of today, fortified with the wisdom of hindsight, to render a negative judgment on the Paris Peace Conference and the five treaties with the defeated powers that were signed in various Parisian suburbs in 1919–1920.* The last great diplomatic gathering of comparable importance, the Congress of Vienna, had established a framework for international order that had prevented the outbreak of a Europe–wide war for a century. The Peace of Paris collapsed within a generation, ushering in a terrible cycle of totalitarianism, genocide, and war on a scale previously unimagined. Nonetheless, it must in fairness be recorded that the Treaty of Versailles proved to be a failure less because of the inherent defects it contained than because it was never put into effect. It is impossible to imagine a Germany that had been compelled to fulfill its treaty obligations in their entirety endangering the peace of Europe. Effectively reduced to a token force and excluded in perpetuity from the Rhineland, the German army would have posed no military threat to France or the newly independent successor states to the east. Payment in full and on schedule of the relatively modest reparation sum fixed in May 1921 would doubtless have defused France's anxiety about its precarious economic condition and probably would have considerably reduced Franco-German tension. Recently uncovered evidence of a genuine French desire to co-

---

* The Treaty of Versailles with Germany, the Treaty of Saint-Germain-en-Laye with Austria, the Treaty of Trianon with Hungary, the Treaty of Neuilly with Bulgaria, and the Treaty of Sèvres with Turkey.

operate economically with Germany, particularly in the critical metallurgical sector (where French iron ore complemented German coking coal), suggests an opportunity for Franco-German reconciliation that was tragically lost.

It is difficult to conclude from a brief review of the territorial losses suffered by Germany after the Great War that the Versailles Treaty was unduly harsh on that score. The cession of Alsace-Lorraine to France merely restored the *status quo ante* of 1870 and was never seriously disputed by anyone of consequence in German official circles. The loss of the Baltic port of Danzig and the "corridor" connecting it to Poland was more objectionable because it separated the German province of East Prussia from the main body of the nation and therefore caused considerable inconvenience in regard to overland transportation to the severed province. But such inconvenience was nothing in comparison to the economic disadvantages that would have been suffered by a landlocked Poland. Furthermore, the formation of the corridor was scarcely a blatant violation of German nationality claims, since a majority of its inhabitants were Polish. Nor did it entail the loss of valuable natural resources that could not easily be compensated elsewhere. The same may be said for the cession to Poland of Upper Silesia, a coal-mining region of mixed Polish-German nationality. Coal output in the Ruhr and Saar covered Germany's domestic needs as well as its reparation obligations to France. Without the coal mines of Silesia, Poland would have been compelled to import enormous quantities of this expensive but essential fuel at a time when that fragile new state was struggling to put its financial house in order. Together with minor border rectifications to the profit of Denmark and Belgium, this constituted the totality of German territorial amputations after the war. Germany lost less territory at the peace conference than did any of her allies save Bulgaria. If any of the defeated nations deserved to complain of immoderate territorial losses, these were Austria, Hungary, and Turkey. But their complaints were of no consequence because they had ceased to be great powers and had lost all chance of regaining their former stature. Germany's treatment at Paris in 1919 was considerably less severe than the project for postwar European reorganization that had been endorsed by all significant political forces in Germany during the war and had been partially implemented in Eastern Europe after the collapse of Russia through the provisions of the Treaty of Brest-Litovsk. Despite her decisive military defeat, Germany emerged from the First World War as potentially the most powerful nation on the continent. Her industrial heartland, in contrast to that of victorious France, survived undamaged and intact because the war had been fought beyond her frontiers. Her territorial losses did not decisively curtail her capacity for recovery, as did those of her hapless allies.

Similarly, the final reparations obligation imposed on Germany hardly constituted the barbaric exploitation that German publicists made it out

Boundary Changes in Europe after the First World War

to be. The London Schedule adopted in May 1921 reduced Germany's total reparation bill so drastically that she could easily have managed the payments with but a moderate reduction of domestic consumption. That the German government, and the German people, refused to accept the reparations schedule and the economic sacrifices it entailed had little to do with the country's "capacity to pay." Rather, it reflected the German belief that *any* reparations, like *any* diminution of national territory, was by definition unjust. They were judged to be unjust because of the prevalent tendency to deny that Germany had lost the recent war. Its armies in the east had defeated the Russian colossus and thrust it back out of Europe, according to plan. Its armies in the west had marched home in orderly formation after their leaders had negotiated what had been fraudulently advertised as an armistice based on the principle of "no annexations, no indemnities." There had been little destruction or military occupation of German land during the four years of the war. Under such conditions, it comes as no surprise that the German people proved responsive to the allegation, repeated ad nauseum by a succession of national leaders after the war, that their fatherland had been deceived and betrayed by the victorious Allies. When all was said and done, the critical shortcoming of the Versailles Treaty was not that it was unjust and unworkable, but that the Germans thought it was and were able to win widespread support for that view at home and abroad.

Once Anglo-American confidence in and support for the peace settlement of 1919 evaporated, the burden thrust upon France and the other continental beneficiaries of the treaty gradually became unbearable. In time the new political order in Europe took on the appearance of an unstable system. By preserving intact the political and economic structure of the German Reich while surrounding it with a collection of politically immature, militarily vulnerable, economically unstable states, the peacemakers had mandated a potentially explosive imbalance of power on the continent. The presence of substantial German-speaking minorities in the eastern successor states and the German majority in the new Austrian Republic constituted a perpetual temptation to the advocates of German expansionism. Their plaintive pleas for the liberation of their oppressed compatriots and the recovery of this "lost" territory challenged the legitimacy of the political settlement of postwar Europe long before Hitler embarked upon his campaign to revise it. The only effective deterrent to German revisionism in Eastern Europe would have been the preservation of the wartime coalition of the United States, Great Britain, and France, fortified by the presence of the inter-Allied military force in the Rhineland. The disintegration of the victorious diplomatic coalition at the beginning of the postwar decade and the premature disappearance of the military deterrent force in the Rhineland at the end of it removed the sole practical means of enforcing the treaty that was supposed to keep the peace in Europe for all time.

CHAPTER 3

The Western World in the Twenties:
The Era of Illusions

The Illusion of Economic Restoration

The extensive economic dislocations caused by the First World War and the painful readjustment to peacetime conditions prompted widespread nostalgia in the Western world for the familiar system of international economic intercourse that had operated with relative effectiveness before 1914. As governments sought, with much wishful thinking, to resurrect the tried-and-true practices of the prewar epoch, a handful of perspicacious observers warned that the revolutionary transformation of the political and economic structures of the world wrought by the war precluded a simple return to the "good old days." But these ominous admonitions went unheeded. A superficial economic recovery during the second half of the 1920s effectively concealed the cracks in the edifice of international economic relations that had been rebuilt on the shaky foundations of the postwar world. The return of prosperity enabled national leaders to ignore the grave systemic weaknesses in the world economy and to avoid fashioning bold new policies to fit the new realities. It required the total unraveling of the network of international trade and investment that occurred in the 1930s to convince the political leaders that the First World War had signified the end of an era, and that a new mechanism for the allocation of the world's productive resources was required.

For the purposes of historical analysis, the postwar decade may conveniently be divided in two. The first five years of peace were marked by severe depression in some countries, hyperinflation in others, and in general a slowdown of international economic activity. The cause of this poor performance was not a decline in production. The physical capacity of the world to produce goods and services had not been appreciably reduced by the destructive effects of the war, except in those unfortunate regions of northeastern France, Belgium, and European Russia that had served as the principal theaters of combat. The problem lay rather in the defective channels for the distribution of productive factors throughout the world, that is, in the international network of trade, investment, and migration. In the most general sense, the principal impediment to postwar economic recovery was the disappearance of the relatively efficient mechanism for the international exchange of products, resources, capital, and labor that had eased the Western world's transition to an international industrial order in the second half of the nineteenth century (see p. 36).

The sluggish recovery of world trade in the early postwar years was directly related to developments in the political and economic relations among the nations of continental Europe. Among the most important of these problems was the spread of economic nationalism. This phenomenon was a natural outgrowth of the war, which had ostensibly revealed the military advantages of economic self-sufficiency and the danger of dependence on foreign markets and sources of supply. Most economic experts, and many political leaders, had recognized the folly of pursuing the elusive goal of autarky in the context of the narrow economic base of the individual nations of Europe. None of the belligerents in the Great War had possessed sufficient food-producing land, raw materials, or markets within their borders to meet its national needs. The recognition of the pressing necessity for some type of continental economic cooperation had prompted such multinational schemes as the German Mitteleuropa plan and the French proposal for an inter-Allied economic bloc. But these wartime projects for European economic integration had been thoroughly discredited by the end of the war. Instead, as we have seen, the political reorganization of Central Europe proceeded according to the principle of national self-determination; the territorial settlement codified in the Treaty of Saint-German-en-Laye with Austria and the Treaty of Trianon with Hungary set in motion the opposite trend: economic disintegration. The number of independent economic units in Europe—within which productive factors could circulate without restriction—increased from twenty to twenty-seven as the integrated economic systems of Austria and Hungary were shattered and parceled out among seven states (including three newly created ones), while five new nations were carved out of the western borderlands of Russia.

A negative economic consequence of this territorial distribution was the disruption of previously complementary regions: Urban centers (such as Vienna) were severed from their food supply in the agricultural hinterlands; industrial sectors (such as the Bohemian region of Czechoslovakia) were separated from their traditional sources of raw materials in those parts of the Habsburg empire that had been allocated to other states; the new frontiers often cut across the existing and most efficient means of transportation. Thus, the railway system of Czechoslovakia was centered on Vienna rather than on the Czech capital, Prague, causing considerable confusion and inefficiency in the economic relations between rump Austria and the new Czechoslovak Republic. Unlike the national unification process of Western Europe in the nineteenth century, which enlarged economic units and increased productivity, the nation-building in Eastern Europe after the First World War reduced the size of existing economic units and thereby decreased the efficiency that has traditionally resulted from economies of scale. The products, resources, capital, and labor that had circulated relatively freely within the two political subdivisions of the Austro-Hungarian Empire before the war encountered all manner of political restrictions enacted by the successor states. For reasons of insecurity and national pride, the political elites of these new nations sought to nurture their infant industries by the usual discriminatory practices—tariffs, import quotas, and government subsidies—thereby inhibiting the revival of intra-European commerce after the war. To make matters worse, access to the extensive natural resources and potentially lucrative markets of Russia was impaired on account of the intense ideological hostility evoked by the Soviet regime.

The clogging of the traditional channels of trade within Europe was a microcosmic version of the commercial crisis that gripped the entire world during the first half of the 1920s. The spirit of economic nationalism that inspired the governing classes of the new or newly enlarged nations in the center of the European continent also appeared in regions far removed from the battlegrounds of the recent war. Nations in the Western Hemisphere and the Far East had established or expanded domestic industries during the war in order to produce substitutes for the manufactured products that were no longer obtainable from the European belligerents. By the end of the war, several countries in Latin America, Canada, Japan, India, and Australia boasted highly developed industrial sectors that produced goods in direct competition with Europe's principal exports. It is no surprise that investors, managers, and labor groups that had acquired a stake in the profitability of those fledgling enterprises clamored for government protection against the anticipated influx of products from an economically revitalized Europe. Even the victorious powers of Western Europe, which had the most to gain from a revival of world trade because of their superior productive capacity, retained a number of wartime restrictions on imports of "luxury items" (defined in the broadest possible sense) to preserve the domestic market for national enterprises struggling to restore their productivity after four years of war-induced economic distortions.

But the necessity of protecting infant industries or to revive economic institutions devastated by war scarcely explains the protectionist policy pursued by the United States after the war. The Emergency Tariff Act of May 1921 and the Fordney-McCumber Tariff of the following year raised duties to their highest level in modern American history. These restrictionist commercial measures were the result of intense pressure exerted on the United States Congress by domestic agricultural and manufacturing interests that feared future competition from the replanted farmlands and re-equipped industries of Europe. Moreover, in conjunction with this new protectionist policy, successive American administrations waged a vigorous campaign to promote the American export trade. The Webb-Pomerene Act of 1918 had exempted American export firms from the Sherman Anti-Trust Act in order to enable them to join forces and compete on equal terms with the European cartels. Soon thereafter several American industrial enterprises joined international cartels that proceeded to allocate world markets, establish minimum prices, and restrict output. Under the Harding administration, Secretary of Commerce Herbert Hoover intensified this government-sponsored effort to increase sales of American products overseas. The Commerce Department's Bureau of Foreign and Domestic Commerce conducted marketing surveys in foreign countries and transmitted lists of prospective customers to American export firms. The State Department, as always devoted to the hallowed American dogma of the Open Door, vigorously supported the efforts of American firms to obtain access to markets and resources previously controlled by European concerns. A prime example of this partnership of business and government to expand American economic power overseas was the successful campaign by American petroleum companies, strongly backed by the State Department, to break the British monopoly on the oil reserves of Iraq, Saudi Arabia, and the sheikdoms along the Persian Gulf. In the meantime the United States mounted a spirited challenge to British domination of the international carrying trade. The Merchant Marine Act of 1920 authorized the sale of government-owned vessels to private shipping companies at bargain prices, while subsequent legislation granted public subsidies for the construction of new merchant ships. Economists warned that it was counterproductive for the United States to compete with European merchant fleets, since shipbuilding in the United States was more expensive than it was elsewhere because of higher labor costs. It would have made much more sense economically to purchase the services of the established European lines at lower prices. But this argument did not deter the advocates of a merchant fleet second to none, who countered with appeals to national pride: American goods should be carried by American ships, regardless of cost.

In addition to the relatively slow recovery of international trade caused by the revival of protectionism and economic nationalism, there occurred an important change in the structure and direction of world trade. We have already noted that the European powers' wartime diversion of productive capacity to the fabrication of munitions and military supplies caused a drastic decline in their export trade, a condition that was aggravated by the blockade policy of Britain and the submarine warfare of Germany. We have also noted that this cutoff of European supplies compelled those neutral nations that possessed the means to do so to create or expand new industries to compensate for the shortfall in imports. But those underdeveloped nations that lacked the productive factors that would have permitted them to replace European imports with their own domestic output increasingly turned to the United States or Japan as alternative sources of industrial products. Consequently, the United States replaced Great Britain as the principal trading partner of Latin America and surged far ahead of Germany and France, while Japan (whose output of manufactured goods doubled between 1913 and 1921) made substantial inroads into British markets in Asia for textile products such as cotton and wool. Similarly, the opening of new coal mines in the United States, India, and South Africa and the emergence of Middle Eastern petroleum as an alternative source of energy caused a serious decline in British coal exports, which, together with textiles, had accounted for the bulk of Britain's prewar export trade. These new commercial relationships persisted after the war. When the European powers sought to recapture their traditional markets abroad, they found themselves excluded by a combination of political restrictions and economic competition from upstart economic powers. During the same period, Europe's share of the previously lucrative American market declined precipitously: Throughout the 1920s, the percentage of the total value of United States imports supplied by Europe averaged about 30 percent compared to over 50 percent before the war.

The extent of this dramatic shift in the direction of international trade away from Europe and toward North America and Japan is recorded in other revealing statistics as well. Between 1913 and 1929, the total value of all of the world's exports increased by two-thirds. During the same period, the total value of British, German, and French exports grew by 15, 33, and 50 percent, respectively. But the total value of American exports doubled while Japan's trebled. What these figures reveal is that Europe was gradually losing its position as the undisputed master of world trade. The acceleration of the two principal prewar trends in international economic development—the economic penetration of Latin America by the United States and Japan's commercial expansion in East Asia—required drastic readjustments in the structure of international economic relationships. Such spectacular shifts in the locus of world economic power need not have produced international economic instability. But they were bound to cause serious disruption unless the newly emergent economic giants of the world grasped the extent of their international responsibilities and displayed a willingness to discharge them in such a way as to promote harmony in international economic exchange.

Unfortunately, the United States proved unwilling to bear its new burden as the leading exporter and international investor of the world. The first sign of this American reluctance to assume its new world obligations was the retreat into political isolation after the legislative rejection of the peace settlement of 1919. Apart from a few minor exceptions, the United States government declined to join the numerous international organizations that had been established to enforce the peace treaties and preserve collective security. American delegates did not participate in the succession of international conferences held in the course of the 1920s to address economic and security problems. The absence of an American voice in these deliberations both diminished their effectiveness and reduced Washington's ability to coordinate its foreign policies with those of the other industrial powers of the world.

Second, as will be seen, the financial and commercial practices of the United States in the postwar years were mutually contradictory and served to undermine America's dominant position in the world economic order. It is wholly inaccurate to apply the term "isolationism" to American foreign economic policy in the 1920s: While America's military and diplomatic presence abroad was drastically reduced, its banking and trading interests were engaged in strenuous economic expansion that definitively established the United States as a world financial and commercial power of the first rank. But the way in which this expansion was managed produced a number of problems that were to damage and eventually unravel the fragile fabric of international economic exchange that was being refashioned after the war.

We have already had occasion to note the resurgence of commercial protectionism in postwar America and its deleterious effect on world trade. But this trend became all the more injurious to the health of the international economy because it occurred at a time when the United States had become the major source of investment capital for the world. The principal movement of capital had ceased, in the course of the war, to be from Western Europe to primary producing regions for the purposes of developing underutilized resources, and went instead from the United States to Europe to finance human and material destruction. In 1914 the United States was a net debtor on international account by $3.7 billion. By 1929 she was a net creditor by more than $10 billion. Though the use to which American foreign lending and investment was put changed after the restoration of peacetime conditions, its direction remained largely the same, namely, to the European continent. That meant that America was lending to and investing in countries whose exports directly competed with American products. Consequently, the protectionist commercial policies adopted by postwar American governments, together with the vigorous campaign to expand American exports and to wrest control of foreign raw materials and the shipping trade from the European nations, made it increasingly difficult for America's European debtors to earn sufficient foreign exchange to repay their creditors across the Atlantic. Throughout the 1920s the United States maintained a balance-of-trade surplus with Europe that averaged a billion dollars annually, and continually enjoyed balance-of-payments surpluses.

Unlike Great Britain in its heyday as the world's premier trading nation, the United States was reluctant to receive large quantities of raw materials, foodstuffs, and semifinished industrial products from abroad to balance its continually expanding exports of finished manufactured goods. The source of this "closed door" policy can be traced to the unique advantage of the

American economy: privileged access to a vast internal market and virtual self-sufficiency in manufactured goods, basic foodstuffs, and most industrial raw materials. Foreign trade therefore accounted for a small proportion of its gross national product—less than 10 percent in 1929. Since American productivity was not significantly affected by the surpluses and deficits in international accounts, there was little incentive for officials in Washington to devise foreign economic policies that would promote the kind of commercial and financial stability that had been one of the principal objectives of British foreign economic policy in the nineteenth century. Instead, Washington responded to domestic pressures to insulate the domestic market even further from foreign competition while at the same time encouraging the expansion of American exports. This combination of import protectionism and export expansionism violated an elementary principle of international economics: Trade is a two-way street. Customers cannot afford to buy your products unless they can sell you the fruits of their own labor. Similarly, your debtors cannot repay you unless they can acquire a sufficient amount of your currency by selling you their products.

As unsettling as this simultaneous pursuit of protectionism and export expansion by the United States proved to be, an equally debilitating influence on international economic stability was price inflation in the industrial countries of the world. During the First World War most of the belligerent and many of the neutral nations had abandoned the gold standard in order to conserve scarce reserves of gold and foreign exchange. The suppression of the free international movement of gold during and immediately after the war disrupted the customary connection between national price systems and permitted prices to fluctuate independently in each nation. Some hapless countries, such as Germany, Austria, and the Soviet Union, suffered such a destructive bout of hyperinflation in the early postwar years that their currencies collapsed altogether. But the scourge of inflation also hit France, whose wholesale prices after the war increased by eight times their 1913 level, and Italy, where they rose about sevenfold. On the international level, exchange instability increased the risks of short-term lending to finance trade and long-term lending to promote economic development: Investors understandably hesitated to transfer their assets into a foreign currency whose value fluctuated wildly against their own. Exporters were reluctant to exchange valuable goods for paper money rendered increasingly worthless by the rise in domestic prices.

In addition to these obstacles to the free international exchange of surplus capital and production, the international movement of labor was severely curtailed by politically imposed restrictions. Just as American producers strove to exclude foreign products from their domestic market, American labor organizations pressed their government to stem the influx of foreign immigrants in order to reduce competition for employment. In 1924 the United States Congress established immigration quotas that discriminated against the very regions of the world (Eastern and Southern

Europe and Asia) that suffered from overpopulation. Before the First World War, people inhabiting densely populated areas with poor economic prospects such as Italy and the Austro-Hungarian Empire migrated to underpopulated regions with plentiful resources and land such as the United States in search of employment opportunities. During the 1920s average annual immigration to the United States dropped by over 50 percent from its prewar level. This meant that overpopulated areas could no longer rely on the safety valve of emigration to relieve internal pressures on land, food, and natural resources. As in the analogous case of tariff protection, this also meant that wages in the United States remained at a higher level than would have been the case had immigrants been permitted to enter the country to compete for jobs.

Free trade and free immigration—the unrestricted international exchange of resources and labor—remained unfulfilled hopes of those who wished to restore the prewar system of international economic relations in the 1920s. But the one significant achievement of this period was the successful restoration of a considerable degree of financial stability in the world. The only obvious solution to the scourge of inflation and exchange instability in the early twenties was a return to the international financial arrangements of the prewar epoch: In that comparatively benign period, a single nation blessed with substantial capital reserves (Great Britain) supplied the necessary liquidity to balance international accounts, while the gold standard assured that national currencies would be convertible into one another on the basis of a fixed relationship to gold.

The temptation to return to the gold standard eventually proved so powerful as to overcome all objections to linking the economic fortunes of the world to what the British economist John Maynard Keynes once contemptuously referred to as "that barbarous relic." The return to gold was not easy for many nations, particularly those whose currencies had drastically depreciated in value during the war; the restoration of the gold standard at prewar parities would have reestablished exchange rates that considerably overvalued their currencies, thereby rendering their exports prohibitively expensive in foreign markets. This was precisely the position of Great Britain, which committed the error of returning to the gold standard at the prewar parity of $4.86. Other nations, such as France and Italy, took the precaution of devaluing their currencies in terms of its prewar parity, so as to bring their external value down to the level of their depreciated value and retain the competitive price advantage of their exports. Between 1925 and 1929 more than forty nations, including all of those with a significant stake in international trade, returned to the gold standard. By the end of the decade, the familiar method of adjusting international accounts had been universally reestablished. But, as always, it depended on the solidity of the principal reserve currencies (in this case, the British pound and the American dollar) and the willingness of the two governments that issued them to buy and sell gold at a specified price to preserve the convertibility of the world's currencies.

Equally important for international monetary stability as the return to the gold standard was the revival of long-term foreign investment. By the middle of the 1920s the total amount of foreign lending had surpassed its prewar level, with the United States replacing Great Britain as the principal source of this international capital flow. Between 1920 and 1929 American private lenders furnished $7.6 billion in dollar loans abroad, of which $7.3 billion were outstanding at the end of 1929. Though on a much more modest scale, Great Britain and France resumed their role as net exporters of capital in the early 1920s. This revival of foreign lending supplied the foreign exchange required for the conduct of international trade, the repayment of existing debts, and the stimulation of economic development.

But the new international financial system forged in the 1920s differed from its prewar predecessor in a number of important respects. The law of supply and demand should have dictated the resumption of large-scale capital flows from those nations with a surplus of savings over domestic investment opportunities as well as high labor costs to regions with abundant but underutilized resources and cheap labor. This would have meant the export of capital from the United States and, to a lesser extent, Great Britain and France, to the primary producing regions of the earth (particularly Latin America and East Asia, which had already begun to receive substantial infusions of investment capital before the war). But as Wall Street replaced the City of London as the "banker of the world," the volume, character, and direction of foreign investment underwent an important transformation.

First of all, the United States lent abroad a much smaller proportion of its gross capital formation than had Great Britain before 1914. The resulting accumulation of gold and foreign exchange in the United States was in large part due to the speculative boom on Wall Street, which drove stock prices to lofty heights entirely unrelated to the real assets that those securities represented. The prospect of selling these stocks at higher prices in a short period of time attracted an inordinate amount of domestic and foreign capital that otherwise would have been available for short-term lending to balance international accounts and long-term credits to increase the productive capacity of America's trading partners and debtors. In short, the lure of instant capital gains on the American stock market prevented the New York banking community from assuming its rightful role as the supplier of liquidity in international economic transactions. To make matters worse, the periodic attempts by the Federal Reserve Board to dampen the speculative boom by increasing interest rates precipitated a flood of foreign capital into the American money market in search of higher returns.

Second, the foreign lending that the United States did undertake in the 1920s differed from previous British lending policy in both character and direction. In the prewar years, most European foreign investments were channeled into the development of productive enterprises and transportation systems (such as railroads, roads, and ports) in developing countries in order to improve their ability to produce, transport, and export products that were desired in Europe. By contrast, most American foreign loans in the 1920s went to European governments and municipalities to finance public works projects such as bath houses, parks, urban housing, and the like. Such consumption-oriented amenities, however much pleasure they may have brought to European citizens weary of their wartime sacrifices, did not increase the productive capacity of the recipient countries or improve their ability to earn the foreign exchange required to finance their imports and service their foreign debts. The proportion of American lending that did go to productive enterprises tended to take the form of short-term loans financing long-term projects. This anomalous arrangement left the debtor countries vulnerable to default in hard times and dependent on the perpetual renewal of American credit.

A great deal has been written about the role of inter-Allied debts and German reparations as disruptive factors in the international economy of the 1920s. It has often been asserted that the intergovernmental obligations left over from the recent war inhibited postwar economic recovery by generating international capital movements that were entirely unrelated to commercial transactions or investment opportunities. Before the war, as we have seen, capital exports resulted from the free choice of individual investors, or of the banks in which they deposited their savings, as they sought the highest return for their funds consistent with safety. But after the war many of the governments of the world owed considerable sums to other governments for debts (either contractual or moral) incurred in the course of the war. In order to discharge these obligations, the debtor governments would have had to raise the funds domestically and then transfer them into the currencies of the creditor nations. Thus, these politically defined debts represented distortions in the normal flow of international payments.

The first category of these intergovernmental debts comprised the roughly $10 billion that had been lent by the American Treasury to the governments of twenty nations during or immediately after the First World War. Over 90 percent of these debts were owed to the United States by its three principal associates in the war: Great Britain, France, and Italy (see Table VI). These sums had been raised by the sale of war bonds to American citizens after the intervention of the United States in April 1917. As we have seen, the proceeds of these bond sales were used to finance Allied purchases of American supplies required for the prosecution of the war and, after the armistice, for the beginning of postwar reconstruction. Though these debts

TABLE VI   Major Wartime and Postwar Foreign Loans of United States Government (In millions of dollars)

Recipient Nation	Pre-Armistice (cash)	Post-Armistice (cash & supplies)	Total Indebtedness
Great Britain	3,696.0	581.0	4,277.0
France	1,970.0	1,434.8	3,404.8
Italy	1,031.0	617.0	1,648.0
Russia	187.7	4.9	192.6
Belgium	171.8	207.3	379.1

Source: Harold Moulton and Leo Pasvolsky, *War Debts and World Prosperity* (New York, 1932), p. 426, and Thomas A. Bailey, *A Diplomatic History of the American People* (Englewood Cliffs, N.J., 1974), p. 657.

were established as sight obligations and therefore were theoretically payable on demand, in the spirit of wartime cooperation the American government did not raise the issue of repayment during the war or its immediate aftermath. But during the first four years of peace the Wilson, Harding, and Coolidge administrations prodded the European debtors to enter into negotiations with the American Treasury Department to devise repayment schedules.

America's erstwhile wartime associates resisted this pressure with vigor. They contended that these loans represented America's contribution to the joint war effort and therefore should be drastically reduced or written off altogether. The United States had basked in isolation during the first three years of combat, and then took over a year to field a fully trained and equipped army on the western front while the European Allies bore the brunt of German military power at great cost to themselves. The French, British, and Italians could not retrieve their dead soldiers. Why should the United States be entitled to recover the funds that it had originally sent in place of men?

To this moral argument were added numerous economic ones. The notion that these loans represented an economic sacrifice on the part of the United States came under harsh criticism. The proceeds had been spent almost entirely in the United States to purchase American products. They therefore increased American profits and employment and even indirectly benefited the American Treasury through the income taxes and excess profits taxes generated by these sales. Moreover, it was universally predicted in Europe that the cancellation of inter-Allied debts would redound to the commercial benefit of the United States. European treasury officials repeatedly reminded their American counterparts that Great Britain had forgiven the debts on the loans it had advanced to its continental allies during the war against Napoleon and had thereafter been repaid many times over by a prosperous Europe that imported British manufactured goods. From a financial point of view, it seemed pure folly for a major creditor nation, which had lent billions of dollars abroad through private channels, to expect repayment of these government obligations. The rules of international financial conduct suggested that the surplus funds that had accumulated in the United States during and after the war ought to be recycled into those war-ravaged countries that required working capital for reconstruction; instead, Europe was being asked to increase the American capital surplus even further through debt payments that would be exceedingly difficult to manage.

The most cogent argument advanced by the European debtors in favor of cancellation centered on the inherent contradiction between America's postwar commercial policy and its insistence on debt repayment. On many counts it resembled the case against reparations presented by Germany and other interested parties. The European debtors possessed insufficient gold reserves to effect payment in that precious metal, and in any case such massive gold outflows would destroy the value of their currencies. But even if they could raise the domestic paper currency equivalent of the amount owed to America, the European debtors lacked the balance-of-payment surplus to purchase the foreign currencies required to service the debt. Their dollar receipts from "invisible exports," such as shipping and insurance services, tourist expenditures, and remittances of European immigrants abroad, were far below the level required to make up the difference. Therefore, the Europeans argued, the only way that they could accumulate the necessary amount of dollars to discharge their obligation was by maintaining a continuously favorable balance of trade, especially with the creditor country. But, as we have seen, the combination of protectionism and aggressive export promotion pursued by the Republican administrations of the 1920s made it difficult for European firms to gain access to the American market, while throwing open European markets to American products. Economists on both sides of the Atlantic scratched their heads to figure out how the European nations, in the midst of this chronic "dollar shortage," could possibly satisfy American demands for debt repayment.

All of the economic arguments in favor of debt cancellation made good sense. What they failed to take into consideration was the extent of America's insulation from the operation of the international economic system in the 1920s. As we have noted in regard to the postwar commercial policy of the United States, the absence of a sense of economic interdependence enabled domestic pressure groups to exercise a decisive influence on their government's foreign economic policy. The same was true with regard to the dispute over inter-Allied debts. American taxpayers refused to bear the burden of higher taxation that would be required to redeem the war bonds at maturity if the European governments failed to pay. Sensational news reports from Europe of lavish spending for armaments and luxury items reinforced this parsimonious state of mind. American war veterans clamored for a "bonus" as a belated reward for services rendered to the Allied cause. They bitterly recalled that their government had generously chosen to forgo the liberal separation allowances and veterans' pensions that had been written into the reparation section of the treaty for the benefit of their British and French counterparts. Agricultural and manufacturing interests in the United States were deaf to the technical arguments of economists about the necessity of permitting European access to the American market in order to facilitate the repayment of the intergovernmental debt. Most importantly, American officials saw no distinction between public and private debts. These loans were regarded as normal business transactions. "They hired the money, didn't they?" asked President Calvin Coolidge. To forgive these intergovernmental obligations would undermine the sanctity of contracts and set a dangerous precedent that European recipients of American private loans might be tempted to invoke at some future date.

Prompted by these domestic pressures, the United States Congress established the World War Foreign Debt Commission on February 9, 1922, and instructed it to reach agreement with the European debtors at a minimum interest rate of 4.25 percent and a maximum maturity of twenty-five years. Bilateral negotiations on the debt settlement dragged on for several years, while the State Department pressured recalcitrant governments to come to terms by encouraging an informal embargo on private loans to nations in default. As a result, all of the major debtors had signed funding agreements by the end of 1926. The total interest charges more than doubled the original debt, though the rates were much lower and the maturities much longer than had been stipulated in the act creating the commission. The annual debt payments came to approximately a third of a billion dollars a year, which represented a significant portion of Europe's current dollar income from merchandise exports to the United States.

France, the major holdout, finally signed a funding agreement in April 1926; but the French parliament delayed ratification until the summer of 1929, when Germany's acceptance of the Young Plan promised sufficient reparation payments to France to cover France's debt payments to the United States. It was the issue of German reparations, more than any other, that poisoned the atmosphere of international relations during the decade of the 1920s. Though recent research has shown that the actual economic consequences of the reparations settlement of 1919 were considerably less dramatic than was supposed at the time, the political passions that this issue engendered on all sides played a major role in undermining the structure of European security that had been fashioned at the Paris Peace Conference. Most of the issues that emerged in the course of France's effort to collect reparation payments from Germany in the first half of the 1920s had already been aired at the peace conference. The first of these, raised repeatedly at the numerous international economic discussions held during this period, was the familiar question of Germany's "capacity to pay." How much of the German people's income could be taxed by its government and applied to the payment of the reparation debt without impoverishing the nation and destroying its productive capacity? No one doubted that a bankrupt, unproductive Germany (however attractive a prospect that might have appeared to neighboring nations fearful of the military consequences of German economic recovery) would be incapable of paying anyone anything. But it was also universally understood that in order for Germany to discharge its reparation obligation, its people would have to reduce their consumption and bear the burden of higher taxes. These measures of austerity would release domestically produced goods for export and reduce domestic demand for imports, thereby enabling Germany to accumulate sufficient foreign exchange to pay the annual reparation installment.

This sacrifice the German people, and the German government, refused to accept. Far from submitting to the deflationary fiscal and monetary policy that such belt-tightening required, the Weimar Republic experienced in the early postwar years one of the most extraordinary bouts of hyperinflation that the world has seen. Whether, as some unfriendly critics have suggested, that inflation was deliberately engineered by the German government to sabotage the reparations settlement, or whether it was caused by economic forces beyond anyone's control, remains a matter of intense historiographical controversy. But the result was unmistakable: The nation that was supposed to consume less and produce more in order to indemnify the French for their wartime losses began falling behind on its reparation deliveries as its currency depreciated and its domestic prices soared. It may have been unrealistic for the French to suppose that a people would freely consent to a reduction in its standard of living in order to compensate former enemies for damage claims it regarded as inflated and unjust. But the only alternative to a mutually acceptable contractual obligation is one based on coercion. When Germany repeatedly defaulted on reparation payments throughout the year 1922, the nationalistic government of French Prime Minister Raymond Poincaré chose the path of military force as a means of compelling payment. On January 9, 1923, the French-controlled Reparation Commission officially declared Germany in default on coal deliveries. Two days later, on the express instructions of the commission, French, Belgian, and Italian technicians protected by a small military force entered the industrial heartland of Germany in the Ruhr Valley to procure the coal owed as reparations. When the Berlin government ordered the miners and railway workers to withhold their cooperation, a much larger contingent of French and Belgian troops was sent in to seal off the Ruhr from the rest of Germany and preserve domestic order while the technical personnel mined the coal and operated the railroads that transported it to the frontier.

All nations concerned profited handsomely from the Ruhr occupation. France obtained the coal she required as the German campaign of passive resistance petered out and finally ended in September 1923. British exports of coal and pig iron soared as continental customers who were cut off from their traditional suppliers in the Ruhr rushed to adopt British substitutes. The German government as well as private heavy industry discharged much of its domestic debt in the worthless currency debased by Berlin's profligate printing of paper money to pay unemployment benefits to the striking workers of the Ruhr. The only major losers amid the resulting hyperinflation that engulfed Germany in 1923–24 were the members of the German middle class living on fixed incomes, who lost their life savings and their confidence in the future.

But the short-term benefits of French coercion in the Ruhr did not alleviate the structural weaknesses of the European economic system. Though there was little evidence that the slow pace of postwar economic recovery was caused by the reparations dispute, official opinion in Great Britain and the United States increasingly came to accept this explanation. In addition to the problem of Germany's capacity to pay, the transfer problem that had bedeviled the financial experts at the Paris Peace Conference loomed large in the thinking of Anglo-American officials as they observed the unilateral French intervention in western Germany. The nature of the problem, according to contemporary financial opinion, had not changed since the debates over reparations at the peace conference: The transfer of such massive quantities of real wealth across national boundaries would inevitably disrupt the economies of debtor and creditor countries alike, discourage foreign investment, and endanger world trade. Domestic producers in Great Britain feared an influx of cheap articles "made in Germany," while British exporters shrank from the prospect of German competition in foreign markets that they were striving to recapture. American trading interests, eagerly eyeing the German market, worried about the decline in Germany's capacity to import that such large reparations payments would inevitably entail. Wall Street investment houses hesitated to commit funds to Germany so long as its government was saddled with a huge reparations burden.

By the end of 1923, a consensus had formed in financial circles of the English-speaking world in favor of a comprehensive reparations settlement that would resolve the problem of Germany's capacity to raise and transfer funds to her creditors. The onset of a severe financial crisis in France at the beginning of 1924—caused mainly by the French government's refusal to increase domestic taxation once it became evident that substantial German reparation payments to finance reconstruction of the northeastern *départements* would not be forthcoming—afforded British and American bankers the leverage they needed to impose a new reparations regime on the reluctant authorities in Paris. A committee of economic experts, headed by the American banker Charles Dawes, had been appointed by the Reparation Commission to study the problem and propose a solution. The Dawes committee report, submitted on April 9, 1924, proposed a complex system of annual payments that could be adjusted to Germany's capacity to pay, provided for a large private international (but mainly American) loan to Germany in order to facilitate the payment, and effectively destroyed France's controlling position in the Reparation Commission. National elections in France during the spring of 1924 led to the replacement of the Poincaré government, which had carried out the occupation of the Ruhr and consistently refused all compromise with Germany, with a cabinet headed by the more conciliatory Edouard Herriot. Alarmed by the collapse of the franc and tempted by the prospect of Anglo-American financial assistance, the new French government officially accepted the Dawes Plan at the London Conference of July 1924.

The Dawes Plan constituted a fundamental modification of the reparation section of the Treaty of Versailles by abolishing France's legal authority to compel German payment by unilateral fiat. The emasculation of the Reparation Commission and the evacuation of French military forces from the Ruhr in August 1925 removed forever the threat of military force as an option in French reparation policy. Through an elaborate financial sleight of hand, voluntary American capital investment had replaced the coerced diversion of German production as the engine of European economic reconstruction. In a certain sense, this represented a modified version of the original French plan for European recovery unveiled at the peace conference and subsequently rejected by the United States. The only major difference was in the source and direction of the capital movements involved. The funds would be supplied by private investment firms in New York instead of by the Treasury Department in Washington. They would be recycled through the German economic system instead of flowing directly to the Allied nations in need of working capital for reconstruction and debt service. Between 1924 and 1931 private American investors lent $2.25 billion to Germany. Germany resumed its reparation payments to the Allied states. The latter in turn forwarded about $2 billion to the United States in repayment for the wartime loans.

There were two important long-term consequences of this modification of the reparation system. First, the economic recovery of Europe became directly dependent on the willingness or ability of American banks and investment houses to maintain this continuous flow of private funds to the national and municipal governments of Germany. Second, the targeting of Germany for the major portion of the American lending effort enabled the defeated nation in the war to discharge its annual reparation debt and reequip its industries almost entirely with capital supplied by the former enemy.

The apparent settlement of the reparations dispute, coinciding as it did with the influx of American capital, greatly assisted Europe in recovering rapidly from the debilitating effects of the Great War. By the end of 1925 industrial production and real wages in most continental nations had returned to their prewar levels and continued to rise for the remainder of the decade. The Europe that in 1923 seemed mired in economic crisis and torn apart by the Franco-German altercation over reparations embarked upon a period of prosperity and economic expansion in the middle of the decade. The only regions of the earth that failed to participate in this burst of economic activity were the primary producing countries of the Southern Hemisphere and Eastern Europe. These nations suffered from a persistent problem of agricultural overproduction that so exceeded world demand for foodstuffs as to cause a catastrophic drop in the price of such commodities as wheat, corn, sugar, coffee, and cocoa.

The causes of this agricultural overproduction can be traced directly to the First World War: The sharp decline in European food production during the war drove up commodity prices on the world market and prompted farmers on other continents to increase their acreage. After the war the fertile farmlands of France and Eastern Europe were quickly restored to their prewar level of agricultural output, in part because the introduction of better fertilizers and mechanization sharply increased the yield per acre. The resulting agricultural surpluses accumulated unsold because of income inelasticity in the industrial world. That is, as incomes rose in the developed countries of Western Europe, North America, and Japan, people did not spend their additional money on more food. At the same time, those regions of the Southern Hemisphere with large undernourished and even starving populations lacked sufficient income to purchase the agricultural production even at depressed prices. It was a tragic paradox of the interwar period that the food-producing regions of the earth, such as the newly independent countries of Eastern Europe, brought to the world market more of their cash crops than the industrial nations could consume and more than the hungry masses of the world could afford to pay for. The resulting agricultural depression in turn applied a brake on the economic expansion of the industrialized nations of Western Europe, which found it increasingly difficult to sell their surplus manufacturing output to the hard-pressed primary producing areas of the world. Thus, the remarkable economic growth experienced by the industrial nations of the North Atlantic region during the second half of the 1920s concealed the ominous global implications of the chronic agricultural crisis that gripped the Southern Hemisphere and Eastern Europe during the same period. The illusion of Western prosperity survived so long as the engine of American financial power and industrial productivity continued to operate at peak efficiency.

The Illusion of Continental Security

The history of the political relations among the nations of Europe in tne 1920s may be reduced to a few essential themes: the German Republic's effort to dismantle the peace treaty that restricted its economic, diplomatic, and military power; the attempt by France and its continental allies to enforce those treaty limitations; and the effort by Great Britain, with the tacit encouragement of the United States, to remove the objectionable features of the peace treaty that were thought to be responsible for Germany's refusal to accept the new European order created at Versailles.

Throughout the first half of the 1920s, French governments of diverse political tendencies devoted their diplomatic skill to the achievement of one overriding objective: the resurrection of the alliance with Great Britain that had lapsed in 1920 after the failure of the United States Senate to consent to the French security treaty signed by President Wilson in Paris. The ostensible reason for Britain's repudiation of its commitment to defend France against unprovoked German aggression was purely a legalistic one: The Anglo-French security pact was to become operational only as an integral component of the ill-fated Franco-American agreement. The explanation of London's subsequent refusal to replace this moribund treaty with a strictly bilateral guarantee of France's frontier with Germany requires a cursory review of Great Britain's conception of its national interest.

As always, British foreign policy after the First World War was dictated by the interrelated objectives of protecting the British Isles, preserving the empire, and controlling the sea communications between them. When Germany's "world policy" after the turn of the century had endangered those vital interests, Great Britain composed its differences with France and Russia in North Africa and southern Asia, respectively, in order to form a common front in opposition to any further accretion of German power. As a result of the First World War and the peace conference that terminated it, the principal threats to the security of Great Britain and its empire had been removed: The abolition of the German air force, the reduction of the German navy to insignificance, and the dissolution of the German colonial empire had the combined effect of denying Germany the capacity to project its power beyond the European continent. The internal disarray of Russia removed the other potential menace to British imperial interests, namely, aggression by land against India, disruption of the British lifeline to Asia, and pressure against British-controlled petroleum resources along the Persian Gulf. In fact, as long as Germany was disarmed and deprived of its naval power and colonial bases, Russia was kept at bay in southern Europe and southern Asia, and Japan remained content to confine its expansionist aspirations to the region north of the Yangtze River in the Far East, the only conceivable peril to Britain's imperial communications came from France itself. France's ambitions in its newly acquired mandates in Syria and Lebanon and its intrigues in Turkey caused considerable friction with Great Britain, which insisted on preserving its undisputed position of dominance in the eastern Mediterranean.

In conjunction with its "empire first" strategy, London reverted to its traditional policy of promoting a balance of power in Europe while striving to prevent any one of the great continental nations from amassing sufficient military might (especially air and naval power) to pose the threat of an invasion across the English Channel. This policy inevitably inspired British opposition to France's quest for an overwhelming margin of military superiority over Germany. It is easy to forget, in light of the subsequent debacle of 1940, that France in the 1920s possessed the most formidable land army and air force in the world. With Germany militarily disarmed by diplomatic fiat and Great Britain and the United States by choice, France was the only one of the former belligerents to retain land and air forces of wartime dimensions. Though unmistakably intended for defense of the eastern frontier, French air power alarmed British strategists, who realized that the English Channel no longer provided the security from attack that it had before the advent of the air age, particularly since Britain had begun to dismantle its own air arm shortly after the armistice.

In light of Germany's disarmament and France's acquisition of undisputed military preponderance in Europe, it comes as no surprise that Great Britain systematically rebuffed French attempts in the early 1920s to secure a British commitment to defend by force of arms the territorial settlement in Western Europe. This refusal to accord France the promise of the military assistance she so ardently sought did not signify any willingness on Great Britain's part to tolerate German aggression against France. On the contrary, officials in London repeatedly reaffirmed that the inviolability of France's eastern frontier was an extension of Britain's own security interests. "Britain's frontier is on the Rhine" appropriately became the slogan of the new era. The problem lay in the conflicting views in Paris and London of how French and therefore British security could best be preserved. The French tenaciously clung to the notion that the only effective means of preventing Germany from endangering the peace of Europe was by compelling its strict adherence to the Versailles Treaty; any modification of the military, territorial, or reparation sections of the treaty was considered inadmissible in Paris on the grounds that it would encourage further efforts at revision. And a Germany freed from the restrictions imposed upon her at the peace conference would inevitably threaten the political status quo on the continent because of her position as the most populous and potentially the most economically powerful nation in Europe. By contrast, British policymakers contended that European security could best be assured by removing those irritants embedded in the Versailles Treaty that prevented Germany from accepting her reduced status in the world. Hence the British refusal to promise military aid to France against Germany as well as Britain's campaign to reduce Germany's reparations burden. Hence also British opposition to French efforts to compel German adherence to the Versailles Treaty by the threat or actual application of military sanctions. Underlying this British approach to European affairs was the conviction that a productive, stable, secure Germany could be enticed to rejoin the community of great powers as a peaceful, cooperative member. A Germany torn by economic chaos, political instability, and military insecurity could only foster sentiments of resentment and revenge.

The disappearance of the Anglo-American guarantee of France's border with Germany in 1920 prompted that nation to begin a compensatory quest for allies among the states on the European continent that shared with her a common interest in preserving the postwar political settlement. On September 7, 1920, France concluded a military alliance with Belgium, whose acquisition of the frontier districts of Eupen and Malmédy from Germany and whose strategic location astride the historic invasion route in northern Europe rendered it a likely object of German aggression in a future war on the continent. This terminated that small country's long-standing status of neutrality and formed the basis of close Franco-Belgian cooperation to enforce the provisions of the Versailles Treaty.

On the opposite flank of Germany lay those states of Eastern Europe that been formed or enlarged at the expense of the Central Powers after the war and therefore were prime candidates for inclusion in the emerging continental coalition organized by Paris during the first half of the twenties. Foremost among these was Poland, which had been carved out of German, Austrian, and Russian territory to form an independent republic on November 3, 1918. Poland had obtained Allied recognition of its western frontiers with Germany in the Treaty of Versailles, acquiring thereby large parts of West Prussia and Posen (the corridor along the Vistula to the Baltic) as well as special economic privileges in the port city of Danzig. German resentment of Poland's acquisition of this territory, exacerbated by Polish designs on Upper Silesia (an important industrial region of mixed German-Polish population that contained Germany's largest coal reserves), predisposed the government in Warsaw to seek the military protection of France. Paris responded favorably to these overtures from a fellow opponent of German revisionism; on February 19, 1921, the two states concluded a military alliance that was followed by extensive French economic assistance to Poland for armaments and national reconstruction.

In the meantime, the three nations in the Danube region that had acquired territory from Hungary after the war—Czechoslovakia, Romania, and Yugoslavia—concluded bilateral alliances with one another to deter Hungarian attempts to regain this lost land. Though this diplomatic association (which came to be known as the Little Entente) was directed against Hungary rather than Germany, French officials actively promoted it in the expectation that its three member states, in combination with Poland, could replace Russia as a counterweight to German power in Eastern Europe. French hopes for such an eastern bloc were pinned on Czechoslovakia, the only signatory of the Little Entente that shared a common frontier with Germany and possessed the industrial and military wherewithal to pose a credible deterrent to German aggression in the region. The presence of some three million German-speaking inhabitants in western Czechoslovakia and the efforts by nationalist elements in Germany to exploit their grievances against the Czech state guaranteed a sympathetic response in Prague to the French attempts at alliance making. On January 25, 1924, the two countries concluded a bilateral pact which provided for mutual assistance in the event of unprovoked aggression. Subsequent treaties of friendship between France and Romania (June 10, 1926) and between France and Yugoslavia (November 11, 1927) completed France's ambitious campaign to compensate for the absence of the Russian alliance by surrounding Germany with a bloc of small Slavic states committed to the maintenance of the political status quo in Europe.

Though formidable on paper, this informal bloc of Eastern European states linked to France was beset with defects that severely undermined its potential value as a peacekeeping coalition on the continent. All of France's partners in the east were multinational states whose discontented ethnic minorities represented an omnipresent threat to their political unity and social stability (see Table VII). Worse still, all of them were locked in bitter conflict over disputed territory either among themselves or with foreign powers other than Germany: Poland had wrested land from Russia after launching an invasion of the Ukraine in 1920. Romania had seized the Russian province of Bessarabia during the latter stages of the world war. Yugoslavia clashed with Italy over competing territorial claims on the Istrian peninsula and the Dalmatian coast of the Adriatic. Czechoslovakia had obtained the coal-mining district of Teschen despite the presence of a Polish majority there, touching off a bitter altercation between Prague and Warsaw that poisoned relations between Paris's two premier allies in Eastern Europe. These internal difficulties and external tensions, legacies of the Paris Peace Conference's hopeless task of reconciling conflicting nationalist aspirations in a region of heterogeneous populations, guaranteed perpetual instability in Eastern Europe that could only redound to the benefit of Germany once it succeeded in emancipating itself from the strictures of Versailles.

In light of the fragility of these medium-sized states in Eastern Europe, why did France not probe further east to seek an understanding with Russia, the historic counterweight to German power on that half of the continent, which boasted a population almost three times that of Poland and the nations of the Little Entente combined? First of all, the ideological antipathy for bolshevism engendered in the Western world by the October Revolution and its aftermath did not abate even after the failure of the Bolshevik-inspired insurrections in Central Europe during the early postwar years. The establishment in March 1919 of the Communist International (or Comintern), together with the subsequent emergence in all European countries of Communist parties that affirmed their allegiance to the Soviet Union and its Marxist-Leninist doctrines of social revolution, struck fear in the hearts of governing elites everywhere. In France this ideological hostility to the Soviet Union, which was particularly acute during the tenure

TABLE VII   The Ethnic Minority Problem in Selected Eastern European
Countries

POLAND
Census of September 30, 1921

Ethnic Group	Number	Percentage of Total Population
Poles	18,814,239	69.2
Ukrainians (Ruthenes)	3,898,431	14.3
Jews	2,110,448	7.8
White Russians	1,060,237	3.9
Germans	1,059,194	3.9
Lithuanians	68,667	0.3
Russians	56,239	0.2
Czechs	30,628	0.1
Others	78,634	0.3

CZECHOSLOVAKIA
Census of February 15, 1921

Czechoslovaks	8,760,927	65.5
Germans	3,123,568	23.4
Magyars	745,431	5.6
Ukrainians (Ruthenes)	461,849	3.5
Jews	180,855	1.3
Poles	75,853	0.5
Romanians	13,794	0.1

YUGOSLAVIA
Census of January 31, 1921

Serbs	5,953,000 } Census of		50.0
Croats	3,221,000 } March 1931		27.0
Slovenes	1,019,907		8.5
Germans	505,790		3.9
Magyars	467,652		3.8
Albanians	439,657		3.6
Rumanians	231,068		1.9
Italians	12,533		0.1
Others	220,220		1.8

Source: Hugh Seton-Watson, *Eastern Europe Between the Wars, 1918–1941* (New York: Harper & Row, 1967), pp. 412 ff. Originally printed in 1945 by Cambridge University Press. Reprinted by permission.

of right-wing governing coalitions during the early 1920s, was reinforced by lingering resentment at the Bolshevik government's premature withdrawal from the war against Germany and its repudiation of the enormous debt owed to French investors by the tsarist regime. Thus France had been the most vociferous advocate of the Allied intervention in the Russian civil war of 1918–20, lending its support to a succession of counterrevolutionary groups that tried in vain to strangle the infant Bolshevik regime and encouraging the Poles during their ill-fated thrust into western Russia in the spring of 1920.

Even more significant than this ideological element in Russia's tense relations with foreign powers was the geopolitical condition that not only rendered it unsuitable as a prospective member of the anti-German bloc but in fact guaranteed Russian opposition on purely national grounds to the postwar political order that France was striving to uphold. Russia had lost more territory and population as a result of the Great War than had Germany. Finland, Estonia, Latvia, and Lithuania had been formed out of Russian territory along the Baltic. Romania had been enlarged by the forcible acquisition of the Russian province of Bessarabia. The eastern frontier of the reconstituted state of Poland, which was fixed by the Treaty of Riga between Poland and the Soviet Union in 1921, included within it large numbers of White Russians and Ukrainians who had previously been subjects of the tsar. The Soviet regime was obliged to acquiesce in these territorial amputations by its smaller neighbors to the west because it was preoccupied with the immediate tasks of internal recovery and reconstruction in the wake of civil war and economic collapse. But the Bolshevik government remained unreconciled to the loss of these European borderlands and therefore shared with Germany a determination to destroy the territorial settlement of 1919 when conditions permitted. The revisionist grievances of Germany and Russia converged over Poland, which had been reconstituted at the mutual expense of these two states and therefore served as a basis for cooperation between them. Indeed, the permanent nightmare of Western statesmen throughout the 1920s was an alliance between these two dispossessed powers against the beneficiaries of the peace settlement. Thus the chain of successor states from the Baltic to the Balkans served in the eyes of French officials not only as a *cordon sanitaire* to shield Western Europe from the infection of Bolshevism but also as a means of keeping the two dissatisfied and potentially most powerful states of Eastern Europe apart.

The rapprochement between the Weimar Republic and the Soviet Union had begun in the winter of 1920–21 in the realm of military cooperation (see p. 120), but these contacts were unknown to Allied leaders at the time. The first overt indication that the two pariah powers of the continent had joined forces hit the world like a bombshell in the spring of 1922 during the international economic conference in Genoa, to which Soviet representatives had been invited for the purpose of discussing means of promoting the economic recovery of Europe in general and Russia in particular. After French officials made it clear that Russia could expect no foreign economic assistance until it had recognized its prewar debt and provided compensation for nationalized foreign property, German foreign minister Walther Rathenau and the Soviet foreign commissar, Georgi Chicherin, retired to the nearby town of Rapallo to sign a bilateral agreement providing for the establishment of diplomatic relations and economic cooperation between the two states. The specific terms of the Treaty of Rapallo—the mutual repudiation of claims for war costs and damages,

Russia's renunciation of reparations from Germany, and Germany's renunciation of claims arising out of the nationalization of German property in Russia—were less important than the fact of the signing itself. It put the Western world on notice that the two most populous powers in Europe, though temporarily hobbled by internal economic problems, territorial losses, and the animosity of their neighbors, were committed to the pursuit of friendly diplomatic and economic relations with each other that could only strengthen their respective positions on the continent.

The normalization of relations between the Weimar Republic and the Soviet Union and the strengthening of their mutually beneficial economic links during the years after Rapallo reinforced other developments that were undermining France's attempt to isolate Germany and compel her to fulfill her obligations under the Versailles Treaty. We have already noted how Washington and London had successfully prodded Paris into granting substantial concessions to Berlin in the matter of reparations. The Dawes Plan, by effectively reducing the German debt and abolishing the coercive power of the French-dominated Reparations Commission, represented the first major revision of the peace treaty to Germany's advantage. But the lightening of the reparation burden in 1924 did not produce the sudden improvement in German behavior that the British and Americans had confidently anticipated and the French had cautiously hoped for. On the contrary, it soon gave way to a drumfire of German invective against the two other major restrictions on German sovereignty incorporated in the treaty: the clauses on disarmament and the inter-Allied occupation of the Rhineland. These two questions were closely interlinked, at least in the minds of French policymakers. In anticipation of American and British repudiation of the security treaties that had been offered to France in place of a permanent occupation of the Rhineland, Clemenceau had insisted on the insertion of article 429 in the Versailles Treaty; this clause stipulated that in the absence of adequate guarantees against unprovoked German aggression, the evacuation of the Rhineland could be delayed until such guarantees were forthcoming. The logic of this precautionary article was peculiar; it seemed to penalize Germany for decisions taken in London and Washington over which it had no control. Nevertheless, French leaders wielded the threat of an indefinitely prolonged Rhineland occupation as a sheathed sword to cajole Germany into fulfilling its disarmament obligations under the treaty; in the absence of the Anglo-American guarantee, only a disarmed Germany would render a perpetual occupation of the Rhineland unnecessary.

The process of effecting the disarmament of Germany presented difficulties that had not been anticipated by Allied statesmen at the peace conference. First of all, the rapid demobilization of hundreds of thousands of young men whose only marketable skill was the bearing of arms placed an intolerable burden on the economic system of the Weimar Republic in its formative years. Even more disturbing was the threat to internal security posed by the existence of organized bands of unemployed veterans who detested the republican regime and periodically conspired to topple it, often with the tacit encouragement of their former superiors in the officers' corps. At the same time, these paramilitary vigilante groups performed a useful function in the service of the German state: They waged a pitiless campaign of intimidation and violence against the revolutionary Left, which itself was plotting to overthrow the parliamentary republic and replace it with a Communist regime modeled on the one recently installed in Russia. The Western powers were prepared to tolerate neither a right-wing military putsch that would rekindle the flame of German expansionism nor a Communist revolution that might inspire proletarian uprisings throughout the continent. The political leadership of the Weimar Republic skillfully exploited both of these Allied fears to extract concessions on the matter of disarmament. In June 1920, after an abortive military coup in Berlin followed by a Communist insurrection in the mining districts of the Ruhr Valley, the German government persuaded the Allies to authorize an increase in the size of the German police forces from 60,000 to 150,000 in order to protect the fledgling republic from its enemies on both extremes of the political spectrum. This beefed-up internal security apparatus, equipped with artillery and armored vehicles and soon quartered in barracks, was to supplement the regular army of 100,000 whose existence had been justified by the need to preserve internal order. Together they represented a potential force of a quarter of a million men under arms. In addition to this formal increase in the level of military manpower to meet the needs of internal order, the formation of numerous private paramilitary organizations, rifle clubs, veterans' organizations, and the like enabled Germany to evade the prohibition against universal military training.

The task of verifying German compliance with the disarmament provisions of the Treaty of Versailles fell to the Inter-Allied Military Control Commission (IMCC). This unarmed inspection team met with continual efforts at concealment by German military authorities and instances of intimidation by the general population. But even without deliberate German harassment, the process of disarmament inspection was rendered exceedingly difficult by the increasingly blurred distinction between the military and civilian sphere. The potential strength of modern armies could no longer be measured simply by the number of men in uniform. Modern warfare depended to a high degree on technology that was equally beneficial to industry, as we have seen in our own time, when nuclear energy can be used both to generate electricity and to fabricate weapons of mass destruction. The postwar German chemical industry manufactured substances that could be used for either fertilizers or explosives. German aeronautics firms built commercial aircraft that could easily be converted to bombers. The Allies found it impossible to discover a justification for prohibiting Germany from producing fertilizers for its farms or developing its civilian aviation industry, especially at a time when the country was expected to recover economically in order to pay reparations. As a consequence, the IMCC was impelled to grant numerous exemptions to those sections of German heavy industry that possessed the capability of developing products that could be readily converted to military use.

The preservation of Germany's technological capacity to wage war was enhanced by secret military arrangements between the Weimar Republic and the Soviet Union. Collaboration between German and Soviet military authorities had begun in the winter of 1920–21 and was expanded after the signing of the Rapallo Treaty in 1922. Deep in the Russian interior, the German army was able surreptitiously to engage in the production and testing of military aircraft, tanks, poison gases, and other weapons outlawed by the Versailles Treaty, as well as the illegal training of military personnel in their use. Though this program of clandestine rearmament was organized and financed entirely by the German military out of secret funds placed at its disposal, its existence was known to and tacitly approved by German governments throughout the 1920s.

In spite of the geographical, political, and economic obstacles to the verification of German disarmament, the IMCC persisted in its thankless task. It had been forced to suspend activities during the Ruhr occupation when the Berlin government refused to guarantee the personal security of its members; it resumed its inspection only after Britain and France informed the German government that the impending evacuation of the Cologne zone in the Rhineland, which was scheduled for January 10, 1925, according to the timetable of the Versailles Treaty, would not begin until the control commission was permitted to verify German compliance with the disarmament sections of the treaty. In December 1924 the commission issued an interim report detailing flagrant German violations of most of the disarmament clauses. As a consequence, the Allies notified Berlin that the evacuation of Cologne would be delayed.

The German government was thereby faced, at the beginning of 1925, with a major foreign policy dilemma: how to achieve the liberation of the Rhineland without interrupting the clandestine rearmament that all of the major political leaders of the Weimar Republic deemed essential to Germany's return to the ranks of the great powers. It was to the solution of this dilemma that Foreign Minister Gustav Stresemann, the architect of German foreign policy during the second half of the 1920s, devoted the remainder of his career. Soon after he became chancellor of the German Republic in the summer of 1923 and terminated the passive resistance in the Ruhr, Stresemann acquired a reputation in Western capitals as a trustworthy advocate of "fulfillment" of the Versailles Treaty. In November 1923 he was replaced as chancellor and assumed the office of foreign minister. For the next six years until his premature death in October 1929 this astute diplomat became the symbol of those democratic forces in the Weimar Republic that ostensibly sought peaceful relations with the victorious Allies and the reintegration of Germany into a stable, prosperous Europe.

In reality, Stresemann was an unreconstructed German nationalist who had never accepted his country's defeat in war and reduced status in peace. His preeminent objective in foreign policy was the destruction of the detested treaty requirements of 1919 that kept Germany in chains. But unlike the nationalist firebrands on the extreme right, Stresemann wisely recognized that Germany's temporary military inferiority in Europe dictated that the first attempts to revise the Versailles Treaty be conducted with diplomatic finesse rather than sterile militarist bluster. He identified two tempting soft spots in the armor of the Anglo-French entente which, if properly probed, might lead to the weakening of the French stranglehold on Germany. To begin with, he accurately surmised that Great Britain would welcome the opportunity to obtain a peaceful resolution of the Franco-German dispute in Western Europe, even if such a settlement were to erase France's margin of military superiority over Germany. He also understood that France, because of its chronically unstable financial situation and fear of diplomatic isolation, would be incapable of resisting British pressure to reach an accommodation with Germany over the most egregious sources of friction.

In accordance with these views, the German foreign minister mounted a bold diplomatic initiative carefully crafted to attain his own country's major foreign policy goals while satisfying the minimum security requirements of Germany's chief antagonist. France craved assurances of security in the form of (1) Germany's acceptance of the territorial status quo in Western Europe as well as the demilitarized status of the Rhineland, and (2) a British guarantee of these two arrangements. Germany sought the evacuation of Allied troops from the Rhineland, but without having to submit to the stringent treaty requirements for disarmament. Throughout the winter and spring of 1925, Stresemann approached London about the possibility of breaking the half-decade-long deadlock between Germany and France. He hinted broadly that Germany was prepared to acknowledge its loss of Alsace-Lorraine to France and affirm the inviolability of the Rhineland demilitarized zone in return for Allied concessions on a number of points. These conciliatory overtures, coming as they did after six years of German intransigence, were received with great enthusiasm in London and were promptly communicated to Paris with the British seal of approval. The consequent flurry of diplomatic activity eventually led to the convocation of the foreign ministers of France, Great Britain, Germany, Italy, and Belgium at the Swiss resort city of Locarno in October 1925. The pact initialed at this gathering and later signed in London committed France and Germany, and Belgium and Germany, to the formal acknowledgement of their mutual frontiers. It also included Germany's endorsement of the permanent demilitarization of the Rhineland. The political status quo in Western Europe and the demilitarized status of the Rhenish buffer zone, thus officially recognized by the three powers concerned, was in turn guaranteed by Great Britain and Italy. In return for acknowledging its territorial losses in the west (Alsace-Lorraine to France and the small frontier districts of Eupen and Malmédy to Belgium), Germany received from France the quid pro quo it had so earnestly sought: the promise of a prompt evacuation of the Cologne zone of the Rhineland, the scaling down of the occupation forces in the two remaining zones, and a reduction in the size and authority of the Allied inspection team, all to begin once Germany displayed some measure of good faith in regard to its disarmament intentions.

The Locarno agreement was universally hailed as an almost miraculous resolution of the conflict between the two powers on the Rhine that had unsettled Western Europe since the end of the war. After six years of disappointment and frustration, France had obtained what it wanted most: from Germany, freely tendered assurances that the Franco-German frontier as well as the demilitarized condition of the Rhineland were inviolate; from Great Britain (as well as Italy), the precious guarantee that had eluded French statesmen ever since the end of the Paris Peace Conference. Germany's prize was the promise of the eventual liberation of the Rhineland plus the assurance that French troops would never return to German soil. Almost as important as the actual text of the treaty was the atmosphere of cordiality that pervaded the meetings that produced it. German, French, and British officials dined together, exchanged pleasantries during leisurely boat cruises on Lake Maggiore, and gave every indication that the acrimony of the past had been buried in a universal enthusiasm for detente. The British foreign secretary, Austen Chamberlain, foreshadowing the misplaced optimism of his younger half-brother thirteen years later at Munich, confidently boasted that his conciliatory influence at Locarno had produced peace for his time. He shared the Nobel Peace Prize with Stresemann and the French foreign minister, Aristide Briand, the following year for this collective achievement of reconciliation.

But the euphoria engendered by the Locarno pact concealed serious deficiencies that were to be found not in what the treaty contained but in what it omitted. Most important of all, the German foreign minister had adamantly refused to affirm the inviolability of Germany's borders with Poland and Czechoslovakia. By acknowledging its territorial losses to France and Belgium while refusing to recognize the political settlement in Eastern Europe, Germany had in effect reserved the right to seek redress of its grievances in that region at some future date. By freezing Germany's frontiers in the west without extracting equivalent pledges to respect the territorial status quo in the east, Briand and Chamberlain seemed to be encouraging Germany to press for territorial compensation in that direction. The fact that neither Poland, Czechoslovakia, nor the Soviet Union had been invited to this important conference on European security aroused justifiable fears in those countries that the Western powers had settled with Germany at their expense.

Equally as ominous was the absence of a specific German commitment to fulfill the disarmament provisions of the Versailles Treaty. Berlin had consistently objected to the principle of unilateral disarmament on the grounds that it left the German people perpetually exposed to invasion from a vindictive France armed to the teeth. By agreeing to the reduction of the military control commission to a token force, the Allies had effectively entrusted to Germany itself the responsibility of self-supervision without requiring even an innocuous verbal commitment to the principle of unilateral disarmament. The clandestine rearmament initiated in the early twenties proceeded thereafter without even the threat of detection by Allied military observers. In the meantime the Allies scrupulously adhered to their part of the bargain. The evacuation of the Cologne zone began on December 1, 1925, the day of the official signing of the Locarno pacts in London, and was completed by January 31, 1926. In time the French and British were moved to increase the concessions made at Locarno in their eagerness to appease Germany.

The most important diplomatic prize that Briand took home from Locarno, the British guarantee of the Franco-German frontier, was rendered worthless by the multilateral character of the commitment: For British military power to be effective in assisting France against unprovoked German aggression, extensive Anglo-French military preparations would have been required. But such privileged contacts would have prejudiced Britain's position as an impartial guarantor of the territorial status quo in Western Europe. Hence London systematically declined to authorize prior military arrangements with any of the beneficiaries of the Locarno guarantee. The most bizarre aspect of the situation was to be found in the fact that the British guarantee could be invoked by Germany against France in the event of a future French military operation in the Ruhr Valley. This meant that Germany was theoretically free to default on reparation deliveries, violate the disarmament restrictions, and exert pressure against France's allies in Eastern Europe, just so long as she refrained from sending troops into France, Belgium, or the Rhineland. Any French military response to these provocations would give rise, according to the language of Locarno, to British (and Italian) intervention against France on Germany's behalf.

The Locarno treaties were to enter into force upon the admission of Germany into the League of Nations. This remarkable event took place on September 10, 1926, after several months of haggling over how to accommodate Stresemann's demand for a permanent seat on the League Council without antagonizing other aspirants for this prestigious position among the second-rank powers. To French critics of Briand's conciliatory policy toward Germany, Stresemann at Geneva seemed equivalent to the fox in the chicken coop. How could an organization dedicated to the maintenance of the political status quo in Europe operate effectively with the most notorious proponents of territorial revision occupying a powerful place in its midst? In fact the question was moot, since the League had ceased to function as the forum for the discussion of matters relating to European security. On the model of the Locarno consultations, the important issues of the day were thereafter settled by the representatives of the four great European powers in private meetings in Geneva hotel suites. No longer a pariah among nations, Germany would participate on an equal footing with the victorious Allies in the deliberations concerning the future of Europe. That the recently elected German head of state, Field Marshal von Hindenburg, was a troublesome reminder of the imperial past; that the German foreign minister, Stresemann, never concealed his disdain for the territorial settlement in Eastern Europe—these were matters of little import in the eyes of a European world basking in the agreeable atmosphere of prosperity and peace. Armies were no longer on the march, intergovernmental debts were being repaid on schedule, production and employment had reached and surpassed the prewar levels. "Away with the rifles, the machine guns, the cannon!" Briand had exclaimed in his welcoming speech on the occasion of Germany's admission to the League. "Make way for conciliation, arbitration, and peace." The almost hysterical enthusiasm that greeted these words signified that the French foreign minister was expressing the hopes of an entire generation weary of war and intent on enjoying the fruits of prosperity and peace.

Yet the shrewd Briand, unjustly reviled by his nationalist critics at home as a gullible dupe of Stresemann, was fully aware of the grave shortcomings of the Locarno settlement as a guarantee of France's security. Indeed, his concessions to Stresemann had been reluctantly given, and only after persistent prodding from Chamberlain. Historians may never discover the true motivations of this incomparably enigmatic architect of French foreign policy in the second half of the 1920s. He seldom committed his most intimate thoughts to writing; even if he had done so, most of his private papers were destroyed and those that survive have remained inaccessible. But his foreign policy initiatives after Locarno reveal the persistence of a profound skepticism about the good intentions of the German leadership with which he had recently made peace. To supplement the new Franco-German rapprochement he had helped to inaugurate, Briand took a number of precautionary steps to enhance France's diplomatic and military position vis-à-vis Germany as insurance against the day when Stresemann's conciliatory policy would be repudiated.

The first of these precautions was taken toward the end of the Locarno Conference itself. After his failure to obtain Stresemann's formal affirmation of Germany's borders in Eastern Europe, Briand hastened to reassure France's nervous allies in that region. He concluded mutual assistance pacts with Poland and Czechoslovakia that reaffirmed and strengthened the bilateral military commitments previously undertaken in 1921 and 1924, respectively. In June 1926 he added a treaty of friendship with Romania and in November 1927 a similar pact with Yugoslavia. By the end of the decade, Briand's passion for bilateral instruments to deter German aggression had provided France with military alliances or political understandings with Poland and the three countries of the Little Entente. Considered in conjunction with the Franco-Belgian alliance of 1920, this eastern alliance system seemed to represent for France a formidable supplement to the Locarno accords. Despite the aforementioned disputes among themselves (see p. 115), all of the members of the French alliance system shared a common interest in preserving the territorial settlement in Europe from which they all benefited. Moreover, these military and political links between France and the nations to Germany's east and south were reinforced by economic connections as well. French capital investment was directed to these countries both to enhance their value as allies and to secure their economic independence from Germany.

On two other occasions after Locarno Briand attempted to reinforce the Franco-German detente by enlisting outside assistance on behalf of European peace and security. The first of these initiatives was launched on April 6, 1927, when the French foreign minister inserted in his message of gratitude to the American people on the tenth anniversary of the United States intervention in the Great War a suggestion that the two nations sign a bilateral treaty forswearing war between them. Since the likelihood of armed conflict between France and the United States was nil at the time, the State Department correctly suspected an ulterior motive behind this curious emanation from the Quai d'Orsay: Briand apparently hoped to ensnare the United States in a privileged relationship with France that might eventually evolve into some kind of commitment to bolster French security in Europe. Consequently, Briand's overtures received a cool reception from Secretary of State Frank Kellogg, who had no intention of permitting his nation to be lured into signing a disguised version of the ill-fated Franco-American security treaty negotiated by Wilson at Paris. But an effective publicity campaign orchestrated by prominent American pacifists, who saw in the French proposal an opportunity to establish peace through international agreement, forced the State Department to respond. The shrewd Kellogg thereupon seized the initiative in December 1927, dispatching to Paris a draft treaty that transformed Briand's project for a bilateral pact into a universal declaration against war that all nations would be invited to sign. When the startled French authorities complained that such a treaty would nullify regional agreements (such as the Locarno treaties) which obliged certain powers to intervene militarily against aggressors, the draft treaty was further weakened by provisions for self-defense and regional security. Just as Clemenceau had earlier seen the French project for a League of Nations empowered to compel German adherence to the peace treaty transformed by Wilson into a universal mechanism for ensuring global peace, the disappointed Briand finally obtained, in place of the bilateral agreement between Washington and Paris that he had originally sought, a multilateral renunciation of war rendered entirely innocuous by the absence of precise commitments and enforcement machinery.

With great fanfare the representatives of fifteen nations signed the Pact of Paris on July 27, 1928, solemnly agreeing to "condemn recourse to war for the solution of international controversies, and renounce it as an instrument of national policy." Eventually sixty-two nations adhered to what became known as the Kellogg-Briand Pact, including all of those whose aggression was to produce a second world war in the near future.

Foiled in his surreptitious effort to obtain American support for French security, the energetic French foreign minister unveiled an even bolder scheme for the maintenance of European peace. In an historic oration from the rostrum of the League Assembly on September 5, 1929, Briand issued a vaguely worded but dramatic appeal for the creation of some kind of supranational confederation linking the sovereign states of Europe. This urgent plan for European union sprang from the same motivation behind the earlier proposal to the United States: Briand hoped to restrain Germany from relapsing into its former aggressiveness, in this instance by submerging that nation in a supranational Europe economically integrated and politically interdependent. He was thereupon invited by the surprised European members of the League to draft a detailed memorandum specifying the organizational structure and function of the "federation" alluded to in his speech. On May 17, 1930, he unveiled a formal proposal for the establishment of inter-European political institutions, a general system of arbitration and security, and a common market in which "the circulation of goods, capital, and persons would be facilitated." What appeared for a brief moment to be an imaginative prescription for European union proved instead to be one of the last gasps of the old order established at Versailles. As the delegates at Geneva debated the Briand plan with ever-decreasing enthusiasm, the German legislative elections of September 14, 1930, increased the Nazi Party's representation in the Reichstag from 12 to 107, making Hitler's wrecking crew the nation's second largest political party. Within a few months the Briand proposal had been permanently pigeonholed in a committee of the League Assembly. The juxtaposition of these two events at the beginning of the 1930s constituted an ominous portent for the future: The continent of Europe was to be unified within a decade not by the free consent of democratic nations but by the military might of a rejuvenated Germany. Briand's project for European union, like his abortive effort to secure an American commitment to European security, was a generation ahead of its time. It required a second world war before the United States would come to regard Europe's security an extension of its own, and before the nations of Western Europe would recognize the advantages of economic integration and political cooperation.

While the Quai d'Orsay sought to bolster France's diplomatic position in Europe through bilateral alliances and multilateral guarantees during the second half of the 1920s, the French Ministry of War was hard at work devising a military strategy that would protect France in case Briand's intricate network of diplomatic safeguards failed to deter German expansionism. The fatal strategic problem that confronted French military planners was the following: All but one of the restrictions on German military recovery that had been written into the Versailles Treaty were of limited duration. Allied inspection of German disarmament was to end (and did end, in 1927) once the inspection commission judged the process of disarmament complete. Allied military occupation of the Rhineland was to be phased out in stages (the Cologne zone in 1925, the Coblenz zone in 1930, the Mainz zone in 1935). But the timetable for withdrawal from the last two zones was shortened in response to a combination of German complaints and pledges of good behavior. Coblenz was evacuated ahead of schedule on November 30, 1929, and the Mainz zone on June 30, 1930, both in exchange for Germany's acceptance of the Young Plan, an American-inspired proposal for the definitive resolution of the reparations problem. The sole permanent guarantee of French security was the demilitarized status of the Rhineland. This, it will be recalled, was the principal substitute for the Rhine frontier that Clemenceau had failed to obtain in 1919. However, the Versailles Treaty did not oblige any nation to render France military assistance in the event of a German move to remilitarize this buffer region. Even the explicit Anglo-Italian guarantee of the demilitarized status of the Rhineland contained in the Locarno treaties was to become operational only in cases of "flagrant violation" of the provisions of the pact. Cases of "non-flagrant violation" were to be referred to the League Council for consideration. It soon became evident that London and Rome defined "flagrant violation" in the narrowest possible sense, namely, the entrance of German troops into the demilitarized zone preparatory to an actual military invasion of France. Before the ink was dry on the Locarno pacts, Great Britain made known her intention of using this semantic loophole to avoid any obligation to assist France against the isolated act of remilitarization itself.

The phased withdrawal of Allied troops from the Rhineland deprived France of its last line of defense against a resurgent Germany. With the Ruhr Valley no longer within range of French heavy artillery and mechanized infantry in the Rhineland, Germany's industrial heartland could no longer be held hostage to Berlin's pacific behavior. The French strategy of offensive military action in western Germany to compel German adherence to the Versailles Treaty, developed by Marshal Foch after the armistice and employed by Poincaré in 1923, underwent a radical transformation during the second half of the twenties. By the end of the decade, the decision was taken to replace the disappearing natural defensive barrier of the Rhine with a manmade substitute: a continuous stationary fortification covering the entire length of the Franco-German frontier which came to be known, after the war minister who authorized its construction, as the Maginot Line.

So much ridicule has been heaped upon this military strategy since the demonstration of its inadequacies in May–June 1940 that it is worth pausing to review the underlying motivations for its adoption. Above all, there was the striking disparity in human and material resources between the two antagonists along the Rhine: There were forty million Frenchmen facing seventy million Germans who were endowed with superior industrial (and therefore military) potential. French strategists accordingly concluded that in the event of a future conflict with Germany, France's only hope for survival as a nation lay in a defensive posture designed to spare as many French lives and as much industrial plant as possible. This inclination was reinforced by the putative lessons of the Great War: The suicidal offensives of 1914–17 were universally blamed for having needlessly squandered precious French manpower and resources. The superiority of firepower afforded by modern weapons, such as the machine gun and heavy artillery, was taken to mean that the war of movement was a relic of a bygone era. In future conflicts the advantage would unmistakably rest with the defensive, as it had during the war of recent memory. Instead of improvising underground shelters to protect against the devastating firepower of the advancing enemy, as had been necessary in 1914, France would construct in advance a permanent network of subterranean fortifications equipped with all of the supplies and amenities that had been lacking in the cramped, disease-ridden trenches of the First World War: barracks, mess halls, ammunition dumps, even movie theaters and canteens, all interconnected by an underground railroad. In these comfortable surroundings the French infantry, protected by shields of concrete and fortified with powerful artillery pieces, would lie in wait for any German military force rash enough to risk a repetition of the bloody offensives of the Great War. The valuable time purchased by this defensive strategy would enable Great Britain to rearm, gather her military forces from their faraway imperial outposts, mobilize her extensive economic resources, and enter the fray alongside France. It was even contemplated, though without good reason, that the establishment of a stationary front along France's eastern frontier would once again result in an influx of the enormous industrial resources of the United States to tip the scale against the German aggressor.

From a purely military point of view, the Maginot Line was brilliant in conception and effective in practice. It functioned precisely according to plan when the German offensive finally came in May 1940. Nowhere along the Franco-German border was it penetrated by Hitler's armies. It was circumvented and taken from behind. France's defensive strategy failed to prevent the German breakthrough not because it was defective but because it was not carried to its logical conclusion. For the system of interconnected fortifications contained two gaps. The first was of secondary importance: A portion of the Lorraine frontier was left uncovered because it was erroneously assumed that the adjacent German district of the Saar, which had been administered by the League of Nations since the coming into force of the Versailles Treaty, would either vote to remain under League auspices or to be annexed by France in the plebiscite scheduled for 1935. The fatal flaw in the Maginot system was the decision to terminate construction of the continuous fortified line at Longwy, leaving the entire Franco-Belgian border unprotected. This omission was a striking one in view of historical precedent and geographical reality, both of which suggested that the Belgian lowland would be the most likely path of a German assault against France, as in 1914.

The decision not to extend the Maginot Line the entire length of the Franco-Belgian frontier to the English Channel was dictated by considerations of foreign policy and domestic politics. To begin with, the military alliance that France had concluded with Belgium in 1920 made it diplomatically inopportune even to discuss the possibility of leaving a trusted ally outside the French defense perimeter. The French war plan presumed that Belgium would request French military assistance at the slightest hint of an impending German invasion; a Franco-Belgian line of defense could easily be improvised behind the only natural barrier to military aggression on the Belgian plain: the confluence of the Meuse River and the Albert Canal. What rendered this theoretically astute strategy fatally vulnerable was that it depended entirely on the willingness of a weak little neighboring state to maintain its commitment to joint defense with France in the face of German intimidation. But even in the unlikely event that Belgium would have cheerfully tolerated the establishment of a fortified line separating it from its ally and protector, the northward extension of the Maginot Line would have presented serious complications in the northeastern corner of France. This highly industrialized, densely populated region was entirely unsuitable for the permanent emplacement of heavy artillery, which requires long stretches of uninhabited territory to operate without obstruction. It was unthinkable, and politically impossible, to locate these weapons of destruction behind or within one of France's principal industrial, urbanized regions. These negative reasons for halting the Maginot Line at the intersection of the French, Belgian, and Luxembourgeois frontiers were reinforced by a positive consideration: French military authorities judged the densely wooded hills of the Ardennes that roll across the Franco-Belgian frontier impassable to tanks, armored personnel carriers, and other mechanized vehicles of modern warfare.

The construction of the costly Maginot Line had to await the definitive stabilization of France's financial situation in 1928. Begun in the following year as French troops prepared to evacuate the Rhineland, it was completed in the midthirties; the elaborate fortifications produced in the security-conscious French a feeling of relative safety amid an increasingly dangerous international environment. It also helped to erase the image of postwar France, by then widespread in the English-speaking world, as a vengeful nation bent on perpetually intimidating a disarmed Germany with its overwhelming military superiority. What more conclusive demonstration of France's defensive intentions than a military strategy of passively awaiting events behind an impregnable fortified line? But the feelings of security in Paris and relief in London were not shared in Prague and Warsaw. France's adoption of a defensive military strategy so soon after the Franco-German reconciliation at Locarno reinforced the skepticism of the Czechs and the Poles about the value of their bilateral alliances with their French protector. The presence of French military forces in the Rhineland during the 1920s had served as an effective deterrent to German meddling in the affairs of France's eastern allies. The evacuation of the Rhineland and the establishment of a stationary position behind the Maginot Line seemed to undermine the basic assumptions of France's ambitious diplomacy in Eastern Europe. Germany's recently acquired immunity from the threat of offensive military action by France seemed an open invitation to maintain a defensive posture on the Rhine while conducting an aggressive policy on the Danube and the Vistula.

The reduced likelihood of effective military assistance from France compelled the Eastern European states to reassess their strategy for protecting themselves from the consequences of German revisionism. Czechoslovakia, the most highly industrialized and financially secure nation in the region, was able to bear the costs of constructing its own miniature version of the Maginot Line. Unfortunately for the ill-starred Czechs, geographical considerations dictated that this defensive line be established in the mountains along the Bohemian frontier region called the "Sudetenland," an enclave of ethnic German settlement that served as a potential object of irredentist ambition across the border. Poland, which possessed neither the economic resources to finance elaborate defensive fortifications nor the natural geographic barriers on which to base them, responded to the devaluation of its French alliance by desperately seeking an accommodation with its two menacing neighbors. As will be seen, nonaggression pacts concluded with the Soviet Union in July 1932 and Germany in January 1934 represented desperate efforts by Warsaw to preserve a precarious balance between the two powers that harbored designs on Polish territory.

The first two years of the 1930s were dominated by the spreading economic crisis and the attempts by various governments to develop means of coping with it. These economic policies, both foreign and domestic, inevitably had important consequences in the political and military realm. This was particularly so in Europe, where political stability and military security were so closely dependent upon the efficient operation of the international network of trade, investment, and intergovernmental debt service. The breakdown of this system in the early thirties delivered a devastating blow to the European security system that had been fashioned in the middle of the previous decade. The death of Gustav Stresemann in the same month (October 1929) that the American stock market began its downward slide was an eminently symbolic coincidence: The era of European detente associated with his name came to a close as the international economic order upon which it so heavily depended began to disintegrate. The man whose deceptively conciliatory diplomacy from 1924 to 1929 had relieved Germany of the burden of military occupation and inspection, drastically reduced its reparation debt, and restored it to the ranks of the great powers, had bequeathed to his successors a golden legacy. They had only to bide their time while the deterioration of world prosperity and stability enabled them to complete what he had begun: the liberation of Germany from the remaining fetters of Versailles.

Yet it would be a grave mistake to conclude, as many historians have been tempted to do, that the disappearance of the "spirit of Locarno," the revival of German revisionism, and the advent of the Nazi dictatorship were direct results of the international economic collapse of the early thirties that will be discussed in the next chapter. The assumption of a causal relationship between economic prosperity on the one hand and political democracy and international stability on the other, widely held by government officials, business people, and financiers in the English-speaking world during the postwar period, may well explain the peaceful, prosperous, democratic years of Europe in the second half of the twenties. But the converse of that causal proposition fails to account for subsequent events. Germany began to terminate its brief experiment with international conciliation and political democracy in 1930, before the effects of the Great Depression had taken their toll. The legislative election campaign of that year, which resulted in the spectacular success of the Nazi Party, was fought largely on issues of foreign rather than domestic policy. All of the major parties competed for votes with nationalistic denunciations of the Versailles system: strident demands for an end to reparations, restoration of the Saar and the former colonial empire, recovery of territories lost to Poland, and the unrestricted right to rearm. Chancellor Heinrich Brüning's proposal for a customs union with Austria in March 1931 was less a measure for economic recovery than a political assault on the Versailles system and a threat to the security of Czechoslovakia. This move toward an economic *Anschluss** (which was torpedoed by France), together with the launching of a heavy cruiser construction program in the same year, were both justified to the apprehensive British and French as necessary ploys to outbid the Nazis in chauvinism in order to win over their supporters in the German electorate. So too were Brüning's insistent demands for a revision of Germany's eastern frontiers and his successor Franz von Papen's decision to default on reparation payments in September 1932. In December of that year German pressure finally obtained from the nervous members of the League formal recognition of Germany's right to achieve equality of armaments. In short, the main features of the foreign policy program of the Nazi party were adopted by the very German statesmen, such as Brüning, Papen, and Hindenburg, who advertised themselves as the only alternative to Hitler.

* German for "union"; used in the 1930s to designate the German annexation of Austria.

The stage for Germany's internal evolution from democracy to dictatorship was likewise set during the three years prior to Hitler's accession. On July 16, 1930, after the Reichstag had rejected the government's budget bill, Hindenburg authorized it by presidential decree, dissolved the Reichstag, and called the new elections that produced the stunning Nazi gains. Within a year Brüning was circumventing the elected legislators altogether, invoking emergency powers to enact unpopular measures of economic austerity. The fierce political infighting of the year 1932, during which Brüning, Franz von Papen, and General Kurt von Schleicher succeeded one another in the chancellor's office, represented abortive attempts to patch together a governing coalition that would preclude Hitler's assumption of power. But the legislative elections of July 1932, in which the Nazis won 37 percent of the vote to become the largest party in the Reichstag with 230 seats, demonstrated the extent of Hitler's popularity among all segments of German society. Though a subsequent election in November of the same year reduced somewhat the Nazis legislative representation, the handwriting on the wall was unmistakable. The guardians of the old order read it accurately and acted accordingly. Their reluctance to embrace the upstart leader of the Nazis did not stem from any distaste for his revisionist foreign policy goals, still less from concern about his antipathy for democratic political institutions. It was the radical social program of National Socialism that alarmed these conservative politicians and the social elites they represented. Once assured of the purely rhetorical nature of the "socialist" element in the Nazi creed, and of Hitler's intention to leave intact the existing socioeconomic hierarchies, the East Prussian landowners, Ruhr and Rhenish industrialists, and upper-echelon military officers hastened to make their peace with him. The Junkers craved assurances that their vast estates would not be expropriated and redistributed to indigent veterans, as had been suggested by some as a means of combating the effects of the depression; the Krupps, Thyssens, and their fellow magnates of heavy industry coveted assured markets and sources of supply in Europe; the military leaders longed for a trained and equipped mass army; all three sought protection against what they feared to be the rising tide of Communism in Germany, as reflected in the improved performance of the Communist Party in recent legislative elections. These things Hitler promised, either directly or through intermediaries, as part of his program of foreign expansion, rearmament, and domestic dictatorship. In return he received the support, both political and financial, of these powerful interest groups in his bid for power. Hitler's appointment as chancellor on January 30, 1933, was engineered by men who believed that they could manipulate him and his extremist movement to obtain what they wanted and prevent what they feared. Instead, as will be seen, the Nazi leader turned the tables on his allies among the industrial, agricultural, and military elites, using them and the resources under their control to realize his ambitious plans for the future of Germany and Europe.

CHAPTER 4

The Western World in the Thirties: The Illusions Dispelled

The Collapse of the World Economic Order

Since the wave of economic prosperity that swept Europe in the second half of the 1920s rested in large part on the industrial and financial strength of the United States, it was inevitable that the crash on the American stock market in the autumn of 1929 would have profound and deleterious effects on the other side of the Atlantic. The new role assumed by the United States in the postwar decade as the largest producer, lender, and investor in the world had rendered the international economic order acutely sensitive to the operation of the American economy. When that economy flourished, as it did with a few minor corrections and adjustments from 1922 through 1929, it served as an engine of prosperity for the rest of the industrial world. During the second half of the twenties the United States, with about 3 percent of the world's population, accounted for 46 percent of its total industrial output. During the same period it produced 70 percent of the world's oil and 40 percent of its coal. Moreover, the flow of American surplus capital to Europe provided a relatively painless solution to the acrimonious disputes over German reparations and inter-Allied debts and supplied the necessary liquidity for the trading nations of the world to balance their international accounts.

We are familiar with the symptoms of weakness in the international economy that were already apparent in the boom years of the second half of the 1920s: the speculative fever on Wall Street that diverted capital investment away from those regions of the world that needed it most to the nation that needed it least; the tendency of those American investments that did go to postwar Europe to be short term rather than long term and speculative rather than productive; declining prices of foodstuffs, metals, and other primary products that prevented the countries of the nonindustrial world from earning enough to pay for imports from industrial countries; the problems of exchange instability, commercial protectionism, and immigration restrictions, which hindered the free exchange of capital, resources, and labor across national frontiers. Once the American engine of world prosperity faltered and proceeded to burn out between 1929 and 1932, all of these ominous symptoms of economic instability, which had been either discounted or ignored during the boom years, developed into a full-blown disease of the international economic order.

The causes of the precipitous decline in the prices of securities on the New York Stock Exchange need not detain us here. What is important for our purposes is the effect of the "Great Crash" on the economic health of the United States and then of the entire industrial world. The mere recitation of United States economic statistics for the three years after 1929 tells the story: Industrial production and national income declined by half; the real gross national product dropped by a third; the unemployment rate approached 25 percent of the work force; one-third of the nation's banks closed their doors; wholesale prices fell by 32 percent. Workers without work; banks without deposits; investors wiped out; home mortgages foreclosed; farmers and small business people unable to sell their wares and therefore unable to pay off their commercial debts—such was the domestic economic condition of the nation upon whose prosperity the entire world had grown accustomed to depend.

The international effect of this sudden and pronounced economic downturn in the United States was devastating. The first and most obvious consequence was the abrupt termination of long-term foreign lending and the repatriation of existing foreign loans as they came due. Long-term foreign lending by private American investors declined 68 percent between 1929 and 1933, and then ceased altogether for the remainder of the decade. From 1934 to 1939 there was actually a net liquidation of foreign assets held by Americans. This massive withdrawal of American funds had an immediate impact on the economies of those nations, particularly in Central Europe, that had become vitally dependent on an uninterrupted influx of American capital for the balancing of their budgets, the expansion of their industrial production, the financing of their trade, and the service of their foreign debts. The repatriation of American foreign loans and investments was soon followed by a massive transfer of foreign gold holdings to the United States in response to the political instability in Europe. Between 1931 and 1938 American banks received a net inflow of gold amounting to roughly $6.6 billion. This liquidation of American assets abroad, the acquisition of American assets by foreigners, and the accumulation of foreign-owned gold in American banks resulted in a total capital inflow into the United States far in excess of the amounts required for the settlement of the world's current account deficit with the United States. This anomalous trend drastically reduced the supply of desperately needed gold and dollars in Europe.

To make matters worse, the decline of purchasing power in the United States sharply curtailed the ability of Americans to pay for imports from abroad. American merchandise imports dropped from $4.463 billion in 1929 to $1.343 billion in 1932, representing a 40 percent decline by volume. Furthermore, to compensate for the collapse of domestic prices, agricultural and manufacturing interests in the United States pressured the Congress into enacting the steepest protective tariff in the twentieth century, the Hawley-Smoot Tariff of 1930, which raised the average duty on protected goods to 59 percent. The combination of reduced demand and tariff protection in the United States precipitated a drastic decline in incomes and widespread unemployment in the exporting countries.

The contraction of world trade during the early 1930s also caused an abrupt decline in British foreign investment. France, the other great international lender, had already begun to divert a substantial portion of its surplus capital to gold purchases in order to bolster its recently stabilized currency. The simultaneous curtailment of foreign lending by the few nations of the world with surplus savings forced the recipient countries to acknowledge a fundamental weakness in their economic position that had been conveniently overlooked during the recent years of prosperity: their inability to service their enormous foreign debt (both private and governmental) without the continued receipt of additional foreign loans.

At first, the major European nations and the United States sought to ride out the storm by reverting to the traditional cure for such economic crises. Instead of repudiating the gold standard and permitting the exchange rate of their currencies to depreciate in order to preserve the competitive price advantage of their exports, they tenaciously clung to the system of fixed exchange rates and prepared to endure the severe deflation that was certain to result. But before this deflationary medicine had a chance to take effect, Europe was plunged into a full-fledged financial panic in the spring of 1931: The largest commercial bank of Austria, the Creditanstalt, was found to be on the brink of insolvency due to the withdrawal of foreign short-term funds. The Austrian government's decision to freeze the remaining assets of the beleaguered bank prompted a precautionary stampede on the financial institutions of Germany and the other nations of Central Europe, as foreign lenders scrambled to recover their deposits before those governments followed the Austrian example. After failing to stem the outflow of foreign funds by the traditional means of raising interest rates to entice foreign investors to keep their assets in marks, the German government imposed exchange controls to halt the capital flight and preclude further bank closings. By the end of the year eleven other European nations had enacted various types of restrictions on the transfer of capital abroad. In the meantime, political and financial authorities had taken steps to relieve the deteriorating economic condition of the Central European nations in general and the German Republic in particular. On June 21, 1931, President Herbert Hoover proposed a one-year moratorium on the payment of reparations and inter-Allied debts to afford Germany sufficient breathing space to get its financial house in order. The central banks of the United States, Great Britain, and France extended short-term loans to Germany, while international bankers undertook a study of the feasibility of arranging new long-term private loans to shore up the faltering economies of Central Europe.

But the financial storm brewing on the continent rapidly crossed the English Channel to engulf Europe's bulwark of monetary stability. Public awareness that British banks were heavily invested in the nations of Central Europe that had frozen foreign-owned assets or imposed exchange controls caused a widespread loss of faith in sterling. So too did the abrupt termination of German reparation payments after the announcement of the Hoover moratorium, which came during a period of chronic budget deficits in Britain. At the same time the need to make large international payments forced foreign creditors to withdraw foreign exchange and gold on deposit in London. What all of these considerations added up to, in the summer of 1931, was a run on the pound sterling that depleted Britain's reserves of foreign currencies and gold. When a large loan to the Bank of England from the Federal Reserve Bank of New York and the Bank of France failed to stem the tide, the British parliament on September 21 took the extraordinary step of suspending the obligation of the Bank of England to sell gold in exchange for the national currency.

Great Britain's repudiation of the gold standard was a landmark in the economic history of the modern world. It exposed the fundamental economic weakness of the nation that had presided for so long over the international monetary system: London was shown to be incapable of retaining sufficient reserves of gold and foreign currencies to function as one of the two financial centers of the world. The explanation of Great Britain's ignominious descent from her previous position of financial preeminence can be found in the shifting patterns of world trade during and after the First World War. The failure to recapture overseas markets lost during the four years of combat prevented the British export trade from resuming the spectacular rate of growth that had attracted the financial reserves of the world to the London banking system during the nineteenth century. The consequence of Britain's abandonment of gold on that historic day in September 1931 was the crumbling of the international monetary system that had been reestablished after the First World War.

The decision in April 1925 to return to the gold standard at the prewar parity of $4.86 was, by the beginning of the 1930s, generally blamed for having aggravated Britain's chronic trade deficit by making British exports too expensive in nations that had returned to the gold standard at a devalued level. Accordingly, British treasury officials hoped that once the exchange rate of the pound was free to fluctuate on world money markets it would drop to a level that would restore the competitive position of British exports. On being cut loose from gold, the British currency rapidly fell from par ($4.86) to about $3.50. But those nations for which Britain was a major customer and British banks the principal center for their surplus reserves could ill afford to allow sterling to continue to depreciate against their currencies for fear that their own exports would be priced out of the British market and the value of their sterling deposits in London would dwindle. Twenty-four such countries were therefore compelled to leave the gold standard and allow their currencies to float freely by the spring of 1932. Thereafter, the trading nations of the world were left to their own devices to adopt temporary expedients to finance their international transactions. The system of fixed exchange rates linked to gold, one of the pillars of postwar economic recovery, was in shambles.

The international monetary system soon disintegrated into three distinct groups of nations, each of which cautiously embraced its own preferred expedient. One set of five countries blessed with relatively healthy financial conditions—the United States, France, Belgium, Holland, and Switzerland—remained on the gold standard while striving to reduce imports by erecting protectionist tariff barriers and imposing restrictive import quotas. A second group, composed of Britain and its major trading partners (including all of the member states of the empire except Canada together with twelve other nations) followed Britain's flight from gold and tied the value of their currencies to the pound sterling. Exchange stability within this "sterling bloc" was maintained through the buying and selling of the British currency by the member governments, while Britain drew upon a stabilization fund to moderate exchange fluctuations between this sterling bloc and the "gold bloc." The third group, dominated by Germany and including many of the impoverished nonindustrialized nations of Central Europe and Latin America, imposed rigid exchange controls that rendered their currencies inconvertible. Since the protectionist policies of the gold bloc countries and the depreciation of the currencies of the sterling bloc countries had the identical effect of reducing imports, the only alternative open to the "exchange control states" was to seek new markets and sources of imports in other nations that had adopted exchange controls. This expedient of bilateral trade was increasingly adopted by Germany after the advent of the Nazi regime. On account of the drying up of foreign loans, the closure of markets abroad, and the inconvertibility of the mark, Germany lacked the means of accumulating foreign exchange to finance the imports of raw materials and foodstuffs that it required. It therefore increasingly strove to obtain its imports from those countries (mostly in Central Europe) that were indebted to Germany on current account or were willing to receive payment in marks that could not leave Germany because of the exchange restrictions. As a consequence, Germany's suppliers of raw materials and foodstuffs were required to import as much from her as they exported to her in order to avoid allowing the marks that they earned from their sales to accumulate unused in German banks. The German government also experimented with old-fashioned bilateral barter arrangements with various countries to circumvent the problem of currency inconvertibility. Thus German coal was shipped to Brazil for an equivalent value of coffee while German fertilizer was exchanged for Egyptian cotton. Even the United States flirted with a barter deal with Hitler's Germany involving an exchange of American cotton for various German products.

The gold bloc and sterling bloc countries themselves turned away from the traditional system of multilateral payments through the London money market in favor of bilateral arrangements for the balancing of international accounts. Great Britain, France, and the Netherlands stepped up their imports from those parts of the world (in particular, their colonial empires) where their extensive capital investments supplied the necessary foreign exchange to pay for those imports. As a consequence, trade between the three large financial-commercial blocs of the earth continued to dwindle.

A related cause of the decline of world trade was the universal appearance of politically imposed restrictions on international commerce that made the protectionist measures of the 1920s pale in comparison. In response to the Hawley-Smoot Tariff of the United States, the major trading nations of Europe hastened to enact protectionist legislation to halt the precipitous decline of prices and the increase of unemployment in their domestic industries. France and Germany erected high tariff walls and imposed strict quantitative restrictions on imports. Even Great Britain, the perennial champion of free trade, succumbed to the protectionist pressures of the era. The Import Duties Act of 1932 terminated three-quarters of a century of free trade by raising duties on a variety of items. At the Ottawa Conference in the summer of the same year, this protectionist policy was extended to embrace the self-governing Dominions of the empire. Britain raised duties on foreign agricultural commodities that competed with Dominion exports to the metropole such as Canadian wheat, Australian wool, and New Zealand dairy products. In return, British manufactured goods received preferential treatment in Dominion markets. Meanwhile, France and Holland had devised similar preferential arrangements with their colonial possessions. The turn toward imperial preference, the protectionist legislation that insulated the vast continental market of the United States from foreign competition, and the bilateral trading arrangements of the exchange control countries, signaled the disintegration of the network of international trade into a half dozen virtually self-enclosed commercial blocs. By 1931 tariff rates in some fifteen European nations had increased 64 percent above the 1927 level. Throughout the 1930s trade in manufactured products between Germany, France, and Great Britain declined to half the level of 1913.

International cooperative efforts to rectify this situation by reviving world trade and the international monetary system on which it depended were uniformly unsuccessful during the 1930s. This was so largely because domestic pressures in each major nation inhibited government officials from adopting policies which, though painful in the short run, might have promoted long-term recovery of international trade and investment. The most graphic instance of this shortsighted, narrow-minded response to the world economic crisis was the initial monetary policy adopted by the new administration of Franklin D. Roosevelt in the United States. In early 1933, the League of Nations issued invitations to an international economic conference to devise a multilateral solution to the chronic instability of the world's currencies caused by the collapse of the gold standard. The United States had previously declined to participate in the international economic conferences at Brussels (1920) and Genoa (1922) and most recently at Lausanne (1932). Moreover, though private American financial experts had played an important role in devising the economic recovery programs of the 1920s, such as the Dawes and Young plans, the United States government had expressly declined any official connection with those measures. It was with considerable relief that European officials learned of the decision of the new American administration to send high-level representatives to the conference scheduled to convene in London during the summer of 1933. But before the conference got under way, Washington cast a pall over the forthcoming talks, first by refusing to permit any discussion of intergovernmental debts and then, on April 19, by abandoning the gold standard. The new president and his advisers, alarmed by the collapse of domestic commodity prices and subject to intense political pressure from the farm bloc, erroneously concluded that American prices could be boosted by deliberately reducing the foreign exchange value of the dollar in order to stimulate demand for American commodities abroad. Roosevelt feared that any agreement on exchange stability reached in London would inhibit his ability to employ monetary measures at home to raise the domestic price level. He therefore jolted the London conference with a July 3 message expressing his unwillingness to consider even a temporary linkage of the dollar exchange rate to any international standard until domestic prices could be raised.

Once the world's major currency was cut loose from gold and permitted to depreciate on world markets, the London Conference's plan for international currency stabilization was nipped in the bud. The United States soon saw the error of its ways and renewed its commitment to exchange stability by returning to a gold exchange standard* in January 1934, but at a fixed price of $35 per ounce compared to the predepreciation price of $20.67. It was only a matter of time before the other gold bloc nations were forced to devalue their own currencies in order to preserve the competitive position of their exports and finally to abandon gold altogether. In the meantime the United States signed the so-called Tripartite Agreement with Great Britain and France, later joined by Belgium, Holland, and Switzerland, by which the member nations agreed to sell each other gold in exchange for the seller's own currency at an agreed upon price.

---

* The gold exchange standard differed from the traditional gold standard in one fundamental respect: Under the old gold standard, each nation's currency was freely convertible to gold on demand; under the gold exchange standard, American citizens were legally prohibited from owning gold.

This temporary expedient kept the exchange rates of the world's strongest currencies within the narrow range of the announced gold support price of each country. This agreement, though serving as an important precedent for the revival of international monetary cooperation after the Second World War, failed to operate as a satisfactory alternative to the gold standard on account of its limited application. In response to these financial machinations, the exchange control countries of Central Europe and Latin America tightened their restrictions on capital transfers to protect their domestic reserves. The absence of a universally recognized mechanism for the convertibility of national currencies, together with the drying up of international investment to facilitate the adjustment of international payments, prevented the recovery of world trade (which stood at 10 percent below its 1929 level at the end of 1936) and the repayment of existing debts (most of which remained in default for the rest of the decade).

Just as the Tripartite Agreement represented the only significant American initiative to restore exchange stability in the 1930s, the Reciprocal Trade Agreement Amendment to the Hawley-Smoot Tariff Act was the sole American effort to unclog the channels of world trade. This legislation, which went into effect on June 12, 1934, authorized the president to reduce existing duties up to 50 percent of their current level in exchange for reciprocal tariff concessions by America's trading partners. It was also based on the unconditional most-favored-nation principle, which meant that any concessions made to one country were automatically extended to imports of the same commodity from all other countries. By 1940 bilateral reciprocal agreements to reduce duties had been signed with twenty-one countries representing 60 percent of the volume of American foreign trade. In principle, this should have produced a general reduction in commercial restrictions and a corresponding expansion of world trade. In practice, American tariff negotiators attempted to limit concessions to items that did not compete with American products. Moreover, even the maximum concession of 50 percent preserved a high degree of protection, since the rates established by the 1930 tariff act had been so steep in the first place. Finally, a number of quantitative restrictions (such as an import quota on sugar) were introduced by the Roosevelt administration. A federal law of March 1933 required United States government agencies to purchase American-made products in preference to foreign imports. In sum, it may be said that the reciprocal reduction of tariff barriers during the New Deal was motivated less by a recognition of the critical relationship between the United States balance of payments and world economic recovery than by the expectation that reciprocity would stimulate American exports and therefore hasten domestic recovery. The bilateral character of these agreements further reflected the American government's reluctance to participate in a genuinely international effort to revive world trade.

The same can be said about the creation of the Export-Import Bank in March 1934. Despite the second term in its title, this government-funded agency initially confined its operations largely to the supplying of credits to American exporters of agricultural commodities and industrial equipment. Its comparatively modest lending for import purposes was dictated by considerations of national interest, such as the procurement of strategic raw materials or the cementing of friendly relations with the primary producing countries of Latin America that sought access to the American market. It was not until 1940 that the bank began to disburse long-term development loans to stimulate industrialization in selected Latin American countries such as Brazil, and then primarily for the national security goal of combating the growing economic influence of Germany in the Western Hemisphere. The expansion of this policy of long-term American government lending to develop the productive capacity of present or prospective trading partners had to await the end of the Second World War and the full recognition of America's veritable global responsibilities.

Finally, the United States government's stubborn refusal to modify its policy regarding the troublesome issue of intergovernmental debts further confirmed the narrowly nationalistic character of American foreign economic policy in the 1930s. It was inconceivable that the economically battered nations of Europe could have been expected to continue to make these large capital transfers once the lubricant of American foreign investment in Central Europe had dried up. Consequently, as Hoover's one-year moratorium on the payment of these government obligations approached its expiration in the summer of 1932, the European powers issued an invitation to the United States to attend an economic conference at Lausanne, Switzerland, to discuss ways of removing these irksome impediments to European economic recovery. After the refusal of the United States to participate, the European debtors proposed what amounted to a mutual cancellation of German reparations and inter-Allied debts. The Hoover administration, which, like its predecessors, had consistently denied the connection between German reparations and the European war debts to the United States, indignantly refused. Since Germany had failed to resume the reparations payments that had been interrupted, temporarily it was thought but permanently as it turned out, by the Hoover moratorium, the European debtors of the United States were forced to the wall. When the next installment on the war debts came due on December 15, 1932, six nations (including France and Belgium) defaulted for the first time. In June 1933 Great Britain and Italy made drastically reduced payments, and within a year all of the European debtors except Finland had ceased payment altogether.

Instead of writing off these intergovernmental obligations left over from the First World War, the United States Congress retaliated with the Johnson Act of April 1934, which prohibited American citizens from purchasing the securities of governments in default on their war debts. All that was accomplished by this measure was the closure of American financial markets to Great Britain and France as they undertook programs of industrial expansion and rearmament to meet the Nazi menace. Similarly, the Neutrality Act of 1935, which banned the sale of munitions to belligerents and required cash payment for all exports to nations engaged in hostilities, denied the Western democracies American supplies on credit once they went to war with Germany in September 1939. As a consequence Britain and France were forced to reduce their imports from the United States to conserve their dwindling gold and dollar reserves. As American public support for the Anglo-French cause increased, Congress lifted the arms embargo in November 1939, but this belated reversal of isolationist policy did not come in time to be of much assistance to France, which collapsed before the Nazi blitzkrieg in June 1940. The cash-on-delivery requirement was not removed until March 11, 1941, with the inauguration of the Lend-Lease Program, which authorized American exports to Great Britain and her allies for which payment was postponed until the end of the war.

In sum, to the extent that the New Deal of Franklin Roosevelt rescued the United States from economic collapse—and historians have increasingly challenged that conventional judgment—it did so by pursuing narrowly conceived domestic remedies rather than by cooperating with the industrial nations of Western Europe to fashion a coordinated program of international recovery. The resumption of industrial expansion in Europe was precipitated by international strategic factors rather than by remedial economic measures: The intensive campaign of rearmament that got under way in the late 1930s generated demand for manufactured products, raw materials, and labor that far surpassed in stimulative effect the modest public works projects and domestic spending programs undertaken earlier in the decade by the Western democracies. It is perhaps the most tragic irony of modern history that organized violence on a large scale, or the preparation for it, has proved to be the most effective remedy for the economic problems of underconsumption and unemployment.

The causal connection between military preparedness and economic recovery was most graphically demonstrated in Hitler's Germany, where strict state control of political and economic life permitted the most efficient mobilization of capital, labor, and resources for military purposes and consequently generated phenomenal economic growth throughout the second half of the 1930s. The Nazi Four-Year Plan of economic development instituted in 1936 was designed to make Germany entirely independent of markets and resources outside its political and economic orbit. As will be seen in greater detail below, this goal of economic self-sufficiency, or autarky, was to be attained through the combination of two strategies. First, the German chemical industry developed a number of synthetic products to substitute for raw materials, such as rubber, cotton, and wool, that could not be produced domestically in sufficient quantity. Second, Germany tightened its economic grip on its weaker neighbors in Eastern Europe that possessed valuable mineral and agricultural resources. By expanding its bilateral trade relations with such countries as Poland, Hungary, and Romania, Germany obtained access to enormous supplies of wheat, lumber, oil, and other raw materials it required as well as markets in which it could dispose of its surplus industrial production.

The Collapse of the European Security System

As we have seen, the rearmament of Germany was already well advanced by the time of Adolf Hitler's rise to power in January 1933. The dramatic announcements of March 1935 confirmed the existence of, rather than the intention of creating, a German army and air force that had been a decade and a half in the making. The patient, subtle efforts of General Hans von Seeckt and his successors in the Reichswehr to evade the disarmament prescriptions of the peace treaty without provoking Allied retaliation had forged an institutional structure of military power that Hitler inherited intact: a general staff, effectively concealed within a labyrinth of government agencies and military bureaus; the nucleus of a well-trained army of several hundred thousand men dispersed among various police forces, paramilitary organizations, veterans' associations, and rifle clubs; the kernel of an air force in the form of hundreds of commercial airline pilots with thousands of hours of flying time; and an elaborate infrastructure of munitions plants, first located in Russia during the period of Allied inspection and later reassembled in the Ruhr, that were capable on short notice of turning out huge quantities of the implements of war that had been proscribed by the peace treaty, including aircraft, tanks, artillery pieces, shells, and poison gas.

The full extent of this German military buildup was not known to the Allies, but enough evidence had been uncovered to cause grave apprehension in European capitals about the consequences of an unlimited increase in Germany's warmaking potential. The removal of the Allied inspection team in 1927 and the evacuation of the Rhineland three years later left the victors of 1918 with little leverage to apply against a Germany that was determined to rearm. As the feasibility of enforcing the unilateral disarmament of Germany began to recede at the end of the 1920s, the alternative of general disarmament began to exert an increasingly powerful attraction on peace-loving folk everywhere. This was particularly true of public opinion in Great Britain and the United States, two countries which had unilaterally demobilized their large land armies, dismantled their munitions industries, and voluntarily accepted limitations to their naval strength in the early years after the war. The concept of universal disarmament* had been endorsed by the Versailles Treaty in accordance with the popular presumption that the very existence of stockpiles of munitions and large standing armies made war more likely. But no progress toward that end had been possible during the first half of the twenties

* A misnomer for "arms control": No one advocated the abolition of *all* military forces and armaments.

because of France's refusal to relinquish its military superiority over Germany in the absence of an iron-clad guarantee of the security of its eastern border.

The insertion of just such a guarantee from Great Britain and Italy in the Locarno treaties paved the way for the convocation of a preparatory commission on disarmament in Geneva in May 1926 to study means of reducing the level of armaments in the world. The tangible results of these deliberations were minimal because of French suspicions of Germany's good intentions. The commission closed up shop in January 1931 with little to show for its five years of disputatious deliberation. But public interest in universal disarmament was revived soon thereafter when the effects of the economic crisis that originated in the United States began to be felt in Europe. As governments hastened to reduce expenditures and shore up their faltering finances, the enormous costs of maintaining defense establishments came under heavy attack from advocates of austerity. It began to seem senseless to divert an ever-increasing proportion of a nation's ever-decreasing supply of resources to the unproductive purposes of military preparedness while businesses failed, banks closed their doors, and the unemployment lines lengthened. Hence, the economic crisis of the early 1930s, together with the mounting apprehension about the clandestine, unilateral rearmament of Germany, prompted the great powers to convene an international conference on land armaments in Geneva in February 1932 in the hope of reaching some definitive agreement on the size of national armies.

At this conference the German delegation reiterated the position that it had taken in informal exchanges with the Allied governments throughout the twenties: either universal disarmament as envisaged by the Versailles Treaty or equality of arms between Germany and the other great powers of Europe. When this demand foundered on the shoals of France's insistence on security prior to disarmament, the German delegates abruptly left the conference on September 16. Desperately intent on getting the German government back to the bargaining table, Britain and France promised on December 11 to grant Germany "equality in a system which would provide security for all other nations." Though this formula simply restated the insoluble dilemma that had prevented previous agreement, it was conveyed in sufficiently conciliatory language to lure Germany back to the conference in February 1933.

But the German delegation that returned to Geneva was under orders from Adolf Hitler, designated chancellor the previous month. The new German leader had already decided upon a massive program of unilateral rearmament which he communicated to the highest-ranking military and naval officers of the Reich on February 3, the day after the reappearance of his delegates in Geneva: Germany would go through the motions of negotiating an agreement for equality of arms with the other great powers while secretly constructing a military force superior to that of all potential enemies. The ostensible purpose of this ambitious rearmament program was principally economic in nature. In the short run, the vast government expenditures for military purposes would stimulate employment and industrial production and therefore rescue the German economy from the depression into which it had recently plunged. The huge government outlays required for this program would be furnished through deficit financing, a drastic departure from the deflationary fiscal policies of Hitler's predecessors that was facilitated by the appointment of the Nazi sympathizer Hjalmar Schacht as president of the Reichsbank* on March 17, 1933. More than one historian has noted the similarities between the remedial measures adopted by the National Socialist government to combat the depression and those of the new Roosevelt administration in the United States, whose domestic recovery program was getting under way at the same time. The key difference, of course, was the object of the deficit financing and stimulative government spending in the two countries. In the German case, it was directed not toward domestic recovery but rather toward the overriding priority of achieving military superiority in Europe.

The long-term objective of this military buildup, as expounded by Hitler with perfect consistency in his major writings and speeches, was also superficially economic in character. To summarize this objective briefly, Germany, with her existing frontiers, suffered from the Malthusian curse of insufficient arable land with which to feed her expanding population. If the territory under German sovereignty were to remain constant, the only solutions to this dilemma were more intensive cultivation of the available land (a possibility Hitler never took seriously) or a reduction of the birthrate through measures of population control such as contraception or abortion. The latter alternative was repellent to Hitler because it signified a deliberately engineered form of racial suicide. In light of Hitler's assumption of German racial superiority, the obvious solution to the problem of overpopulation and insufficient agricultural resources was emigration. But the type of emigration that he envisioned differed, both in its object and its methods, from that employed by Great Britain to ease its population pressures in the nineteenth century. Instead of directing German settlers to overseas lands, where they were likely to lose their consciousness of their racial and national origins and therefore represent a net loss to the mother country, they were to be relocated in the adjacent land area to Germany's east that was populated by inferior races that would be subdued and then expelled or annihilated to make way for the German pioneers.

None of these ideas was new in Germany. In somewhat less brutal form they had been aired since the turn of the century in circles of Social Darwinists, geopoliticians, and racist thinkers. In the guise of the Mitteleuropa concept, they had played a part in the more extravagant schemes of military conquest and continental domination entertained by expansionist think-

* The central bank of Germany, analogous to the Federal Reserve Board in the United States.

ers in Imperial Germany during the First World War. Hitler's signal contribution to this hitherto inchoate mélange of nationalistic doctrines was to give them a specific geographical focus. The Nazi leader never deviated from his insistence that the living space, or *Lebensraum,* that Germany required was to be found in Eastern Europe and western Russia. The fertile agricultural land and valuable mineral resources located in this region could supply Germany with the food and raw materials she needed to survive and prosper as well as affording her an outlet for her surplus population. It was inhabited by two "racial" groups that, for personal reasons, Hitler detested and was determined to liquidate: The majority population of Slavs was so racially decadent as to be incapable of organizing this valuable territory politically, exploiting it economically, or defending it militarily; and the minority of Jews dispersed throughout the region, together with their coreligionists in Germany itself, constituted a cancer on the body of Europe that had to be removed.

Hitler's policy toward the other great powers of Europe, as it unfolded in the early months of his rule, can be understood in the context of this single-minded goal of extending Germany's living space eastward at the expense of the Slavic and Jewish populations of Eastern Europe and Western Russia. Since France was the self-appointed guarantor of the existing territorial distribution in Europe and protector of those states in the east that stood in the way of Germany's *Drang nach Osten,* Hitler's foreign policy envisioned the prior destruction of France as a prelude to his eastern conquests. With England the German dictator had no quarrel so long as it could be induced to remain disinterested in continental affairs. Indeed, his project of eastward expansion on land was entirely compatible with the maintenance of friendly relations with the British. Recalling the disastrous consequences for Germany of the Kaiser's bid to challenge Britain's position outside Europe, Hitler hoped and expected that Germany's abstention from an aggressive colonial and naval policy would remove any basis for Anglo-German friction and therefore any reason for British support of France. So far as Italy was concerned, Hitler's genuine admiration for Mussolini on ideological grounds was reinforced by realistic reasons for Italo-German friendship: Italy was in perpetual conflict with France over naval and colonial matters in the Mediterranean, while Germany's ambitions in Eastern Europe and Russia posed no direct threat to Italy's vital interests (save Hitler's designs on Austria).

Because of the Eurocentric nature of his foreign policy concerns, the German chancellor took only a passing interest in the affairs of the other continents. It bears repeating: His overriding goal was the conquest of living space in Eastern Europe and Russia. He expected to achieve this objective after the prior destruction of France with the cooperation of Italy and the abstention of Great Britain. Once this primary goal had been reached, the land mass of Eurasia under German auspices could then enter into global competition with the remaining two imperial blocs of the world, those of Great Britain and the United States, perhaps with the cooperation of Japan, whose political system and national dynamism he vaguely admired. In the meantime, the two English-speaking powers were expected to remain aloof from the continent of Europe while Germany proceeded to subdue, organize, and exploit it for its own needs.

It is worth pausing at this juncture to remark upon the extent to which this program for continental domination diverged from the foreign policy objectives of the political elite of the Weimar Republic. The superficial similarity between the immediate foreign policy goals of Stresemann and Hitler has led some historians to emphasize the continuity of German foreign policy throughout the interwar period. Some have been tempted to view Hitler as a traditional German nationalist pursuing the policy that had been adopted in the 1920s by his republican predecessors: the recovery of the territory lost by Germany at the Paris Peace Conference, the annexation of adjacent regions with substantial German populations on the basis of the principle of national self-determination, and the restoration of military parity for Germany with the other powers of Europe. The plausibility of this interpretation stems from the incontestable fact that all of Hitler's official diplomatic initiatives from his accession in January 1933 to March 1939 were aimed at securing these traditional objectives of German foreign policy. What this interpretation overlooks are Hitler's numerous unofficial references to the expansionist program delineated above. The reversal of the "unjust" verdict of the Paris Peace Conference, which implied the recovery or annexation of all German-speaking regions of Central Europe, was but the first step in Hitler's grand design. In truth he cared nothing about the fate of the German-speaking citizens who had been incorporated within half-a-dozen neighboring states in the peace settlement of 1919–20. Their grievance merely served as a pretext for destroying the territorial settlement, and therefore the balance of power in Europe, as a prelude to conquering and exploiting the vast expanses of territories to the east where few Germans lived but where German colonists were to be sent in some distant future. Though his grandiose ambitions beyond the regions of German settlement were not openly pursued until as late as March 1939 with the absorption of the non-German sector of Czechoslovakia, they were frequently and forcefully expressed in speeches and writings that were well known to the world's political leaders.

In the light of this program of eastward expansion, the disarmament talks in Geneva to which the German representatives returned in February 1933 were exercises in futility. Even the compromise plan drafted by British Prime Minister Ramsay MacDonald that projected parity of national armies in Europe at 200,000 men each, to be achieved by the gradual reduction of French forces over five years, failed to secure the approval of Hitler's hand-picked delegation, which had been instructed to reject any multilateral restrictions on the German rearmament program already underway. When the German demand for the immediate right to construct proscribed weapons and increase the size of the standing army encountered the anticipated French opposition, Hitler summarily withdrew Germany from the disarmament conference and the League of Nations on October 14, dissolved the Reichstag, and staged a plebiscite on November 12 which produced a 90 percent vote of confidence in his recent actions in Geneva. The Führer was thereupon free to pursue a foreign policy independent of both domestic opinion (represented by an impotent Reichstag that functioned merely as a forum for his periodic harangues against Versailles) and world opinion (represented by an irrelevant League that functioned as a forum for the expression of helpless rage and alarm by the representatives of those nations most endangered by Germany's new independent posture in foreign affairs).

Germany's simultaneous withdrawal from the disarmament conference and the League of Nations dealt a devastating blow to the principle of collective security that was soon to prove fatal. Though that principle had already been severely undermined in the Manchurian affair (see p. 243), an incident in far-off Asia that did not involve the vital interests of the great powers in Europe could be conveniently overlooked. But the advent of an independent German foreign policy in the autumn of 1933 compelled French officials to abandon whatever hopes they may have entertained of restraining Germany by the application of the pressure of world opinion through the instrument of the world body in Geneva.

Following closely on the heels of Hitler's abandonment of Geneva was an equally dramatic reversal of German foreign policy that dealt a severe blow to France's defensive alliance system in Europe: the conclusion of a German-Polish nonaggression pact on January 26, 1934. Berlin's approach to Warsaw for an improvement of their traditionally frosty relations was prompted by Hitler's realization that in its present condition of partial rearmament Germany was unprepared for war: A relaxation of tension with its traditional adversary in Eastern Europe would facilitate Germany's internal consolidation and military preparation. The two outstanding sources of friction between the two countries were a tariff war that had raged for over eight years and the political conflict between the German-speaking majority of the free city of Danzig (Gdańsk) and the Polish government, which maintained a customs union with the city as well as authority over its relations with foreign states. The German dictator promoted a temporary resolution of the Danzig issue by imposing tactical restraints on the National Socialist municipal government that had been elected in 1933 by the German-speaking majority. Warsaw's desire to improve its relations with Berlin, in order to enhance its balancing act between its two powerful neighbors as well as to gain access to the German market for its coal and agricultural surpluses, cemented the friendship. The pact of January 1934 committed each signatory to a bilateral resolution of their mutual problems and the avoidance of the use of force against each other for a period of ten years. A commercial agreement concluded on March 7, 1934, terminated the tariff war and opened up the possibility of improved trade relations between the two countries. Though the Polish government was careful to insert a reservation in the nonaggression pact acknowledging its treaty obligations to France, the German-Polish rapprochement inaugurated a diplomatic revolution in Europe. In his first foray into bilateral diplomacy since divesting Germany of the constraints imposed by membership in the League, Hitler had punched a hole in the French alliance system and obtained what appeared to be a considerable measure of security on Germany's eastern flank.

The dramatic announcement of the German-Polish nonaggression pact prodded the Quai d'Orsay into action. The successors of Briand, whose death in March 1932 had marked the end of an era in French diplomacy, hastened to bolster France's sagging security arrangements on the continent through bilateral approaches to two great powers that had been allies of France in the Great War but had been alienated from her ever since.

The first of these was Italy. Even before the advent of the Fascist regime in 1922, Italy had nurtured deeply felt grievances against France. All of these were related in one way or another to the frustration of Italian aspirations to become an imperial power in the Mediterranean basin. Italian Prime Minister Vittorio Orlando's failure to obtain Allied support for Italy's territorial ambitions along the Dalmatian coast at the Paris Peace Conference, though largely due to President Wilson's endorsement of Yugoslavia's competing claims, had caused a serious breach in Franco-Italian relations because of Clemenceau's reluctance to champion the Italian cause. The long-simmering Italian resentment at France's acquisition of Tunisia, a North African territory across the Mediterranean from Sicily, came to a boiling point after the war when France repudiated its earlier pledge to respect the special privileges of the large Italian population there. Reinforcing these territorial and colonial disputes was an intense Franco-Italian naval rivalry that developed in the course of the 1920s. Though France had been compelled to accept parity in capital ships with Italy at the Washington Naval Conference of 1921–22 (see p. 232), she offended Italian sensibilities by insisting that the necessity to divide the French fleet between the Mediterranean and the oceanic routes to the French empire in Africa and Asia entitled her to superiority in auxiliary craft such as cruisers and submarines. Added to these Mediterranean tensions was an incipient Franco-Italian conflict in Central Europe: Paris endeavored to weld together a diplomatic coalition including Poland and the nations of the Little Entente (Czechoslovakia, Romania, and Yugoslavia) through defensive alliances, treaties of friendship, and financial subsidies. Italy simultaneously sought predominant influence in the Danubian basin by extending political protection and economic assistance to

Austria and Hungary while undermining its Adriatic rival (and France's diplomatic partner), Yugoslavia, by supporting Croatian separatist agitation against the Serb-dominated government in Belgrade.

In spite of these numerous obstacles to Franco-Italian cooperation, the two countries shared one common objective that French officials hoped would serve as the basis of reconciliation. This was the preservation of the political independence of the German-speaking rump state of Austria. The periodic calls for the political unification of Austria and Germany, or *Anschluss,* that had emanated from pan-German circles since the end of the war had caused considerable alarm in Rome throughout the 1920s. That sense of alarm was increased after January 1933 when a pan-German zealot of Austrian birth came to power in Berlin. The source of Italy's anxiety about the extension of German sovereignty to its northern frontier was its potential effect on the German-speaking inhabitants of the south Tyrol region in the Alps that had been ceded by Austria to Italy at the Paris Peace Conference. France opposed the *Anschluss* both because of the threat that it would pose to its ally Czechoslovakia (which would be caught in the vise of an enlarged Germanic state) and because of the increase in Germany's population and industrial potential that such a union would entail.

Officials at the French foreign ministry hoped that this shared interest in preserving Austria's independence could be expanded to unite the two antagonistic blocs in Central Europe into some sort of economic federation and political association under the joint tutelage of Paris and Rome. The prospects of Franco-Italian cooperation in the defense of the territorial status quo in Central Europe were enhanced by Italy's reaction to the Austrian crisis of July 1934, during which local Nazis in Vienna assassinated Chancellor Engelbert Dollfuss (a determined foe of *Anschluss*) and appealed to Hitler for assistance in their prospective coup d'état. Italian troops which had coincidentally been on maneuvers near the Austrian border staged a show of force at the Brenner Pass, prompting Hitler to repudiate the plot that his own embassy in Vienna had played a role in hatching. The ignominious collapse of the venture enabled Mussolini to take credit for having deterred Germany from interfering in Austria's internal affairs. Suitably impressed, Parisian authorities hastened to seek formal arrangements with Italy to deter any future German initiatives of similar stripe. In January 1935, Foreign Minister Pierre Laval of France journeyed to Rome to sign an agreement with Mussolini which settled most of the outstanding Franco-Italian differences in Africa to the Duce's satisfaction in return for an Italian pledge to consult with France in the event of German violations of the Versailles clauses on disarmament and the independence of Austria.

The emerging Franco-Italian entente received its first test in March 1935, when Hitler formally repudiated the disarmament provisions of the Versailles Treaty. It had long been apparent that the military forces that the German dictator considered essential for his foreign policy objectives could no longer be forged in secrecy. The construction of a navy, an air force, and a mechanized army could not escape detection. After the plebiscite in the Saar, which was held on January 13, 1935, and resulted in the return of that territory to the German Reich on March 1, Hitler was free to remove the remaining legal restrictions on Germany's military recovery. On March 9 he revealed the existence of a German air force as well as plans to expand its size and strength. On March 16 he decreed the reintroduction of universal military conscription with the announced goal of creating a thirty-six-division army (compared to the seven divisions permitted by the Versailles Treaty and the thirty divisions of the existing French army). A week later the French, British, and Italian prime ministers met to fashion a coordinated response to Germany's flagrant repudiation of the Versailles military restrictions. At the conclusion of this conference, held from April 11 to 14 at the Italian resort city of Stresa, the three powers issued a joint communiqué that sternly condemned the German action and threatened joint opposition to any further treaty violations. Moreover, France and Italy secretly exchanged pledges of military assistance to counter German violations of either the Rhineland demilitarized zone or the independence of Austria. Italy's commitment to cooperate with France in resisting further German revisionist bids reached its apex in June 1935, when Franco-Italian military conversations were resumed for the first time since the end of the war.

These fruitful French approaches to Fascist Italy were paralleled by simultaneous overtures to the Soviet Union. From the vantage point of ideological consistency, it may seem astonishing that a parliamentary democracy such as France could hope to base its system of continental security upon diplomatic links with Fascist and Communist dictatorships. But the realities of international power in Europe seemed to dictate just such an ideologically contradictory policy during the interwar period. In its frantic search for an effective anti-German coalition in the mid-1930s, France expressed an eagerness to obtain allies wherever it could find them, regardless of the character of their domestic political institutions. The approach to Italy, though distasteful to democratic opinion in France, was pursued with minimal domestic opposition. The overtures to Soviet Russia predictably provoked some agitation in the ranks of the anti-Communist right in France, but not enough to derail the Quai d'Orsay's efforts to reach an accommodation with the Kremlin. The national interest, which was thought to require a diplomatic strategy of encircling Germany with hostile powers associated with France, prevailed over the promptings of ideological preference in the minds of all but the most vociferously anti-Fascist and anti-Communist Frenchmen. Moreover, the simultaneous approach to Rome and Moscow was favored by the surprising record of compatibility between France's two potential allies: Mussolini had been one of the first Western leaders to recognize the Soviet regime in the early twenties, and Italy and Russia had maintained remarkably cordial relations ever since.

The possibility of a diplomatic understanding with Russia had long tempted Parisian officials because of the obvious advantages of confronting Germany with the prospect of a war on two fronts after the fashion of 1914. But the obstacles to a resurrection of the prewar Franco-Russian alliance were even more formidable than those that had hindered a Franco-Italian rapprochement: On the French side there was lingering resentment at the Soviet government's conclusion of a separate peace with Germany during the First World War and its repudiation of the enormous debt to French investors that had been contracted by the tsarist regime; on the Russian side there was bitterness at France's anti-Bolshevik posture in the Russian Civil War and its support of Poland's military offensive against Soviet Russia in 1920. Added to these historical animosities was the underlying incompatibility of foreign policy between the two states throughout the 1920s. As the major beneficiary of the peace settlement of 1919, France vigorously defended the postwar status quo in Europe by extending its financial support and political protection to the states of Eastern Europe that had also profited from the defeat of the Central Powers. Russia, which had lost a considerable portion of its territory in Europe to these new or enlarged states on its western frontier, accordingly favored the destruction of the postwar European system and had not hesitated to cooperate with the other great revisionist power, Germany, in an effort to bring about that result during the twenties.

But the rise of Hitler and the stalling of the disarmament talks in Geneva precipitated a simultaneous reversal in official French and Soviet attitudes toward each other. Hitler's oft-stated intention of seeking living space in Eastern Europe at Russia's expense, together with his frequent denunciations of communism as a political philosophy, were well known to the leaders of the Kremlin. In February 1933, the Soviet foreign minister, Maxim Litvinov, officially reversed his government's long-standing support for revision of the peace treaties by openly endorsing the French position on collective security at the disarmament conference. In subsequent remarks the Russian diplomat clearly enunciated his government's new official line: Treaty revision meant war and therefore had to be avoided at all costs. The French government responded with alacrity to this stunning Soviet volte face. For the first time since Russia's withdrawal from the world war, a French military attaché was dispatched to Moscow on April 8, 1933, as a gesture of interest in the Kremlin's new anti-German orientation. By the summer of 1933 the secret collaboration between the Reichswehr and the Red Army came to a halt, all German military facilities in Russia were closed, and visits of Soviet officers to Germany were cancelled. With an eagerness he could scarcely conceal, Foreign Minister Paul-Boncour of France took the occasion of Germany's withdrawal from the disarmament conference in the autumn of 1934 to approach Litvinov in Geneva about the possibility of creating some formal mechanism for Franco-Russian cooperation to preserve collective security in Europe. Conversations about a possible commercial agreement between France and Russia to pave the way for friendlier political relations foundered on the problem of the mutual incongruity of the two economic systems: Russia required massive infusions of industrial technology for which she could export only agricultural products in exchange; France was agriculturally self-sufficient and had begun to restrict imports of foodstuffs to protect her politically powerful farmers from a further decline in domestic agricultural prices. But these increasing diplomatic, military, and economic contacts between the two governments helped to clear the air of mutual suspicion that had kept them apart to Germany's profit since the end of the war.

The accession of Louis Barthou as French foreign minister in February 1934 marked the real beginning of the French quest for a Russian connection. A conservative lawyer with impeccable nationalist credentials, Barthou was ideally suited to the task of allaying right-wing suspicions of a closer relationship with the Soviet regime. In resuming Paul-Boncour's overtures to the Kremlin, Barthou concocted the scheme of a dual alliance system in Eastern Europe designed to refurbish the existing French security arrangements in the region that had been recently weakened by Poland's accommodation with Germany in the month before he took office. The first part of this proposed association was a pact of regional assistance in Eastern Europe, modeled on the Locarno treaties for Western Europe, in which Germany, Russia, Poland, Czechoslovakia, Finland, and the Baltic states would mutually guarantee their frontiers. The second part of the proposal was a bilateral agreement between France and Russia in which Russia would render a commitment to France as though it were a member of the Locarno Pact while France would offer a guarantee to Russia as though it were a member of the proposed eastern pact. Later, at British insistence, Barthou invited Germany to join this bilateral agreement in order to preserve the multilateral principle of European security. As expected, Hitler contemptuously refused to become a party to France's bold campaign to freeze the territorial status quo in a region earmarked for absorption by Germany.

Barthou's effort to forge an "Eastern Locarno" failed not because of Germany's refusal to join, which had been anticipated because of Hitler's well-known aversion to multilateral agreements that would restrict German freedom of action, but rather by the announcement by Poland on September 27, 1934, that it would refuse to grant Russian troops transit rights across Polish territory to fulfill Soviet commitments under the proposed eastern security pact. Polish motives for this obstructionist posture were not difficult to discern. For Warsaw to permit a Soviet military advance across Polish territory to engage the forces of a nation with which Poland had just signed a nonaggression pact would have contradicted

Poland's policy of balancing Germany against Russia. Moreover, no one, least of all France at the other end of the continent, could guarantee that a Red Army on Polish soil would not take the opportunity to enforce Russia's own extensive territorial claims against the Polish state. The French project for an "Eastern Locarno" was consequently torpedoed by Poland's unwillingness to endanger its recent rapprochement with Germany and compromise the security of its frontier with Russia. The accidental assassination of the architect of that policy on October 9 in Marseilles ended the matter for good.*

But Barthou had always intended to pursue the bilateral pact with the Soviet Union regardless of the fate of the multilateral scheme for Eastern European security. The continuing recalcitrance of the Poles, together with the announcement of German rearmament, brought the issue to a head in the spring of 1935. Barthou's successor at the Quai d'Orsay, Pierre Laval, was profoundly skeptical of both the desirability and the value of an alliance with Russia. He favored instead a policy of cementing relations among France, Great Britain, and Italy as a prelude to luring Germany into a four power pact to manage the affairs of Europe that had first been proposed by Mussolini in March 1933 but never acted upon. But the declaration of German rearmament in March 1935 frightened the French government into forcing the reluctant foreign minister to complete the arrangements with Moscow that Barthou had begun: On May 2, 1935, France and Russia concluded a pact of mutual assistance that was followed on May 16 by a similar agreement between the Soviet Union and France's principal Eastern European ally, Czechoslovakia. For a brief moment, Germany seemed isolated by a powerful coalition of states determined to resist further violations of the peace treaty. This impression was enhanced by a dramatic policy reorientation at the Seventh Congress of the Comintern, the international organization of Communist parties loyal to the Soviet Union, in August 1935. Whereas the Communist parties outside Russia had previously been instructed to refuse all political cooperation with "bourgeois parties" (including the Socialists), Hitler's liquidation of the German Communist party had revealed the dangers of this sectarian strategy. The new Comintern line called for Communist participation in a "popular front" with all political groups opposed to fascism at home and German expansion in Europe.

But the revival of Franco-Russian cooperation to restrain Germany was a pale shadow of the military alliance that had compelled the Kaiser's armies to fight a war on two fronts in 1914–17. Laval had taken the precaution of ensuring that the bilateral agreement was strictly compatible with the multilateral provisions of the League Covenant and the Locarno treaties. What this meant in practice was that military assistance could be rendered by one signatory to the other only after an allegation of unpro-

---

* Barthou was killed while traveling with the king of Yugoslavia, who was assassinated by a Macedonian terrorist operating in league with Croatian separatists.

voked aggression had been submitted to the League, and only after prior approval of the other signatories of the Locarno Pact (Great Britain, Italy, and Belgium) had been obtained. The effectiveness of the pact was undermined even further by the French government's insistent refusal to accept a military convention stipulating the way in which the two armies would coordinate actions in the event of war with Germany. These critical qualifications and omissions reduced the Franco-Soviet Pact to little more than a bilateral extension of the Stresa declaration of the previous month. The effectiveness of the Czech-Soviet pact was similarly weakened by a provision subordinating it to the prior application of the Franco-Soviet Pact as well as by the failure to resolve the problem posed by the absence of a common border between the two signatories.

The reasons for France's hesitation to enter into an authentic military alliance with the Soviet Union to deter Nazi Germany were manifold. Not to be discounted was the notable upsurge of ideological hostility to the Soviet regime and its international organization, the Comintern, that was caused by the formation of the Popular Front coalition in France. The French Communist Party's electoral alliance with the parties of the non-communist left in a united front against fascism, which had been intended to strengthen the basis for Franco-Russian cooperation in the face of the German threat to both countries, had precisely the opposite effect in France: The Popular Front was denounced by conservative critics as a Trojan horse for Soviet interference in domestic French politics which, in conjunction with the Franco-Soviet pact, threatened to drag France into a suicidal war with Germany for Russia's benefit. This domestic opposition was reinforced by the intense hostility of France's Locarno partners, England and Belgium, to the idea of becoming embroiled with Germany on behalf of the Soviet regime. Even apart from this ideological distaste for Communist Russia, the dictates of geography and military strategy inspired French caution. The military value of the Red Army to French security remained problematical because of Poland's refusal to budge on the question of granting transit rights to Soviet troops in the event of war with Germany. Moreover, the defensive military strategy of France adopted at the end of the twenties precluded the type of offensive thrust into western Germany that a mutual defense treaty with Russia would imply.

Why, in view of all of these complications, did the governments of Paris and Moscow conclude the pact of May 1935? It appears that the most that France expected from the agreement was that it would discourage further German misbehavior merely by raising the alarming prospect of a two-front war. It also seems probable that Laval planned to use the threat of a Franco-Russian rapprochement as a means of enticing Germany into a West European diplomatic grouping and then to leave Russia out in the cold. Since the Kremlin does not open its diplomatic archives for inspection, one can only speculate about Stalin's motives for concluding the pact with France. It is possible that he welcomed the international publicity attendant upon Russia's dramatic adherence to the anti-German coalition as a diversion from the domestic turmoil that eventually resulted in the political purges he was to launch against putative internal enemies. It is also likely that the Russian dictator hoped to demonstrate to Hitler the value of an understanding with the Soviet Union. Ever since Hitler's rise to power the Kremlin had repeatedly sought an accommodation with Berlin, both because of Soviet anxieties about the Nazi leader's intentions and because the menace from a militaristic Japan on Russia's eastern flank dictated a quest for security in Europe. Though Hitler was willing to allow the mutually profitable trade relations between Germany and Russia to continue, he rebuffed these Soviet overtures because he was unwilling to sacrifice the propagandistic value of his anti-Communist posture in Europe or to antagonize the Poles, whose acquiescence in German rearmament he valued.

In any event, the issuance of the Stresa declaration in April 1935, the signing of the Franco-Soviet pact in May, and the advent of Franco-Italian military talks in June collectively gave the impression that France was well on the way toward fashioning the system of European security that had eluded her since the end of the last war. In addition to her alliances with Belgium, Poland, and Czechoslovakia and her treaties of friendship with Romania and Yugoslavia, France finally seemed about to resurrect the old wartime coalition of Great Britain, Russia, and Italy in an effort to prevent further German transgressions of the peace treaty.

Yet within less than a year, that coalition was in shambles as a result of the defection of Great Britain, Italy, and Belgium, France's three Western friends. The first chink in the armor of the anti-German coalition appeared on June 18, 1935, the 120th anniversary of the Battle of Waterloo, the date which the British government tactlessly chose to unveil a bilateral naval agreement that it had secretly negotiated with Germany behind the backs of the French. The accord permitted Germany to exceed the naval limitations of the Versailles Treaty in exchange for a promise not to increase its total tonnage beyond 35 percent of that of the combined fleets of the British Commonwealth. This Anglo-German naval agreement torpedoed the Stresa front by providing for precisely what the Stresa declaration had forbidden, namely, a further violation by Germany of its treaty obligations. London's motivation for acquiescing in Germany's repudiation of the last remaining disarmament restriction of the Versailles Treaty was obvious: It was known from intelligence sources that while Hitler planned to build a navy that would eventually enable Germany to play a global role, the German naval construction program for the immediate future was geared to the limited objectives of assuring control of the Baltic against the Soviet Union and harassing France's oceanic communications with her colonies and foreign sources of supply. In April 1935 the German government had informed the British of a construction program of twelve destroyers, two cruisers, and twelve submarines. Faced with this evidence of Hitler's intention to violate the treaty restrictions with impunity, the British judged it opportune to obtain at least the assurance that Germany would not threaten Great Britain's supremacy in the Mediterranean and the North Atlantic. The agreement had no effect whatsoever on Germany, which constructed as many ships as its resources permitted and continued to develop plans for ultimately contesting British naval power on the high seas once its predominance in Europe had been assured.

The second dramatic defector from the anti-German front established in the spring of 1935 was Italy. This defection was caused by Mussolini's invasion of the East African empire of Ethiopia, one of only two African states (the other being the Republic of Liberia) which had successfully resisted absorption by European powers during the imperial expansion of the prewar years. Italy's interest in Ethiopia dated from the last two decades of the nineteenth century. After a humiliating military defeat at the hands of Ethiopian warriors in 1896, Italian colonial forces retreated to the coastal enclaves of Eritrea on the Red Sea and Somaliland on the Indian Ocean. In 1906 an agreement concluded by Italy and the two other colonial powers in the region, Great Britain and France, guaranteed the territorial integrity of Ethiopia and demarcated European spheres of influence there. But by the mid-1930s, Mussolini's grandiose design for a new Roman Empire around the Mediterranean inspired a revival of the dormant territorial claims against the independent East African state. Great Britain and France, which had minimal interests in the area and were intent on securing Italian support for resistance to German adventurism in Europe, did nothing to discourage Italy's belated colonial aspirations. During his meeting with Mussolini in Rome in January 1935, Foreign Minister Laval of France formally renounced his country's minor economic interests in Ethiopia and gave the Italian leader verbal assurances of a free hand there. At the Stresa Conference in April, Mussolini's subtle intimations of Italian ambitions in East Africa elicited no objections from the French and British heads of government. In August 1935 London and Paris went so far as to offer Rome a privileged economic position in Ethiopia together with the right to appoint Italian advisers to the country's civil service, army, and police, the traditional prelude to the establishment of a protectorate.

These extensive Anglo-French concessions to Italian ambitions in Ethiopia clearly indicate that Mussolini could have obtained effective control of that country through patient diplomacy. But the prospective leader of the new Roman Empire was interested less in acquiring this barren territory in East Africa than in obtaining military glory with a minimum of risk. He therefore launched a full-scale armed attack against Ethiopia on October 3 with the expectation that Italy would encounter little military resistance from the ill-equipped forces of the Ethiopian emperor, Haile Selassie, and no diplomatic opposition from the European powers. On the first count he was correct. The rugged mountains in the interior slowed the Italian advance, but the introduction of air power and poison gas routed the Ethiopian forces in the spring of 1936. But on the diplomatic front in Europe, the Duce was to be first disappointed and then outraged by the unsympathetic response of his friends in London and Paris. Since Ethiopia was a member of the League of Nations, public opinion in Great Britain lashed out at this overt violation of national sovereignty and pressured the government into invoking the principle of collective security. To Mussolini's astonishment, Britain and France prodded the League into condemning the Italian offensive as an act of aggression and voting for the imposition of economic sanctions against the aggressor state on October 18. The hypocritical policy of the two powers that had divided up most of the continent of Africa between them before the First World War, and had recently given Italy the green light belatedly to obtain its share of the spoils, left a lasting negative impression on the Italian leader. His feelings of betrayal and annoyance were not assuaged by subsequent efforts by London and Paris to undermine the very policy that they had promoted at Geneva. A secret Anglo-French agreement in December providing for the cession of most of Ethiopia to Italy and the reduction of the remainder to the status of an Italian client state had to be disavowed when its embarrassing contents were leaked to the press by unsympathetic personnel in the Quai d'Orsay. But the abortive Hoare-Laval pact, named for the British and French foreign ministers who devised it, accurately reflected the true policies of the two governments, as had the earlier efforts to placate Mussolini. This is shown by their refusal to extend the economic sanctions to an embargo of oil, which Italy required to fuel her mechanized army and air force in Ethiopia and which she had to import from foreign sources. The imposition of an effective oil embargo would have required a British naval blockade in the Mediterranean, since Italy was receiving the bulk of her petroleum from the United States (whose oil exports to Italy more than doubled during the Ethiopian conflict). But a naval blockade would surely have meant war with Italy and complications with the United States, obviously unacceptable risks on behalf of a country of no importance to Britain or France.

The most important consequence of the Ethiopian affair, apart from the military defeat of Haile Selassie's empire and its annexation by Italy in May 1936, was the deterioration of relations between Italy and her erstwhile partners in the Stresa front against Germany. By supporting economic sanctions against Italy and verbally condemning its actions in the League, Britain and France had antagonized Mussolini without succeeding in denying him the objectives he sought in East Africa. The Hoare-Laval scheme and the half-hearted application of sanctions also undermined the principle of collective security. If such an unmistakable instance of aggression against a member of the League could go unpunished, what was to prevent the more subtle forms of aggression practiced and planned by Germany in Europe?

In the meantime, Hitler remained neutral in the Italo-Ethiopian struggle while expressing his willingness to supply Mussolini with iron, coal, steel, and other scarce materials. Berlin's benevolent neutrality was greatly appreciated in Rome. Thus, with the two guarantors of the Locarno treaties (Great Britain and Italy) at loggerheads over East Africa and Mussolini grateful for Germany's acquiescence in his imperial policies, the Führer correctly gauged that the time was right for a daring probe of the anti-German diplomatic coalition. The submission of the Franco-Soviet Pact to the French Chamber of Deputies for ratification in February 1936 supplied the perfect pretext for Hitler's first provocative move since his announcement of German rearmament a year earlier. Though France had prudently obtained prior assurances from Great Britain and Italy that the bilateral arrangement with Russia would not be deemed incompatible with the multilateral agreement signed at Locarno, Hitler warned that he would regard the Franco-Soviet alliance as a violation of Locarno and a grave threat to Germany's security; he would therefore feel free to renounce Germany's end of the Locarno bargain by reintroducing German military forces and fortifications into the demilitarized zone of the Rhineland. In fact Hitler regarded the Franco-Soviet pact as a great advantage for German foreign policy. Useless to France as a military deterrent because of its geographical contradictions, it was immensely valuable as a propaganda tool to Germany. Its unpopularity in anticommunist circles in all European states, especially England, enabled the German dictator to raise the bogey of the "Red menace" while citing the innocuous pact as justification for tearing up the Locarno agreement. The French Chamber, as expected, ratified the treaty on Feburary 27, and on the morning of March 7 three battalions of German infantry, accompanied by antiaircraft guns and air force squadrons, moved into the Rhineland.

As we have seen, the demilitarized status of the Rhineland was widely regarded as the most important guarantee of German good behavior in Europe. It was thought to preclude a German advance against France and Belgium and, by exposing Germany to invasion from the west, to deter German aggression eastward. Its disappearance in March 1936 ought therefore to have elicited a strong response from France. But no such response was forthcoming. The reasons for France's inaction are perfectly obvious: French military strategy as developed over the past several years dictated just such a posture of passivity. By constructing the Maginot Line France had in effect already written off the Rhineland as indefensible. It would make little difference on which bank of the river the German line of defense was situated so long as France retained its impregnable bastion of concrete and gun emplacements along the Franco-German frontier. Accordingly, the French army possessed no mobile force that could be dispatched to the Rhineland to expel the German battalions and had devised no advance plan for such an operation, despite extensive intelligence information indicating that remilitarization was imminent. The creation of such a force and the development of such a plan, suggested a year earlier by the politician Paul Reynaud on the advice of Colonel Charles de Gaulle, was rejected as incompatible with the defensive strategy so tenaciously pursued by the French general staff. So long as the German forces in the Rhineland did not give any indication of preparing for a military attack against France, which Hitler shrewdly forbade them to do, the French high command warned the government in Paris that a military response to the recent German action would be both unnecessary and foolhardy. It was thought unnecessary for the strategic considerations mentioned above. It was deemed foolhardy because of the exaggerated estimate of German military strength in French military circles at the time.

It is curious that the civilian government in Paris, a caretaker ministry in power pending the legislative elections scheduled for the following month, displayed greater interest in an offensive operation to expel the German forces from the Rhineland than did the military authorities. Foreign Minister Pierre-Etienne Flandin flew to London to discuss the possibility of a joint Anglo-French countermove. He was greeted with the news that the British government did not view the remilitarization of the Rhineland as a "flagrant" violation of the treaty of Locarno because it was not accompanied by menacing German moves toward the French frontier; consequently Britain would neither participate in any military response nor approve of a unilateral French action. Beneath this narrow, legalistic interpretation of the language of Locarno lay the real reason for Britain's hesitation: its desire to avoid at all costs the European war that it believed would inevitably result from a French or Anglo-French advance into the Rhineland. In this perception the British were quite correct. Though the commanders of the German forces in the Rhineland were under orders to withdraw in the event of military opposition, that withdrawal was to be only a tactical retreat preparatory to a renewed offensive. The oft-repeated assertion that Germany would have backed off in the face of French resistance is a myth. Hitler was prepared to risk war over the issue in March 1936, largely because he correctly anticipated that his willingness to go to the brink of war would make war unnecessary by paralyzing the Western powers. Consequently, the response of London and Paris was confined to the issuance of stern protests, the sponsorship of a pro forma condemnation of the action by the League of Nations, and the authorization of joint Anglo-French military conversations. Though the latter development satisfied a long-standing objective of French foreign policy, these staff talks were confined to meaningless generalities because of British reluctance to discuss detailed plans of operations. Even the advent of British rearmament in the aftermath of the Rhineland crisis gave little comfort to France, since it concentrated on upgrading naval and air forces for home and imperial defense instead of on establishing a land army that could be dispatched to the continent. In subsequent public statements the British government forcefully expressed its desire that France and Germany seek some type of arrangement to freeze the territorial *status quo* in Europe. Thus the remilitarization of the Rhineland was rapidly to become a *fait accompli.*

As noted above, the remilitarization of the Rhineland did not appreciably alter the strategic balance between France and Germany in Western Europe, since France's previously adopted defensive posture along her eastern frontier had rendered the Rhenish buffer zone irrelevant to French military calculations. Nor did it suddenly negate the value of France's security commitments to Poland and Czechoslovakia. Those had previously been rendered incapable of realization once construction of the Maginot Line had begun half a decade earlier. But the failure of France to react firmly to Hitler's unilateral repudiation of the Locarno pact had a devastating psychological impact on all of the smaller countries on the continent that had expected France to take the lead in restraining Germany.

The result of this French abstention was a radical reorientation of the foreign policies of all of these minor powers. The chiefs of staff of the Little Entente, meeting in June 1936 to reassess the strategic situation in Central Europe in the light of recent events, concluded that their countries' future security might well require a choice between subservience to Germany or to Russia. The Polish government, which faced that unpleasant predicament even more directly, resumed with greater enthusiasm its policy of detente with Germany that had been inaugurated at the beginning of 1934. But at least these countries of Central and Eastern Europe retained their diplomatic arrangements with France in the illusory hope that some element of French protection could be furnished to them. It was Belgium, France's neighbor in Western Europe and its earliest and staunchest ally against Germany, that drew the appropriate conclusions from French inaction during the Rhineland crisis and acted accordingly. On October 14, 1936, after a lengthy reappraisal of its security situation, the Belgian government formally renounced its military alliance with France and reverted to its prewar status of neutrality. The dramatic Belgian reversal stemmed in part from domestic political tension between the French-speaking Walloons and the Flemish population, the latter of which had long resented their country's diplomatic subservience to France. It also reflected the reluctance of anti-Communist elements to see their nation dragged into a war with Germany on behalf of France's new Russian ally. But the principal reason was the belief that neither France nor Great Britain could or would afford Belgium the kind of protection she required for the preservation of her security. The military consequences of the Belgian defection were critical: Anglo-French forces were no longer guaranteed transit rights across Belgian territory in case of war with Germany. Franco-Belgian military coordination, a key element in France's strategy for the defense of her unfortified northeastern frontier, was abruptly terminated.

By the autumn of 1936, Germany had thus obtained geographical protective screens on her western and eastern borders that effectively insulated her from the threat of military intervention from the great powers in alliance against her. In the west, a neutralized Belgium and a remilitarized Rhineland (which was in the process of being reinforced by the construction of elaborate fortifications along the French frontier) shielded Germany's industrial heartland in the Ruhr Valley from French military power. To the east, an increasingly cooperative Poland served as a for.ni-dable barrier against the Soviet Union. To the south, the nations of the Little Entente, geographically separated from their undependable French patron, were driven to seek improved relations with Germany in the hope of stabilizing the political situation in that region. Hitler wasted no time in profiting from Germany's enhanced position on the continent to expand his nation's economic and diplomatic influence in those nations of Central and Southeastern Europe whose cooperation or acquiescence he desired in the fulfillment of his short-term objectives in foreign policy, which were the annexation of Austria and the destruction of Czechoslovakia. At the same time he took steps to accelerate the pace of German rearmament and to reorient the economy in such a way as to prepare his nation for the major war that he planned to launch in the more distant future.

The failure of the Western powers to recognize the implications of this process of consolidation, both within Germany and between Germany and its neighbors to the south and east, was in large part due to the fixation of world attention on the civil war that erupted in Spain in the summer of 1936. On July 17 of that year, military officers in command of the garrisons in Spanish Morocco rebelled against the left-leaning government in Madrid that had been elected the previous February and proceeded to organize an uprising on the Spanish mainland. When the navy and air force remained loyal to the Republican government, the leader of the coup, General Francisco Franco, was compelled to look abroad for assistance in transporting his forces in Morocco across the Straits of Gibraltar to the Iberian peninsula. This appeal from the Spanish rebels, or Nationalists, as they called themselves, received a sympathetic response in Berlin and Rome. By the end of July German and Italian planes were ferrying Franco's troops to the mainland, where they quickly established contact with the rebel-held sector in the northeast. By the autumn of 1936 the quantity of German and Italian aid markedly increased. Hitler dispatched a special air force unit, the Condor Legion, to provide air cover for the rebel forces, while Mussolini contributed large contingents of Italian infantry in the guise of "volunteers" in the struggle against international communism.

Hitler's decision to assist the military rebellion in Spain was determined by a number of factors. The most important military advantage to be gained, apart from the opportunity to test the tactic of terror-bombing of civilian population centers that would later be used against Warsaw, Rotterdam, and London, lay in the promise of access to Spain's abundant supply of strategic raw materials. With Germany engaged in a massive rearmament program at a time when it suffered from a severe shortage of foreign exchange, Hitler hoped to obtain Spanish iron and copper ores without having to pay for them in scarce foreign currency. An arrangement to this effect was reached in the summer of 1937, once the major iron- and copper-producing regions of Spain had fallen under Franco's control. Large quantities of these strategic materials, which had previously been exported to Great Britain, were diverted to the German rearmament program in payment for the military supplies that Hitler was furnishing Franco. In addition to this expectation of economic advantage, two diplomatic considerations dictated Germany's active support of the Nationalist insurrection in Spain. The first was the likelihood that cooperation with Italy on Franco's behalf would cement the friendly relations between Berlin and Rome that had been established during the Ethiopian affair. This became all the more apparent when France and Great Britain organized a nonintervention committee in September 1936 to curb all foreign involvement in the Spanish conflict. Once Mussolini had committed his personal prestige to a rebel victory in Spain, the Western democracies' expressions of displeasure at the Italian intervention, though no more effective than their exhortations during the Ethiopian affair, dashed whatever chances may have existed of reconstituting the Stresa coalition and drove Mussolini even closer to Hitler. But the most obvious benefit that Germany derived from the Spanish Civil War was the diversion of French and British attention from the process of German rearmament and continental economic consolidation that was underway. For this reason it was to Hitler's advantage to prolong the military conflict on the Iberian peninsula as long as possible instead of helping the rebels to achieve a quick victory. This was accomplished by refusing Franco's urgent request for large German infantry units after the failure of the rebel offensive against Madrid at the end of 1936, as well as by restricting the Condor Legion to its original size for the duration of the conflict.

The ideological overtones of the Spanish Civil War were apparent from the outset and contributed to its image in the popular imagination as an epic confrontation between the forces of international fascism and the defenders of the democratic cause. Franco's tactical alliance with the small Spanish fascist movement, the Falange, viewed in the context of his dependence on Mussolini and Hitler for military support, seemed to herald the spread of the ideological doctrine hatched in Italy and perfected in Germany to the western tip of Europe. Conversely, the arrival in Spain of the "International Brigades," groups of volunteers organized in various foreign countries to fight on behalf of the beleaguered Republic, expressed the democratic world's commitment to oppose fascism in all its forms. The conspicuous presence of the small Spanish Communist Party in the Popular Front coalition in Madrid and the flow of military aid from the Soviet Union reflected the Kremlin's newly adopted policy of defending parliamentary institutions against the Fascist menace.

In fact, this ideological dichotomy was deceptive. Franco and the military, clerical, and landowning groups that formed his base of support were reactionary devotees of a premodern era who shared little in common with the Falangist firebrands, who were reduced to insignificance when the marriage of convenience with them had outlived its usefulness. Once Franco's military victory in the spring of 1939 relieved the Spanish dictator of the need to rely on German and Italian assistance, he displayed little interest in joining a "Fascist crusade" in league with Hitler and Mussolini. Fears of a menace to France from a Nationalist regime across the Pyrenees proved ill founded. The Spanish Caudillo was to remain neutral for the duration of the Second World War despite strenuous German efforts to secure his active cooperation with the Axis war effort.

In the opposite camp, all manner of internal tensions and contradictions undermined the political unity and ideological consistency of the antifascist cause. Within Republican Spain itself, Communists, Anarchists, Trotskyists, Socialists, and Liberals repeatedly clashed over matters of political ideology and military strategy, with differences often being settled by a burst of machine gun fire. Outside of Spain, the nations supposedly committed to the defense of democratic government against the menace of fascism behaved in ways ill suited to that objective. The Conservative government in Great Britain could scarcely conceal its distaste for the leftist regime in Madrid or its unwillingness to lift a finger in its defense. Even the recently elected Popular Front government in France, dominated by Socialists with Communist support, refused Spanish Republican appeals for military supplies for fear of antagonizing Great Britain and further inflaming domestic Catholic opinion already agitated by reports of monasteries looted and nuns murdered by defenders of the regime in Madrid. The Soviet Union, though the only European power to furnish supplies to Republican Spain, kept the flow of aid to a minimum and demanded immediate payment in gold or raw materials. It is possible, as some historians have speculated, that Stalin's parsimony was prompted by the same considerations that caused Hitler to restrict his assistance to Franco, namely, to keep the Spanish pot boiling as a diversion from domestic turmoil, in Russia's case the purge trials that began a month after Franco's insurrection.

While the Spanish Civil War occupied the attention of the world, Germany proceeded to inaugurate a program to put its economy on a wartime footing while mounting a diplomatic offensive in several directions to facilitate the realization of Hitler's two immediate objectives: the annexation of Austria and the annihilation of Czechoslovakia.

The economic situation of Germany in 1936 was marked by superficial signs of prosperity that concealed a structural weakness of alarming proportions. The major achievement of the Nazi economic policy was the elimination of unemployment by the rearmament boom fueled by the deficit financing of the government. But an underlying weakness of the German economy began to occupy the attention of Hitler's economic policymakers at the beginning of 1936: Because of its heavy reliance on foreign imports of raw materials required by the rearmament program, Germany had begun to suffer from a severe shortage of foreign exchange. Previous efforts to resolve this problem through the requisitioning of domestic savings, restrictions on imports, and coerced diversion of exports to countries whose raw materials were in demand proved only partially successful. If present trends continued, the remilitarization of Germany and the economic recovery that it had stimulated risked being halted in its tracks by the inability of the German government to pay for the continued importation of strategic raw materials that could not be produced domestically.

The crisis of raw material imports that loomed in the winter and spring of 1936 reminded the Nazi leaders of Germany's plight in the Great War, when its dependence on foreign supplies had exposed it to the crippling effects of the British blockade. Hitler's proposed solution to this threat to his future plans took the form of a short-term program of economic development designed to render Germany self-sufficient in the strategic materials she required to prepare for the European war that was expected to begin no later than the summer of 1940. The Four-Year Plan, launched on October 18, 1936, under the supervision of Hermann Göring, aimed at establishing Germany's absolute independence from foreign trade by fostering the production of synthetic materials as substitutes for the natural resources unobtainable domestically. In time the German chemical industry developed artificial rubber, textiles, and plastics. A synthetic fuels program was expanded, whereby oil was extracted from Germany's abundant coal supplies. The utilization of Germany's low-grade iron ore for the production of steel was intensified in order to reduce the nation's dependence on the high-grade ores of Sweden and Spain.

The unfolding of Hitler's military strategy in the mid-1930s reflected the precarious position of the German economy at that time. The shortage of raw materials, even with the compensation provided by the development of synthetic substitutes, meant that Germany could not hope to win a long war of attrition against Russia and the British Empire, especially if American assistance were eventually thrown in the balance against her. Such was the lesson of the 1914–18 war. Hence the adoption of the strategy of "blitzkreig," a series of short, swift engagements against isolated opponents. The principal weapons to be used were tanks and airplanes, both of which required large quantities of oil, rubber, and other products that Germany was preparing to produce synthetically. But the brief duration of these "lightning wars" would permit victory with only a modest mobilization of Germany's economic power. The territory conquered by Germany in these mechanized thrusts against isolated opponents would eventually afford her access to the raw materials of the European continent that would bring self-sufficiency at last.

The diplomatic counterpart of this economic-strategic program developed by Hitler in the course of 1936 was the campaign to weaken the French alliance system in Eastern Europe and to discourage the other great powers of Europe—Italy, England, and Russia—from joining France and her remaining Eastern European clients in resisting Germany's bid for hegemony in that region. Since the annexation of Austria was the first item on Hitler's agenda for Germany's continental expansion, it is no surprise that he endeavored to solidify Germany's friendly ties with Italy, the traditional guarantor of Austrian independence, that had been established during the Ethiopian invasion and the early stages of the Spanish Civil War. On October 26, 1936, following cordial discussions between the Italian foreign minister, Galeazzo Ciano, and his German counterpart, Konstanin von Neurath, in Berlin, the two governments announced the conclusion of an agreement on Italo-German cooperation that was soon being touted as the "Rome-Berlin Axis." This agreement, in conjunction with a secret understanding concluded on July 11 between Germany and Austria with Mussolini's blessing, in effect signaled the Italian leader's tacit acceptance of Germany's freedom of action in Austria in particular and southeastern Europe in general. The reorientation of Italian foreign policy toward an accommodation with Germany reflected Mussolini's conversion to Hitler's conception of the geopolitical basis of Italo-German cooperation: the complementary expansion of Italian power southward into the Mediterranean basin and of German power eastward into the heartland of Central Europe and beyond. The formation of the Rome-Berlin Axis on this basis afforded Hitler two crucial advantages: It removed the Italian veto of Germany's annexationist designs on Austria, and it increased the likelihood of tension in the Mediterranean and North Africa between Italy and the two dominant powers in that region, Great Britain and France.

Throughout the year 1937 Hitler steadily increased the pressure on the Austrian government to align its foreign and domestic policies more closely with those of the Third Reich. In the meantime he encouraged the Austrian Nazis to step up their subversive activities in preparation for a peaceful takeover in Vienna that would lead to a voluntary unification with Germany. But when the Austrian chancellor, Kurt von Schuschnigg authorized police raids on the headquarters of the Austrian Nazis that uncovered embarrassing evidence of collusion with their counterparts in Germany, Hitler reversed his earlier strategy for an evolutionary move toward *Anschluss* and prepared to achieve that result quickly through direct intimidation of the government in Vienna. In a meeting between Hitler and Schuschnigg at Berchtesgaden on February 12, 1938, the Führer berated the Austrian chancellor for failing to pursue pro-German policies in conformity with the July 11, 1936, agreement and threatened immediate military intervention unless Schuschnigg allowed the Austrian Nazis to play a major role in his government. Though the Austrian leader acceded to this demand on the advice of Mussolini, he boldly decided to preempt Hitler's plans for a peaceful takeover of his country by seeking an expression of national support by means of a plebiscite to be held on March 13 in which the Austrian people would be asked to vote on the question of their nation's independence. Though a plebiscite conducted before the advent of the Nazi regime in Germany would probably have resulted in an overwhelming vote for unification of the two German-speaking states, anti-Nazi sentiment in Austria was sufficiently strong to prevent Hitler from risking the embarrassment of a negative vote. Thus, after securing the tacit consent of Mussolini, the Führer sent German troops into Austria on March 12, where they met no resistance from Austrian military forces. Schuchnigg's request for advice from the British and French governments had revealed that neither London nor Paris was any more willing to intervene on Austria's behalf than was Mussolini. Neither power was bound by treaty obligation to defend Austria, and neither was prepared to risk war by enforcing the provision of the Versailles Treaty that forbade the *Anschluss*. On April 10 a rigged plebiscite resulted in an overwhelming vote for the unification of Hitler's adopted nation and the land of his birth.

Germany's success in securing Italian consent for its expansionist policy in Central Europe was matched by the gradual evolution of a cordial relationship with the rising imperial power in the Far East (see p. 245). The German-Japanese rapprochement that developed in the years 1936–38 was actively promoted by Hitler for reasons similar to those that had prompted his fruitful overtures to Italy: By encouraging Japanese imperial ambitions in East Asia, Germany stood to benefit from the pressure that such expansion would exert on the Asian possessions of Germany's principal antagonists in Europe. Great Britain would be less likely to interfere with Germany's eastern policy on the continent if confronted with the simultaneous challenge to her imperial interests from Japan in the western Pacific and from Italy along her Mediterranean lifeline. The Soviet Union would be deterred from fulfilling its treaty obligations to France and Czechoslovakia in the face of a Japanese threat from Manchuria.

But the coordination of German policy in Europe and Japanese policy in Asia was not an easy task. Just as the related issues of Austrian independence and the status of the German-speaking inhabitants of the South Tyrol had delayed the establishment of the Rome-Berlin Axis, the close relationship between Germany and the Chinese Nationalist regime of Chiang Kai-shek represented a serious impediment to the formation of a Berlin-Tokyo Axis. Since the mid-1930s Germany had participated in a mutually beneficial relationship with China. In exchange for military advisers who helped Chiang modernize his armed forces and military equipment, Germany received strategic raw materials required for its rearmament without having to expend foreign exchange. The presence of German military advisers in Nanking and the flow of German arms to Chiang's army understandably annoyed the Japanese government and impeded the development of German-Japanese cooperation. But the ratification of the Franco-Soviet pact by the French parliament in February 1936 highlighted the obvious congruity of interest between Tokyo and Berlin. In combination, Germany and Japan could restrain the Soviet Union on its European and Asian flanks to the benefit of both. Accordingly, on November 25, 1936, the two governments unveiled with much fanfare an agreement designated as the Anti-Comintern Pact. Its ostensible purpose was to promote cooperation to combat the subversive activities of the Communist International and its political apparatus in each country. But since both Germany and Japan had long since suppressed their domestic Communist parties, the agreement was widely and correctly suspected of containing secret provisions directed against the Soviet Union. With the adhesion of Italy to the agreement on November 6, 1937, the world was confronted with the nightmare of an impending global alignment of the three expansionist powers.

But the transformation of the Anti-Comintern Pact into a full-fledged military alliance was delayed by two considerations. The first was Germany's reluctance to sacrifice its lucrative economic relations with China at a time when Japan was launching an undeclared war against the Nanking government. This obstacle was finally removed in the winter and spring of 1938, when Hitler recognized the Japanese puppet state of Manchukuo, terminated all military assistance to China, and recalled the German military advisers to Chiang Kai-shek as a prelude to proposing a military alliance to Japan the following summer. Despite these concessions, Tokyo balked at the German overture because of Berlin's insistence that the proposed alliance be directed at Great Britain as well as the Soviet Union. Japan's goal was to transform the Anti-Comintern Pact into a German-Japanese alliance against Russia, its major rival in East Asia, but hesitated at this stage to risk a war with Great Britain for fear of drawing the United States into the conflict. Berlin, on the other hand, was less concerned about the threat of Russia than about Anglo-French opposition to Germany's policy of continental expansion. This conflict of priorities was to delay the conclusion of the long-awaited alliance with Japan until after the beginning of the Second World War. But the absence of a formal military understanding among Germany, Italy, and Japan did not prevent Hitler from exploiting the Anti-Comintern Pact to deter the principal opponents of German aggression in Europe from pursuing a steadfast policy in defense of the territorial status quo that he intended presently to destroy.

While Fascist Italy and Imperial Japan gradually gravitated toward the German orbit in the years 1936–38, Hitler mounted a successful campaign to undermine the French alliance system in Eastern Europe and establish German predominance in that region in preparation for the war of annihilation against Czechoslovakia that he had planned for some time. His principal aim in this policy was to accelerate Germany's tactical rapprochement with Poland and Hungary and to establish ties with Czechoslovakia's two partners in the Little Entente, Yugoslavia and Romania. The courtship of Poland and Romania was intended to secure their services in blocking the Soviet Union's access route to its Czechoslovak ally. The simultaneous approaches to Hungary and Yugoslavia were designed to encourage those two countries to settle their long-standing dispute over the status of the large Magyar minority in Yugoslavia so that Hungary could concentrate its revisionist ambitions against the easternmost provinces of the Czech state, Slovakia and the Carpatho-Ukraine (Ruthenia), with their 750,000 Hungarians.

To secure Poland's acquiescence in this plan to destroy Czechoslovakia Hitler had only to remove the major source of friction between Berlin and Warsaw while emphasizing the one issue that was likely to foster Polish-German cooperation against his intended victim. The principal source of friction was the city of Danzig, where the Nazi municipal government caused considerable trouble for Polish authorities. Directives from Berlin had effectively restrained the anti-Polish agitation of the Danzig Nazis during the period that Hitler solicited Warsaw's friendship. The positive basis for German-Polish cooperation at the expense of Czechoslovakia was the Teschen district of Silesia, a rich industrial area awarded to Czechoslovakia in 1920 despite the presence of almost 80,000 Poles. At Hitler's urging the Polish government added its demand for Teschen to Hitler's insistence that the German-speaking Sudetenland be ceded by Czechoslovakia to Germany. It may have seemed hypocritical if not dangerous for the Poles, who presided over a collection of discontented minorities in their own multinational country, to issue terriorial demands on the basis of the principle of nationality. But this inconsistency caused them little concern at a time when the prospects seemed excellent, as a silent partner of Germany, to acquire at no cost economically valuable territory at Czechoslovakia's expense.

The task of obtaining the consent of Romania and Yugoslavia for the destruction of Czechoslovakia was fraught with many more difficulties. Neither had territorial claims on Germany's prospective victim and therefore could not be rewarded for their indulgence as Poland was to be. Both were associated with Czechoslovakia in the Little Entente and closely identified with that country's protector, France. On the other hand, neither nation shared a common border with Germany and therefore had relatively little reason to quarrel with or fear her. Their common adversary was Hungary, which had lost much of its territory to them at the Paris Peace Conference and had never ceased to agitate for its restitution. Indeed, it was only the fear of Hungarian revisionism that served as the basis of diplomatic cooperation among Yugoslavia, Romania, and Czechoslovakia. This fear was particularly profound in Yugoslavia because of its strategic position blocking Hungary's only outlet to the sea. But since Hitler was actively soliciting Hungary's participation in the partition of Czechoslovakia by dangling Slovakia and the Carpatho-Ukraine before the authorities in Budapest, this diversion of Hungarian attention served to allay fears in Belgrade. Accordingly, Yugoslavia and Hungary, with Berlin's encouragement, were able to reach agreement in August 1938 on the major issues of dispute between them, in the process dealing a serious blow to the anti-Hungarian basis of the Little Entente. Simultaneous German efforts to detach Romania from Czechoslovakia were facilitated by the bitter territorial struggle between Romania and Czechoslovakia's ally, Russia, in regard to Bessarabia, a former province of the tsarist empire annexed by Romania during the Russian Revolution. Just as Poland, with its large holdings of former Russian territory, needed little prodding from Germany to block Soviet access to Czechoslovakia, Romania's own national interest prompted it to deny the Red Army the ability to circumvent the Polish barrier to Central Europe.

Hitler's diplomatic campaign to isolate Czechoslovakia from its neighbors was bolstered by a series of commercial policies designed to subordinate the shaky economic systems of the nations of Central Europe to the expanding economy of Germany. This economic advance into Central and Southern Europe had begun in the early 1930s, when the predominantly agricultural economies of those regions had began to suffer from the catastrophic collapse in world commodity prices. Germany, with its chronic deficit in food production, became the major customer for the agricultural surpluses that were piling up in these nations. With the advent of the Nazi regime, as we have seen, the introduction of exchange controls and bilateral barter arrangements compelled these nations to import an ever-increasing quantity of German industrial products in exchange for their agricultural exports. Subsequent political developments increased this dependence on Germany as a market for their primary products and a supplier of their industrial needs. Yugoslavia's avid participation in the League-sponsored economic sanctions against Italy during the Ethiopian campaign deprived her of a major market for her grain exports, caused her severe economic damage, and forced her to reorient her trade toward Germany. The German annexation of Austria, a major trading partner of Yugoslavia and Hungary, increased Germany's domination of those nations' foreign trade. German economic penetration of Romania was prompted by increasing interest in that nation's abundant supplies of oil, which was required by the mechanized army and air force that Germany was constructing. A German-Romanian agreement of December 1937 provided for the exchange of German military equipment for Romanian oil to supplement the synthetic petroleum production quota of the Four-Year Plan. These commercial connections between Germany and the nations of Central and Southern Europe, though developed for rational economic reasons that promised benefits to both partners, helped to smooth the path toward more cordial political relations at a time when German diplomacy was loosening the bonds of the Little Entente to isolate the Czechoslovak prey.

Germany's diplomatic and commercial offensive in Central Europe severely undermined the security of Czechoslovakia. The enlistment of Poland and Hungary in Germany's campaign of territorial revision and the de facto collapse of the Little Entente left the Czech state bereft of defenders and surrounded by predators. Its bilateral alliances with France and the Soviet Union, though technically operational, had been gravely weakened by the diplomatic revolution wrought by Hitler in the two and a half years after the remilitarization of the Rhineland. Profiting from the Belgian-Rhenish screen in the west, the Polish-Romanian screen in the east, and the deterrent effect that the new alignment with Italy and Japan could be expected to exercise on Great Britain, Hitler proceeded to lay the political groundwork for his projected blitzkreig against Czechoslovakia.

The furious propaganda campaign that the Nazi leader unleashed against the Prague regime in the summer of 1938 was directed at its alleged persecution of the three million German-speaking inhabitants of the Bohemian borderlands. Though better treated than any of the other Germanic minorities throughout Europe, the Sudeten Germans harbored genuine grievances against the government in Prague. A prime instance of these was the preference accorded Czech-speaking citizens in the recruitment of government employees, a discriminatory practice that engendered considerable resentment among the German-speaking minority during the depression years and was skillfully exploited by Berlin. But Hitler cared little about the plight of the Sudetenlanders. The last thing he wished was an amicable resolution of their dispute with Prague that would remove the pretext he required to destroy the Czech state by force. He accordingly instructed the leader of the Sudeten German Party, Konrad Henlein, to demand from the Czech government what he knew it could not grant, namely, concessions that would lead to the political autonomy of the German-speaking region as a prelude to secession and eventual annexation by Germany. This solution was predictably unacceptable to Czechoslovakia for two reasons: First, the loss of the Sudetenland would deprive it of its defensible frontiers and the elaborate border fortifications constructed behind them, leaving the truncated nation exposed to invasion by a German military force unimpeded by natural or artificial barriers; second, the granting of autonomy to the Germans of Bohemia would establish a precedent for similar demands by the other national minorities in the polyglot republic—the Poles of Teschen, the Hungarians in southern Slovakia and the Carpatho-Ukraine, even the increasingly dissatisfied Slovaks. The result was bound to be the dissolution of the multinational state erected in 1918.

As German intimidation of Czechoslovakia intensified, and as it became increasingly evident that Hitler was fully prepared to resort to force in pursuit of his annexationist aims, the French and British governments were compelled to clarify their policies toward the impending crisis in Central Europe. In July the Czech minister in Paris was privately informed that France was unwilling to go to war over the issue of the Sudetenland, though it would remain publicly committed to the Franco-Czech alliance for the sake of appearances. The deplorable condition of the French air force, the refusal of Belgium to allow the transit of French troops to Germany's most vulnerable industrial targets, and exaggerated estimates of the size of the German army and the strength of the Rhineland fortifications all contributed to this French failure of nerve. The British government, unaware of Paris's repudiation of its obligation to Prague, became greatly alarmed at the prospect of being dragged into a war between France and Germany over an issue of no importance to British national interests. With memories of the Luftwaffe's bombardment of the Spanish Basque towns fresh in their minds, British leaders exerted every diplomatic effort to avert a war that might bring German air attacks on British cities still inadequately protected by the antiaircraft artillery system and radar installations then under construction. Anglo-French pressure on Prague to reach a settlement with the Sudeten Party compelled Czech President Eduard Beneš to grant all of that party's main demands in a major concession on September 5. But since war rather than a political settlement on *any* terms was Hitler's goal, he instructed the Sudeten German Party to fabricate a new list of grievances that could be exploited when preparations for the invasion were complete.

The German dictator was deprived of his goal, and dealt what he later complained was his first diplomatic setback, because of the eagerness of the British prime minister, Neville Chamberlain, to take him at his word. Like many British statesmen of his generation in both major parties, Chamberlain was profoundly influenced by memories of the two major events of his younger years, the Great War and the Paris Peace Conference. He shared the widespread conviction that the great powers had blundered into a terrible war that might well have been averted by a more skillful, active diplomacy. He also believed that the victorious Allies had mistreated Germany at the peace conference by refusing to apply the principle of national self-determination to the delimitation of the defeated nation's eastern frontiers. The convergence of these two issues during the Czech crisis of September 1938 prompted Chamberlain to make one last effort to prevent a second world war by means of face-to-face negotiations with Hitler to reach a definitive solution of what he conceded to be Germany's just grievance against Czechoslovakia. On September 15, two days after Hitler approved the Sudeten German leader's withdrawal from the negotiations with the Czech government in preparation for war, Chamberlain boarded an airplane for the first time in his life and flew to Hitler's private retreat at Berchtesgaden in a frantic quest for a settlement.

He received there Hitler's demand for the transfer of the Sudetenland to Germany on the basis of national self-determination and returned to London to try to persuade the representatives of France and Czechoslovakia to accept this peaceful solution. At first the French premier, Edouard Daladier, rejected the use of self-determination through plebiscites in German-speaking areas as a dangerous precedent that would expose the remainder of Central Europe to German revisionist intrigues. But his knowledge of France's weak military position caused him to withdraw his objection after Chamberlain dramatically reversed a century of British foreign policy by promising to guarantee Czechoslovakia's redrawn frontiers. The government in Prague angrily rejected the Anglo-French proposal but was quickly forced into line by the threat of an end to British peacemaking efforts and a bluntly repeated refusal of French assistance if war broke out. When Chamberlain returned to the German city of Godesberg on September 22 to inform Hitler that his demands had been accepted by all interested parties, the Führer reneged on the agreement that he himself had earlier proposed; the deteriorating political situation in the Sudetenland required immediate German intervention. The grievances of Poland and Hungary on behalf of their own oppressed minorities in Czechoslovakia, now being raised with great fervor by Warsaw and Budapest in line with their prior arrangement with Berlin, would have to be redressed as well.

Both the tone and the substance of the new German demands conveyed the unmistakable message that Hitler was intent on war with Czechoslovakia and would not be deprived of military conquests by diplomatic concessions of any kind. Accordingly, the British and French governments could hardly avoid retracting their previous opposition to Czechoslovakia's right to prepare for its own defense, and Prague mobilized its armed forces on September 24 as the Godesberg talks ended in deadlock. Public opinion in Britain and France had congealed in support of the agreement proposed by Hitler at Berchtesgaden and accepted by Beneš at Anglo-French insistence. The German retraction at Godesberg turned many British and French appeasers into hard-liners and momentarily stiffened the resolve of Chamberlain and Daladier to hold to their position even at the risk of war. France began to mobilize its army and Great Britain announced the mobilization of its fleet on September 27. In London and Paris trenches were dug in parks, gas masks were distributed, and children were evacuated to the countryside. Hitler ordered the attack on Czechoslovakia to begin on the morning of September 30.

Few doubted that war would eventually lead to the defeat of Czechoslovakia for the strategic and geographical reasons summarized above. The French war plan envisioned a token advance into the Rhineland to be followed by a tactical withdrawal behind the Maginot Line for the winter. The British government could only hold out the possibility of sending two underequipped divisions to the continent. The Soviet Union, whose treaty with Czechoslovakia was due to go into effect once France had come to that country's assistance, had no way of assisting its ally except by air because of the Polish-Romanian barrier and therefore did not even take the precaution of a general mobilization. As the hopelessness of Czechoslovakia's position regardless of British, French, and Russian support became apparent, the tragic absurdity of the situation began to dawn on officials in Paris and London: Czechoslovakia was about to be crushed and Europe about to be embroiled in a war over the trivial details of how and when a previously agreed upon plan of territorial transfer was to take place.

While resuming their preparations for war, therefore, Chamberlain and Daladier desperately cast about for ways to arrange a negotiated settlement. The British prime minister persuaded Mussolini to intervene with Hitler to arrange for a final meeting to avert war. For reasons known only to himself, the Führer agreed to postpone his mobilization plans and to host a conference of the leaders of Britain, France, and Italy at Munich on September 29. His decision to stop at the brink of war may have been influenced by the hesitations of Mussolini, the reluctance of his generals, or the refusal of Chamberlain and Daladier to stand idly by if Germany attempted to settle the Sudeten crisis by military means. In any event, he had every reason to assume that his Godesberg demands would be accepted and he knew that their implementation would spell the early demise of the Czechoslovak state.

The Munich Conference, from which both Czechoslovakia and its ally the Soviet Union were excluded at German insistence, produced an agreement that provided for the evacuation of Czechoslovak military forces from the Sudetenland between October 1 and 10 to be followed by its occupation by German troops in four stages. An international commission would administer plebiscites in disputed areas and fix the new frontier. Britain and France undertook to guarantee the redrawn borders of Czechoslovakia against unprovoked aggression while Germany and Italy promised similar guarantees once Polish and Hungarian territorial claims had been satisfactorily adjudicated. The Czech government was presented with this agreement in the form of an ultimatum on September 30 and denied even the right to submit written objections that Germany had enjoyed at the Paris Peace Conference in 1919. Abandoned by its Western allies and threatened with a war it could not hope to win if it resisted, the Prague government dutifully signed what its leaders knew to be its death warrant.

Upon their return to their respective capitals, Chamberlain and Daladier received euphoric expressions of public gratitude for having prevented the arcane dispute in far-off Czechoslovakia from plunging Britain and France into a war with Germany that neither nation wanted nor was prepared to fight. For those who believed Hitler's oft-repeated assurances that his objective in Eastern Europe was the absorption of territory populated by citizens of German descent, the Munich Pact promised the end of Germany's claims against what remained of Czechoslovakia and seemed to herald the advent of stability in the region. They ignored those passages in the Führer's speeches and writings that clearly enunciated his ultimate goal, which was not to liberate oppressed Germans from foreign rule but rather to subject the non-German peoples of all of East Europe and western Russia to direct or indirect domination from Berlin. There were those in England and France who were willing to tolerate and even to encourage the diversion of Germany's expansionist energies eastward at the expense of states for which they had little concern or, in the case of Soviet Russia, considerable aversion. But the leaders of Great Britain and France who struck the bargain with Hitler at Munich did not belong to this group of enthusiastic appeasers. They appear genuinely to have believed, Chamberlain with greater confidence than the more skeptical Daladier, that the annexation of the Sudetenland would remove the last obstacle to the peaceful reintegration of Germany into the Versailles system thus modified to her benefit. They both recognized that German domination of all of Eastern Europe would inevitably pose a grave menace to the security of their own countries and at no time were prepared to tolerate such a radical imbalance of power on the continent.

Far from securing the territorial status quo on the continent, the Munich settlement accelerated the process of disintegration that would tip the balance of power in Eastern Europe toward Germany. The territorial amputations had condemned the rump state of Czechoslovakia to such a precarious existence as to preclude its operating as an independent political unit. Germany's annexation of the Sudetenland, together with the subsequent acquisition of the Teschen district by Poland and parts of Slovakia by Hungary, shattered the political authority of the government in Prague. The Slovaks, who inhabited the eastern region of the state and resented the politically dominant Czechs, seethed with separatist agitation that was actively encouraged by Berlin. The loss of the formidable string of fortifications along its western frontier—the "eastern Maginot Line" as it was sometimes called—exposed the truncated Czech state to unimpeded military invasion from Germany. Once the Munich Agreement was put into effect, the political disintegration of Czechoslovakia and its gravitation toward the German orbit could have been prevented only by Hitler's willingness to abide by its terms or the determination of the Western powers to enforce them. The first possibility was ruled out by the German leader's plan to destroy Czechoslovakia preparatory to waging a war in the west to crush France and forcibly remove Britain from the continent in order to free German military forces for the land grab in the east that remained the ultimate goal of his foreign policy. The second prospect—that of an effective Anglo-French military deterrent to German violations of the Munich accord—was precluded by the geographical and strategic impossibility of bringing such Anglo-French military power as there existed to bear against Germany.

The devastating consequences of the Munich pact for rump Czechoslovakia were also felt in the other countries of Eastern and Southern Europe. France's willingness to sacrifice its strongest and most trusted ally in the region encouraged Czechoslovakia's partners in the Little Entente to hasten the reorientation of their foreign policies toward greater cooperation with the emerging German colossus. Shocked by France's abandonment of Prague and uneasy about threats to its own territorial integrity from Hungary and the Soviet Union, Romania resumed its rapprochement with

Germany that had begun in response to earlier indications of the recession of French power in Eastern Europe. An economic agreement signed on December 10, 1938, guaranteed German access to Romanian oil (to supplement the insufficient synthetic production from domestic coal) as well as surplus wheat (to help compensate for Germany's annual shortfall in agricultural output). Yugoslavia, also subject to Hungarian revisionist demands and alarmed at the perpetual threat of Italian territorial ambitions along the Adriatic, strengthened its economic ties with Germany and solicited Hitler's restraining influence on its two revisionist neighbors. Hungary, which had hesitated to throw in its lot with Germany during the Munich crisis (and consequently received from Hitler a much smaller share of the Slovakian spoils than it had coveted), rapidly adjusted to the new political realities in Eastern Europe. Budapest dramatically demonstrated its alignment with Berlin's foreign policy by joining the Anti-Comintern Pact and withdrawing from the League of Nations. As a reward it received Germany's approval to annex Czechoslovakia's easternmost province, the Carpatho-Ukraine (Ruthenia), which contained numerous Hungarians.

The process of German economic and political domination of the smaller states of Eastern and Southern Europe was completed by Hitler's destruction of the Munich Agreement on March 15, 1939. On that day the grievances of the Slovak minority against the Czech ruling elite were seized upon as a pretext for the German military occupation of Prague. The western half of the country, inhabited by the Czechs, was promptly transformed into a German protectorate while the eastern half was converted into the satellite state of Slovakia. In response to this spectacular and effortless extension of German military power into the Danube basin, all of the states of Eastern and Southern Europe, with one important exception, were either seduced or intimidated into accepting German hegemony on the eastern half of the continent. Romania and Yugoslavia, the former allies of Czechoslovakia and clients of France, relapsed into a policy of diplomatic and economic subservience to Germany. Lithuania was reduced to the status of a de facto satellite when its port of Memel with its German-speaking majority was annexed by Hitler a few days after the dismemberment of Czechoslovakia. Hungary and Bulgaria, already firmly in the German orbit, resumed their active support for Hitler's aggressive moves.

It is ironic that the single exception to this pro-German reorientation in Eastern Europe after Munich was the policy conducted by the earliest supporter and principal beneficiary of Germany's eastern revisionism: Poland. Berlin's tactical flirtation with Warsaw, inaugurated by the nonaggression pact of 1934 and confirmed by the two governments' collaboration in the territorial amputation of Czechoslovakia in the autumn of 1938, reflected Hitler's intention of using Poland first as an accomplice in removing the Czech menace and later as a geographical barrier to possible Soviet interference with his planned military offensive in the west. But the government in Warsaw consistently rebuffed Hitler's demands that Poland pub-

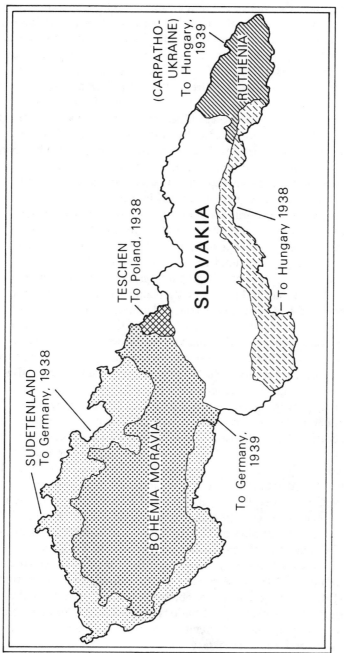

SUDETENLAND
To Germany, 1938

TESCHEN
To Poland, 1938

(CARPATHO-
UKRAINE)
To Hungary,
1939

RUTHENIA

SLOVAKIA

To Hungary 1938

BOHEMIA MORAVIA

To Germany,
1939

The Partition of Czechoslovakia, 1938–1939

licly confirm its subservience to German foreign policy by adhering to the Anti-Comintern Pact. Though staunchly anticommunist and implacably hostile to the Soviet Union, the Polish ruling elite stubbornly withheld this symbolic gesture because it would signal the end of the precarious balancing act between Germany and Russia that Poland had conducted since its rebirth as a nation after the Great War. The Warsaw regime became even more intransigent after March 1939, when the outflanking of Poland's western defenses by the establishment of a German military presence in Slovakia to the south reminded it of the way in which Czechoslovakia's defensive fortifications had been circumvented by the German annexation of Austria two years earlier. For reasons of national pride, the Poles were unwilling to accept the same fate as the Czechs or to tolerate the establishment of German hegemony in Eastern Europe.

Poland's refusal to affirm its subservience to German foreign policy after Munich, and especially after the German march on Prague, caused Hitler to revise his attitude toward Poland and therefore to reverse his timetable for European domination. With an unreliable Poland to the east, he could ill afford to resume his preparations for the war against France and Great Britain that he had originally planned to launch after removing the military threat of Czechoslovakia and obtaining that country's valuable munitions plants and raw materials for the German war machine. The Führer accordingly decided that the war in the west would have to await the prior defeat of Poland, the only recalcitrant power on Germany's eastern flank. Since the authorities in Warsaw could be neither enticed nor intimidated into acquiescing in Germany's plans for continental conquest, as all of its neighbors in Eastern Europe had been, Poland would have to be eliminated before rather than after the inevitable showdown with the Western democracies. Once the decision to attack Poland ahead of schedule was taken in the spring of 1939, the old grievances that had been deemphasized during the period of German-Polish detente were suddenly revived. The alleged maltreatment of the Germans in Danzig and the economic difficulties caused by the separation of East Prussia from the rest of the Reich once again gave rise to heated protests from Berlin. German demands for the restoration of Danzig to German sovereignty and an extraterritorial road and railroad across the corridor to East Prussia (ostensibly to conserve the foreign exchange expended for transit payments to Poland) were met with the same polite but firm refusals in Warsaw that had greeted Hitler's earlier efforts to obtain Polish adherence to the Anti-Comintern Pact. Alone among the nations of Eastern and Southern Europe, Poland seemed prepared to defend its territorial integrity and national independence, by force if necessary.

A major factor contributing to the stiffening of Polish resolve after the collapse of the Munich settlement was the abrupt change of British and French foreign policy from appeasement to resistance. Shortly after returning from Munich, Chamberlain and Daladier had taken a number of precautions against the possibility that the recent agreement to preserve the peace in Eastern Europe would come unglued. In the early months of 1939, Great Britain greatly accelerated the pace of its rearmament and finally began to formulate precise plans for the creation of a large expeditionary force for deployment on the continent. France took steps to rectify the serious deficiencies in its air power by placing orders for warplanes in the United States after obtaining the tacit consent of the Roosevelt government. But it was the German occupation of Prague that precipitated the fundamental reversal of Anglo-French policy toward Hitler's Germany. Unlike all previous instances of German territorial expansion during the thirties, this one was executed at the expense of non-Germans and therefore could not be justified by the principle of national self-determination that Hitler had previously invoked in regard to the Rhineland, Austria, and the Sudetenland. Public opinion in Britain and France had rallied behind the Munich pact because it was advertised by all of its signatories as the definitive resolution of Germany's nationality grievances in Eastern Europe. Its unilateral repudiation by Hitler less than half a year later produced a profound sense of betrayal in London and Paris as well as the determination not to repeat the same mistake in the future. As the principal architect of the Munich settlement, Chamberlain was instantly transformed into a firm opponent of further German territorial claims. He abruptly recalled the British ambassador to Berlin, issued a stern note of protest, and suspended the Anglo-German trade talks that had dragged on inconclusively for months. On March 18, only three days after the fall of Prague, the British Foreign Office, in concert with the Quai d'Orsay, approached the governments of Russia, Poland, Romania, Yugoslavia, Greece, and Turkey about the possibility of forming a coalition to oppose further German aggression. Initially it was feared that Germany's next move would be against Romania to secure control of its oil wells and grain resources as a means of evading the consequences of a British blockade in the event of war. But it rapidly became evident that the most likely victim of Hitler's next aggressive move was Poland, the only nation in Eastern Europe that had refused to align its policies with Germany and therefore denied Hitler the luxury of concentrating the bulk of German military forces in the west. In accordance with this perception, the British government took two unprecedented steps in the spring of 1939 that expressed its newfound determination to halt German aggression in its tracks. On March 31 it publicly pledged to guarantee the territorial integrity of Poland. On April 26 it announced its intention to request parliamentary authorization for the introduction of universal military conscription. Never before had Great Britain been willing to promise military assistance to a nation in Eastern Europe and to institute conscription during peacetime. Such measures were unnecessary for France, with its existing treaty commitment to Poland and its large conscript army. It had only to support the British campaign to organize an anti-German coalition among Poland's neighbors that could deter Hitler from taking the plunge.

The minor powers of southeastern Europe whose adhesion to an anti-German bloc Great Britain belatedly sought in the spring of 1939 were by then entirely unsuited for such service. Romania and Yugoslavia had drawn so close to Germany, both economically and politically, as to render them unwilling, while Greece and Turkey were so geographically remote as to render them unable, to play a role in Poland's defense. Only the Soviet Union was in a geographical position, and had previously expressed the willingness, to join Britain and France in a common front against Germany. But the Anglo-French overture of March 18 was foredoomed by the refusal of Poland and Romania to be associated with the Soviet Union and the reluctance of London and Paris to press them on this point. A month later, on April 17, Stalin offered the alternative of a military alliance among France, Great Britain, and Russia—the old Triple Entente of 1914—to guarantee all of the independent nations of Central and Eastern Europe against German aggression. On the same day, however, he authorized the Soviet ambassador to Berlin to broach the subject of a Russo-German rapprochement to officials in the German Foreign Office. In short, a month after the German absorption of Czechoslovakia, the Soviet leader had simultaneously floated two trial balloons to assess the intentions of the two contending blocs that were forming in anticipation of the impending showdown over Poland. In the absence of reliable documentation of Soviet decision making during this critical period, one can only reach the conclusion that common sense suggests: that the two conflicting traditions of postwar Soviet foreign policy, the Popular Front collective security strategy of cooperation with the Western powers to restrain Germany and the Rapallo policy of collaboration with Germany against the west, hung precariously in the balance.

There is no need to review the manifold reasons for Moscow to fear the consequences of German hegemony in Europe. Hitler's brutal suppression of the German Communist party, his periodic outbursts against the menace of international communism, and the well-known project sketched in his book *Mein Kampf* and reiterated frequently thereafter for the seizure of Russian land for German agricultural development and resettlement—all of this had made a profound impression on Stalin and converted him to the cause of collective security and the Popular Front during the period 1935–38. But the refusal of the French to transform the Franco-Soviet Pact into a military alliance, the hesitation of Great Britain to commit itself to guaranteeing the territorial status quo in Eastern Europe, and above all the exclusion of the Soviet Union from the Munich conference, left Stalin with the impression (whether accurate or not) that the Western powers looked with favor on Germany's eastward expansion. That some influential publicists and statesmen in France and England believed that their nations stood to profit from, and therefore should promote, a struggle to the death between Teuton and Slav in the expanses of Eastern Europe there is no doubt. It is also undeniable that anti-Communist sentiment in the Western democracies, which ironically was exacerbated by the very Popular Front policy that Stalin had invented to reconcile the capitalist world with Russia, made the London and Paris governments reluctant to respond to the numerous overtures for cooperation against Germany that had emanated from the Kremlin. The private comments of key policymakers in Great Britain and France suggest that a lack of faith in the efficacy of the Red Army, with its decapitated command structure* and its inadequate transportation facilities, together with the refusal of Poland and Romania to tolerate the presence of Russian troops on their soil, outweighed ideological hostility as a motive for this cautious posture. But whatever the reason, by the time the British and French governments had overcome this reluctance to make common cause with the Kremlin against Hitler in the spring of 1939, Stalin had decided, for a number of reasons to be summarized presently, that the best hope for Russia to protect the security of its western frontier lay in rapprochement with rather than resistance to Germany.

The first of these reasons was the Kremlin's discovery of evidence that Hitler's plans for the destruction of Poland were preparatory to a war not against Russia but rather against the Western powers. This conclusion emerged from intelligence reports from a well-placed Soviet spy in Tokyo, which detailed the acrimonious dispute between Germany and Japan during secret negotiations to transform the Anti-Comintern Pact into a triparte military alliance of the Axis powers. As we have seen, the Japanese steadfastly insisted that any such association be directed specifically and exclusively at the Soviet Union (their primary antagonist on the mainland of Asia), while Berlin had tried and failed to lure Tokyo into a military alliance aimed solely at France and Great Britain. Had the impending assault against Poland represented merely the first stage of a German invasion of Russia, a Germano-Japanese alliance against the Soviet Union would have obviously represented the most effective means of diluting Moscow's military strength by forcing it to fight a war on two fronts. Yet this was precisely the alignment that Hitler, in spite of unmistakable indications of Japanese interest, was unprepared to contemplate at this time. The announcement of the "Pact of Steel" between Germany and Italy on May 22 confirmed the breakdown of the German-Japanese negotiations and signaled Hitler's intention to direct his aggressive policies against France and Great Britain (the only powers against which Italian assistance would count).

Thus the Soviet Union could hope to escape the trauma of an immediate German invasion, which did not fit into Hitler's plan for a westward ad-

---

* Four hundred officers from the rank of colonel up had been executed during the purges of 1937–38.

vance after the destruction of Poland. It followed that Russia had much to gain from assuming a defensive posture on its western frontier and much to lose from joining a military alliance with Britain and France that might provoke the German dictator into revising his timetable for European conquest and dispatching his forces eastward after Poland's demise. Herein lies the obverse of the sinister intention that Stalin imputed to Western leaders after Munich. An accommodation with Hitler in Eastern Europe would deflect German aggression westward. Russia could obtain considerable advantage by abstaining from a war between the capitalist powers that was likely to result in their mutual exhaustion. In the meantime, such an abstention would afford a precious breathing spell that would enable the Russian leader to reorganize the command structure of the Red Army that had been decimated by his own paranoic purges of 1937–38; it would also permit the gearing up of the Russian economy for the war with Germany that was bound to come once Hitler had secured his western flank by defeating France and forcibly removing British power from the continent.

It was these considerations of national advantage that determined the Kremlin's double game in the spring and summer of 1939, when Britain and France belatedly solicited Soviet assistance in the containment of Germany. Russian criticism of the German occupation of Prague, followed up by the intimations of Soviet interest in the formation of a new Triple Entente, kept the door to London and Paris open. But various exploratory gestures from the Kremlin simultaneously kept the door to Berlin ajar. The most spectacular of these signals came on May 3. The Soviet foreign minister, Maxim Litvinov, whose Jewish ancestry and passionate advocacy of the pro-Western policy adopted in the mid-1930s rendered him inappropriate for the task of negotiating an accommodation with Nazi Germany, was abruptly replaced by Stalin's loyal henchman Vyacheslav Molotov. This unmistakable signal to Hitler that Stalin was prepared to do business was followed up by an intensification of the contacts between Moscow and Berlin initiated on April 17. On May 20 Molotov himself informed the German ambassador of Stalin's interest in exploring a "political basis" for greater Russo-German cooperation. For the next three months, as Hitler's propaganda war against Poland reached a fever pitch, the low-level discussions between the Germans and the Russians resumed their leisurely pace. It is likely that Stalin's mind was not yet made up when, on July 25, Britain and France finally agreed to dispatch military missions to Moscow to explore the basis of an alliance with the Soviet Union against Germany. The German ambassador to Moscow was convinced that the Kremlin was at that time "determined to sign with England and France, if they fulfill all Soviet wishes."

But the manner in which the two Western governments conducted their negotiations with the Kremlin conveyed neither a sense of urgency nor a determination to secure Soviet membership in the anti-German coalition as an equal partner. The departure of the Anglo-French negotiating team was postponed for eleven days and then sent on its way not by airplane, which would have got the mission to Moscow in a day, but rather by the slowest possible means of oceanic transport, a 9,000 ton passenger-cargo vessel. When it finally reached Moscow on August 11 after six days at sea, it consisted of low-ranking officers uncertain of their negotiating powers. When the talks got underway, the Anglo-French delegates evaded searching questions from the Soviets about troop strength, military plans, and means of persuading Poland and Rumania to permit the passage of Russian military forces across their territory. The Russians could not help but compare the desultory behavior of the British and French governments to the eagerness of Chamberlain and Daladier to fly to Munich to deal directly with Hitler. It also contrasted dramatically with the strong expressions of interest in a Russo-German rapprochement that had begun to emanate from Berlin during the first three weeks of August. The strenuous efforts by the German foreign minister, Joachim von Ribbentrop, to secure an audience with Stalin as soon as possible were prompted by Hitler's concern about the timing of the Polish campaign, which had to be completed before the onset of winter would interfere with mechanized transport and aerial operations.

Stalin's decision to receive Hitler's foreign minister on August 23 marked the end of the double game that Russia had played since the spring of 1939. During the two meetings conducted in the Kremlin on that historic date, the German and Russian representatives reached a series of understandings that were codified in two documents—one for public consumption, the other for the confidential reassurance of the two signatories. The public document committed Germany and Russia to the observance of strict neutrality toward one another should either become involved in war. Hitler thereby secured Russian acquiescence in Germany's forthcoming campaign against Poland as well as relief from the threat of a two-front war once he turned his forces westward against France and Britain. Stalin obtained what Chamberlain and Daladier had earlier secured at Munich: the postponement of a war with Germany that their countries were at the time unprepared to fight, which afforded them precious time to upgrade their strategic capabilities as best they could. The "secret additional protocol" confirmed the geopolitical reality that had, since the end of the Great War, represented a potential basis of collaboration between Germany and Russia and an obstacle to Russia's rapprochement with the west: While France and, belatedly, Britain, had been driven by the dictates of national interest to support the independence of the successor states in Eastern Europe, Germany and Russia were impelled by the promise of territorial aggrandizement to cooperate in their destruction. Thus the two signatories secretly agreed to the fourth partition of Poland. Finland, Latvia, and Estonia—all, like the eastern sector of Poland, former provinces of the Tsarist Empire—were allotted to the Russian sphere of influence.* Germany recognized Russia's right to recover the province of Bessarabia, whose seizure by Romania during the Russian Revolution had never been recognized by the Soviet regime. Except for the reannexation of Bessarabia, the motive for this Soviet expansionism may be summarized in a single phrase: the quest for security. Soviet domination of Finland and the two northernmost Baltic states would reduce the vulnerability of Russia's second capital, Leningrad, by providing it with a defensive buffer in the path of the traditional northern invasion route. The recovery of the territory lost to Poland in the war of 1920 would restore the historic buffer between the Germanic and Russian populations in Eastern Europe.

The Nazi-Soviet Pact of August 23, 1939, sealed the fate of Poland and enabled Hitler to launch the European war he had planned since coming to power. Last minute British efforts to promote a peaceful resolution of the German-Polish crisis had no chance of success: Hitler's military time-table required the war against Poland to begin no later than September 1 in order to permit the annihilation of that country before the autumn rains could interfere with the operations of his tank columns and dive bombers. He would not again be cheated out of a victorious war against a despised victim, as he had been at Munich. His evasive reply to Britain was therefore designed to split the Western powers from Poland—since he preferred to engage his enemies seriatim if that could be arranged—rather than to serve as the basis for a negotiated settlement he was determined to avoid at all costs. On the eve of August 31, a fabricated border incident involving German S.S.† men in Polish uniforms was used as the justification for mounting a massive armor and air assault against Poland the following morning. The British and French governments, which had previously warned Berlin that the rapprochement with Russia would not alter their determination to honor their commitment to Poland, dutifully declared war on Germany on September 3 following the expiration of their ultimatum demanding the evacuation of German forces from Polish soil. With the temporary abstention of Russia and Italy (the latter on the grounds of unpreparedness), only four European powers were involved in the military drama that unfolded at the beginning of September 1939 on the Polish plains. But the limited number of participants and the geographically localized theater of combat did not prevent journalists from soon referring to a second world war.

* Lithuania, assigned to Germany's sphere in the Nazi-Soviet Pact, was transferred to the Soviet sphere in a subsequent agreement on September 28.

† *Schutz Staffeln*, Hitler's black-shirted secret police led by Heinrich Himmler.

CHAPTER 5

Germany's Second Bid for European Dominance (1939–1945)

The six-year war that began in the autumn of 1939 may be conveniently divided into three chronological periods. The first phase started with the successful blitzkreig against Poland and ended with the establishment of a deceptively stable front along Germany's western frontier during the winter of 1939–40. The second phase opened with a German offensive in the west through the Low Countries that resulted in the rapid collapse of France and the evacuation of British military forces from the continent according to plan, and ended with the failure of German aerial bombardment of Great Britain to knock that country out of the war. The third phase marked the transformation of the European war into a veritable world war, in which first the Soviet Union and then the United States were drawn into the global conflict which eventually destroyed Nazi Germany and its two Axis allies, Fascist Italy and Imperial Japan.

The collapse of Poland after less than a month of fighting was foreordained by the Nazi-Soviet Pact, which denied Poland the hope of military assistance from Russia against Germany and partitioned that geographically cursed nation between the two powerful states that adjoined it to the east and the west. Though the Russo-German agreement of August 23, 1939, did not stipulate Soviet participation in the military destruction of Poland, Stalin prudently dispatched troops westward on September 17 to lay claim to the territory allotted to the Soviet Union. Following the surrender of Warsaw on September 27, Poland once again simply disappeared from the map of Europe as Germany and Russia absorbed their respective shares of the spoils.

Both Great Britain and France were obliged by their treaty commitments to mount a military offensive against Germany in the event of a military attack by that country against Poland. Such an offensive failed to materialize. The French general staff had devised no operational plans for a drive into western Germany, believing as it did that such a strike against Germany's heavily fortified French frontier was inconceivable and knowing that an offensive against Germany's greatest point of vulnerability in the Rhineland bordering Belgium was precluded by the latter country's refusal to compromise its neutrality by granting transit rights to French troops. As for the British, they had begun to rearm in earnest and to organize a land army on the basis of compulsory military service less than six months before the outbreak of the war in Poland. They therefore possessed neither the weaponry nor the manpower to mount a credible deterrent on Germany's western flank even if they could have solved the geographical riddle of how to project such military force as they did possess into enemy territory.

The efficacy of the blitzkreig—the rapid thrust of massed tank formations supported by aerial assaults from dive bombers—was so brilliantly confirmed in the Polish campaign that Hitler prematurely issued an order on October 9 for the preparation of an early offensive with identical tactics through the Low Countries against France. Originally scheduled for November 12, then twice postponed on account of bad weather, the date for the great western offensive was definitively set for the second week in May to take advantage of the spring thaw. As the winter set in, German military forces transferred from the Polish front massed along the Dutch and Belgian frontiers while British and French forces dug in along France's eastern border. The absence of actual fighting led journalists to dub this second phase of the European struggle for hegemony the "phony war." Blitzkreig, observed one wag, had given way to Sitzkreig.

Amid this eerie atmosphere of inactivity in the west, world attention was suddenly turned to events in the frozen terrain of northern Europe. In September and October the Soviet Union began to exercise the prerogatives accorded it by the secret protocols of the Russo-German Pact to reassert Russian authority over the former European domains of the tsarist empire that had been lost after the revolution. The governments of the Baltic states of Latvia, Estonia, and Lithuania were compelled to authorize the garrisoning of Russian troops on their territory and to sign treaties of mutual assistance with the Soviet Union. When Finland refused both to grant Russia the strategic bases it sought for the protection of Leningrad and to regard itself as part of the Soviet "sphere of interest," Stalin launched a military attack against that country on November 30 in the expectation that Finnish resistance would collapse in short order after the fashion of Poland. But subzero temperatures and rugged terrain—advantages that had been unavailable to the hapless Poles—helped the Finns to hold out for over three months against a Russian army three times larger than their own.

With public opinion in Britain and France clamoring for military intervention on behalf of valiant little Finland, authorities in London and Paris concocted a scheme ostensibly designed to relieve the Finns but in reality aimed at a soft spot in the strategic arsenal of Germany. As noted earlier, Germany depended heavily on imports of high-grade iron ore from Sweden for its armaments production. During the winter months, when much of the Baltic Sea was frozen, the ore had to be transported overland by rail to the ice-free port of Narvik in Norway for transshipment through Norwegian territorial waters to ports in northern Germany. Plans were drawn up for an Anglo-French expeditionary force to be landed at Narvik and sent across Norway and Sweden to assist Finland while seizing the Swedish ore fields along the way. When the Finnish capitulation on March 12 foreclosed this project, it was replaced by an earlier British scheme to mine Norway's territorial waters in order to cut Germany off from its iron ore supplies. Though both of these schemes were fraught with diplomatic complications caused by the refusal of Norway and Sweden to compromise their neutrality, the British proceeded with the plan anyway. But the day after the British mining operation began, German amphibious and paratroop forces seized the capital and major ports of Norway and occupied Denmark on April 9. Contingents of Anglo-French troops hastily landed on the Norwegian coast failed to secure defensible beachheads and eventually had to be withdrawn. Germany had instantaneously obtained at virtually no cost a string of strategically located bases in Scandinavia that would subsequently be used for submarine warfare against Great Britain in her home waters. By refusing to coordinate their defense plans with Great Britain and France, and by denying the Anglo-French armies transit rights across their territory, the Nordic neutrals facilitated the abrupt expansion of German power into Northern Europe. Norway and Denmark paid for their policy of aloofness by being forced to submit to German military occupation and all of the privations that that entailed. On account of its previously demonstrated willingness to cooperate economically with Germany, Sweden was spared the agony of its neighbors. From its posture of absolute neutrality it continued to supply the German war machine with all of the high-grade iron ore it required at a handsome profit.

After Germany had secured its northern flank, the long-awaited western offensive finally unfolded on May 10. The buffer states of Holland and Belgium, which like their Scandinavian counterparts had consistently rebuffed Anglo-French overtures for joint military planning, were rewarded for their scrupulous adherence to neutrality with a brutal combination of aerial bombardment and mechanized invasion that rivaled the Polish campaign in its rapidity as well as its destructiveness. On paper the two sides were of roughly equal strength in manpower (134 German divisions versus 94 French, 10 British, 22 Belgian, and 8 Dutch divisions). Germany's three-to-one advantage in air power was partially offset by the numerical superiority of the Western Allies in the decisive weapon of the moment: 3,200 Anglo-French versus 2,500 German tanks. But sheer numbers of men and machines do not tell the whole story. The training and equipment of the German motorized infantry units were vastly superior to that of the Western powers. Moreover, the Allies squandered their numerical superiority in armor by dispersing their tank formations among the regular infantry divisions as support groups instead of concentrating them in separate armored divisions to serve as spearheads for motorized infantry units. It is supremely ironic that this tactic for the most efficient use of armor in offensive warfare had been conceived by a British military theorist, B. H. Liddell Hart, and popularized by a young French tactician, Colonel Charles de Gaulle, only to be put into practice by the German Generals Fritz Erich von Manstein and Heinz Guderian. Dutch resistance collapsed in five days and Belgian forces retreated in total disarray before the German juggernaut as it rolled toward the French frontier. Panzer spearheads with dive-bomber support cleared the way for motorized infantry units to slash through the Ardennes hill country in southern Belgium (which had been considered "impassable" to armor by those French military planners who vetoed the extension of the Maginot Line to the North Sea). The German forces breached the French defenses at Sedan on May 16, then veered northward toward the Channel coast to sever the supply lines and communications of the main Anglo-French armies in northeastern France and Belgium. After reaching the sea on May 20, this advance German tank contingent swung eastward toward the isolated Allied forces that had reassembled at the French port of Dunkirk near the Belgian frontier. On May 28 the British government, refusing the urgent request of the French prime minister, Paul Reynaud, that the remainder of the Royal Air Force be dispatched to the continent for the defense of France, ordered the evacuation of the Anglo-French troops trapped in the vicinity of Dunkirk. During the next eight days 200,000 British and 130,000 French soldiers were ferried across the Channel by a hastily improvised flotilla of vessels while the German armies turned southward to deliver the knockout blow to the remnants of the French army. By June 16 the French cabinet, which had abandoned Paris five days earlier and headed south, reluctantly concluded that further resistance was pointless. Reynaud resigned in favor of the octogenarian war hero Marshal Henri-Philippe Pétain, who assembled a ministry favorable to a prompt end to the war. On June 22 the French government capitulated after less than six weeks of resistance, signing an armistice that provided for the disarmament of the French forces and the delivery of the northern three-fifths of the country to German military occupation.

Four days before the French capitulation, the recently promoted Brigadier General Charles de Gaulle, a prewar critic of the French high command's defensive military doctrines and an undersecretary of defense in the Reynaud government who had opposed the decision for an armistice and had fled to London, broadcast a message to the French people over British radio urging resistance to the German occupation and inviting French military and political authorities to join him in England to resume the struggle against the invader. When no one in high office responded to this appeal, he promptly formed a French National Committee in London which operated alongside the other governments in exile that had fled the overrun countries of the continent. Great Britain subsidized and encouraged this "Free French" movement and severed relations with the collaborationist regime of Marshal Pétain established on July 2 in the unoccupied sector of southern France at the resort city of Vichy. Unlike the other European governments in exile that had reassembled in London after the defeat of their armies in the field, de Gaulle's organization had no claim to political legitimacy since the legally elected French parliament had voted to confer emergency powers on the Pétain regime on July 9. Nonetheless, de Gaulle assembled a ragtag military force, composed of French soldiers, sailors, and airmen who had escaped from the continent, which participated in many of the important campaigns against the Axis during the rest of the war.

The fall of France in the summer of 1940 completed the revolution in the balance of power in Europe that had begun with the remilitarization of the Rhineland. In just four years Germany had come from nowhere to dominate the entire continent, controlling roughly the same geographical area as Napoleon at the height of his power. Nine formerly independent states had submitted to the domination of Berlin in various guises, ranging from outright annexation in the case of Austria to a fictitious independence in the case of the Vichy regime in France. The remaining nations of the continent had become either military allies or economic vassals of Germany, except for a handful of states—Spain, Portugal, Switzerland, and Sweden—that managed to cling to a precarious neutrality. The sympathetic collaboration of the Soviet Union in Germany's drive toward the west, originally confined to the joint partition of Poland but soon expanded to include the exchange of Russian grain and oil for German manufactured products, seemed to afford Germany the advantage it had gained too late in the last war: protection against economic strangulation by the British blockade through access to Russia's inexhaustible supply of food and fuel.

The end of the battle of France on June 22 was followed by hasty preparations for the Battle of Britain. Plans for a Channel crossing were drawn up on July 2: Germany assembled troop transport ships along the French Channel coast and organized thirteen divisions in preparation for what Hitler christened "Operation Sea-Lion," the first attempted invasion of the British Isles since the Norman Conquest. But Churchill's decision to hold in reserve the bulk of the Royal Air Force (RAF) during the French campaign forced a postponement of the projected amphibious landing until the Luftwaffe could remove the threat of aerial harassment of the trans-Channel invasion force. Emboldened by its astonishingly effective performance against Poland and France, Air Marshal Hermann Göring assured his Führer that the numerically superior German fighter force, after several days of precision bombing of the British fighter bases, could remove the enemy's air arm from the skies within a month.

Apart from the courage and skill of the pilots of Britain's Fighter Command, three technological factors enabled the RAF to foil German plans for achieving the control of the air deemed necessary for a successful amphibious invasion. The first was the qualitative superiority of British air power that helped to compensate for its numerical inferiority. In this respect, Britain's belated entry in the aerial arms race had proved to be an advantage; the new Spitfire and Hurricane fighters fresh off the assembly line were faster, more maneuverable, and possessed much greater firepower than the older German Messerschmidts. The second was radar, the technique of employing the reflected echo of radio waves to detect distant objects in the atmosphere. Perfected in 1935 by the British scientist Robert Watson-Watt, this technological breakthrough resulted in the construction of twenty early warning stations along Britain's Channel coast by the spring of 1939 from which observers could locate approaching aircraft soon after their departure from continental bases and measure their range with uncanny accuracy. This radar network enabled the RAF fighters to conserve precious fuel by remaining on the ground until an attack was underway and then heading straight for the incoming German planes, whose limited fuel supply often forced them to return prematurely to their French or Belgian bases. The third factor in the British air victory was the acquisition by British intelligence of an electrically operated cipher machine capable of decoding German radio messages. This device, which had been captured in Germany by the Polish Secret Service and transported to England in the utmost secrecy before the war, enabled British cryptographers to crack the German code and therefore gave the RAF command advance knowledge of the German air force's operational instructions and targeting schedule.

But the major responsibility for the Luftwaffe's failure to gain control of British air space in the autumn of 1940 must also be placed squarely on the shoulders of Hitler himself. When the RAF raided Berlin in retaliation for the accidental bombing of London by German planes, the Führer angrily ordered round-the-clock bombardment of the major British metropolitan areas as punishment. He apparently persuaded himself that such brutal tactics would serve a good military purpose by sapping British morale and inciting civilian opposition to Churchill's policy of resistance. Hitler's faith in the efficacy of massive aerial bombardment of civilian population centers (rather than military installations) was shared by an entire generation of strategists inspired by the writings of the Italian general Giulio Douhet, who had forecast the total breakdown of social order and mass uprisings leading to demands for capitulation by the terrorized civilian victims of such air power. Though German bombing raids killed 51,509 British civilians and damaged or destroyed one out of five British homes, they did not produce the widespread demoralization and civil unrest that the theorists of strategic bombing since Douhet had predicted. On the contrary, the Blitz, as these bombing raids were collectively called in Britain, galvanized the population behind its leadership and stiffened its resolve to carry on the war. The campaign to terrorize the metropolitan centers of Britain proved counterproductive in strategic terms also, because it diverted German air power from the military targets that really counted: the fighter bases of the RAF, which had been severely damaged by the initial onslaught and might very well have been wiped out by a continuation of the precision bombing that Göring had initiated in the late summer.

The postponement of Operation Sea-Lion and the dispersal of the cross-Channel invasion flotilla in mid-September did not signify the end of the Luftwaffe's bombardment of British cities, which continued through the spring of 1941. But the air war in the British skies thereafter took second place to the project that had remained the touchstone of Hitler's foreign policy: the annihilation of the Soviet Union. On July 31, two weeks before the beginning of the bombardment of Britain, Hitler informed his generals of his plan to invade Russia the following May. In the early autumn the redeployment of German forces from occupied France to the east began. But "Operation Barbarossa" against Russia was unexpectedly delayed when Mussolini, who had entered the war against France and Britain in June, imprudently embroiled Italy in conflicts in the Balkans and North Africa, which required the diversion of German forces southward in rescue operations. Italian troops based in the recently acquired protectorate of Albania had attacked Greece in October 1940 in search of a quick, cheap victory. Instead they encountered fierce resistance from the Greek army and by March 1941 faced the prospect of a humiliating military defeat when British troops landed in Greece at the invitation of the Athens government. The sudden reappearance of a British army on the continent elicited a swift response from Berlin. When the new government of Yugoslavia bravely repudiated its predecessor's pledge to grant transit facilities to the Germany army, Hitler launched an invasion from bases in Hungary and Bulgaria which crushed Yugoslav and Greek resistance in three weeks and forced a hasty evacuation of the British force from the Greek peninsula.

In the meantime, an offensive mounted in mid-September by Italian forces in Libya against the lightly defended British garrison in Egypt (which protected the Suez Canal and the Middle Eastern oil fields) ground to a halt and then was tranformed into a rout as British forces counterattacked deep into Libyan territory. In February 1941 Hitler was compelled to dispatch an Afrika Corps of an armored and a light-armored division under General Erwin Rommel to relieve the battered Italian forces in North Africa. Within two months Rommel's panzers had hurled the British back to the Egyptian frontier. Though successful in the short run, these two Mediterranean diversions caused a six-week delay in Hitler's timetable for the invasion of Russia. The loss of precious time during a season of favorable weather caused little concern in Berlin because of Hitler's confident expectation, based on the French precedent, that Russian resistance would crumble within three months, before the onset of winter.

So confident was the German military command of a speedy victory in the east that it had ordered winter clothing only for the few men who were to remain in Russia for occupation duty after the withdrawal of the victorious invasion force.

The German invasion of the Soviet Union began on June 22, 1941, the 129th anniversary of the launching of Napoleon's ill-fated expedition to Moscow. Four million men, 3,300 tanks, and 5,000 aircraft were sent eastward to wage what was to become the greatest land war in history. Ignoring warnings from British, American, and even Soviet intelligence sources about the impending attack, Stalin and his military advisers were totally unprepared for the German onslaught. As the Soviet armies reeled in confusion before the offensive in the summer and fall of 1941, the consequences of Stalin's purge of the officers' corps in 1937–38 were graphically revealed in the tactical incompetence of the inexperienced junior officers who had replaced the executed members of the high command. In the first three months of battle, over half of the Soviet army was killed, wounded, or captured. Its tank force was reduced from 15,000 to 700. At the farthest extent of the German army's three-pronged advance—toward Leningrad in the north, Moscow in the center, and the Ukrainian grain fields and Caucasian oil wells in the south—almost half of Russia's industrial resources and cultivated land were under enemy control.

It has often been asserted in justification of Stalin's separate peace with Hitler in August 1939 that the Soviet Union gained valuable space and time to prepare for its defense. But the space gained in the Baltic states and eastern Poland proved of no strategic value and was overrun by the invading German armies in the first few days of the eastern offensive. The time gained by Stalin for the reorganization of the Red Army and the construction of munitions factories far to the east of Russia's exposed western frontier was also time gained by Hitler that the latter put to good use. Freed from the threat of a two-front war by Russia's indulgence, Germany forcibly acquired the economic and strategic resources of a dozen countries for use against the Soviet Union. With the fall of Kiev and the siege of Moscow and Leningrad in the autumn of 1941, the benefits of Russia's abstention from the war in Europe that had begun in September 1939 were difficult to identify. Space and time counted for little in the type of war that Germany was waging against the Soviet Union—a blitzkreig whose aims were to rout the Red Army and topple the Stalinist regime before the arrival of the winter snows.

The failure of the German army to deliver the decisive blow before the Russian winter ground its mechanized offensive to a halt in December 1941 has been traced by some military historians to the six-week delay caused by the Balkan and Mediterranean diversions of the previous spring. Others have blamed Hitler's decision to detach armored divisions from the Center Army Group advancing along Napoleon's road to Moscow in order to bolster the drive against Leningrad in the north and the Ukraine in the south. But whatever its tactical cause, the strategic result of the stalled eastern offensive was unmistakable: Hitler's swift war of annihilation became a long war of attrition. This change upset the calculations of the German leader, which rested on the presumption of total victory in Russia within three months. It also enabled Stalin's Machiavellian diplomacy during the 1939–41 period of Russian abstention to yield its anticipated dividends. The industrial output of the newly constructed factories east of the Urals that had been shielded from the effects of the European war by the nonaggression pact with Hitler began during the winter of 1941–42 to compensate for the lost production in the regions of European Russia that had been overrun by the invading German armies. The nonaggression pact that Stalin had signed with Japan on April 13, 1941, freed Russia from the threat of a war on two fronts and permitted the redeployment of large numbers of troops from the Far East to replenish the depleted ranks of the defenders of Moscow. Once the promise of a quick German triumph was buried in the snows of December, the scales gradually began to tip in favor of the Soviet Union, whose seemingly inexhaustible reserves of military manpower and strategic raw materials represented a formidable advantage in a long war of attrition.

The potential vulnerability of Germany in a conflict of long duration became evident during the six months that it waged war against two powers, Great Britain and Russia, which together commanded almost a quarter of the world's resources. The imbalance became all the more pronounced with the transformation of the European conflict into a world war upon the entry of the United States a few days after the Russian counteroffensive from Moscow began. Though the brunt of America's military power could not be hurled against the Third Reich for another two and a half years, its vast economic resources were placed at the disposal first of Great Britain and then of Russia just as they had been in the period before the active participation of the American Expeditionary Force in the earlier war against Germany.

During the twelve months after the fall of France that Great Britain faced Germany alone, the isolationist policy of the Roosevelt administration gradually evolved into a pro-British strategy as the damaging consequences to American national interest of a German victory against England became apparent to Roosevelt and his foreign policy advisers. On September 2, 1940, as the Luftwaffe began its furious air assault on the British Isles, the United States transferred fifty overage destroyers to Great Britain in exchange for a ninety-nine-year lease of naval and air bases on eight British possessions in the Western Hemisphere. This arrangement supplied the Royal Navy with desperately needed ships with which to wage the Battle of the Atlantic against German submarines, while the sale of surplus American munitions enabled the British army to replace the materiel abandoned on the beaches of Dunkirk. On December 20 Roosevelt established a Defense Board to plan and coordinate American assistance to the embattled British, a move that was denounced by the German government as an unwarranted intervention in the European war that compromised America's neutral status. But the "cash and carry" provisions of American neutrality legislation, which prohibited American merchant vessels from entering the war zone in Europe and required advanced payment for purchases by belligerents in the American market, had brought Britain to the brink of bankruptcy by the end of the first year and a half of the war. The decline of Britain's foreign trade, caused by the conversion from production for export to production for warmaking and aggravated by German submarine attacks on British merchant shipping, left that country without a sufficient reserve of dollars to finance its mounting purchases from the "arsenal of democracy" across the Atlantic. Even the sale of its remaining foreign assets and the depletion of its gold stocks would not bridge the gap for very long. The American response to the exhaustion of British dollar reserves was the enactment on March 11, 1941, of the so-called Lend-Lease Act. This legislation repealed the "cash" part of the cash-and-carry requirement, authorizing the sale of American products on credit to "any country whose defense the President deems vital to the defense of the United States." Under the authority granted by this law, a million tons of American agricultural surpluses were shipped across the Atlantic between April and December 1941 to alleviate Great Britain's serious food shortage caused by the German submarine campaign. On November 6, 1941, the Roosevelt administration extended a $1 billion lend-lease credit to the Soviet Union, which was struggling to defend its major cities against the German attack that had been launched that previous summer. In this way a considerable proportion of the strategic arsenal and economic resources of the United States was made available to the two major powers in the anti-Axis coalition during the remaining months of American neutrality.

The intervention of the United States in the Second World War was precipitated not by any quarrel with Nazi Germany but by Japan's surprise attack on the American Pacific fleet based at Pearl Harbor, in Hawaii, on December 7, 1941.* By the spring of 1942, all of East Asia had come under the domination of Japan. American forces had been expelled from the Philippines, Britain's major East Asian base at Singapore had surrendered, and Japanese military and naval power began to fan out in three directions—toward Australia, India, and the Aleutian Islands off Alaska (see p. 253). Yet in the face of the expanding power of Japan across the Pacific, and despite the absence of any immediate German threat to America's vital interests, Roosevelt resolved to pursue a "Europe-first" strategy in the war. By the summer of 1942 the United States had replaced Britain as the major foreign supplier of the Soviet Union, shipping foodstuffs, clothing, and mechanized vehicles across the

* Germany and Italy declared war on the United States on December 11, 1942.

Atlantic to the northern ports of Murmansk and Archangel as well as to the Persian Gulf for transshipment by rail across Iran to the embattled cities of European Russia. The menace of German submarines, which had sunk a third of Britain's merchant fleet tonnage by the time of the Pearl Harbor attack, was removed by the spring of 1943 with the help of American convoys and reconnaissance planes equipped with microwave radar to detect U-boats. In April German naval authorities conceded defeat in the Battle of the Atlantic by recalling the submarines to their bases along the Norwegian and French coasts. Anglo-American control of the sea lanes to Europe enabled Allied strategists to envision for the first time an invasion of the continent.

Yet that invasion was not soon in coming. For three full years—from June 1941 to June 1944—the Russian army fought the German army on the continent virtually unaided. The British government's enthusiastic expressions of solidarity with and tendering of economic assistance to its newly acquired ally against Germany* were not translated into concrete actions on behalf of the common struggle in the form of direct military intervention. Despite urgent pleas from Stalin for some kind of diversionary action in Western Europe to relieve the pressure on the Soviet armies, Churchill steadfastly declined to risk such a direct assault on the western flank of the German-controlled continent. The British preferred to engage the vulnerable Italians in their ersatz empire in the Mediterranean basin rather than challenge the formidable German forces ensconced in their *Festung Europa,* except for long-range bombing raids on German cities that had no discernible effect on Germany's capacity to wage its land war in the east. The American intervention did not change the situation, in spite of Roosevelt's professed enthusiasm for an Anglo-American landing in northern France, for the British prime minister was able to persuade the American president that such an operation was inopportune. The extensive inter-Allied discussions about the opening of a "second front" in France appear to have been intended mostly to placate the increasingly insistent Stalin. Why it took the Western powers so long to organize and execute such an operation has remained a point of intense historiographical controversy. Defenders of the Soviet Union have detected a cynical motive behind this Anglo-American hesitation, namely, the desire to see Russia bled white while her Western allies conserved their military and economic resources in order to step in at the last moment to replace defeated Germany and preempt exhausted Russia as the dominant power on the continent. To judge from the statements of the principals themselves, what prompted Churchill to oppose an early Allied landing in Western Europe, and what persuaded Roosevelt to acquiesce in this postponement, were two considerations. The first was the insufficient number of landing craft, the risks of transporting large numbers of American troops to Brit-

---

* On July 13, 1941, London and Moscow concluded a pact of mutual assistance.

ain while German submarines still roamed the North Atlantic with impunity, and the entrenched position of the German forces along the French
Channel coast. This caused Churchill to fear that a premature landing of
ill-equipped, undermanned Allied forces in northern France would suffer
the same fate as the suicidal amphibious operation at Gallipoli that he had
organized during the First World War and which had almost cost him his
political career. The second consideration was the existence of a much
more attractive alternative: an Allied landing in the lightly defended North
African colonies of Vichy France, which could then serve as a springboard for the invasion of Fortress Europe through its back door in the
Mediterranean.

The revival of the German offensive in Russia in the summer of 1942
placed a considerable strain on the Grand Alliance,* as Stalin vainly
badgered the Anglo-American leadership to open the much-discussed
second front in the west. The invasion of French North Africa, which
took place in November 1942, was a spectacular success from the Western
Allies' point of view. It led to the surrender in the following May of the
Axis armies in Libya, which were caught in the vise between the Allied
forces landed in Morocco and Algeria and the British army in Egypt that
had pierced the German-Italian front at El Alemein. It also brought
southern Italy within range of Allied bombers stationed in Tunisia just
across the Mediterranean narrows. But the liberation of North Africa was
accomplished at the expense of the long-delayed cross-Channel invasion of
France. To the suspicious Stalin it seemed a disappointing diversion of
Anglo-American military power from where it was needed in Western
Europe. The trans-Mediterranean landing on Sicily in July, which paved
the way for the Allied invasion of the Italian mainland in September, did
little to calm Soviet anxieties about the implications of Allied strategy. It
merely increased Stalin's exasperation at his allies' reluctance to engage
the German army directly while Soviet troops were mounting their own
ferocious counterattack in the east.

The professed objective of the Anglo-American Mediterranean strategy
was to force an Italian surrender and to pin down as many German troops
as possible on the Italian peninsula in preparation for the invasion of
France. In this the British and the Americans were signally successful.
The landing of Allied troops in Sicily, coming as it did amid desperate
shortages of food, fuel, and munitions and mounting evidence of social
unrest in Italy, compelled Mussolini to convene on July 24, 1943, a meeting of the Fascist Grand Council, his rubber stamp "parliament" which
had not met for years, to shore up the deteriorating prestige of his regime.
Instead, the Council voted to confer emergency powers on King Victor
Emmanuel, who the following day replaced Mussolini with Marshal Pietro
Badoglio and had the Duce arrested. The new Italian leader promptly

* The popular term for the American, British, and Soviet coalition against Germany.

dissolved the Fascist party, approached the enemy for an armistice (which was finally concluded on September 8), and announced his country's adherence to the Allied cause. The German military forces in Italy, which had been increased to twenty-five divisions in anticipation of just such a turnabout, proceeded to disarm the Italian army, occupy the northern two-thirds of the peninsula, and install Mussolini as head of a new "Italian Social Republic" in the city of Saló after his spectacular rescue from prison by German paratroopers. The subsequent squandering of Anglo-American lives and supplies in the long and costly advance up the Italian peninsula, which took almost two years after the landing in Sicily, was unquestionably one of the greatest strategic blunders of the Allied campaign in Europe.

As the Anglo-American forces cleared North Africa of Axis troops, gained effective control of the Mediterranean, and began their Italian campaign, the Soviet armies in the east finally turned the tide of battle against the German invaders. The German army in southern Russia had been advancing toward the strategically situated city of Stalingrad on the Volga throughout the summer of 1942, threatening to sever the direct railway and river connections linking the major Soviet armies to their sources of fuel in the oil wells of the Caucasus. By mid-September the German Sixth Army had reached the outskirts of the city that bore Stalin's name, the industrial and communications hub of southern Russia, and proceeded to place it under siege. But the gradual buildup of a numerically superior Russian defense force in the autumn prompted the German commander, General Friedrich von Paulus, to request authorization to fall back to a more defensible position. Refusing to countenance what would have been regarded as a humiliating retreat, Hitler ordered a fight to the finish. After three months of what one military historian has called "the most senseless example of human slaughter in history," von Paulus disobeyed his Führer's orders and surrendered the tattered remnant of his army on February 2, 1943. The loss of half a million Axis soldiers dead, wounded, or captured, and the opening of a massive Soviet counteroffensive in the spring, signaled the beginning of the end of Hitler's obsessive drive for German *Lebensraum* in European Russia. By the end of the year two-thirds of the Russian territory under German occupation had been reconquered by the advancing Red Army.

As the Soviet counteroffensive from the east gathered momentum, Roosevelt, Churchill, and Stalin met together for the first time at Teheran, Iran, in November 1943 to plan the timing and strategy of the projected invasion of Western Europe. Churchill, true to form, unveiled an elaborate proposal for an Anglo-American landing at selected points in the Balkans that would have once again deferred the long-delayed invasion of France. Stalin had little difficulty in persuading Roosevelt and his military chiefs that such an indirect assault on Hitler's Europe was a poor substitute for a cross-Channel operation on France's Normandy coast, which would place the Anglo-American armies on the shortest and most direct route to the center of Germany's industrial and warmaking power in the Ruhr. Thus the American and Soviet heads of state turned aside the British leader's Balkan scheme in favor of an amphibious landing in northern France to be followed by a crossing from North Africa to the French Mediterranean coast. On June 6, 1944, five seaborne and three airborne divisions of American, British, and Commonwealth troops were put ashore along the Normandy coast, quickly securing four beachheads. They were supplied by two massive floating docks that had been prefabricated in England and towed across the Channel to compensate for the absence of good harbors in the invasion zone. Within a week and a half the initial Allied invasion force had swollen to 640,000 well-equipped soldiers. The greatest amphibious operation in history was facilitated by the absence of effective resistance from the two arms of Hitler's war machine that had enabled it to subdue the entire continent of Europe four years earlier: the air force and the armored divisions. The Luftwaffe had been driven from the skies for lack of gasoline by the U. S. Army Air Corps' precision bombing of Germany's oil supply in the spring of 1944. The German tank units in northern France had been held in reserve until it was too late on the mistaken assumption that the Normandy invasion was an elaborate feint to lure the panzers into a trap. At the end of July the Allied forces smashed out of their coastal enclave and began a relentless offensive which, in conjunction with the northeastward advance of Anglo-American and Free French forces landed in southern France on August 15, cleared France of the German occupation army by the end of the year.

After flirting with the idea of subjecting liberated France to an Allied military occupation on the grounds that Marshal Pétain's collaboration with Germany had qualified his country for treatment as a defeated enemy, the United States government reluctantly recognized de Gaulle's French Committee of National Liberation as the de facto civil government of France on July 11. Roosevelt had long been contemptuous of the imperious leader of "Free France," suspecting him of harboring authoritarian plans for postwar France scarcely less objectionable than the current policies of Pétain. For his part, de Gaulle deeply resented the American president's decision to maintain diplomatic relations with the Vichy regime after the fall of France, his refusal to inform de Gaulle in advance of the Normandy invasion or to assign Free French forces an active role in it, and his ill-disguised efforts to promote the candidacies of rivals to de Gaulle within the French army. De Gaulle succeeded in elbowing his way into a position of supreme political authority in liberated France during the summer of 1944 and forced the United States to acknowledge his fait accompli. But his wartime dispute with Roosevelt left a legacy of bitterness and ill will which, as we shall see, was to have an unsettling effect on Franco-American relations in later years.

As the American, British, and Free French armies approached Germany's western frontier in the autumn of 1944, Soviet forces overran Bulgaria and Romania and advanced deep into Polish territory. In the winter of 1944–45, desperate German counteroffensives against the Western Allies in Belgium and against Soviet forces approaching Hungary temporarily postponed the inevitable collapse of Hitler's tottering empire in Central Europe. But in February 1945 the offensives on Germany's two flanks resumed. In early March the Anglo-American armies became the first military force to cross the Rhine in combat since Napoleon's day. The Soviet army in southern Europe took Budapest on its way to Vienna, while Soviet forces in the north decimated retreating German contingents along the Baltic coast in preparation for the march on Berlin.

The disintegration of the exhausted German armies before the advancing forces of the United States and its allies from the west and the Soviet Union from the east produced a vast military vacuum in the center of the European continent. The question inevitably arose: Which of the two invading armies would fill it? This was a question that was fraught with political as well as strategic overtones. In light of the radically dissimilar political, social, and economic systems of the Anglo-Americans and the Russians, which had given rise to intense mutual antagonism before they were thrown together in the joint crusade against Nazi Germany, it was inevitable that this ideological hostility would resurface once the military collapse of Germany removed the only important reason for them to continue to cooperate. On the Russian side, as we have seen, Stalin's distrust of his Western allies had originally been engendered by their hesitation to open a second front in France while the Red Army engaged nine-tenths of the German army in the east. It was increased in the spring of 1945 when Nazi military leaders approached American agents in neutral Switzerland with proposals for a separate peace in the west that would preserve a part of Germany's empire in the east. Neither the stellar performance of the American army in crushing German resistance in the west nor Washington's repeated promises to observe the policy of unconditional surrender, adopted by Roosevelt and Churchill at the Casablanca conference of January 1943, appeared to allay Stalin's fear that the Western capitalist powers planned to allow the doomed German army to engage Soviet forces in the east while Anglo-American troops prepared to thrust deep into the continent and dictate a political settlement in Eastern Europe at Russia's expense. Had Churchill's been the decisive voice in Allied military planning, the Russian dictator's assessment would not have been wide of the mark. Fervently anti-Communist and alarmed at Soviet designs on Eastern Europe, the British prime minister wanted the Allied forces that had penetrated western Germany to march as far east as Berlin and as far south as Prague, whence they would be in a strong position to bargain with the Russians over the political future of the former Nazi satellites.

But the American government rejected the Englishman's plan, as it had earlier turned down his project for a Balkan landing during the confer-

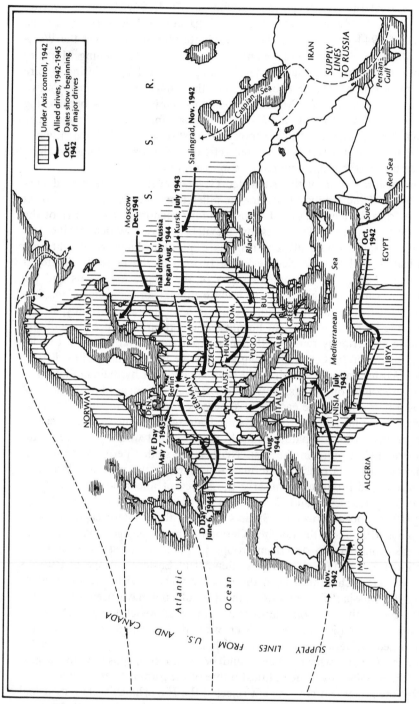

The Second World War in Europe, 1941–1945

ence in Teheran, on the grounds that it was unwise from a military point of view. The American president was counting on Russian assistance in the war against Japan in the Far East, which his generals told him could not be won before November 1946. He also assumed that the American people would not tolerate a continued American military presence in Europe for very long after the war and therefore regarded the Red Army as a useful deterrent to the resurgence of German military power. Consequently, Eisenhower's forces in Germany were instructed to halt their eastward march at the Elbe River while the Soviet army proceeded to liberate Berlin and Prague. On April 25 American and Russian soldiers shook hands at Torgau on the Elbe just northeast of Leipzig, and on May 1 Eisenhower and the Russian commanders agreed on a temporary military occupation line that left Soviet forces in control of all of Eastern Europe including the eastern halves of Germany and Austria. Hitler's suicide on April 30 in his Berlin bunker brought his thousand-year Reich to an end twelve years after its birth. German military authorities surrendered unconditionally at Eisenhower's headquarters in Rheims, France, on May 7, and again to the Russians in a separate ceremony in Berlin two days later.

The last year of the war against Hitler brought to the fore the question of how Germany and the vast territory on the continent that it had subjugated should be politically reorganized. It is scarcely surprising that little serious thought was devoted to the question of the postwar political settlement in Europe while the outcome of the military struggle remained in doubt. Before the summer of 1943, when the defeat of Germany looked likely with the Anglo-American landings in southern Italy and the Russian counteroffensive in eastern Europe, the war aims of the Allies were confined to vague generalities. Meeting at sea off the coast of Newfoundland in August 1941, Churchill and Roosevelt had signed the Atlantic Charter, which committed to the two English-speaking powers to work for a postwar international order reminiscent of the one that Wilson had vainly attempted to forge a generation earlier. They agreed to oppose all postwar territorial changes that violated the wishes of the populations concerned, to support the establishment of democratically elected governments in the regions emancipated from German rule, and to favor the creation of an international peacekeeping organization to supplant the moribund League of Nations. It was easy enough for the Soviet Union to endorse these neo-Wilsonian platitudes as a gesture of solidarity with its new British partner in the common struggle against Germany. But when London sounded out Moscow on its attitude toward specific matters, such as the principle of territorial transfer, it encountered Stalin's blunt assertion of his nation's right to retain the territory in Eastern Europe that it had forcibly acquired under the terms of the Nazi-Soviet Pact. Churchill reluctantly agreed to this concession to Stalin's understandable obsession with the security of Russia's western frontiers, even though it violated the Atlantic Charter's prohibition of forcibly imposed territorial changes.

After Pearl Harbor the American government, while shrinking from an official endorsement of Soviet claims on the Baltic states, eastern Poland, Rumania, and Finland, tacitly accepted them as inevitable in recognition of Russia's critical role in the Grand Alliance against Hitler.

The turning of the tide of war in the summer of 1943 forced the leaders of the anti-German coalition to confront seriously for the first time the long-deferred question of Europe's postwar political future. At the first joint meeting of Allied foreign ministers in Moscow in October 1943, plans were drawn up for the inter-Allied military occupation of Italy after the war. Despite Soviet efforts to obtain equal participation, effective power was placed in the hands of Anglo-American administrative authorities who accompanied the American and British armies on their northward march up the Italian peninsula. At the Teheran conference a month later, Stalin stubbornly reiterated his intention to retain Russia's territorial acquisitions of 1939–41 in Eastern Europe. The two Western leaders grudgingly gave way, on the condition that Poland's territorial losses in the east to Russia be compensated by the annexation of German territory in the west. No one thought to propose a plebiscite to consult the Poles earmarked for inclusion in the Soviet Union or the Germans to be incorporated in the reconstituted Polish state as it "moved west." Thus did the high-sounding idealism of the Atlantic Charter succumb to the practical requirements of Realpolitik in the midst of total war.

Once Roosevelt had definitively rejected Churchill's proposal at Teheran for an Anglo-American landing in the Balkans as a prelude to an offensive into the Danube Valley, Soviet domination of southeastern Europe was assured, just as Western primacy in Italy, France, the Low Countries, and Scandinavia had been foreordained by the liberation of those countries by American and British forces. By September 1944 Rumania and Bulgaria had capitulated to the Red Army, which was poised for an advance into Yugoslavia, Hungary, and Greece. The British prime minister thereupon hastily flew to Moscow in October to confirm and extend an informal understanding with the Russian leader on the future political orientation of the Balkan nations that had first been suggested by the British in June 1944. The architect of the Atlantic Charter and its principled commitment to national self-determination obtained Stalin's consent to a gentlemen's agreement allotting Romania, Bulgaria, and Hungary more or less to the Soviet sphere of influence, Greece to the Anglo-American sphere, with Yugoslavia to be split between them. President Roosevelt, though prevented from attending the Moscow conference by political obligations in his reelection campaign, was kept fully informed of the proceedings by his ambassador to Moscow, W. Averill Harriman. Roosevelt's subsequent failure to raise objections to this cynical bargain may be taken as a signal of Washington's tacit acceptance both of the sphere-of-influence approach to the political future of southeastern Europe and of the specific geographical divisions agreed to by Churchill and Stalin.

But the spirit of cooperation that had enabled the Allies to agree on the de facto partition of Southern Europe and to recognize Russia's right to retain her western borders of 1941 began to evaporate when the question arose concerning the fate of Germany and Poland, the two nations whose quarrel had precipitated the conflict in Europe that was drawing to a close. When the question of Germany's future status had been informally addressed at Teheran, the Big Three had seemed to agree that political disintegration represented the only effective solution to the "German problem" that had plunged Europe into two great wars in the first half of the century. Reviving proposals first aired by French right-wing publicists during the Paris Peace Conference in 1919, Churchill spoke of detaching from Germany its industrial heartland in the Rhineland-Westphalia region, of establishing a Central European federation linking the south German states, Austria, and Hungary. Stalin forcefully pressed for the political dismemberment of the nation whose expansionist policy had brought such ruin to his own country. The original American proposal to solve the German problem was equally harsh, but characteristically economic in character. At the Anglo-American conference in Quebec in September 1944, Roosevelt obtained Churchill's tentative agreement to a scheme devised by Treasury Secretary Henry Morgenthau that envisioned the destruction of Germany's industrial plant and the reduction of the country to agricultural status. But by the time of the summit meeting at the resort city of Yalta on Russia's Crimean peninsula in February 1945, the Anglo-American position on the political and economic future of Germany had undergone a fundamental shift from the vindictive schemes entertained at Teheran and Quebec. With Allied military forces deep in German territory and the Third Reich on the brink of collapse, British and American officials began to have second thoughts about the consequences of Germany's political and economic disintegration. Some of the same considerations that had prompted Wilson and Lloyd George to oppose Clemenceau's harsh plans for postwar Germany at Paris a quarter of a century earlier inspired Roosevelt's and Churchill's resistance to Stalin's stringent demands for reparations and political dismemberment at Yalta: The total disappearance of German power in Central Europe would leave a vacuum in that region that Russia was bound to fill; and the crippling of the German economic system through excessive reparation demands would have a deleterious effect on the rest of the industrial world. While no definitive decision was reached on the twin issues of reparations and the political future of Germany, the Yalta Conference produced an agreement on the temporary partition of the country into military occupation zones. The Soviet army would occupy the territory east of the Elbe that it was in the process of liberating from Hitler's retreating forces. The remainder would be occupied by the armies of the United States, Great Britain, and France (whose participation Churchill demanded for fear that American military forces would be withdrawn from

Europe as they had been after the last war, leaving Britain facing Russia alone). As in 1919, the controversial issue of reparations was submitted to a commission for recommendations.

The long-simmering dispute over the political future of Poland became the major bone of contention between the western and eastern members of the Grand Alliance at Yalta. In April 1943 Stalin had abruptly withdrawn diplomatic recognition of the pro-Western Polish government in exile headquartered in London when it appeared to give credence to Nazi accusations that Soviet military forces in Poland had massacred ten thousand Polish officers during the period of Soviet cooperation with Germany. Shortly thereafter Stalin gave his official blessing to a rival group of Polish exiles in Russia which disputed the London Poles' claim to political legitimacy. On July 23, 1944, a pro-Soviet Polish Committee of National Liberation was established in the Polish city of Lublin after its capture by the Red Army. On August 1, in response to an appeal from the London Polish group, the 46,000 members of the Warsaw underground rose against the German occupation army and were joined by most of the city's civilian population. At the time of the Warsaw uprising the Red Army had smashed through the German defenses to within six miles of the city while Radio Moscow broadcast messages of support for the insurrection. But the Soviet forces abruptly halted their advance and withdrew several miles from the city, permitting the German occupying army to crush the uprising by the end of September. Churchill's appeal to Stalin for permission for Anglo-American planes based in Italy to land on Soviet airfields after bomb attacks and parachute drops in support of the Warsaw uprising fell on deaf ears in the Kremlin. The consequent death of thousands of Polish partisans wiped out the impressive political and military organization that the London Poles had succeeded in establishing in the occupied country, thereby paving the way for the pro-Soviet rival group that accompanied the advancing Red Army. In January 1945, with Soviet military forces in occupation of the entire prewar territory of Poland, the Kremlin installed the pro-Russian Polish faction in Warsaw and accorded it formal diplomatic recognition.

At Yalta, Roosevelt and Churchill obtained Stalin's agreement to add non-Communist resistance leaders to the recently established provisional government. They also wrested from him the pledge that free elections, Western style, would be conducted in Poland after the end of the war to enable that country to determine its own future form of government. This promise was subsequently extended to the entire continent through the adoption by the Big Three of the American-sponsored Declaration on Liberated Europe. Roosevelt returned home to die in April from the mortal illness that was already in evidence during the Crimean meeting, apparently convinced that the "spheres of influence" formula adopted by Stalin and Churchill at Moscow four months earlier had been superseded by a neo-Wilsonian principle of national self-determination that revived the spirit of the Atlantic Charter. His successor, Harry S Truman, believed even more resolutely in this version of the wartime agreements concerning the political future of Europe.

Stalin returned to his capital apparently assuming that the informal understanding on the spheres of influence previously reached with Churchill remained in effect and that the Yalta declaration represented nothing more than rhetorical window dressing, perhaps to placate voters of East European descent in the United States. Western journalists and politicians had often spoken of the need to establish a postwar consortium consisting of the three great powers in the anti-German coalition, each of which would ensure peace and stability by exercising paramount influence in its own orbit. At Teheran, Roosevelt had broached to Stalin his neo-Metternichian project of the "Four Policemen"–the United States, Great Britain, the Soviet Union, and China–that were to maintain order in the world after the defeat of the Axis. The decision at Teheran to permit the Russian army to liberate the Balkans, the bargain in Moscow delineating the victors' respective spheres of influence in that region–all of this apparently led Stalin to believe that the old concept of the concert of great powers would continue to operate in peacetime as it had during the war. Thus, the Soviet leader proceeded to execute the provisions of the Moscow accord, which had formed the basis of the armistice agreements concluded with the former Nazi satellites in Eastern Europe that lay within the Soviet sphere. Russian members of the control commissions in Romania, Bulgaria, and Hungary bypassed their Anglo-American colleagues to assure Soviet predominance, just as the British and Americans ignored the Soviet representatives on the control commission in Italy, which, although not covered by the percentages agreement, clearly lay within the Western sphere of influence. When a civil war spontaneously erupted in Greece during the winter of 1944–45 between Communist and anti-Communist factions within the resistance movement, Stalin withheld support from the Greek Communist insurgents, thereby enabling the pro-Western government in Athens to retain its power with British military assistance. The Communist parties in France and Italy, whose ideology had previously prevented them from participating in "bourgeois" political administrations, were urged by the Kremlin to accept subordinate positions in non-Communist coalitions and to behave with unaccustomed moderation despite their newly acquired status as the strongest political parties in their respective countries. This was because Stalin recognized those two countries, which had been liberated by Anglo-American military forces, as belonging within the Western zone of influence. As the European war drew to a close in the spring of 1945, the impending military triumph of the Grand Alliance necessitated a resolution of these contradictory versions of the wartime decisions regarding the political reorganization of liberated Europe. Would the spirit of Metternich or the spirit of Wilson prevail?

CHAPTER 6

The Confirmation of United States Supremacy in Latin America

The Era of Direct Domination (1914–1932)

We have earlier noted how the Caribbean Sea was transformed into a veritable American lake between the end of the Spanish-American War and the beginning of World War I. Through a combination of financial supervision, commercial penetration, diplomatic agreements regulating relations with foreign nations, and the occasional application of military force, the United States had acquired effective control of the political and economic systems of some of the islands in the Caribbean and the mainland republics of Central America that had achieved independence from their European colonial masters in the course of the nineteenth century. The European powers, particularly Great Britain, acquiesced in this extension of American hegemony because their national energies were absorbed by their own colonial rivalries in Africa and Asia as well as by the power struggles in Europe that resulted in the First World War. It was the war itself that confirmed American supremacy in the Caribbean region and facilitated the expansion of American economic power to the continent of South America as well, for reasons presently to be discussed.

Historians have often remarked upon the irony that Woodrow Wilson, champion of national self-determination and critic of his Republican predecessor's "dollar diplomacy" in Latin America, conducted more military and diplomatic interventions south of the border than any American president before or since. It is apparent from his private observations as well as his public declarations that Wilson had genuinely persuaded himself of the essential morality of his interventionist policies in the Caribbean: A passionate proponent of good government, he cringed at the widespread corruption, inefficiency, autocracy, and social unrest that was conspicuously in evidence among America's southern neighbors. Just as he had sought to cleanse the political institutions of New Jersey and then of Washington, this progressive idealist set out to impose order, honesty, and efficiency on the Caribbean republics for their own good.

But beneath this disinterested idealistic position lay the same preoccupation that had prompted the interventionist policies of Roosevelt and Taft in the era of Republican supremacy: the fear that political revolution, social instability, and financial collapse in the Caribbean region would tempt the great powers of Europe to intervene to protect the lives and investments of their citizens. The prospect of European powers militarily ensconced, or even financially engaged, in a region critical to the security of the canal that had been opened in the summer of 1914 as the war clouds appeared in Europe was more than any American president could tolerate.

Consequently, behind a smokescreen of progressive rhetoric about America's obligation to foster good government in its own hemisphere, Woodrow Wilson resumed the Roosevelt-Taft policies of military intervention and dollar diplomacy in Latin America. The first beneficiary of this new form of American heavyhandedness couched in the language of Wilsonian benevolence was Nicaragua. The Bryan-Chamorro Treaty (signed on August 5, 1914, and ratified two years later) transferred supervisory authority over the finances of that nation from American private banking interests to a commission controlled directly from Washington. The United States government advanced funds to the financially strapped Nicaraguan regime to reduce its public debt in return for an exclusive concession to construct a trans-Isthmian canal and to establish naval bases at its two termina. The object of this agreement was to protect the northern land approach to the Panama Canal, preclude any future European-constructed canal along the alternative Nicaraguan route, and rehabilitate the finances of this perpetually insolvent nation so as to remove any possible pretext for European intervention. The American marine contingent that had been landed in 1912 was retained and augmented to provide the requisite armed support for the policy of financial reorganization then undertaken.

Similar instances of social unrest and financial instability in the adjacent states of the Dominican Republic and Haiti on the island of Hispaniola elicited similar intimations of European intervention and, consequently, a similar preemptive response from Washington. The reader will recall that a default on foreign loans by the Dominican government in 1904 had resulted in the establishment of a customs receivership in the hands of an agent appointed by the president of the United States who was empowered to distribute the customs receipts of Dominican ports to foreign creditors. As in so many of previous and subsequent instances of American financial intervention in the Caribbean, this policy was motivated by the obsession with removing any pretext for intervention by European nations on behalf of their aggrieved bondholders. The rapid breakdown of social order and the attendant possibility of financial collapse in the Dominican Republic during Wilson's first term once again raised the prospect of European intervention in that beleaguered country. To avert such a possibility the United States undertook to supervise national elections in 1914 and then to dispatch marines in 1916 to preserve order and assure American financial control.

In the contiguous republic of Haiti, the possibility that Germany would exploit that nation's perennial political unrest and financial difficulties by seizing control of its customs houses to ensure the service of its huge foreign debt inspired great unease in Washington. So too did the prospect of German naval bases in Haiti that would command the passage between Hispaniola and Cuba to the Panama Canal. When revolutionary disorders continued to rage, Wilson resolved to act unilaterally to preempt any such European involvement in Haitian affairs. Marines were dispatched in 1915 to protect foreign lives and property, American banks were persuaded to lend funds to the Haitian government to enable it to consolidate and refund its foreign debt, an American financial adviser assumed control of the national finances, an American receiver-general was installed to supervise the collection of customs receipts, and American military officers took charge of the Haitian police forces. A new constitution (drafted by Assistant Secretary of the Navy Franklin D. Roosevelt) transformed Haiti into an American protectorate. In the same year the Wilson administration reintroduced military forces into Cuba (from which they had been withdrawn in 1909) and purchased the Danish West Indies (renamed the Virgin Islands) from Denmark under the implied threat of seizure, all in the interest of keeping the European belligerents out of the "American lake."

Wilson's most spectacular intervention in Latin America ironically took place in a nation that had been relatively well disposed to the United States and was scarcely in danger of falling under the sway of the European powers. Of all the nations of Latin America, Mexico had retained the most cordial relations with the United States since the end of the American Civil War. Resentment at the territorial losses to its northern neighbor in the mid–nineteenth century had been attenuated by the American government's decisive role in pressuring France to withdraw its military forces from Mexico in 1867. This led to the overthrow by Mexican nationalists of the French satellite empire headed by the Austrian archduke Maximilian. As we have seen, between 1876 and 1910 Mexican dictator Porfirio Diaz eagerly solicited American capital investment in Mexican land, natural resources, railroads, and public utilities. But the Mexican Revolution of 1910–11 which ousted Diaz had plunged that nation into a social and political upheaval that seriously menaced these American properties and investments. The assumption of dictatorial power by President Victoriano Huerta in February 1913 offended the democratic sensibilities of President Wilson, who withheld diplomatic recognition and attempted to topple the new Mexican strongman by permitting American arms shipments to his "Constitutionalist" enemies who controlled most of the northern sector of the country. The arrest in April 1914 of American sailors on shore leave in the Caribbean port of Tampico, though in fact nothing more than a spontaneous indiscretion by an overly zealous subordinate, was viewed in Washington as a retaliatory action by the Mexican president that deserved and required punishment. Consequently, American naval units occupied the port of Vera Cruz and war between the two countries was narrowly averted before a compromise settlement facilitated their evacuation seven months later. In March 1916 one of the Constitutionalist leaders, Pancho Villa, eager to provoke American intervention in the Mexican civil war so that he could unite his divided country against the common enemy to the north, launched a raid on an American border town in New Mexico. In retaliation, Wilson dispatched a punitive military expedition under General John J. Pershing deep into the Mexican interior in pursuit of the "bandit" leader. The ostensible purpose of this quixotic adventure was to impress upon the Mexicans the necessity of establishing a democratic government capable of preserving social order. After angry protests from the Mexican government and clashes with Mexican military forces, the American troops were finally withdrawn on February 5, 1917, two days after Washington's severence of diplomatic relations with Berlin over the issue of unrestricted submarine warfare foreordained America's intervention in the European war.

The Wilson administration's resumption of the Roosevelt-Taft policy of military intervention and financial supervision in the Caribbean occurred at a time when the United States was rapidly expanding its economic power to the continent of South America. In the aftermath of the Spanish American War, United States commercial and financial involvement in Latin America was concentrated almost exclusively in the neighboring Caribbean islands and the nations of Central America. Between 1898 and 1914, American investment south of the border had increased from $320 million to $1.7 billion, with Mexico and Cuba together accounting for almost a third of the total. Despite the beginning of American economic activity in the larger nations of South America, the foreign trade and financial relations of those republics were still centered on Europe. At the turn of the century, Great Britain was still the prime source of foreign capital for Latin America as a whole, its direct and portfolio investments in the region totaling $2.5 billion. By 1914 total British investment in Latin America had increased to about $3.7 billion, with Argentina and Brazil receiving 60 percent of the total and Chile, Peru, Mexico, and Uruguay taking most of the remainder. France became a major investor in Latin America after 1880, increasing its total commitment in the region threefold between 1900 and 1914 to $1.2 billion. Approximately $900 million of German foreign investment was in Latin America by 1914, principally in Argentina, Brazil, Chile, and Mexico. Thus, at the beginning of the First World War, the value of Britain's investment in the region roughly equalled that of her three principal foreign competitors combined (Table VIII).

Collectively, the major European economic powers supplied the Latin American republics with the largest proportion of their investment capital and manufactured products while receiving in exchange the bulk of their

TABLE VIII   Nominal Value of Foreign Investment in Latin America in 1914

Creditor Country	Billions of Dollars
Great Britain	3.7
United States	1.7
France	1.2
Germany	0.9
Others	1.0

Source: Marvin D. Bernstein, ed., *Foreign Investment in Latin America* (New York: Alfred A. Knopf, 1966), p. 40.

agricultural and mineral exports. But the First World War abruptly severed these financial and commercial connections between Latin America and the old world. The British blockade and the German submarine campaign, together with the diversion of European industrial production, capital investment, and merchant shipping to war-related purposes, deprived Latin America of the foreign trade and financial assistance that had previously flowed across the Atlantic.

Into the economic vacuum in Latin America produced by the reduction of European trade and investment during the war stepped the powerful, prosperous, neutral state from the north. American manufacturers captured markets previously dominated by European exporters. American agricultural, mining, and petroleum interests wrested control of Latin American land and subsoil resources from British, French, and German firms. When Great Britain and France were forced to curtail their investments in Latin America in order to finance their war effort and German holdings in the region were either sold or confiscated, American lenders promptly replaced their European competitors as the prime source of investment capital. During the war the dollar value of American investments in the region increased by about 50 percent. By the end of the war, the inflow of American capital had paved the way for the spectacular expansion of United States investment in and trade with Latin America during the 1920s as the European powers found it impossible to regain their prewar position as bankers and trading partners of the region.

The spurt of American investment in the economies of the Latin American republics after the war was facilitated by the passage in 1919 of the Edge Act, which authorized for the first time the establishment of foreign branches of American banking institutions. This legislation afforded American investors, who had previously been required to conduct their financial operations through the British banking system and its vast network of international affiliates, direct access to the money markets of the various Latin American states. Wall Street banks lent ever-increasing sums to national and municipal governments, as well as to private corporations, whose securities could no longer find a market in a Europe struggling to satisfy its own substantial capital requirements in the period of postwar reconstruction. During the second half of the 1920s Latin America absorbed 24 percent of the new capital issues floated for foreign account.

Accompanying this notable increase in United States portfolio investment in Latin American countries was a spectacular upsurge in direct investment. Channeled principally into electrical utilities, railroads, mining, petroleum, and tropical plantation agriculture, American direct investment in Latin America increased almost threefold between 1914 and 1929. By the latter date it had come to represent 44 percent of total United States direct investment abroad. The combined total nominal value of American direct and portfolio investment in Latin America had more than doubled in the decade after 1919, while British investments in the region remained roughly unchanged and those of France and Germany declined dramatically.

This strong investment position enabled the American financial community to acquire a large measure of control over the fiscal and monetary policies of the recipient nations. The effects of this economic power were naturally felt most directly in those countries, such as Nicaragua, Haiti, and the Dominican Republic, whose financial institutions had come under direct American supervisory control. But even such nominally independent states as Cuba, Brazil, Chile, and Venezuela became so dependent on American investment that most of their tax revenues were generated from economic activities directed by American banks and corporations. Decisions taken in the boardrooms of these American-based institutions often had an immediate and decisive impact on the budgetary policies of Latin American governments (and therefore on the distribution of national wealth). The sharp increase of American capital investment in Latin America during the First World War transpired amid a remarkable expansion of inter-American trade. The three years of American neutrality hastened the process whereby the United States replaced Britain as the region's principal trading partner for the reasons sketched above. After the war, operating under the provisions of the Webb-Pomerene Act (which exempted firms engaged in the export trade from the application of antitrust laws), American conglomerates continued to supplant weaker European export firms in the Latin American market. United States exports to Latin America tripled in value from 1914 to 1929 and by the latter year accounted for almost 40 percent of the region's total imports. In exchange for its sales of manufactured goods, the United States became the major customer for Latin America's primary products (principally subsoil minerals and tropical foodstuffs), taking almost a third of Latin America's total exports by the end of the 1920s.

In different circumstances this inter-American commercial relationship might have matured into a mutually beneficial exchange of surplus products between complementary economic systems. Instead, it degenerated into a neocolonial relationship from which one party derived extensive benefits while the other became locked into a system of abject dependence.

The unequal nature of inter-American trading patterns that emerged in the postwar period can be traced to several sources. The first of these was the tendency of American firms and their financial backers to acquire through direct investment a controlling interest in the principal export industries of many Latin American nations. Examples of this overwhelming domination abound. American capital came to represent 92 percent of the total investment in Chilean copper mines. American oil companies, after forcing out their European competitors, acquired control of over half of Venezuela's petroleum production. Two-thirds of the Cuban sugar crop was owned by American producing and refining corporations. Two American firms, the United Fruit Company and the Standard Fruit Company, together enjoyed a monopoly of the banana plantations of Guatemala, Honduras, Nicaragua, and Panama. This extraordinary degree of foreign ownership resulted in the repatriation of profits generated from the exploitation of these national resources rather than reinvestment in the infrastructure of the host country. This diverted scarce capital that might otherwise have financed projects of domestic economic development that would have increased the nation's productive capacity and raised the standard of living of the indigenous population.

The second adverse feature of this pattern of inter-American commercial exchange from the Latin American point of view was the propensity of United States direct investment to promote the intensive development of a single export crop or commodity in each country at the expense of product diversification. This tendency to "put all one's eggs in one basket" rendered most Latin American nations tragically vulnerable to the wild fluctuations of commodity prices that characterized the 1920s. When the world prices of sugar, coffee, copper, and other commodities dropped precipitously, as they frequently did during this period, the national economies for which exports of these primary products represented virtually the only source of hard currency were plunged into severe crises.

Finally, the commanding share of the Latin American export trade acquired by the United States during and after the First World War created a relationship of dominance-subservience that naturally extended to other matters as well. The extent of this export dependence was to reach incredible extremes in some cases: In the year 1937 the United States was purchasing 80 percent of Cuba's exports, 88 percent of those of Honduras, and 91 percent of those of Panama. No nation whose domestic prosperity depended so heavily on unimpeded access to the American market could be expected to withstand pressure from Washington to adjust their foreign and internal policies to the requirements of the national interest of the United States.

Were the independent states of Latin America condemned to languish in a position of perpetual subservience to their powerful northern neighbor? As noted earlier, the reduction of Europe's economic stake in Latin America as a consequence of the First World War removed whatever advantage the Latin republics had derived from United States-European rivalry in the region. In light of the striking imbalance of economic and military power in the Western Hemisphere, the only alternative to a destiny of continual inferiority for the individual states south of the North American giant was progress toward the type of political and economic integration on a continental scale that the United States had achieved in North America.

Sentiment for the unification of Latin America had surfaced soon after the expulsion of Spanish and Portuguese authority in the first quarter of the nineteenth century. Under the inspiration of the great liberator, Simon Bolivár, the Congress of Panama in 1826 produced a number of resolutions aimed at amalgamating the Spanish and Portuguese successor states in order more effectively to combat the anticipated menace of intervention by the European powers. But only four Latin American republics sent representatives to that conference, and only Bolivár's Colombia ratified the agreements on continental cooperation that were concluded. Three more Latin American congresses met during the nineteenth century, usually in response to the threat or reality of foreign intervention in the hemisphere. But these four conferences (1826, 1847–48, 1856, and 1864–65) produced nothing more promising than a single, innocuous consular convention ratified by the few states that bothered to send delegates. Instead of advancing toward some form of continental integration, the successor states of Latin America were plagued by the opposite tendency of political disintegration after the withdrawal of Spanish and Portuguese authority. The United Provinces of Central America seceded from Mexico in 1823, then shattered into five small republics in 1840. The Gran Colombia of Bolivár eventually split into Venezuela, Colombia, and Ecuador, and the rump state of Colombia subsequently lost its province of Panama in 1903. The Dominican Republic seceded from Haiti in 1844. As we have seen, Mexico lost half its territory to the United States at midcentury. The combination of geographical isolation, poor communications, and fierce national rivalries nipped in the bud all integrationist tendencies, even when the advantages of Latin American cooperation became so apparent during the achievement of United States supremacy in the twentieth century.

The persistence of these centrifugal forces suggested that the unification of Latin America stood the best chance of success under the aegis of one or the other of those regional powers that exhibited some of the characteristics traditionally associated with a leadership role. Brazil, comprising almost half of the territory and over a third of the population of the South American continent, was the obvious candidate to become the "Prussia" of Latin America. But Brazil's historic rivalry with the other potential unifier of the continent, Argentina, not to speak of the linguistic barrier separating the only Portuguese-speaking nation of the hemisphere from its Spanish-speaking neighbors, prevented it from assuming continental leadership. Instead of becoming an instigator of Latin American integrationist sentiment in opposition to North American domination, Brazil was to become the United States' most loyal supporter in the region. This political cooperation was enhanced by a profitable economic relationship based on American purchases of Brazil's principal export crop, coffee, a commodity which enjoyed great popularity in the United States and was not grown domestically.

Brazil's reluctance to spearhead a movement of Latin American solidarity in resistance to American hegemony left Argentina as the sole aspirant to such a position after the First World War. The special geographical and economic advantage enjoyed by Argentina enabled it to adopt an independent posture in hemispheric affairs that frequently brought it into direct conflict with Washington. Its geographical location at the southern extremity of South America rendered it less susceptible to American military and naval intimidation. Moreover, unlike any other South American country, its major exports (beef and grain) competed with rather than complemented American exports and therefore precluded the type of cooperative economic relationship that had developed between the United States and Brazil. On the contrary, American farmers obtained extensive tariff protection against Argentinian grain and Western ranchers were insulated against competition from Argentinian cattle in the form of a stringent sanitary prohibition of beef imports from regions infected by foot-and-mouth disease (a persistent condition in the Pampas). This closure of the American market impelled Argentina to preserve and extend its commercial relationship with Europe during the very period that her sister republics were submitting to the domination of American trade. As late as 1937, Argentina's imports from the United States accounted for only 16.1 percent of its total foreign trade while it received 59.1 percent of its imports from Europe. In the same year Argentina shipped only 12.8 percent of its exports to the United States compared to 74.3 percent to Europe. This European commercial orientation was reinforced by the presence of substantial numbers of first-generation immigrants in Argentina from countries of the old world (principally Germany and Italy) who retained close ties to their homelands. The combination of these geographical, economic, and cultural factors helped to place Argentina beyond the reach of American power in Latin America and enabled her to mount a spirited challenge to American hemispheric hegemony.

The rallying cry of Argentina's campaign to organize Latin American sentiment in opposition to United States domination was the ideology of pan-Hispanic solidarity, which it trumpeted as a preferable alternative to the Pan-American ideology that the United States had employed since the end of the nineteenth century as a means of mobilizing its Latin American clients. But in light of the patent inequality of power in the Western Hemisphere, the likelihood of Latin American solidarity and independence was problematical so long as the United States continued to enjoy the prerogative of intervening directly in the domestic affairs of Latin American nations to protect the lives of American citizens, preserve social order, and collect public debts from governments that refused to submit disputes with foreign investors to international arbitration. Consequently, it was the issue of the right of intervention that became the focal point of the Argentinian-led assault on United States hegemony that enlivened the periodic Pan-American conferences of the 1920s. This prerogative, which was both generally recognized in international law and specifically codified in the Roosevelt Corollary of the Monroe Doctrine, was periodically reasserted by the American government. The right of foreign intervention was deeply resented by the nations of Latin America as a humiliating limitation to national sovereignty much in the same way that the principle of extraterritoriality engendered fierce opposition in China (see p. 238). In vain did the southern republics endeavor to secure acceptance by the United States of the Calvo Doctrine (after the Argentinian jurist Carlos Calvo) which asserted the principle of a sovereign state's absolute immunity from external intervention and recognized the judicial system of the host nation as the final authority in disputes involving foreign citizens or corporations. Though most Latin American nations customarily inserted a "Calvo clause" in contracts signed with foreign investors (to preclude their appealing to their home governments for diplomatic support in disputes with the host government), the United States stubbornly declined to relinquish its right to intervene on behalf of its aggrieved citizens if the host country refused to arbitrate.

The Latin American states just as resolutely refused to recognize the obligation to submit to international arbitration disputes between a host government and citizens of a foreign government, denouncing it as an intolerable infringement on national sovereignty. They pressed instead for the codification of an inter-American system of international law that would enshrine the principle of absolute equality and sovereignty of the nations of the Western Hemisphere. The United States, for its part, opposed the concept of a regional international law that would deprive it of the traditional right of intervention sanctioned by international legal precedent. Between 1889–90 (the meeting of the first Pan-American Conference) and 1928 (the sixth conference at Havana), the Colossus of the North and its Latin American clients periodically sparred over this divisive issue. At the Havana Conference, in response to the introduction of a formal resolution prohibiting intervention, United States delegate Charles Evans Hughes mounted his country's last defense of its absolute right to intervene in its hemisphere to preserve internal stability and national independence. That this dispute represented more than mere legalistic wrangling was attested to by the conspicuous presence of American military forces in Nicaragua and Haiti as well as by the legal constraints on the sovereignty of Cuba and Panama that remained in force as the delegates deliberated.

In addition to this Latin American campaign on behalf of the doctrine of absolute nonintervention, there were other indications of mounting resistance to American hemispheric hegemony. The first of these was the refusal of most Latin American states to follow the lead of the United States in the First World War. In contrast to the British Dominions, which enthusiastically rallied to the side of the mother country and made important contributions to the British victory, only eight of the twenty Latin American republics (of which seven were tiny Caribbean and Central American nations under direct American domination) declared war on Germany. Such geographically strategic states as Mexico, Colombia, and Venezuela maintained a position of strict neutrality.

This spirit of independence from American foreign policy resurfaced in the postwar period. All of the Latin American republics joined the League of Nations at one time or another after that world body had been repudiated and shunned by the United States. Fifteen of them sat in the first Assembly of the League; the presidency of the Assembly was often occupied by a Latin American delegate; Latin American nonpermanent seats in the League Council increased from one to three in the course of the 1920s. The very fact of Latin American membership and active participation in the international organization signified a defiant repudiation of the United States' conception of a self-enclosed inter-American security system. But Latin American efforts to employ the League as a counterweight to United States power in the Western Hemisphere were uniformly unsuccessful. It was precisely such a possibility that had inspired American insistence on the inclusion in the League Covenant of article 21, which specifically denied League jurisdiction over matters within the purview of the Monroe Doctrine. Latin American attempts to persuade the League to repudiate this endorsement of American hegemony in the Western Hemisphere failed to budge the cautious European governments that dominated the League Council and were reluctant to antagonize the United States. As a consequence, the League was able to intervene in inter-American conflicts on only two occasions (and then only after having secured the prior approval of Washington), successfully in the Letitia conflict between Peru and Colombia (1932–35), unsuccessfully in the Chaco War between Bolivia and Paraguay (1928–38).

To recapitulate: Between 1914 and 1929 the United States definitively replaced Great Britain as the dominant commercial and financial power in Latin America after having successfully challenged British diplomatic and naval supremacy in the region at the end of the nineteenth century. Direct American military domination and financial control of Cuba, Panama, Haiti, the Dominican Republic, and Nicaragua, together with the acquisition of the Virgin Islands from Denmark, completed the process of domination of the Caribbean region begun before the First World War. The establishment of undisputed strategic mastery of the Caribbean and economic preponderance in South America was facilitated by the weakening of European economic power in the Western Hemisphere during the war and then confirmed by the inability of the exhausted European states to recapture their prewar position in the 1920s. Latin American efforts to counter the southward advance of American power through some form of continental cooperation were frustrated by Brazil's reluctance to renounce its privileged relationship with the United States and the unwillingness of the other republics to follow Argentina's lead in directly challenging American encroachments on Latin American sovereignty. The promise of collective security represented by the League of Nations proved illusory because of the European powers' hesitation to risk Washington's displeasure by supporting the extension of the League's protection to the nations within the inter-American security system formed and dominated by the United States.

The Era of Indirect Hegemony (1933–1945)

The United States' acquisition of undisputed hegemony over Latin America during the First World War and the succeeding decade removed the traditional justification for the employment of military force to forestall European intervention in the Western Hemisphere. This new situation of absolute immunity from trans-Atlantic threats, which was confirmed by the abolition of the German navy at the Paris Peace Conference of 1919 and the limitations on naval construction adopted by the other maritime powers at the Washington Conference of 1921–22, enabled Washington to adopt less overtly coercive means of preserving its position of hemispheric dominance. As Latin American criticism of heavy-handed American intervention and the legal principles upon which it was based reached a crescendo toward the end of the 1920s, the direct methods of military force and diplomatic intimidation gradually gave way to a more subtle, but scarcely less effective, mechanism for maintaining control of the client states south of the border.

The first direct challenge to American power in Latin America was to come from the contiguous nation of Mexico, that once proud country that had lost half of its territory to the United States in the middle of the nineteenth century, endured American military and naval interventions between 1914 and 1917, and seen most of its natural resources and valuable land fall into the hands of American investors and corporations. Memories of past humiliations, mingled with the daily experience of economic subservience, rekindled the spirit of resentment toward the powerful neighbor north of the Rio Grande. These long-suppressed grievances bubbled to the surface as the last contingent of American troops that had been dispatched southward by President Wilson to suppress "banditry" was withdrawn in February 1917 once the American chief executive was satisfied that representative government was about to be restored. It is supremely ironic that the democratic government that Wilson had insisted upon with such unbending determination proceeded in one of its first official acts to adopt a national constitution that contained a number of articles designed to liberate Mexico from the economic domination of foreign nations in general and the United States in particular. The most controversial of these constitutional safeguards vested in the Mexican nation ownership of all the subsoil resources of the country (of which petroleum was indisputably the most valuable). Soon thereafter this constitutional provision was judged by the Mexican government to apply retroactively: This signified the loss of title to hundreds of millions of dollars worth of oil reserves owned by American petroleum companies. It is worth pausing to record that this unilateral action by the Mexican government constituted a landmark in the history of the relations between the developed and the underdeveloped world; it was the first attempt by a country whose economic system had fallen under the *de facto* control of foreign interests to assert its prerogative to exercise exclusive legal authority over its own natural resources.

This unprecedented gesture of defiance did not immediately produce the desired result. The American government, under intense pressure from petroleum interests with extensive Mexican holdings, wielded every diplomatic weapon short of economic retaliation—including the policy of non-recognition—to induce Mexico City to reverse its course. A compromise of sorts was reached in 1923, whereby the United States acknowledged Mexico's right to exercise authority over its subsoil resources in return for Mexican acknowledgment of the legal sanctity of contracts held by American oil companies prior to the adoption of the 1917 constitution. A similar compromise was struck in 1927, following a temporary revival of the dispute over retroactivity, which remained in force until 1938. In the latter year the Mexican government settled the matter for good by expropriating the property of British, Dutch, and American oil companies after they refused to abide by the ruling of the Mexican judicial system in a labor dispute.

Efforts by the expropriated American oil companies to organize an international boycott of Mexican crude in retaliation failed because of the eagerness of Germany, Italy, and Japan to purchase this critical source of energy as their rearmament programs got into high gear. American concern about the potential threat to national security posed by the development of intimate economic ties between Mexico and the Axis powers eventually took precedence over the parochial interests of the oil firms. A mutually acceptable agreement was signed a few weeks before Pearl Harbor whereby Mexico retained control of its oil reserves in return for a promise of financial compensation to the dispossessed American companies. Having extracted this major concession from the United States, Mexico was to become a loyal supporter and supplier of the American war effort, in sharp contrast to its defiant posture of absolute neutrality during the First World War.

Mexico's persistent (and eventually successful) campaign to reassert control of its national economic resources became an inspiration for burgeoning nationalist movements in other Latin American countries, which brought increasing pressure to bear on their governments to challenge the United States' refusal to acknowledge the prerogative of a sovereign nation to exercise political authority over people and property within its borders. We have seen how Latin American attempts to gain American recognition of this right at the Pan-American conferences of the 1920s met with failure. At the sixth conference of the American states in 1928, United States delegate Charles Evans Hughes' reference to a "breakdown of government" as sufficient justification for American intervention seemed so broad and imprecise as to justify virtually unlimited interference in the domestic affairs of the sovereign states of Latin America.

Yet, by the early 1930s, the presence of American military forces in the Caribbean region had become a source of acute embarrassment to the United States as it endeavored to mobilize world opinion against Japan's expansionist policies in the Far East. The Japanese incursion in Manchuria had been officially justified by Tokyo as a necessary step to protect Japanese citizens and property endangered by Chinese lawlessness; such language was uncomfortably reminiscent of the rationale invoked by the United States in defense of its military interventions south of the Rio Grande. Sensitive to the mounting allegations of hypocrisy that emanated from the world community, the new administration of Franklin Roosevelt that took office in 1933 inaugurated a dramatic modification of the Latin American policy of the United States. The groundwork for this change had been laid by the Hoover administration in 1930, when the State Department published a lengthy memorandum composed by Under Secretary of State J. Reuben Clark that repudiated the Roosevelt Corollary to the Monroe Doctrine as a justification for the American right of intervention in Latin America. Though the Clark Memorandum was replete with qualifications and did not receive much serious attention from American officials, it heralded a new attitude toward inter-American relations that had begun to crystallize in Washington. Before leaving office, the Hoover administration undertook a systemic reevaluation of the interventionist policy that had been pursued by every American president since Theodore Roosevelt.

In his inaugural address on March 4, 1933, Franklin Roosevelt declared that in the field of foreign policy he "would dedicate this Nation to the policy of the good neighbor who resolutely respects himself, and, because he does so, respects the rights of others." There was no reason for his listeners to believe that this innocuous phrase applied specifically to Latin America, since no geographical region was mentioned in the speech. But a month later, speaking at the office of the Pan American Union, the new American president mentioned the need for hemispheric cooperation in such conciliatory tones that commentators were soon hailing the new "good neighbor policy" of the United States toward Latin America. Later in 1933, at the seventh conference of the American states in Montevideo,

Uruguay, this presidential rhetoric was translated into government policy. The new secretary of state, Cordell Hull, abruptly reversed a long-standing American policy by supporting a resolution prohibiting any nation in the Western Hemisphere from intervening "in the internal or external affairs of another." By this historic act the Calvo doctrine, resisted so long by the United States, was incorporated in an official document endorsed by Washington. Though Hull insisted on reserving the rights of the United States conferred by international law, the American reversal at Montevideo marked a turning point in inter-American relations. Soon thereafter, the United States proceeded to relinquish, one by one, its treaty rights to intervene in the de facto protectorates in the Caribbean basin. During the first two years of the Roosevelt administration, American military forces were withdrawn from Nicaragua and Haiti. In 1934 the United States Senate abrogated the notorious Platt Amendment of 1901, which had restricted Cuba's treaty-making power and established the prerogative of American military intervention to protect Cuba's independence and preserve domestic order. In July 1935 an agreement was concluded with the government of Haiti enabling it to regain control of its finances by purchasing the Haitian national bank from the National City Bank of New York. A year later a treaty with Panama terminated the American right of military intervention outside the Canal Zone (though Senate ratification was delayed until 1939, when an exchange of notes authorized "emergency" military action by the United States to protect the canal).

The Roosevelt administration had thus resumed and accelerated the radical transformation of the traditional policy of the United States toward Latin America initiated by President Hoover. By 1934 no American troops were stationed in the region (except at the military and naval bases retained in Guantanamo Bay, Cuba, and the Panama Canal Zone). Washington had specifically relinquished its claim to the right of intervention to protect persons and property. Financial supervision of Haiti, the Dominican Republic, and Nicaragua was phased out between 1936 and 1940. Mexico had successfully nationalized American-owned petroleum properties without suffering the effects of American retaliation. It truly seemed that the previous relationship of dominance and subservience between North and Latin America had been replaced by a relationship of equality and mutual respect.

But the modification of American policy toward Latin America was more apparent than real. While the Good Neighbor Policy terminated the practices of military intervention and financial supervision, it replaced this discredited diplomacy of the gunboat and the dollar with a more indirect form of American control. In essence this consisted of the utilization of noncoercive means of enlisting the assistance of indigenous political, military, and business elites in preserving the United States' grip on the economic resources of the region. The judicious use of American Export-Import Bank loans to tie the economic systems of the individual Latin

American republics even more closely to the American economy, the training and equipping of national constabularies to suppress social insurrection against pro-American regimes, and financial assistance to autocratic governments to balance budgets and stabilize currencies—these were the alternative means for perpetuating American hegemony once the employment of direct military force and financial control were abandoned.

The experiences of Nicaragua and the Dominican Republic furnish typical illustrations of this evolution from direct to indirect control. The United States had retained military forces in Nicaragua from 1912 to 1933 (except for a brief interlude in 1925–26). During the last years of the American occupation, American officials trained and equipped a National Guard to assume the function of preserving internal security upon the withdrawal of American troops. After the American evacuation in 1934, Cesar Augusto Sandino, leader of the rebel forces that had been harassing American marines throughout the twenties, signed a truce with the Nicaraguan government only to be murdered by members of the National Guard. Two years later the head of the American-trained security forces, General Anastasio Somoza, seized power and instituted a dictatorial regime that brutally repressed revolutionary elements in the country and maintained close relations with the United States. The Somoza family remained in power either directly or through puppets until being overthrown by the ideological heirs of Sandino in 1979.

A similar transfer of power from American military occupation authorities to an American-trained indigenous elite occurred in the Dominican Republic. After ruling that nation under martial law since 1916, the United States withdrew its military forces in 1924 after establishing a national constabulary to replace the departing marines. In 1930 General Raphael Trujillo, who had moved up the ranks of the national guard to become its chief in 1928, assumed the presidency after a fraudulent electoral campaign. With the financial assistance of American sugar interests, the National City Bank, and the government in Washington, Trujillo ruled his country with an iron hand for the next thirty-one years until his assassination in 1961. Within a few days after Pearl Harbor all four of the former American protectorates—Nicaragua, Cuba, Haiti, and the Dominican Republic—displayed their continuing loyalty to the United States by declaring war on Japan, Italy, and Germany.

In conclusion, it may be said that Franklin Roosevelt abandoned the "Big Stick" first wielded by his cousin in the years before the First World War for a number of economic and strategic reasons. First of all, the economic recovery of the United States in the depths of the depression required guaranteed and continuous access to the raw materials and markets of Latin America. This became all the more important as the revival of economic nationalism and the increased likelihood of war in Europe and Asia threatened to disrupt American trade with those distant continents. Second, the rearmament of Germany, not to speak of the increasing bellig-

erence of Italy and Japan, revived the long-dormant issue of foreign interference in the Americas. In order to counter this new menace posed by
the informal "unholy alliance" of Nazi Germany, Fascist Italy, and Imperial Japan, the United States sought to strengthen the peacekeeping machinery of the Pax Americana. But the traditional methods of military
coercion and diplomatic intimidation had been rendered increasingly difficult to countenance in the face of sustained resistance from the Latin American republics and the accusations of hypocrisy from the world community.
By substituting indirect for direct methods of hemispheric domination, the
Roosevelt administration cast off the embarrassing albatross of old fashioned imperialism. It was thereafter free to act as the defender of peace
and national sovereignty in the world at large as well as to mobilize its
clients in Latin America in a hemispheric security system based on the
voluntary cooperation of juridically equal nations.

After the announcement of German rearmament and the Italian invasion of Abyssinia in 1935, the United States government launched its first
initiative aimed at establishing a system of hemispheric solidarity amid the
collapse of collective security across the Atlantic. On January 30, 1936,
President Roosevelt proposed the convocation of a special inter-American
conference to devise procedures for protecting the Western Hemisphere
from the new threat to world peace brewing in Europe. At this conference, held in Buenos Aires in December 1936, the American and Argentinian delegations clashed head on over the question of how such hemispheric security could best be assured. Foreign Minister Carlos Saavedra
Lamas of Argentina, the leading proponent of Latin American resistance
to United States domination, trotted out a proposal for cooperation with
the League of Nations to implement sanctions against aggressor states anywhere in the world. Predictably, the Argentine plan struck at the very
heart of the Pan-American ideology propounded by the United States. It
linked the security of the Western Hemisphere to the international organization headquartered in Europe, dominated by the European powers,
and repudiated by the United States. The American plan, introduced by
Secretary of State Cordell Hull, preserved the principle of Pan-Americanism
by seeking to organize the republics of the Americas in a common defense
of hemispheric security. It proposed the creation of an inter-American
consultative committee comprising the foreign ministers of the twenty-one
republics which would be authorized to hold consultations during international emergencies. In the event of war involving any of the member states,
the neutral nations of the Americas would be obliged to enforce an embargo of credits and arms supplies on all belligerents.

Determined Argentine opposition to this United States effort to circumvent the League of Nations by establishing an exclusively inter-American
security system resulted in the passage of a seemingly innocuous compromise: The principle of mutual consultation in the event of a threat to
the peace of the Americas was embodied in the Treaty for the Mainte-

nance, Preservation, and Reestablishment of Peace, but no institution was designated to hold such consultations and the obligation to embargo credits and munitions to belligerents was dropped. The absence of effective peacekeeping machinery notwithstanding, the mere affirmation of the principle of inter-American consultation represented a significant victory for Washington in its diplomatic confrontation with Buenos Aires. It established the precedent for the policy of hemispheric neutrality and collective defense that was later to be adopted by the American states at the outbreak of war in Europe. The price that the United States had to pay for this unanimous declaration of hemispheric solidarity was the Special Protocol Relative to Non-Intervention, which overrode the Hull reservation to the Montevideo resolution by prohibiting any of the signatories from intervening "directly or indirectly, and for whatever reason," in the internal or external affairs of the others. It was unimaginable that the United States, which was earnestly endeavoring to mobilize its Latin American clients against the menace of aggression from abroad, could cling to the last vestige of its own prerogative to violate their national sovereignty. The abrogation of all of the treaty rights authorizing United States military intervention and financial supervision in the Caribbean by the end of the 1930s fulfilled the solemn promises of the Buenos Aires protocol.

In the two years after the Buenos Aires Conference of December 1936, the deteriorating political situation in Europe underlined the necessity of institutionalizing the principle of hemispheric security that had been endorsed by the American republics. The failure of the League of Nations to restrain Italian aggression in East Africa and the inability of Great Britain and France to halt German revisionism in Central Europe raised the possibility of a new European war that would inevitably affect the economic and strategic interests of the Western Hemisphere. Most ominous of all was the apparent increase of Axis-inspired subversion in those Latin American states, such as Argentina, Brazil, and Uruguay, with substantial numbers of first-generation immigrants from Germany and Italy. Hitler's agents had seized control of the major organizations and publications of the Latin Americans of German descent. In some cases German immigrants were blackmailed into serving the Nazi cause under the threat of reprisals against their relatives at home. The resulting upsurge of subversive activity in these countries was accompanied by a propaganda broadside launched from Berlin in the form of radio broadcasts, press subsidies, and cultural exchange programs that was aimed at promoting Latin American support for German foreign policy. In the meantime, the Nazi regime made a determined effort to improve Germany's economic position in the region through the granting of foreign credits to and the conclusion of barter agreements with a number of Latin American states.

In the aftermath of the Munich conference, the Roosevelt administration began to exert pressure on the Latin American republics to tighten the bonds of hemispheric solidarity in the face of the threat of war in Europe and the increase in German political and economic activity in the Americas. At the Eighth Conference of the American States in Lima, Peru, in December 1938, Secretary of State Hull obtained unanimous consent to a pledge of joint cooperation to defend against "all foreign intervention or activity" that might threaten any of the twenty-one American republics. To facilitate the process of joint consultation endorsed at the Buenos Aires conference, a consultative organ composed of the foreign ministers of the signatory states was formed to handle emergencies. As was customary, Argentina resisted this United States-inspired movement toward closer hemispheric cooperation and held out for the maintenance of close relations with Europe; but the mounting anxiety in Latin America about the threat of a European war enabled Secretary Hull to win the day while the Argentine delegate remained incommunicado after having prematurely stalked out of the conference.

The consultative machinery established by the Declaration of Lima was first put into operation in response to the outbreak of the European war in September 1939. The first ad hoc meeting of the foreign ministers, held in Panama September 23–October 3, 1939, produced a series of recommendations that were unmistakably detrimental to the Axis and favorable to the Anglo-French cause. These included the proscription of domestic activities on behalf of any belligerent state (a measure aimed at German and Italian nationals residing in Latin America) as well as the revision of maritime legislation to enable neutral ports in the Western Hemisphere to receive armed merchant ships (thereby affording an advantage to Great Britain's large surface fleet) and to exclude belligerent submarines (thereby discriminating against the principal naval weapon of Germany). Less successful was the Panama conference's designation of a neutral zone around the Western Hemisphere extending several hundred miles from shore as far north as Canada. This presumptuous redefinition of the laws of naval warfare deterred none of the European belligerents as they launched the Battle of the Atlantic in the winter of 1939–40.

In addition to passing these blatantly anti-Axis resolutions, the Panama conference strengthened the existing machinery of hemispheric solidarity by creating an Inter-American Financial and Advisory Committee to promote economic cooperation among the American republics. Behind the euphemism of inter-American cooperation lay a concerted (and ultimately successful) campaign waged by the United States to reduce Latin American trade with the Axis powers and to reserve for itself the markets and the strategic raw materials of the region. This American effort to forge a hemispheric economic bloc was the culmination of a long and bitter trade dispute that had threatened to undermine United States commercial predominance in Latin America. During the second half of the 1920s, the traditionally protectionist Republican administrations in Washington had resisted Latin American initiatives, led by Argentina, to eradicate artificial trade barriers (such as the notorious sanitary prohibition that excluded most Argentine beef from the American market). The Hawley-Smoot Tariff of 1930 placed additional obstacles in the path of Latin American exports to the United States. This upsurge of American protectionism ultimately forced many of the states of Latin America (with Argentina typically leading the way) to turn to Europe for alternative trading partners. The Roca Convention of May 1, 1933, established a privileged commercial relationship between Argentina and the British Empire (which had recently been reorganized into a virtually closed economic bloc by the imperial preference agreements signed in Ottawa in the summer of 1932). Great Britain agreed to purchase a prescribed annual quantity of Argentine beef and grain in return for assurances that Argentina would spend the proceeds from these sales on British manufactured products. This preferential trade arrangement, which adversely affected both American agricultural exports to Britain and American exports of manufactured goods to Argentina, was followed by other bilateral commercial agreements between various Latin American states and the increasingly closed economic systems controlled by Britain, France, and Germany.

It was in response to this threat to inter-American commercial relationships that American Secretary of State Hull promoted his pet project for the reciprocal lowering of trade barriers to revive foreign commerce in the midst of the Depression. Though originally proposed to all of the major trading partners of the United States, the lack of enthusiasm on the part of the European powers (which were busy forming autarkic trade zones out of the extensive territory under their political control) caused Hull to concentrate on reducing trade barriers between the United States and the twenty other American republics. The American secretary of state tirelessly pressed for the adoption of reciprocity at the conferences of the American states, first in Montevideo in 1933, and with even more determination after the passage by the United States Congress of the Reciprocal Trade Agreements Act in June 1934, which authorized the president to negotiate reciprocal reductions in tariff duties with individual countries. During the last half of the 1930s a number of such bilateral agreements were signed with the nations of Latin America. This lowering of barriers to trade, together with the extension of commercial credits by the Export-Import Bank, forged a tight-knit commercial relationship between the United States and its Latin American clients that intensified the economic solidarity of the Western Hemisphere.

The sudden collapse of the Low Countries and France in May–June 1940 presented the first direct challenge to the security and neutrality of the Americas. The uncertain fate of the Dutch and French possessions in the Caribbean and on the northeast coast of South America raised the unnerving possibility of Germany's extorting rights to bases in this region from the helpless Dutch and French authorities. To avert such an eventuality, the United States Congress passed a joint resolution on June 18, 1940, reaffirming America's traditional opposition to the transfer of territory in the Western Hemisphere from one non-American power to another. The hastily convened second conference of foreign ministers of the American states, held in Havana July 21–30, 1940, endorsed the "no transfer" principle and authorized the seizure and joint administration by the American republics of any European possession judged to be in danger of falling into hostile hands. The most momentous act of the Havana conference was the Declaration of Reciprocal Assistance and Cooperation for the Defense of the Americas, which defined an act of aggression by a non-American state against any one of the twenty-one republics as an act of aggression against them all. This declaration in effect represented the formal multilateralization of the Monroe Doctrine. The principle of regional collective security, based on the mutual consent of the twenty-one American republics, thereby replaced the unilateral prerogative of the United States to prevent foreign intervention in the hemisphere.

The Declaration of Reciprocal Assistance enabled Washington to proceed with its plans to organize the defense of the Americas in the face of the Axis threat. The way in which hemispheric defense was to be managed became a subject of intense debate within the Roosevelt administration in the year before Pearl Harbor. The State Department, led by Undersecretary Sumner Welles, advocated the extension of the multilateral principle underlying the Good Neighbor Policy to the realm of regional military cooperation. Such an approach would furnish a solid foundation for the recent trend toward hemispheric unity in political and economic matters by giving all twenty Latin Republics an equal stake in the cause of regional defense. The War and Navy Departments preferred to organize the defense of the Americas on the basis of the United States' own special security requirements as defined by its service chiefs. This implied a series of privileged bilateral military relationships with a handful of countries (Mexico, Panama, Ecuador, and Brazil) strategically situated along the southern extension of the United States' defense perimeter (which was thought to run from the Galapagos Islands eastward to the Brazilian bulge). This approach would avoid overextending American resources to the peripheral southern portion of Latin America, which in any case contained two countries (Argentina and Chile) that maintained relatively cordial relations with the Axis powers and therefore were unlikely to be reliable partners in a hemisphere-wide security system led by the United States. It would permit military planners in Washington to concentrate on the two most pressing objectives of American strategy: the defense of the Pacific approaches to the Panama Canal against Japan and the protection of Brazil's northeastern bulge from the potential naval threat from bases that Germany might obtain in French West Africa.

Even before the entry of the United States in the Second World War, it became apparent that American military authorities were prevailing in their bureaucratic struggle with the advocates of a genuinely multilateral or collective security system for the defense of the hemisphere. The Roosevelt administration concluded bilateral defense agreements with the strategically situated republics within the United States' defense perimeter. Bilateral commissions modelled on the United States–Canadian Joint Board of Defense were established with Mexico and Brazil to coordinate those two countries' contribution to hemispheric defense. Negotiations were begun with Brazil and several states in the Caribbean region to secure air and naval base facilities for the United States to supplement those obtained in the British possessions in the new world by virtue of the destroyers-for-bases exchange of September 1940. American military and naval missions were dispatched southward to assist the individual states in their defense preparations while Latin American army and navy officers were invited to either the United States or the Panama Canal Zone for training. Lend Lease agreements for the delivery of military supplies were eventually signed with every Latin American nation except Argentina and Panama (which received American aid under a separate arrangement for the protection of the canal zone).

Washington's success in assuming the role of the sponsor of strategic and economic coordination in the Western Hemisphere was facilitated by the common sentiment of danger from Axis-controlled Europe that gripped the ruling elites of Latin America after the fall of the Low Countries and France. That sense of a foreign menace, together with the abandonment of overt coercion within the hemisphere by the United States, secured the cooperation of the Latin American republics (always excepting Argentina) in the cause of hemispheric solidarity that was championed and dominated by the senior partner to the north.

This is not to suggest that this wartime expansion of America's hegemonic position in its hemisphere occurred without any resistance on the part of the weaker nations to the south. Even two such pro-American states as Brazil and Panama, for example, dragged out for many years their negotiations with the United States for base rights on their territory. But the behavior of Latin America as a whole after the United States' entry in the Second World War exhibited a cooperative spirit unprecedented in the history of inter-American relations. In contrast to the First World War, all of the twenty republics of Latin America eventually followed the United States into war, although Chile and Argentina held out until the last minute. At the third conference of foreign ministers in Rio de Janeiro, January 15–28, 1942, all of the American republics except Argentina and Chile severed diplomatic relations with the Axis powers, undertook to cooperate in the suppression of German espionage in the Americas, and adopted an extensive program of inter-American economic coordination and the pooling of strategic materials. Strategically located states such as Ecuador, Brazil, and the Caribbean republics eventually furnished base facilities to American military and naval forces, which accommodated over 100,000 United States troops by the end of the war.

These developments collectively reflected the unequal distribution of inter-American military and economic power that had been evident for so long. Notwithstanding the ubiquitous references to multilateral cooperation and collective security in the rhetoric of American officials concerned with Latin America during the war, the Roosevelt administration engineered the military buildup in the Western Hemisphere according to the specific strategic requirements of the United States. The most notable exception to the general trend toward bilateralism in the United States' security relations with its Latin American clients was the establishment in 1942 of the Inter-American Defense Board. But that sole surviving symbol of the State Department's original project for multilateral hemispheric defense was reduced to an innocuous advisory role as the United States military establishment pursued its preferred policy of bilateral links with the military elites of the individual states to the south.

But Latin America's most important contribution to the war effort was economic rather than military. Under the procurement programs drawn up by the War Department in Washington, the Latin nations were induced to step up production of raw materials essential to the struggle against the Axis and to export them northward at artificially low prices in exchange for the extension of Export-Import Bank loans. This emergency program of wartime production led to the almost total reorientation of the economies of the Latin American states toward the United States, placing them in a position of great dependence on the American market for the specific strategic commodities involved. Once the demand for these war-related exports abruptly declined after 1945, most of the supplier countries were condemned to endure a painful readjustment to peacetime conditions. In the meantime, the reciprocal trade agreements (which reduced Latin American tariff barriers to United States exports) and Export-Import Bank loans strengthened the bilateral commercial ties between each of the individual Latin American countries and their powerful and prosperous neighbor to the north at the expense of the region's former trading partners in wartorn Europe and Asia. Thus the Second World War and the intense inter-American cooperation it generated reinforced the long-term trend toward United States dominance of economic relations in its hemisphere and launched the process of bilateral military cooperation between the armed services of the individual Latin states and their sources of military aid and training in Washington.

CHAPTER 7

The Confirmation of Japan's Supremacy in East Asia

The Period of Peaceful Penetration (1914–1930)

The First World War afforded the Japanese empire a golden opportunity to consolidate and expand its economic penetration and political domination of East Asia without incurring the diplomatic risks that would earlier have accompanied such an aggressive policy. In its capacity as an ally of Great Britain, Japan had declared war on Germany in August 1914 and proceeded to seize all of the German possessions in the Far East. By the end of the year, Japanese military forces were in occupation of Tsingtao and the province of Shantung on the Chinese mainland as well as the German-controlled island chains in the northern Pacific (the Marianas, Marshalls, and Carolines).

The effortless absorption of the former German colonial possessions in Asia and Oceania, when added to the territories and privileges previously obtained as the spoils of victory after wars with China and Russia, enabled Tokyo to direct its expansionist energies toward the historic object of Japanese designs: China itself. The Chinese revolution of 1911–12, which overthrew the decrepit Manchu dynasty, had sparked Japanese fears of losing the economic toehold on the mainland that had been acquired as a result of those earlier military triumphs. While the Manchu regime had relied heavily on Japan for financial assistance and political advice, the successor government in Beijing turned to Europe for support in an apparent attempt to loosen the mainland's ties of dependency to its powerful island neighbor. Anxious about losing its privileged position in southern Manchuria and Inner Mongolia, Japan profited from the military stalemate in Europe (which distracted the powers that had previously combined to restrain Japanese ambitions in East Asia) to present the Chinese government with the infamous "Twenty-One Demands" in January 1915. In its original form, this harsh ultimatum stipulated Japanese control of China's principal natural resources (especially the extensive iron and coal reserves located in the central part of the country) as well as the establishment of a de facto protectorate in the form of Japanese advisers attached to the Chinese government. Though energetic protests from the United States and Great Britain induced Tokyo to rescind its demand for a protectorate, it succeeded in extracting a number of economic concessions from the helpless Chinese government that significantly improved Japan's economic position on the mainland.

By 1916 Japan's major European allies, Great Britain, France, and Russia, granted formal recognition of Tokyo's wartime gains in East Asia, thereupon conferring the stamp of legitimacy on this unilateral extension of Japanese power. The sole obstacle to Japanese expansionism was the United States, which had expressed profound displeasure at the imposition of the Twenty-One Demands on China. Washington's mounting concern about the developments across the Pacific was not due to any fear for the security of the American homeland. The opening of the Panama Canal in the summer of 1914, which permitted the rapid concentration of American naval power in the eastern Pacific, had virtually eliminated a Japanese naval threat to the American west coast. But America's longtime commitment to the preservation of the territorial integrity of China and the "Open Door" for trade and investment in that country, coupled with the concern for guaranteeing the security of the Philippines, gave rise in 1916 to the passage of an ambitious naval construction program designed to ensure American naval supremacy in the western as well as the eastern Pacific. Japan's equally insistent preoccupation with securing its privileged position in Manchuria and northern China seemed to preclude an amicable resolution of this impending trans-Pacific rivalry. Finally, on November 2, 1917, a mutually satisfactory compromise was reached by the American Secretary of State and the Japanese ambassador to Washington. The so-called Lansing-Ishii Agreement affirmed the territorial integrity of China and the principle of the Open Door while recognizing Japan's "special interests" in China that were conferred by geographical proximity. This ambiguous accommodation—an executive agreement that was not submitted for legislative ratification—enabled the two countries to cooperate in the common struggle against Germany while postponing the inevitable showdown over China until after the end of the war.

In Japanese eyes, this reference to the "special interest" in China represented something akin to the Asian counterpart of the Monroe Doctrine, with Japan playing the role of hegemonic power in this instance. Such an interpretation gained even wider acceptance in Tokyo after the military collapse and political disintegration of Russia, Japan's traditional rival for the Chinese spoils. Following the Bolshevik Revolution and the signing of the Treaty of Brest-Litovsk, the French government persuaded President Wilson to approve a Japanese military intervention in eastern Siberia; its ostensible purpose was to restore order and promote the reconstitution of a Russian political and military authority capable of renewing offensive operations against Germany's eastern front in order to relieve the embattled Allies in the west. Japanese expansionists welcomed the opportunity to strengthen Japan's economic and political position in eastern Siberia and to create a buffer zone between Russia and Japanese-dominated Manchuria. Wilson reluctantly bowed to French pressure for a Japanese intervention on the condition that the expeditionary force be limited to seven thousand officers and soldiers, approximately the size of the American contingent that was earmarked for the Siberian campaign. But the Japanese army in eastern Siberia mushroomed to seventy-two thousand by the end of the war. There it was to remain until 1922, long after the defeat of Germany and the evacuation of the small American contingent that had been stationed in Vladivostok. The political authority of Russia, the traditional counterweight to Japan in the northern border-lands of China, was virtually nonexistent in the region just as Japanese power there reached its height.

Japan's conspicuous presence at the Paris Peace Conference as one of the five dominant powers was a fitting tribute to that small island nation's remarkable rise from backwardness and obscurity in less than half a century. Though disinterested in the redistribution of territory and resources in far-off Europe, the Japanese delegation pressed for and obtained substantial advantages within its own geographical sphere. These included the acquisition of the former German Pacific islands north of the equator in the form of a League of Nations mandate as well as Germany's former economic privileges on the Shantung peninsula of China. The latter region was viewed by expansionist business elites in Tokyo as a stepping stone for further economic penetration of China similar to the one acquired earlier in Korea, the other peninsula extending from the mainland toward the Japanese islands. These territorial and economic gains firmly established Japan as a major economic force on the Asian mainland and the principal naval power in the western Pacific at a time when Russia still reeled from the effects of civil war and economic chaos and Great Britain was struggling to recover financially and commercially from the consequences of the Great War.

Once again, it was the United States that posed the most formidable challenge to Japan's expansionist moves in the Far East. America's growing apprehension about Japan's imperial ambitions across the Pacific was caused not only by the latter's territorial and economic gains at the peace conference but also by the alarming growth of Japanese naval power. The Tokyo government's spending on naval construction tripled from 1917 to 1921 and came to represent over a third of the imperial budget. Though possessing a fleet that ranked a distant third behind the formidable armadas of Great Britain and the United States, Japan's distance from North America rendered it virtually immune to the deterrent effect of American naval power (which in any case had to be divided between two oceans) while its alliance with Great Britain (concluded in 1902 and renewed in 1905 and 1911) neutralized the Royal Navy as a potential constraint on

Japanese imperial ambitions. In response to the increase of Japanese naval strength, the United States transferred the bulk of its fleet from the Atlantic to the Pacific after the end of the war in Europe (in order to achieve virtual parity with Japan in that ocean) and proceeded to open the dry dock at Pearl Harbor in Hawaii. Relieved of the German naval menace in the Atlantic by the disarmament provisions of the Versailles Treaty, American naval strategists began for the first time to develop contingency plans for the projection of American naval power across the Pacific to the vicinity of Japan.

The prospect of a costly naval race so soon after the termination of the world war was anathema to all powers concerned. Great Britain, still the mistress of the seas but in danger of being surpassed by the United States and equaled by Japan in the near future, was plagued by chronic unemployment and industrial stagnation; these domestic ills dictated a policy of austerity and budgetary restraint that was incompatible with a large naval construction program. The American administration of President Warren Harding presided over a serious postwar recession in the early twenties and was dominated by conservative isolationists committed to drastic reductions in taxation and government spending as well as retrenchment from President Wilson's ambitious global commitments. Japanese leaders, while continuing to believe that national prosperity depended on privileged access to markets and raw materials abroad, displayed a willingness to adopt a strategy of peaceful economic expansion and cooperation with the two great English-speaking powers rather than incur the domestic costs and foreign policy risks of a naval arms race. It was in the context of this widespread apprehension about the economic and strategic consequences of unrestrained naval rivalry that President Harding invited the foreign ministers of eight maritime nations to the first international conference on naval arms control in the history of the world. Held in Washington during the winter of 1921–22, this unprecedented conclave produced a number of agreements to limit the naval arms race in general and to reduce Pacific tensions in particular.

The principal achievement of the Washington Conference, the so-called Five Power Treaty, established a tonnage ratio for existing capital ships (defined as warships over 10,000 tons carrying guns larger than eight-inch) of 5:5:3:1.75:1.75 for Great Britain, the United States, Japan, France, and Italy, respectively, and decreed a ten-year moratorium on the construction of new ships in the same category. The three great naval powers agreed to refrain from building new fortifications on their Pacific possessions (excluding Singapore and Pearl Harbor, the principal forward bases of Britain and the United States, respectively). Japan consented to evacuate eastern Siberia, to restore to China sovereignty over the Shantung peninsula, and to permit its bilateral alliance with Great Britain—which was strongly opposed by the United States—to be replaced by a multilateral agreement to respect the political status quo in Asia. The

Washington Conference was widely acclaimed as the opening of a new era in international relations. Never before had the great powers freely consented to limit the size of a portion of their armed forces and to refrain from constructing new fortifications. Advocates of universal disarmament regretted the exclusion of land armaments from the agenda—a concession to the nervous French, who insisted on the right to retain undisputed military superiority over Germany in the absence of effective security guarantees. But this omission did not dampen the spirit of exhilaration that greeted the publication of the Washington treaty provisions. The vague commitment to universal disarmament that had been inserted in the Paris peace treaties finally appeared to be on the brink of realization, at least in the limited sphere of naval power.

The agreements specifically relating to East Asia also engendered considerable optimism about the prospects of peace and stability in that unsettled region, in Washington as well as in Tokyo. American Secretary of State Charles Evans Hughes, the host and guiding spirit of the conference, had achieved his three principal objectives—the termination of the Anglo-Japanese alliance, the recognition of American naval parity with Great Britain and superiority over Japan, and the evacuation of Japanese military forces from eastern Siberia. Tokyo had accepted the inferior position in the 5–5–3 ratio for capital ship tonnage because the nonfortification agreement seemed to represent an adequate guarantee of Japan's security in its home waters as well as its control of the sea approaches to the Asian mainland. These mutually acceptable compromises in strategic matters were supplemented by a series of informal pledges by Japan to abandon its unilateral quest for preferential rights in China in favor of a multilateral approach to the economic development of that country in cooperation with the Western powers.

Domestic developments within Japan after the conclusion of the Washington Conference appeared to confirm the new orientation of Japanese foreign policy and facilitated the rapprochement between Tokyo and the Western powers possessing colonial holdings in East Asia. The passage of progressive social legislation and the adoption of universal male suffrage in 1924 helped to dispel the lingering image of Japan in the Western democracies as an authoritarian, militaristic society. This apparent evolution toward enlightened administration and representative government caused many American bankers and business executives to reassess their attitudes toward economic opportunities in the Far East. China, the traditional object of American commercial and financial interest in the region, seemed hopelessly mired in political chaos and social unrest and therefore came to be regarded as a poor risk for trade and investment. By contrast, Japan acquired the well-deserved reputation as an island of stability in a turbulent part of the world that offered a much more hospitable environment for American economic interests. A close Japanese-American commercial relationship had developed during the First World War, when American exports to Japan increased fivefold and Japanese exports to the United States almost tripled. These economic contacts were expanded throughout the 1920s, during which the United States remained Japan's biggest customer and supplier. Throughout the decade the United States was exporting to Japan most of the island empire's automobiles, machinery, building-construction materials, and oil. Conversely, the American market absorbed 40% of Japan's total exports, including 90 percent of its raw silk products (a major source of foreign exchange for the export-dependent Japanese economy). During the same period American banks supplied Japan with 40 percent of its foreign investment. These commercial and financial connections, reinforced by the mutually advantageous agreements on naval arms limitation concluded in 1922, produced an atmosphere of cordiality and cooperation between Tokyo and Washington which in turn promoted stability in the Western Pacific for the remainder of the 1920s.

But the structure of economic interdependence and multilateral security for East Asia depended, in the final analysis, on Japan's willingness to continue to pursue its national aspirations by peaceful means; that is, through economic rather than military rivalry with the Western powers. The limitations written into the Five Power Treaty at Washington confirmed Japan's naval superiority in its geographical sphere. By agreeing not to construct additional fortifications between Pearl Harbor and Singapore, the United States and Great Britain had significantly reduced their capability of deterring future Japanese aggression on the Chinese mainland or in southeast Asia. The vulnerability of British and American possessions in the Far East was increased by the advent of air power as a decisive factor in naval warfare. Four months before the opening of the Washington Naval Conference, the United States Army Air Corps had sunk a captured German battleship in an experimental test off the Virginia capes with foreign (including Japanese) military observers in attendance, conclusively demonstrating that gravity-propelled bombs could send a heavily armored vessel to the bottom. In strategic terms, this suggested that capital ships could no longer safely operate in waters within range of land-based enemy aircraft or aircraft carriers. Gone were the days when great battle fleets could roam about the oceans with impunity, intervening anywhere at will. Anglo-American superiority in battleships, which Japan had conceded at Washington, was therefore a deceptive advantage. The comforting vision of the great white fleet advancing westward from Pearl Harbor to liberate the Philippines and blockade the Japanese home islands, the basis of American naval strategy since the early 1920s, was chimerical. Japan had obtained a string of potential air bases in the form of the German mandate islands that lay sprawled across the western Pacific between the Philippines and Hawaii. From these safe bases, or from the aircraft carriers that were under construction, Japanese bombers could conceivably block American naval access to the western Pacific, thereby isolating the vulnerable Philippine islands from the principal American Pacific base at Hawaii.

This potential imbalance of power in the western Pacific, though continually decried by American naval authorities, generated little concern among policymakers in Washington. Preoccupation with European and Latin American affairs in the 1920s resulted in a relatively nonchalant attitude toward Asia. American trade with and investment in Japan continued to increase, while Tokyo gave every indication of honoring its pledges to refrain from exploiting the advantage conferred by geographical proximity and technological innovations in naval warfare to upset the balance of power of the region. But the demographic, geographical, and economic sources of Japanese expansionism that had prompted the foreign adventurism of the past remained. The fatal combination of a rapidly expanding population, a limited supply of arable and habitable land, and a dearth of mineral resources and fossil fuels represented in the minds of worried officials in Tokyo a potentially insuperable barrier to future Japanese economic growth. Unless a remedy to this predicament could be devised by the ruling elite of the nation, Japan faced the prospect of a drastic reduction in its standard of living and the social tensions and political instability that often accompany economic stagnation and decline.

The solution to this dilemma sought by the Japanese government in the 1920s was reminiscent of the path chosen in the previous century by Great Britain, that other island nation that was plagued during its developing phase by overpopulation and inadequate natural resources. This involved (1) the encouragement of emigration to relieve domestic pressures on land, food, and natural resources; (2) the promotion of exports of manufactured products to finance imports of essential raw materials and foodstuffs; and (3) the pursuit of political accommodation with the other great powers in order to facilitate this policy of peaceful economic expansion. During the period of the so-called Taishō democracy, a progressive governing coalition of bankers, industrialists, and civil servants successfully combined a domestic program of social and political reform with a conciliatory foreign policy toward the other great powers and a drastic reduction in military expenditures.

But this turn toward moderation never commanded the support of the powerful military, naval, and bureaucratic elites in Japan that had shaped the expansionist policies of the recent past. Like their counterparts in Weimar Germany, these stalwarts of the old order remained unalterably opposed to their government's domestic reform program and its foreign policy of accommodation. They continued to dream of an East Asia dominated by an authoritarian Japanese empire free of Western influence. Their cause was strengthened by a series of international developments in the course of the 1920s that gradually undermined the basis of the government's cooperative relationship with the Western powers and enabled its military critics to mobilize popular opposition to that policy. The first of these was the appearance of legal restrictions on Japanese immigration in the English-speaking world. Opposition to Oriental immigration in the United States, Canada, and Australia, which had surfaced at the turn of the century, sharply curtailed the opportunity of Japanese nationals to migrate to low-population-density countries bordering the Pacific. In 1924, the American Congress went so far as to enact legislation that singled out Japanese immigrants as ineligible for American citizenship.

Though the practical effect of this punitive legislation was minimal—the previously existing quota system had allowed only a few hundred Japanese immigrants a year—its emotional impact on the proud Japanese people was considerable. Not only did it imply an American assumption of racial inferiority: Considered in the context of similar exclusionary restrictions imposed in Canada and Australia, it suggested a white man's conspiracy to deny Japan the opportunity to relieve its population pressures through emigration to the underpopulated regions of English-speaking settlement across the Pacific. Earlier Japanese hopes for the large-scale colonization of Korea, Formosa, and Manchuria after those nearby areas had been brought under direct or indirect Japanese control before the war had failed to materialize: Less than half a million Japanese had migrated to Korea in the decade following its annexation and less than 200,000 had settled in Formosa. Twenty years after the acquisition of special privileges in Manchuria, less than a quarter of a million Japanese had resettled there. The reluctance of Japanese citizens to relocate to these neighboring areas, in spite of lavish inducements from their government, has generally been attributed to the overpopulated conditions and unsuitable climate that were to be found there. But whatever the explanation, and regardless of the alternatives to emigration that were available, expansionist-minded zealots in Japan began to raise the alarm: Their country and its people were being boxed in by the racist policies of the white, English-speaking nations.

The erection of barriers to the exportation of surplus population was soon followed by the appearance of obstacles to the expansion of Japanese trade with the English-speaking world. Commercial intercourse between Japan and the United States, which (as we have seen) increased steadily since the end of the war, began to decline sharply at the beginning of the 1930s because of the sudden collapse of purchasing power in depression-ridden America. By 1930 Japan's raw silk prices had fallen to one-fourth of the previous year's level and silk exports to the United States fell by over 40 percent, causing the ruination of many peasants who depended on this important cash crop for their livelihood. The abrupt decline of the Japanese export trade caused by the contraction of demand in the United States was aggravated by the increase in American protectionism during the world economic downturn. Producers for the domestic market and labor organizations in the United States sponsored boycotts of

Japanese goods and waged a "buy American" campaign to protect domestic profits and jobs. The Hawley-Smoot Tariff of 1930 raised duties on Japanese products by an average of 23 percent. The government in Tokyo made matters worse by returning to the gold standard at the existing exchange rate in January 1930. Intended as a measure to integrate the Japanese economy more closely into the international monetary system that was dominated by other nations that had long since returned to gold, this belated decision caused a dramatic overvaluation of the yen and therefore increased the price of Japanese exports at the very moment that the decline in purchasing power and the rise of protectionism abroad was closing foreign markets. All of these developments contributed to a rise in unemployment, a sharp decrease in the real income of agricultural and industrial workers, and the beginnings of social unrest in Japan.

As opportunities for increased trade and emigration across the Pacific vanished, certain interest groups in Japanese society revived the old dream of establishing a neocolonial relationship with the gigantic neighbor on the Asian mainland. At the end of the Great War, Japan had seemed ideally positioned to exploit the political divisions and economic distress of China to establish its predominance there. Though the Western powers had induced Tokyo to join them in reaffirming the Open Door policy concerning equality of commercial opportunity in China, the agreement lacked an enforcement mechanism. This meant that Japanese economic domination of China, even if it were to violate the protections agreed upon at the Washington conference, was unlikely to elicit more than verbal protests from the other great powers.

The internal political situation in China constituted an open invitation to Japanese intervention. The Chinese revolution of 1911–12 that had toppled the Manchu dynasty failed to establish a viable government capable of unifying the country and liberating it from foreign interference. From 1912 to the mid-1920s, administrative authority in China was divided among a number of regional military commanders or political leaders, most of whom passively tolerated the humiliating system of economic and legal privileges enjoyed by Japanese, European, and American trading companies. Manchuria was dominated by a local figure beholden to the Japanese; an ineffectual regime in Beijing, recognized by the Western powers as the nominal "government" of China, was powerless to prevent foreign restrictions on Chinese sovereignty and the assumption of regional authority by local warlords. Only Sun Yat-sen, the spiritual leader of the 1911 revolution who had established a rival "government" in Canton in 1917, represented a potential inspiration for Chinese national unity and sovereignty. But his regime lacked the military strength to enforce its will on the regional warlords and to command the respect of the foreign powers.

Enfeebled by these centrifugal forces, China submitted to an ever-increasing degree of Japanese economic domination. In the course of the

1920s Japanese capital accounted for 90 percent of all new foreign investment in China while 25 percent of Japan's total exports went to that country. The offshore island was rapidly developing a neocolonial relationship with the mainland analogous to that of the United States with Latin America, exchanging manufactured goods and investment capital for coal, iron, rice, soybeans, and other mineral and agricultural resources. Japan's economic penetration of China was facilitated by the system of commercial privileges inherited from the previous century. Restrictions on China's tariff autonomy prevented increases of duties on imports without the approval of the great powers. The principle of extraterritoriality exempted foreign residents of China from the jurisdiction of Chinese legal authorities and permitted foreign powers to maintain their own infrastructure (such as postal, communications, and transportation services) within their concessions. Both constraints on Chinese sovereignty were justified by the foreign powers on the grounds that China's chronic political instability prevented it from exercising the legal authority that is normally associated with sovereign states. Though the European nations and the United States also benefited from these privileges, Japan drew the greatest economic advantage from them and accordingly became the principal object of Chinese resentment against these blatant instances of foreign intrusion.

Chinese demands for the restoration of tariff autonomy and the abolition of extraterritoriality fell on deaf ears in Western circles whenever they were voiced. Despite the high-sounding endorsement of Chinese administrative and territorial integrity at the Washington conference, none of the great powers was prepared to accord China the full political sovereignty she craved. The United States was concerned almost exclusively with the preservation of the principle of equal opportunity for foreign nations seeking to trade with China and displayed little interest in restoring tariff and judicial autonomy to that country. Frustrated by the Washington Treaty powers' refusal to recognize China's sovereign rights, Sun Yat-sen turned for support to the Soviet Union, a country which had not been invited to the Washington conference and which had renounced all of the special privileges in China that it had inherited from the Tsarist regime. The Canton government's overture to Moscow came at a propitious moment in the evolution of Soviet foreign policy after the First World War. Surprised and disappointed at the failure of the Communist revolution to spread to the industrialized countries of Europe, Lenin and his successors turned their attention to the nonindustrialized regions of Asia in the hope of exploiting for Russia's benefit the anti-imperialist discontent of the subjugated masses there. In 1924 Russian representatives of the Communist International (Comintern) were dispatched to Canton to reorganize Sun's political movement, the Kuomintang, into a disciplined revolutionary organization capable of leading a mass movement in alliance with the small Chinese Communist Party that had been founded three years earlier. The death of Sun Yat-sen in 1925 eventually brought to power in Canton a young military officer named Chiang Kai-shek who had visited the Soviet Union and remained in close touch with the Comintern agents in China. Chiang promptly mounted a campaign to unify the country as well as to liberate it from the detested system of foreign economic privileges. He proclaimed the Kuomintang the national government of China and on July 4, 1926, formally launched a northern military expedition to destroy the power of the regional military authorities, promote the administrative unification of the country, and expel foreign interests from Chinese territory. In the same year popular outbursts of xenophobia resulted in attacks on foreign citizens and property, revealing widespread support for Chiang's dynamic policy of national unification and liberation.

But unlike the Communists in his Nationalist coalition, Chiang was willing to distinguish among the various foreign powers that were encroaching on Chinese sovereignty. He expressed an eagerness to negotiate bilaterally with any one of them that was prepared to consider phasing out the despised treaty privileges. As it happened, public and official attitudes toward China in the United States had been gradually evolving toward greater sympathy for China's predicament. This new departure in American policy was publicly confirmed on January 27, 1927, when Secretary of State Frank Kellogg issued a statement affirming Washington's willingness to consider granting tariff autonomy to a central government of China that could command the allegiance of the Chinese people and protect American lives and property. The new Chinese strongman soon began to pursue policies and display personal traits that endeared him to public opinion in the United States. In April 1927 he turned against his erstwhile Communist allies, expelling Comintern advisers from the country, ruthlessly suppressing the Chinese Communist Party, and denouncing the Soviet Union as a "red imperialist." At the end of the year he married a Wellesley College–educated daughter of a wealthy Christian businessman from Shanghai, who converted him to the Christian faith. In July 1928 Kuomintang forces successfully completed their northern expedition by occupying Beijing and bringing most of China under their effective control. In the meantime, the Nationalist government had caused a furor in Tokyo by announcing plans to construct a railroad in Manchuria in competition with the existing Japanese line, actively encouraging thousands of Chinese to emigrate to the northeastern province, and harassing Japanese economic interests there. Soon thereafter boycotts were organized against Japanese goods, and on December 29, 1928, Manchuria was formally reunified with China.

This nationalist revival hastened the process whereby the United States revised its paternalistic attitude toward China. The military successes, administrative reforms, and anti-Communist political orientation of the Nationalist regime appealed to those elements in American society that had longed for a stable, pro-Western, Christianized China open to American trade and investment. In recognition of these changed circumstances, the United States unilaterally accorded tariff autonomy to China on July 25, 1928, in exchange for a reciprocal most-favored-nation agreement; thus ended one of the humiliating economic privileges that had been extracted from the impotent Chinese during the age of imperial expansion. American business executives and bankers began once again to ponder the potential value to American trade and investment represented by the vast mainland of China, politically unified and protected from internal instability by a vigorous national government.

This revival of Sino-American friendship, together with the impending collapse of the system of foreign privileges in China and the challenge to Japanese interests in Manchuria, inflamed expansionist opinion in Tokyo. Japan's privileged position on the mainland seemed in danger of being swept away by a resurgent Chinese nationalism aided and abetted by the United States, which could be expected to obtain economic advantages from its recent rapprochement with Kuomintang China to the detriment of Japanese interests. Indeed, Japanese exports to China dropped by one half between 1929 and 1931, and by the latter year the United States had supplanted Japan as China's principal supplier of foreign products. The collapse of Japan's export trade in Asia, together with the sharp decline in Japanese-American commerce noted above, provoked widespread anxiety among merchants, bankers, and government officials. Their principal concern was the prospective loss of foreign exchange to pay for the supplies of coal, iron, oil, rubber, rice, and soybeans from the Chinese mainland and the offshore islands of southeast Asia that Japan depended upon for survival. The deepening of the world depression prompted the United States and the industrialized nations of Europe to insulate their domestic markets from foreign competition, while the Asian and African empires of the European powers were rapidly becoming inaccessible to Japanese commercial penetration. The United States and the Soviet Union with their vast continental domains, and Britain and France with their worldwide empires, boasted a sufficiently diverse base of raw materials and sufficiently large markets to ride out the storm. Japan, by contrast, seemed isolated and economically vulnerable, without a market and resource base equal to its needs at a time when closed economic blocs were being formed throughout the world.

Added to this fear of economic strangulation was a growing concern about Japan's security interests in the western Pacific. At the London Naval Conference of 1930, which had been convened to reduce naval competition in categories of ships not covered by the Washington Treaty limitations—destroyers, cruisers, and submarines—the Japanese delegation was persuaded to accept a compromise agreement which was viewed in naval circles as a serious threat to Japan's position of naval superiority in its region. Patriotic organizations in Japan bitterly denounced this "sell-out" to the Western powers and mounted a nationwide campaign against the government for compromising the safety of the nation. The military and naval critics of the civilian government's conciliatory policy at London effectively exploited the widespread social discontent that had been caused by falling farm incomes and expanding urban unemployment. High-ranking military and naval officers perceived an ominous connection between the economic and security problems that the empire faced at the beginning of the thirties: Many were convinced that a global war was inevitable in the not-so-distant future; they believed that Japan's only hope of defending its interests lay in forging a domestic consensus behind a program of foreign expansion in order to create a self-sufficient strategic-economic bloc in East Asia controlled from Tokyo. In short, the conciliatory, pro-Western orientation of Japan's postwar civilian leadership appeared in the eyes of its naval, military, and nationalist critics to be leading Japan down the path of national suicide and economic decline.

The Period of Military Expansion (1931–1941)

The collapse of Japanese democratic political institutions and the abandonment of the moderate foreign policy of the Taishō period did not occur overnight. There was no march on Rome, no Reichstag fire, whereby the antidemocratic elements in Japanese society abruptly overthrew the democratic regime. The transformation of the Japanese political system from a Western-type parliamentary system into a military dictatorship transpired in almost imperceptible gradations between 1931 and 1936. There were ample domestic reasons for the collapse of Japanese democracy amid the social tensions and economic distress caused by the depression. The plight of the peasantry in particular rendered it susceptible to demogogic appeals from political groups that promised deliverance from the deepening agricultural crisis. But the substance of the militaristic movement's program was concentrated on foreign policy issues because the world outside was seen both as the cause of Japan's mounting economic problems as well as the most promising source of salvation. The weak, vacillating policy of the government had brought the empire to its current perilous position. National renewal and economic prosperity were to be found in the rediscovery of Japanese pride at home and in the reassertion of Japanese power abroad.

The spearhead of this revolt against the established political order in Japan was a conspiratorial coterie within the officers' corps of the army known as the "Imperial Way" faction (so called because of its devotion to the principle of emperor-worship); it was composed mainly of younger officers stationed in Manchuria to guard the Japanese-owned South Manchurian Railway together with their supporters and promoters at home. This cadre tended toward ideological fanaticism, conceiving of foreign conquest as the most effective mechanism for the spiritual regeneration of a Japan that had become corrupted by Western cultural and commercial influences and was menaced by Western naval power. Passionately intent on purifying their society and restoring national glory, the young zealots of the Imperial Way launched a number of violent attacks on the political leadership and its foreign policy that paved the way for the collapse of the Japanese parliamentary regime and the abandonment of its conciliatory foreign policy.

The first of these challenges to the political elite came on September 18, 1931, when middle-echelon officers on duty in Manchuria blew up a section of the South Manchurian Railway, attributed that act to unnamed Chinese terrorists, and proceeded to use it as a pretext for occupying the rest of the Chinese province. This plot, which had been hatched in consultation with sympathetic officers in the war ministry in Tokyo, represented a response to the encroachments in Manchuria by the reinvigorated Chinese government of Chiang Kai-shek. Though the emperor, the business leaders, and high government officials continued to preach caution and restraint in Japan's relations with the mainland, an outpouring of public support for the army's independent action forced the political authorities to acquiesce in the military fait accompli. In March 1932 a "Manchurian independence movement" financed and controlled by the Japanese occupation army established the sovereign state of Manchukuo, which was detached from China and placed under Japanese military protection. This virtually bloodless subjugation of Manchuria, a region with a land area greater than that of Japan, a population of 30 million, and valuable agricultural and mineral resources, had a profound repercussion on Japanese domestic politics. The wave of euphoria that swept the country confirmed the army's predominance in political affairs and relegated the elected government officials to a subordinate role, particularly in the formulation of foreign policy.

The response of the Western powers to this egregious violation of the principle of collective security was timid and vacillating. The American president, Herbert Hoover, was averse to the imposition of economic sanctions against Japan, fearing that they would lead to war (an attitude evidently shared by the majority of the American people at the time). Instead, Secretary of State Henry Stimson dispatched a note to Tokyo on January 7, 1932, expressing the American government's refusal to recognize any "treaty or agreement" that was brought about by means contrary to the Kellogg-Briand Pact. This nonrecognition doctrine enabled the Hoover administration to uphold the sanctity of international law without running the risk of imposing economic sanctions. This cautious American response was dictated by a number of considerations. To begin with, American economic and strategic interests in northern China were minimal; they certainly were insufficiently important to warrant retaliatory measures against Japan that might result in a diplomatic and perhaps even military showdown. Second, as noted above, American commercial and financial concerns had developed a substantial stake in the Japanese economy in the course of the 1920s; they were understandably reluctant to jeopardize their current trade and investment interests, not to speak of future opportunities, and did not hesitate to make their views known to the American government. Third, Congressional refusal to appropriate funds to bring American naval strength up to the Washington and London treaty limits had deprived the United States of a credible deterrent force in the western Pacific to back up a strong diplomatic response to the Japanese action.

The circumspect policy adopted by the Hoover administration was resumed by President Franklin Roosevelt upon his inauguration in March 1933. The ambitious program of economic reconstruction launched in the first few years of the New Deal absorbed the attention and energies of the new administration, leaving little room for bold initiatives in foreign affairs. Moreover, the advent of the Nazi regime in Germany distracted world attention from the expansion of Japanese power in East Asia. Consequently, rumors of clandestine Japanese efforts to fortify the mandated Pacific islands in violation of the Five Power Treaty went uninvestigated. The State Department continued to discourage American trade with and investment in the vulnerable remnant of China under Kuomintang control. American exports of strategic materials to Japan continued unabated throughout the remainder of the 1930s.

Great Britain displayed even less of an inclination to risk antagonizing Japan by seeking to dislodge it from an area of no particular importance to Britain's national interests. Some officials in London even welcomed Tokyo's increasing military involvement in northern China as a useful diversion from the region of East Asia—which stretched from Hong Kong southward to Singapore—that was of substantial concern to Britain on economic and strategic grounds. Throughout the Manchurian episode British policy toward East Asia was dominated by the aspiration to reach a mutually satisfactory division of the entire region into Anglo-Japanese spheres of commercial and strategic interest. The tame condemnation of Japanese aggression in Manchuria by a League of Nations commission headed by Britain's Lord Lytton reflected London's inclination to placate Tokyo: On the basis of the Lytton Commission report, the League's "sanctions" against Japan were confined to symbolic gestures of disapproval, such as the refusal to recognize the passports and postage of the newly installed Japanese puppet state of Manchukuo that Tokyo had imposed on the Manchurians.

But it soon became evident that the Japanese military's thirst for foreign conquest could not be quenched by the de facto absorption of Manchuria. The collapse of parliamentary democracy in many nations of Europe and the deepening of the world depression had undermined the credibility of that section of the Japanese ruling elite that had attempted to transplant Western type political and economic practices to Japan and to cooperate with the Western powers in fostering international stability and prosperity. In its place emerged the dynamic young cadre of the army—the "Imperial Way faction—that had launched the spectacularly successful coup in Manchuria. Gradually the power of the political parties and the Diet waned. Real authority was assumed by a small group of cabinet ministers beholden to the military chiefs. Army and naval officers infiltrated the middle and upper echelons of the civil service in increasing numbers, bringing great pressure to bear on the surviving remnants of the old governing elite to adopt more authoritarian measures at home and aggressive policies abroad. Internal repression mounted. Leftist politicians and labor leaders were imprisoned, newspapers were censored, and Western influences in Japanese culture came under attack from the proponents of the new nationalism.

But the beneficiaries of this political transformation in Japan were not to be the fanatical young officers of the Imperial Way. Their romantic reverie of a purified Japanese society untainted by the evils of the industrialized West was patently inappropriate to the launching of the war of conquest that all significant factors of the Japanese ruling elite had come to favor by the middle of the 1930s. The more sober and practical-minded members of the Japanese military establishment recognized that the time had long since passed when spiritual virtues were sufficient to win wars, nor could they promote the economic growth upon which military success in the modern world depended. The more conservative modernizers among the army leaders, while equally committed to the cause of military grandeur, realized that discipline, organization, and technological innovation were the most suitable means of achieving that end. The so-called Control Faction of older, maturer officers therefore resolved to harness the energies of their exuberant younger colleagues and redirect them into more effective channels. The opportunity for coopting the program of the radical firebrands of the Imperial Way arose in February 1936, when fifteen hundred junior officers and soldiers in Tokyo seized government buildings and assassinated several current and former government leaders and a high-ranking army general before being captured by loyalist forces in the military. This abortive putsch provoked a response by the modernizing faction of the army high command, which hastened to restore discipline in the armed forces and suppress the Imperial Way cabal.

The modernizing faction of the military, while acting against the excesses of the junior officers, had been converted to the cause of foreign conquest that the latter group so energetically espoused. Domestic authoritarianism and foreign expansion were endorsed by the army leaders not as a means of spiritual renewal, but rather as means of mobilizing domestic support for military modernization and an increase in the political power of the army high command. Similarly, the business and financial oligarchy that had presided over Japan's industrial revolution was gradually won over to the cause of rearmament and foreign expansion for reasons of economic self-interest. The Zaibatsu elite—comprising the conglomerates Mitsui, Mitsubishi, Sumitomo, and Yasuda—which had previously cooperated with the civilian governments' policy of domestic liberalization and peaceful economic expansion aboad, joined forces with the modernizing sector of the army to form a vast military-industrial cadre devoted to massive rearmament in preparation for overseas conquest. The army leaders recognized the necessity of obtaining the services of this business elite for the exploitation of the extensive economic resources of Manchukuo. Japanese heavy industry in turn reaped lavish rewards from the remilitarization of Japanese society and the increased economic penetration of the mainland. Industrial production skyrocketed from 6 billion yen in 1930 to 30 billion yen in 1941. The four Zaibatsu conglomerates more than tripled their total assets during the same period. It is ironic that a movement of national regeneration launched by a radical faction of disgruntled junior officers who sought to realize their nostalgic vision of a return to the preindustrial way of life was appropriated by the technologically minded elite of the army and heavy industry. Historians have drawn the parallel between the February 1936 abortive coup in Japan and the "Night of Long Knives" of Nazi Germany in 1934, when Hitler turned against the anticapitalist, romantic youth of the Sturm Abteilung (S.A.) and forged an alliance with the conservative elite in the officers' corps and the business community.

Once the Control Faction of military technocrats and their allies in the Zaibatsu industrial and financial empires consolidated their authority in Tokyo, plans were laid for the extension of Japanese power in East Asia beyond the frontiers of the new client state of Manchukuo. In August 1936 the cabinet adopted the "Fundamental Principles of National Policy," which foresaw the economic integration of Japan, Manchukuo, and northern China, the economic penetration of southeast Asia, and the acquisition of undisputed naval primacy in the western Pacific. In order to protect its northern flank from possible Soviet interference with this southward expansion, the Japanese government signed the so-called Anti-Comintern Pact with Nazi Germany in November 1936 to intimidate Moscow.

The first stage of this plan for regional hegemony was put into operation in July 1937, when an accidental clash between Chinese and Japanese troops on maneuvers near Beijing escalated into a full-fledged (though undeclared) war between the two states. Japanese military forces swept south and west from their bases in northern China, defeating the best divisions of the Kuomintang army around Shanghai and capturing Chiang's capital city of Nanking in December. Hankow and Canton fell in the autumn of 1938, by which time all of the major cities, ports, railway lines, and productive parts of northern and central China had fallen under Japanese control. On the heels of the victorious Japanese armies followed industrial officials who organized "development companies" to exploit the mineral resources and run the basic industries of the newly occupied regions. In December 1938 the Nationalist Chinese government retreated to the mountain redoubt of Chungking in the west to carry on the fight, while a guerrilla resistance movement was organized by the Communist Party in Yenan in the northwest. The Japanese occupation authorities established a puppet government in northern China and then in March 1940 formed a collaborationist regime in Nanking to rival the Nationalist stronghold in Chungking.

It is surprising that the United States government continued to pursue a wait-and-see attitude toward Japanese aggression in China. Japan had launched an ambitious program of naval construction after the expiration of the London Treaty in 1936 that unmistakably upset the balance of naval power in the western Pacific. The economic penetration in north and central China that followed in the wake of the military advance clearly endangered existing American commercial interests and foreclosed future opportunities there. Yet the Roosevelt administration persistently rebuffed British entreaties for joint diplomatic pressure against Tokyo to force a halt to the southward advance in China. The American president was content to issue stern verbal warnings, such as the vaguely worded "Quarantine the Aggressor" speech of October 5, 1937, in which he called for "positive endeavors to preserve peace." This phrase, linked as it was to the quarantine metaphor, was taken to imply Washington's willingness to consider the imposition of economic sanctions against Japan, until the public outcry from isolationists in the United States forced the president to beat a hasty retreat. But within a year, the Japanese onslaught in China precipitated a change in American policy toward the undeclared war in the Far East. By purchasing Chinese silver, the American government supplied the hard-pressed Nationalist government with dollars to pay for American military equipment. Secretary of State Hull announced a "moral embargo" on aircraft sales to Japan. Congress authorized the construction of two new aircraft carriers and a twofold increase in the number of naval aircraft.

But the greatest leverage that the United States exercised over Japan was its ability to mount a full-scale campaign of economic retaliation. Despite the drop in Japanese exports to the United States during the 1930s, Japan remained America's third best customer in world trade (behind Great Britain and Canada), receiving over 40 percent of its imports from the United States. We have noted how these close commercial ties constituted one of the main causes of Washington's reluctance to consider the imposition of economic sanctions on Japan in retaliation against the Manchurian invasion. American export interests feared the loss of lucrative markets that would result from an American embargo. But this commercial interdependence worked both ways: Japan's heavy reliance on American suppliers for strategic materials such as petroleum, iron, copper, steel, and industrial machinery rendered that nation vulnerable to American economic pressure. A cutoff of these supplies would seriously jeopardize the continuation of Japan's economic expansion and rearmament.

After a fierce struggle within the Roosevelt cabinet between supporters and opponents of economic retaliation, the advocates of sanctions prevailed. On July 26, 1939, the United States gave Japan the required six-months notice of its intention to abrogate the Japanese-American commercial treaty of 1911, thereby removing the legal obstacles to the adoption of trade restrictions. Before the expiration of the six months, the outbreak of the European war in September 1939 presented the Japanese with a fortuitous opportunity similar to the one they had enjoyed in 1914. Events across the world again diverted attention from Tokyo's expansionist designs in the Far East. The Asian colonies of Britain, France, and Holland were left virtually undefended as most available forces were redeployed to Europe to participate in the forthcoming confrontation with Hitler's armies. Then the fall of Holland and France in May–June 1940 enabled the Japanese to extort extensive economic and strategic concessions from those weakened European powers. The Dutch government finally bowed to Japanese pressure in June and removed many restrictions on petroleum exports from the Dutch East Indies to Japan. In the same month the Vichy government of France was pressured by Japan into closing the supply route through Indochina to Chiang Kai-shek's besieged regime in Chungking. In September Japanese forces occupied the northern half of French Indochina for the ostensible purpose of ensuring the isolation of the Chinese Nationalists' stronghold. Recognizing that further expansion southward risked a confrontation with the United States, Tokyo sought and obtained the conclusion of a Tripartite Pact with Germany and Italy in the hope of intimidating Roosevelt into granting Japan a free hand in Asia.

Confronted with this unmistakable Japanese bid for primacy in the Far East, the American government mounted a campaign of retaliation that unfolded in graduated stages in response to each Japanese transgression. Reports of Japanese efforts to corner the market on American oil exports prompted President Roosevelt to impose an embargo on aviation fuel and the highest grades of iron and scrap steel in July 1940. As Japanese troops poured into northern Indochina and Tokyo prepared to sign the Tripartite Pact in September, the embargo was extended to include all scrap metals. While Japan consolidated its position in northern Indochina, the American president finally agreed in October 1940 to authorize joint Anglo-American naval staff talks (though he stubbornly resisted London's suggestion that the American Pacific Fleet be transferred from Pearl Harbor to Singapore to bolster British naval power in the Far East).

Japan's objectives in pursuing its southward campaign were both economic and strategic in nature. The economic planners in Tokyo hoped to achieve national self-sufficiency in strategic materials by obtaining control of the oil, rubber, tin, and nickel resources located in the European colonial possessions in southeast Asia (British Malaya, French Indochina, and the Dutch East Indies). When the Dutch government rebuffed Japanese demands for the right to import unlimited quantities of oil from the East Indies, the Imperial Council adopted on July 2, 1941, a grandiose scheme for the definitive expulsion of European power from Asia and the establishment of a confederation of Asian nations under the economic control, political tutelage, and military protection of Japan. In the minds of officials in Tokyo, this "Greater East Asia Co-Prosperity Sphere" would concretize the Oriental Monroe Doctrine that had been ineffectually advanced by earlier Japanese officials: The vacuum produced by the withdrawal of European power from East Asia, like the vacuum produced by the withdrawal of European power from Latin America in the nineteenth century, would be filled by the regional power whose cultural, economic, and military superiority entitled it to exercise hegemony in its geographical sphere. In pursuit of this objective, Japanese troops advanced into the southern part of Indochina on July 24, 1941. The acquisition of naval and air bases on the Indochinese coast immediately posed a grave menace to the British naval base at Singapore and the petroleum reserves of the Dutch East Indies. The American government's retaliatory response to this dramatic extension of Japanese power marked the decisive turn in relations between Tokyo and Washington: President Roosevelt froze Japanese assets in the United States and imposed an embargo on high-octane gasoline, effectively terminating all trade between the two countries and depriving Japan of the fuel she needed to resume mechanized military operations on the Asian mainland.

The mounting concern in Washington about the deteriorating situation in the Far East was accompanied by growing public support in the United States for the embattled population of China. Pearl Buck's best-selling novel, *The Good Earth,* later made into a popular motion picture, evoked widespread sympathy through its portrayal of the sturdy, virtuous Chinese peasant. Such an image stood in glaring contrast to wire service photographs and news stories of Japanese troops looting and pillaging throughout China. The American support for China had come in the form both of official government loans ($20 million in the spring of 1940, $100 million in November 1940) and of unofficial expressions of solidarity with the suffering Chinese. In 1937 Captain Claire Chennault, a retired Army Air Corps officer, had become the chief adviser to the Chinese Air Force; he brought with him a group of mercenary American pilots, the "Flying Tigers," whose services on behalf of a foreign power were tacitly tolerated by the American government. In April 1941, Roosevelt signed an executive order legalizing this mercenary activity and in October 1941 dispatched an official American military mission to Chiang's government in Chungking.

The imposition of the American embargo, together with the stepped-up American economic and military support for the Chinese resistance, left

Japanese officials in a quandary: Japan possessed less than a two-year supply of oil at a time when the seemingly interminable struggle on the Asian mainland absorbed huge quantities of aviation and motor fuel. In light of severe shortages of other vital minerals, the cutoff of American oil exports forced Tokyo to consider the alternative of seeking a negotiated settlement with China and evacuating Indochina (the conditions upon which American oil shipments would be resumed). Such a reversal would have constituted a return to the policy adopted during 1914–18 of peacefully seeking advantages in Asia by capitalizing on the Western powers' involvement in the European war. This option unmistakably represented the most promising one from a purely economic point of view.

But withdrawal from the mainland would have caused a humiliating loss of face for that group of army officers that had spearheaded the expansionist policy of the thirties. It would also have weakened the domestic position of the military and would have abruptly halted the momentum of the movement of national regeneration launched in the aftermath of the Manchurian expedition.

The second option available to Japan was a southward thrust to break the American-imposed embargo by seizing the petroleum reserves of the Dutch East Indies and the other raw materials of southeast Asia. In the end the lure of the extensive natural resources and territory in southeast Asia left unprotected by the European colonial powers induced the military party in Japan to risk war with the United States.

It is necessary here to review the conflicting pressures operating in Tokyo and Washington during the evolution of foreign and military policies toward East Asia. In Japan army planners were continually preoccupied with the traditional victim, China, and the traditional rival on the Asian mainland, Russia. Japanese military leaders, together with most of the prominent civilian leaders, favored the preservation of normal relations with the United States. They failed to realize, or realized too late, that the offensive operations in China were likely to alienate American opinion and provoke measures of retaliation from Washington. Even after the decision to expand toward southeast Asia was taken, high-ranking generals in Tokyo hoped to exclude the Philippines from the new Asian economic bloc that would be formed under Japanese leadership out of the former British, French, and Dutch possessions in the region. They entertained the hope that the new East Asian bloc would thereafter compete peacefully with the Russian, American, and European economic systems on relatively equal terms.

The Japanese navy, on the other hand, had regarded the United States as the most probable enemy since the end of the First World War. After the London Naval Conference of 1930, naval authorities in Tokyo forcefully pressed for parity with the United States in order to assure undisputed Japanese control of the western Pacific and permit an eventual advance southward. The army's lack of enthusiasm for this "southern" strategy was prompted by its obsession with protecting the newly acquired empire on the Chinese mainland from the predatory grasp of Russia. An advance toward the South Seas would necessarily denude Japan's northern defenses and conceivably tempt Moscow to intervene at the Japanese rear.

But two developments in the spring and summer of 1941 relieved this source of anxiety about Russian intentions. In April 1941 the Japanese government succeeded in signing a neutrality treaty with the Soviet Union in order to remove the possibility of a two-front war. Two months later Hitler launched his full-scale military assault on Russia from occupied Europe, compelling Stalin to transfer several divisions from Siberia to European Russia to repel the Nazi advance against its major metropolitan areas. These two events removed the threat of Soviet pressure in Manchuria and helped to convert the Japanese military to the cause of the southern strategy championed by the navy. The cabinet's decision in July 1941 to acquire the bases in Indochina preparatory to a strike against Singapore and the East Indies reflected this confluence of strategic opinion in the two services.

American policy toward East Asia was subjected to similar pressures from various sources within Roosevelt's entourage. The internecine struggle in the cabinet between advocates of economic sanctions (led by Treasury Secretary Henry Morgenthau and Interior Secretary Harold Ickes) and opponents (such as Secretary of State Cordell Hull and his undersecretary, Sumner Welles) was reenacted within the leadership of the armed services. Naval authorities had targeted Japan as America's most likely enemy since the early twenties. War Plan "Orange," formulated in 1924, envisioned a westward sweep of the American battle fleet from Pearl Harbor to liberate the lightly defended Philippines, destroy the Japanese navy, and blockade the home islands. But the spectacular increase in German naval power in the North Atlantic astride the critical trade route to Western Europe forced a reversal in American naval thinking. In the spring of 1939 American naval officials began to shift toward a defensive strategy in the Pacific: They took it for granted that economic pressure would suffice to deter Japanese aggression in that ocean. The military collapse of France and the German air assault on England hastened this reorientation. On November 4, 1940, a revised war plan, dubbed "Plan Dog," became the official basis of American naval strategy. It identified Germany as the foremost naval threat and presumed that Japan would never risk war with the United States by attacking its possessions in the Pacific. Even in the event of a Japanese invasion of the Philippines, the combination of economic warfare and a defensive naval task force was deemed sufficient to protect American interests in the region while the brunt of American power was to be deployed against Germany. The Lend-Lease Agreement with the European powers fighting Germany, the acquisition of bases in Greenland, the increase in the American naval presence in the North Atlantic, and the refusal to dispatch the American fleet to Singapore constituted additional evidence of the European orientation of American naval strategy and the hesitancy to become embroiled in Asian complications. As Roosevelt himself graphically put it, in response to the pleas of those favoring a hard-line policy toward Japan: "I simply have not got enough navy to go around—and every little episode in the Pacific means fewer ships in the Atlantic."

By the time of the seizure of the Indochinese bases and the imposition of the American oil embargo, negotiations had gotten underway between Tokyo and Washington to reach a mutually acceptable compromise. In the course of these talks, which had begun in February 1941, the incompatability of Japanese and American demands became apparent. The United States insisted on the prior withdrawal of Japanese forces from *all* of the territories occupied since 1931 as a *precondition* to a settlement in East Asia. Certain sections of official opinion in Tokyo, aware of the increasing naval cooperation between Great Britain and the United States, disheartened by the failure of the German army to deliver the knockout blow against Russia, and anxious about Japan's dwindling oil reserves, were prepared to support a retreat from Indochina in exchange for a resumption of trade with the United States and the assurance of an adequate flow of strategic raw materials. But no Japanese leader in a position of authority was prepared to relinquish the special position in Manchukuo and China that had been acquired at such great cost. Yet American Secretary of State Hull stubbornly reiterated the original American demand for a total Japanese withdrawal from the Asian mainland.

By the autumn of 1941 the Japanese naval forces in the western Pacific had attained virtual parity in the region with the combined fleets of the United States and Great Britain. At the same time, the productive capacity, and therefore the warmaking potential, of the Western powers was many times greater than that of the island empire. Moreover, the United States had recently embarked on a massive naval construction program that threatened to erase Japan's margin of safety in the western Pacific within a few years. Such a fatal combination of short-term advantage and the prospect of long-term inferiority, as we have seen in the case of Imperial Germany in the years before 1914, tends to increase the temptation to resort to preventive war. While the Japanese diplomats sought to moderate the more extreme features of the American negotiating position in the fall of 1941, the military and naval commands prepared for the worst. On October 16 General Hideki Tojo replaced the civilian Prince Fumumaro Konoe as prime minister, and proceeded to set a deadline for a settlement with Washington that would lift the embargo on strategic materials. When that deadline, after two extensions, expired on November 30, a task force of six aircraft carriers and two battleships steamed eastward toward the headquarters of the American Pacific Fleet at Pearl Harbor. A few minutes before 8 A.M. (Hawaiian time) on Sunday, December 7, planes transported by this flotilla struck the American vessels moored in the harbor. Within two hours eight battleships went to the bottom, depriving the United States of the bulk of its Pacific fleet.

American intelligence, thanks to the cracking of the Japanese code in August 1940, was aware of Tokyo's plans to move against Singapore, the Dutch East Indies, and Thailand. There was also some evidence in these intercepts that Japan planned an assault on the Philippines. But no one in a position of authority in Washington expected an attack on Pearl Harbor; the Japanese government's instructions to its consul in Honolulu contained strong hints of an impending attack against the naval base, but code machines (which had been dispatched to the Philippines) had unaccountably not been sent to Hawaii. Intercepted instructions cabled to Japanese negotiators in Washington contained sufficiently menacing language that Chief of Staff General George Marshall dispatched a last minute warning to Pearl Harbor on December 7, but he sent it by Western Union instead of by the overloaded government cable; the messenger boy carrying the news was pedaling his bicycle toward the American military compound when the Japanese planes struck. That there were numerous examples of mistaken judgment on the part of American officials in the Pearl Harbor affair is indisputable. But despite the claims of conspiracy-minded critics, there is no hard evidence that President Roosevelt knew in advance of the plan to attack Pearl Harbor and deliberately exposed the Pacific fleet to destruction in order to bring the United States into a war against Japan and its European allies.

It is safe to conclude that neither the United States government nor the Japanese government looked forward to a Pacific war. Influential sections of the governing elites in both countries had good reason to press for a restoration of the amicable diplomatic relations and reciprocally profitable economic intercourse that had transpired during the 1920s. But it is equally true that the two governments developed foreign policies in the course of the following decade that guaranteed an eventual confrontation. The ruling elite in Tokyo, despite Japan's spectacular economic advances of the interwar period, came to regard hegemony over China and the French, British, and Dutch empires in East Asia as the only alternative to economic decline and subservience to the European powers that controlled the vital resources of the region. Conversely, a consensus gradually developed in Washington that the addition of China and the European possessions in Asia to the Japanese empire would constitute an unacceptable alteration of the balance of forces in the western Pacific as well as a severe menace to American economic interests in the region. Once these mutually incompatible perceptions of national interest became the basis of foreign policy, it was only a matter of time before the two powers on opposite sides of the Pacific would come to blows.

The War in Asia (1941–1945)

Japan's surprise carrier raid on the American naval base at Pearl Harbor effectively erased the naval power of the United States in the western

Pacific. Three days later land-based Japanese planes sent two of Great Britain's premier battleships to the bottom off the coast of Malaya. In his memoirs Winston Churchill recalled that in those dark days of December, "There were no British or American capital ships in the Indian Ocean or the Pacific except for the American survivors of Pearl Harbor, who were hastening back to California. Over all this vast expanse of waters Japan was supreme, and we everywhere were weak and naked." These crippling blows to Anglo-American naval strength in East Asia were soon followed up by rapid Japanese military advances against the Western powers' imperial outposts in the region. On February 15, 1942, Britain's naval base at Singapore, the supposedly impregnable Gibraltar of the Far East, was taken from behind by a Japanese land army that had advanced down the jungles of the Malay peninsula. By the spring of 1942 the major colonial possessions of the Western powers in Asia—the Philippines, Malaya, most of the Dutch East Indies, and Burma—had come under Japanese military occupation, while nominally independent Thailand became an ally and subservient client state of Tokyo. An area encompassing 100 million people and sufficient food-producing land, strategic minerals, and petroleum reserves to assure Japan the economic self-sufficiency it had previously lacked and had desperately sought was organized as the Greater East Asia Co-Prosperity Sphere. With Japanese forces advancing westward toward India and southward toward Australia, the remnant of the British Empire in Asia was exposed to mortal danger at a time when Britain's power was concentrated in the North Atlantic and the Mediterranean to combat the German threat closer to home. America's only ally in Asia, the Chinese Nationalist government holed up in its Chungking mountain redoubt, was cut off from land communications with the outside world when the Japanese closed the Burma road to India.

From the beginning of the Pacific war it was certain that Japan could pose no serious threat to the national existence of Great Britain and the United States. Britain's Mediterranean–Indian Ocean lifeline to Asia had been superseded in importance by her Atlantic lifeline to North America, which was kept open by Allied convoys and antisubmarine warfare against Hitler's U-boats. Not even the most fanatical warlord in Tokyo deluded himself into believing that Japan had the capability of projecting its power across the Pacific to the American west coast. That delusion was confined to California politicians, who persuaded the Roosevelt administration to authorize on February 9, 1942, the forced evacuation and internment of 120,000 Japanese-Americans in California, Oregon, and Washington on the grounds that they represented a fifth column of potential value to a Japanese invasion force. In the aftermath of Pearl Harbor, the American and British governments agreed that Germany was the main enemy. The Europe-first strategy relegated the Pacific war to the background. The Anglo-Americans waged their bombing campaign against Germany in preparation for the cross-Channel assault on Hitler's Fortress Europe, while the Soviet Union honored its nonaggression pact with Japan in order to concentrate its forces against the German armies in European Russia.

The expanding Japanese empire reached its limit within the first year of the Pacific war. In June 1942 the Japanese fleet suffered its first major defeat at the hands of the American navy as it vainly attempted to seize Midway Island west of Hawaii. From September 1942 to February 1943 Japanese efforts to reach Australia, the principal base of Anglo-American operations in the South Pacific theater, were turned back in a fierce jungle campaign in New Guinea and Guadalcanal. The strategy of the American counteroffensive against Japan consisted of a two-pronged drive. The first was an island-hopping campaign by the navy across the central Pacific spearheaded by the aircraft carriers that had been missed at Pearl Harbor by the Japanese bombers. The second was a drive by the American army under General Douglas MacArthur along the northern coast of New Guinea and other islands in the vicinity toward the Philippines. By the summer of 1944 American naval forces advancing westward had reached the island of Saipan in the Marianas, from which the first land-based bombing raids of Japanese cities were launched by the autumn of that year. In October MacArthur's forces landed on Leyte Island in the Philippines, and retook Manila in February. The two prongs of the American counteroffensive converged on the island of Okinawa in April; then, as the defeat of Germany in Europe permitted the redeployment of Allied troops and materiel to the Pacific, the Americans used the Okinawa base to launch the greatest air offensive in history against the major cities of Japan. During the spring and summer of 1945 these bombing raids from land- and carrier-based aircraft, supported by shelling from United States battleships operating with impunity off the Japanese coast, destroyed or immobilized the remnants of the Japanese navy, shattered Japanese industry, and cut off the Japanese home islands from their supplies and military forces abroad.

Acknowledging the certainty of defeat, the emperor formally urged the Supreme Council in June to approach the Allied governments for peace terms. The military and naval leaders in power refused to face the inevitability of the collapse of their grandiose dreams: They vainly attempted to arrange for Soviet mediation in favor of a conditional surrender that would enable them to preserve their positions of prestige and authority. In the meantime, a peace faction within Japan cautiously advocated ending the war on the sole condition that the titular authority of the emperor be preserved. But the United States government reaffirmed its demand for the unconditional surrender of Japan that had been formulated at the wartime conferences in Casablanca and Cairo in 1943. The formal definition of this unconditional surrender was issued on July 26, in the so-called Potsdam Declaration: Japan was to be stripped of its empire and occupied militarily until it had been transformed into a peaceful nation. The future status of the emperor, that symbolic issue of such emotional importance to

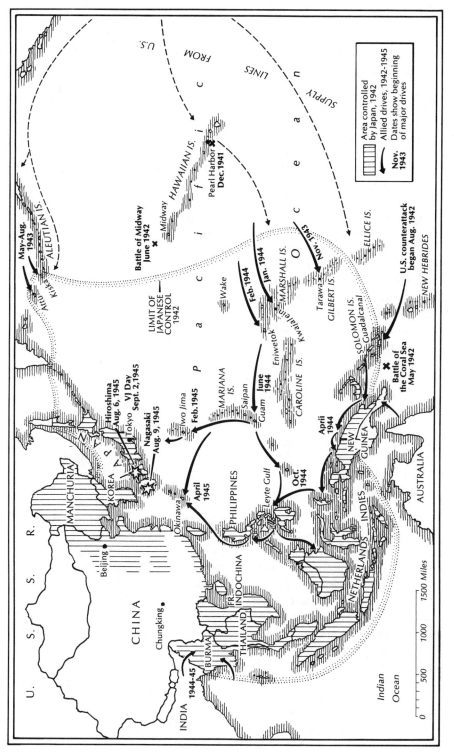

Far East and Pacific, 1941–1945

the Japanese people, was left ambiguous, but the consequence of a Japanese refusal was not: It was to be "prompt and utter destruction."

The government in Tokyo failed to respond to this ultimatum, probably because such ominous threats were common fare in the propaganda warfare of the time. In any case, the military and naval policymakers who wielded decisive authority in Japan were determined to wage a pitiless struggle to the finish in defense of the home islands, while the position of the moderate peace faction had been undermined by the uncompromising language of the Potsdam Declaration. The United States thereupon proceeded to unleash upon Japan a devastating weapon of destruction that had been developed in total secrecy by American and European émigré scientists in the course of the war. On August 6 the first atomic bomb was detonated over Hiroshima, Japan's eighth largest city, with a population of 200,000, killing over 50,000, seriously injuring as many more, and leveling four square miles of homes and factories. Three days later a second bomb was dropped on Nagasaki with similar results. In the meantime the Soviet Union, honoring its pledge made at the Yalta Conference to enter the conflict in the Far East within three months of Germany's surrender, declared war on Japan and dispatched military forces to Japanese-occupied Manchuria.

Spurred by these devastating events into assuming authority he had previously shrunk from exercising, Emperor Hirohito broke a deadlock in the Supreme Council on August 10 by voting to accept the Potsdam Declaration as the basis for Japan's surrender. The sole condition specified by Tokyo was that the emperor's right to retain his throne as the titular leader of his people not be prejudiced. Upon receiving American assurances to this effect, the Japanese government accepted the terms of surrender and formally capitulated to General MacArthur on September 2 aboard the American battleship *Missouri* in Tokyo Bay.

President Truman's decision to drop two atomic bombs on Japan in August 1945 ushered in the nuclear age. It was the first and, thus far, only time that nuclear weapons have been used in combat. The question of whether, once available, they would be employed seems never to have been raised by officials in Washington, from the advent of the $2 billion nuclear weapons research program in August 1942—the so-called Manhattan Project—to the first successful test explosion in the desolate mesa at Alamogordo, New Mexico, on July 16, 1945. Truman had been solemnly warned by his military advisers that an amphibious invasion of the Japanese islands would cost at least half a million American casualties and prolong the war for another six months. The temptation to terminate the conflict immediately in a manner that would sacrifice not a single American life outweighed whatever moral qualms American policymakers may have entertained about the particular type of weapon used. In any case, the indiscriminate slaughter of civilian populations by conventional aerial bombardment had become an acceptable form of warfare during the Second World War, confirming the Douhet school's hair-raising prophecies of terror rained upon defenseless civilians from the skies (see p. 190). More people perished in the conventional bombing raids on Dresden and Tokyo than at Hiroshima or Nagasaki.

Subsequent critics of Truman's decision have contended that the same military objective could have been achieved by unveiling the new weapon in a demonstration test on an uninhabited Pacific atoll in the presence of Japanese observers. Defenders of the decision counter this argument with the reminder that (1) the scientists who had developed the two bombs were unable to guarantee that they would detonate, and (2) at the time the Nagasaki bomb was dropped no others were available; the highly publicized testing of a "dud" would, according to this argument, have seriously damaged the credibility of American military power, stiffened Japanese resistance, and prolonged the war. Apart from these hypothetical disagreements about the feasibility of a demonstration nuclear test as a means of terminating the Asian war without the devastation that actually transpired, one thing is certain: The capitulation of Japan could have been assured by the imposition of a total naval blockade coupled with precision bombing of her internal transportation network. This would most likely have starved her into submission within a few months by depriving her people of the food and fuel they needed to survive.

But in two or three months time the United States might well have been compelled, as it had been in Europe, to share the prerogative of filling the power vacuum created by the collapse of the defeated enemy with the Soviet Union. By the end of the war, the Red Army had swept into Manchuria and into Korea down to the 38th parallel, and had occupied the Kurile Islands and the southern half of Sakhalin Island. Stalin's conditions for Russian entry in the war against Japan, which had been earnestly sought by the United States before the development of the atomic bomb, included the recovery of all of the territory and privileges that had been lost by Russia after its defeat by Japan in 1905.

Thus, in addition to the demonstrable military advantages of compelling a Japanese capitulation without the necessity of mounting a costly invasion of its home islands, a diplomatic factor may have reinforced the American government's determination to employ its powerful new weapon as soon as it was operational, which was assured by the successful test explosion in New Mexico in July 1945. The diplomatic tug-of-war between the United States and its Russian ally concerning the political reorganization of the postwar world had already begun. Upon learning of the test during the Potsdam Conference of the Big Three wartime leaders, Truman informed Stalin that the United States had developed a new weapon "of unusual destructive force," a fact already known to the Russian leader through his espionage network. Some historians have suggested that Truman was eager to wield the atomic weapon against Japan in order to frighten the Soviet Union into granting political concessions in Europe as well as to terminate the war in the Far East before Russia could participate in the victory in that theater and therefore claim a role in the postwar military occupation of Japan.

In contrast to the situation in defeated Germany, the United States was able to assert its unchallenged position of primacy in defeated Japan. Beginning on August 28 American military forces were landed on the home islands to occupy key cities and supervise the disarmament of Japanese military forces. With the formal surrender on September 2, supreme authority passed into the hands of General Douglas MacArthur in the name of the Allied powers. Soviet requests for the right to share in the occupation of the northern Japanese island of Hokkaido, which lay only twenty-five miles from the Russian-occupied Sakhalin Island, were turned aside. Though ostensibly acting on behalf of the victorious coalition, the United States proclaimed its intention to manage the occupation of Japan without the assistance of its wartime allies and administer it as a single political unit. The acrimonious Soviet-American disputes over the treatment of postwar Germany would not be reenacted over the treatment of postwar Japan: The overwhelming American air and naval superiority in the western Pacific enabled Washington, through its powerful proconsul in Tokyo, to enjoy undisputed supremacy there.

PART TWO

The Thirty-Year "Cold War" Between the Superpowers (1945-1975)

CHAPTER 8

The Formation of the Bipolar World in the Truman-Stalin Era (1945–1953)

The Political Division of Europe

When the advancing armies of the United States and the Soviet Union met at the Elbe River in the heart of Germany on April 25, 1945, the exhilarating prospect of victory and peace momentarily overshadowed the political disagreements between their respective governments that had surfaced at the Crimea conference two and a half months earlier. Within a week word had arrived of Hitler's death by his own hand and the capitulation of the German armies in Italy and Austria. The formal surrender by German military authorities on May 7 merely confirmed what had been known for months to be a foregone conclusion: the collapse of the Nazi imperium in Europe. Though the Allied soldiers encamped along the opposite banks of the Elbe and in other liberated regions of the continent anticipated redeployment to the Far East for the final drive against the receding military forces of Japan, the end of the most destructive military contest in history was, at long last, in sight. The promise of a return to civilian pursuits and the renewal of familial attachments engendered the customary euphoria that attends the conclusion of great wars. For a brief moment, in the afterglow of triumph for what was universally felt to be a supremely worthy cause, the peoples and political leaders of the two preeminent powers in the victorious coalition could celebrate the dawn of a new era of world peace.

But the convergence of American and Russian military power at the center of the devastated continent of Europe in the spring of 1945 signified something of critical significance for the future of the world beyond the immediate reality of Germany's defeat. Amid the universal expressions of relief on "Victory in Europe" day, or VE day, as it was to be widely called, there remained a number of disturbing facts about the way in which the war against Hitler had been brought to a close that were to prevent the restoration of the peacetime conditions for which all of the belligerent populations yearned.

Foremost among these postwar realities was the disappearance of all forms of indigenous political authority and military power in Central Europe as the German state disintegrated and its war machine ground to a halt. This condition had been foreordained by the Allied leaders' decision to impose upon the vanquished enemy an unconditional surrender that would assure the instantaneous destruction of all German political and military institutions. The unprecedented brutality of the Nazi occupation of Europe had inspired in the victorious coalition the determination to rid the continent once and for all of the scourge of German power. The war against Hitler had assumed the character of a moral crusade against a monstrous evil that had to be subdued and then permanently eliminated for the benefit of humanity. In striking contrast to Wilson's discriminating policy at the end of the First World War, Roosevelt declined to distinguish between the objectionable regime of the enemy state and the civilian population that it had ruled. The Führer was regarded merely as the agent of a German people whose instinctual propensity for aggression disqualified it from playing any role whatsoever in the postwar reorganization of Europe.

This moralistic justification of the American war effort, developed for domestic consumption to justify the painful public sacrifices required for the waging of total war, camouflaged the principal reason for America's intervention in the European struggle, which was to redress the balance of power on the continent that had been disturbed by Germany's bid for hegemony. But the dissolution of the Nazi administrative and military apparatus by the Allied powers, followed by their refusal to countenance the prompt reconstitution of a German successor regime, produced the vacuum in Central Europe that Churchill had foreseen before the Yalta Conference. This vacuum was inevitably to be filled by the military power of the advancing armies that converged upon the center of the continent from west and east in the spring of 1945.

In this way the informal partition of liberated Europe into pro-Western and pro-Soviet spheres was dictated by the military situation at the moment of Germany's collapse. Each of the two zones eventually adopted political institutions, economic practices, and foreign policies that reflected the preferences and influences of its liberator. France, Belgium, Greece, and Italy, in spite of the presence of powerful Communist movements that had played a significant role in resisting the German occupation of their countries, reestablished Western-style parliamentary systems and capitalist economic structures while adapting their foreign policies to the Anglo-American vision of the postwar world. The states on the eastern half of the continent, despite the ideological hostility to Communism and nationalistic antipathy for Russia that characterized the recent history of most of them, adopted Soviet political and economic models and supported the Kremlin's foreign policy goals under the watchful eyes of the Russian occupation armies and their civilian collaborators among the indigenous population.

This ideological bifurcation of Europe did not occur overnight. In the Soviet sphere, non-Communist political parties were permitted to operate and non-Communist leaders to participate in coalition governments in all of the Eastern European states for a few years after the war; similarly, the Communist parties of France, Italy, and Belgium were not only tolerated but allowed to hold cabinet posts in the early postwar coalitions in those countries. But one salient feature of the postwar political situation in Europe eventually caused the division of that continent into two mutually antagonistic blocs of states respectively identified with the superpower whose military forces had emancipated them from German rule: This was the unwavering determination of the Soviet government to establish a ring of subservient client states in Eastern Europe along the broad invasion route stretching from the western shore of the Black Sea to the eastern shore of the Baltic that had brought marauding armies to the heart of Russia twice within the memory of most of its citizens still alive in 1945.

We have seen how Stalin's insistence on securing border rectifications at the expense of Finland, Poland, and Romania to enhance the security of Russia's western frontier had won the reluctant assent of the Western powers. But the Kremlin's subsequent attempt to promote, through political intimidation backed by the presence of the Red Army, the installation of pro-Soviet regimes in the states of Eastern Europe beyond the newly expanded frontiers was to provoke increasing opposition from Washington. In time a momentous evolution in the strategic thinking of policymakers in the Truman administration took place. American officials began to ponder the implications of the developments unfolding on the eastern half of the European continent in light of historical precedent and geographical context. Great Britain and, belatedly, the United States had intervened in the two European wars of the twentieth century to restore the balance of power that had been upset by Germany. The temporary elimination of German power at the end of the First World War had been preceded a year earlier by the temporary disappearance of Russian power. The simultaneous weakness of Germany and Russia in the decade of the 1920s had enabled the small states of Eastern Europe to preserve their independence from both of their potentially powerful neighbors with the support and encouragement of France. Hitler's subsequent bid for German hegemony in Europe had also resulted in the erasure of German power, but this time Russian power had been projected into the political and military void of Eastern Europe at a time when no nation or coalition of nations on the Western half of the continent was strong enough to balance it. The tough-minded realism of geopolitics, so familiar to European strategists and statesmen, began to replace the Wilsonian reveries of Roosevelt in the minds of the foreign policy advisers of the new American president: Russia was rapidly acquiring control of the heartland of Eurasia. The military exhaustion and economic distress of the nations along the western rim of Europe exposed them to the threat of Soviet domination as well. A Russian-controlled continental empire stretching from the Sea of Japan to the Atlantic and from the Arctic to the Aegean would be better positioned to mount a drive for world dominion than Nazi Germany had been at the height of its power. What may have appeared to Stalin as a legitimate attempt to bolster the security of Russia's vulnerable western frontier by the formation of compliant buffer states beyond it was increasingly interpreted in Washington as the beginning of a Russian drive for continental hegemony on the road to mastery of the globe. The ominous prophecy of Mackinder returned to haunt those who had confidently expected that the end of the fighting would bring the peace and security earnestly sought by all: "Who rules east Europe commands the Heartland; who rules the Heartland commands the World-Island; who rules the World-Island rules the world."

The establishment of Russian hegemony over the reconstituted states of Eastern Europe from 1945 through 1948 was accomplished with impunity because the only nation capable of preventing it had disengaged militarily from the European continent. At the time of Germany's defeat the numerical strength of the armed forces of the United States exceeded 12 million. By the end of 1947 that number had fallen to 1.4 million as a consequence of the abolition of universal military conscription and a drastic reduction in the size of the professional armed services. The demobilization of America's military forces and the dismantling of its war industries transpired at a time when the Soviet Union kept over 4 million battle-seasoned veterans under arms—down from the 12 million wartime level—and retained the formidable arsenal of weaponry with which it had driven the German army from Moscow to Berlin.

The reasons for this precipitous disengagement of American military power from Europe after the Second World War are easy to appreciate, as ill advised as it may have appeared in retrospect. The American public, accustomed to small volunteer armies in peacetime, had no inclination to tolerate the retention of an American military presence in postwar Europe beyond the token forces required for occupation duty in Germany, Austria, and Italy.* The United States had entered the European war for the purpose of destroying the Nazi regime and eliminating German military power from the continent. Once those two objectives had been achieved, only an American government endowed with superhuman powers of persuasion could have induced its war-weary citizens to bear the enormous costs and manifold inconveniences of maintaining large military forces across the Atlantic solely for the purpose of balancing the undiminished

---

* Allied military forces remained in occupation of northern Italy until December 1945, notwithstanding that country's status as a "cobelligerent" after the overthrow of Mussolini in 1943.

military might of a nation that had so recently been hailed as a trusted ally against Hitler.

The American public's inclination to "bring the boys home," reflected in expressions of Congressional sentiment and recorded in the opinion polls of the period, was entirely consistent with the Roosevelt administration's master plan for the political organization of the postwar world. The American commander in chief during the Second World War shared the optimistic expectation of his predecessor during the First World War that the defeat of Germany would herald a new era in which international conciliation would supplant the operation of the balance of power as the mechanism for the preservation of world order. The United Nations Organization, conceived by American, British, and Russian representatives at the Dumbarton Oaks Conference in the autumn of 1944 and formally established by the delegates of fifty states meeting in San Francisco from April through June 1945, was designed to supersede the discredited League of Nations and resume its noble purpose with more effective means. Since both the United States and the Soviet Union shared, along with Great Britain, France, and China, permanent representation on the new organization's decision-making body, the Security Council, it was widely assumed that such disagreements as might arise among the great powers over the postwar political settlement could be amicably adjudicated in the United Nations without recourse to the old practices of power politics and regional alliance systems that had been so decisively discredited in the course of the previous decade.

Furthermore, the American monopoly on nuclear weaponry in the early postwar years reinforced the traditional sense of invulnerability to external aggression that had long nourished the national proclivity for isolationism. The United States had intervened in the two world wars on the assumption that the subjugation of Europe and the control of its resources and Atlantic bases by a single aggressive power would perforce pose an unacceptable threat to the security of the Western Hemisphere. In the first few years after Hiroshima and Nagasaki, America's ability to devastate the principal cities of any potential aggressor without the slightest risk of retaliation against its own territory seemed to afford a greater degree of protection than even the Atlantic Ocean ever could. Such a condition of strategic omnipotence was scarcely conducive to the sentiment of national insecurity that would have been required to generate broad public support for the assumption of extensive military commitments abroad so soon after the end of the war. Particularly in light of Roosevelt's tacit endorsement of Soviet predominance in the half of Europe that was liberated by the Red Army, his successor was in no position to contest the Kremlin's exercise of that prerogative beyond innocuous expressions of displeasure at the inevitable violations of the rights of the populations concerned.

The Truman administration forcefully challenged the expansion of Soviet power only when it appeared to surpass the demarcation line separating the two spheres of influence that had been tacitly recognized by the Allied leaders at the wartime conferences. During the years 1946 and 1947 a series of political developments along the southern rim of Eurasia was viewed by Western leaders as evidence of a coordinated Soviet effort to attain one of the traditional objectives of Russian foreign policy: expansion southward toward the Eastern Mediterranean and the Persian Gulf, a region historically under the sway of British power.

The site of the first direct confrontation between the Soviet Union and the Western powers was Iran, a country whose strategic location had rendered it the object of Russian and British rivalry as early as the end of the nineteenth century. As we have seen, these two imperial powers had jointly partitioned the country into spheres of influence in the decade prior to the First World War. The collapse of the Tsarist empire and the advent of the Bolshevik regime had temporarily resulted in a diminution of Russian influence in Iran; Great Britain proceeded to organize and supervise the exploitation of the vast reserves of petroleum that had recently been discovered there while striving to establish predominant political influence over the government in Teheran. In August 1941, as Hitler's armies advanced deep into the Soviet Union, Russian and British military forces simultaneously entered Iran and promptly replaced the increasingly pro-German regime of Reza Shah with a more compliant government headed by his teenaged son, Mohammed Reza Pahlevi. According to the terms of an Anglo-Russian-Iranian treaty concluded on January 29, 1942, Russian troops were stationed in northern Iran and British troops in the south to protect the vital supply route from the Persian Gulf to the Russian frontier along which British and American arms were transported to the Soviet Union. Both foreign occupation forces, as well as the American contingent that later joined the British troops in the southern zone, were to be withdrawn within six months of the end of the war. Shortly after the cessation of hostilities, the Communist-controlled Tudeh party fomented a separatist revolt in the northwestern province of Azerbaijan bordering on the Soviet Union. The Russian occupation army prevented the Iranian government from suppressing the insurgency by denying its military forces access to the rebellious province. In November a provincial assembly dominated by the Tudeh party was elected in Azerbaijan and promptly declared its autonomy, a move that was widely regarded as the first step toward the absorption of the province by the Soviet Republic of Azerbaijan across the border. The Iranian prime minister received a set of demands from Moscow which included indefinite retention of Soviet troops in northern Iran, recognition of the autonomy of Azerbaijan, and the formation of a Russian-Iranian joint stock company to develop the petroleum resources of the northern provinces.

Interpreting these Soviet moves as the beginning of a campaign to obtain effective control of the entire country, including its rich petroleum reserves and its ports on the Persian Gulf, the British and American governments applied vigorous diplomatic pressure on the Kremlin to terminate its Iranian adventure. Tough speeches by British Foreign Secretary Ernest Bevin on February 21 and American Secretary of State James Byrnes on February 28 signaled the intention of London and Washington to resist further Soviet advances in the region. When the Red Army, alone among the three wartime occupation forces, delayed its evacuation beyond the March 2, 1946, deadline, the resulting firestorm of criticism from the British and American governments prompted the Kremlin to withdraw its forces prior to the Iranian parliament's ratification of the agreement on Azerbaijan autonomy and the joint oil venture. After the Red Army completed its evacuation in May 1946, the Iranian parliament, apparently emboldened by the vigorous expressions of Anglo-American support, declined to ratify the agreement that had been concluded under duress with the Kremlin. In the meantime an American military mission had arrived in Teheran and arrangements had been made for the purchase of American military equipment by the Iranian government. The diplomatic setback suffered by the Soviet Union in the Iranian crisis of 1946 was a direct consequence of the Truman administration's decision to join Great Britain in protecting this historic object of Russian expansionist ambition. Washington's determination to bolster the Pahlevi regime set the stage for the establishment seven years later of an intimate security link between Washington and Teheran that was to last for a quarter of a century. In a more general sense, it heralded America's determination to resist the expansion of Soviet influence throughout the world.

Just as Soviet activities in northern Iran during 1946 were viewed in Washington as evidence of the Kremlin's renewal of traditional Russian expansionism toward the Persian Gulf, simultaneous Soviet pressures on Iran's neighbor Turkey appeared to rekindle Russian ambitions for a geopolitical offensive into the eastern Mediterranean. On March 19, 1945, Moscow had formally denounced the Turko-Soviet treaty of friendship concluded in 1925, which had established close political and economic collaboration between these two historic enemies and included reciprocal pledges of nonaggression. On June 7, 1945, Foreign Commissar Vyacheslav Molotov presented the Turkish ambassador to Moscow with a set of demands that collectively constituted a substantial infringement on Turkish sovereignty. These included the cession of territory in the Caucasus annexed by Russia in 1878 and reacquired by Turkey after the First World War, the revision of the Montreux Convention of 1936 governing the Turkish Straits so as to establish joint Russian-Turkish jurisdiction over this vital waterway, and the leasing of Soviet bases on its shores to ensure its defense.

Readers of these pages need no reminder of Russia's historic interest in obtaining effective control of the outlet of the Black Sea to the Mediterranean. As had been the case with Soviet advances in Eastern Europe at the expense of Finland, the Baltic states, Poland, and Romania, as well as in Manchuria at the expense of China, Stalin's diplomatic offensive against Turkey represented an attempt to restore territory or privileges previously possessed by or promised to the Russian state. Not even the demand for de facto control of the Dardenelles was new. In a modified form it had been secretly granted to the Tsarist regime by its Anglo-French allies during the First World War before the Bolshevik Revolution resulted in its repudiation. More recently, Molotov had tried in vain to secure Germany's endorsement of Russian designs on Turkey's Caucasian frontier and the Straits during the period of the Nazi-Soviet Pact. Stalin had insistently raised the matter of the Straits with Churchill at Moscow in October 1944, with Roosevelt at Yalta, and with Truman at Potsdam, all without concrete result. His argument was framed in entirely defensive terms: Turkey, which had remained neutral during the war despite British and Russian bids for an alliance and permitted the sale of strategically important chrome to Germany until the spring of 1944 for fear of antagonizing Hitler, was too weak to prevent powers unfriendly to the Soviet Union from sending their warships into the Black Sea. But to the United States, Stalin's demand represented nothing less than the revival of the old dream of a Russian breakthrough to the Mediterranean at Turkey's expense, and therefore had to be resisted with the same firmness that had been displayed by Great Britain in the days when it was still capable of playing such a role.

In short, the Truman administration's response to the Turkish crisis of 1945–46 reflected the same determination to replace Britain as the principal guarantor of Russia's confinement along the southern rim of Eurasia that had prompted its vigorous resistance to Soviet pressure on Iran. To Washington, as to London during the era when the "eastern question" had preoccupied the architects of British foreign policy, Russian control of the Straits would entail domination of the eastern Mediterranean. This in turn would signify command of the vital commercial waterway linking Europe to the Orient and afford easy access to the valuable mineral resources of North Africa and the Middle East. Accordingly, when Ankara's indignant rejection of Moscow's demands precipitated a violent campaign against Turkey in the Soviet press and the deployment of twenty-five Russian divisions on the Caucasian frontier, the Truman administration resolved to bolster the beleaguered Turkish regime. In response to a harshly worded Soviet note of August 7, 1946, reiterating the Russian claims, Washington dispatched a naval task force to the eastern Mediterranean as a demonstrative show of force and on September 30 announced that a portion of the American fleet would be permanently stationed there. In the face of this ostentatious display of American naval power, which was implicitly reinforced by the American monopoly on atomic weapons, Moscow backed down at the Turkish Straits just as it was being dislodged from northern Iran, though the extent of the Soviet retrenchment was not apparent until much later.

During the Russian-American showdown over Soviet demands on Turkey, acute domestic unrest across the Aegean in Greece was viewed in London and Washington as a third aspect of the putative Russian campaign of southward expansion already in evidence in Iran and Turkey. It will be recalled that upon the evacuation of German occupation forces in Greece in November 1944, a fierce internal struggle had erupted between the conservative faction of the Greek resistance movement loyal to the monarchy and the Communist partisan organization. The intervention of British military forces in the winter of 1944–45 resulted in a truce concluded between the two factions in February 1945 as well as an agreement stipulating a referendum on the question of the restoration of the monarchy and national elections under Allied supervision. The elections of March 1946 were boycotted by the leftist political organizations and therefore produced a comfortable majority for the royalist party that was actively supported by the British. In the summer of 1946, at the height of the Turkish crisis, thousands of Greek Communists concentrated in the north renewed their guerrilla warfare against the pro-Western government in Athens with the encouragement and material assistance of the newly established Communist states across the border, Yugoslavia, Albania, and Bulgaria. When the national referendum in September resulted in a large majority in favor of the restoration of the monarchy, the conflict raging on the Greek peninsula assumed the aspect of an ideological confrontation pitting the British-backed royalist regime in Athens against the Communist guerrilla movement in the north that was supplied and supported by the adjacent Communist states.

In this sense the Greek drama was reminiscent of the earlier struggle in Poland between the pro-Western and pro-Soviet factions of the resistance movement. But there were two critical differences between the Polish and Greek situations that determined their divergent outcomes. First of all, the geographical position of Greece was decisively favorable to the pro-Western government and its British protectors. Whereas Poland's common border with Russia and its forbidding distance from the Western powers foreordained the triumph of the pro-Soviet Polish faction backed by the Red Army, the proximity of the Greek peninsula to the British bases in the Mediterranean constituted a major liability for the Communist partisans in their struggle with the Athens regime. Moreover, it will be recalled that Stalin had excluded Greece from the Russian sphere of influence in his wartime bargain with Churchill and had displayed no enthusiasm for the Communist insurrection there in the winter of 1944–45. On the contrary, the Soviet leader instructed the Greek Communists to cooperate with the British-backed government in the same way that he had urged restraint upon the Communist parties of France and Italy that were participating in governing coalitions dominated by pro-Western groups. The principal foreign supporter and supplier of the Greek Communist insurgency was Yugoslavia, which, under the leadership of its charismatic strongman, Marshal Tito, was already displaying the taste for independent activity that was soon to result in a total break with Moscow.

It may be supposed, in the absence of confirmation from the appropriate files in the Kremlin, that the motivation for this Soviet caution in the Greek civil war was twofold. It probably reflected Stalin's disinclination to favor the establishment by indigenous partisan forces of an independent Communist state beyond the effective reach of Russian military power and political control. This tendency appears to have determined his simultaneous reluctance to offer unqualified support to the Communist forces of Tito in Yugoslavia and Mao Zedong in China in their respective struggles for power against anti-Communist rivals. An additional source of Soviet hesitation seems to have been the apprehension that a Communist takeover in a country specifically allotted to the Western sphere of influence was certain to provoke sharp reactions from Washington and London with potentially unpleasant consequences for the Soviet Union.

As it turned out, the capacity of Great Britain to fulfill its historic function as the guardian of Greek independence had been severely impaired by the economic crisis that gripped this erstwhile world power at the end of the Second World War. The drain on British reserves of gold and foreign exchange occasioned by the requirements of financing the war against the Axis had been partially mitigated by Lend-Lease assistance from the United States. Following the termination of this wartime aid, an American emergency loan of $3.75 billion was extended to Britain in 1946 on the assumption that this would suffice to cover its short-term needs until the restoration of its export trade would produce the foreign exchange required to finance essential imports. But the proceeds of this loan were promptly spent for the consumption of food and fuel rather than invested in productive enterprises that would revive the country's export capability. The result was the rapid exhaustion of British reserves, a potentially catastrophic condition that was exacerbated by the onset of the worst weather conditions in recorded history during the winter of 1946–47. The national transportation system ground to a halt, the shortage of coal forced the closing of factories and temporary cutoffs of electricity, and the freezing of winter crops led to the rationing of food.

A nation in such dire straits was hardly in a position to furnish the military and economic assistance required by the Greek government to quell the Communist insurrection in the north. At the same time, the United Nations Organization was prevented from intervening in the Greek civil war to restore order by the Soviet veto in the Security Council. Once it had become apparent that neither Great Britain nor the United Nations was able to act in its defense, the government in Athens appealed to the United States several times in 1946 for financial aid and military equipment. The Truman administration furnished such meager economic assistance as was available under existing authority, but by the beginning of

1947 it had become evident that only large-scale assistance over a long period would avert a total collapse of the Greek economy and the probable seizure of power by the Communist guerrilla movement. But such a massive program of economic aid to a financially unstable regime seemed inconceivable in the domestic political climate of postwar America. The Republican party, which had recently won control of the Eightieth Congress, had consistently opposed all of the major foreign economic aid programs devised by Democratic presidents up to and including the British loan in 1946. The opposition party, which had rallied to the cause of internationalism during the period of America's participation in the Second World War, seemed poised to return to its prewar isolationist tradition of economic nationalism, which meant support for high tariffs and hostility to foreign loans that did not directly promote American exports.

Then, on the twenty-first of February, 1947, the British Foreign Office officially informed the American State Department of its intention to terminate all financial assistance to Greece and Turkey and to remove the forty thousand British troops from Greece as of the following March 31 on account of Britain's own economic trauma. Remarking that both of the recipient countries were desperately in need of foreign loans to stave off total economic collapse as well as to finance the reorganization and reequipment of their armed forces to preserve their security, the British government expressed the hope that the United States would be able to assume the obligation it was about to relinquish. In this dramatic diplomatic communication the government of the greatest empire the world has ever seen conceded the beginning of its demise. The dissolution of British power along the vulnerable lifeline to that empire, from Gibraltar to Singapore, had produced a vacuum along the southern shores of Eurasia comparable in importance to the vacuum in Eastern Europe produced by the crumbling of German power there. Britain's inability to continue to bear the financial burden of maintaining its far-flung garrisons and bolstering friendly regimes along the lifeline seemed to present the United States with the choice of substituting American for British power in that region or of passively permitting Soviet power to fill the void.

The American president took up the challenge on March 12, 1947, in a historic address before a special joint session of Congress: The United States government declared its intention to supplant Great Britain as the guarantor of the economic viability and military security of Greece and Turkey. Congressional authorization was sought, and duly obtained, for the disbursement of $250 million and $150 million worth of military and economic assistance to the governments of Athens and Ankara, respectively, as well as for the dispatch of American advisers to these troubled regimes to assist in their economic stabilization and military reorganization. As noted above, the Soviet claims on Turkey simply disappeared from public discourse after the American show of force in the eastern Mediterranean. In Greece, the civil war petered out during the years

1948–49, as the Royal Greek Army, organized in close collaboration with the American military mission and lavishly supplied with American munitions, swept northward to occupy all of the rebel strongholds in the mountains and force the Communist partisans into exile in Bulgaria and Albania. The Greek Communists' chief benefactor, Tito's Yugoslavia, had sealed their fate by closing its frontier and terminating all assistance to the insurgents in July 1948 in retaliation against its exclusion from the world Communist movement the previous month.

Embedded in Truman's speech of March 12 was a single sentence that affirmed that the American government had no intention of confining its newly adopted program of foreign assistance to the narrow objective of helping the governments of Greece and Turkey to overcome their immediate difficulties: "I believe," Truman declared, "that it must be the policy of the United States to support free peoples who are resisting subjugation by armed minorities or by outside pressures." Implicit in this presidential declaration, which subsequently acquired the designation "Truman Doctrine," was the pledge to employ the economic resources of the United States to bolster friendly nations all along the periphery of the Soviet bloc that appeared susceptible to pressure from their powerful neighbor or to insurgency by domestic Communist movements connected by ideological affinity to the Soviet Union. The power vacuum in the Balkans and south Asia created by the collapse of the Pax Brittanica seemed in danger of being filled by Soviet power. This circumstance presented the Truman administration with an emergency that was promptly met, as we have seen, by the dispatch of American assistance to the governments of Greece, Turkey, and Iran. But the power vacuums at the two opposite ends of the Soviet empire, in Europe after the collapse of Germany and in East Asia after the defeat of Japan, represented even more serious threats to American security than did the prospect of Soviet domination of the eastern Mediterranean and southern Asia in the eyes of those highly placed officials in the Truman administration who were engaged in this fundamental reshaping of American foreign policy.

It therefore became the task of this handful of men—led by George Kennan, Dean Acheson, and William Clayton at the State Department and James Forrestal at the Pentagon—to develop a rationale for a coordinated response to Soviet expansionist pressures wherever they might occur that would persuade the Republican-controlled Congress and the American public at large of the pressing necessity to abandon the tradition of peacetime isolationism. The most articulate and influential enunciation of the case for an activist American foreign policy appeared anonymously in the July 1947 issue of the journal *Foreign Affairs* under the heading "The Sources of Soviet Conduct." Composed by Kennan, the director of the newly created Policy Planning Staff of the State Department who had observed Soviet behavior at firsthand in his former post as deputy chief of mission at the American Embassy in Moscow, it summarized official government policy as distilled from the high-level discussions conducted in Washington during the recent crises in Iran, Turkey, and Greece. Its message was straightforward and simple:* The Soviet Union, for reasons related more to the traditional Russian sense of insecurity than to the messianic goals of Marxist-Leninist ideology, could be expected to probe the weak points beyond its frontiers in an effort to extend the reach of Soviet power in the world. It is in the national interest of the United States to conduct a firm but patient policy of containing the expansion of Soviet power beyond the limits informally established at Yalta by strengthening the political, social, and economic institutions of those countries that had or might become subject to such expansionist pressures. Through the application of such counterpressure the Kremlin would gradually be brought to realize, over a period of ten to fifteen years, that the cost of such aggressive policies would greatly outweigh any conceivable benefits they might yield. The ultimate result, Kennan confidently predicted, would be the attenuation of the Soviet threat to the vital interests of the United States and the front-line nations which his policy of "containment" was designed to protect.

While this bold reformulation of American policy toward the Soviet Union was being put in press, a dramatic public statement by Secretary of State George C. Marshall delivered at the Harvard University graduation ceremonies on June 5, 1947, directly addressed the particular problem that had preoccupied Kennan as he drafted what came to be known as the doctrine of containment: This was the vulnerability of the Western European countries to Soviet domination caused by their inability to recover from the war-induced dislocations of their economic systems. We have already had occasion to ponder, in connection with the Greco-Turkish crises of 1946–47, the catastrophic consequences of the postwar financial crisis in Great Britain for the recovery of that country's industrial productivity and the resumption of its foreign trade. Economic conditions were far worse in those nations on the continent that had served during the occupation as the victims of German economic exploitation and then as the final battleground for the war in Europe. The continued impoverishment of the countries of Western Europe seemed an open invitation to the Soviet Union to extend its political dominion over them with the connivance of the powerful Communist parties and Communist-controlled labor organizations in countries such as France, Italy, and Belgium. To meet this presumed threat the American secretary of state invited the nations of Europe, including the Soviet Union and its satellites, to prepare a plan for European economic recovery with massive American assistance on the basis of permanent economic cooperation among themselves.

---

* Though apparently not sufficiently so as to prevent its being misrepresented in subsequent years by advocates of policies that Kennan lived to abhor, such as the American intervention in the Vietnamese civil war to "contain" Russian (or Chinese) expansion.

The inclusion of the Soviet Union in this unprecedented offer of foreign economic assistance from Washington prompted the governments of France and Great Britain to solicit the Kremlin's participation in a conference in Paris at the end of June to draw up a collective response to the American initiative. On June 26 Soviet Foreign Commissar Molotov arrived in the French capital accompanied by eighty-nine economic specialists, apparently prepared to give serious consideration to the American proposal. But after a few days of fruitless negotiation, Molotov and his entourage abandoned the conference while the Soviet government denounced the project and forbade the governments of its East European satellites to have anything to do with it.

The grounds for the Soviet rejection of what came to be known as the Marshall Plan were twofold. First, in order to collect the pertinent economic statistics and to ensure that the funds disbursed were spent for the purposes intended, the American government had insisted on access to, and some degree of advisory authority over, the internal budgets of the recipient states. These are conditions customarily required of impoverished countries by their prudent foreign bankers, from the era of financial imperialism before the First World War to the current tight-fisted lending policies of the International Monetary Fund. But it was too much to expect of a victorious great power, particularly one as secretive and suspicious as the Soviet Union, to open its books to the prying eyes of American financial officials and to adjust its budgetary policies to spending priorities established in Washington. This requirement was denounced in Moscow as an intolerable infringement on the national sovereignty of the participating states. The investigations of the Marshall Plan administrators would doubtless have revealed how vulnerable the postwar economy of the Soviet Union was, a circumstance that the Kremlin was desperately trying to conceal for reasons of Communist ideology as well as national pride. Moreover, the proviso that most of the Marshall aid be spent for the purchase of American exports prompted Soviet suspicions of an ulterior motive beneath the facade of humanitarian largesse. It appeared to confirm the Leninist prediction of the impending collapse of capitalism and the capitalists' frantic efforts to prevent it: American corporate monopolies, squeezed by the drastic decline in domestic demand for their products as war-related orders dried up, now strove to save themselves by obtaining markets in Europe and subjecting the shattered economies of that continent to American commercial domination. This interpretation even received some confirmation from the mouths of American officials themselves, who tried to sell the Marshall program to Congress by warning that Europe's huge trade deficit with the United States was bound to cause serious difficulties for American exporters unless the chronic "dollar shortage" across the Atlantic could be rectified through the granting of government credits.

Responding to the invitation of the foreign ministers of Britain and

France, representatives of all the sixteen European nations outside the Soviet sphere except Spain* assembled in Paris on July 12 to lay the groundwork for a coordinated response to the American government's offer of economic assistance. On September 22 a committee formed at this gathering submitted a plan for a four-year recovery program which specified the anticipated combined budget deficit of the sixteen participating states. On the basis of the plan, the United States congress voted by lopsided majorities on April 3, 1948, to appropriate $6 billion to cover the combined deficit for the first year and agreed to make three annual grants later. In mid-April the recipient nations established the Organization for European Economic Cooperation to supervise the allocation of the American aid and promote coordination among the nations that were to receive it. Between 1948 and 1952 the European Recovery Program (as Marshall's brainchild was officially known) supplied grants and credits totaling $13.2 billion. The largest amounts went to Great Britain and its dependencies ($3.2 billion), France ($2.7 billion), Italy ($1.5 billion), and West Germany ($1.4 billion).

The economic consequences of the Marshall Plan surpassed the most optimistic expectations of its authors. By 1952, the termination date of the American aid program, European industrial production had risen to 35 percent and agricultural production to 10 percent above the prewar level. From the depths of economic despair the recipient nations of Western Europe embarked on a period of economic expansion that was to bring a degree of prosperity to their populations unimaginable in the dark days of 1947. In the meantime, the donor nation derived great commercial benefits from its financial largesse, as the Marxist-Leninist critics had forecast; more than two-thirds of the European imports under the plan came from the United States, which meant higher profits for American firms engaged in the export trade as well as more jobs for the workers they employed. It is doubtful that the phenomenal growth of the American economy in the prosperous era of the fifties and early sixties would have occurred without the stimulus provided by orders for its goods and services from the other nations of the industrial world across the Atlantic that were rebuilding their war-torn economies. One must not exaggerate the extent of the American economy's export dependence in the early postwar years. With a huge internal market still capable of absorbing most of its industrial production and a considerable proportion of its agricultural output, the United States still exported less than 10 percent of its gross national product compared to much higher percentages for the genuinely export-dependent nations of Western Europe and Japan. Nevertheless, postwar America had begun to develop an important stake in international trade for the first time in its history. In 1946 America's

* Spain was excluded from participation in the Marshall Plan on account of its autocratic political system as well as its pro-Axis sympathies during the Second World War.

total exports were almost four times the prewar average of $4 billion per year, and certain sectors of the economy had come to depend on foreign sales for a major proportion of their earnings. The dollars lent or given to the importing nations to finance this expansion of trans-Atlantic trade were repaid many times over in the form of a mutually beneficial system of commercial links between Western Europe and the United States that complemented their increasingly intimate political ties.

The postwar recovery of the industrialized countries of the Western world was facilitated by the relatively efficient operation of the new international monetary system that had been established at a meeting of forty-four allied nations at the Bretton Woods resort in the White Mountains of New Hampshire during July 1944. Recognizing that the low level of international trade and investment represented a serious impediment to postwar economic growth in all countries, the financial representatives of the states at war with the Axis devised at Bretton Woods a number of measures to promote the resumption of world trade and capital movements. The International Monetary Fund (IMF) was created to restore the network of multilateral international payments that had broken down in the early thirties as countries left the gold standard and adopted temporary expedients such as exchange controls and devaluations that disrupted world trade. The IMF consisted of a pool of currencies contributed by member states upon which any member could draw in order to correct temporary balance-of-payments difficulties without having to resort to exchange controls or devaluation. The chronic problem of exchange instability was addressed through the reestablishment of a modified system of fixed exchange rates: The dollar became the world's principal reserve currency and was rendered freely convertible into gold at a fixed price. The exchange rates in operation at the opening of the Bretton Woods conference were recognized as the par values for the new system, and any subsequent adjustment of the exchange value of a member country's currency required the prior approval of the governing board of IMF. The West European economies were not strong enough to accept convertibility of their fixed-rate currencies until 1958, and there were occasional exchange problems for Britain and France. Nonetheless, Bretton Woods ushered in a quarter century of relative exchange stability, which enabled exporters, importers, lenders, and borrowers to transact their foreign business with much less concern about the relationship between the world's currencies.

An additional stimulus to the postwar recovery of world trade was the creation of a multinational institution empowered to establish rules for the international exchange of goods and services to replace the beggar-thy-neighbor protectionism of the thirties. America's increasing involvement in world trade after the war had led the Truman administration to importune other nations, particularly those wartime allies who were deeply in debt to the Treasury Department and therefore particularly susceptible to Washington's pressure, to dismantle the trade barriers inherited from the Depression years that blocked American access to foreign markets. The major trading nations of the world were finally induced by the United States to adhere in the summer of 1947 to the General Agreement on Tariffs and Trade (GATT). In subsequent years GATT served as a forum for periodic negotiations between trading partners aimed at reducing the bewildering array of trade restrictions that had accumulated over the years. The stipulation that all agreements concluded under GATT's auspices include the most-favored-nation clause ensured that trade concessions negotiated bilaterally would automatically be extended to all members. The reduction of tariffs and other trade barriers during GATT bargaining sessions nourished and sustained an unprecedented increase in the international exchange of goods and services. World trade grew at an annual rate of almost 7 percent in real terms between 1948 and 1970 after almost two decades of stagnation, while many of the prewar trade restrictions were scrapped.

The principal disappointment of the Marshall Plan was its failure to promote the economic integration of Western Europe along the lines originally envisaged by its architects. Though one-sixth of Marshall aid was employed to finance trade within Western Europe itself, and trade among the recipient countries did in fact increase by 70 percent, few efforts were made to remove impediments to the free movement of goods, capital, and labor across national frontiers for the duration of the program. The creative initiatives in the direction of economic integration were later to spring from disappointed European administrators of Marshall aid, such as France's Jean Monnet and Belgium's Paul-Henri Spaak. But their integrationist campaign was to be undertaken independent of, and in a certain measure at the expense of, the American benefactor of 1948–52.

The political consequences of the Marshall Plan were to prove as far-reaching as the economic ones for the future of Europe. The Soviet bloc's repudiation of the program not only foreclosed the possibility of restoring prewar economic, and therefore political, relations between Eastern and Western Europe; it also accelerated the ideological polarization within each European state. The deterioration of political relations between Communist and non-Communist parties in all countries of the continent had already begun by the time of Secretary Marshall's offer of economic assistance. In the spring of 1947, the Communist ministers in the coalition governments of France, Italy, and Belgium were either excluded from or chose to leave office because of mounting ideological differences with the dominant pro-American parties. In the meantime, the Communist parties of Eastern Europe were systematically eliminating all non-Communist organizations from positions of power. The advent of the American-sponsored European Recovery Program hastened this trend toward the ideological bifurcation of the continent. In the eyes of the Soviet leader-

ship, a formal organization of European Communist parties to ensure
their subservience to Moscow in the face of the American economic penetration of Europe was called for; thus was created on September 22,
1947, the Communist Information Bureau (or Cominform), the successor
to the Communist International (or Comintern) that had been dissolved
by Stalin in 1943 to allay the ideological fears of his capitalist allies in the
war against Hitler. Though successful in liquidating all non-Communist
political forces in Eastern Europe that might prove susceptible to American influence, the Cominform failed to generate effective opposition to
the Marshall Plan in Western Europe. Strikes and disorders fomented by
the Communist-controlled labor organizations of France and Italy in the
autumn of 1947 failed miserably. The governing coalitions in those two
countries, from which the respective Communist parties had been expelled
the previous spring, resumed their eager solicitation of American economic assistance and tendered active support for the new anti-Soviet foreign policy adopted in Washington.

Thus, by the beginning of 1948 the European continent had been
reorganized into two political and economic blocs, the one dependent on
the United States, the other subservient to the Soviet Union. This was soon
to be followed by the division of the continent into two military blocs
joined in a commitment to common defense against the other and backed
by the overwhelming armed might of their respective patrons. Since the
end of the war, Western and Soviet representatives had engaged in regular
if not cordial communication in successive conferences at the foreign
minister level, in the Allied Control Council for Germany and in the
United Nations, in an effort to settle by diplomatic negotiation the outstanding matters in dispute. But the February 1948 Communist takeover
in Czechoslovakia, which symbolically and literally blocked the last major
avenue in Europe linking East and West, precipitated a final rupture in
relations between the two victorious powers that had been building since
the end of the war. Thereafter, the economic reconstruction of Western
Europe that was about to get under way seemed futile unless the nations
of that region could adequately protect themselves against what had come
to be viewed, in the aftermath of the Communist-inspired unrest in France
and Italy and the Prague coup, as Moscow's imminent bid to project its
power westward beyond the sphere of interest informally allocated to it at
the end of the war.

On March 17, 1948, two events occurred on opposite sides of the
Atlantic that together signified the determination of the Western nations
to supplement their emerging trans-Atlantic economic partnership with a
commitment to collective self-defense. The first of these was the signing
of the Brussels Pact and the formation of the Brussels Pact Organization,
a military alliance of fifty years' duration, binding Great Britain, France,
and the three small countries now collectively designated as Benelux
(Belgium, the Netherlands, and Luxembourg) in a joint pledge to repel

"an armed attack" against any one of the signatories. The second was President Truman's special message to the United States Congress requesting authorization to reinstate conscription and universal military training, which had been allowed to expire after the war in keeping with the traditional American preference for a small volunteer army during peacetime. These two simultaneous actions were obviously not unrelated. The Brussels Pact was designed to demonstrate the West European nations' willingness to cooperate in their own defense and therefore facilitate Truman's task of securing Congressional approval of American participation in that effort.

These first tentative steps toward American rearmament and West European collective defense were to provoke a Soviet response of such belligerence as to confirm the worst fears of the Western leaders and therefore to accelerate the trend toward military preparedness and trans-Atlantic cooperation in security matters. The site of the first direct confrontation between Western and Soviet power was, appropriately, the region of Europe where it collided head-on: occupied Germany. The partition of Germany, Austria, and their respective capitals into four military occupation zones under American, British, French, and Soviet jurisdiction had been intended as a temporary expedient pending the emergence of indigenous political elites untainted by Nazi connections that would be prepared to undertake the governance of their reunified sovereign state. In the meantime Germany (like Austria) was to be administered as a single political and economic unit by the Allied Control Commission sitting in its capital, Berlin, which itself, though divided into four occupation sectors, was to be governed as a single municipal unit.

But a number of developments during the three years after the end of the war had converged to sabotage the Potsdam plan for eventual German unification. All of these were related to the determination of the Soviet Union to profit from its military control of the eastern part of Germany to procure by force the reparations that had been allocated to it in principle at Yalta but remained uncollected. The Soviet occupation authorities peremptorily requisitioned German machinery, power plants, railway track and rolling stock, as well as substantial quantities of coal and other raw materials for delivery to Russia. They also repudiated their pledge to furnish agricultural products from their own zone to the three Western zones in exchange for the industrial equipment they had already received from them. These unilateral measures, as understandable as they may have been in light of the desperate economic condition of the Soviet Union that had been caused by the German invasion, elicited sharp criticism from the American government and its representative on the Control Commission in Berlin. The Truman administration had no intention of permitting the Russians to strip their zone of all of its portable economic assets and continue to receive reparation deliveries from the Western zones while the United States was footing the bill for the sustenance of the impoverished populations of postwar Germany. Convinced that Germany's economic recovery was vital to the economic recovery of Europe as a whole, the United States pressed the Soviet Union in vain to treat the matter of reparations as part of a comprehensive plan for the orderly management of the entire economy of the country. When the Russians resumed their unilateral requisitions, the United States terminated the transfer of reparations to the Soviet zone in May 1946. In the meantime, the Russians had introduced measures of economic reform in their own zone—such as the confiscation without compensation and the redistribution of all large landholdings—which not only contradicted American principles of free enterprise but also further undermined the agreed-upon policy of treating all of Germany as a single economic entity.

Then, in an abrupt shift in strategy, the Kremlin abandoned its vindictive policy toward Germany in favor of a conciliatory approach. At the Paris meeting of Allied foreign ministers in July, Molotov violently accused the United States of reintroducing in disguised form the long-since repudiated Morgenthau Plan for the de-industrialization of the Reich by imposing restrictions on Germany's coal and steel production. The Soviet Foreign Commissar proposed the establishment of a single German government and denounced the French plan for the separation of the Ruhr from Germany. Molotov's remarks apparently signified a Soviet bid to curry favor with the starving and suffering German masses by portraying the Western occupying powers as their tormentors and the Russians as their friends. Did this startling departure portend a return to the policy of Russo-German collaboration at the expense of the West? Did the same Soviet premier and foreign minister who had concluded the pact with Hitler in 1939 have in mind a scheme to turn the German people against the Americans, British, and French and convert them to the cause of friendship with Russia?

Not to be outbid in the "struggle for Germany," American Secretary of State James Byrnes responded to Molotov's ploy in a speech before an audience of 1,400 German dignitaries in Stuttgart on September 5 that signified a critical turning point in American policy toward the occupied country. He announced his government's intention to promote the economic rehabilitation of Germany in order to enable it to contribute to the economic recovery of Europe as a whole. He rejected the idea of splitting off the Ruhr from the rest of the country. He called for the prompt formation of a provisional government with authority to administer the entire country so that Germans could once again manage their own affairs. Most important of all, from the standpoint of German public attitudes toward the Soviet Union, Byrnes specifically refused to recognize the Oder-Neisse frontier between Germany and Poland. That boundary, which deprived Germany of a considerable portion of its prewar territory, had been unilaterally established by the Russians in 1945 in order to compensate Poland for the seventy thousand square miles of its own territory that it had been forced to cede to the Soviet Union. By throwing American support behind the German people's demand for the restoration of that lost land, Byrnes had shrewdly smoked out the Kremlin, forcing it to choose between its client state in Poland and its prospective friends in Germany. Stalin sided with Poland, and by doing so irretrievably lost whatever opportunity may have existed for wooing the Germans away from the West.

The Truman administration proceeded to make good on the commitments to the German people that had been sketched by Byrnes in his Stuttgart speech. It promoted greater coordination of the occupation policies in the three western zones and granted a greater measure of economic and political authority to the pro-Western German elites that were emerging there. On January 1, 1947, the Americans and the British formally merged their two zones into a single economic unit, and in the following May established an economic advisory committee consisting of fifty-two delegates from the regional (*Land*) assemblies that the two occupying powers had permitted to be elected in their zones. In July the United States decided to extend Marshall Plan aid to the three Western occupation zones. The French, who had at first steadfastly opposed all measures favoring German political or economic integration (for obvious historical reasons), acceded to Anglo-American pressure in the summer of 1947 and began to participate in a common economic policy for the three Western zones. Soon the rudiments of a West German administration appeared in the form of a Supreme Economic Council, which adopted a bold plan for industrial recovery that was to pave the way for the West German economic "miracle" of the fifties. On March 1, 1948, a central bank serving all three western zones came into being; on June 18 France finally agreed to fuse its zone with the Anglo-American zone ("Bizonia") to create a "Trizonia"; and on June 20 an all-West German currency, the deutsche mark, was established to cure inflation, curb black market activities, and restore faith in paper money after three years of quasi-barter in which cigarettes had been the hardest currency. These reforms signified the allies' acknowledgment that Western European prosperity depended on Germany's economic recovery, that the reunification of the entire country was impossible under current circumstances, and that the most suitable alternative was to amalgamate the three German zones under American, British, and French control and to integrate the new entity into a Western European community linked to the United States.

This process of economic integration in western Germany—the removal of all restrictions on the circulation of labor, capital, and products within the three zones, the formation of German-controlled trizonal economic bodies with broad decision-making powers, and the establishment of a trizonal central bank and currency backed by American financial power under the Marshall Plan—can only have been interpreted by Moscow as what indeed it proved to be: a prelude to the political integration of the three western zones in the form of a West German state dependent on and loyal to the United States. Since the newly consolidated western occupation zones of Germany contained three quarters of that country's population as well as the most productive industrial region of prewar Europe (the Ruhr-Rhineland-Westphalia complex), the prospect of a politically unified, economically advanced west German state associated with the United States produced predictable uneasiness in the Kremlin: It might exert a magnetic attraction on German nationals within the eastern zone, which was being drained of its resources and compelled to endure acute economic privation by its Soviet occupiers; it might serve as a center of Western intrigue against the East European satellites; worst of all, in light of the simultaneous request by Truman for the restoration of conscription in the United States and the formation of a West European military alliance, the emerging West German state might become a launching pad for aggression by America and her West European clients in the Brussels Pact against the Soviet motherland.

Moscow chose to counteract the American decision to establish a west German political and economic entity by applying pressure at the point of greatest Western vulnerability: the western sector of Berlin, situated 110 miles inside the Russian zone and tenuously linked to the western zone by a highway and a railroad. On June 24, 1948, the Soviet authorities in Germany halted all surface traffic crossing from the Western zone through the Soviet zone to West Berlin, whose 2.4 million inhabitants thereupon faced the prospect of starvation, having food stocks for only thirty-six days. Though ostensibly undertaken in retaliation against the establishment of a strong currency in the western zone (which was bound to destroy the weak German currency in the Soviet zone), the evident purpose of the Berlin blockade was to expel the Western occupation forces from the city. If the formation of a west German state could not be forestalled, at least the last open hole in the "iron curtain" that Churchill had decried in his famous address in March 1946 could be plugged. But the American and British governments responded to this direct challenge to their occupation authority in Berlin by organizing an airlift which supplied the beleaguered citizens of the city with the food, fuel, and other basic commodities they required. On May 12, 1949, Stalin acknowledged the failure of the blockade and terminated it with a face-saving gesture that fooled no one. (The Kremlin announced that the roads and railroads, which had been closed "for repairs" for a year, would be reopened to traffic from the West.) The Soviet Union's failure to remove this anomalous island of Western influence within a region firmly under its control and subject to its overwhelming military superiority was due to a single overriding fact: The United States possessed nuclear weapons that could be dropped on Russian cities by the sixty B-29 bombers that had been transferred (though without their bombs) to British bases at the height of the crisis.

The Berlin blockade accelerated the progressive involvement of the

United States in the defense of Western Europe that had begun on the rhetorical level with the proclamation of the Truman Doctrine and the adoption of the containment policy during the Greek and Turkish crises in 1947. On April 23, 1948, a few weeks after President Truman's request to the United States Congress for the reintroduction of conscription and universal military training and the simultaneous formation of the Brussels Pact in Europe, Foreign Secretary Ernest Bevin of Britain had sounded out the State Department about the possibility of forming a North Atlantic security system linking the United States, Canada, and the five signatories of the Brussels Pact. The imposition of the Berlin blockade in June strengthened the position of those officials within the Truman administration who had reached the conclusion that the United States had to make a clean break with its isolationist heritage and supplement its support for European economic recovery with some kind of concrete commitment to European defense.

The two measures that were required for the United States to assume such an unprecedented foreign commitment were both in the hands of the legislative branch of the government, as had been the case thirty years before, when a Democratic president's plans for America's global responsibilities were dashed on Capitol Hill. American participation in European defense required a sufficiently powerful military force to assure the credibility of the pledge as well as legislative authorization to adhere to whatever system of regional defense that Bevin and his European colleagues had in mind. As it turned out, Congressional Republicans who had been converted to the cause of "internationalism" outnumbered the remaining guardians of the isolationist heritage by a wide margin. On June 24, 1948, the Congress repudiated the tradition of a small volunteer peacetime army by enacting the euphemistically named Selective Service Act. This legislation laid the basis for a sharp increase in American military manpower by subjecting all able-bodied males from nineteen to thirty-five years of age to compulsory military service of twenty-one months. Like their counterparts in the Brussels Pact nations, which had also reinstituted conscription after the war, millions of American young men would be trained in the martial arts not to fight a war in Europe but to deter the Soviet Union from starting one there.

The concept of extending American military protection to the European signatories of the Brussels Pact that came under active consideration in Washington during 1948 seemed to contradict the essential purpose of the United Nations Organization, which was to provide a global network of collective security that would render such regional defense arrangements superfluous. Whereas the British wartime government had pressed for the decentralization of the projected world body in the form of regional associations, it had been overruled by an adamant Roosevelt who had insisted on the Wilsonian concept of a single universal organization without regional subdivisions. But shortly after Roosevelt's death, as delegates from fifty countries assembled in San Francisco to draw up a charter for the United Nations Organization, American officials concerned with Latin American affairs expressed the fear that the projected global system of collective security might endanger the United States' special relationship with its clients south of the border. Just as the Wilson administration had insisted on exempting the region covered by the Monroe Doctrine from the purview of the League of Nations Covenant, the Truman administration arranged for the insertion of Article 51 in the United Nations Charter, which preserved the right of member states to establish regional security organizations outside the United Nations. The first such regional agreement to be concluded was the Rio Pact of September 2, 1947, which established the principle of collective self-defense for the Western Hemisphere by defining an attack against one of the American republics as an attack on them all, and providing for a joint response to aggression. The aforementioned Brussels Pact for Western Europe's joint defense was also based on the provisions of Article 51. Armed with the precedent of the Rio and Brussels pacts, Republican Senator Arthur Vandenberg (a former isolationist turned internationalist who had helped to formulate Article 51 and had subsequently become chairman of the Senate Foreign Relations Committee) introduced a resolution in the United States Senate that was designed to circumvent the Soviet veto in the United Nations Security Council on matters relating to European security without violating the United Nations Charter. The Vandenberg resolution in effect repudiated the Monroe Doctrine and its guiding principle of hemispheric exclusivity by affirming Washington's willingness to join the Western European regional security system that was in the process of formation.

Acting under the authority of the Vandenberg resolution, which passed the Senate with only four dissenting votes, the State Department opened discussions with representatives of the Brussels Pact countries on July 5; by the end of the year Italy, Norway, Denmark, Iceland, Portugal, and Canada had joined the talks. After months of intensive negotiations, delegates of these twelve nations signed on April 4, 1949, the North Atlantic Treaty, a regional security arrangement modeled on the Rio Pact which obligated each signatory to render assistance to any of the others that sustained an armed attack. The Senate ratified the North Atlantic Treaty by the lopsided margin of 82 to 13 and President Truman signed it on July 25. On the same day he requested Congressional approval of the Mutual Defense Assistance Program, a one-year military aid package of $1.5 billion earmarked for America's new allies in Europe that represented the financial underpinning of the military commitment.

It was in this way, and for these reasons, that the mythical concept of a North Atlantic Community was born. It was a myth because it included countries such as Italy (not to speak of Greece and Turkey, which adhered to the pact in 1952) whose shores were far removed from the waves of the Atlantic Ocean. It was a myth because it did not include geographically eligible states such as Spain (on account of its abhorrent form of government and its past associations with the Axis powers)* and Sweden and Ireland (which insisted on retaining their traditional neutrality). Nor could it be represented as a coalition sharing a cooperative spirit of long standing, since it was to comprise two states, Italy and later West Germany (which joined in 1955), with which most of the other members had recently been at war. The new myth of Atlanticism superseded, at least in the minds of the American proponents of the alliance, the older myth of hemispheric solidarity that had governed American diplomatic behavior from the promulgation of Monroe's Doctrine to the pursuit of Roosevelt's Good Neighbor Policy. The Atlantic Ocean ceased to be regarded as an aquatic buffer between two distinctly separate if not mutually incompatible civilizations, the old world and the new, which protected the latter from the nefarious influences of the former. Instead the sea was seen as uniting the peoples of European heritage, those whose forbears had traversed it and those who had remained at home, in a community of shared principles and values. In fact the Atlantic alliance, as we have seen, was forged not by a common devotion to shared beliefs but rather by the sentiment of danger: What united the signatories of this pact was the fear of Russian aggression, which had been exacerbated by the Berlin blockade, and the determination to deter or resist it with the assistance of the American guarantee bolstered by the atomic bomb.

Another important consequence of the Berlin blockade was the formal partition of Germany into two separate political entities, each intimately linked to one of the two superpowers. Shortly after the formation of the North Atlantic alliance and during the final week of the blockade, in May 1949, the three Western occupation powers permitted the establishment of the Federal Republic of Germany with its capital in the Rhenish city of Bonn. The first postwar elections conducted on August 14, 1949, throughout the three Western zones resulted in a plurality for the conservative, pro-Western Christian Democratic Party, whose leader, Konrad Adenauer, became chancellor of the new Federal Republic, a position he was to occupy continuously for the first fourteen years of its existence. Resolutely anti-Communist, profoundly suspicious of Soviet intentions, and firmly committed to the free market policies pursued by his minister of economics, Ludwig Erhard, this shrewd Catholic politician from the Rhineland was ideally suited to guide his fledgling state toward closer cooperation with the United States and support for its policy of containment and economic recovery in the non-Communist half of Europe. Though still formally an occupied country with a number of restrictions on its political

* Though Franco's Spain was denied membership in NATO, largely at the insistence of the British Labour government, the United States and Spain concluded a bilateral agreement in September 1953 which provided for the establishment of American naval and air bases on Spanish territory as well as American military and economic assistance to Franco. After the death of the dictator and the restoration of a constitutional monarchy, Spain was admitted to NATO in 1982.

sovereignty, the Federal Republic, from the very day of its birth, in fact ceased to be treated as a former enemy. It came to be regarded instead as a bulwark against the Communist bloc and as a potentially valuable contributor to the economic reconstruction of Western Europe as a whole. Thus restrictions on Germany's economic sovereignty were relaxed and Marshall Plan assistance to Bonn was increased. Erhard's policy of promoting savings, investment, and the revival of industrial production and foreign trade generated a phenomenal economic boom in this war-ravaged country. By November 1949 the prewar level of production was attained, and by the beginning of the 1950s West Germany entered a period of sustained economic growth that was to restore it to the front rank of the world's industrial powers by the end of the decade.

As the three western occupation zones of Germany united to form the Federal Republic, the eastern zone was transformed by its Soviet occupiers into the nominally independent state of the German Democratic Republic in October 1949 without the formalities of an election. In this way the eastern and western parts of Germany achieved separate statehood by the end of the 1940s, each adopting the political and economic systems of its respective protector. Hitler had set out to unify all of Europe under German auspices. Instead, his policies resulted in the division of Europe, the division of Germany, and the division of the city where he had directed his armies and finally met his own end.

The Korean War and Western Rearmament

It would be premature to designate the Berlin blockade and the formation of NATO as the decisive events that produced the rearmament, remobilization, and remilitarization of the United States and its allies in Western Europe. The North Atlantic Treaty represented merely a statement of intention, and a rather vague one at that. Though obliging each signatory to take up arms "immediately" in the event of an armed attack on any of them, it left each member to decide for itself if an armed attack had in fact occurred, whether it threatened the security of the region covered by the treaty, and what appropriate responses (if any) were called for. In light of the overwhelming conventional military superiority in Europe that the Soviet Union and its clients were thought to enjoy at the time—175 divisions compared with 14 divisions for the Western powers*—it was unclear how the promised American protection would be extended to the transatlantic allies in the event of a Soviet attack. It was originally assumed that by throwing a "nuclear cloak" over Western Europe, the United States could dissuade Moscow from interfering with the economic recovery and political stabilization of the countries receiving Marshall

---

* Intelligence estimates of eastern bloc troop strength at this time were grossly exaggerated, as the American government itself conceded many years later. But the disparity between the two blocs was still significant.

Plan assistance. The grossly outnumbered armed forces of the European members of NATO would serve as the "shield" of the Western alliance that would slow up a conventional Soviet assault until the "sword" represented by the American nuclear arsenal could be unsheathed and plunged into the heart of Russia. But the deterrent power of America's ultimate weapon was compromised before the ink on the North Atlantic Treaty was dry. On July 14, 1949, the Soviet Union exploded its first atomic bomb, signaling the end of the American nuclear monopoly on which the "shield and sword" strategy of the alliance was based and which American intelligence experts had expected to last for several years.

Shocked by the Soviet nuclear test and apprehensive about its implications for the future of Western defense, President Truman ordered the National Security Council to undertake a comprehensive reevaluation of American policy toward the Communist bloc. The product of this high level investigation was a top secret document known as NSC-68, which was submitted to the president in April 1950. It portrayed the Soviet Union as an inherently aggressive power, fired by a messianic faith that was antithetical to the American way of life, whose unquenchable thirst for expansion had led to the subjugation of Eastern Europe and China and threatened to engulf the remainder of the Eurasian land mass. Moscow's acquisition of atomic weapons would enable it to browbeat its nonnuclear neighbors into submission unless the United States took immediate steps to remedy this potentially catastrophic imbalance of power in the world. A continuation of the containment policy adopted in 1947 would no longer be sufficient. The economic reconstruction of Western Europe and Japan and the stockpiling of American atomic weapons thousands of miles from the flashpoints of East-West confrontation had failed to stem the inexorable advance of Communism in the world. What was called for instead was a global offensive against the Soviet bloc that would restore the initiative to the non-Communist world.

The specific recommendations of NSC-68 included the prompt development of the thermonuclear (hydrogen) bomb, the expansion of American and West European conventional forces, the mobilization of America's economic resources to sustain this military buildup, and the tightening of the bonds between the member states of the Western alliance system in order to meet the Communist threat. Three proposals designed to strengthen NATO and give more concrete form to the American military commitment to Western Europe had been under active consideration ever since the explosion of the Soviet bomb. The first of these was the stationing of large numbers of American ground forces in Europe (beyond the two divisions in West Germany) to supplement Allied manpower as well as to enhance the credibility of America's pledge to participate in the defense of the western half of the continent. The second was the installation of air bases on the continent to accommodate the bombers that carried the American nuclear deterrent. The third was the closer integration of the national armies of the alliance and the development of procedures for joint military planning in order to remove the logistical inefficiencies that are endemic to a loosely organized coalition of sovereign states. The general proposals included in NSC-68, together with its specific prescriptions for the buildup and projection of American military power abroad, implied nothing less than a revolutionary transformation of the manner in which the United States had managed its national defense in peacetime. These proposed innovations predictably engendered a fierce internal debate within the foreign policy establishment of the Truman administration, with Secretary of State Dean Acheson emerging as the staunchest proponent of the new approach. The prospect of sharp increases in taxation to finance this massive rearmament program alarmed a number of officials, including even Secretary of Defense Louis Johnson, who opposed the recommendations of NSC-68 on the grounds that they would undermine the economic health of the country. The State Department's two senior specialists on Soviet affairs, George Kennan and Charles Bohlen, argued that the project was based on a simplistic view of Soviet foreign policy goals and would run the risk of imposing an excessively rigid form on American policy toward the Communist bloc.

While Acheson strove to overcome mounting internal opposition to the new departure in American military policy implied by NSC-68, the Kremlin launched a propaganda campaign in Western Europe that threatened to dampen Allied enthusiasm for the massive program of rearmament under consideration. In early 1950 a "peace offensive" organized by the West European Communist parties and endorsed by notable public figures of various political persuasions denounced the Atlantic alliance as an unwarranted, American-inspired plot to intimidate the Soviet Union, a plot likely to result in the nuclear devastation of the very region that the alliance had supposedly been formed to protect. For the first time since the advent of the Cold War, spokesmen for the non-Communist Left in France, Italy, and West Germany began to hail the advantages of neutrality for Western Europe in the global contest between the two superpowers. Neutrality was advertised as a way not only of avoiding total nuclear destruction but also of preserving for Western Europe a margin of choice between the two antithetical political ideologies that competed for Europe's favor.

What prevented the West Europeans from indulging in the luxury of such a choice was the unexpected outbreak of hostilities between Communist and anti-Communist armies thousands of miles from Europe in the summer of 1950. Though the peninsula of Korea was terra incognita to most Europeans, enough was known about its political situation to cause widespread uneasiness about its similarities to the postwar position of Germany. Formerly a part of the Axis coalition, Korea had been partitioned in 1945 between the United States and the Soviet Union. After three years of fruitless Soviet-American efforts to agree on measures of reunification, each occupying power had established in its own zone a government that claimed authority over the entire country. Now, the Communist half, armed and presumably encouraged by the Soviet Union, had attacked the non-Communist half. Like South Korea, West Germany confronted an adversary who enjoyed decisive military superiority. The Soviet command in East Germany had recruited over fifty thousand "military police" from its occupation zone and had reorganized these paramilitary units into a powerful fighting force that could be hurled against the disarmed Federal Republic. Consequently, the diffuse feeling of anxiety about the theoretical possibility of nuclear annihilation aroused by the Soviet atomic test in the summer of 1949 was instantaneously replaced by a more precisely focused apprehension about the prospect of a Korea-type conventional assault across the north German plain that could radically transform the balance of power on the continent.

Whether the Kremlin ever seriously entertained the notion of making such an aggressive move in Europe—and no evidence has ever surfaced to indicate that it did—is beside the point. What mattered is that the governing elites of the NATO powers at the time made the mental connection between Korea and Germany at the height of the Korean emergency in the summer and fall of 1950. Moreover, the Truman administration's prompt and effective response to the North Korean invasion removed any lingering doubts in Europe about the capacity and determination of the United States to honor its commitments abroad: A nation that did not hesitate to fight a war in an obscure country that had been excluded from its defense perimeter in the western Pacific could scarcely be suspected of reluctance to defend the European members of the Western alliance system to which the United States had enthusiastically adhered.

The long-range geopolitical implications of the war in Korea were felt less on that strife-torn peninsula—where a permanent military stalement developed in the summer of 1951 roughly along the original political demarcation line separating north from south—than in the United States and Western Europe (see p. 377). The transformation of the Cold War into a shooting war in Asia led to the militarization of the containment policy in Europe. The Truman administration seized upon the alarm caused by the aggression in Korea to push forward the ambitious program of military spending as well as the extension of unprecedented American security pledges to Western Europe that had been contemplated during the high level discussions of the NSC-68 memorandum. The provisions of the North Atlantic Treaty, as we have seen, represented little more than a vaguely worded commitment to common defense, implicitly fortified by the existence of the American atomic arsenal and the large pool of American military manpower produced by the introduction of peacetime conscription. But the concrete American contribution to European defense was initially to be confined to the provision of munitions and materiél, and even those were in short supply because of the reduction in American military spending in the years after the Second World War. The Korean War abruptly changed all of this. In September 1950, the council of NATO foreign ministers assembled in New York and unanimously adopted a "forward-looking strategy" for the defense of Western Europe, which was to be facilitated by the formation of an integrated military force under a unified command. In the same month President Truman dispatched four divisions of American combat troops to Europe and announced plans to augment even further the size of the American military contingent on the continent. On December 19 the NATO foreign ministers announced the creation of an integrated defense system under the supreme command of General Dwight D. Eisenhower. When the United States Senate endorsed the principle of an integrated command and approved Eisenhower's nomination on April 4, 1951—two years to the day after the signing of the NATO Treaty—it endorsed the transfer of the four divisions of American ground troops to Europe.

In the meantime the Truman administration had undertaken a massive military buildup designed to increase America's nuclear and conventional capability as well as to furnish the European allies with the military equipment that they required. At the beginning of 1951 the President submitted a $50 billion defense budget, compared to the $13.5 billion budget of six months before, and increased the size of the standing army by half to 3.5 million men. In the last year of the Truman presidency, the institutional structure of the Western alliance system was rationalized: the Lisbon conference of the Atlantic Council in February 1952 created a NATO secretariat under a secretary general and centralized all alliance activities in headquarters located in and around Paris. Plans were drawn up to increase the number of divisions from 14 to 50, the combat readiness of existing forces was improved, and concrete steps were taken to centralize the command structure and integrate the national armies of the alliance. Negotiations were begun, and a number of agreements concluded, with various European states for the establishment of bases for American ground, air, and naval forces.

It is impossible to exaggerate the precedent-shattering significance of the new American defense policy that gradually unfolded from the formulation of the Truman Doctrine in 1947 to the establishment of a full-fledged American military presence in Europe by 1952. By assuming the supreme command of NATO, by furnishing armaments to its allies, and by stationing its own ground forces on the other side of the Atlantic, the United States had undertaken the task of preserving the postwar political status quo in Europe. The original emphasis on containing Russia's westward expansion by promoting the economic recovery and political stability of the nations of Western Europe was superseded by the commitment to project American military power to the very heart of the continent in an effort to achieve the same objective.

But the assumption of such unprecedented global responsibilities was not without cost. The American economy, notwithstanding its spectacular rate of growth in the early fifties, could not have been expected to sustain unlimited demands on its productive capacity. Particularly during the Korean War, when the American public was required to endure austerity measures such as wage and price controls and various restrictions on consumption, it was not surprising that the Truman administration began to press the European allies for greater contributions to their own defense. In July 1950 the five signatories of the Brussels Pact consented to increases in arms spending and the prolongation of military service. But there were limits to what they could do. Their economic recovery was not yet complete. Moreover, France, Britain, Belgium, and Holland were still obliged to maintain large military forces abroad to preserve order in the remnants of their colonial empires, while tiny Luxembourg's contribution was insignificant. Europe's greatest reserve of potential military strength was West Germany, with its large pool of manpower and its latent economic capacity. It was unrealistic to expect the United States, which had assumed the major obligation to defend the Federal Republic, to continue its military buildup in that country without requiring the Germans themselves to contribute to their own protection, especially since any conceivable Soviet military advance in Europe would of necessity take place on German territory.

At the height of the Korean emergency American officials began to prod the West European governments to confront the issue that they had previously preferred to postpone: the rearmament of West Germany and its adhesion to the Atlantic alliance. On September 12, 1950, Secretary of State Acheson formally proposed to his British and French counterparts that German divisions be added to NATO. Though explicitly forbidden by the Potsdam agreement and resolutely opposed by the governments of those nations, such as France, that had recently endured the painful consequences of German military power, German participation in Western European defense had been informally discussed since the formation of the alliance. "Germany's rearmament is contained in the Atlantic Pact as the embryo is in the egg," warned the Parisian newspaper *Le Monde* on the very day the NATO treaty was signed. French officials remained resistant to the idea of resurrecting German military forces, even with the assurance that their guns would be pointed east this time. "Germany has no army and cannot have one," declared French Foreign Minister Robert Schuman during the parliamentary debates on the ratification of the pact. "It has no armaments and it will not have any." But the increased pressure from Washington had its effect on Germany's apprehensive neighbors in the West. Particularly in France, public opinion began to accommodate itself to the idea of Germany's reintegration into the Western European system. Many French people had ceased to regard Germany as the hereditary enemy as they began to view Russia as the principal threat to national security. Moreover, that portion of Germany under Western influence, which contained over three quarters of the country's industrial plant, came to be regarded as a valuable economic asset to Western Europe as a whole: The enormous productive potential of the Federal Republic, if permitted to develop to its full capacity, could serve as the engine of economic recovery for the entire western half of the continent. All that remained was to devise some means of assuring that West Germany's economic recovery would be managed without endangering the security of its non-Communist neighbors.

Even before the stimulus provided by the Korean War, the French government had launched a bold initiative that was eventually to provide such assurance. On May 9, 1950, French Foreign Minister Robert Schuman formally proposed that the coal and steel production of France and West Germany be combined and supervised by a supranational authority, which would be open to the participation of the other countries of Western Europe. Great Britain declined the invitation to join in discussions of this proposal because of its reluctance to compromise its privileged relationship with North America and the Commonwealth. But representatives of West Germany, Italy, and the Benelux nations joined French officials in negotiations that produced in 1951 an agreement to form a European Coal and Steel Community. When the Schuman Plan officially went into effect in the summer of 1952, the new supranational entity had been endowed with a political organization to complement its economic apparatus: an executive body, a parliamentary assembly, and a court of justice. Moreover, the specified objective of gradually abolishing all politically imposed obstacles to trade within the community (such as tariffs, quantitative restrictions, and import quotas) in coal and steel products implicitly established a precedent that could (and would) be extended to other and eventually all sectors of the economy. Thus the Schuman Plan contained the seeds of European economic integration that would later germinate during the second half of the fifties.

But the Schuman Plan was pregnant with strategic implications as well: it seemed to offer a masterly solution to the question of German rearmament that had been insistently raised by the United States since the beginning of the Korean War. Schuman's proposal, like the abortive scheme for European union advanced by another French foreign minister, Aristide Briand, a generation earlier, had been prompted by the hope of enmeshing Germany in a web of European economic integration that would forever remove both the incentive and the opportunity to make war on its partners in such a cooperative enterprise. It was inevitable that a proposal to domesticate Germany's industrial power by integrating it into a European economic community would give rise to the idea that Germany's war-making potential could similarly be harnessed to the cause of joint European defense. Schuman's original hope was that an economically integrated, politically unified Europe, led by France and its junior partner across the Rhine, could emerge as a "third force" capable of managing its own defense without depending on either of the two superpowers or be-coming embroiled in their global struggle for hegemony. But the outbreak of the Korean War five days after representatives of the six interested states had assembled in Paris to consider the French proposal abruptly transformed the nature of the discussion. The concept of Franco-German partnership within a Europe disengaged from the two superpowers van-ished amid the prospect of all-out war with the Communist bloc. On Oc-tober 24, 1950, as the governments of Western Europe groped for a con-structive response to Acheson's proposal for the addition of West German divisions to NATO, French Premier René Pleven unveiled a plan that was carefully crafted to satisfy the American demand for German rearmament while allaying the fears that such an event was bound to engender in Ger-many's West European neighbors. The Pleven Plan provided for the for-mation of an integrated European military force, equipped and financed by the member states, with the integration of national contingents at the lowest possible level. The virtue of the scheme was that it would mobilize French, German, Italian, and Benelux forces without actually creating a German army or a German high command. Instead, German soldiers would be thinly diffused through the ranks of a genuinely European army, under the jurisdiction of a European defense minister who would be re-sponsible to a European parliament.

The American government initially hesitated to endorse the French pro-posal for a unified European military force for fear that it was merely a diversionary maneuver to delay or forestall German entry in NATO. But Washington was gradually won over to the Pleven Plan as the most suit-able formula for including Germany in the common European defense ef-fort without inspiring apprehension in the other allied countries. At a time when the conflict in Korea was widely regarded as a prelude to a general war, the governments of Western Europe displayed an uncharacteristic willingness to accept the restrictions on their national sovereignty implied by the Pleven Plan. On May 27, 1952, after long and arduous negotia-tions, representatives of the six nations concerned signed the treaty estab-lishing the European Defense Community (EDC). Thus was born the concept, if not yet the reality, of a supranational military organization un-der the supreme command of NATO, with common armed forces wearing a common European uniform, a common defense budget, and common political institutions including a Council of Ministers, an Assembly, and a Court of Justice. The EDC treaty diverged from the original Pleven Plan in one important respect: Instead of providing for the dispersion of na-tional forces in small units throughout the military organization, it estab-lished national contingents on a divisional scale (ostensibly for reasons of efficiency). This meant that German divisions would contribute to the defense of Western Europe after all, belonging to a multinational force and taking orders from "European" commanders. In recognition of West Germany's proposed adherence to the military alliance directed against

Russia, the three Western occupying powers took the requisite steps to remove the anomalous reminders of its status as a vanquished enemy. A day before the signing of the EDC pact in Paris, the American, British, and French governments concluded an agreement with the Adenauer regime in Bonn providing for the termination of the military occupation and the restoration of political sovereignty to the Federal Republic upon the entry into force of the treaty.

As the parliaments of the six member states of the EDC ratified or began debate on the ratification of the treaty to create a European army, two momentous political transformations occurred almost simultaneously in Washington and Moscow. In January 1953, the Democratic administration of Harry S Truman, which had inaugurated the policy of containing the Soviet Union and brought America into the Atlantic alliance, turned over the reins of power to the Republican administration of Dwight D. Eisenhower. On March 6, less than two months after the new American president took office, the Kremlin announced that Joseph Stalin had died the previous day. It soon became evident that the Soviet dictator would be replaced by a cadre of political and military personalities who would rule Russia on the basis of collective leadership and that the upper echelons of the Soviet government and Communist party had undergone the most sweeping reorganization since the purges of the late thirties. The simultaneous disappearance of the two governing elites that had between them presided over the destinies of the entire globe since the end of the Second World War engendered a universal sense of uncertainty in the world. This sense of uncertainty increased once it became evident that the new American administration would resemble its new Russian counterpart in the degree to which power and responsibility would be delegated and diffused rather than centralized at the top. No one could predict with confidence whether the foreign policies conducted by the two decisive leaders of the superpowers would be perpetuated by their unfamiliar and untested successors.

What *was* certain, however, was that Truman had left an impressive legacy of solid achievements in the realm of foreign policy. The underlying objective of that policy, the containment of Soviet expansion beyond the regions that had come under Russian military domination at the end of the war, had been met everywhere. In Iran, Turkey, Greece, West Berlin, South Korea—wherever the Soviet Union probed or was alleged to have probed Western intentions—American diplomatic, economic, or military power had been exercised in such a way as to preserve the non-Communist character and pro-Western inclinations of those disputed regions. The countries of Western Europe, on the brink of economic collapse and reputedly vulnerable to Soviet military aggression in 1947, had made spectacular strides toward economic recovery and collective defense under American inspiration. And American economic assistance to Yugoslavia after its defection from the Soviet bloc in 1948 facilitated Marshal Tito's campaign against Moscow's primacy in the Communist world.

In view of the success of this containment policy it must be regarded as ironic that the Republican party's victory in the presidential election of 1952 was in large part due to its success in portraying the Truman administration as "soft on communism." The strength of this paradoxical assertion rested on the supposed advance of Soviet power in Asia rather than in Europe. China, the most populous country on earth, had apparently been absorbed into the Soviet empire. The Korean War dragged on inconclusively while American soldiers died and their commanders were shackled. The Communist insurgents in Indochina threatened to dislodge America's French allies and open all of Southeast Asia to the domination of the Kremlin and its puppets in the region. Added to this perception of Soviet gains across the Pacific was the widespread suspicion, incited by legislative demagogues such as Wisconsin's Senator Joseph R. McCarthy, that Communist agents had infiltrated American political, diplomatic, and even military institutions and were promoting Soviet interests there. The new American administration promised in certain ill-defined ways to remedy these defects in American policy toward the Soviet bloc and to halt what was viewed by the Republicans as the trend toward retrenchment and retreat.

CHAPTER 9

Coexistence and Confrontation (1953–1962)

Eisenhower's "New Look"

After having languished in impotent political opposition for twenty years, the Republican party took control of the White House at the beginning of 1953 ostensibly committed to a reversal of the foreign policy of its Democratic predecessor. But it was not to be a reversal toward the direction of isolationism and "America first." That wing of the party, led by Senator Robert Taft, had been decisively defeated by the "internationalist" faction that had adopted General Eisenhower as its standard-bearer and chosen as its foreign policy spokesman the New York attorney John Foster Dulles, who was to become Eisenhower's secretary of state. Prior to and during the presidential campaign, Dulles had articulated his party's alternative to the Truman administration's foreign policy. He denounced the containment doctrine as excessively passive in the face of the greatest threat of global aggression that the world had ever faced; moreover, it represented an immoral abandonment of the populations of Eastern Europe that had been permitted to fall under Soviet domination. Instead of striving to preserve the balance of power in Europe that had been established at the end of the war, Dulles asserted, the United States should make every effort to liberate the satellite states and "roll back" Soviet power to the Russian frontier. Inspired by a Manichean conception of good and evil and a messianic devotion to advance the boundaries of what he called the "free world," the new American secretary of state challenged all foreign nations to choose between enlisting in the American crusade for global righteousness or submitting to Soviet domination. Observers at the time did not fail to detect the similarity between this ideologically charged conception of American foreign policy and the orthodox doctrines of Marxist-Leninism. Both regarded the other side as so intrinsically evil as to preclude mutual accommodation, and each exhibited the unshakable confidence that its eventual triumph over the other was inevitable.

Such a dynamic vision of America's role vis-à-vis its principal rival in the world obviously implied a considerable augmentation of American military power. Yet the requirement of a drastic increase in defense spending to lend credibility to the American challenge to Soviet power contradicted the orthodox economic platform of the Eisenhower presidential campaign, which promised tax relief, a reduction in government expenditures, and a balanced budget. The resulting paradox was resolved by a high-level decision to inaugurate what was dramatically labeled a "new look" in America's defense policy. In January 1954, Dulles unveiled the Eisenhower administration's new innovation in strategic doctrine that was designed to increase American military power while reducing defense expenditures: Since the most expensive component in the defense budget was represented by spending on conventional forces (mainly pay and equipment for the army and navy), this would be reduced in the interests of cost efficiency. The old idea of increasing NATO's troop strength to fifty divisions, which had been formally adopted by the alliance in 1952 but was never taken seriously by anyone in light of the enormous costs involved, would be abandoned. Instead, the United States would place greater reliance on its nuclear arsenal and delivery system (which at the time consisted of a powerful bomber force based in the United States and abroad). In this way a parsimonious Republican administration could plan to hold down the costs of defense without sacrificing the security interests of the Atlantic alliance. The inferiority of the Western allies' conventional forces in Europe would be compensated for by upgrading the capacity of American strategic airpower to deliver a retaliatory nuclear blow "instantly, by means and at places of our own choosing," in Dulles's own forceful formulation. This highly touted new look in American defense policy was advertised by the American secretary of state as a way of providing "more basic security at less cost," or, as one of his colleagues in the administration put it, more crudely—"more bang for the buck."

The strategy of "massive retaliation," as it came to be known, could remain a credible deterrent to aggression only so long as the Soviet Union lacked the means to retaliate in kind. At the time that Dulles proclaimed his policy, the United States possessed the wherewithal to inflict extensive damage to Russian territory by means of long-range bombers based at home or medium-range bombers deployed in allied countries along the periphery of the Soviet empire. The Soviet Union had exploded its own hydrogen bomb on August 20, 1953, only nine months after the first successful American nuclear test. But it possessed neither long-range bombers capable of making the round-trip flight from Russian territory to North American targets nor air bases abroad. Thus the United States could count on devastating the major urban areas and industrial sectors of its enemy without fear of reprisal.

The deterrent value of massive retaliation also depended on the ability of the United States to assure its adversary that aggressive activity in certain strategically situated areas of the globe would automatically trigger an

American nuclear response. The dynamic military strategy associated with Dulles's name therefore also gave birth to an equally aggressive diplomatic strategy intended to ring the Soviet bloc with hostile powers linked to and protected by the United States through a series of mutual defense treaties. The Atlantic alliance and its emerging regional subgroup, the European Defense Community, that had been inherited from the Truman administration formed the keystone of the global security system that Dulles was striving to construct. Confronted with a rearmed West Germany within a rearmed Western Europe backed by the invulnerable American nuclear deterrent, the Soviet Union would be dissuaded from risking further probes of the soft spots beyond the Western borders of its empire.

But the Dulles strategy for Europe was dealt a devastating blow on August 30, 1954, when the French parliament declined to ratify the treaty establishing the European Defense Community two years after it had been signed by the leaders of the six member states. The grandiose project for a supranational West European military force came to an ignominious end at the hands of the very nation that had originally proposed it. French opposition to EDC sprang from a variety of impulses, apart from the predictable hostility to the restrictions on national sovereignty implied by the treaty. Foremost among these was the apprehension that Great Britain's refusal to adhere to the pact signified a return to the traditional aloofness of that island nation that would condemn France to a lonely and vulnerable position of inferiority on the continent vis-à-vis a rearmed, prosperous, self-confident Germany. London's pledge on April 13, 1954, to assign to the projected European army one armored division as a token of British involvement was to no avail. Neither was Dulles's veiled threat in December 1953 of an "agonizing reappraisal" of American support for European defense if France rejected the EDC. An additional cause of France's dwindling enthusiasm for the project it had initiated was the mounting hope of detente with the Soviet Union that had been stimulated by the death of Stalin and the increasingly amicable comportment of his successors. During a period when Soviet and Western statesmen cordially negotiated a settlement to the Indochinese war at Geneva and no less an avid anti-Communist than Winston Churchill was urging East-West discussions to settle the world's problems, it was more difficult to preserve the cohesion of the Western bloc than in the period of high tension.

For a brief moment the French rejection of the EDC threatened the unity of the Atlantic alliance, upset the plan of integrating West Germany into the system of European defense, and derailed the movement toward European unity. But after the initial flurry of recriminations, the interested parties settled down to explore alternative arrangements for salvaging the cause of Europe's common defense. This time the initiative was to come from London. British Foreign Secretary Anthony Eden suggested, as a practicable alternative to the supranational defense organization that had recently been repudiated, the enlargement of the more conventional type of military alliance that had been created by the Brussels Pact of 1948 to include Germany and Italy. Since Britain was a charter member of the Brussels Pact and maintained four infantry divisions and air force units on the continent in that capacity, such a transformation would entail the British commitment to European defense that the French had so earnestly sought as a counterweight to German power. In October 1954, representatives of the Brussels Pact nations plus Germany and Italy signed an agreement enlarging the six-member Brussels Pact organization into the eight-member Western European Union (WEU). Britain, France, and the United States formally agreed to terminate the occupation regime in West Germany and restore full sovereignty to the Federal Republic (including the right to rearm, on the sole condition that it promise never to manufacture atomic, biological, or chemical weapons on its territory). Thus did Germany finally cease to be treated as an "enemy" by the three Western powers that had occupied it since 1945, though the "state of war" technically continued in the absence of a formal peace treaty. Installed as a full-fledged member of the expanded WEU, West Germany was forthwith proposed for membership in NATO, which she officially joined on May 9, 1955.

The Soviet Union responded to these momentous events five days later by assembling representatives of its seven East European satellites in Warsaw for the signing of a twenty-year mutual defense treaty that established a formal military alliance as a counterpart to NATO. The "Warsaw Pact Organization," as this multinational security system came to be called, superseded the separate bilateral arrangements concluded between the Kremlin and its clients during the Stalin era. Though formally a military alliance protecting the eastern bloc against a threat from NATO, and particularly from its newest member, the Warsaw Pact functioned principally as an instrument of Soviet political domination of Eastern Europe for the remainder of the 1950s. Joint military exercises were not conducted until 1961, and even thereafter the pact continued to be employed more as a means of promoting political cohesion within the bloc and ensuring the signatories' subservience to Soviet foreign policy objectives than as a military alliance on the NATO model.

Thus only a few months after the collapse of the ambitious scheme for a supranational West European army, the cause of joint European defense had been rescued by the more modest alternative of a traditional alliance of sovereign states fielding national armies under the aegis of NATO. From the ashes of the EDC emerged a reinvigorated Western alliance system of which a rearmed West Germany, contrary to every expectation, had become a member on an equal basis.

But the objective of military collaboration against the Soviet Union had been reaffirmed at the cost of sacrificing the cause of European unity that many had hoped would be facilitated by the formation of the EDC. Exponents of the European idea such as France's Jean Monnet, though chas-

ICELAND

NORWAY

FINLAND

SWEDEN

GREAT
BRITAIN

DENMARK

NETHER-
LANDS

IRELAND

ATLANTIC

OCEAN

SOVIET

UNION

GER.
DEM.
REP

POLAND

GER.
BELG FED.
REP

CZECHOSLOVAKIA

FRANCE

SWITZ.

AUSTRIA HUNGARY

ROMANIA

Black Sea

ITALY

YUGOSLAVIA

BULGARIA

PORTUGAL

SPAIN

TURKEY

ALBANIA

GREECE

Mediterranean   Sea

Neutral Country

Warsaw Pact Organization

Communist Country, *Not Members of Warsaw Pact*

North Atlantic Treaty Organization   *Plus Canada and The United States*
Greece and Turkey joined in 1952   Germany joined in 1955   Spain joined in 1982
France withdrew from Integrated Military Command in 1966

Europe in the Cold War

tened by this setback, redirected their energies toward promoting *economic integration* as a basis for political integration by strengthening and expanding the sole survivor of their earlier integrationist hopes, the European Coal and Steel Community. The relative ease with which the six member states of the ECSC (France, West Germany, Italy, and Benelux) had consented to the removal of most restrictions on the exchange of coal and steel products within the community inspired considerable optimism among the proponents of supranationalism about the prospects of extending the concept to other economic sectors. Intensive negotiations were conducted during the mid-fifties to that end. Finally, on March 25, 1957, representatives of the six ECSC states signed the Treaty of Rome establishing the European Economic Community (EEC).

The two overriding purposes of the EEC, which formally entered into operation on January 1, 1958, were the gradual elimination of all legal restrictions on trade, capital movements, and labor migration within the community as well as the establishment of a common external tariff to protect member states from foreign competition during the difficult transitional stage leading to the creation of a genuine free trade zone. As had been the case during the formation of the ECSE, Great Britain declined to join the emerging economic bloc on the continent for fear of jeopardizing its "special relationship" with the United States as well as its preferential trade arrangements with Commonwealth countries (which enabled it to import cheap, duty-free food). The long-range goal of political integration was facilitated through the creation of a complex apparatus of embryonic political institutions as well. The most important of these were the Council of Ministers representing the six countries, a Commission of thirteen "European" civil servants appointed by the member governments, and a "European" parliament empowered to oversee the Commission's activities. Though originally endowed with minimal administrative authority and budgetary autonomy, the institutions of what was in 1967 to be renamed the European Community presided over a process of economic integration that survived all subsequent attempts by some member states (especially France) to reassert the old prerogatives of national sovereignty. Though the goal of political federation proved much more elusive, the "idea" of Europe continued to exercise a powerful attraction on Europeans weary of the old national antagonisms and cognizant of the advantages that West European political unity would bring in the global contest for power, influence, and prosperity.

The Post-Stalinist "Thaw"

It was a considerable feat for NATO to absorb West Germany without sacrificing its internal cohesion during a period of reduced tension with the very power whose ostensibly aggressive behavior had given rise to the formation of the alliance in the first place. Ever since Stalin's death in

March 1953, signals had been emanating from the new collegial leadership in the Kremlin that implied compromise and conciliation. One by one, divisive issues that had given rise to acrimonious exchanges between East and West during the Stalin era suddenly proved susceptible to settlement. The armistice negotiations in Korea, which had been hopelessly deadlocked for two years, were expeditiously completed in July 1953 on terms that denied the Soviet client state in the north the political gains it had sought in the south. A year later, in July 1954, the victorious Vietnamese nationalist movement was compelled by its Soviet patron to swallow a cease-fire agreement at the Geneva Conference on Indochina that left it in control of only the northern half of Vietnam (see pp. 390–91). In the spring of 1955 the Kremlin astonished even the most truculent anti-Communists in the West with a flurry of conciliatory gestures. The Austrian State Treaty, which was signed on May 15, 1955, after a decade of bickering, stipulated the withdrawal of all Allied (including Soviet) occupation forces from Austria and the restoration of that country's political sovereignty on the condition that it adhere to a policy of strict neutrality. The Porkkala naval base wrested from Finland in 1947 was returned to that country. The Manchurian naval base at Port Arthur that Stalin had obtained in exchange for the Russian declaration of war against Japan in 1945 was evacuated and turned over to China. Normal diplomatic relations were restored with the renegade Communist regime of Yugoslavia and the initiative was taken to establish them for the first time with West Germany. This series of dramatic diplomatic concessions prompted speculation in Western capitals that the Soviet Union had renounced its aggressive intentions and was prepared to negotiate a settlement of East-West differences.

This new Soviet posture of accommodation appears to have been prompted by a number of considerations. Foremost among these was the uncharacteristic primacy of domestic politics over international affairs in the thinking of the post-Stalinist governing elite during the succession struggle of 1953–57. While the first secretary of the Communist Party, Nikita Khrushchev, gradually outmaneuvered half a dozen rivals for the top leadership post, he was obliged to bargain with and sometimes concede to various blocs and constituencies within the Soviet political hierarchy in order to amass and then consolidate his power.* At the same time, the fluidity of the political situation during the transitional phase following the death of a despot in a country with no institutionalized mechanism for succession permitted the emergence of a kind of public opinion, which clamored for better living conditions and a relaxation of the stifling political repression inherited from Stalin. In such an uncertain

* Khrushchev acquired political primacy in June 1957 by engineering the expulsion of his three principal rivals, Malenkov, Molotov, and Kaganovich, from the Presidium and the party Central Committee, though he did not become head of government until March 1958.

domestic political environment, the Soviet leadership was understandably inclined to avoid confrontation and conflict with its foreign antagonists in the West, particularly after having failed to forestall the emergence of a rearmed Germany allied to the United States and its European partners. It is also possible that the Kremlin's quest for stability in Europe during the mid-1950s reflected a positive consideration as well: the opportunity to exploit and possibly profit from the mounting difficulties experienced by the European powers in Africa and Asia occasioned by the outburst of revolutionary agitation in those regions that remained under their control (see p. 308). A Soviet diplomatic offensive in the colonial world on behalf of the subject populations that were struggling to rid themselves of British or French rule would certainly have dictated a defensive strategy in Europe to avoid antagonizing the United States and its continental protégés.

This trend toward the relaxation of East-West tensions in Europe reached a crescendo at the first postwar meeting of the Soviet and Western heads of government in Geneva during July 1955. The four days of personal conversations among the four plenipotentiaries—President Eisenhower for the United States, Premier Nikolai Bulganin of the Soviet Union, Prime Minister Anthony Eden of Great Britain, and Premier Edgar Faure of France—transpired amid an atmosphere of cordiality that contrasted dramatically with the rhetorical fulminations of the previous ten years. As titular head of the Western coalition, President Eisenhower set the tone of the conference with an earnest appeal for a cooperative new approach to the substantive problems of European security that would obviate the arms race and dispel the fear of nuclear annihilation. His "open skies" proposal, which envisioned a full exchange of blueprints of American and Soviet military installations and mutual aerial photoreconnaissance, was designed to circumvent the traditional Soviet objection to onsite inspection. Bulganin in turn unveiled a project for disarmament stipulating an absolute prohibition of the fabrication and use of atomic weapons as well as a ceiling on the size of the conventional forces of the world's principal military powers. The heads of government were even able to agree on an innocuous pledge to seek a solution to the touchiest issue of all—the political future of Germany—on the basis of the principle of reunification of the two German states by means of free elections.

None of this meant anything in practical terms. Neither arms limitation proposal was acceptable to the other side for the usual reasons—the Soviets were not about to expose their secretive military planning to intelligence reconnaissance by air, while the Americans were averse to participating in reciprocal prohibitions or limitations of military capability without adequate provisions for inspection. Bulganin's vaguely worded endorsement of "the reunification of Germany by means of free elections" was diluted by all sorts of qualifications, including the condition that such a development be compatible with "the interests of European security." Both the Soviet prime minister and the behind-the-scenes master of the Kremlin, party boss Nikita Khrushchev, returned to Moscow by way of East Berlin to reassure the leaders of the German Democratic Republic that their nation's sovereignty would never be sacrificed. But despite the absence of any concrete achievements, the very fact that the leaders of the West and the East were bargaining face to face with polite language represented a significant departure from the confrontational style of the past. The sweet reasonableness of Eisenhower won him accolades at home and abroad as a "man of peace," while the Soviets conveyed an uncharacteristic image of sincerity and trust. To Eisenhower's earnest pledge that "the United States will never take part in an aggressive war," Bulganin solemnly replied, "We believe that statement." Newspaper columnists in the West spoke with wistful optimism about the "spirit of Geneva" while the Soviet press repeated the catchword "peaceful coexistence" that had been bandied about in the early post-Stalin years.

After the conclusion of the summit conference, the foreign ministers of the great powers were scheduled to assemble in October for a more intensive and prolonged exchange of views in an effort to give concrete form to the vague generalities advanced by the heads of government. But before the opening of the foreign ministers' conference, American Secretary of State Dulles made it unmistakably evident that he had no intention of granting the Soviets the concessions in Europe that they sought as the price for a relaxation of East-West tensions. Convinced as he was that the Russians had come to the conference out of weakness, Dulles preferred to increase the pressure rather than resume the conciliatory initiatives of the president, who was convalescing from a heart attack suffered in September. Accordingly, he lost no opportunity, before and during the conference, to berate the Soviet Union for its oppression of Eastern Europe and demand a settlement of the German problem before the questions of disarmament and East-West security could be taken up, a reversal of the Kremlin's well-publicized set of priorities. Though the meeting dragged on for three weeks, its fate had been sealed by the provocative behavior of the American secretary of state, who appeared incapable of abandoning his dream of rolling back Soviet power from the European continent. To give Dulles the credit that is his due, it must be said that he interpreted the Kremlin's uncharacteristically cooperative attitude at Geneva and elsewhere as nothing more than a tactical ploy to lull the West into a false sense of security while it pursued its aggressive goals in disguised form.

In fact, the new conciliatory gestures emanating from Moscow in the midfifties reflected the beginning of what appears to have been a genuine change of attitude at the highest levels of the Soviet hierarchy. As Khrushchev began his bid for uncontested authority toward the end of 1955, he inaugurated a fundamental reassessment of Soviet policy, foreign as well as domestic. This reassessment rapidly developed into a full-scale indictment of the Stalinist legacy as well as of those Soviet political personalities who sought to perpetuate it. As always, the absence of original documentation and reliable memoirs precludes an accurate reconstruction of the specific steps leading up to this significant shift in Soviet policy, let alone of the underlying motivations that prompted it. One is entitled to speculate that the ambitious party secretary, sensing the prospect of political victory, eagerly embraced the cause of "de-Stalinization" as a weapon in his campaign for primacy within the collective leadership. In any case, once the transformation had been effective and the new Soviet line displayed in public view, it was to shake the Communist world to its very foundations. At a closed meeting of the twentieth congress of the Communist party of the Soviet Union in February 1956, Khrushchev delivered a long, rambling address which startled the assembled delegates and then the entire world once its contents had been leaked to the press. The titular head of the international Communist movement berated Stalin for his repressive policies and called for the establishment of less arbitrary rules of political procedure in the Soviet Union. Implicit also in his speech was an endorsement of liberalization in the satellite states of Eastern Europe and a relaxation of the Soviet Union's tight grip over their domestic politics. This impression was confirmed two months later by the dissolution of the Communist Information Bureau (or Cominform), which had been created by Stalin at the beginning of the Cold War to promote the unity of the Communist parties of Europe and to ensure their subservience to the Soviet state.

As noted above, it is probable that Khrushchev's desecration of Stalin's image and his implicit endorsement of liberalization were primarily motivated by his determination to score a definitive victory in the internal power struggle with the unreconstructed Stalinists who remained in positions of power within the Soviet hierarchy; but the de-Stalinization campaign also reflected considerations of foreign and domestic policy beyond the realm of petty political infighting. It is apparent that the emerging leadership faction identified with Khrushchev had come to regard the domestic political repression imposed during the Stalin years as counterproductive in so far as it stifled the very process of economic development that the Soviet dictator had inaugurated in the interwar period. In the realm of foreign affairs, the ascendant authorities in the Kremlin had evidently concluded that Stalin's postwar policies had dangerously overextended Soviet power to the detriment of Russia's national interests. This was particularly true in Eastern Europe, where his obsession with erecting a compliant satellite empire as a protective buffer along Russia's western frontier had united the West in armed opposition to the Soviet Union, incited the defection of Yugoslavia, and led to violent outbursts of anti-Russian agitation within the bloc, such as the East Berlin riots of 1953.

Even before Khrushchev's denunciation of Stalinist repression and the dissolution of the Cominform in 1956, the post-Stalinist leadership had taken tentative steps to relax the rigid economic and political constraints on the satellites of Eastern Europe in an effort to placate the patently discontented subject populations of that region. The objective seems to have been the setting in motion of a gradual, orderly process of retrenchment and liberalization that would remove the most objectionable features of Russian control over the daily lives of the subject populations without impairing the status of the satellites as ideological confreres and military allies of the Soviet Union. But Khrushchev's dramatic repudiation of the Stalinist legacy nearly transformed this cautious retreat into a rout. He had shattered the myth upon which the monolithic unity of the Communist bloc was based, namely, the infallibility of the Soviet Communist party as the undisputed interpreter of Marxist-Leninist doctrine and keystone of the international Communist movement. In so doing he unleashed the forces of "polycentrism," which meant that individual Communist parties throughout the world were free to pursue their separate paths independent of dictates from Moscow. The challenge of Communist pluralism that Tito had hurled at Stalin in 1948 now seemed to have received the tacit endorsement of Stalin's successor, who invited the renegade Yugoslav leader to Moscow and was treated to a lecture from Tito on the necessity for liberalization in the satellites.

The anti-Stalinist reaction in Russia itself quickly spread to Eastern Europe and became a source of acute danger to Soviet interests there, first in Poland and then in Hungary. In June 1956 labor unrest engulfed the Polish city of Poznan as thousands of workers noisily demonstrated for better economic conditions. By October this isolated outbreak of social protest had evolved into a nationwide expression of resistance to Soviet interference in Poland's internal affairs. The trials of the Poznan rioters ended abruptly, several Communist leaders publicly urged that Soviet officers be removed from the Polish army, and Wladyslaw Gomulka, a symbol of nationalist Communism who had been jailed in 1951 by the pro-Soviet puppet regime in power, rejoined the central committee of the Polish Communist party. On October 20 Khrushchev hastily flew to Warsaw to plead for the continuation of pro-Soviet policies only to be rebuffed by Gomulka, whose election as first secretary of the Polish Communist party the following day signified the advent of "national Communism" in Poland. As Russian tanks rolled toward Warsaw and the Polish government began to distribute arms to the workers of the city, the Soviet leader recognized the imminence of a national war between two Communist neighbors and abruptly capitulated: He announced full support of Gomulka, arranged for the return of Soviet troops stationed in Poland to their barracks, and flew back to Moscow. The consequences of the Polish October were the removal of many restrictions on individual liberties, the curtailment of Russian military authority within Poland, and the formation of a de facto alliance between the "national" Communist party of Gomulka and the Polish Catholic Church headed by Stefen Cardinal Wyszynski, who, like Gomulka, had been released from prison during the upsurge of political unrest. Recognizing that Poland's geographic position between

Germany and Russia precluded a totally independent course, Gomulka prudently sought to consolidate the gains of October while affirming his country's loyalty to the Soviet bloc. By preventing the newly won domestic liberalization from getting out of hand and by remaining committed to the goals of Soviet foreign policy, this shrewd Polish patriot preserved for his country a considerable measure of independence and dissuaded the Kremlin from resorting to military means to enforce its will.

Not so prudent, and not so fortunate, was the political leadership of Communist Hungary that had assumed power in October amid circumstances superficially similar to those in Poland. Hungary had been one of the last Eastern European states to succumb to Soviet domination, and the Communist system had never succeeded in enlisting mass support there. The Communist party barely managed to cling to power, as its economic policies resulted in a lowering of living standards and therefore generated considerable resentment among the population. The anti-Stalinist revelations at the Soviet Communist Party Congress in 1956 undermined the authority of the hard-line, pro-Soviet leadership in Budapest; then the events in Poland inspired a popular insurrection in Hungary that rapidly exceeded the limits to dissent that had been imposed by Gomulka. The new Hungarian prime minister, the liberal Communist Imre Nagy, promptly formed a coalition government which, for the first time since the advent of the Cold War, included non-Communist elements. He then announced his intention to conduct free elections in the near future that were certain to result in the defeat of the unpopular Communist party. On October 30, Nagy obtained from the Kremlin a remarkable public pledge of support for Hungary's national independence, which included promises to remove immediately the Soviet troops that had been dispatched to Budapest to quell the incipient insurrection and eventually to evacuate all Russian military forces from Hungarian territory. For a fleeting moment it appeared that the trend of the previous decade had been reversed, that the liberal policies adopted by Stalin's successors would actually result in a significant degree of political independence for the nations in Russia's East European satellite empire.

But as Soviet troops streamed out of Budapest on November 1, Nagy took an extraordinarily provocative step that was to precipitate an abrupt reversal of the Russian retrenchment. Spurred on by the newly liberated forces of anti-Soviet public opinion, he announced Hungary's withdrawal from the Warsaw Pact, the military alliance concluded in May 1955 between the USSR and the seven Communist satellites of Eastern Europe in response to the inclusion of a rearmed West Germany in NATO. The prospect of a politically independent and militarily neutral Hungary was evidently too much for the Soviet leadership to entertain with equanimity: It would establish a dangerous precedent which, if followed by the other East European states, could only bring about the disintegration of the buffer zone between Russia and the West that Moscow had so insistently established after the collapse of Hitler's Reich. The "liberation" of the Soviet East European empire and the "rollback" of Communist power to the Russian frontier suddenly seemed imminent not because of American pressure but because of the explosion of unrestrained nationalism in Hungary. Thus on November 4, the 250,000-man Russian army, which had earlier delayed its withdrawal from Budapest, returned to that city with 5,000 tanks and inaugurated a reign of terror that undid all that had been accomplished during the previous month: The Nagy regime was forcibly replaced by a puppet government under Janos Kadar, whose authority rested entirely on the presence of Soviet troops that were to remain, at the request of that compliant regime, to guard against a repetition of the recent unpleasantness.

The Kremlin's decision to abandon the policy of gradual retrenchment in Eastern Europe that had begun after Stalin's death and was confirmed by Khrushchev's famous speech was occasioned not only by apprehension about the dangerous precedent of a defiant Hungary but also by the tempting opportunity fortuitously presented by the simultaneous eruption of the crisis along the Suez Canal in October 1956 (see p. 313). With the United States and its allies preoccupied with events in Egypt, the Soviet Union could risk a military intervention in Hungary with greater confidence that it could be accomplished without opposition from the Western powers, despite all of the talk on Western transmitters pledging support for the anti-Soviet resistance.

The relaxation of Moscow's iron grip on Eastern Europe and the recession of Soviet power in the Far East in the years after Stalin's death coincided with the revival of Russian ambitions in those regions of the Middle East and southern Asia that were emancipating themselves from the colonial domination of Great Britain and France. Earlier Soviet attempts to establish an ideological affinity between Russian Communism and the cause of national liberation in the colonial world during the 1920s had met with failure and were virtually abandoned during the Stalin years. But the Leninist doctrine of imperialism, according to which the capitalist nations of the West were ineluctably driven by the dynamics of their own internal economic development to seek cheap sources of raw materials as well as markets for surplus production and capital in the non-white regions of the earth, remained a potentially powerful weapon in the ideological arsenal of the Soviet leadership should it attempt anew to compete for influence there. In November 1955 this long-dormant policy of anti-imperialism was revived by Khrushchev and Soviet Premier Nikolai Bulganin during an extended sojourn in southern Asia. The two Soviet leaders vociferously denounced the evils of European imperialism, endorsed the principle of national liberation, and extended the promise of Russian economic, technical, and military assistance to the newly independent nations that were struggling to overcome the debilitating legacy of European rule. This new Soviet ideological offensive toward the south, and the American effort to counter it, was destined to drag the region stretching from the eastern Mediterranean to the Indian Ocean into the Cold War between East and West. Just as the collapse of German power in Europe and Japanese power in Asia in 1945 had left power vacuums in those areas that invited Soviet-American competition for influence, the retreat of British and French power in the Middle East and Asia during the 1950s resulted in a politically unstable situation that inevitably tempted the two superpowers to intervene to promote their respective interests there.

The ruling elites of the newly independent nations of the postcolonial world were confronted with the choice of either declaring their allegiance to one or the other of the two global coalitions or remaining formally non-aligned in the East-West struggle. None of them chose to throw in their lot with the Soviet bloc in the course of the 1950s, in spite of the Kremlin's determined efforts to curry their favor. On the other hand, a number of them were induced by the United States and its European allies to join Western-oriented regional security systems that were specifically directed against the Soviet Union and its allies. In the aftermath of France's military defeat in Indochina (see pp. 389–90), Secretary of State Dulles masterminded a collective defense system for southeast Asia to contain Soviet and Chinese expansion in that region. Established on the NATO model (though without provisions for automaticity of defense collaboration), the Southeast Asia Treaty Organization (SEATO) embraced the United States, Great Britain, France, Australia, New Zealand,* Pakistan, Thailand, and the Philippines.† To bridge the geographical gap between NATO in the west and SEATO in the east, the British government responded favorably to a Turkish initiative in the spring of 1955 and joined the Baghdad Pact (reorganized in 1959 as the Central Treaty Organization, or CENTO, after a revolution in Iraq that brought to power an anti-Western regime). This regional security organization included Turkey, Iraq, Iran, Pakistan, and Great Britain (which remained a power in the region by virtue of the military and naval bases that it retained in the Persian Gulf). The formation of this southwest Asian defense system was actively encouraged by the United States, which acquired observer status in the new regional organization's policy-making body. In this way the Atlantic powers had succeeded by the mid-1950s in forging a network of alliances spanning the southern rim of Eurasia that linked many of their former dependencies or client states in the common purpose of containing the Soviet Union in that area. The states of the Middle East and of southwestern and southeastern Asia that adhered to these Western-sponsored regional pacts received, in

---

* The United States, Australia, and New Zealand had already concluded a tripartite security treaty (ANZUS) in September 1951.

† The United States had been granted a ninety-nine-year lease of Philippine military and naval bases in March 1947. The two countries concluded a bilateral mutual defense treaty in August 1951.

addition to the pledge of protection in the event of an external threat to their security, an increasing amount of technical assistance to promote their economic development and enhance their military capability.

The alternative of nonalignment in the Cold War was most articulately expressed by the principal spokesman for the developing world, the prime minister of India, Jawaharlal Nehru. Long regarded as Great Britain's most valuable colonial possession, the Indian subcontinent had obtained its independence on August 15, 1947, following its partition into the predominantly Hindu state of India and the separate Moslem state of Pakistan. Though embroiled in a costly regional conflict with its Moslem neighbor over the disputed province of Kashmir and plagued by religious strife between its Hindu majority and its Moslem minority, Nehru's India aspired to a world role commensurate with its size and population. Its remarkable chief of state, who acted as his own foreign minister throughout his long tenure in office, pursued a policy of nonalignment in the East-West struggle and urged the other newly independent nations of the Southern Hemisphere to do likewise. He tirelessly warned of the misfortunes that were bound to befall states that were enticed to join one or the other of the two blocs in their global contest for power. Nehru did not hesitate to extract tangible benefits for his own poverty-stricken country from the Soviet-American competition for influence in the postcolonial world, so long as it was understood that no political strings were attached to the economic assistance. In January 1952 he concluded a five-year "Point Four" agreement with Washington for development aid for the Indian subcontinent. In December 1953 he signed a five-year trade pact with Moscow and in June 1955 a long-term agreement for Soviet economic and technical assistance to India. But Nehru's brand of neutralism, which stemmed in large part from his Gandhian abhorrence of war, led to his country's virtual abstention from the hurly-burly game of East-West global rivalry, except insofar as its pacifist influence could be projected as a sort of moral force upon the world. The ultimate objective of Nehru and his disciples was the formation of a cohesive bloc of Third World nations recently emancipated from European rule which would promote the cause of world peace by declining all participation in the Cold War between the superpowers. Such was the message emanating from the first international conference of independent African and Asian nations held at Bandung, Indonesia, in April 1955.

A very different version of Third World neutralism was espoused by the charismatic military officer who had acquired dictatorial power in Egypt by the midfifties, Colonel Gamal Abdel Nasser. Whereas the pacifist Nehru preached nonalignment as a virtuous end in itself, the soldier Nasser considered it as a means to two objectives, one short term and the other long term, that he had embraced with an all-consuming passion. His immediate goal was the promotion of a crash program of economic development and military rearmament for his own country that would establish it as the dominant power in North Africa and the Middle East in the wake of the Anglo-French withdrawal from that region. In the long term he envisioned a vast pan-Arab empire from the Atlantic to the Persian Gulf under his own leadership. In pursuit of these objectives the Egyptian strongman shamelessly played off the two superpowers against one another, soliciting economic and military assistance from both while hinting to each that he was about to strike a bargain with its rival in order to increase the total amount obtained. From the Communist bloc he procured in September 1955 a pledge of military supplies to equip the Egyptian army in exchange for cotton and rice. From the United States and Great Britain came a joint offer of financial assistance in the amount of $70 million for Nasser's pet project of economic development, the construction of a new dam at Aswan on the Nile that would increase Egypt's cultivable land by one-third and its electric power by one-half. Egypt rapidly developed into a microcosm of the East-West competition for influence in the Third World, with American and Soviet missions vying for the privilege of furnishing Nasser the funds he sought to modernize his backward country and its primitive armed forces.

At the same time the Egyptian leader devoted his energies to removing from North Africa and the Middle East three political forces that constituted the principal obstacles to the realization of his pan-Arab dreams. The first of these was French colonial authority in Algeria, which had been forcefully contested since the autumn of 1954 by a guerrilla movement dedicated to the cause of national independence. Unlike France's other overseas territories, Algeria contained a large French colonial population—estimated to exceed one million by the 1950s—that had traversed the Mediterranean to settle as early as the mid-nineteenth century in the coastal cities and their agricultural hinterlands. These Christian, Caucasian "French Algerians" dominated the economic life of the country through ownership of its urban businesses and its fertile agricultural land. The monopoly of political power by these *colons* was assured by a complicated electoral system which, though granting legal equality to all citizens, had the practical effect of disenfranchising most of the Arab Moslem majority. Thus the insurrection against French rule that erupted in 1954 assumed the character of a bloody civil war between two peoples of different ethnic and religious heritage, both of whom claimed Algeria as their homeland as well as the right to control its political and economic life. To the Moslem Arab insurgents Nasser of Egypt promptly furnished all manner of assistance including sanctuary for their political leaders, acquiring thereby immense prestige in the Arab world as the champion of its liberation from European colonial rule. The granting of independence to France's two other North African possessions, Morocco and Tunisia, in March 1956 appeared to confirm the inevitability of decolonization in the region, a prospect which Nasser anticipated with undisguised alacrity.

In order to remove a second major vestige of colonialism, this one in his own country, the Egyptian strongman wrested from Great Britain on October 19, 1954, a pledge to relinquish its right to maintain a military base on the Suez Canal and to evacuate the canal zone entirely within twenty months. In exchange, Egypt guaranteed freedom of navigation through the waterway and promised to permit the reentry of British military forces in the canal zone in the event of an armed attack by an outside power against any Arab state or Turkey. By the summer of 1956, therefore, Anglo-French colonial authority in the Arab world had either disappeared or, in the case of Algeria, was challenged by a powerful insurrection whose ultimate triumph was doubted by no one save the most unrealistic devotees of Algérie française. The future seemed to hold the promise of Arab self-determination and unity after so many years of subservience and disunity under various European masters and their strategy of divide and conquer; such, at least, was the vision of the ambitious soldier-statesman in Cairo.

The third stumbling block to the realization of Nasser's Pan-Arabist dream was the state of Israel, formed in May 1948 by Jewish refugees from European oppression out of the territory of Palestine previously administered by Great Britain under a mandate from the League of Nations. A resolution by the United Nations General Assembly on November 29, 1947, proposing the partition of Palestine into two sovereign political entities, one Jewish and the other Arab, had been rejected by the neighboring Arab states. Consequently, the proclamation of the Jewish state of Israel upon the termination of the British mandate resulted in a war between Israel and the Arab states that was temporarily interrupted by an uneasy truce in the summer of 1949. To its Jewish inhabitants and their coreligionists abroad, the new state of Israel represented the fulfillment of a two-thousand-year-old dream of returning to the land of their ancestors. In more concrete terms, it offered a haven from the type of persecution they had encountered in Central and Eastern Europe, from the pogroms of the Russian tsars to the Holocaust of Hitler. The political movement of Zionism, founded in the 1890s by the Austrian journalist Theodor Herzl in reaction to the resurgence of European anti-Semitism occasioned by the Dreyfus Affair in France, was based on a single principle that has continued to guide the creators of Israel in 1948 and its defenders thereafter: This is the conviction, reinforced by the indelible memory of the concentration camps of the Third Reich, that the Jews scattered throughout the world would never enjoy security in any nation where they constitute an ethnic minority. Their only hope lay in the establishment of a state populated, controlled, and defended by Jews. But to the proponents of Pan-Arabism, the emergence in 1948 of a state dominated by citizens of European descent in the very heart of the Arab world signified a return to the colonial past and posed a serious challenge to the cause of Arab unity. Thus, Nasser took the lead in organizing the Arab states in opposition to Israel, barring Israeli ships from passing through the Suez Canal or using the Straits of Tiran and providing bases for the Arab refugees from Palestine who launched hit-and-run raids across the Israeli border.

In the summer and fall of 1956 these disparate developments—Soviet-American competition for influence in the Middle East, the Arab-Israeli conflict, and Egyptian efforts to hasten the departure of Anglo-French power from the Arab world—converged in an international crisis that was to damage the solidarity of the Western alliance at the very moment that the unity of the Soviet bloc was being shaken by the events in Poland and Hungary. On June 13, 1956, Great Britain formally terminated its seventy-four-year military occupation of the Suez Canal as stipulated in the agreement of October 1954, leaving Egypt with full responsibility for the defense of that important waterway. On July 20 the United States government, annoyed at Nasser's increasing dependence on military assistance from the Soviet bloc and attentive to pro-Israel sentiment in Congress, abruptly withdrew its offer to finance the construction of the Aswan Dam. Stung by this threat to his personal prestige and his plans for the economic development of his country, the Egyptian ruler retaliated six days later by nationalizing the Suez Canal Company (which remained under the financial control of British banking interests) and announcing his intention to employ the revenue from the canal to defray the costs of building the dam. After three months of fruitless diplomatic efforts to bring the pressure of world opinion to bear on Nasser to accept multinational control of this vital artery through which the bulk of European trade and Middle Eastern oil shipments passed, the British prime minister, Anthony Eden, concluded that his only recourse was military force. He hoped to topple Nasser, whom he had come to view as an incarnation of Hitler who, if not restrained, would accomplish in the Middle East what Hitler had done in Europe. Nasser's prior support for the Algerian rebellion against France and the Palestinian guerrilla campaign against Israel guaranteed that the British leader's scheme would find a sympathetic audience in Paris and Tel Aviv. Without consulting their American ally in advance, the British and French governments concocted and executed an elaborate hoax involving three nations that was designed to achieve for each the objectives it sought at Egypt's expense. By prior arrangement the Israeli army attacked Egypt on October 29, 1956, and within a few days had routed the Egyptian army on the Sinai peninsula and ominously approached the Suez Canal. On November 5 British and French paratroops were dropped in Suez and Port Said for the ostensible purpose of separating the two armies and protecting the canal in the interests of its international clientele. The real goal of this coordinated military operation against Egypt was the forcible replacement of the Nasser regime with one that would abstain from menacing British interests in the canal, French authority in Algeria, and Israel's security along its western frontier. The Suez intervention failed not because of Egyptian military resistance, which crumbled before Israeli tanks in the Sinai and Anglo-French paratroopers along the canal, but rather because of the unexpected and vigorous opposition of the United States. For reasons related as much to personality conflicts between Dulles and Eden as to divergences of national interest, the American government exerted sufficient pressure on its two European allies to compel a humiliating withdrawal of the three military forces that had converged by prior arrangement on the Suez Canal at the end of October.

The Suez fiasco was pregnant with long-range consequences for the future of the international balance of power. It spelled the end of Anglo-French pretensions to an imperial role in the Middle East. It undermined the political cohesion of the Atlantic alliance by revealing to the Europeans that they no longer enjoyed the prerogative of pursuing foreign policies that did not have Washington's blessing. It immeasurably bolstered the prestige of Nasser in the Arab world and solidified his reputation as the spokesman for the developing nations in their struggle to eradicate the remaining vestiges of European colonialism. The Soviet Union, which had energetically intervened on Egypt's behalf to the point of threatening nuclear retaliation against Britain and France at the height of the crisis, acquired a reputation as the champion of Arab aspirations at the expense of the Western powers and their Israeli ally. Thus, just as the Soviet Union's undisputed predominance in Eastern Europe appeared threatened by the outbreak of nationalist agitation in Poland and Hungary, the Suez affair enabled the Kremlin to renew its ideological offensive in the Third World under the most favorable of circumstances. Moreover, while the polycentrist tendencies within the Communist bloc were abruptly curbed through Polish prudence in Warsaw and Soviet repression in Budapest, America's abandonment of its allies at Suez strengthened those Western European forces, which were particularly strong in France, that favored the pursuit of military, diplomatic, and economic policies independent of the United States.

The trans-Atlantic tensions generated by the Suez crisis were fed by the mounting anxiety felt in Western Europe about the reliability of American military protection against the Soviet menace. As we have seen, the strategy of nuclear deterrence embraced by the Eisenhower administration consisted of the threat of a massive nuclear strike against the population centers of Russia in retaliation against a conventional Soviet military advance into Western Europe. Its credibility rested on the capability of the United States to unleash its nuclear arsenal without fear of a Soviet counterblow against its own cities. During the first decade of the Cold War the Soviet Union had made considerable progress in narrowing the lead of the United States in the nuclear arms race; it exploded its first atomic bomb four years after the United States in 1949 and its first hydrogen bomb only nine months after the United States in 1953. What Russia conspicuously lacked were either bases in the Western Hemisphere from which to threaten American territory with nuclear bombardment or an intercontinental delivery system to transport nuclear weapons from Russian territory to their targets in North America. During the second half of the 1950s the Soviet Union acquired just such a delivery system that promised to neutralize the American deterrent. By mid-1955 it had perfected a long-range bomber which had the round-trip capacity to strike at American territory; but the United States possessed five times as many such planes as well as an efficient radar system to detect those of the enemy. The major Soviet breakthrough in nuclear delivery systems occurred as a consequence of advances in rocketry associated with the early efforts at space exploration. On October 4, 1957, the Kremlin astonished the world with its announcement that Russian scientists had successfully launched the first man-made space satellite, the Sputnik. It was evident in the minds of all competent observers that a rocket capable of projecting a metal object into orbit around the earth would be capable of delivering a nuclear warhead to targets anywhere on the surface of the globe. Indeed, on August 26 of the same year the Soviet news agency Tass had announced the first successful test of an intercontinental ballistic missile (ICBM). The United States quickly followed suit by successfully testing a five-thousand-mile range Atlas ICBM in December 1957 and then launching its first space satellite, the Explorer, in February 1958. But until the Americans could construct a large number of ICBMs, they would be forced to rely on obsolete long-range bombers (which, unlike the ICBMs, were vulnerable to interception by enemy aircraft before reaching their targets) and on intermediate-range ballistic missiles (IRBMs) launched from bases in friendly countries close to the Soviet Union.

As it turned out, the United States rapidly erased the Soviet lead in the technology of nuclear delivery systems. By the early 1960s it had begun to deploy its own ICBM system, upgraded its long-range bomber force, and expanded its arsenal of medium-range bombers and IRBMs based in allied countries. Nervous talk in Washington about a "missile gap" during the presidential campaign of 1960 proved excessively pessimistic, largely because Soviet nuclear technology was not up to the ambitious task assigned to it by the Soviet leadership. But the fact remained that, for the first time since the advent of the atomic age, the United States was vulnerable to a surprise nuclear attack from missiles launched from Soviet territory. A successful Soviet first strike against the American retaliatory force (that is, the long-range bombers and ICBMs on American territory as well as the medium-range bombers and IRBMs based on Allied soil) could instantly disarm the United States and leave its principal population centers exposed to annihilation. From this ominous transformation of the nuclear balance America's European partners drew two conclusions, both of which were destined to create serious tensions in the Atlantic partnership. The first was the growing suspicion that in a genuine crisis the United States would decline to sacrifice American cities for the sake of defending Western Europe against a conventional Soviet attack. The second was that by consenting to the deployment of American medium-range missiles and bombers on their own territory, as several of the NATO allies had been persuaded to do by the end of the 1950s, the nations of Western Europe would be exposing their own populations to total nuclear destruction in the event of a Soviet-American nuclear exchange. In time, the realization that the densely populated countries of Western Europe that hosted American bomber bases or missile installations would be automatic targets for any surprise attack by Russia provoked widespread discontent within the Western bloc. In England, which had launched its own modest nuclear armament program in the midfifties and integrated it with the much larger American deterrent force, groups such as the Campaign for Nuclear Disarmament and the Committee of 100 loudly demanded withdrawal from NATO, the removal of American air bases and missile sites, and the abandonment of British nuclear armament. On the continent, official voices were raised in favor of a reciprocal disengagement of American and Russian forces from their forward positions in Central Europe in order to avert a superpower confrontation in that region that could lead to a nuclear holocaust. At the same time, skepticism about the reliability of the American "nuclear umbrella" prompted some Western leaders to call for greater European efforts at self-defense and independence from the United States.

The Crisis Years: From Berlin to Cuba

The disarray of the Western alliance in the wake of Suez and Sputnik emboldened the recently entrenched leadership group in the Kremlin to test the resolve of the United States and its European partners at their most vulnerable point. This was West Berlin, which remained a perpetual irritant for the Soviet Union and its East European satellites and remained militarily indefensible by the small American, British, and French garrisons stationed there. The former capital of Hitler's Reich once again became the focus of East-West tension in November 1958: Khrushchev abruptly demanded the total evacuation of all four occupation forces from Berlin within six months, failing which the Soviet Union would unilaterally transfer its functions in the city to its East German puppets sitting in the Berlin suburb of Pankow. Since the Allies had neither diplomatic relations nor an access agreement to Berlin with the Pankow regime, acceptance of the Soviet ultimatum would have isolated the Western enclave from its protectors and doubtless led to its absorption by East Germany. The Kremlin reopened the "Berlin question" that had lain dormant for a decade after the abortive blockade of 1948–49 because of its uneasiness about the growing military power of West Germany, which was well on its way to possessing the strongest European military contingent within NATO. The enthusiasm with which the fervently anti-Communist chancellor of the Federal Republic, Konrad Adenauer, and his aggressive young defense minister, Franz-Josef Strauss, endorsed the tough line of Dulles and welcomed the presence of American ground forces and nuclear weapons on West German territory provoked great alarm in Moscow. Added to the ominous implications of the German-American military partnership for the Soviet Union were the devastating consequences of the West German economic "miracle" for the economically depressed East German state. The promise of a much higher standard of living, not to speak of a less repressive political climate, had induced over two million East Germans to escape to the Federal Republic during the first decade of its existence. The inordinately large proportion of highly skilled professionals in this mass migration westward jeopardized the economic recovery of the German Democratic Republic. By 1958 the long border separating the two Germanies had been effectively sealed. But the brain drain continued through the last remaining hole in the iron curtain: the unobstructed passage between the eastern and western sectors of Berlin.

The Khrushchev ultimatum on Berlin was not only designed to achieve the narrow objective of removing this irritating challenge to Soviet control over its East European satellite empire and East German opportunities for economic development. It was also intended to serve two more ambitious purposes. The first was to disrupt the increasingly intimate connection between the United States and West Germany. The Adenauer regime had come to regard Berlin as the preeminent test of America's determination to defend Bonn's security interests. If the Western allies, whose token garrisons in that city were outnumbered five to one by Communist military forces in the vicinity, could be pressured into surrendering their patently indefensible position deep within the Communist sphere, the emergent Washington-Bonn axis would be severely damaged, perhaps beyond repair. The second objective was the disengagement of the other NATO allies from Washington's embrace. At the height of the Berlin crisis in the winter of 1958–59, Moscow explicitly warned half a dozen West European nations that their military partnership with the United States guaranteed their total destruction in the event of a nuclear war between the two superpowers. This admonition was unmistakably intended to discourage the European members of NATO from agreeing to the establishment of medium-range missile bases on their own soil.

The Western powers unanimously rejected the Soviet ultimatum, reaffirming their access rights to Berlin and refusing to recognize the transfer of Russia's authority to the East German regime. Faced with this united front by the West, the Kremlin finally backed down in March 1959. Khrushchev revoked the deadline for the transfer of sovereignty to East Germany, acknowledged allied rights in Berlin, and proposed a summit meeting to settle the Berlin issue once and for all. By the summer of 1959, Great Britain, Italy, and Greece had formally authorized the establishment of bases for American medium-range missiles on their territory. On August 3, 1959, during a conference of foreign ministers in Geneva, the American and Soviet governments announced that Chairman

Khrushchev and President Eisenhower had agreed to exchange state visits. The most recent crisis over Berlin seemed to have been resolved by the Russian government's unilateral retreat.

During the last two weeks of September 1959, Nikita Khrushchev became the first Russian leader in history to visit the United States. After a whirlwind tour of the American hinterland, the Soviet visitor settled down for a series of private discussions with Eisenhower at Camp David, the presidential retreat in the Maryland mountains. Nothing of substance seems to have resulted from these confidential talks, save a tacit agreement to put the Berlin problem on ice pending the convocation of a summit conference of the great powers in the following year. Nevertheless, the state-controlled Soviet press began to wax lyrical about the "spirit of Camp David," just as it had celebrated the "spirit of Geneva" after the inconsequential exchange of pleasantries at the summit four years earlier. The tenor of cordiality that marked East-West communications greatly improved the prospects for genuine detente as the tension-filled decade of the 1950s drew to a close. The death in May 1959 of John Foster Dulles, the preeminent symbol of the Cold War mentality in the American government, seemed to signify the end of the era of Soviet-American confrontation. The moratorium on the Berlin question that had been effortlessly agreed to at Camp David provided a welcome respite from a tension-filled dispute. In a speech from the rostrum of the United Nations General Assembly in New York, Khrushchev unveiled a proposal for general and complete disarmament within four years—an appealing if unrealistic solution to the arms race that the Kremlin has periodically reiterated ever since. A few months after his return to Moscow the Russian leader announced that the Soviet Union would reduce its standing armed forces by a third in an apparent gesture of goodwill. From the brink of war over Berlin, the two superpowers had advanced a considerable distance toward mutual accommodation.

The summit conference that was to transform the conciliatory spirit of Camp David into a comprehensive settlement of the remaining issues of the Cold War was scheduled to open in Paris in the spring of 1960. On the fifth of May, eleven days before the discussions were to begin, the Kremlin cast a pall over the forthcoming proceedings by announcing that a high-altitude U-2 American spy plane had been shot down over Soviet territory on the first of the month, and it angrily demanded an explanation. After a clumsy effort by the State Department to deny the intelligence-gathering purposes of the flight, President Eisenhower accepted full responsibility for the embarrassing incident. Khrushchev thereupon announced that he would refuse to participate in the Paris meeting unless Eisenhower formally apologized for the violation of Soviet air space, punished those responsible, and promised to discontinue the flights. Since the intelligence-gathering function of these high-altitude planes was soon to be assumed by satellites orbiting the earth, it was a small matter for the United States to accede to the final Soviet demand. But for reasons of domestic politics in an election year as well as of international prestige, the American president was in no position to apologize to the Russian leader, let alone to penalize subordinates who were merely following instructions. This supplied Khrushchev with the pretext he had apparently been searching for to close down the Paris summit conference on May 16, the very day it had begun, and to revoke Eisenhower's invitation to the Soviet Union.

The Kremlin had been aware of and had publicly denounced the U-2 reconnaissance flights across Soviet territory since their inception in the summer of 1956, but had been unable to prevent them because their altitude put them beyond the range of Russian fighters and surface-to-air missiles (SAMs).* Why, then, did Khrushchev seize upon this relatively trivial incident as an excuse to sabotage the summit conference and cancel Eisenhower's return visit of goodwill to Moscow, both of which the Soviet leader had been active in promoting?

Khrushchev had come under intense pressure from sources within the Communist camp to reverse the policy of rapprochement with the West that he had inaugurated in the late 1950s. A hard-line faction within the Soviet Politburo strongly opposed a negotiated settlement of the German problem in general and the Berlin issue in particular for fear that Soviet concessions would further undermine Russia's hegemonic position in Eastern Europe that had earlier been challenged in Warsaw and Budapest. At the same time, the Communist regime in China had become openly antagonistic toward Khrushchev's conciliatory posture in world affairs. In the eyes of the Maoist leadership in Beijing, the prospect of a Soviet-American rapprochement in Europe violated the revolutionary principles of Marxist-Leninism, of which the Oriental branch of the international Communist movement had ironically become the most orthodox devotee. In place of the relentless struggle for the triumph of world communism, Khrushchev had substituted the policy of peaceful coexistence through disarmament negotiations and summit talks with the enemy. To counter this apparent renunciation of the messianic goals of world communism, Beijing let it be known after the Camp David talks that it would not be bound by such international agreements to reduce tensions as might be concluded by the two superpowers and their partners. Reinforcing this ideological dispute was Beijing's mounting displeasure at Moscow's failure to support with sufficient vigor the Chinese position on a number of critical issues; these included its border dispute with India (a country with which Russia maintained excellent relations), its campaign to reacquire by military force the Chinese Nationalist offshore haven of Formosa (which enjoyed the military protection of the United States), and its goal of acquiring nuclear weapons (a prototype of which had been promised by the Russians to the Chinese in October 1957 only to be cancelled by Khrushchev in June

* The U-2 plane was shot down by a Soviet SAM on May 1, 1960, because it had lost altitude due to engine trouble.

1959). Herein lay the early indications of what was soon to be called "the Sino-Soviet split," which would shatter the monolithic unity of the Communist bloc (see pp. 383–86).

Thus, the opposition of domestic hard-liners within the Soviet ruling elite, combined with the Chinese threat to challenge Soviet leadership of the Communist bloc on the issue of Khrushchev's attempt to relax East-West tensions, had placed the Russian leader in a vulnerable position as the Paris summit conference approached. The U-2 incident fortuitously played into the hands of those in Moscow and Beijing who had been resisting a comprehensive settlement in Europe. Eisenhower, whom Khrushchev had praised upon his return from Camp David as a man who "sincerely wants, like us, to end the Cold War," was suddenly exposed as an organizer of spy missions for which, when caught red-handed, he lacked the good grace to apologize. In light of the American president's damaged credibility, it is also probable that Khrushchev preferred to await the change in American administrations that was due to occur the following winter. In any case, within a week of the Paris meeting's premature demise, the man who had virtually declared the Cold War to be at an end during his American tour issued a threat to conclude a separate peace treaty with East Germany, repeated the warning to European nations hosting American bases that they were inviting nuclear destruction, and flew to Beijing to reassure his Chinese critics of Soviet toughness.

This brusque reversion to an aggressive posture continued for the remainder of Eisenhower's tenure in office. Khrushchev appeared intent on seizing every available opportunity to challenge the West, no doubt to disarm his critics at home and in Beijing, perhaps also to confront the new American president with a challenging set of foreign policy crises upon his inauguration. Once again, the temptation to fish in the troubled waters of the Third World proved irresistible. In Laos, a landlocked kingdom in southeast Asia formerly attached to the French Indochinese empire, the Soviet Union sent massive military supplies to the pro-Communist guerrilla movement that challenged the authority of the right-wing government forces that were being trained and equipped by the United States. The Soviet leader even took the gamble of extending Russian influence to the heart of sub-Sahara Africa, a large portion of which was in the process of obtaining national independence from the European colonial powers. When civil war erupted in the former Belgian Congo soon after its independence in the summer of 1960, the Kremlin provocatively hinted at the possibility of Soviet military intervention on behalf of the central government against a secessionist regime in the mineral-rich province of Katanga that was backed by Belgian copper and cobalt interests. When an international police force under the auspices of the United Nations was dispatched at the request of the Congolese government to restore order and supervise the withdrawal of Belgian troops that had been rushed back to the country to protect Belgian nationals, Moscow accused U.N. Secretary General Dag

Hammarskjold of prejudice against the leftist regime of Patrice Lumumba. Khrushchev promptly sent the Congolese leader military equipment, technicians, and advisers while threatening to dispatch Russian "volunteers" in a bold plan to establish the first Soviet foothold beyond the Eurasian continent. The collapse of the Lumumba regime and the expulsion of Soviet personnel by its successor dealt Khrushchev's newly aggressive policy in Black Africa a humiliating setback. He retaliated with a spirited assault against the Western bloc's controlling position in the United Nations, proposing the dismissal of Hammarskjold and the replacement of the office of secretary general by a *troika* representing the Western, Communist, and nonaligned states.

Though nothing ever came of either project, Khrushchev's shoe-banging performance at the U.N. General Assembly meeting of October 1960 signified his appreciation of the revolutionary implications of the decolonization process then in full swing. By 1960 the membership of the United Nations had doubled, as newly independent states with unfamiliar names emerged from the ashes of the European colonial empires in the Southern Hemisphere. From an exclusive club dominated by the powerful white nations of the West, the world organization was becoming a forum for over a hundred sovereign political entities from Africa and Asia. Combined with the nations of the Communist bloc, these erstwhile victims of European imperialism formed a solid majority in the United Nations General Assembly that might prove useful in forthcoming diplomatic contests with the United States and its allies in that forum of world opinion.

Yet despite the sudden emergence of the postcolonial developing world as an arena for Soviet-American competition, the center of the Cold War remained in Europe; and the center of Europe remained Germany; and the center of Germany remained Berlin. Accordingly, it was in that perennial trouble spot that Khrushchev strove to regain the initiative in foreign affairs that had been lost amid the abortive efforts to establish a Soviet foothold in sub-Sahara Africa and to reorganize the United Nations. We know enough about the simmering discontent within the Soviet leadership and the increasingly bitter recriminations from Beijing to surmise that Khrushchev desperately needed a triumph in foreign policy to shore up his faltering position at home and within the international Communist movement. The hemorrhage of East Germany's skilled labor force through the Berlin gap would continue so long as the Western allies remained in military occupation of the western sector of that city. With the new, untested administration of President John F. Kennedy recently installed in Washington, Khrushchev resolved once and for all to settle the Berlin issue on Moscow's terms. He took the occasion of a Soviet-American summit conference at Vienna in June 1961—the fourth such face-to-face encounter since the advent of the Cold War—to present the new American chief executive in the most menacing of terms with another ultimatum demanding a German peace treaty, an end to the occupation regime, and the transformation of West Berlin into a free city. Upon his return to Moscow he set the end of the year as the deadline for his ultimatum and announced a one-third increase in the military budget to underline his determination to dislodge the Allied garrisons from Berlin. On July 25 Kennedy responded in kind, reaffirming America's commitment to defend West Berlin by armed force if necessary and requesting Congressional authorization for an additional $3 billion increase in defense expenditures and the doubling of draft calls. At the end of the tension-filled summer of 1961, the Kremlin announced the resumption of nuclear tests that had been suspended by mutual agreement of the Soviet Union, the United States, and Great Britain since the fall of 1958; a series of Soviet nuclear tests in the autumn was capped by the detonation of a 58-megaton device, three thousand five hundred times more powerful than the Hiroshima bomb. American entrepreneurs promoted family-size fallout shelters to protect against the nuclear radiation that was sure to come, while the American and British governments responded by resuming nuclear testing to avoid falling behind in the arms race.

But in the meantime the Soviets and their East German clients had devised a stopgap solution to the Berlin problem that avoided the risk of a nuclear showdown. On the morning of August 13, East German police sealed the border separating the two sectors of the city and began construction of a concrete-and-barbed-wire barrier that eventually blocked all access between East and West Berlin except through a handful of closely guarded checkpoints. The Western response to this imaginative method of unilaterally nullifying the intercity access arrangements was confined to sharp diplomatic protests and a token reinforcement of Allied garrisons in the Western sector of the city. No attempt was made to remove the wall, which, though an embarrassing symbol of East Germany's prison-like status, admirably served its purpose: the torrent of East German refugees pouring through the escape-hatch of Berlin to the West was reduced to a trickle. Over 103,000 had fled during the first six months of 1961 alone. In succeeding years the annual outflow averaged 6,000.

The improvisation that had been intended as a temporary solution of the festering problem of divided Berlin became a permanent one. On October 17, by which time it had become evident that the Western allies had acquiesced in the fait accompli of the wall, Khrushchev again lifted his deadline for the resolution of the related issues of Germany and Berlin; Russian and East German authorities allowed the Allied military forces in the Western sector to remain unharassed and refrained from interfering with their access to the Federal Republic across the East German autobahn. On June 12, 1964, the Soviet Union concluded a bilateral treaty with East Germany formally recognizing its sovereignty but without challenging the special status of West Berlin and the presence of the Allied military forces stationed there. Never again would the anomalous position of Germany and Berlin seriously disturb relations between the two superpowers. In the interest of averting a nuclear confrontation, Washington and Moscow had become reconciled to the permanent partition of the German nation and its erstwhile capital.

But the solution to the Berlin problem reached in 1961 had fallen far short of the spectacular success in foreign policy that Khrushchev had coveted as a means of stifling the rumblings of discontent within the Communist bloc. Though the problem of East German emigration had been resolved, the Americans had stood firm in Berlin, with the unqualified support of their NATO allies (including even the increasingly independent-minded French regime of President Charles de Gaulle). The Kremlin's resumption of nuclear testing may be viewed as both a compensatory and an intimidating gesture: it was compensation for the patent Soviet strategic inferiority and vulnerability to the United States (as revealed by the U-2 flights over Russian territory and subsequently confirmed by the Pentagon's public references to the small number of ICBMs the Soviets had managed to produce since Sputnik) and intimidation of the increasingly hard-headed Kennedy and the increasingly recalcitrant Mao Zedong. The resumption of nuclear testing during the autumn of 1961 shattered the hopes for strategic arms control that had been nurtured by the 1958 moratorium and kept alive by the atomic disarmament negotiations conducted in Geneva. Thus, instead of serving as the first step in a comprehensive resolution of East-West differences, the stalemate over Berlin resulted in heightened international tensions and rekindled Soviet-American competition in nuclear weaponry.

It was in this context of strategic rivalry that Khrushchev felt impelled to take his most reckless gamble in foreign policy, one that brought the two superpowers to the brink of a nuclear exchange that would surely have annihilated a large proportion of the people in the two belligerent countries. In one of the most notable ironies in the history of international relations, the Soviet-American confrontation that came closest to transforming the Cold War into the nuclear Armageddon that the prophets of doom had been predicting since the advent of the atomic age occurred not in one of the usual distant flashpoints of East-West conflict in Europe or the Far East, but in the one region of the world which had been entirely off limits to Soviet influence because of its proximity to and historic connections with the United States.

The position of the United States vis-à-vis the twenty independent republics of Latin America from the end of the Second World War to the beginning of the 1960s can best be characterized as one of undisputed domination. The world war and its aftermath had definitively confirmed the economic preeminence of the United States in the Western Hemisphere. Europe's commercial and financial stake in Latin America had declined dramatically as Great Britain, Germany, and France squandered their human and material resources during the war and then struggled to rebuild their own shattered economies after 1945. In the meantime, as we have seen, the economic systems of most of the Latin American countries had been closely tied to the expanding economy of the United States as it geared up for and then sustained the global war against Germany and Japan. American military power was projected southward with the explicit consent of the Latin American states for the purpose of protecting them from the menace of Axis aggression. As the end of the war approached, many Latin American governments expressed concern that the United States' new global responsibilities as well as its sponsorship of a new international organization for the maintenance of peace and security would undermine the solidarity as well as the effectiveness of the inter-American regional security system that had been forged during the war. In order to allay Latin American anxieties on this score, United States delegates at the founding conference of the United Nations Organization in the spring of 1945 inserted a provision in the U.N. Charter authorizing the formation of regional security organizations with powers of enforcement that would not be subject to the approval of the U.N. Security Council.

With the advent of the Cold War in Europe, the United States and its Latin American clients moved to give concrete form to the informal regional security arrangements agreed to during the war. The Inter-American Treaty of Reciprocal Assistance, signed in Rio de Janiero in September 1947 and eventually ratified by all of the twenty-one American republics, established a permanent defensive alliance against aggression originating both outside and inside the hemisphere. In the spring of 1948 the American republics endowed this military alliance with a formal political structure by transforming the loosely organized Pan American Union into the Organization of American States (OAS). The peacekeeping machinery of the OAS thereafter operated with unanticipated effectiveness in settling a number of regional disputes between member states, such as those between Nicaragua and Costa Rica in 1949, 1955, and 1959 as well as a flareup between Nicaragua and Honduras in 1957.

But whereas the Latin American members of the OAS regarded the inter-American system as a multilateral mechanism for the maintenance of regional peace and security, the United States came to view it in much narrower and more explicit terms, particularly after the outbreak of the Korean War and the resulting American preoccupation with the spread of Communism throughout the world. From Washington's perspective, the OAS-Rio Pact structure was designed to serve the same purpose that was being served by the other regional security systems that the United States had sponsored, namely, the defense of the free world against the expansionist ambitions of the Soviet bloc.

We have seen how the fear of Communist insurgency in the war-ravaged countries of Western Europe had led to the provision of large amounts of American aid to cure the socio-economic ills on which Communist was thought to thrive. But in spite of the persistence of such problems in Latin

America on a scale much larger than in Western Europe, and in spite of urgent requests from Latin American countries for economic assistance to address them, there was to be no Marshall Plan for the Western Hemisphere in the early postwar years. Secretary Marshall himself had pledged at the Rio Conference of 1947 that serious attention would be devoted to Latin American pleas for development assistance. But no progress was made in the few discussions of inter-American economic affairs that were conducted in subsequent years. Whereas the Latin American countries hoped to secure United States government assistance after the fashion of the European Recovery Program, Washington insisted that such development aid as might be forthcoming would have to emanate from private sources. Whereas the Latin states called for international agreements to stabilize world commodity prices in order to halt the drastic price fluctuations of the region's principal exports, the United States consistently opposed any measures that would interfere with the operation of the free market as a price-setting mechanism.

The economic stagnation suffered by all Latin American countries after the Second World War, caused partly by long-term structural problems (treated at length in earlier chapters) and partly by the abrupt termination of war-induced demand for their raw materials after 1945, exacerbated acute social tensions that stemmed from the extreme maldistribution of land and capital. The landowning, commercial, and financial oligarchies, in alliance with the military caste and the hierarchy of the Catholic Church, maintained a monopoly on political authority and resisted social and economic reforms that would curtail their wealth and power to the profit of the landless, impoverished *campesinos* in the countryside and the small but expanding working class in the cities. Such a volatile situation was a classic prescription for social instability; many of the republics of Latin America were shaken by a seemingly endless cycle of popular upheaval and repressive conservative reaction in the years after 1945. And in view of the extensive involvement of United States firms in the economies of Latin America, not to speak of the United States government's expanded postwar security commitments in the region, it is scarcely surprising that the domestic turmoil there would eventually engage the attention of the authorities in Washington.

This is precisely what was to happen in the Central American republic of Guatemala, where, after the thirteen-year-old dictatorship of General Jorge Ubico was overthrown in 1944, a mild-mannered university professor named Juan Arevélo was elected president on a program of sweeping social renovation. From 1945 to 1951 Arevélo undertook to narrow the gap between rich and poor as well as to improve the educational and economic conditions of the large Indian population through a series of government-sponsored reforms that antagonized landowners, foreign investors, and military officers alike. In March 1951 Arevélo was succeeded by the fiery spokesman for the ruling party's left wing, thirty-seven-year-old Colonel Jacobo Arbenz Guzmán. After pushing through the Guatemalan parliament a far-reaching program of agrarian reform, Arbenz announced his intention to expropriate 225,000 acres of undeveloped land belonging to the American banana concern, the United Fruit Company, and to redistribute it to the peasantry. As United Fruit solicited the support of its government against the Guatemalan regime, the new Eisenhower administration was becoming greatly alarmed at what its ambassador in Guatemala City was describing in ominous terms as the mounting influence of Communists in Arbenz's entourage.

By the beginning of 1954, representatives of United Fruit as well as agents of the Central Intelligence Agency were approaching right-wing Guatemalan exiles in Nicaragua and Honduras with schemes to overthrow Arbenz while Washington organized a boycott of arms to the country. When evidence surfaced that the Guatemalan leader had attempted to circumvent the boycott by contracting for a shipment of 2,000 tons of light arms from Czechoslovakia, Washington had the pretext it required for initiating remedial action to forestall the spread of Communist-bloc influence to its own backyard. In June the American-backed Guatemalan exiles reentered the country with air support furnished by planes piloted by CIA operatives and instigated a military coup that toppled Arbenz and sent him into exile. The new military junta that assumed power promptly revoked most of the land reforms enacted by its predecessor and inaugurated a campaign of repression against left-wing organizations in the country.

The unilateral intervention of the United States in Guatemala had been undertaken with the tacit acquiescence of the OAS, which had issued a declaration during the Caracas conference in March 1954 condemning the domination of any member state by "the international Communist movement" as a "threat to the sovereignty and political independence" of them all. But this new inclusion of anti-Communism in the definition of Pan-Americanism was opposed by most of the civilian-ruled republics, and even some of the military dictatorships had to be threatened with American economic reprisals before they cast their affirmative vote. The prospect of United States interference in Latin America, notwithstanding the principle of non-intervention enshrined in the OAS Charter, remained a much greater source of concern to the Latin republics than the remote danger of a Communist takeover. The CIA-sponsored coup in Guatemala seemed to demonstrate that the principle of non-intervention, for which Latin American governments had fought so hard and so long, had become a casualty of the Cold War.

As a symbol of the resurgence of unilateral, if covert, United States interference in the internal affairs of Latin American states, the overthrow of Arbenz rekindled widespread resentment among nationalistic groups throughout the region. The central role of the United Fruit Company in the Guatemalan episode also played into the hands of left-wing political agitators, who mobilized mass support by attributing Latin America's chronic economic problems to the nefarious influence of United States corporations operating there. The extent of Latin American discontent with the United States came to light in dramatic fashion during Vice President Nixon's good-will tour to eight Latin American countries in May 1958. The startled Vice President and his entourage were confronted by hostile demonstrations at every stop. In Caracas his motorcade was almost overwhelmed by angry, stone-throwing mobs hissing "Yankee go home."

The embarrassment of the Nixon tour alerted the Eisenhower administration to the simmering grievances that the Latin American masses harbored against the United States. A few weeks later, an imaginative proposal issued by Brazilian President Juscelino Kubitscheck envisioning a joint program of economic development for the hemisphere caught the eye of United States officials alarmed by the upsurge of anti-American sentiments south of the border. The final year of the Eisenhower presidency was marked by a notable modification of United States economic policy toward Latin America. Washington finally withdrew its opposition to the formation of a government-funded regional financing agency, a longstanding objective of several Latin American states. In October 1960 the Inter-American Development Bank was established to disburse development loans to Latin American countries. Though a mere drop in the bucket compared to the region's enormous financing requirements, the advent of IADB lending signified an important symbolic departure from Washington's traditional insistence on referring Latin American borrowers to the private capital markets.

The Kennedy administration promptly transformed this tentative Eisenhower initiative into a full-fledged program of hemispheric economic development along the lines originally proposed by Kubitschek in 1958. In his inaugural address on January 20, 1961, the new American chief executive spoke of forming an "alliance for progress" with the United States' sister republics to the south in order to help them overcome the debilitating effects of economic backwardness. In a speech on March 13 to an assembly of representatives from the Latin American states, Kennedy outlined in detail an ambitious project of United States public assistance to the region. At the Inter-American Economic and Social Conference in Punta del Este, Uruguay the following August, the Alliance for Progress was formally brought into existence. As originally conceived, it included features that responded to two concerns that the Latin American countries had been voicing for decades. The first, and by far the most important, was the pledge of a 10-year, $20 billion project of United States government aid to promote the economic development of Latin America and to raise its per capita income 2.5 percent annually. The second was an agreement to seek means of preventing the wild fluctuation of foreign exchange earnings from commodity exports that had plagued the Latin American economies for so long.

This radical reversal of United States economic policy toward Latin America was undertaken with the enthusiastic support of all of the twenty republics to the south save one. Ironically, it was the one that had over the years been most closely linked, economically, politically, and militarily, to the "Colossus of the North." In January 1959 the autocratic Batista regime in Cuba, which had preserved that impoverished nation's traditionally subservient relationship with the United States and with the private American sugar companies that controlled its single-crop economy, was toppled by an insurrectionary movement headed by a charismatic revolutionary in the Latin American style named Fidel Castro. Once ensconced in Havana, the new Cuban ruler took a number of steps to eliminate American economic influence in his country amid a flurry of rhetorical outbursts against "Yankee imperialism." In June 1960 he expropriated the extensive landholdings of the American sugar firms. The following October he nationalized all of the banks and large industrial enterprises on the island, a considerable proportion of which were American-owned. This egregious challenge to American economic interests in Cuba provoked a graduated response from Washington that was originally confined to measures of economic retaliation, including a 95 percent reduction of the sugar quota (by which Cuba's exports of its major cash crop were allowed to enter the United States at prices above those obtainable on the world market) on July 6 and an American embargo on all exports to the island except medical supplies and most foodstuffs on October 19. As the once-intimate economic relationship between the United States and Cuba approached the breaking point during 1960, the Soviet Union grasped this unprecedented opportunity to contest the hegemonic position of the United States in its own hemisphere. In February 1960 the USSR agreed to purchase one-fifth of Cuba's sugar production, subsequently raising the proportion to a half in December of that year. It also granted $200 million in low-interest loans to the financially hard-pressed Havana regime. By the end of the year, Cuba was receiving substantial arms shipments from the Soviet bloc.

As President Eisenhower prepared to vacate the White House during the winter of 1960–61, it had become unmistakably evident that American economic pressure on the Castro regime was doomed to fail because of the Soviet Union's eagerness to replace the United States as Cuba's primary customer for its sugar and principal supplier of its foreign credits. Moreover, the Cuban leader had explicitly endorsed the general foreign policy goals of his new economic benefactors, most dramatically during a four-and-a-half hour harangue in full battle dress from the rostrum of the United Nations General Assembly on September 26, 1960. While the size of America's diplomatic representation in Havana was systematically reduced at Cuban insistence to such minimal levels as to provoke a rupture in relations in January 1961, thousands of Soviet technicians, military advisers, and diplomatic personnel poured into the country to lend assistance to Castro's revolutionary regime. To nervous observers in Washington, it appeared that the small island that had long been regarded, in strategic and economic terms, as an extension of the Florida keys in the Caribbean, was on the verge of becoming a client state of the Soviet Union.

To obviate that ominous possibility, the outgoing Eisenhower administration had bequeathed to its successor a plan for the forcible overthrow of the Castro government. Under the supervision of the American Central Intelligence Agency, an exile army composed of refugees from Cuba had been armed and trained at clandestine camps in Florida, Guatemala, and Nicaragua in preparation for an invasion of the island. The organizers of the expedition were confident that the mere appearance of these paramilitary freedom fighters would incite an internal uprising by the disgruntled victims of Castro's oppression. Though skeptical about its chances of success, the new American president authorized the projected invasion. On April 17 a brigade of about fifteen hundred Cuban exiles transported in American ships from training camps in Guatemala disembarked on the island and established a beachhead at a place called the Bay of Pigs. The anticipated revolt against Castro failed to materialize, and within three days the entire invasion force had been either killed or captured by Castro's military forces.

As embarrassing as this misadventure proved to be to the new American president at the very beginning of his term, its most important consequences were felt in Cuba itself. Convinced that the abortive landing at the Bay of Pigs was merely the opening salvo in America's campaign to dislodge him, Castro earnestly solicited Moscow for what it had previously refrained from according him: the promise of military protection against the United States. Khrushchev's earlier threats of reprisal for any American effort to unseat Castro had been taken seriously by no one. His circumspect behavior in the aftermath of the Bay of Pigs fiasco seemed to signal an understandable reluctance on the Soviet leader's part to challenge the United States militarily in a region recognized by all to be so vital to its security. But for reasons that will doubtless remain forever obscure, the Kremlin decided sometime in the spring of 1962 to accede to the request of its protégé in Havana for the deployment of ballistic missiles in Cuba as a means of deterring what Castro professed to fear most of all—another American-sponsored invasion of his island by Cuban exile commandos who were still being trained on American territory without even an effort at concealment.

Notwithstanding all of its professions of concern for the security of its new client state in the Caribbean, Moscow's decision to begin the construction of sites for forty-eight medium-range ballistic missiles (MRBMs) and twenty-four intermediate-range ballistic missiles (IRBMs) in Cuba during October 1962 must certainly have been prompted by considerations more directly related to the Soviet national interest. Some have speculated that the missiles were intended to serve as bargaining chips in the global poker game that the Cold War between the two superpowers had become. Perhaps Khrushchev envisioned a Cuba-for-Berlin deal that would finally remove the embarrassing showcase of Western economic prosperity and political liberty from the center of East Germany. Or perhaps the Soviet leadership genuinely expected Kennedy to acquiesce in the fait accompli of nuclear weapons in America's own backyard, as the Russians themselves had learned to live with the American intermediate-range missiles across the border in Turkey. In such a case Khrushchev stood to regain for his country the strategic advantage that had been lost by the impressive buildup of American ICBMs since Sputnik: Missiles based in Cuba with ranges of eleven hundred to twenty-two hundred miles would have constituted ersatz intercontinental missiles, reducing the American warning time to virtually nothing and exposing the entire territory of the continental United States save a corner of the Pacific Northwest to a Soviet first strike.

In any case, the discovery of the Soviet missile sites by American reconnaissance planes overflying Cuba in mid-October 1962 provoked an American rejoinder of such unyielding firmness as to preclude whatever high-level horse-trading or strategic gains the Soviet leader may have had in mind. Smarting from partisan Congressional criticism of his inaction in the face of the Soviet military buildup in Cuba, President Kennedy flung down the gauntlet to Khrushchev in a nationally televised address on October 22. After citing the irrefutable evidence of the missile sites in the process of installation, he announced his intention to impose an air and naval "quarantine"—avoiding the term "blockade" because it signified an act of war according to international law—to prevent the arrival of additional nuclear armaments in Cuba. He proceeded to warn Moscow that any nuclear missile launched from Cuba against any nation in the Western Hemisphere would be considered a Russian attack on the United States and would trigger American nuclear retaliation against the Soviet Union. He demanded the prompt removal of the missile sites already completed or in the process of construction. After obtaining the unanimous support of America's allies in NATO and in the Organization of American States, Kennedy ordered the naval blockade into effect on October 24. Nineteen warships of the American Second Fleet took their stations along the arc of a five hundred mile radius around the eastern tip of Cuba with instructions to intercept and search all vessels suspected of carrying the proscribed missiles to the island. On the same day, twenty-five Russian cargo ships were steaming across the Atlantic for Cuba while construction work on the missile sites continued at a hastily increased pace. Suddenly, after a decade of careless rhetoric about "massive retaliation" in Washington and "winnable nuclear war" in Moscow, the two superpowers appeared poised for an epic confrontation from which neither seemed able to back down.

The first break in the tension-filled impasse came on the evening of the twenty-fourth, when a dozen of the twenty-five Russian ships en route to Cuba (presumably those carrying the contraband) either altered or reversed course. The remaining problem of the missile sites already in place was resolved in the following few days through an exchange of written communications between Kennedy and Khrushchev. Confronted with the genuine possibility of all-out nuclear war, the Soviet leader capitulated to the Kennedy ultimatum on the basis of a single condition: The missile installations would be dismantled and returned to Russia in exchange for an American promise not to invade Cuba. By the end of the year, the Soviet missile sites had disappeared from the Cuban earth, the American naval quarantine had been lifted, and Moscow had signaled to Washington its earnest desire to settle all of the outstanding issues in dispute between the two superpowers across the globe. Both sides managed conciliatory gestures in recognition of the necessity to keep alive the spirit of cooperation that had been forged in the fires of the Cuban crisis. The Soviet Union, which could easily have blockaded Berlin in revenge for the American blockade of Cuba, refrained from even the slightest provocation in that region of maximum American vulnerability. In the following year the United States inconspicuously dismantled its Jupiter missiles based in Turkey. Such a step had been proposed by Khrushchev during the Cuban crisis as a quid pro quo for the removal of Soviet missiles from Cuba. It had been rejected at the time by Washington on the grounds that, though the Jupiters were obsolete and had been slated for removal in the near future, the acceptance of such an exchange under duress would have undermined the credibility of America's commitment to its allies.

The Kremlin gamely attempted to put the best possible light on its humiliating setback in Cuba in order to reassure allies and prospective clients alike of its reliability as a patron: By extracting the no-invasion pledge from Kennedy, Khrushchev had rescued Castro from a terrible fate. The missiles were therefore no longer required as protection against Yankee aggression. But the American Secretary of State, Dean Rusk, supplied the most accurate assessment of the Cuban missile incident in a pithy, unforgettable line: "Eyeball to eyeball, they blinked first."

CHAPTER 10

Detente and Multipolarity (1962–1975)

Inter-American Relations After the Cuban Crisis

If we define a global power as a state capable of exercising decisive influence anywhere in the world through economic, political, and military means, then the United States alone deserved that designation at the time of the Cuban missile crisis of 1962. With a gross national product three times that of its nearest competitor, the Soviet Union, America's economic preponderance in the world was beyond dispute. So too was the ubiquity and potency of its political influence in the non-Communist world. America's political preeminence in Western Europe had been secured once President Truman assumed the leadership of the Atlantic bloc at the end of the 1940s and Eisenhower reaffirmed the ideological unity of what he and Secretary of State Dulles were wont to call the "free world" during the 1950s. In the early 1960s the political influence of the United States was extended to the nations of the Third World by means of the elaborate projects of foreign assistance—bearing such attractive titles as "Peace Corps" and "Alliance for Progress"—that had been inaugurated by the charismatic new occupant of the White House. As the unchallenged protector and benefactor of the non-Communist portions of the earth, the United States could, at least until the mid-1960s, confidently count on commanding a comfortable majority for its policies in the General Assembly of the United Nations to supplement the preeminent position occupied by itself and its three loyal allies among the permanent members of the Security Council.

In sum, Washington's political standing in most of the non-Communist part of the developing world had risen dramatically during the first half of the 1960s. The progressive rhetoric of the Kennedy administration endowed American foreign policy with a positive ideological component that it had lacked during the rigidly anti-Communist Eisenhower–Dulles years. The professed commitment to "nation building," to the provision of United States economic and technical assistance to promote modernization in the

Third World, exerted a powerful attraction on the impoverished masses of the earth and their political spokesmen. The other part of the Kennedy policy toward the developing world was the counterinsurgency feature. This was designed to ensure that the sweeping socioeconomic reforms that were supposed to be catalyzed by the American aid programs would be managed in an evolutionary rather than a revolutionary manner. This aspect of American policy naturally appealed to the ruling elites of the developing countries who feared insurrection and welcomed American assistance in quelling it. As the United States behaved during the first half of the sixties as the champion of peaceful social reform and economic modernization in the developing world, Moscow had emerged from the Cuban missile crisis with the tarnished reputation of a patron who could or would not stand firm behind its client when the chips were down. It appeared, however briefly, that America was winning what President Kennedy was fond of calling the contest "for the hearts and minds of the underdeveloped and uncommitted peoples of the world."

Arms Control and Strategic Parity

It was only in the realm of military power that the Soviet Union was widely thought to be capable of challenging America's global supremacy, and even that threat proved to be illusory. As we have seen, the alarmist talk about a "missile gap" following the firing of the first Soviet intercontinental ballistic missile in August and the launching of the Sputnik earth satellite in October of 1957 was based on a gross overestimation of the Russians' capacity to translate technological potential into strategic achievement. In December of the same year the United States launched its own five-thousand-mile-range Atlas ICBM, and by 1960 the American nuclear arsenal consisted of about fifty strategic missile warheads compared to the Soviets' thirty-five. Eisenhower's embarrassment over the U-2 affair of May 1960 was surpassed by Khrushchev's own humiliation at seeing the hollowness of his inflated strategic claims exposed: A nation that had launched the world's first earth satellite and tested the first ICBM could not prevent American spy planes from overflying its territory at 75,000 feet for four years until engine trouble forced one to descend. At the time of the showdown over Cuba, the Soviet Union was outclassed by the United States in every category of nuclear armament and delivery system; moreover, Russia boasted neither an oceanic navy capable of projecting Soviet power beyond its coasts nor overseas bases to accommodate such a "blue water" fleet, while the United States boasted a naval presence and base facilities all over the world. The Russian colossus remained the premier land power in Eurasia, capable of reaching the Rhine or the Mediterranean or the Persian Gulf in a few weeks by dint of its overwhelming conventional superiority vis-à-vis weak and vulnerable neighbors. But it was dissuaded from even seriously considering such a conventional military breakthrough by the American nuclear deterrent composed of ICBMs and long-range bombers based on American soil and IRBMs, MRBMs, and medium-range bombers arrayed along the Russian frontier in countries allied to the United States.

Khrushchev's attempt to leapfrog the American defense perimeter along the periphery of Eurasia by implanting a Soviet nuclear armament system in Cuba may have in part represented a desperate gamble to rectify this strategic imbalance in a single decisive blow. The humiliating conditions of the Soviet retreat in Cuba produced precisely the opposite effect from the one presumably intended. Instead of establishing a more stable balance of nuclear power between the two superpowers, the Cuban crisis graphically revealed to the world the extent of Soviet military inferiority. Instead of rallying the Communist bloc behind a newly invigorated Soviet Union, it prompted the Chinese leadership to accelerate its defection from the Soviet orbit that had begun two years earlier. Instead of enhancing Khrushchev's standing in the eyes of the Soviet military establishment and its allies in the civilian leadership, it aggravated the internal dissatisfaction that eventually led to his downfall.

The lessons learned by the Kremlin from the Cuban fiasco resulted in the adoption of two strategies—one diplomatic and the other military—that were to remain the basis of Soviet policy after Khrushchev's departure. The first was the resumption of the quest for "peaceful coexistence" with the Western bloc that had been initiated by Stalin's successors in the mid-fifties but had been interrupted by the bellicose Soviet probes in Berlin and Cuba during 1958–62. Its purpose was to minimize the possibility of a nuclear confrontation such as had almost occurred in 1962—a contest that the Soviet Union, in its current state of strategic inferiority, was bound to lose. The second was the acceleration of a long-range program, also begun in the mid-fifties but postponed for a variety of domestic reasons, to transform Russia from a Eurasian land power into a global sea and air power capable of defending its interests anywhere in the world. *Its* purpose was to achieve an approximate parity in nuclear and naval forces that would neutralize the American strategic deterrent and naval superiority that had been exercised so effectively at Russia's expense in the autumn of 1962.

The most dramatic consequences of the policy of peaceful coexistence were to become evident in the realm of strategic arms control. Since the end of the Second World War, fruitless discussions on nuclear disarmament had been conducted in the United Nations and proposals to that effect had periodically issued from Washington and Moscow. At the first meeting of the United Nations Atomic Energy Commission in June 1946, the United States, at the time enjoying a nuclear monopoly, offered to turn over its stockpile of atomic weapons to an international agency under United Nations auspices on the condition that all other countries pledge not to produce them and agree to an adequate system of inspection. The

Soviet Union, hard at work on the development of a nuclear capability of its own, rejected the so-called Baruch plan on the grounds that the United Nations was dominated by the United States and its West European partners and therefore could not be trusted to exercise authority over atomic weaponry in an evenhanded manner. Once the Soviet Union became a nuclear power in September 1949, it began to display greater interest in the cause of atomic arms control, particularly after the death of Stalin and the beginning of the pursuit of peaceful coexistence. At the 1954 session of the UN General Assembly, the Soviet delegate called for a moratorium on the manufacture of nuclear weapons and suggested the creation of a UN commission to consider means of controlling those already in existence. On May 10, 1955, the Kremlin formally proposed a gradual reduction of conventional forces to fixed levels and the destruction of nuclear stockpiles once those levels had been reached. In his speech to the UN General Assembly in 1959, as we have seen, Khrushchev advocated general and total disarmament within four years. But all of the disarmament proposals that emanated from the Soviet Union in the course of the fifties foundered on the question of verification: Washington firmly insisted on the principle of onsite inspection to certify compliance with such disarmament agreements as might be concluded, while Moscow adamantly rejected the presence of foreign observers as an intolerable infringement of its national sovereignty. Even Eisenhower's "Open Skies" proposal at the Geneva summit conference in 1955, which provided for mutual aerial surveillance of the two superpowers' military installations, was denounced by the Soviet delegation as a ploy to legalize espionage against the USSR.

But if superpower disarmament in an unstable world proved to be an impossible goal, the nuclear alarm sounded by the Cuban missile crisis prompted the two sides to concentrate on a more modest and attainable objective: the imposition of limitations on the testing, deployment, and proliferation of nuclear weapons in the future. In August 1963 the Soviet Union joined the United States and Great Britain in signing a treaty banning nuclear tests in the atmosphere and in the sea. In January 1967 the same three nations together with France, which had become the fourth nuclear power in 1960, agreed to keep outer space free of nuclear weapon. Later in the same year, Latin America was declared a nuclear-free zone by its member states with the approval of both Washington and Moscow.*

The establishment of direct teletype communications between the White House and the Kremlin after the Cuban missile crisis—the "hot line" agreement of June 20, 1963—was an expression of Soviet-American determination to reduce the risk of accidental nuclear war. But an even greater concern shared by the two superpowers was the potential threat to the delicate strategic balance posed by the acquisition of nuclear weapons by other

* The only precedent for regional nuclear demilitarization was a treaty in 1959 that declared Antarctica a nuclear-free zone.

countries. The Soviet Union had adamantly refused to share its nuclear technology with its European satellites and its Asian allies or even to supply them with nuclear weapons under Russian control. The United States had done its best to dissuade its Atlantic partners from developing nuclear capabilities of their own by refusing to share nuclear information while assuring them adequate protection under the American nuclear "umbrella." But the advance of scientific knowledge and the consciousness of national sovereignty were not limited to the United States and the Soviet Union. What had been a nuclear duopoly at the beginning of the 1950s had become a nuclear club of ominously expanding membership by the middle of the 1960s. Great Britain had tested her first atomic device in 1952 and her first hydrogen (or thermonuclear) bomb in 1957. France and China, two nations that began to pursue foreign and defense policies independent of the wishes of their erstwhile superpower allies in the early 1960s, joined the nuclear club in 1960 and 1964, respectively.

With the intention of curbing the further expansion of the nuclear fraternity, the United States, the Soviet Union, and Great Britain signed in July 1968 the Nuclear Non-Proliferation Treaty, which came into force on March 5, 1970, when ninety-seven countries had signed it and forty-seven (including the original signatories) had ratified it. According to its provisions, the nuclear powers (minus China and France, both of which refused to sign) pledged never to furnish nuclear weapons or the technology to fabricate them to nonnuclear powers, while the nonnuclear countries promised never to produce or acquire them. An international inspection team was established in Vienna under the auspices of the United Nations International Atomic Energy Administration to verify compliance with the treaty.

The spate of international agreements in the 1960s had the effect of forbidding the testing, development, or deployment of nuclear weapons by nonnuclear powers and by nuclear powers in certain specified regions. But these treaties did nothing to limit the stockpiling of strategic weapons and the expansion and perfection of delivery systems by the two countries that alone possessed the capacity to unleash nuclear devastation on the world. It was in the realm of superpower arms control that the decision makers in Washington and Moscow confronted their greatest challenge. The USSR had had no incentive to endorse strategic arms control during the twenty-year period after the Second World War when its nuclear capability remained decisively inferior to that of its principal adversary. To freeze the nuclear forces of the two competitors in the Cold War at a level of such strategic imbalance would have permanently relegated the Soviet Union to the position of military vulnerability that had enabled Dulles to threaten massive retaliation against conventional Soviet moves during the 1950s.

In the very period (the aftermath of the Cuban missile crisis) when the Soviet Union cooperated with other nations to impose limits on the nuclear arms race, it earnestly pursued the goal of strategic parity with the United States. When the Brezhnev–Kosygin faction toppled Khrushchev on October 15, 1964, it inherited an ambitious project for military expansion begun in 1960 that was designed to erase the Soviet Union's strategic inferiority by the end of the decade. This program included a buildup of the Strategic Rocket Forces (which were created as an independent arm of the military forces), the development of medium- and intermediate-range ballistic missiles for deployment in the European theater, and the upgrading of antiaircraft and civil defense capabilities. In all of the categories of military strength, the new leadership in the Kremlin achieved its goals. During the second half of the 1960s, while America's costly conventional military operation in Indochina diverted funds that might otherwise have been spent to increase the size of its nuclear arsenal, the Soviet Union tripled the number of its land-based ICBMs and greatly expanded the number of its submarine-launched ballistic missiles (SLBMs). Consequently, the missile gap that had forced Khrushchev to back down during the Cuban crisis had been bridged by the end of the decade: Whereas the United States had possessed 294 ICBMs compared to 75 for the Soviet Union in 1962, by 1969 the Soviet arsenal of long-range missiles numbered 1,050 as against 1,054 for the United States. During the same period the Soviets had surpassed the American submarine force of 656 SLBMs and were challenging U.S. superiority in long-range bombers. In short, the two superpowers had achieved what President Richard M. Nixon later termed "essential equivalence" in their strategic forces. In the chilling language of defense analysts, they had acquired the capacity for "mutual assured destruction" (MAD). This meant the ability to destroy a quarter of the enemy's population and over half of its industry in a surprise attack.

During the same period, Soviet naval power was expanded with the intention of contesting America's hitherto undisputed supremacy on the high seas. Since, unlike the United States, Russia's seaborne trade was insignificant and she could reach all of her major allies by land, the Soviet leadership had never before felt impelled to contruct a fleet capable of operating on the oceans and remained content with a naval force geared to coastal defense. But in the course of the 1960s the Soviet navy acquired the capability to intervene far from its shores in defense of Soviet interests. This feat was accomplished under the leadership of Admiral Sergei Gorshkov, who had been appointed head of the navy by Khrushchev in 1957. In 1964 a Soviet Mediterranean squadron made its first appearance and in 1968 a regular Soviet naval presence was established in the Indian Ocean just as British naval power was being withdrawn from that region. A large Soviet nuclear submarine fleet was roaming the ocean depths by the late 1960s. By the early 1970s, the Soviet Union was able to project its naval power and its nuclear deterrent to all of the strategically important regions of the world. All that stood in the way of its becoming a global naval power was the lack of overseas bases and refueling stations to accommodate its oceanic fleet, a problem that would, as we shall see, be overcome in the course of the following decade.

This narrowing of the strategic gap between the two superpowers in the late 1960s supplied the stimulus for the first successful arms control negotiation since the advent of the Cold War. There had been some serious talk of convening Soviet-American arms limitation talks in the mid-1960s. But the American military escalation in Vietnam, the Arab-Israeli conflict in the Middle East, and the Soviet intervention in Czechoslovakia embittered relations between Washington and Moscow during the years when Lyndon Johnson occupied the White House and Leonid Brezhnev and Alexei Kosygin jockeyed for primacy in the Kremlin after Khrushchev's removal in 1964. It required the inauguration of a new American president, Nixon, and the emergence of an undisputed master of the Politburo, Brezhnev, in the year 1969 before the hopes of bilateral talks on strategic arms control could be translated into reality. For a complex set of political and economic reasons to be summarized below, Nixon and Brezhnev had simultaneously developed an appreciation of the numerous advantages that were likely to accrue to both sides from a relaxation of Soviet-American tensions in the world. The military context of the evolution toward improved relations between Washington and Moscow was the rough parity in strategic weaponry cited above: In the face of the certainty of mutual destruction, both superpowers shared a common interest in curbing an arms race that, it was now unmistakably plain, neither side could win. The economic advantages to be gained from a deceleration in military spending need scarcely be cited: The swollen defense budgets of both superpowers had diverted financial resources that might otherwise have been available for the funding of domestic social programs and productive enterprises that would increase the standard of living of the Russian and American people. Accordingly, on the day of Nixon's inauguration (January 20, 1969) the Kremlin publicly proposed Soviet-American negotiations for the reciprocal limitation and reduction of nuclear delivery vehicles and defensive systems. A week later the new American chief executive endorsed the Soviet proposal in a speech that also contained a significant modification of the traditional American position concerning the strategic balance that was bound to smooth the path toward accommodation with the USSR: For the first time, an American president accepted the principle of strategic parity in place of the customary insistence on American strategic superiority. On November 17, 1969, the first formal talks began in Helsinki between Soviet and American officials. Six subsequent sessions were held alternately in Vienna and Helsinki under the formal title, Strategic Arms Limitation Talks (SALT).

After two years of tortuous negotiations over the complexities of strategic weaponry, an interim arms control agreement was signed on May 26, 1972, during President Nixon's unprecedented official visit to Moscow. Instead of attempting to impose limits on the number of nuclear bombs that had been stockpiled by the two superpowers in the course of the previous two decades, the SALT negotiators concentrated on two other components of the strategic balance that proved more susceptible to agreement. The first was the delivery vehicles that would carry the warheads to their targets. A ceiling was placed on the number of ICBMs that each side could deploy for a period of five years (October 3, 1972, to October 3, 1977). The effect of this limitation was to freeze the existing number of American ICBMs at 1,054 while permitting the Soviet Union to expand its ICBM arsenal from 1,530 to 1,618. A moratorium of equivalent duration was declared on the construction of submarine-launched missiles (SLBMs), leaving the Soviet Union with 950 missiles in sixty-two submarines compared to 710 American missiles in forty-four submarines. These two agreements represented the first successful effort by the two superpowers to establish quantitative limits on their strategic delivery systems.

The second issue to be addressed at the SALT I talks was the so-called Antiballistic Missile System (ABM) that was designed to intercept and destroy incoming missiles before they reached their targets. The United States had been experimenting with a variety of antimissile defense systems since 1956, a year before the Soviets launched their first ICBM. The first successful test of an interceptor missile was conducted in New Mexico in 1959. Between 1962 and 1967 Robert S. McNamara, the secretary of defense under presidents Kennedy and Johnson, presided over the development of an ABM system that consisted of two principal components: a long-range, high-altitude missile (the Spartan) designed to intercept an incoming ICBM above the atmosphere, and a short-range missile (the Sprint) for use within the atmosphere against whatever might elude the Spartan. Shortly before he left office in 1967 McNamara publicly described the purpose of this antimissile system, renamed "Sentinel" by President Johnson, as that of defending cities exclusively against the relatively minor nuclear arsenal that *China* could be expected to deploy in the near future. This was a tacit admission that no antimissile system could conceivably provide an airtight defense of densely populated areas against the formidable nuclear arsenal of the Soviet Union: A single missile eluding interception could destroy Washington, New York, or Los Angeles. In recognition of this fact, President Nixon in 1969 abandoned the concept of defending cities (except for Washington, the nation's command center) in favor of protecting America's land-based retaliatory missiles, which, because they were housed in concrete underground silos, could be expected to survive damage that would prove lethal to an entire population of an unprotected urban area. The Nixon ABM system, renamed "Safeguard" and partially operational by 1972, prompted great uneasiness in Moscow, while the simultaneous development of a Soviet ABM system (Galosh) aroused similar apprehension in Washington. The reason that what appeared to be a purely defensive weapons system evoked such anxiety on both sides is that it threatened to upset the delicate balance of mutual deterrence that had been established by the end of the 1960s. The future deployment of an impenetrable ABM system by either side, capable of defending all of that side's large cities from nuclear attack, could readily be interpreted by the other side as a prelude to a surprise first strike that could be launched without fear of retaliation. In recognition of this, the SALT I agreement limited each side to the deployment of 100 ABM launchers and interceptor missiles in two sites, one to be the national capital and the other to be an ICBM missile base (in the American case, the Minuteman silos located near Grand Forks, North Dakota). The logic underlying this feature of the SALT I agreement was that it preserved the stability of the strategic balance by reducing the incentive for either side to gamble on a first strike: If one side could protect its command center* and one of its land-based ICBM sites, it would thereby retain the capacity to retaliate in spite of the total destruction of its remaining nuclear arsenal by a surprise attack.

The preceding comparative figures reveal that the Soviet Union retained superiority in the total number of missiles covered by the SALT I agreement (ICBMs and SLBMs). Nevertheless, President Nixon was able to assure his domestic constituency that the United States enjoyed overall parity with its principal adversary because of American superiority in strategic weapons systems not covered by the treaty limitations. First of all, the United States retained a considerable advantage in the number of long-range bombers. Second, the Soviet Union had no counterpart in the Western Hemisphere to the American intermediate-range missiles stationed in Europe that could reach cities in western Russia. Third, the British and French nuclear forces, however inconsequential in comparison to those of the two superpowers, provided an additional incremental advantage to the United States unavailable to the Soviet Union, which refused to permit its East European satellites to develop independent nuclear forces and could scarcely count the Chinese nuclear armament on the plus side of its strategic ledger. But the decisive equalizer for the United States was its technological superiority in the development of warheads. Many of the American land-based (Minuteman) and submarine-based (Poseidon) missiles had been fitted with multiple warheads, each of which could be targeted for a different site. These so-called Multiple Independently Targetable Reentry Vehicles (MIRVs) greatly increased the destructive power and reduced the vulnerability to interception of each American missile that was included in the SALT I numerical limitations. Moreover, while it was relatively easy to detect through satellite reconnaissance the number

---

* A protocol signed in 1974 restricted each side to a single ABM deployment, thereby abandoning the original idea of protecting the two national capitals. Since then, even the plan to protect the American Minuteman silos has been scrapped, though President Reagan revived the idea in 1983 with his "Strategic Defense Initiative" (see page 409).

of land-based and submarine-based missiles a nation possessed, it was virtually impossible to verify the number of independently targetable warheads each missile contained.

In sum, the two superpowers remained roughly equal in their strategic capability as a consequence of the SALT I treaty concluded in May 1972. Each side's ability to destroy the other many times over remained unimpaired. The exclusion of long-range bombers, MIRVs, intermediate- and medium-range missiles, and other important components of the strategic balance left the two superpowers free to expand their nuclear capability by those and other means. Yet it must be reemphasized that the treaty represented the first successful effort to impose some restraints on the nuclear arms race since that race had begun at the end of the 1940s. Moreover, it was specifically recognized as an interim agreement of five-years' duration, to be succeeded by a more comprehensive treaty. The forced resignation of President Nixon in August 1974 did not impede the ongoing Soviet-American negotiations for an arms control treaty to replace the SALT I agreement that was due to expire in 1977. Continuity of policy had been assured through the retention of Henry Kissinger as secretary of state by Nixon's successor, Gerald Ford. Ford and Brezhnev were able to conclude an interim agreement at the Vladivostok summit conference on November 24, 1974, which established guidelines for a SALT II treaty that would limit categories of strategic delivery vehicles not covered by SALT I (such as MIRVs and long-range bombers).* For the first time since the advent of the Cold War, officials in Washington and Moscow were confidently forecasting an end to the unrestrained competition for strategic superiority between the two superpowers.

The development of Soviet-American cooperation to impose restraints on the nuclear arms race during the first half of the 1970s would have been inconceivable without prior success in the reduction of political tensions between the two superpowers in those parts of the world where their interests directly collided. The most visible flashpoint of superpower confrontation at the time was southeast Asia, where half a million American troops combated a Vietnamese army supplied and supported by the Soviet Union. The Nixon administration's decision to terminate America's direct involvement in the war in Indochina, however protracted that disengagement turned out to be, removed a major irritant in Soviet-American relations. But in the context of the global rivalry between Washington and Moscow, the war in Southeastern Asia was overshadowed by the salient geopolitical feature of the 1960s, which was the gradual disintegration of the two rigid power blocs that had coalesced in the early years of the Cold War. Throughout the previous decade a majority of the countries of the

---

* In addition to placing an upper limit of 2,400 on each side's ICBMs, SLBMs, and heavy bombers, the Vladivostok agreement (which was never ratified) established a ceiling of 1,320 MIRVed missiles.

world were aligned in one or the other of the two armed camps. The two superpowers had been able to count on the almost unswerving allegiance of those nations that remained under their tutelage and protection. The dissolution of this bipolar international system during the 1960s was precipitated by three important developments in the world. The first, already alluded to in Chapter 9, was the appearance of dozens of newly independent nations in the Third World that swelled the ranks of the nonaligned bloc. The second was the increasingly assertive and independent posture of America's allies in Western Europe, who began to chafe at their position as pawns in the Cold War and eagerly sought a *modus vivendi* with the Communist states to the east in order to reduce the risks of nuclear annihilation. The third was the defection of China from the Communist camp and its emergence as an independent force in world affairs. These three converging developments helped to produce a more fluid international environment than had existed when two tightly organized blocs dominated by two superpowers confronted each other across the great ideological divide in Europe and Asia. In the end, as we shall see, the evolution of a multipolar international system enabled the United States and the Soviet Union to break the impasse of the Cold War and approach the hitherto impossible goals of arms control, disengagement, and detente.

France's Assault on the Bipolar World

The first direct challenge to America's preeminent position in Western Europe was to come from France after the return to power in June 1958 of Charles de Gaulle, Roosevelt's old wartime nemesis who had disappeared from the political scene in 1946. The occasion of his reappearance was France's costly, foredoomed struggle to retain control of its North African colony of Algeria in the face of an insurrection by its majority Arab population. Armed with emergency powers to settle this bitter dispute, which had brought his own country to the brink of military insurgency and civil war, de Gaulle proceeded to divest France not only of the albatross of Algeria but also of its remaining colonial possessions in Africa. By 1962 France's painful process of postwar decolonization was virtually complete, while a fundamental constitutional reorganization had placed extensive authority in the hands of the chief executive. These two developments freed France from the debilitating political and colonial burdens of the recent past and set the stage for a series of bold diplomatic initiatives aimed at securing an objective that had been dear to de Gaulle's heart since the end of the Second World War: the transformation of Europe into a political, economic, and strategic bloc independent of both the United States and the Soviet Union and capable of acting as a third force in world affairs. Though the outcome of this bid for European independence of superpower domination fell far short of the excessively ambitious expectations of its architect, the foreign policy of Gaullist France from

1962 to 1969 left a lasting imprint an East–West relations by loosening the ties that had bound the signatories of the North Atlantic Treaty in a position of subservience to American authority and unqualified support for American global objectives.

De Gaulle's foreign policy stemmed from a fundamental dissatisfaction with the international order envisioned by the leaders of the United States and the Soviet Union at the wartime conferences in Yalta and Potsdam and formalized during the heyday of the Cold War in the 1950s. The postwar division first of Europe and then of the entire world into a bipolar system under the shared hegemony of the two non-European superpowers was regarded by de Gaulle as an intolerable condition for France in particular and Europe in general for a number of reasons.

First of all, it deprived the once proud and independent states of the continent of the freedom of action that de Gaulle regarded as the prerequisite of great power status. No nation condemned to rely on the military protection of another for its security, he declared, could hope to aspire to a role beyond that of compliant protégé. The understandable resentment that had been engendered by this condition of subservience was especially widespread in France, with its vivid memories of a glorious heritage as a continental and imperial power of the first rank. But de Gaulle's blatant appeal to national pride struck a sensitive nerve throughout Western Europe, whose postwar economic and political recovery had erased the sense of despair and vulnerability that had prevailed in the early years of the Cold War and led to its dependence on American military protection and economic assistance. The European Economic Community that had been formed in 1957 was rapidly developing into the most formidable economic bloc in the world, with a combined gross national product approaching and eventually surpassing that of the United States. Many Europeans who basked in the economic prosperity and political stability of the 1960s began to wonder why they should continue to feel obligated to adapt their foreign and defense policies to the global strategy of their transatlantic patron, particularly at a time when the Russian threat to Western Europe appeared to have receded.

In addition to this appeal to national pride, de Gaulle's denunciation of Western Europe's military dependence on the United States exploited the sentiment of fear stimulated by the nuclear arms race. Since the two superpowers were engaged in a global contest for hegemony, Soviet-American tensions in regions of secondary concern to Europe could readily escalate into a nuclear confrontation that would inevitably engulf the western half of that continent by virtue of its alliance with the United States and the presence of American military bases and missile installations on its territory. Dulles's saber-rattling during the Quemoy crisis shortly after de Gaulle's return to power in 1958 raised the prospect of a nuclear showdown over a worthless island thousands of miles from France (see p. 381). The war scare over Cuba in 1962 reinforced such apprehensions, as did the subsequent American military escalation in Vietnam during the mid-1960s.

The obverse of this fear of being dragged by the United States into a nuclear Armageddon over issues unrelated to Europe's vital interests was the fear of being abandoned by the United States in the case of Soviet aggression on the continent. Ever since the development of Soviet intercontinental ballistic missiles in 1957, the credibility of the American pledge to deter a Soviet attack in Europe by threatening nuclear retaliation against Russia itself encountered mounting skepticism across the Atlantic. During the last years of the Eisenhower administration, European doubts about the future of the American commitment were fed by the writings of influential American defense theorists who severely criticized the "all or nothing" strategy of massive retaliation in favor of a more discriminating approach that would permit a graduated response to a Soviet attack in Europe. Under the Kennedy administration, the outmoded doctrine of massive retaliation was formally supplanted by a new approach of "flexible response," which envisaged reliance on a variety of military measures—conventional, tactical nuclear, or strategic nuclear—to counter Soviet aggression in Western Europe. The new strategy was a tacit acknowledgement that the threat of nuclear retaliation was no longer a credible deterrent when American cities were within range of Soviet missiles. Its professed intention was to induce uncertainty, apprehension, and therefore caution in Moscow, since the precise nature of the American response could not be known in advance. But by reserving maximum flexibility for the American president to determine the time, place, and manner of a military response to Soviet actions, it inevitably heightened insecurity among America's European allies, who had become accustomed to depending on the certainty of an unconditional American guarantee. Many observers in Europe interpreted the new doctrine as a thinly disguised effort to renege on the pledge of military assistance in case of war in Europe.

In anticipation of the day when the risk of nuclear retaliation from Russia would weaken America's resolve to defend Western Europe, French officials since the mid-fifties had considered alternative means of providing for their country's defense. One possibility, which had been broached by Prime Minister Pierre Mendès-France in 1954 and subsequently revived by de Gaulle in 1958, was the formation of a three-power directorate consisting of the United States, Great Britain, and France that would share control of NATO's nuclear force and jointly plan its political and military strategy. Such an arrangement was designed to calm French fears of losing the American nuclear guarantee, but both initiatives were rebuffed by the Eisenhower administration. In the meantime the alternative solution of an independent French nuclear force was inherent in the ambitious nuclear energy program that had been launched in the mid-fifties. Shortly before the demise of the Fourth Republic in the spring of 1958, the French government authorized preparations for the testing of a nuclear device. De

Gaulle accelerated this weapons-related research program upon his accession in June, convinced as he was that no nation could hope to play an influential role in the modern world without a nuclear capability of its own. On February 13, 1960, France became the fourth member of the nuclear club with the announcement that it had tested its first atomic bomb in the Algerian Sahara.

Ever since the passage of the McMahon Act in 1946, the United States government had been legally precluded from assisting other countries, even its most trusted allies, in developing an independent nuclear capability. In 1957 this prohibition was modified in order to permit the sharing of nuclear technology with Great Britain, which had exploded her first atomic bomb in 1952 and her first hydrogen bomb in 1957. But American support for the modest British nuclear force was tendered on the unstated condition that it remain under indirect American control and conform to American strategic doctrine. France's acquisition of a nuclear capability, on the other hand, posed a serious challenge to the incoming Kennedy administration because of de Gaulle's undisguised intention to develop a fully independent nuclear strike force, or *force de frappe*. The prospect of a French nuclear force operating under national rather than NATO (hence American) auspices directly contradicted the new strategic doctrine embraced by Kennedy and his defense secretary, Robert McNamara, which depended on a centrally controlled mechanism of retaliation against Soviet aggression.

Since the one component lacking in the British and French nuclear forces was a credible delivery system, Kennedy sought to exploit this weakness in order to ensure American control over them. At the Nassau conference in December 1962 between President Kennedy and Prime Minister Harold Macmillan, the United States offered to supply Great Britain with Polaris missiles for deployment on British submarines as a replacement for its obsolete and vulnerable long-range bomber force. The offer was contingent on Macmillan's pledge that the modernized British force would be assigned to a projected Multilateral Nuclear Force (MLF) within NATO. Upon Macmillan's acceptance, Kennedy tendered a similar offer to de Gaulle on the same condition, but was rebuffed with the reply that French military independence was incompatible with supranational control of its emerging nuclear armament. The American concept of a Multilateral Nuclear Force for NATO was spelled out in March 1963 in the form of a proposal for a multinational fleet of surface ships armed with Polaris missiles under the joint supervision of the member states of NATO. To Washington this represented a concession to European misgivings about the American monopoly of the alliance's nuclear decision-making authority. In Paris it was perceived as an attempt to dissuade France from proceeding with its plans to deploy an independent nuclear force by raising the frightening possibility of West German participation in an all-European nuclear force. The MLF proposal finally died in December 1964 on account of the reluctance of the other NATO powers to antagonize France for fear of provoking a full-fledged crisis in the alliance.

But by the time of the MLF's demise, France had already begun to deploy a rudimentary delivery system, which eventually consisted of long-range bombers as well as land-based and submarine-based missiles.* The strategic rationale for France's *force de frappe* was the theory of "proportional deterrence" developed by General Pierre Gallois and implicitly endorsed by President de Gaulle in July 1964. According to this doctrine, the two superpowers each required a massive deterrent capability because a deficiency in either one might tempt the other to risk the destruction of a large proportion of its population for the grand prize of total victory over its only global adversary and therefore absolute security in the future; but the modest nuclear force that France had begun to deploy was sufficient as a credible deterrent because the damage it could inflict on a few Russian cities represented a patently unacceptable sacrifice for the minimal rewards that Moscow could expect to obtain by the conquest of a second-rank power such as France. A supplementary justification for France's *force de frappe* was furnished by General André Beaufre's doctrine of "multilateral deterrence," which held that the proliferation of small independent nuclear forces increased Soviet uncertainty and therefore enhanced the deterrent value of the American strategic arsenal. Also implicit in this latter theory was the conception of the French nuclear force as a trigger of the American deterrent: If the United States were ever tempted to counter a conventional Soviet thrust in Europe by merely conventional means rather than the promised nuclear retaliation against Russian territory, as the flexible response doctrine appeared to permit, the unleashing of the French nuclear force against targeted Soviet cities would ensure that a conventional war on the continent would rapidly escalate into a nuclear exchange between the two superpowers.

The incompatibility of these Gaullist strategic doctrines and the American conception of a tightly knit Atlantic alliance under the centralized direction of Washington needs no reemphasis here. Underlying the esoteric Franco-American debate over technical matters of military strategy was a more fundamental divergence of views concerning the emerging supranational European entity. The formation of the European Economic Community in 1957 and the subsequent progress toward European economic integration inevitably posed the question of America's future relationship to this powerful West European economic bloc, with its potential for political and even military integration. The Kennedy administration had devised a "grand design" for the improvement of relations between the United States and Western Europe. It hailed the emerging economic

---

* By the end of 1982 the French *force de frappe* was composed of eighteen land-based ballistic missiles, thirty-six Mirage IV bombers, and five nuclear submarines armed with missiles (with a sixth brought into operation at the end of the 1980s).

community across the Atlantic as a welcome sign of vitality in valued allies, despite the potential menace to American commercial interests implied by the formation of an integrated, protectionist trading bloc on the continent. But in the realm of defense policy, as we have seen, the United States declined to relinquish its ultimate authority over the nuclear armament of the Western alliance. It was therefore on the sensitive issue of European military security that de Gaulle sought to mobilize his continental partners in support of his own competing "grand design," which envisioned the disruption rather than the strengthening of the transatlantic partnership.

It seemed ironic that the soldier-statesman of France whose career had been dominated by fear and distrust of Germany would turn first to his country's traditional adversary for assistance in his ambitious plan to emancipate Europe from the American embrace after Washington's rejection of his tripartite scheme for the management of the Western alliance. As head of the provisional government of France in the immediate postwar years, de Gaulle had pressed for punitive measures against defeated Germany, including political dismemberment and harsh economic exactions, to ensure that it would forever remain subservient to France in Europe. After the establishment of the West German state, de Gaulle out of power strongly opposed its reintegration into the Western system on the basis of equality for the fear that it would one day overshadow France. But by the early 1960s, two aspects of the Franco-German relationship proved conducive to a political reconciliation of these two historic adversaries. The first was the strengthening of the economic ties between them during the 1950s to the point where they had become each other's most important trading partner by the end of the decade. The fond hopes of integrationists like Jean Monnet in France and Walter Hallstein in West Germany that mutually beneficial economic relationships would promote political reconciliation were confirmed as the ancient hostility between these two countries dissolved amid economic partnership and shared prosperity. The second factor favorable to a Franco-German rapprochement was France's newly acquired status as Western Europe's only nuclear power. Since West Germany was prohibited from acquiring a nuclear capability of its own by agreement with its allies, France was assured of a decisive advantage in military power to compensate for its eastern neighbor's superior economic strength. From this position of strategic preeminence de Gaulle felt secure enough to conclude with Chancellor Konrad Adenauer a Franco-German treaty of reconciliation, which was signed by these two elder statesmen in Paris on January 22, 1963. It specified bilateral cooperation on security matters (including regular meetings of defense ministers, exchanges of military personnel, and cooperation in arms production) and provided for prior consultation between Paris and Bonn on all important subjects relating to European defense. De Gaulle's motivation for establishing a privileged bilateral relationship with West Germany within NATO was the hope of weaning Bonn away from the American-controlled alliance as the first step toward the formation of a truly independent West European security system based on France's national nuclear deterrent. Adenauer's flirtation with de Gaulle's projected Paris–Bonn axis seems to have stemmed from his fears that the Kennedy administration's flexible response doctrine and its insufficiently belligerent posture during the Berlin crisis of 1961–62 heralded a weakening of America's resolve to defend West Germany's security and political interests in Central Europe.

To de Gaulle's disappointment, the Franco-German entente did not yield the benefits that he had anticipated; it lapsed into insignificance after Adenauer's replacement in October 1963 by the more resolutely Atlanticist Ludwig Erhard, who reaffirmed Bonn's close ties to Washington while holding Paris at arm's length. De Gaulle's project of a Paris–Bonn axis ultimately failed because he was unable to persuade the Germans that the independent French nuclear force, or any future European nuclear system that might evolve from it, would represent a more reliable source of protection than the American strategic deterrent. As French criticism of American preeminence in NATO mounted in intensity during 1964–65, West German officials began to fear that it might provoke a resurgence of isolationism in the United States that would result in an American withdrawal from Europe. Such a prospect struck fear in the hearts of a people bordering on the Soviet East European empire; the Germans recognized that the only reliable guarantee of their security was the one tangibly offered by the superpower across the Atlantic rather than the one vaguely proposed by the increasingly assertive but nonetheless second-rank power across the Rhine.

Frustrated in his attempt to cement a Franco-German partnership as a prelude to the reorganization of a French-led Europe detached from the United States, de Gaulle proceeded to provoke a serious crisis within the Atlantic alliance in pursuit of the same end. The central issue that de Gaulle seized upon in this campaign was the intolerable infringement on France's national independence represented by the integration of its armed forces in a supranational military organization whose supreme commander had always to be an American general and whose nuclear armament was under the sole control of the American president. The French leader's dissatisfaction with the integrated command structure of NATO had been expressed in earlier gestures of noncooperation, such as the refusal to permit the deployment of American-controlled tactical nuclear weapons on French territory in 1959, the removal of the French Mediterranean fleet from NATO jurisdiction in the same year, and the detachment of the French Atlantic Fleet from the alliance command in 1963. This incremental disengagement from NATO activities had prompted speculation that de Gaulle was laying the groundwork for a major proposal for a fundamental restructuring of the alliance that would transfer more decision-making authority to its European members. Thus the fourteen other NATO states were unprepared for the shock to allied unity administered by the French president in March 1966, when he announced the withdrawal of all French land and air forces from the NATO military command, demanded the removal of the alliance's military headquarters from the Paris region, and required the departure of the thirty American and two Canadian military bases located on French territory.

As the Western governments reeled from these French blows to the cause of unified Western defense, de Gaulle provocatively embarked on a state visit to the Soviet Union in June 1966. In Moscow the renegade in the Western camp was showered with honors, including an invitation to become the first Western leader to visit the top secret space-launching site in Kazakhstan. Soviet Premier Kosygin returned the visit in December and received an equally cordial welcome in Paris. The Kremlin had actively encouraged France's estrangement from the United States in the expectation of deriving valuable benefits from the resulting turmoil in the Atlantic alliance. For his part, de Gaulle accompanied his broadsides against the United States, which included harsh criticism of the American interventions in Vietnam and the Dominican Republic, with an ostentatious bid for an improvement in France's bilateral relations with the Soviet Union.

By means of these two interrelated policies—disengagement from NATO and detente with Moscow—the French president evidently dreamed of establishing his nation as the self-appointed spokesman for Western Europe in its relations with the Communist bloc. A French-dominated Western Europe detached from the United States would be in an advantageous position to negotiate directly with the Russians to resolve the outstanding political disputes on the continent that had perpetuated the Cold War, particularly those concerning the status of divided Germany and its eastern frontiers. Since a French-led Europe unencumbered by the American nuclear guarantee would pose no menace to Russia's security interests, the Kremlin could be more easily induced to relax its iron grip on the East European buffer states and reach an acceptable accommodation with West Germany. Conversely, Paris's privileged bilateral relationship with Moscow would endow it with sufficient leverage over Bonn to pressure the nervous, recalcitrant Germans into settling the boundary disputes in Eastern Europe on terms acceptable to the Communist bloc. The ultimate goal of this ambitious project was a mutual disengagement in Europe that would leave the Russian satellites in the east free to pursue their autonomous course as Western Europe resumed its evolution away from the United States. A continent partitioned into two rigid power blocs at Yalta and Potsdam would thereafter be emancipated from superpower domination and be free to reassert its authority and influence in the world.

The military consequences of France's withdrawal from NATO were trivial: The headquarters of the alliance were transferred from Paris to Brussels with relative ease. Neither the forced evacuation of American and Canadian military personnel nor the loss of French territory as a staging area for the provisioning and reinforcement of Allied troops in West Germany caused serious difficulties. The bases in France had always played a subsidiary, supportive role in NATO strategy, which envisioned West Germany as the principal battlefield for a conventional engagement with Warsaw Pact forces and presumed a nuclear response before they reached the Rhine. Supplies could be and had for years been channeled through Benelux and West German ports to the forward area in Central Europe. The only three indispensable French contributions to NATO's defense capability—the stationing of French ground and air forces in West Germany as a guarantee of France's participation in the defense of that country, the granting of access to the pipeline across France that carried oil and fuel to NATO forces in Germany, and overflight rights in French air space that connected the northern and southern half of the alliance— were all preserved by special agreement. Moreover, France retained representation on the exclusively political organs of the alliance (the North Atlantic Council and its subsidiary bodies) as well as liaison officers attached to some of the military organs. Thus the dire predictions of Western disarray in the wake of de Gaulle's disengagement were not borne out. The Atlantic alliance proved capable of withstanding the assertion of French independence and of adapting to the increasingly pluralistic international environment that it heralded.

Similarly, the bid for a bilateral rapprochement with Moscow that accompanied de Gaulle's diplomatic warfare with Washington failed to produce the anticipated realignment of power in Europe: The monetary and financial crisis that engulfed France following the student–worker unrest in the spring of 1968 revealed how poorly endowed that country was to play the powerful, independent role envisioned for it by its leader. The Soviet invasion of Czechoslovakia in the summer of the same year had the dual effect of enhancing the cohesion of the Western bloc and undermining the assumption of Soviet retrenchment in the east upon which de Gaulle's hopes for a free and independent Europe rested. The abrupt abdication of the idiosyncratic French president in April 1969 brought to an end his grand design for France and Europe, which had overestimated French power and Europe's willingness and ability to defend itself without American assistance.

The Political Settlement in Europe

But if de Gaulle's excessively grandiose conception of a new *international* system proved ephemeral, the Gaullist vision of a new *intra-European* order survived the demise of its author with profound consequences for Europe, Russia, and America. Beneath the spectacular rhetorical flourishes of this quixotic advocate of a French-led Europe emancipated from superpower domination lay a much more practical prescription for the solution of the political antagonisms on that continent that had perpetuated its partition into two political, economic, and military blocs. Foremost among these were the outstanding matters of dispute between the Federal Republic of Germany and its Communist neighbors to the east. These nettlesome issues, de Gaulle asserted, had to be settled by patient diplomacy before the Cold War in Europe could be brought to a close and the superpowers' grip on their respective halves of the continent loosened. The French president's mistake was to imagine that his own country, on the strength of its military supremacy and powerful diplomatic influence in Western Europe, was capable of orchestrating such a relaxation of tensions in the center of the continent as the West's privileged interlocutor of the eastern bloc. This Gaullist strategy overlooked two fundamental elements of European power politics: The first was that the only continental state capable of granting the Soviet Union and its satellites the assurances they required as a prerequisite for genuine detente in Europe was West Germany; the second was that Bonn, unlike Paris, would never dare to seek an accommodation with the Eastern bloc without obtaining the prior consent of Washington, on whose military protection and diplomatic support it utterly depended for its security.

The Cold War in Europe had begun over the issues of Germany and Berlin and persisted into the mid-sixties because those two related questions remained unresolved. The principal obstacle to their resolution was West German Chancellor Konrad Adenauer's stubborn refusal to abandon the dream of the political reunification of the two German states that had been established in 1949. This was a cause that continued to exercise great emotional appeal upon West German voters, but was anathema to the Soviet Union and its East European satellites, particularly the East German regime in Pankow that understandably feared being submerged in the larger, more populous, and more prosperous West German entity. Bonn's denial of East Germany's sovereignty and its insistence on enjoying the exclusive right to represent all Germans was formally expressed in December 1955 with the promulgation of the Hallstein doctrine (named after the then-secretary of state of the West German foreign office). This declaration affirmed Bonn's intention to regard diplomatic recognition of the East German regime as an unfriendly act because it implied acceptance of Germany's permanent division. Accordingly, West Germany severed diplomatic relations with the Eastern European states that recognized Pankow except for the Soviet Union, which it prudently exempted from the purview of the doctrine. A related source of antagonism between West Germany and its eastern neighbors was its refusal to recognize Germany's frontiers with Poland and Czechoslovakia that had been redrawn in 1945 to the advantage of those two countries; to acknowledge these territorial losses would be to antagonize the large and vocal political constituency composed of German refugees who had been expelled from these regions after the war and who dreamed of regaining their lost lands. The twin prospects of unification of the two Germanies and territorial revision in the east understandably alarmed the East European states and their Soviet patron. No two issues had done more to keep the embers of the Cold War burning throughout the fifties and into the following decade.

In December 1966, as de Gaulle was administering his shock treatment to the Western alliance, a governing coalition was formed in West Germany that brought to the foreign ministry the Social Democratic leader Willy Brandt, a passionate proponent of world peace who was fired by the determination to normalize his country's relations with the Communist bloc even at the cost of renouncing the cherished goals of national unification and recovery of the lost territories. Brandt's new "eastern policy," or *Ostpolitik,* reflected a profound shift in West German attitudes toward these overriding foreign policy issues. Majority opinion within the two parties that formed the new coalition had concluded that the old "policy of strength" toward East Germany and Eastern Europe had failed to yield the desired results: Instead of promoting the collapse of the Communist system in Eastern Europe, the reunification of the German peoples, and the recovery of the former German territories, the unyielding approach inherited from the Adenauer years had left the Federal Republic isolated in the Western camp as the last stronghold of orthodox policies of the Cold War amid a general evolution toward the acceptance of the political status quo in Europe and the permanent division of the two Germanies. The alternative that Brandt proposed was the normalization of West Germany's relations with its East European neighbors as a means of facilitating a continentwide relaxation of tensions that might, at some distant date in the future, lead to the peaceful reunification of the two German states. In short, the once-central component of Bonn's foreign policy, the insistence that all-German reunification was the precondition for detente, was abandoned and the priority reversed: Detente became the means of achieving the ultimate goal of the reconciliation of the two Germanies on a stable, peaceful continent.

After prudently informing and obtaining the tacit approval of his NATO allies (including the United States), Brandt embarked on a cautious campaign to improve West Germany's relations with the nations of Eastern Europe. In January 1967 Bonn restored diplomatic relations with Bucharest in direct violation of the Hallstein doctrine. By 1968 West German trade missions had been dispatched to several East European capitals to lay the groundwork for an unprecedented commercial penetration of the Communist bloc that was financed by West German banks. The Soviet military intervention in Czechoslovakia in the summer of 1968 temporarily set back West Germany's opening to the east, as Bonn joined other NATO nations in condemning the Warsaw Pact's action. But the West German elections of October 1969 brought Brandt to power as chancellor in a coalition cabinet dominated by his Social Democratic Party. As head of government he promptly renewed and intensified his efforts to reach a

comprehensive settlement with the East. In response to his earlier overtures, the Warsaw Pact states had specified the price for such a rapprochement: acknowledgment of the territorial status quo in Eastern Europe and
the recognition of East Germany's sovereignty. Before tackling these difficult issues, the West German leader paved the way for a mutual accommodation by signing the Nuclear Non-Proliferation Treaty on November
28, 1969; he then concluded a nonaggression pact with the Soviet Union
on August 12, 1970, (thirty-one years after the signing of the Hitler–Stalin
pact) by which both parties affirmed the existing frontiers in Eastern Europe and forswore the use of force against one another. These two gestures helped to alleviate Moscow's ultimate fear of a revisionist West Germany armed with nuclear weapons. The festering dispute concerning
Germany's border with Poland was disposed of with astonishing ease
in view of the quarter-century deadlock over this troublesome issue. On
December 7, 1970, Brandt journeyed to Warsaw to sign a nonaggression
pact with Poland that formally renounced Germany's territorial claims by
recognizing the German-Polish frontier at the Oder-Neisse line.

The more emotionally charged matter of East German sovereignty required more time and patient diplomacy to resolve. Since the establishment of the two German political entities in 1949, the West German people and their political leaders had steadfastly adhered to the principle of
German reunification on the basis of Western-style free elections. If such
a goal seemed within the realm of possibility during the 1950s, it had
ceased to be anything but a chimera after the construction of the Berlin
Wall in 1961 and the West's failure to contest its existence. No longer able
to escape their condition of servitude by voting with their feet, the remaining inhabitants of East Germany had to resign themselves to permanent
citizenship in the Communist state and build their future as best they
could. In tacit acknowledgment of the irreversibility (at least in the near
future) of Germany's partition into two sovereign states, Brandt had
broached the novel suggestion that Germany be considered "two states
within one nation." This concession failed to elicit the approval of East
German leader Walter Ulbricht, who repeated his demand for formal recognition of his regime's sovereignty in exchange for improved relations
with Bonn. But Ulbricht had been installed and maintained in power by
his masters in the Kremlin, and therefore had no hope of conducting a
foreign policy that contradicted their wishes. As we have seen, by the beginning of the 1970s Moscow was actively pursuing a policy of rapprochement with Washington, partly out of fear of China, partly in the expectation of obtaining economic assistance from the West; to complement the
projected agreement on arms control between the two superpowers, Brezhnev and company pushed for political detente in Europe that would clear
up all the sources of East–West friction there. Since Ulbricht's recalcitrance
represented the major stumbling block to agreement with the new conciliatory government in Bonn, the old East German hard-liner had to go. On

May 3, 1971, he was replaced as first secretary of the party by the more compliant functionary Erich Honecker.

The removal of this aged symbol of the Cold War era paved the way for the European political settlement that both sides had come to favor. In September 1971 the four occupying powers in Berlin—the United States, the Soviet Union, Britain, and France—signed an agreement recognizing each other's existing rights in their respective sectors of the city and affirming the special political relationship between West Berlin and the Federal Republic. The Kremlin had thereby sacrificed in the interests of detente the long-standing demand of its East German client for total control of access routes to the city that had precipitated the Berlin crises of 1958–61. Finally, on December 21, 1972, East Germany was compelled to accept and sign a Basic Treaty with the Federal Republic that failed to accord Pankow the formal diplomatic recognition it had always demanded as a precondition for inter-German reconciliation. The Basic Treaty provided for increased commercial, cultural, and personal relations between the two German states as well as the exchange of permanent missions rather than embassies. In September 1973, twenty-four years after they had emerged as de facto nations, the two Germanies were admitted into the United Nations as separate sovereign entities. Three months later the last remaining issue in dispute between West Germany and the Eastern bloc, the frontier between Germany and Czechoslovakia, was resolved by mutual agreement: On December 11 Bonn signed a treaty with Prague that nullified the Munich Agreement of 1938, thereby acknowledging the loss of the Sudetenland whose German-speaking inhabitants had been forcibly repatriated after the collapse of the Third Reich. In this piecemeal, *ad hoc* fashion, the unresolved issues of the Second World War were settled insofar as the countries of Central Europe were concerned.

All that remained was for the two superpowers who had won the war and were simultaneously pursuing improved relations in other ways to put their seal of approval on the European settlement negotiated bilaterally between West Germany and its eastern neighbors. Ever since the mid-fifties the post-Stalinist leaders in the Kremlin had issued periodic proposals for the convocation of a European Security Conference to break the political impasse on the continent and reduce the likelihood of a military confrontation between NATO and the Warsaw Pact. The nations of Western Europe had consistently rebuffed these Soviet overtures on the grounds that political agreements were meaningless unless accompanied by a mutual reduction of military forces on the continent; that was an idea that had little appeal in Moscow (presumably because of Soviet apprehension about the political consequences in Eastern Europe of such troop withdrawals). But by the early 1970s two developments in the global balance of power forced the West European nations on the one hand and the Soviet Union on the other to reconsider their incompatible positions in the interests of promoting an all-European conference that now seemed advantageous to both sides. Western Europe's enthusiasm for an agreement to reduce the size of the military forces on the continent was increased by the ominous signs of retrenchment that had appeared in the United States in reaction to the traumatic experience of Vietnam. The Mansfield resolution calling for the withdrawal of most American military forces from Europe, though defeated in the Senate in 1970, had elicited sufficient public and Congressional support to cause anxiety in Europe about the future of the American military presence there. The abolition of American conscription after the Vietnam pullout foreshadowed a reduction in American military personnel that would require politically unpopular increases in European defense spending if the military forces of the two alliance systems were to remain at their current levels. The key to Russia's new conciliatory posture in Europe was to be found in Beijing. Russo-Chinese border clashes along the Amur-Ussuri rivers in March 1969 highlighted the increasingly bitter territorial disputes between those two erstwhile Communist allies; the spectacular visit to China in July 1971 by President Nixon's national security adviser, Henry Kissinger, forshadowed an improvement of Sino-American relations at Russia's expense (see p. 397). Confronted by a hostile, independent China on its Asian frontier, the Soviet Union could not fail to recognize the advantages of detente and stability on its European flank.

Two months after Kissinger's China sojourn, Brezhnev agreed in principle to participate in a conference on Mutual and Balanced Force Reductions (MBFR) in exchange for the Western nations' endorsement of the Soviet proposal for a European Security Conference (CSCE). After a year of preparatory discussions these two parallel conferences began, the CSCE in Helsinki on January 15, 1973, and the MBFR in Vienna on October 30. While the talks on military reductions bogged down in technical matters and led to nothing of consequence, the political discussions in Helsinki achieved remarkable progress largely because of the preparatory groundwork laid by the bilateral agreements concluded between West Germany and the Communist bloc. Though Nixon and Brandt, the two Western architects of detente, were forced from office by domestic scandals in 1974, their successors resumed their efforts to reach a comprehensive political settlement in Europe. What Moscow hoped to obtain at the Helsinki conference was the West's formal recognition of the postwar political status quo in Europe, including the sovereignty of East Germany that had already been conceded de facto by Bonn through its bilateral Basic Treaty with Pankow.

In addition to these cherished political goals, economic considerations played an important role in the Soviet Union's bid for detente in Europe: The Polish riots against food price increases in December 1970, which toppled Communist party boss Gomulka from power, marked the culmination of a decade of growing economic unrest within the Soviet Union's East European empire. In January 1949 Moscow had established the

Council for Mutual Economic Assistance (Comecon) to develop an integrated economic bloc in Eastern Europe as a counterweight to the Marshall Plan and the Organization for European Economic Cooperation in the West. But as Western Europe edged toward genuine economic integration with impressive results during the 1950s, Comecon remained little more than an instrument for perpetuating the Soviet Union's stranglehold on the economic life of its Eastern European satellites. The economies of the region were exploited to accelerate the economic recovery of the Soviet Union by means of reparation exactions from former enemy states, the formation of joint stock companies under Russian control, and the forced diversion of trade on advantageous terms to the Soviet Union. Khrushchev's efforts in 1962–63 to emulate the success of the European Economic Community by welding Comecon into a supranational integrated economic bloc with a division of production failed largely because of Romania's refusal to accept the role of grain and oil producer assigned to it. As Romania defiantly pressed on with its plans for rapid industrialization in violation of the Comecon blueprint, Czechoslovakia, Poland, and Hungary expressed dissatisfaction at having to pay for Soviet raw materials at prices far above those prevailing on the world market. There were also bitter complaints from the economically hard-pressed satellites about the necessity of supplying free of charge or on advantageous terms military and industrial equipment to Third World countries where the Soviet Union was seeking political influence. These rumblings of discontent within the Communist bloc reflected a growing awareness of the marked disparity between the prosperity of Western Europe and the economic stagnation of Eastern Europe. From Molotov's abandonment of the Paris meetings on the Marshall Plan in 1947 through the 1960s, the Kremlin had strenuously opposed the only obvious solution to this problem, namely, the opening of its satellite empire to trade and investment from the West, for fear that economic penetration would bring ideological contamination and the attendant menace of political unrest within the bloc. But by the early 1970s Brezhnev and his associates had come to believe that the only hope of satisfying the mounting consumer demands of the Eastern European peoples, and indeed of the Russian population itself, was a massive influx of foreign industrial products, technology, and investment capital that only the advanced economic powers of the non-Communist world could provide.

Agreements on trade and technical cooperation concluded with France and West Germany in the early 1970s had set the stage for this economic opening to the West, which was given a tremendous boost by the conclusion on August 1, 1975, of the two-year-long European Security Conference in Helsinki. On that historic date, representatives of thirty-three European countries (all but the perpetually isolated Albania), the United States, and Canada signed the Final Act of the European Security Conference. Among its most important provisions were those that formally recognized the existing political frontiers of Europe (including the border separating the two Germanies), provided for an increase in economic and cultural relations between the two blocs, and specified prior notification of and the exchange of observers at large-scale military exercises conducted by the two alliance systems. The major concession made by Moscow in exchange for the West's implicit acknowledgment of its domination of Eastern Europe was the so-called basket three, which guaranteed respect for human rights and political freedoms in a manner reminiscent of the Yalta Declaration on Liberated Europe.* Thus, thirty years after the defeat of Hitler, the war he had started was brought to an end (though without the formalities of a peace treaty, since the Final Act of the Helsinki conference was officially only a political statement of intent rather than a legally binding document). The political division of Europe, which had precipitated the Cold War between the two victors in the struggle against Nazi Germany, was finally acknowledged as a *fait accompli*. By obtaining international recognition of its preeminence in the East European buffer zone as well as the *de facto* division of Germany, the Soviet Union now enjoyed a degree of political security that reinforced the military security that had resulted from its acquisition of strategic parity with the United States in the course of the 1960s.

Complementing the political and military detente of the mid-1970s was an informal "economic detente" consisting of the unclogging of commercial and financial channels between East and West. The bifurcation of Europe into two closed economic blocs, itself both a cause and a consequence of the Cold War, gave way to a notable increase in trade and investment between them. West German and French banks poured hard-currency loans into the economies of Eastern Europe, which enabled these states to purchase Western consumer goods and industrial products in unprecedented quantities. Italy opened a Fiat automobile plant in the heart of Russia. The United States became the Soviet Union's principal foreign supplier of grain after the conclusion of a five-year sales agreement on October 25, 1975. But as political and economic intercourse between the two blocs in Europe intensified and Soviet-American negotiations on strategic arms limitation progressed during the first half of the 1970s, the deteriorating situation in that volatile part of the world known as the Middle East threatened to nip in the bud this promising trend toward East–West reconciliation.

The Middle East as Perennial Hotspot

The engagement of the two superpowers in this perennial trouble spot had begun toward the end of the 1950s. The United States sought to counter

* The "basket three" provisions encouraged dissidents within the Soviet bloc to campaign openly for measures of political liberalization during the remainder of the 1970s. But the absence of effective enforcement machinery condemned the Helsinki human rights principles to a fate similar to that of the Yalta declaration.

what it saw as Moscow's efforts to exploit for its own benefit Arab opposition to the lingering presence of European colonial power in the region and to the existence of the state of Israel that had been carved out of the former British mandate in Palestine. We have seen how the Suez crisis in the autumn of 1956 marked a critical turning point in the history of foreign involvement in the Middle East. Chastened by Washington's refusal to endorse their attempt to retain an influential position in the region, Great Britain and France were compelled to follow the lead of the United States as it strove to exclude the Soviet Union from this strategically located, oil-rich part of the world. This transfer of authority was formalized on January 5, 1957, by the proclamation of the Eisenhower Doctrine, which affirmed the responsibility of the United States to assist any nation in the Middle East that was judged to be threatened by Communist aggression. Since the Soviet Union at the time had neither the capacity nor, so far as was known, the inclination to expand militarily into the region, the Eisenhower Doctrine served as the justification for American action against the one power there that did entertain expansionist ambitions at the expense of states friendly to the United States and its European allies, namely, Nasser's Egypt. In July 1958 Anglo-American troops intervened to rescue the pro-Western regimes of Jordan and Lebanon from the presumed threat of a pro-Nasser coup such as the one that had recently toppled the government of the British client state in Iraq. It was Nasser's professed goal to unite all the Arab states of the Middle East and North Africa under his leadership, and his increasingly intimate political and economic relations with the Communist bloc made him appear in American eyes as the stalking horse for the Kremlin in what had come to be regarded as an area of vital interest to the United States.

Apart from the economic benefits that he obtained from the Soviet Union, such as development aid for the Aswan Dam project to replace the funds previously withheld by the United States and Great Britain, the Egyptian leader's principal reason for cultivating Russia's friendship was the hope that it would assist him, diplomatically and militarily, in removing what he considered the major roadblock to the realization of his Pan-Arab project: the state of Israel. In the aftermath of the Suez affair, and particularly after the promulgation of the Eisenhower Doctrine, the two superpowers had become indirectly embroiled in the bitter dispute between the Jewish state and its Arab neighbors that had festered ever since its formation in May 1948. The Soviet Union furnished military assistance to Egypt and dispatched Russian officers to train the army of Syria, Israel's northeastern neighbor, which had fallen under the control of an anti-Western ruling elite that cultivated close ties with Moscow. The fear that a pro-Communist Syria would also threaten the adjacent pro-Western regimes of Jordan, Lebanon, and Turkey prompted Washington to step up military assistance to those states, while American arms supplies flowed into Israel to counter the ominous buildup of Russian weaponry in Egypt.

When these links with the Soviet Union failed to produce the Middle East settlement that Egypt and Syria desired, these two states jointly endeavored to break the deadlock by force. Armed with Soviet tanks and planes, Nasser demanded and obtained the removal of the United Nations peacekeeping force that had been deployed between Egypt and Israel on the Sinai peninsula after the Suez incident in 1956. On May 22, 1967, he closed to Israeli shipping the Straits of Tiran, the narrow waterway that afforded access to Israel's only port on the Red Sea. Interpreting this partial blockade as a prelude to war, Israel launched a preemptive strike against Egypt and Syria on June 5. Within six days Israeli forces had captured the strategic buffer zones of the Golan Heights from Syria, the entire Sinai peninsula including the east bank of the Suez Canal from Egypt, and the west bank of the Jordan River including the Jordanian sector of the holy city of Jerusalem (which had been partitioned after the 1948–49 war). By one bold stroke in three directions, Israel had decimated the military forces of her most determined adversaries and obtained defensible borders on all sides. To these she defiantly clung for more than a decade, in spite of Resolution 242 passed by the United Nations Security Council on November 22 which called for Israel's withdrawal from the recently occupied territories in exchange for assurances from the front-line Arab states that her sovereignty within secure frontiers would be recognized and her freedom of navigation in international waters assured.

The Six Day War of June 1967 represented a humiliating setback for the Soviet Union and its two client states in the Middle East. Moscow's credibility as a reliable and effective patron had been undermined. Its armaments in Egypt and military advisers in Syria had failed to halt the advance of the outnumbered Israeli forces in their victorious war of six days on three fronts. The United States, distracted by its deepening military involvement in Southeast Asia and therefore reluctant to be drawn into a second conflict with Soviet client states on the other side of the world, maintained a neutral posture in the Arab-Israeli showdown. The hot line established by Kennedy and Khrushchev after the Cuban missile crisis was used during this conflict for the first time to assure that neither the Kremlin nor the White House would miscalculate the other's intentions regarding the Six Day War. But Washington's prior military assistance to Israel was sufficient proof of where its sympathies lay, as was the ostentatious sale of fifty American F-4 Phantom jets to Israel in December 1967 while Egypt and Syria were still licking their wounds inflicted the previous June.

Half of the Arab states severed diplomatic relations with Washington during the Six Day War, and a number of them promptly granted the Soviet Union the use of their ports in retaliation against America's support for the hated Zionist entity in their midst. In early 1970 the Soviet Union supplied some three hundred surface-to-air (SAM) missiles to Egypt to help it counter Israel's air superiority, which had been decisively demonstrated in the war three years earlier and more recently during Israeli raids over the Suez Canal. Moscow also dispatched twenty thousand advisers and technicians to man the missile sites and reorganize Egypt's shattered military forces. The completion of the Russian-financed Aswan Dam in January 1971 was followed by new Soviet commitments of economic assistance to Cairo. In exchange the Soviet Union obtained naval facilities at the Egyptian ports of Alexandria, Port Said, and Mersa Matrûh to accommodate its Mediterranean fleet—a prime Soviet objective ever since Albania's eviction of the Russians from the naval base at Vlone on the Adriatic in May 1961 just as the United States prepared to deploy Polaris submarines in the Mediterranean—as well as the use of Egyptian airfields for reconnaissance flights along NATO's southern flank. On March 28, 1971, Egyptian President Anwar Sadat, who had succeeded to the presidency after Nasser's death in September 1970, concluded a fifteen-year treaty of friendship and cooperation with the Soviet Union—the first Soviet military commitment to a Third World country—in the hope of obtaining much larger quantities of sophisticated weaponry that would enable his country to regain by force the Sinai territory it had lost to Israel in 1967.

Those Egyptian hopes were to be gravely disappointed, however, just as Israel failed to secure Washington's unqualified endorsement of its newly expanded frontiers. The two superpowers patiently attempted to restrain their respective protégés in the Middle East by restricting arms deliveries and prodding them into seeking a mutually acceptable resolution of their differences. Neither Washington nor Moscow wished to be dragged into a confrontation in this volatile part of the world at a time when Nixon and Brezhnev were jointly striving to reduce East–West tensions. But neither was capable of controlling its Mideastern client because the stakes in this regional conflict had become so high for both Cairo and Tel Aviv. Sadat required a military success against Israel that would recover at least a portion of the lost land in the Sinai in order to shore up his sagging domestic popularity and divert public attention from the precarious state of the Egyptian economy. The leaders of Israel were driven by a sense of mistrust and anxiety to refuse any concession that might undermine the recently acquired security afforded by the Sinai buffer. On the contrary, plans were drawn up to populate the occupied territories with Jewish settlers, a policy that was viewed by the Arab states bordering on Israel as a prelude to de facto annexation.

The tension between Egypt and Israel, which boiled over in intermittent skirmishing along the Suez Canal during the early seventies, was exacerbated by the plight of the 2.75 million stateless Palestinian Arabs, half of them refugees from the area incorporated in the new Jewish state after the 1948–49 war. The government of Israel had declined to permit their repatriation after the conclusion of the armistice, unwilling to allow the Jewish citizens of the new state to be numerically overwhelmed by a million

TABLE IX   Unofficial Estimates of Palestinian Residence in the Middle East
as of March 1973

Jordan	700,000
West Bank	675,000
Israel	350,000
Gaza	375,000
Lebanon	275,000
Syria	175,000
Egypt	25,000
Iraq	10,000
Persian Gulf countries	170,000
	2,755,000

Source: Dana A. Schmidt, *Armageddon in the Middle East* (New York: The John Day Company, 1974), p. 148. © 1974 by the New York Times Company. Reprinted by permission.

discontented Arabs returning to a land they considered their own. Since no neighboring Arab state was prepared to resettle them permanently within its own frontiers, these hapless souls had been "temporarily" dispersed in squalid refugee camps located in Syria, Jordan, and the Egyptian-controlled Gaza strip, where they festered in poverty and idleness. The more politically active among them formed in 1964 the Palestine Liberation Organization (PLO), which operated from Jordanian territory until it was expelled in September 1970 by the military forces of King Hussein, who feared that his kingdom would be overwhelmed by its Palestinian majority. As the PLO reassembled in Lebanon in the early 1970s, its commandos sponsored spectacular acts of terrorism to publicize the Palestinian grievances, such as the hijacking of airplanes and the murder of Israeli athletes at the 1972 Olympic games in Munich.

When President Sadat failed to secure from the Soviet Union the offensive weapons that would have assured Egyptian military superiority over Israel, he abruptly turned against his less-than-accommodating benefactors. On July 18, 1972, shortly after the Nixon–Brezhnev summit talks in Moscow appeared to confirm the Kremlin's commitment to East–West detente at the expense of its clients in peripheral regions such as the Middle East, the Egyptian leader angrily ordered most of the Soviet advisers and technicians out of his country (though he permitted the Russians to retain access to Egyptian naval facilities). In the ensuing months he had come to believe that Egypt stood a good chance of recapturing at least some of the lost territory on the Sinai even without the sophisticated military hardware withheld by Moscow. He also became convinced that a renewal of armed struggle in the Middle East was necessary in order to involve the two superpowers in a Middle East peace settlement. Thus in early October 1973, on the Jewish holy day of Yom Kippur, Egypt in concert with Syria launched a well-coordinated surprise attack against Israel. Egyptian forces drove across the Suez Canal into the Sinai peninsula, overrunning Israel's

Bar-Lev defense installation with furious infantry and artillery assaults. In the meantime a large Syrian force equipped with eight hundred tanks swarmed onto the Golan Heights overlooking Israeli settlements in the valley below. After two weeks of the fiercest tank battles since World War II on the Sinai and the Golan, Israel gained the upper hand. An Israeli force counterattacked into Syria and drove to within twenty miles of Damascus, while another landed on the west bank of the Suez Canal to encircle the Egyptian Third Army on the east bank in the Sinai, sever its supply lines, and block its retreat.

The two superpowers, though reluctant to become involved in another Middle East confrontation that might unravel the fragile fabric of detente fashioned by Nixon and Brezhnev, did not want to be defeated by proxy. They therefore supplied military equipment to their respective clients while vainly seeking to arrange a ceasefire in the United Nations. When an Egyptian defeat appeared imminent after Israeli forces crossed the Suez Canal on October 16, the Kremlin endorsed Sadat's request that the United States and the Soviet Union jointly intervene to separate the belligerents. Once President Nixon refused to countenance the unprecedented deployment of Russian troops in a region of such strategic and economic importance to the United States, the Kremlin thereupon declared its intention to introduce its own forces in the area unilaterally. In response, Nixon ordered a worldwide nuclear alert of American forces and the Soviet Union promptly followed suit. For a moment it appeared that Moscow's desire to exploit the Arab-Israeli conflict in order to gain a foothold in the Middle East, and Washington's determination to prevent such a radical shift in the global balance of power, outweighed both superpowers' commitment to the Nixon–Brezhnev policy of detente.

But the escalation of the fourth Arab-Israeli war into a global confrontation between the United States and the Soviet Union was averted by a compromise resolution passed by the UN Security Council on October 22 that authorized the interposition of a seven-thousand-man United Nations emergency force between the combatants to supervise a ceasefire. In December 1973 the Israelis and Arabs, under intense pressure from the superpowers (and with American and Soviet participation), conducted their first face-to-face negotiations in a quarter of a century at a peace conference in Geneva. Thereafter, the energetic American secretary of state, Henry Kissinger, shuttled between Cairo and Tel Aviv intermittently for two years in an effort to bring Israel and Egypt together while freezing the Soviet Union out of the negotiating process. In September 1975, the two sides finally concluded an agreement that provided for a partial Israeli withdrawal in the Sinai to create a buffer zone manned by American and United Nations observers operating technical equipment to detect violations of the ceasefire. Though the Soviet Union did not recognize this American-sponsored interim solution to the Israeli-Egyptian conflict, it refrained from interfering with the peace process in the Middle East. Thus, the superpower detente appeared to have survived its first serious test, while the prospects for stability in the Middle East seemed more promising than ever before by the middle of the 1970s.

Despite the apparently satisfactory outcome of the October War from the standpoint of the United States and its Israeli client, the Western world's stake in the Middle East conflict had taken on an ominous new dimension during the most recent outbreak of violence. In retaliation against Washington's airlift of supplies to Israel to replace losses of tanks and planes, the oil-producing states of the Arab world imposed a five-month embargo on petroleum shipments to the United States, which caused gasoline shortages and considerable inconvenience to American consumers. More serious than the inconvenience of long lines at the gasoline pumps was the severe shock to the world economy administered by the oil-producing cartel, the Organization of Petroleum Exporting Countries (OPEC), which quadrupled the price of crude oil between 1973 and 1975. These sharp and sudden price increases of this essential commodity produced the most serious economic downturn that the world had experienced since the Great Depression of the 1930s.

The oil embargo and the precipitous price increases exposed the industrial nations of the Northern Hemisphere (the United States and Canada, Western Europe, and Japan) to an unprecedented type of economic warfare waged by a coalition of developing nations in the Southern Hemisphere. OPEC's ability to increase at will the world price of its precious product highlighted the industrial world's dependence on foreign sources of energy—the United States imported 40 percent of its petroleum in the mid-1970s while the nations of Western Europe and Japan satisfied over 80 percent of their energy needs through purchases abroad. As the first commodity cartel to employ its raw material assets as an effective economic and political weapon, OPEC set a precedent that other primary producing nations could be expected to follow. The industrial world of the north depended on the nonindustrial world of the south for over half of its supplies of a whole range of raw materials—cobalt, copper, chrome, manganese, tungsten, tin, bauxite, aluminum, and others—without which its economic prosperity would grind to a halt. The specter of Third World producer cartels dictating sharp price increases of these essential commodities as a means of forcibly redistributing the world's wealth haunted officials in the non-Communist industrial world during the mid-1970s. Nervous statesmen in Western Europe began to call for the opening of a north–south dialogue to establish orderly procedures for the exchange of economic assets between the industrialized and the commodity producing regions of the earth. Others, especially naval and military strategists in the United States, reemphasized the necessity of safeguarding the sea lanes to these vital mineral resources and ensuring the security and the pro-Western orientation of the regimes that controlled them through increased American military assistance and protection.

In conclusion, the danger of a Soviet-American confrontation in the Middle East was averted by the Kremlin's decision to abstain, presumably in the interests of preserving East–West detente, from interfering with the unilateral American effort to promote a reconciliation between Israel and Egypt. By the middle of the 1970s that American campaign was well on its way to fulfillment as Secretary of State Kissinger, preserving the continuity of American foreign policy throughout the tumultuous transition from the disgraced Nixon to the untested Ford, firmly established the United States as an ostensibly disinterested arbiter of the Arab-Israeli conflict. Both superpowers had apparently learned to appreciate the advantages of stability in the Middle East as a complement to the relaxation of tensions in Europe and the strategic arms control agreement recently achieved. Moscow, though periodically proposing a return to the "Geneva forum," seemed resigned to Washington's unilateral sponsorship of a Middle East peace, while the United States prodded its Israeli client into relinquishing the Egyptian territory it held in exchange for Cairo's pledge to respect Israel's right to exist as a sovereign and secure state in the midst of the Arab world.

CHAPTER 11

The Rise of China and the Cold War in Asia

The Communist Victory in the Chinese Civil War

The total collapse of the Japanese empire in August 1945 left a vast power vacuum in Asia comparable to the one created in Europe by the German capitulation three months earlier. But the political consequences of the Allied military victory in the Far East differed from the postwar situation in Europe in one crucial respect: The United States had waged the Pacific war almost singlehandedly and had been able to compel the enemy's surrender without having had to rely on the military assistance of the Soviet Union. By the time the Red Army had begun to consolidate control of its prescribed occupation zones on the Asian mainland (Manchuria and northern Korea) and its offshore islands (the Kuriles and the southern half of Sakhalin), the predominance of the United States and its European associates in the rest of Japan's former East Asian empire was assured. American forces under General Douglas MacArthur unilaterally undertook the military occupation and political administration of the Japanese home islands despite Soviet pleas to participate. British, French, and Dutch forces returned to their old outposts of empire in Southeast Asia either to reassert colonial authority or to grant political independence to successor regimes controlled by non-Communist, pro-Western indigenous elites.

The reestablishment of Western power in East Asia after 1945 appeared to thwart whatever ambitions Stalin may have entertained of extending Soviet influence over the populous, economically valuable region recently liberated from Japanese domination. A crucial exception was the new state of Indonesia, which was formed out of the former Dutch East Indies in 1949 and maintained friendly relations with the Communist bloc under the leadership of its charismatic president, Achmed Sukarno, until his overthrow in 1966 by anti-Communist elements in the armed forces. A far more spectacular exception to this record of postwar Russian setbacks in the Far East was the establishment in October 1949 of the People's Republic of China, a Communist state comprising a quarter of the world's population that promptly became a military ally and economic beneficiary of the Soviet Union.

The installation of a Communist government in China in late 1949 terminated a civil war that had raged intermittently in that country since 1927 between the pro-Western government of Chiang Kai-shek and the Communist guerrilla movement operating in the countryside. Since the victory of communism in China occurred in the year following the Soviet-inspired coup in Czechoslovakia and the attempt to dislodge the Western allies from Berlin, the new People's Republic in Beijing was viewed by many officials in Washington as an Asian counterpart of the Soviet satellite empire in Eastern Europe. But the handful of American foreign service officers who had spent time with the Chinese Communist guerrilla forces in the caves of Yenan in Shensi province during the war understood a signal fact about this movement that was entirely ignored by official and public opinion in the United States amid the indiscriminate anti-Communism of the 1950s: They knew it to be a thoroughly indigenous organization whose ideological affinity with and material dependence on the Soviet Union was minimal, and whose political relations with the Kremlin and its representatives in Asia had long been marked by stresses and strains.

Such a conclusion was inescapable from a study of the history of the Chinese Communist party from the mid-1930s to its spectacular triumph in 1949. That history was replete with instances of ideological and tactical differences between the dedicated band of revolutionaries in China and the agents of the Comintern who had been dispatched there by Moscow to organize an insurrection on the Soviet model. Prominent among those was the ideological contradiction between the Marxist-Leninist emphasis on the revolutionary role of the urban working class and the growing recognition on the part of the Chinese Communist leadership of the revolutionary potential of the landless peasantry in a preindustrial country where less than 1 percent of the work force toiled in factories. Lenin, who had relied on the impoverished rural masses of Russia to ensure the success of his own revolution, nevertheless had regarded the peasantry as only an auxiliary force in the proletarian revolution. In line with this theoretical conception, the Soviet Comintern agents in China and their protégés in the Chinese Communist party concentrated their energies throughout the 1920s on organizing labor in preparation for a workers' insurrection that would begin in the cities and eventually spread to countryside, where it would receive the support of the discontented peasantry. But in China the workers' vanguard had no workers. This lesson had been learned at great cost to the Chinese Communist movement in 1927, when, at the suggestion of their Russian advisers, they incited proletarian uprisings in several cities that were easily suppressed by the government because of their isolation from the genuine class struggle that was brewing in the Chinese countryside. In the same year a brilliant Communist organizer named Mao Zedong had independently concluded that the only hope for social revolution in his country lay in mobilizing its hundreds of millions of oppressed peasants against their exploitative landlords and the political and military elites who sustained them. By the middle of the 1930s Mao had effectively assumed control of the Communist party apparatus. Though he slavishly adhered to the Stalinist line in international matters and refrained from disputing the applicability of Soviet Communist ideology to the peculiar conditions of his own country, Mao charted an increasingly independent course for the Chinese variant of communism and began to assume the role of the infallible interpreter of Marxist-Leninist doctrine in China. Such a posture was anathema to Stalin, who was accustomed to dealing with foreign Communist leaders who were entirely dependent on the Kremlin for their positions and respectful of its absolute authority within the international Communist movement.

The principal source of friction between the Communist regime in Moscow and the Communist revolutionary movement in the Chinese countryside was Stalin's subsequent determination to maintain friendly relations with the very government in China that Mao's movement was striving to overturn. The Russian leader's solicitude for the fervently anti-Communist Chiang during the 1930s stemmed from considerations of national interest, namely, the concern that the two strongmen shared about the increasing military menace to their respective countries posed by Japan. During that country's undeclared war against China from 1937 to 1945, the Soviet Union pressured the Communist guerrilla movement ensconced in northern Shensi province to observe a temporary truce in its insurrectionary challenge to Chiang's nationalist government in Nanking (and later Chungking) in the interests of waging a common struggle against the foreign invaders. The Kremlin supplied considerable military and financial assistance to the Nationalist forces and persuaded Mao to place his Red Army under the nominal jurisdiction of the Chinese government. The removal of the Japanese threat in 1945 neither dampened Stalin's enthusiasm for preserving cordial relations with Chiang nor produced an increase in direct Soviet support for the Chinese Communist movement. On August 14, 1945, the day before Japan accepted the Allied terms of surrender, the Soviet Union concluded a treaty of friendship and alliance with the Chinese Nationalist government. By its terms Moscow formally recognized Chiang's regime as the legitimate government of China and pledged to send it military and economic aid in exchange for joint Sino-Soviet management of the Manchurian railway and the port of Dairen, the right to construct a Soviet naval base at Port Arthur, and Chinese recognition of the "independence" of the Soviet client state of Mongolia. In the meantime the Kremlin advised the Chinese Communists to dismantle their independent military apparatus and to join the Nationalists in a political coalition as junior partners. By the time that Russian military forces evacuated Manchuria in 1946 (after having stripped it of all portable industrial equipment), it had become evident that Moscow was playing off the two rivals in the Chinese civil war against each other in order to forestall what Stalin wanted most to avoid: the creation of a unified China under a single political authority. Thus, the Soviet occupation forces turned over captured Japanese weapons to Mao's partisans in Manchuria while acceding to Chiang's request that the Soviet troops remain in the region until the Nationalist forces could arrive in sufficient numbers to prevent a Communist takeover.

Moscow's equivocal policy toward the Chinese civil war continued after hostilities resumed in 1946 following the failure of an American mediation mission headed by General George C. Marshall. As the Nationalist armies in northern China disintegrated before the Communist onslaught in 1948, Stalin urged Mao to halt his southward advance at the Yangtze River in order to permit the regrouping of Chiang's forces and the creation of a non-Communist enclave in southern China. After the Chinese Communists rejected that advice and burst into the southern cities in early 1949, the Soviet embassador remained with the retreating Nationalist government almost to the bitter end. The reason for the Kremlin's reluctance to tender its unqualified support to the Communist insurrection in China was evidently the same that had prompted the recent exercise of its restraining influence on the Communist insurgents in Greece: the fear that a local Communist triumph over forces supported by the West would provoke an American response that could escalate into a global confrontation with the Soviet Union for which she was at the time entirely unprepared. It probably also reflected Stalin's concern that a vigorous new Communist regime established without the assistance of the Red Army in a country with almost three times the population of Russia would inevitably become a competing pole of attraction within the world Communist movement.

Ironically, while the Soviet Union attempted to restrain the Chinese Communists and preserved its diplomatic contacts with the doomed Chinese Nationalist regime as it collapsed during the summer of 1949, the United States announced on August 5 the termination of all economic and military assistance to Chiang Kai-shek on the grounds that through corruption and inefficiency his government had forfeited its claim to American support. Upon the establishment of the People's Republic of China on October 1, 1949, Washington appeared prepared to accept the *fait accompli* of a Communist victory in the Chinese civil war. In January 1950, a month after the last tattered remnants of Chiang's military forces and political administration had retreated to the island of Formosa, President Truman reaffirmed the Allied declarations of Cairo and Potsdam that Formosa was to be regarded as an integral part of China and announced that he had no intention of resuming American military assistance to the Nationalist authorities that had been suspended the previous August. The implication of these declarations was that Washington would do nothing to prevent the new regime on the mainland from completing its victory by forcing Chiang's forces to surrender their vulnerable offshore redoubt.

The Communist leadership in Beijing, though triumphant in its twenty-two-year struggle without significant Soviet assistance and in spite of Soviet counsels of restraint, was compelled by the disastrous economic conditions it inherited to look toward Moscow for economic assistance to recover and rebuild. The extensive damage wrought by the Japanese occupation and the civil war required a massive infusion of foreign capital and technological expertise. Correctly anticipating that the prospects of Marshall Plan-type assistance from the United States were slight as American anti-Communist sentiment increased in response to events in Europe, Mao left his country for the first time in his life at the end of 1949 to visit the Soviet capital hat in hand. After being kept waiting in the cold Moscow winter for two months, the new ruler of the world's most populous nation was persuaded to sign on February 14, 1950, a thirty-year Treaty of Friendship, Alliance, and Mutual Assistance that was directed at Japan and, implicitly, at the United States. By the terms of other agreements, Stalin secured Chinese recognition of the independence of Mongolia under Soviet tutelage as well as the continuation of Russian participation in the management of the Manchurian railroad and Soviet base rights in the two Yellow Sea ports of Dairen and Port Arthur until 1952. Mao also had to consent to the formation of joint stock companies to develop the mineral resources of Manchuria and Xinjiang, two historic objects of Russian economic ambition. Moscow thereby obtained the assurance of a friendly power on Russia's Asian frontier together with temporary naval privileges and long-term economic concessions that can only be labeled imperialist in character. Such was the price that Mao had to pay for the Soviet economic assistance that turned out to be paltry in comparison to the lavish subsidies he had hoped to receive: $300 million in long-term credits, less than half a dollar for each Chinese citizen. Significantly, no military assistance flowed from Moscow at a time when Chiang's armies were regrouping on Formosa in preparation for an invasion of the mainland.

In light of this inauspicious beginning of the Sino-Soviet entente and Stalin's earlier tendency to hold the Chinese Communists at arms length, one is tempted to pose the question: Could Washington have disrupted the emerging partnership between Moscow and Beijing by extending diplomatic recognition and economic assistance to the new ruling elite in China once its authority on the mainland had been confirmed in the early months of 1950? As we have seen, the United States has traditionally considered itself the benefactor and protector of the Chinese people and American export interests had long coveted the "China market" for American goods. During the Second World War President Roosevelt's overestimation of China's status as one of the world's five great powers had led him to secure for it, over the objections of a skeptical Churchill, a permanent seat in the Security Council of the United Nations. We have seen how the Truman administration, after the failure of its mediation efforts in the winter of 1945–46, had disengaged from the Chinese civil war by withdrawing its support of the Nationalist regime. There is some evidence, though sparse and inconclusive, that Mao entertained the possibility of establishing correct if not cordial relations with Washington at the end of the war, while he was still in close contact with American diplomatic and intelligence agents attached to the Chinese Communist movement during the common struggle against Japan. The Truman administration's cultivation of friendly ties with Yugoslavia after Tito's defection from the Soviet bloc in 1948 furnished an instructive precedent for Washington's willingness to temper its indiscriminate antipathy for Communist regimes. The United States government was in no hurry to join the East European Communist states, most of the Asian countries, Scandinavia, Switzerland, and Great Britain* in extending formal recognition to the Beijing government at a time when it was mistreating American citizens and seizing American property in China. But officials in the State Department were patiently preparing for a time when, after a suitable interval, the Communist triumph in the Chinese civil war would receive explicit acknowledgment from the United States.

The Korean War and America's Reengagement in the Far East

That acknowledgment was to be postponed for two and a half decades because of the unforeseen outbreak of hostilities on the Korean peninsula in the summer of 1950, which eventually brought the military forces of Communist China and the United States into armed conflict. We have already noted the ways in which postwar Korea resembled postwar Germany: Temporarily partitioning the country along the 38th parallel of latitude into a northern Soviet zone and a southern American zone, the two superpowers failed to reach agreement on the conditions of reunification and thereupon permitted the establishment in their respective zones of a government that claimed sovereignty over the entire country. In August 1948, after free elections conducted under the supervision of the United Nations, the Republic of Korea was formed in the south with Seoul as its capital and the conservative anti-Communist Syngman Rhee as its president. In the following September a People's Democratic Republic of Korea was established in the northern city of Pyongyang under the leadership of the revolutionary Communist militant Kim Il Sung. But whereas the mutual disengagement of Soviet and American military power from divided Germany proved to be an impossible goal, the two superpowers had little difficulty in withdrawing from divided Korea, the Russians by December 1948 and the Americans by June 1949. But what they left behind was a bubbling cauldron of political instability: two separate

* London's hasty recognition of the People's Republic appears to have been prompted by concern about the status of the British crown colony of Hong Kong, a coastal showcase of Western capitalism that was tolerated by Beijing because of its value as a "window" to the non-Communist world. On Hong Kong's future status, see page 472.

Korean governments, each armed and supplied by one of the two contestants in the Cold War, each claiming authority over the territory ruled by the other.

On the early morning of June 25, 1950, this unstable political situation on the Korean peninsula boiled over into war when more than 100,000 North Korean troops launched a surprise attack across the 38th parallel against South Korea. Profiting from their numerical superiority and the element of surprise, the North Korean forces hurled back the South Korean army, capturing the capital city of Seoul on June 27. On the same day the United Nations Security Council, meeting in the absence of the Soviet delegate (who had been boycotting its sessions since January 1950 in protest against the refusal of the United Nations to assign the Chinese seat to the newly established Communist regime in Beijing), adopted an American-sponsored resolution that requested all member states "to provide the Republic of Korea with all necessary aid to repel the aggressors." Even before the adoption of this resolution, President Truman had instructed the commander of the American occupation forces in Japan, General Douglas MacArthur, to furnish naval and air support to a South Korean army that was reeling in disarray from the North Korean onslaught. On June 29, in the face of an imminent South Korean collapse, he ordered the transfer of two American infantry divisions from Japan to Korea. On July 4 the Security Council, still in the absence of the Soviet delegate, established a United Nations expeditionary force for deployment in Korea, which the following day was placed under MacArthur's command with instructions "to repel the armed attack and to restore international peace and security." By the middle of September twenty member states had contributed token ground forces to the United Nations army. But the United States troops stationed in Japan bore the main brunt of the fighting, accounting for half of the ground forces (compared to 40 percent contributed by South Korea), 86 percent of the naval forces, and 93 percent of the air forces.

It is evident from his remarks at the time that President Truman's decision to intervene militarily in Korea was prompted by his conviction that the North Korean attack was a Soviet-inspired probe of Western resolve in Asia similar to those in Europe that had given rise to the American doctrine of containment. "This is the Greece of the Far East," he announced to reporters on June 25 as he pointed to the Korean peninsula on a large globe in his office. "If we are tough enough now, there won't be any next step." The evidence for Soviet collusion in, if not inspiration for, the North Korean aggression is circumstantial but compelling: The North Korean leader, Kim Il Sung, had lived in Russia for years, had returned to his country in the company of the Soviet liberation army in 1945, and had been installed in power three years later on the express orders of Stalin. Russian military advisers were attached to the North

Korean army down to the battalion level. It was therefore inconceivable that the Pyongyang regime could have planned and executed the attack on South Korea without the prior approval of the Kremlin.

Stalin's motives for endorsing the North Korean action are less clear. But the prospect of a speedy victory at minimal cost for his Asian client state over the outmanned, underequipped South Korean army must have represented a nearly irresistible temptation to the Soviet leader. The lure of South Korea's warm water ports after Moscow's pledge to restore Port Arthur and Dairen to China by 1952 may well have influenced Stalin's decision to give North Korea the green light. In any case, he had no reason to suspect that the United States would interfere with the Pyongyang regime's bid to unify the Korean peninsula under its auspices. On the contrary, in a highly publicized speech before the National Press Club in Washington on January 12, 1950, Secretary of State Dean Acheson had specifically refrained from including South Korea within America's "military defense perimeter" in the Far East.

The swift and massive intervention of the American-dominated United Nations army in Korea appears to have caught the Kremlin entirely off guard. Its failure to wield its veto in the Security Council to prevent the authorization for such an action can only be regarded as a serious blunder with unfortunate consequences for its North Korean protégés. By September 15 the North Korean forces had conquered practically the entire peninsula, driving the demoralized South Korean army into a small corner around the port of Pusan on the southern coast. But on the same day MacArthur's UN force executed a successful amphibious landing behind enemy lines at Inchon, the port of Seoul. Within two weeks MacArthur's troops had driven the North Korean army all the way north to the 38th parallel, killing or capturing half of its soldiers in the process. The daring debarkation at Inchon, and the prompt liberation of South Korea that followed it, had fulfilled the United Nations mandate to "repel the armed attack" by restoring the military *status quo ante*. The accompanying instructions to "restore international peace and security" seemed to suggest as the next step the opening of negotiations with North Korea with a view toward securing its pledge to respect the sovereignty and security of its southern neighbor.

But the disorganized retreat of the North Korean invasion force presented the Truman administration with an opportunity too tempting to pass up: that of forcibly reunifying the peninsula by erasing the artificial dividing line that neither Korean regime had ever accepted as permanent and that had never been recognized by the United Nations. In pursuit of this objective, the United States pushed through the General Assembly of the United Nations on October 7 a resolution authorizing MacArthur to "take all appropriate measures to insure a stable situation in the whole of Korea." Acting on the authority of this resolution, which technically lacked the force of law because it had emanated from the General Assembly rather than the Security Council,* MacArthur ordered his troops to cross the 38th parallel into North Korea on October 9. Within three weeks they had captured the northern capital of Pyongyang and were approaching the Yalu River on the Chinese border.

The extension of the war to North Korea in the autumn of 1950 inevitably raised the question of Communist China's attitude toward the bloody conflict that was raging across its Manchurian frontier. Excluded from membership in the United Nations by the American veto and elbowed out of North Korea by the Soviet Union, Beijing had taken no part in the flurry of diplomatic activity during the early stages of the war. But even before the ominous advance of MacArthur's forces toward Manchuria, the United States government had taken a decisive step that was guaranteed to provoke a hostile response from the new Communist government on the mainland. This was the decision taken by President Truman on the evening of June 26, 1950, to interpose the American Seventh Fleet between China and the island of Formosa, where the battered armies of Chiang Kai-shek had reassembled after their expulsion from the mainland. The interposition of American naval power in the Formosa Strait was undertaken for an entirely precautionary reason and in a scrupulously evenhanded manner: It was ostensibly designed to prevent mainland China and the Nationalist Chinese on its wayward island province from further complicating the unstable situation in the western Pacific by renewing their own bitter conflict. But to the regime in Beijing this American action appeared as a flagrant intervention in the Chinese civil war that effectively prevented the victors from consolidating their triumph. Beijing's suspicions of Washington's motives were hardly allayed by MacArthur's provocative and highly publicized visit to Chiang on July 31, particularly in view of the Nationalist strongman's previous offer to contribute thirty-three thousand soldiers to the crusade against the Communists in Korea.

It was MacArthur's counteroffensive deep into North Korea and his rapid advance toward the Manchurian frontier that finally spurred Beijing into action. On October 2, Chinese Premier Zhou Enlai warned the United States through an intermediary that if American forces crossed the 38th parallel, China might well be obliged to intervene in defense of its vital interests. When that warning was ignored by Washington, almost 200,000 Chinese "volunteers" crossed the Yalu River into North Korea during the month of October, traveling stealthily at night to avoid detection by the United Nations forces that were advancing northward. After a series of inconclusive engagements with MacArthur's troops, the Chinese attacked

---

* The General Assembly possesses no decision-making power, according to the UN Charter. Once the Soviet Union, realizing its error in boycotting the Security Council, resumed its seat on August 1 it was in a position to veto any resolution presented to that body. Hence, the United States was driven to endow the General Assembly with an authority it did not legally possess.

along a broad front on November 26, forcing a United Nations retreat southward. By the end of the year the counterattacking Chinese and North Korean forces had crossed the 38th parallel and on January 4, 1951, the southern capital of Seoul fell for the second time to the northern invaders.

The Truman administration was confronted with the equally unattractive alternatives of waging a protracted ground war on the Korean peninsula or of adopting MacArthur's strategy of extending the conflict to China itself by bombing the Manchurian sanctuary. Anticipating that the latter course would risk escalation of this regional conflict into a world war in view of China's alliance with the Soviet Union, Truman decided in early March to confine UN military operations to Korea while simultaneously pursuing a negotiated settlement that would restore the political partition of the peninsula at the 38th parallel. By the beginning of April the United Nations troops had halted the Communists' spring offensive and counterattacked once again into North Korea. MacArthur thereupon issued on his own authority a provocative proclamation that in effect presented Beijing with the ultimatum of accepting an armistice at the parallel or enduring attacks on its own territory across the Yalu. On April 5 the Republican leader of the House of Representatives caused a sensation by publishing a letter from MacArthur dated March 20 that revived the prospect of employing Nationalist Chinese troops in Korea and advocated total victory in the war. Stung by this egregious challenge to his presidential authority by his independent-minded proconsul in Asia, Truman abruptly dismissed MacArthur for insubordination on April 11 and replaced him with General Matthew B. Ridgway.

The removal of MacArthur and the repudiation of his bellicose recommendations by Washington cleared the way for the pursuit of a negotiated settlement to the war in Korea. Both the United States and the Soviet Union had been brought to the realization that the risk of escalation was too great to allow it to continue without serious efforts to bring peace to the peninsula. On June 25 Truman accepted a Soviet suggestion for a ceasefire and the beginning of armistice discussions. The first meeting between representatives of the United Nations and the Communist commands took place on July 9, 1951. These talks dragged on intermittently for two more years until an armistice was finally signed on July 6, 1953, at the tiny farm village of Panmunjom near the 38th parallel. It provided for a demilitarized zone along the redrawn frontier separating the two Korean states and a joint UN-Communist military armistice commission to meet periodically for the purpose of resolving matters in dispute. The new boundary line gained South Korea fifteen hundred square miles of territory, a paltry reward for a three-year conflict that cost a million South Korean, a million North Korean and Chinese, and thirty-three thousand American lives.

The importance of the Korean War as a catalyst of rearmament and remobilization in Western Europe has already been remarked upon. No less dramatic were its effects on the political and military situation in the Far East. What had begun as a regional conflict between rival Korean contenders for sovereignty on the peninsula had ended in the extension of the Cold War into the entire area of East Asia and the western Pacific. The United States, confronted by what it viewed as a calculated bid by a monolithic Communist bloc to expand into the power vacuum of an Asia recently liberated from Japanese domination, hastened to reengage its power there by extending military protection and economic assistance to the non-Communist states of the region just as it had done to the non-Communist states of Europe in the previous decade.

The retention of American military forces in South Korea and the conclusion of a mutual security agreement with that country, which pledged American armed intervention in its defense, was merely one of a number of similar commitments that were undertaken in the early fifties. During the Korean emergency in 1951 the United States concluded in rapid succession military agreements with island nations in the westen Pacific to bolster their security in the face of the presumed menace of Communist aggression. On August 30 a treaty with the Philippines (which had gained independence from the United States in 1946) reaffirmed American air and naval base rights in that country, which had been granted in March 1947, and committed the United States to its defense. On September 1 Washington concluded a tripartite security treaty with Australia and New Zealand (the ANZUS Pact), thereby replacing Great Britain as the protector of those two transplanted European states in the Pacific.

But the most important addition to the American-sponsored East Asian security system that was being formed in the autumn of 1951 was to be the country whose aggressive acts had brought the United States into the Far Eastern war a decade earlier. The American military occupation of Japan, like the American military occupation of Germany, had originally been established for the purpose of preventing the vanquished power from ever again threatening the security of its neighbors. This meant the total demilitarization of the country, the abolition of all nationalistic societies, the purging of public officials and business leaders who had cooperated with the military authorities in planning and waging the recent war, and the dissolution of the large industrial conglomerates that had promoted and profited from the seizure of the markets and resources of the "Co-Prosperity Sphere" in East Asia. It also meant the imposition of restraints on Japan's economic recovery and the supervision of reparation payments to those countries in the Far East that had endured the painful consequences of Japanese conquest. The imperious commander of the American military occupation regime in Japan, General Douglas MacArthur, instructed his staff to draft a new constitution for the country, which went into effect on May 3, 1947. It established a parliamentary form of government on the British model, safeguarded civil liberties, and included a provision renouncing war as well as the maintenance of land, sea, and air forces. But the Soviet-American confrontation in Europe at the end of the 1940s prompted the Truman administration to reconsider and eventually to reverse its stern occupation policy in Asia for fear that an economically weak, militarily vulnerable Japan would become a tempting target for Soviet intimidation once the American occupation forces had been withdrawn. Thus in 1948–49 the United States removed all restrictions on Japan's economic recovery, halted the requisition of capital equipment for reparations, abandoned plans for the forced decentralization of Japanese industry, and began to furnish financial assistance to promote Japan's economic growth and social stability.

The outbreak of the Korean War accelerated the transformation of Japan from impoverished enemy to prosperous ally by demonstrating that country's value to the United States as a counterweight to Soviet and Communist Chinese power in the Far East. American military procurement expenditures during the war stimulated an economic boom in Japan that by the mid-fifties was to bring its people the highest standard of living in Asia. Capital investment and technology transfers from the United States increased sharply, enabling Japanese industry to replace its war-damaged equipment with the most up-to-date machinery. Japan's export trade rapidly recovered, first in textiles and other light industries, and later in advanced sectors such as electronics, automobiles, and shipbuilding. The spectacular economic revival sparked by the Korean War was accompanied by an expansion of Japan's defense capabilities. In the summer of 1950 the government in Tokyo secured American authorization to create a 75,000-member National Police Reserve to replace the American occupation troops that were being redeployed in Korea. A rudimentary Japanese navy was created in August 1952 to ensure coastal defense. In February 1954 the existing ground and naval forces were expanded and a small air force was brought into being. All of these were designated as "self-defense" forces in deference to the constitutional renunciation of war and the means of waging it. But whatever their euphemistic designation, they collectively constituted the nucleus of Japan's rearmament during a period when the Cold War was being extended to Asia.

The rearmament and economic recovery of Japan during and after the Korean War transpired behind the protective shield of the United States, which hastened to terminate Japan's status as occupied enemy and restore it to full political sovereignty. On September 8, 1951, the United States and forty-eight other nations (excluding the Soviet Union and China) signed a peace treaty with Japan in San Francisco, which ended the state of war and brought the American occupation to an end on April 28, 1952. On the same day the treaty was signed, Washington and Tokyo concluded a security pact providing for the indefinite retention of American military forces in Japan as well as the maintenance of a major base under direct American administration on the Japanese island of Okinawa. Thus the former enemy Japan, like the former enemy Germany at the other end of the Eurasian land mass, had come to be regarded by the United States as an indispensable asset in its campaign to contain the global expansion of Soviet power.

A similar function was soon to be fulfilled by the outpost of the anti-Communist Nationalist Chinese on the island of Formosa. In the course of the Korean conflict, the United States had abandoned its evenhanded policy toward both sides in the Chinese civil war by resuming the deliveries of economic and military assistance to Chiang's government in exile that had been discontinued in the final stage of the Nationalist collapse on the mainland. Throughout the 1950s this American assistance to Taiwan averaged $250 million per year. In early 1953 President Eisenhower announced that the Seventh Fleet, which continued to patrol the Formosa Strait, would no longer interfere with Chiang's efforts to "liberate" the mainland from Communist rule. In time Nationalist bombing raids were conducted against the Chinese coast and commandos were dispatched to the mainland. On December 2, 1954, the United States concluded a mutual defense treaty with Taiwan (which continued to be recognized by most non-Communist countries as the "Republic of China" and retained the Chinese seat in the United Nations). In 1955 the United States Congress voted by large majorities to authorize the president to commit American military forces to the defense of the island. When China in 1954–55 and again in 1958 shelled Quemoy and Matsu, two small islands a few miles off its coast that had been occupied by Nationalist troops and used for commando raids against the mainland, the United States pledged to defend the islands by force. Throughout the 1950s Washington enforced a trade embargo on mainland China and forbade American citizens to travel to that country. The exotic land that had once exercised such an irresistible attraction for American merchants in search of markets and American missionaries in search of converts abruptly disappeared from the public consciousness of the United States.

Russia and China: From Partnership to Rivalry

All of these measures understandably poisoned Sino-American relations and forestalled the rapprochement between Beijing and Washington that may have been a fleeting possibility during the brief interlude between the Communist victory on the mainland and the outbreak of the Korean War. In the meantime Moscow and Beijing drew closer together in the face of what they jointly viewed as Washington's attempt to erect an anti-Communist bastion in Asia composed of nations armed, assisted, and protected by the United States. The American-sponsored rehabilitation of Japan, the former enemy of Russia and China that had risen to power at their expense, was a special source of common concern. Though prohibited by its own constitution from ever again becoming a military power of the first rank, Japan's security pact with the United States, its willingness to host American bases on its national territory, and its rapid progress toward economic recovery raised fears in the Communist-controlled portion of East Asia similar to those simultaneously engendered in Eastern Europe by the revival of an economically powerful West Germany supported by the United States.

The Sino-Soviet partnership that matured during the first half of the 1950s took the form of Russian economic and diplomatic support for China in exchange for Beijing's continued recognition of Moscow's undisputed authority in the world Communist movement. The Soviet Union had supplied China with roughly $2 billion worth of military equipment during its undeclared war in Korea. Thereafter, by the terms of an agreement concluded by the two governments in September 1953, Soviet economic aid and technical advisers poured into China to assist that country in its crash program of industrialization. By the middle of the decade the Soviet Union had become China's principal trading partner, taking about half of its exports. On October 11, 1954, Moscow removed the last vestiges of Russian imperialism in China by pledging to evacuate the Soviet naval base at Port Arthur by the end of 1955* and transferring to Beijing the Soviet share of the joint-stock companies that had been formed in 1950 to exploit Xinjiang's mineral resources. The Russians also consented to a long-term development loan of $250 million and promised to assist the Chinese in a number of industrial projects. In the meantime the Soviet Union led the unsuccessful campaign in the United Nations to transfer the Chinese seat from the "Kuomintang clique on Formosa" to the Communist regime on the mainland and strongly supported China's claim to sovereignty over the island. This strengthening of bilateral ties between the two giants of the Communist bloc confirmed American fears of a monolithic Communist conspiracy to conquer the world, fears that were aggravated by the spread of McCarthyite hysteria in the United States during the same period.

But as American Cassandras bemoaned the "loss of China," the "nowin policy in Korea," and the rising tide of Communism in Asia, cracks were already evident in the supposedly sturdy edifice of Sino-Soviet friendship. As already noted, China drew close to the Soviet Union during the first half of the fifties because it needed Russian economic aid for its industrialization and Moscow's diplomatic support in its disputes with hostile neighbors, particularly the American-backed Nationalist regime on Taiwan. Throughout the entire period of the Soviet economic assistance program, however, the authorities in Beijing were disappointed with the amount furnished and the strings attached. The military aid during the Korean conflict had to be repaid in full at a time when China was struggling to recover from the effects of its civil war and launch its industrial takeoff. The economic aid that was forthcoming thereafter fell far short of

---

* The Russian withdrawal from Port Arthur, which had been scheduled to take place in 1952, was postponed by joint agreement because of the Korean War.

Chinese expectations. Once Khrushchev mounted his campaign to extend Soviet influence in the nonaligned countries of the Third World in 1955, Russia was supplying more development assistance to non-Communist states such as India and Egypt than to its Communist neighbor in Asia. Similarly, Soviet support for China's military preparedness was half-hearted and always tendered on the condition of Beijing's absolute sub-servience to Moscow. On October 15, 1957, Khrushchev had secretly agreed to furnish a modest amount of aid to the Chinese nuclear program that was about to get underway and offered to supply China with a pro-totype of an atomic bomb provided that Beijing consent to joint coordina-tion of foreign policy and Soviet control of Chinese nuclear warheads. After two years of fruitless efforts to obtain Mao's consent to these in-fringements on China's freedom of action, Khrushchev unilaterally can-celled the atomic agreement with Beijing in June 1959.

These disagreements and disappointments over the quantity and charac-ter of Soviet aid to China transpired against the background of a growing ideological dispute between Moscow and Beijing during the second half of the 1950s. The sources of this friction within the Communist world was Mao's insistence on reaffirming the orthodox Leninist belief in the inevita-bility of war with the capitalist powers at a time when Khrushchev, fearful of the consequences of a nuclear exchange for his own country, was pur-suing peaceful coexistence with the West in the form of arms control nego-tiations and summit meetings with "enemy" leaders. China's mounting dissatisfaction with the Soviet Union's "revisionist" pursuit of an accom-modation with the capitalist world stemmed less from a divergence of opinion regarding interpretations of Communist ideology than from a more practical concern involving Chinese national interests: Economically un-developed, militarily weak, diplomatically isolated, China was dependent on Soviet support for its security in East Asia. Thus each time Russian and American chiefs of state met face-to-face, in Geneva in 1955, at Camp David in 1959, in Paris (however briefly) in 1960, Beijing feared a rap-prochement between the superpowers that would leave China exposed to the threats to its sovereignty and territorial integrity that emanated from its unfriendly neighbors.

The most serious of these threats continued to come from the Nation-alist regime on Taiwan. In May 1957 Chiang Kai-shek had concluded an agreement with Washington for the installation on Formosa of Matador missiles armed with nuclear warheads that were capable of reaching the Chinese mainland. In the meantime Chiang continued to fortify the coastal islands of Quemoy and Matsu and increased to almost 100,000 the num-ber of Nationalist troops stationed there. When China resumed its heavy shelling of Quemoy in August 1958 as part of its campaign to dislodge the Nationalists from their island fortress five miles from the mainland, Presi-dent Eisenhower ordered American planes to airlift supplies to Chiang's troops and arranged for ships from the American Seventh Fleet to escort a Nationalist convoy to the beleaguered island. The State Department issued a veiled threat of an American military intervention should China seek to recapture Quemoy and Matsu. At the height of the Quemoy crisis, Beijing was displeased to note an official Russian silence instead of the customary expressions of support, a silence that was broken only after China had agreed to participate in direct negotiations with representatives of the United States at Warsaw to seek a peaceful solution to the crisis.

In the following year, Khrushchev's meeting with Eisenhower at Camp David reignited Chinese fears of a Soviet-American accommodation at their expense. This suspicion was not allayed by Khrushchev when, returning from his American tour via Beijing, he publicly warned Mao to avoid a confrontation with the United States over Taiwan. This admonition on behalf of peaceful coexistence, coming as it did three months after the Soviet leader had rescinded his pledge to help the Chinese develop a nuclear armament and only a few days after his cordial tête-à-tête with Eisenhower, brought into question the value of Russian support for China's grievances against the American-backed regime across the Taiwan Strait. It was apparent that Khrushchev had left Camp David with the expectation of a prompt and amicable settlement of the Berlin issue, which could pave the way for a mutual recognition of the European status quo, and was not prepared to allow Sino-American tensions in the Far East to interfere with that development.

A simultaneous source of Sino-Soviet friction as the 1950s drew to a close was the conflict between China and India over Tibet, once a Chinese province that since 1914 had enjoyed de facto independence under its divine ruler, the Dalai Lama, until in 1950 it was forcibly restored to Chinese sovereignty by the new Communist regime. During the spring of 1959, China ruthlessly quelled an armed insurrection in favor of Tibetan independence and accused India, which had given sanctuary to the Dalai Lama and his entourage, of having fomented it. Sino-Indian border clashes were accompanied by conflicting territorial claims along the rugged Himalayan frontier. Suddenly in September 1959, as Khrushchev prepared for his American visit, Moscow infuriated Beijing by declaring its neutrality in the Sino-Indian dispute and then announcing its intention to grant New Delhi a loan much larger than any that had ever been furnished to its Communist ally in Asia. Just as Khrushchev had placed a higher priority on reaching agreement with the West over Berlin and Europe than on supporting China at the Taiwan Strait, he was apparently willing to sacrifice China's security in the Himalayas in the interests of cultivating closer relations with India, the titular leader of the nonaligned states of the Third World.

The Sino-Soviet quarrel first became public, albeit in disguised form, at the Third Congress of the Romanian Communist party in June 1960. Responding to Khrushchev's defense of the policy of peaceful coexistence and his implicit criticism of the Maoist claim that war with the capitalist states was both inevitable and winnable, the Chinese delegate asserted that the recent U-2 incident and the breakup of the Paris summit meeting (to which China had not been invited) revealed the evil nature of imperialism and indirectly chided the Kremlin for attempting to coexist with it. This seemingly fraternal debate over the proper interpretation of Communist doctrine was soon followed up by direct action: Three months later, in August 1960, Khrushchev abruptly recalled the 1,390 Russian technicians who had been dispatched to China to assist in its economic modernization, ordering them to return with their industrial blueprints. At the conference of world Communist parties in Moscow in November 1960, the Chinese delegation, joined by the Albanians, assailed the Soviet Union for betraying the cause of world revolution. The Kremlin retaliated against this challenge to its authority in typically indirect fashion by striking at China's only supporter in the Communist bloc: In April Khrushchev ordered the termination of all Soviet economic assistance and the withdrawal of all Soviet technicians from Albania.

The deterioration of relations between the two states remained an internal affair within the Communist bloc until the autumn of 1962, when the simultaneous outbreak of three unrelated crises strained the Sino-Soviet relationship to the breaking point. The outcome of the Soviet-American showdown over Cuba precipitated an outburst of criticism from Beijing, which in March 1963 denounced the Soviet Union's humiliating retreat before the imperialist aggressor. The Partial Nuclear Test Ban Treaty signed by the two superpowers and Great Britain in August 1963 was assailed by Mao as an attempt by the nuclear powers to frustrate the efforts of countries such as China to provide for their own defense. Refusing to sign the treaty, China proceeded to explode its first atomic bomb without Soviet assistance on October 16, 1964 (coincidentally within a few hours of Khrushchev's fall from power in the Kremlin).

The second source of conflict between Moscow and Beijing was the renewal of hostilities between China and India along their common frontier in the Himalayas at the height of the Cuban missile crisis in October 1962. India had disclosed the previous August the conclusion of an agreement whereby the Soviet Union had promised engines for Indian jet planes. During the border skirmish the Kremlin again took pains to affirm its absolute neutrality, brushing aside Beijing's attempts to secure a Soviet endorsement of its position. On February 27, 1963, the Chinese Communist party publicly denounced the Soviet Union for furnishing military assistance to its enemy India after having terminated its aid to China in 1960.

The third occasion of Sino-Soviet tension was potentially the most ominous of all: a border dispute between the two Communist powers themselves in China's northwestern province of Xinjiang, which had formerly been within the Russian sphere of interest. Little is known about this initial frontier clash, but it marked the beginning of China's assertion

of territorial claims against the Soviet Union, which had retained possession of almost a million square miles of former Chinese territory in central
Asia and the maritime provinces of Siberia that had been forcibly acquired by the tsars under treaties imposed on imperial China in 1858,
1860, and 1881. As the problem of overpopulation began to be recognized
as a serious impediment to China's hopes for rapid industrialization in the
course of the 1960s, the sparsely inhabited spaces of the former Chinese
domains in the Soviet Far East exerted an understandable attraction on
the economic modernizers in Beijing.

By the end of 1964 the Sino-Soviet rift had become embarrassingly
public and apparently irreversible. China's entry into the nuclear club as
its first nonwhite member in October of that year had given a tremendous
boost to its prestige in the Third World, where it was by then avidly
competing with the Soviet Union for influence. Within the international
Communist movement, pro-Chinese factions had broken away from the
regular Communist parties and professed a more radical brand of Marxist-
Leninism in practically every country in the world. Though no other Soviet
satellite in Eastern Europe followed Albania's lead in repudiating Moscow's authority and transferring its allegiance to Beijing, the Chinese defection presented the other satellites with the opportunity to pursue a
more independent course by playing off the two Communist giants against
one another. The two most notable East European beneficiaries of this
polycentrist trend within the Communist camp were Romania and Czechoslovakia. Romania refused the role of agricultural and petrochemical producer assigned to it by the Eastern bloc's economic organization, Comecon, in 1962, as we have seen, and expanded its trade with the West to
more than a third of its total. It also pursued an increasingly independent
foreign policy, establishing diplomatic relations with West Germany and
retaining them with Israel in 1967 in violation of Eastern bloc policy.
Czechoslovakia during the first half of 1968 experimented with various
forms of economic liberalism and political democracy that contradicted
the basic tenets of Communist doctrine.

Romania's assertion of independence was tolerated by Moscow because
the government of Nicolai Ceausescu in Bucharest maintained a harshly
repressive political system that spared the Kremlin what it feared most:
the proliferation of liberal ideas that could infect Romania's partners in
the Warsaw Pact. It was the failure of the government of Alexander Dubček
in Czechoslovakia to keep the lid on domestic dissent during the "Prague
spring" of 1968 that precipitated the Soviet-led invasion of that country
the following August and the termination of its brief flirtation with liberal
communism and national independence. The Soviet intervention in Czechoslovakia predictably prompted a torrent of invective from Beijing against
this blatant interference in the domestic affairs of a sovereign Communist
state. So did the enunciation by the Soviet first secretary in November
1968 of the Brezhnev Doctrine, which justified intervention by Commu-

nist bloc forces in any Communist country threatened by internal or external elements "hostile to socialism." Though ostensibly directed at the Soviet satellites in Eastern Europe, this assertion of the right of intervention (or the "Doctrine of Limited Sovereignty," as it was euphemistically called) could easily have been interpreted as a veiled threat to China, then in the midst of a domestic "cultural revolution" with unmistakable anti-Soviet overtones.

From the vantage point of global power politics, the Sino-Soviet quarrel in the 1960s afforded the United States a rare opportunity: By playing off the two rivals for leadership in the Communist camp against one another, as Romania was doing with remarkable success within the limited context of its own special circumstances, Washington might have been in a position to exploit to its own advantage the divisions within the formerly monolithic Communist bloc. Instead, just as the divergence between China and the Soviet Union was approaching the breaking point in the middle of the decade, the United States became deeply involved, for the second time since World War II, in a military operation in Asia that temporarily reunited the entire Communist world against it.

The United States and Indochina

Between 1862 and 1897 France had established political control over the region of southeastern Asia known as Indochina (today's Vietnam, Laos, and Cambodia). As was frequently the case in late nineteenth-century imperial expansion, the motives for the French colonization of this distant land were mixed. Commercial interests were attracted by the valuable raw materials of the region—rubber, tin, tungsten, and rice—which could be shipped to European markets. Catholic missionaries flocked to this outpost of empire on the other side of the earth in search of converts. Military and naval officials envisioned garrisons and bases that would enable France to challenge Great Britain's preeminence in the Far East. Indigenous resistance to French domination developed after the First World War under the leadership of a charismatic nationalist leader widely known by the pseudonym Ho Chi Minh. In 1919 Ho appeared at the Paris Peace Conference to press for the application of the Wilsonian principle of self-determination, currently being invoked on behalf of the former subjects of the Austro-Hungarian Empire in Europe, to the Indochinese victims of French colonial domination in Asia. Upon learning that the Wilsonian principle of liberal nationalism was to be restricted to white European peoples, the disappointed Vietnamese nationalist turned to the only alternative ideology that appeared to offer the promise of national liberation for his compatriots. In 1920 he became a founding member of the French Communist party, traveling to Moscow to receive instruction in the techniques of revolutionary agitation, and in 1930 he formed the Vietnamese Communist party. After the fall of France in 1940 and the Japanese oc-

cupation of Indochina with the tacit consent of the Vichy French adminis-
tration, Ho organized in China a League for the Independence of Vietnam,
or Vietminh, a coalition of nationalist groups led by the Communist party.
In cooperation with the American intelligence organization, the Office of
Strategic Services (forerunner of the Central Intelligence Agency), the
Vietminh spearheaded the underground resistance to the Japanese occupation. At the end of the war in the Far East, Ho appealed to the United
States government to support the independence of his country on the basis
of the neo-Wilsonian principles of national self-determination incorporated in the Atlantic Charter and reaffirmed in many of President Roosevelt's wartime pronouncements. In September 1945, following the surrender of Japan and the evacuation of its occupation forces from the Asian
mainland, the Vietminh formally declared the independence of the Democratic Republic of Vietnam and established its capital in the northern city
of Hanoi. But Great Britain, whose military forces had temporarily occupied
the southern portion of the country, permitted French troops to reenter
the zone under its jurisdiction. Throughout 1946, Vietminh efforts to negotiate national independence within the French empire (renamed the
French Union in October of the same year) along the lines of the self-
governing Dominions of the British Commonwealth foundered on the unwillingness of France to relinquish sovereignty. In November 1946, after
the refusal of the Vietminh to obey a French order to evacuate Hanoi and
its port of Haiphong, the French military and naval forces in the vicinity
bombarded the two cities, causing six thousand casualties. The Vietminh
responded by taking to the countryside, organizing a guerrilla movement
modeled on that of Mao Zedong's in northern China, and engaging the
French army in a full-fledged war of national liberation.

The policy of the United States toward the Franco-Vietnamese conflict
underwent a profound transformation during the second half of the 1940s.
Toward the end of the Second World War President Roosevelt, who was
personally opposed to the restoration of European colonial power in Asia
after the war, toyed with the idea of placing Indochina under international
trusteeship as a means of removing French authority from the region and
preparing its constituent states for independence. Some historians have attributed Roosevelt's anticolonialist inclinations to his eagerness to thrust
open the European possessions in Southeast Asia to American economic
penetration. Others credit the American chief of state with a genuine desire to apply the progressive principles of the Atlantic Charter to the postwar world. In any event, the Truman administration turned a deaf ear to
Ho Chi Minh's postwar appeals for American economic assistance and
diplomatic support for the political independence of his country. Ho's
Communist affiliations became a matter of great concern in Washington as
the Soviet-American wartime partnership degenerated into the Cold War,
despite the fact that Moscow had given little support or encouragement to
the Vietminh. The victory of Mao Zedong's Communist faction in the Chi-

nese civil war in 1949 left the impression in Washington that all of Asia was under the threat of a coordinated Communist advance masterminded by Moscow. France shrewdly played upon these American fears, arguing that its military operation in Vietnam, which shared a common border with newly communized China, represented the Far Eastern counterpart to the containment policy that the United States and its Western partners were currently pursuing in Europe.

The first formal expression of American support for France's effort to retain its colonial authority in Indochina came in February 1950. Following the diplomatic recognition of Ho Chi Minh's government by China and the Soviet Union in January, Washington established formal diplomatic relations with the puppet regime of Emperor Bao Dai in Saigon that had been established by the French in the previous year as a nominally independent state (along with Laos and Cambodia) within the French Union. But it was the outbreak of the Korean War in June 1950 that prompted the United States to intervene actively on behalf of the French against the Communist-led insurgency in Indochina. In the following autumn a team of American military advisers and $150 million in military equipment were dispatched to Vietnam to assist the French effort there.

By 1954 the United States was paying 78 percent of the costs of the French military operations and had over three hundred military advisers on the spot. By the spring of that year, in spite of the increase in American support for the French forces, the Vietminh had gained effective control of the countryside through daring guerrilla tactics borrowed from the teachings of Mao Zedong. The French military commander, General Henri Navarre, concluded that the only hope of crushing the enemy, who struck from ambush only to disappear into the jungles, lay in luring him out into the open to fight a conventional war that the French, with their superiority in artillery and air power, fully expected to win. Accordingly, the French deployed eighteen thousand of their best troops in the fortress of Dien Bien Phu on the Laotian border in the hope of engaging the Vietminh in a fight to the finish on open terrain. A fight to the finish it was, after a fifty-five day siege of the fortress, but it was the French army that was finished. Employing artillery furnished by the Chinese to shell the beleaguered French ground troops from the hills surrounding their self-made trap, and using Chinese antiaircraft guns to neutralize French air power, the Vietminh killed over seven thousand French soldiers at Dien Bien Phu and captured the remaining eleven thousand on May 7.

During the siege of Dien Bien Phu, on April 26, the conference of the Big Four (the United States, the Soviet Union, Great Britain, and France) that had been meeting in Geneva to discuss German affairs was authorized to open negotiations for a ceasefire in Indochina, to which the governments of the three Associated States of Indochina and China were invited. By a tragic coincidence (from the French perspective), the talks on Indochina began on May 8, the day after the fall of Dien Bien Phu. The United

States had consented to participate in the Geneva conference in the hope of reaching a settlement that would preserve the non-Communist character of Indochina, with or without a continuing French presence there. In a press conference on April 7 President Eisenhower had compared the situation in Southeast Asia to a line of dominoes: If Indochina were to fall to a Communist insurrection, the remainder of non-Communist Asia, as well as America's extensive security interests in the region, would be gravely threatened. But opinion polls and expressions of Congressional sentiment clearly revealed the absence of public support for an American military intervention to rescue the embattled French. Requests from Paris for the use of B-29 American bombers based in the Philippines, though endorsed by the chairman of the Joint Chiefs of Staff, the vice president, and the secretary of state, were turned down by President Eisenhower in the face of Congressional opposition and in the absence of British approval for such a rescue operation. Ironically, in light of subsequent events, one of the most outspoken opponents of an American intervention in Vietnam was the Democratic leader in the Senate, Lyndon Baines Johnson.

The surrender of Dien Bien Phu dashed France's hopes of negotiating a settlement in Indochina from a position of strength, especially once American air support had been ruled out. The final blow to France's imperial position in Southeast Asia came in mid-June when the Laniel government in Paris was replaced by one headed by Pierre Mendès-France, a longtime critic of the war who took office on the basis of a pledge to obtain a cease-fire within a month or resign. Acting as his own foreign minister, Mendès-France hastened to Geneva to fulfill his electoral promise. Ignoring the various factions that were jockeying for position in the Indochinese civil war, he approached directly the representatives of the powers that really counted. In conversations with Russia's Molotov and China's Zhou Enlai he worked out the basis for a settlement that would afford France the opportunity of a graceful exit from a lost cause. On July 21 the Geneva Accords terminating the eight-year war in Southeast Asia were signed and sealed: Vietnam was to be temporarily partitioned along the 17th parallel of latitude; the Vietminh would administer the northern zone; the southern zone would be governed from Saigon, where the discredited Emperor Bao Dai had been replaced a month earlier by an American-educated Catholic mandarin named Ngo Dinh Diem. Neither sector was to sign military alliances, permit foreign bases on its territory, or receive military assistance from abroad. Within two years the entire country was to be reunified on the basis of general elections conducted by secret ballot under the supervision of a United Nations Control Commission. The sovereignty of the royalist governments of Laos and Cambodia was formally recognized by all signatories.

The Geneva Accords concluded France's colonial adventure in Indochina that had begun under Napoleon III in the 1860s. But they did not ratify the independence of Vietnam under the auspices of the Vietminh.

Ho Chi Minh had been persuaded by his Soviet and Chinese patrons to surrender roughly 20 percent of the territory that he controlled to an anti-Communist, American-backed regime in Saigon and to accept the temporary partition of his country. Why did Moscow and Beijing induce a fraternal Communist movement in Vietnam to accept a diplomatic settlement that denied it the fruits of the military victory that it was about to achieve against an exhausted European colonial power? It may have been that Soviet Premier Malenkov was sufficiently alarmed by Dulles's loose talk about "massive retaliation" in January 1954 to shrink from antagonizing the United States over a region of secondary strategic interest to Russia, especially at a time when the post-Stalinist leadership in the Kremlin was avidly exploring ways of settling East–West differences in Europe. It is likewise possible that the long history of ethnic antagonism between the Chinese and Vietnamese tempered Beijing's enthusiasm for assisting in the formation of a politically unified Vietnam to its south, even one under a Communist regime.

In any case, the United States promptly signaled its determination to prevent the unification of Vietnam and to protect the royalist regimes in Cambodia and Laos against insurgencies mounted by their own indigenous Communist movements. Having declined to sign the Geneva Accords, Washington felt under no obligation to honor their prohibition against foreign military involvement in Indochina. In September 1954 Secretary of State Dulles orchestrated the formation of the South East Asia Treaty Organization (SEATO), a regional security arrangement that committed the United States and other countries to the defense of Laos and Cambodia against Communist aggression or insurgency as well as of South Vietnam against North Vietnam. By the end of 1954 Washington had replaced Paris as the anti-Communist bastion in the region. American military advisers were sent to train the South Vietnamese army while American economic assistance was supplied to the Saigon regime in ever-increasing amounts.

These egregious violations of the Geneva Accords were justified by the Eisenhower administration on the grounds that by not signing them the United States was not bound by them. Similarly, the South Vietnamese government's refusal to sign the agreement enabled it to evade the provisions for the holding of nationwide elections for the unification of the country. In the summer of 1955 Hanoi twice formally asked Saigon to designate representatives to the electoral commission envisaged by the accords. On August 9 Diem declined to do so on the grounds that such elections would be pointless as long as North Vietnam refused to grant democratic liberties to its own citizens. The United States government, convinced that the Vietminh would win all-Vietnamese elections, publicly endorsed the cancellation of the electoral provisions of the Geneva Accords. As the date for the projected elections passed in the summer of

1956, the provisional demarcation line along the 17th parallel hardened into a de facto political frontier separating two ideologically antagonistic states. By the end of the decade the 275 American military advisers attached to the South Vietnamese army at the time of the armistice had grown to 685, and about $300 million worth of military aid was flowing into Diem's coffers annually. In the meantime, the Soviet Union and China began to furnish economic and military assistance to North Vietnam.

At the time of the ceasefire in 1954, thousands of Vietminh guerrillas had remained in the southern zone in anticipation either of political victory at the polls two years later or of a renewal of the armed struggle in the absence of a politically mandated national unification. The cancellation of the elections prompted a renewal of the guerrilla campaign, which took the form of the selective assassination of officials appointed by the Saigon regime. In the meantime the corruption, nepotism, and repressive policies of the Diem government had engendered widespread discontent among non-Communist interest groups in the south. On December 20, 1960, a coalition of anti-Diem dissidents—Communist and non-Communist alike—formed a National Liberation Front dedicated to social reform, political liberalization, and neutrality for South Vietnam. Capitalizing on this indigenous discontent, Hanoi extended support to this opposition group in the south, which was contemptuously labeled "Viet Cong" (Vietnamese Communist) by Diem.

The administration of John F. Kennedy had inherited from its predecessor a commitment to help the non-Communist regimes of the former French Indochina—particularly Laos and South Vietnam—to preserve their independence from the Communist regime in Hanoi and to protect them from domestic insurgencies mounted by the indigenous Communist organizations in their midst. Landlocked Laos, granted independence from France in 1954, had been torn by civil strife for the remainder of the decade. After a bewildering succession of government changes, during which the United States furnished military assistance and advisers to various right wing factions while Moscow and Beijing backed a coalition of neutralists and the pro-Communist Pathet Lao forces, the great powers reconvened the Geneva Conference on Indochina in May 1961 to explore a solution to what the outgoing President Eisenhower had glumly described to his successor as "the Laos mess." After a year of disputatious diplomatic wrangling, the Geneva conference finally produced an agreement in June 1962 that ostensibly guaranteed the neutrality of Laos (by prohibiting it from signing alliances with, furnishing bases for, or receiving military aid from foreign powers) under the authority of a coalition government composed of the pro-Western, pro-Communist, and neutralist factions. But by late 1962 the United States had resumed shipments of arms to the coalition government in violation of the neutralization agreement; by 1964 American planes were conducting clandestine bombing raids against the Pathet Lao insurgents, which had abandoned the tripartite co-alition in power as that shaky government turned increasingly to Washing-ton for support.

The collapse of the Laos accords was inevitable because that country, which shared a long common border with Vietnam, could not remain iso-lated from the escalating level of violence that wracked the latter nation in the course of the 1960s. When President Kennedy took office in Janu-ary 1961, almost 900 American military advisers were stationed in South Vietnam to train that country's army in the techniques of conventional and counterinsurgency warfare. By the end of the year that number had in-creased to about 2,600; by the end of 1962 it stood at 11,000; at the time of Kennedy's assassination in November 1963 it had swollen to 16,500. In the meantime the amount of American military aid to Saigon had in-creased dramatically and continued its upward spiral through his final year in office. Amid this escalating American involvement, the Kennedy administration vainly attempted to prod the increasingly corrupt and dic-tatorial Diem to institute land reform to appease the impoverished peas-antry, grant greater political freedom to the non-Communist opposition groups, and accord religious toleration to the Buddhist majority (which suffered systematic discrimination at the hands of the French-converted Catholic elite that dominated the government in Saigon). But the South Vietnamese strongman, convinced that the mounting political and reli-gious opposition to his rule was instigated by Hanoi and its agents in the south, rebuffed Washington's pleas for conciliation in favor of even more repressive policies that only stimulated greater opposition to his regime. As Vietnamese army units fired on unarmed protestors and stormed Buddhist pagodas in 1963, the Kennedy administration publicly expressed displeasure with its recalcitrant protégé by reducing economic assistance to Saigon. Assuming from this signal that Diem had lost Washington's favor, senior South Vietnamese military officers toppled his regime on November 1 with the tacit approval of the American ambassador in Saigon, Henry Cabot Lodge, and murdered Diem.

After the deaths of Diem and Kennedy in November 1963, South Viet-nam experienced great political instability as the various contending fac-tions in the military maneuvered for positions of power. Between Novem-ber 1963 and the end of 1965 Saigon saw twelve changes of government. The succession of generals and marshals who occupied the top post in South Vietnam displayed little inclination to seek public support for the regime by instituting land reforms or expanding political and religious liberties. Nevertheless, the new Johnson administration in Washington resumed and intensified the American military engagement in South Viet-nam on behalf of the anti-Communist forces there. As the insurgents in the south began to receive large quantities of supplies from North Viet-nam, China, and the Soviet Union, the character of the American involve-ment began to change. In February 1964 the American-advised South

Vietnamese army launched covert commando raids into North Vietnam while air strikes were carried out in neighboring Laos to interdict the supply line from north to south. In the summer of 1964, as President Johnson came under intense political criticism from his opponent in the forthcoming presidential election, Senator Barry Goldwater, for waging a "no win" military operation in Indochina, an incident occurred off the coast of North Vietnam that provided the president with a convenient pretext to disarm the Republican opposition by escalating the American military involvement: On the evening of August 4, North Vietnamese torpedo boats allegedly fired on two American destroyers in international waters in the Gulf of Tonkin. Though the Vietnamese vessels promptly retreated and neither American ship suffered damage, Johnson took the occasion of this provocation to submit to the United States Congress a previously drafted resolution requesting Congressional authorization to combat North Vietnamese aggression by all appropriate means. On August 7 the "Tonkin Gulf Resolution" passed unanimously in the House and with only two dissenting votes in the Senate. In the absence of a formal declaration of war, this overwhelming expression of legislative approval afforded Johnson the authority he required to begin the first bombing raids against North Vietnam and to dispatch large numbers of ground troops to the south.

Following Johnson's landslide victory in the presidential election of November 1964, his preestablished plans for the intensive bombardment of North Vietnam were implemented. On February 9, 1965, when a Viet Cong night raid on the barracks of an American airfield at Pleiku resulted in nine American deaths and over a hundred casualties, Johnson ordered retaliatory air strikes against North Vietnam from carriers of the Seventh Fleet. Less than a month after these first large-scale bombings, Washington announced (on March 6) that two battalions of marines were being dispatched to South Vietnam. By the end of 1965, the man who had promised during his reelection campaign that he was "not going to send American boys 15,000 miles away from their homes to do what Asian boys should do for themselves" had sent over 184,000 American ground forces to Vietnam to shore up the sagging Saigon army. That number was to reach 385,000 by the end of the following year, 535,000 by the end of 1967, and a high point of 542,000 in February 1969. Neither the bombing of the north nor the escalation of American troop strength in the south succeeded in quelling the insurrection against the South Vietnamese regime. Hanoi increased its flow of arms and men to the south while the indigenous forces of the Viet Cong gained effective control of almost all rural areas.

The turning point of the war in Vietnam came on January 30, 1968, the day that the Vietnamese celebrate as the beginning of the Lunar New Year, or Tet. On that day Viet Cong guerrillas and North Vietnamese regulars launched a well-coordinated surprise offensive against thirty-six of the forty-four provincial capitals of South Vietnam as well as Saigon itself, where they penetrated the presidential palace, the radio station, the airport, and even the heavily fortified American embassy. The apparent military objective of the Tet offensive was to spark an uprising in the South Vietnamese cities against the Saigon regime and its American protectors. In this strictly military sense it was a failure, and a costly one at that. Over forty-five thousand Communist troops were killed compared to two thousand South Vietnamese and one thousand Americans. The insurgents had failed to hold any of the cities they had overrun in the face of a furious American-South Vietnamese counterattack. But Hanoi and its supporters in the south had won a psychological victory of imposing dimensions by revealing that no part of South Vietnam was secure—not even the government buildings in the capital—thereby discrediting the excessively optimistic claims of the American government about the imminence of victory in a war that was becoming increasingly unpopular at home.

Domestic opposition to the war in Vietnam had begun in the United States on a small scale during the year 1965, at the time of Johnson's escalation of the American military operations there. At that point the voices of dissent were largely confined to the campuses of American universities in the form of "teach-ins" to acquaint the public with the history and character of the conflict. But as the increase in American troop strength required the dispatch of large numbers of conscripts in 1965–68, opposition to the war began to surface in Congress. The casualty figures and "body counts," meticulously recorded by American television correspondents reporting directly from the battlefield, helped to fan the flames of discontent at home. In 1966 and 1967 President Johnson, feeling the sting of political criticism from members of his own party, tried to induce Hanoi to negotiate an end to the conflict by temporarily suspending the bombing of North Vietnam. The North Vietnamese government consistently refused to enter into negotiations until Washington agreed in advance to a permanent bombing halt. After each bombing "pause" failed to lure the North Vietnamese to the conference table on American terms, the bombing was resumed on an intensified scale in an effort to force them to talk. Then the Tet offensive appeared to demonstrate that the ground war in the south was unwinnable, that the bombing of the north had done nothing to bring the contending forces closer to a negotiated settlement, and that the only way out of the "quagmire" in Southeast Asia was a halt to the bombing coupled with overtures to Hanoi.

The mounting public opposition to Johnson's Vietnam policy, unmistakably indicated in the opinion polls, was graphically symbolized by the strong showing of antiwar Senator Eugene McCarthy in the first of the state primary elections of the 1968 presidential campaign. When Senator Robert Kennedy, the younger brother of the slain president, entered the race for the Democratic nomination on an antiwar platform, the discouraged Johnson abruptly decided to reverse his course and leave the Vietnam mess to others. On March 31, 1968, he announced that he would not run for reelection, that future bombings of North Vietnam would be confined to the sparsely populated region below the 20th parallel, and that only token reinforcements of ground troops would be sent to the south. In return he asked Hanoi to enter into negotiations for the termination of hostilities. On May 3 the North Vietnamese government agreed to send a delegation to meet with American negotiators at a peace conference in Paris. For the remainder of this fateful year the two sides haggled over procedural issues, such as the shape of the conference table, as Hanoi awaited the replacement of the lame-duck Johnson administration by one possessing the authority to conclude the war.

The new president, Richard Nixon, had spoken vaguely during his campaign of a "peace plan" that would bring an end to America's military involvement in Indochina. At Guam in July 1969 Nixon finally unveiled what he touted as his country's new foreign policy for East Asia in general and Vietnam in particular. At the heart of this "Nixon Doctrine" was the concept of "Vietnamization," which meant the gradual strengthening of the South Vietnamese military forces in order to permit them to assume the burden of national defense that was gradually to be relinquished by the United States. The number of American military personnel in South Vietnam was reduced from 540,000 at the end of 1968 to 139,000 by the end of 1971 and 25,000 by the end of Nixon's first term. But in an effort to "buy the time needed to make our ally self-sufficient," the Nixon administration simultaneously escalated the level of violence in response to each North Vietnamese success on the battlefield. In April 1970 American ground forces invaded neutral Cambodia with the intention of interdicting the supply routes to the south and driving the North Vietnamese regulars from their Cambodian sanctuaries. In the spring of 1972 North Vietnamese infantry units spearheaded by tanks burst through the demilitarized zone separating the two Vietnams and directly menaced Nixon's Vietnamization program. The American president responded in May by issuing orders to bomb transportation facilities and military installations in North Vietnam and to mine the principal harbors of that country in order to cut off the flow of supplies from China and the Soviet Union. In December 1972, shortly after Henry Kissinger's announcement of the imminence of a peace settlement, Nixon ordered a massive B-52 bombing raid on Hanoi and Haiphong to force North Vietnam closer to the American negotiating position.

Since assuming his position as national security adviser to the president, Kissinger had met secretly with North Vietnamese negotiator Le Duc Tho to explore the basis for an agreement to end the war. By the end of 1972 the United States made the crucial concession: a ceasefire in place instead of the total withdrawal of North Vietnamese forces from the south that it had previously insisted upon. Agreement was finally reached on January 27, 1973, shortly after Nixon began his second term after a spectacular electoral triumph. The United States agreed to remove all of its armed forces from South Vietnam within two months. The two sides agreed on an exchange of prisoners of war. The vague political terms of the accord provided for a coalition government in the south that would conduct free elections there. No serious discussions to that end were ever held, and within two years of the American evacuation all three of the pro-Western regimes of Indochina collapsed to Communist-led insurgencies. The Saigon government fell to North Vietnamese forces on April 30, 1975, two weeks after the Cambodian Communist organization, the Khmer Rouge, toppled the pro-American government that had replaced the neutralist regime of Prince Norodom Sihanouk in 1970. On August 23 the third domino of the former French Indochina fell when the Communist Pathet Lao dissolved the non-Communist administration in Laos.

Between 1961 and 1973 a total of 57,939 Americans died in the Indochina conflict, the longest and costliest foreign war in American history. The United States Air Force dropped on Vietnam over three times the tonnage of bombs that had been dropped on Germany during the Second World War. The financial burden of the war, including military aid to Saigon, has been estimated at approximately $150 billion, with another $200 billion earmarked for the future in the form of veterans' benefits. The escalation of the American military involvement in Vietnam during 1965–68 coincided with a sharp increase in domestic government spending to finance the social programs of Johnson's "Great Society," yet he eschewed politically unpopular increases in taxation to pay for both "guns and butter." The resulting budget deficits produced a rampant inflation whose damaging effects on the American economy persisted for a generation. The social and political consequences of America's long involvement in Indochina, though more difficult to gauge with precision, were scarcely less significant: skepticism bordering on cynicism toward government, fueled by the enormous "credibility gap" between the idealistic, optimistic pronouncements of administration officials and the sordid reality in the Vietnamese jungles that could be seen on the daily television newscasts; a public distaste for foreign entanglements of any kind that threatened to revive the isolationist tradition of the distant past; a host of war-related social and psychological afflictions among returning veterans, such as drug abuse, criminal behavior, and a mental illness designated by psychiatrists as the "Vietnam syndrome."

Why? In the light of the enormous costs paid by the United States for its abortive effort to prevent the three states of the former French empire in Southeast Asia from falling under Communist domination, how does one explain the tenacity and persistence with which this adventure was pursued by four successive administrations of divergent political tendencies? The lure of economic advantage does not come close to justifying the expenditure of money, lives, and prestige; neither the raw materials of the region nor the potential markets for American exports or capital investment played an important role in decision making concerning Indochina. The military threat—actual or potential—posed by a unified Communist Vietnam to the United States and its allies in Asia was nonexistent in light of the preponderance of American naval and air power in the region. Imponderables such as bureaucratic inertia, personal involvements of military and civilian policymakers, and concern about loss of prestige in the eyes of allies and adversaries alike all doubtless played their part in preventing the United States from extricating itself from the morass of Indochina for so many years. But one is also inevitably drawn to the conclusion that an important motivation for the American war in Southeast Asia was concern about China. In April 1965 President Johnson publicly accused Beijing of masterminding the North Vietnamese effort to absorb the south, and Secretary of State Dean Rusk repeated that allegation on several occasions during the legislative hearings on the Vietnam conflict conducted in 1966.

Though Beijing undeniably supplied Hanoi with military equipment during its war with the United States, it did so primarily to compete with the predominant Soviet influence in the north rather than to promote the establishment of a militarily powerful, politically unified Vietnam. Centuries of ethnic antagonism between the Chinese and Vietnamese peoples had left a legacy of mutual mistrust that even the common ideological bond of communism could not overcome. The very idea of Vietnam as a stalking horse for an expansionist China bent on conquering all of Southeast Asia and its offshore islands, so prevalent in the public pronouncements of American officials seeking to justify their nation's military intervention in Indochina, was an absurdity that would have astonished specialists in the region's history (of whom there were precious few in the State Department during the 1960s, owing in part to the McCarthyite purges of the previous decade following the "loss" of China). In any case, the rationale for the Vietnam intervention as a means of containing Chinese communism in Asia lost the last vestige of its credibility in the early 1970s, when Beijing severed the tenuous thread that still connected it to Moscow and began to explore the possibility of improved relations with Washington.

The Development of the Sino-American Rapprochement (1969–1975)

The split between the Soviet Union and China continued to widen during the second half of the 1960s in spite of their joint efforts on behalf of North Vietnam during its military struggle with the United States. In the autumn of 1966 Mao expelled all Soviet exchange students from China and the Kremlin promptly responded in kind. By the end of the decade the Sino-Soviet quarrel had degenerated from a doctrinal dispute between rival claimants to leadership of the Communist world into a fierce diplomatic and, briefly, even military clash between two sovereign powers over traditional matters of territory and regional security. Into this breach between Moscow and Beijing plunged the new administration in Washington that had taken office in January 1969. After initiating the negotiations with North Vietnam that were to produce the American disengagement from Southeast Asia in 1973, the Nixon government undertook to profit from the Sino-Soviet split to open an amicable dialogue with the Communist regime of mainland China that had been ostracized by successive American administrations for the past twenty years. The result was a dramatic transformation of the global relationship between the Communist and non-Communist world.

The deterioration of Sino-Soviet relations finally erupted into violence on March 2, 1969, when Chinese military forces ambushed a contingent of Soviet troops near the disputed Damansky (or Chenpao) island at the confluence of the Amur and Ussuri rivers. Thirty-one Russians and an unknown number of Chinese perished in this border clash; subsequent skirmishes in the same region as well as along the frontier of Chinese Xinjiang during the spring and summer were accompanied by a renewal of Chinese territorial claims against the Soviet Union. In response to these provocations, Moscow took a number of steps to reinforce its defenses on the Chinese border. In April 1969 East European military contingents were detached from the Warsaw Pact command and transferred to the Far East. The number of Soviet divisions deployed along the Chinese frontier was increased from fifteen in 1967 to twenty-one in 1969 and thirty in 1970. Tactical nuclear weapons were stockpiled in Soviet-controlled Mongolia, while officials in the Kremlin apparently considered launching a preemptive strike against China's infant nuclear installation at Lop Nor in Xinjiang.* In the summer of 1969 Moscow sounded out the governments of India, Thailand, and Indonesia about the possibility of concluding an Asian defense pact directed against Beijing. Though neither the preemptive strike nor the diplomatic encirclement materialized, the nervous authorities in China ordered the construction of nuclear fallout shelters in anticipation of a Soviet attack. Negotiations over the disputed frontier, which had begun in September, broke down three months later amid acrimonious exchanges. By 1972 forty-four Soviet divisions stood guard along the 4,500-mile border with China (compared to thirty-one divisions in Eastern Europe), while a quarter of the Soviet air force had been redeployed from west to east.

In the meantime, the new American administration of Richard Nixon had undertaken a fundamental reevaluation of American policy toward China in light of the Sino-Soviet split and the consequent breakup of the

---

* China had exploded its first atomic bomb in October 1964 and its first hydrogen bomb in June 1967. But by the end of the 1960s its delivery system consisted only of missiles with a 2,000-mile range and medium-range bombers, a circumstance which left it vulnerable to a Soviet preemptive strike.

monolithic Communist bloc. In 1969 the first tentative gesture of reconciliation emanated from the White House in the form of a relaxation of certain trade and travel restrictions that dated from the Korean emergency. The Chinese reciprocated a year later by reopening the informal Sino-American talks in Warsaw that had been suspended in early 1968 because of the American bombing campaign in Vietnam. In April 1971 the Chinese government caused a minor sensation by inviting an American table tennis team competing in Japan to try its skills against the championship Chinese team. While newspaper columnists remarked upon Beijing's circuitous "ping pong diplomacy," the American government hastened to follow up this unofficial Chinese overture. In June Nixon formally revoked the twenty-one-year-old trade embargo on China. On July 9 Kissinger, after establishing contact with Chinese authorities through the government of Pakistan (which enjoyed cordial relations with both the United States and China), secretly flew to Beijing. Six days later President Nixon astonished the world with the announcement that he would personally travel to China to "seek the normalization of relations" between the two governments. To impress upon his future hosts the seriousness of his quest for an improvement in Sino-American relations, Nixon inaugurated two changes in American foreign policy that were guaranteed to win approval in Beijing. On October 25, 1971, the United States refrained from exercising its customary diplomatic pressure to prevent the United Nations from expelling the Chinese Nationalist government on Taiwan and transferring its seat on the Security Council to the Communist regime on the mainland. Then Washington openly sided with Pakistan against India, China's perennial antagonist, in the war of December 1971 that led to the creation of the new state of Bangladesh out of former East Pakistan.

Having smoothed his path to Beijing with these gestures of goodwill, Nixon journeyed over twenty thousand miles in February 1972 to become the first American president in history to set foot on Chinese soil. After several days of intensive negotiations, punctuated by an hour-long meeting between top American officials and the ailing seventy-eight-year-old Mao Zedong, the two governments issued a joint communiqué in the city of Shanghai on February 27. This declaration candidly recorded the differences that continued to separate the United States and China. Beijing demanded the withdrawal of American military forces from Taiwan and reaffirmed its intention to support "the struggles of all oppressed peoples" (presumably including the Vietnamese, who were currently engaged in a bloody struggle with China's new friend in the capitalist world). For its part the United States agreed to reduce its military installations on Taiwan, but it also insisted that the dispute between the two Chinas could be resolved only by peaceful means. While committing itself to the total withdrawal of American military forces from Indochina once a negotiated settlement could be reached in Paris, Washington reaffirmed its treaty commitments to South Korea and Japan. On a positive note, both governments agreed to foreswear the pursuit of "hegemony" in East Asia as well as to oppose any other nation's efforts to that end (an unmistakable warning to Moscow). The communiqué also endorsed the expansion of cultural and commercial contacts between the two nations to complement the normalization of political relations that was underway.

The visit by the preeminent symbol of American anti-communism to the center of militant revolutionary opposition to the capitalist world was in itself an almost inconceivable event. The respectful, almost deferential, behavior exhibited by each delegation toward the other during the public ceremonies stood in glaring contrast to the mutual distrust and ideological antipathy that had characterized Sino-American relations since 1950. American reporters observing Nixon and Kissinger embracing their Chinese hosts remarked how far the two governments had progressed since the Geneva conference in 1954, where Secretary of State Dulles brusquely declined to shake the hand of Chinese Foreign Minister Zhou Enlai. It was evident that both Washington and Beijing had been prompted by the most compelling of motives to jettison the bitter legacy of two decades and seek a durable basis for rapprochement.

The primary concern that both governments shared, of course, was that of restraining and containing the Soviet Union. Nixon and Kissinger hoped that the Kremlin's willingness to reach agreement on strategic arms control and political detente in Europe would be hastened by the emerging Sino-American understanding in the Far East; that development, in conjunction with the disengagement of American military forces from mainland Asia that had been heralded in 1969 by Nixon's Guam declaration and was currently being negotiated in Paris, could be expected to increase Soviet uneasiness by releasing Chinese military forces in the southern region for redeployment along the northern frontier. Moscow's subsequent eagerness to conclude the SALT I treaty and settle the remaining East–West political differences in Europe was undeniably influenced by Nixon's willingness to "play the China card" and confront the Soviets with a potential Chinese menace to their eastern borderlands. For their part, Mao and Zhou presumably welcomed the normalization of relations with Washington and the prospective American disengagement from Indochina and Taiwan for the same reason, that is, to permit the concentration of Chinese military strength in the north to counteract the massive Soviet buildup in Siberia, Mongolia, and the maritime provinces.

In addition to these overriding considerations of military strategy and Realpolitik, the economic motivations for the Sino-American rapprochement must not be overlooked. It is hardly surprising that the hoary myth of the China market reasserted its almost magical attraction on American business interests during the early 1970s, when the spectacular postwar economic expansion of the United States had begun to peter out. Increased competition from Japan and the European Economic Community had eaten into America's share of the world market for manufactured goods, while the deficit financing of the Great Society at home and the military intervention in Southeast Asia during the previous decade had generated the highest rates of American inflation since the Second World War. The suspension of the dollar's convertibility into gold in August 1971 shattered the edifice of international monetary relations erected at Bretton Woods in 1944 and exposed the weaknesses of America's financial position in the world. The prospect of gaining entrée to a virtually untapped market comprising a quarter of the world's population fueled extravagant expectations on the part of certain American export interests in the early years of the Sino-American courtship. Within months of Nixon's historic visit, American business executives were flocking to China in search of orders for their products. American exports to China increased from $5 million in 1969 to $700 million in 1973. From the Chinese perspective, the increase in trade with the United States, as well as with its ally Japan, offered an attractive alternative to the economic connection with the Soviet Union that had been severed at Moscow's behest in the 1960s. By January 1975 Chinese Premier Zhou Enlai was publicly advocating closer economic relations among China, Japan, and the United States; he was at pains to dissuade Tokyo from succumbing to the allure of Siberian oil and raw materials, which could be exchanged for the Japanese technology that the Soviet Union desperately needed. At the same time Chinese officials were urging the European Common Market to resist Soviet overtures for more intimate commercial and financial relations.

Neither the Nixon administration nor the interim successor government of Gerald Ford was eager to take the final step of establishing regular diplomatic relations with Beijing for fear of traumatizing the already nervous Nationalist Chinese regime on Taiwan. Following the exchange of "liaison offices" in 1973, a rather clumsy "two Chinas policy" was attempted by Washington in lieu of the formal diplomatic recognition of Beijing that it was as yet unprepared to contemplate. But the remarkable increase in Sino-American trade; the influx of American journalists, scholars, and tourists to China; and numerous return visits by Kissinger and the Ford trip of 1975 confirmed the seriousness of America's courtship of China. No longer would the most populous country in the world be treated as a pariah by the most prosperous country in the world. No longer would China be regarded in the United States as the Far Eastern agent of a monolithic, Moscow-based Communist conspiracy intent on absorbing the remainder of non-Communist Asia. Instead, it would be viewed, and would come to view itself, as a middle-rank power of great potential but modest achievement pursuing regional rather than global objectives. When American military power was engaged on the mainland of Asia during the fifties and sixties, waging two wars against fraternal Communist states bordering on China and protecting the Nationalist Chinese regime on an island that Beijing regarded as its own, China's vital interests seemed most directly threatened by the capitalist superpower across the Pacific. But the American withdrawal from Asia and the simultaneous increase of Soviet military power along China's northern border during the first half of the 1970s brought the two Communist behemoths into direct conflict with one another and spelled the end of the Cold War in the Far East.

PART THREE

From Detente to Detente: The International Order Since 1975

CHAPTER 12

The Resurgence of East–West Tension (1975-1985)

The Prospect for Pluralism and Interdependence

In the year 1975, as the Helsinki conference formally recorded the end of the Cold War in Europe, the Cold War in Asia drew to a close as the pro-Western regimes in South Vietnam, Cambodia, and Laos succumbed in rapid succession to Communist-led insurgencies with only *pro forma* protests from the American government that had abandoned them to their fate two years earlier. In the meantime the People's Republic of China and the United States accelerated their rapprochement that had begun in the early years of the decade. Just as Washington tacitly recognized the permanence of Soviet hegemony in Eastern Europe, it acknowledged the triumph of national Communist movements in China and Indochina. The thirty-three thousand ground forces in South Korea and the token air units stationed in that country and in Thailand constituted the sole remnants of the once-formidable American military presence on the mainland of Asia that had been established for the ostensible purpose of containing Chinese expansionism in that part of the world. In the meantime, signs of progress toward regional detente had even begun to appear in the boiling cauldron of the Middle East after so many false alarms of superpower confrontation there had been sounded. The Soviet Union refrained from interfering with American Secretary of State Henry Kissinger's successful efforts to lay the groundwork for a *modus vivendi* between Israel and its principal antagonist, Egypt, that promised to bring a measure of peace and stability to that chronically unstable area. All the ghosts of the past three decades appeared to have been interred by the arms control agreements concluded between the two superpowers and the signs of political detente that surfaced almost simultaneously in Europe, Asia, and the Middle East, the three historic flashpoints of the Cold War. One is hard put to imagine the reaction of a Dulles or a Stalin had they been resurrected in the middle of the 1970s to witness the fundamental transformation in East-West relations that these momentous developments collectively entailed.

TABLE X   Shares of Gross World Product (percentages)

	1960	1970	1980
European Community	26.0	24.7	22.5
United States	25.9	23.0	21.5
Soviet Union	12.5	12.4	11.4
Japan	4.5	7.7	9.0
China	3.1	3.4	4.5
Less Developed Countries	11.1	12.3	14.8
Other	16.9	16.5	15.8

Source: "International Systems Structure and American Foreign Policy" in Kenneth A. Oye, Robert J. Lieber, and Donald Rothchild, eds., *Eagle Defiant: United States Foreign Policy in 1980s.* Copyright © 1983 by Kenneth A. Oye. Reprinted by permission of Little, Brown and Company.

Underlying the American pursuit of stable relations with the two quarreling giants of the Communist world and the simultaneous reduction of America's overseas role during the first half of the 1970s was the Nixon–Kissinger vision of a new global order that rapidly acquired the designation of the "pentagonal multipolar system." In place of the rigid, ideologically defined bipolar system that had operated during the first quarter century following the end of the Second World War, Nixon and his influential foreign policy adviser envisaged a looser multipolar system in which five rather than two power centers—the United States and the Soviet Union joined by Western Europe, China, and Japan—would function as the principal actors on the stage of world politics. The split within the Communist bloc and China's bid to play an independent role in the world, together with the impressive economic power of the newly enlarged Common Market* and Japan, all seemed to render obsolete the familiar conception of a world divided into two monolithic power blocs directed from Washington and Moscow.† By the time of his forced resignation in the summer of 1974, Nixon, an unabashed admirer of Charles de Gaulle, had left in place an American foreign policy adapted to the new pluralistic international environment that had been prematurely heralded by the French president à decade earlier. For the remainder of the seventies and beyond, the countries of the world were compelled to adjust to the international realities of this new world order.

In regard to Europe, we have seen how the Final Act of the Helsinki European Security Conference in 1975 resolved to the apparent satisfaction of all parties concerned the thorny disputes over borders and sovereignty that had poisoned East–West relations on the continent since 1945.

---

* In January 1973 Great Britain, Denmark, and Ireland joined the European Economic Community. Greece was admitted as the Community's tenth member in January 1981, Spain and Portugal followed in 1986.
† For estimates of the comparative economic power of the five "poles" of the pentagonal world order, see Table X.

Likewise, the economic benefits of this relaxation of political tensions proved so substantial to both sides that the process of conciliation set in motion by Willy Brandt in the early 1970s had acquired a momentum of its own during the second half of the "decade of detente." Trade contacts between East and West expanded significantly in the course of the 1970s (see Figure I). The new willingness on the part of Moscow and its satellites to abandon the traditional quest for bloc autarky in favor of foreign trade contacts outside the Communist world opened up markets and resources that had been virtually inaccessible to Western trading interests.

Accompanying this significant expansion of interbloc commercial relations was a remarkable increase in West European private and public lending to the Communist states to the east. These hard currency loans helped the Soviet satellites to pay for their imports of Western technology and industrial products; German, French, and British banks, whose reserves had been greatly expanded by the influx of petrodollar deposits from the OPEC states after the oil price increases of the mid-seventies, eagerly grasped the opportunity to recycle these funds through high-interest loans to Communist states whose political stability and centralized management of economic activity seemed to render them excellent risks. At the same time, however, the industrial world's economic slowdown caused by the oil shocks of the 1970s shrank markets for products from the Eastern bloc. Consequently, many Comecon countries had to borrow even more heavily to finance their growing trade deficit with the West. The combined foreign debt of the Soviet satellites increased from $19 billion in 1975 to about $62 billion by the end of 1981. The government of Poland alone had run up a foreign debt of $28 billion, of which about $25 billion was held by West European banks and governments, while

FIGURE I   NATO Nations' Exports to the East Bloc (in billions of dollars)

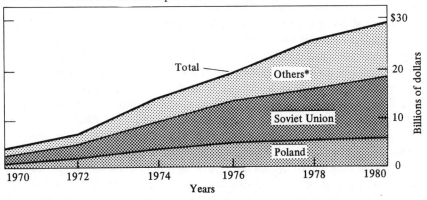

*Includes East Germany, Romania, Hungary, Czechoslovakia, and Bulgaria.

Source: *New York Times,* January 17, 1982. © 1982 by the New York Times Company. Reprinted by permission.

Romania, East Germany, and Hungary became deeply indebted to Western financial institutions. These commercial and financial connections across the iron curtain had the effect of fostering an unprecedented degree of economic interdependence between Western and Eastern Europe (including the Soviet Union). According to the advocates of detente in the West, this web of interdependence was guaranteed to enhance the prospects of continued peace and stability in Europe by giving the West valuable leverage over the East: The economic benefits of trade, technology transfer, and hard currency credits would demonstrate to the Communist bloc the value of cooperation with the non-Communist world and would therefore discourage a reversion to Cold War policies. As Eastern bloc consumers gradually became dependent on the economic resources of the West for their increasing standard of living, the argument ran, their political leaders would be obliged to preserve friendly relations with the West in order to assure continued access of those resources or risk the widespread public discontent that a cutoff of Western goods and capital would probably produce.

The Renewal of the Arms Race

The notable progress toward political conciliation and economic interdependence in Europe during the second half of the 1970s and beyond was accompanied neither by a reduction in tensions between the two superpowers nor by the successful conclusion of their earlier efforts to impose restraints upon the nuclear arms rivalry between them. As we have seen, the retention of the Kissinger foreign policy team following Nixon's ignominious departure enabled the process of Soviet-American detente to proceed on schedule during the interim administration of Nixon's hand-picked successor. The Ford–Brezhnev interim agreement signed at the Vladivostok summit in November 1974 had sketched the basic outlines of a replacement for the SALT I treaty that was due to expire in 1977. But by the advent of the administration of President Jimmy Carter in Washington and the expiration of the SALT I treaty, negotiations for a successor agreement had been thrown off track by a number of technological innovations in the Soviet nuclear arsenal that were denounced by American Congressional critics as a serious threat to the delicate balance of strategic forces that had been confirmed by SALT I: During the Ford interregnum the USSR had tested a MIRVed missile for the first time and deployed a new long-range bomber called the "Backfire." These two developments seemed to suggest that the Soviets were bent on competing with the Americans in the two categories of delivery vehicles in which the United States enjoyed a decisive lead to compensate for its inferiority in the size and number of ICBMs. To meet this Congressional criticism and to offset the perceived menace of the Soviet Union's acquisition of qualitative superiority to match its quantitative advantage in delivery vehicles, the Carter administration accelerated the development of several new weapons systems: the "Missile Experimental," or MX, considered by many weapons analysts at the time to be virtually invulnerable to attack because the ICBMs could be continually shuttled along 10,000 miles of rails in and out of 4,600 shelters in a kind of nuclear shell game; the small, inexpensive "cruise" missile, a pilotless miniature aircraft with its own guidance system that could slide beneath radar and reach Soviet targets undetected; and the new Trident submarine intended to replace the aging Polaris, whose missiles would be within range of any important target in the Soviet Union. President Carter also authorized deployment of the B-1 bomber, an improved supersonic intercontinental aircraft designed to replace America's obsolete B-52 bomber force, and the so-called Enhanced Radiation Weapon, or neutron bomb. The latter was a tactical nuclear weapon whose low heat and blast characteristics combined with its high short-range radiation effects were claimed to offer the advantage of minimizing collateral damage to civilian targets in densely populated, friendly states (such as West Germany) that might have been subjected to a conventional Soviet attack.

The threat to deploy the B-1 bomber and the neutron bomb was apparently little more than a bargaining ploy in the stalled negotiations on SALT II: Carter cancelled the former in June 1977 and deferred deployment of the latter in April 1978, presumably to allay Soviet fears of an American strategic buildup and to facilitate Brezhnev's task of persuading his colleagues in the Kremlin to accept the limitations imposed by the prospective agreement. In any event, the American and Soviet chiefs of state signed the SALT II treaty in Vienna on June 18, 1979. The agreement limited each side to 2,250 delivery vehicles of which no more than 1,320 could be MIRVed missiles. In theory this permitted the Soviet Union approximately 9,000 warheads on land-based missiles, more than enough to place the American Minuteman arsenal in jeopardy, a circumstance that confirmed the Carter administration's determination to accelerate development of the mobile (and theoretically invulnerable) MX missile system.

But as the second treaty on strategic arms control was being debated in the United States Senate in preparation for a ratification vote, the issue of theater nuclear weapons in Europe suddenly emerged as a matter of grave concern to the member states of the Atlantic alliance. While the negotiations on strategic arms were progressing, the Soviet Union had begun to replace its obsolete SS-4 and SS-5 intermediate range missile force by deploying SS-20 land-based missiles whose three-thousand-mile range put them within reach of any target in Western Europe. Unlike the older missiles, the SS-20 was MIRVed, carried three 150-kiloton, independently targetable warheads, and was capable of reaching West German targets in twenty minutes. Moreover, the SS-20 was mobile, which made it difficult to locate and destroy. Viewing this as a prelude to Soviet nuclear superiority on the continent, the NATO Council decided on December 12, 1979, to deploy a new generation of intermediate-range missiles in Western Europe to offset the Soviet SS-20s, unless the United States could reach an agreement with the Kremlin to eliminate the threat posed by the new Soviet deployment. According to this plan, 108 Pershing II missiles would be deployed in West Germany to replace the shorter range Pershing Is that had been there since 1969, while 464 land-based Tomahawk cruise missiles would be deployed in Great Britain, Italy, Belgium, and the Netherlands as well as West Germany by the end of 1983. In the absence of an arms control agreement, these new missiles would serve both as a counter to the Soviet SS-20 force as well as a deterrent to a Warsaw Pact conventional assault against Western Europe.

The NATO decision to modernize the nuclear weapon force in Europe provoked an agitated response from the Kremlin as well as an outpouring of anti-nuclear sentiment in those West European countries that were designated to receive the new missiles. This public opposition increased in intensity after January 1981 when the Reagan administration came to power. The new occupant of the White House was widely perceived to be much less committed than his predecessor to an agreement with the Russians that would remove the justification for deploying the controversial intermediate-range missiles.

But the president surprised allies and adversaries alike by bringing the United States into the Intermediate-range Nuclear Forces (INF) talks with the Soviet Union in Geneva in November 1981. He also upstaged Soviet Premier Leonid Brezhnev, who had won widespread approval in NATO countries for his call for a moratorium on nuclear weapons in Europe, by proposing a simple, definitive solution to the nuclear arms race on the continent. This was the so-called zero option, whereby the United States would cancel deployment of the 572 cruise and Pershing II missiles in exchange for the dismantling of the 600 Soviet intermediate-range missiles. The Kremlin adamantly rejected this scheme, which would have required it to scrap a formidable missile force already in place in exchange for an American promise not to deploy missiles whose effectiveness had yet to be demonstrated and whose deployment was strongly opposed by a significant segment of public opinion in Western Europe. Little progress was made in the INF negotiations, in part because the Russians insisted on counting the 162 British and French intermediate-range missiles as part of the American atomic arsenal in Europe while the United States refused to negotiate on behalf of other sovereign states. At the end of 1983, the Soviet delegates walked out of the INF talks and the United States began to deploy the Pershing and cruise missiles at the designated European sites.

While the two superpowers failed to reach agreement on nuclear weapons in Europe, the complex issue of strategic arms control also continued to elude a mutually acceptable solution. A spirit of ambivalence seemed to characterize the Reagan administration's attitude toward strategic arms control. On the one hand, the new American chief of state presided over the largest peacetime military buildup in history in an effort to overcome what he ominously described as the Soviet Union's commanding lead in nuclear weaponry, while officials in his entourage indulged in blood-curdling rhetoric about the possibility of surviving a nuclear war and the necessity of preparing to fight one. The administration pressed Congress to authorize construction of the MX missile system as an alternative to the ostensibly vulnerable Minuteman ICBM force. After scrapping Carter's plan for a mobile basing mode when domestic opposition developed in the states designated as the sites for the "racetrack" network, Reagan proposed in late 1982 the so-called "dense pack" basing scheme, which envisioned 100 MX missiles in superhardened silos clustered so close together that incoming Soviet missiles would destroy each other trying to hit them. When Congress rejected this basing mode as technically unfeasible, Reagan finally won legislative approval in May 1983 for a scaled-down, fall-back plan to base the MX in existing silos. Two months earlier the president had raised eyebrows by floating the idea of abandoning the existing defense policy of reciprocal deterrence (or "mutual assured destruction") in favor of con-structing an air-tight anti-ballistic missile system composed of satellite-launched laser beams that could intercept and destroy all Soviet missiles before they reached the territory of America or its allies. Such an innova-tion would not only have violated the ABM provisions of the SALT I Treaty of 1972 but would also, according to many experts, have promoted acute instability in the strategic balance and therefore increased the possi-bility of preventive nuclear war.

On the other hand, the Reagan administration took two steps that belied its reputation as a collection of cold warriors. After having denounced the unratified SALT II agreement for freezing the United States into a danger-ous position of strategic inferiority, the president subsequently pledged to follow his predecessor's policy of abiding by the treaty's limitations pro-vided that the Soviet Union did likewise. Reagan thereupon surprised many observers by agreeing to resume strategic arms negotiations with the Soviet Union. In a May 1982 speech he suggested that the new round of discus-sions be designated as Strategic Arms Reduction Talks (START) to sig-nify a break with the SALT II Treaty (which had languished unratified in the U.S. Senate ever since it was signed by Carter and Brezhnev in June 1979) as well as to express his preference for deep reductions in rather than limitations of the nuclear arsenals of the two superpowers. The START talks, which began in Geneva on June 29, 1982, yielded no con-crete results by the end of the first Reagan term, but at least kept the process of arms control negotiations alive amid a deterioration of relations between the two superpowers. The failure of arms control talks during Reagan's first term was in no small measure due to the instability in the Soviet leadership. Yuri Andropov, who replaced Brezhnev in November

1982, died in February 1984. His successor, Konstantin Chernenko, in turn died in March 1985 to be succeeded by the unknown, untested Mikhail Gorbachev.

The poisoning of relations between the United States and the Soviet Union began during the Carter administration, when a significant segment of American official opinion had concluded that detente was virtually dead because Moscow had reneged on its implicit pledge to pursue peaceful coexistence with the West and promote stability in the world. This evolution of American attitudes was prompted less by the destabilizing effects of the new Soviet delivery vehicles on the balance of power than by a succession of Soviet gains and U.S. setbacks in the non-nuclear area during the second half of the 1970s that appeared to signal a return to the confrontational spirit of the Cold War era.

The first of these was the projection of Soviet military influence into a part of the world where it had never existed before: the continent of Africa. The emergence of Soviet client states in Africa, which will be treated in detail below (see page 444), occurred in the middle of the 1970s. Then, at the very beginning and the very end of 1979, the American geopolitical position was further threatened by important developments in two adjacent states in the part of southern Asia that blocked Soviet access by land to the Persian Gulf and the Arabian peninsula.

Turmoil in South Asia

The first of these geopolitical transformations occurred in Iran. The regime of Shah Mohammed Reza Pahlevi, installed by the British and the Russians in 1941 and rescued from a Soviet-backed insurgency in its northernmost province in 1946 by Anglo-American pressure on Moscow, had become America's staunchest ally in the region after 1953, when the Central Intelligence Agency masterminded a coup that restored the Shah to power after his ouster by the nationalist politician Mohammed Mossadegh. By the mid-1950s American firms had acquired equal control with the British-owned Anglo-Iranian Oil Company of the rich petroleum reserves of the country under an arrangement that supplied the government in Teheran with substantial oil royalties, which it used to finance a crash program of industrialization. In the early 1970s the Nixon administration began to equip the Shah's military and naval forces with sophisticated weapons in order to enable Iran to replace Great Britain as the principal peacekeeping force of the anti-Communist bloc in the Persian Gulf. But throughout the year 1978 fierce opposition to the Pahlevi dynasty developed among a broad-based coalition of Shi'ite Moslem fundamentalists who detested the Shah's secular policies and the Westernized life-stye of his entourage, small merchants who resented the overwhelming and distorting influence of American multinational corporations on the Iranian economy, and progressive opposition politicians disenchanted with the repressive methods and corrupt practices of the regime. In January 1979 massive street demonstrations forced the Shah into exile and in the following month political power in Teheran was assumed by a fundamentalist Islamic movement loyal to the octogenarian Shi'ite clerical leader Ayatollah Ruhollah Khomeini.

Though neither the Soviet Union nor the small but influential Iranian Communist party, the Tudeh, had played a significant role in the Iranian revolution, its increasingly anti-American character dealt a devastating blow to Western interests in this strategically and economically important region. Pro-American elements in the Iranian political and military elite were executed, the extensive American economic interests in the country were confiscated, and American military installations (including the radar network deployed along the northern frontier to monitor Soviet military activity) were closed down. The abrupt cutback in Iranian oil production caused by the continuing domestic unrest in that country and the war with neighboring Iraq that broke out in December 1980, though of minimal concern to the United States (which received only 5 percent of its oil imports from Iran), produced serious economic difficulties for America's allies in Western Europe and Japan that were much more dependent on Persian Gulf oil. Moreover, the upsurge of Moslem fundamentalism in Iran threatened to spread throughout the Middle East, causing political instability and undermining pro-Western regimes in Saudi Arabia, Egypt, and elsewhere. The affair of the sixty-nine American embassy hostages in Teheran, seized by Iranian militants in November 1979 in an effort to blackmail the United States government into extraditing the exiled Shah (who had been admitted to a New York hospital for treatment of the cancer that finally killed him in July 1980), further embittered relations between Washington and Teheran.* In the meantime, fundamentalist Moslems attacked the United States consulate in Tripoli, Libya, and the U.S. embassy in Islamabad, Pakistan, raising the specter of a jihad, or holy war, against American interests throughout the Islamic world.

As the United States saw its longtime client state in Iran transformed throughout the year 1979 into a center of anti-American agitation, the Soviet Union embarked on its first overt military operation beyond the confines of its East European empire since the end of the Second World War by dispatching paratroops and armored columns to Afghanistan to quell a Moslem insurrection against the pro-Soviet government in Kabul in December 1979. Afghanistan, like its neighbor Iran, had been the site of acute rivalry between tsarist Russia and Great Britain before the First World War and was formally recognized as a neutral buffer between Russia and British India in 1907. During the Cold War it continued to occupy this nonaligned status between the Soviet Union and the newly created state of Pakistan, the West's principal ally in south Asia. But unlike Iran, which

---

* In December 1979, the Iranian militants released sixteen female and black hostages, but the remaining fifty-three were not freed until Carter vacated the White House in January 1981.

as we have seen, was brought into the American-dominated security system after the evacuation of Soviet forces from its northern provinces in 1946, Afghanistan gravitated toward the Soviet orbit during the 1950s to become a kind of Finland of Asia, renewing an earlier nonaggression pact with Moscow and receiving substantial Russian economic aid. Then in April 1978 the Marxist Nur Mohammed Taraki led an insurrection that overthrew the leftist but nominally neutralist regime in Kabul and established an openly pro-Soviet government, which in turn was toppled in September 1979 by the Marxist Hafizullah Amin. In the meantime a fundamentalist Moslem insurgency against the Soviet-backed regime, which received covert military assistance from the United States, China, and Pakistan, obtained such broad support among the Afghan population as to prompt the Soviet intervention of December 1979. By the spring of 1980 almost 100,000 Soviet soldiers had poured into the country to bolster the new regime of Babrak Karmal, an Afghan exile in Eastern Europe who had been brought in by the Russians to replace the murdered Amin.

Moscow's military operation in Afghanistan did not significantly alter the East–West balance of power in south Asia, since that country had always been recognized by the United States and its allies as lying within the Soviet sphere of influence and had already been ruled by a Soviet puppet government for three years before the intervention. But Washington reacted to the Soviet action with such harshness as to cause observers to wonder whether detente had definitively come to an end. President Carter increased the 1981 defense budget by 5 percent in real terms, imposed an embargo on grain deliveries to the Soviet Union in excess of the minimum quantities specified in the 1975 agreement, restricted Soviet access to American fishing waters and high technology exports, and organized a boycott of the Olympic Games held in Moscow in July 1980. Carter also advised the United States Senate, which by then needed no prodding from the White House, to delay consideration of the SALT II treaty that had been signed in 1979 but was still unratified. Apparently fearing that the invasion of Afghanistan represented an attempt by the Soviets to profit from the American expulsion from Iran to position themselves for a future offensive toward the oil resources of the Persian Gulf and the Arabian peninsula as well as the warm waters of the Indian Ocean, President Carter announced in his January 1980 State of the Union Address that the United States considered the Gulf vital to its national interest and therefore would intervene directly to defend the region against Soviet aggression. Carter then took a number of steps to shore up the deteriorating American position in that part of the world. Relations with the military regime of General Zia ul-Haq of Pakistan, which had cooled because of his repressive internal security policies and his apparent interest in acquiring an independent nuclear capability in violation of the nonproliferation treaty, were improved. Plans were prepared for the creation of a Rapid Deployment Force for use in the Persian Gulf–Red Sea region. Washington approached a number of pro-Western states in the vicinity about the possibility of granting base facilities to American air and naval forces to compensate for the loss of the Shah's formidable military and naval apparatus as the Western-backed policeman of the region. In June 1980 Oman and Kenya granted the United States access to naval and air facilities at Masirah Island and the port of Mombasa, respectively. In August Somalia agreed to allow American warships to use the former Soviet bases at Berbera and Mogadishu. The American naval base on the British-owned island of Diego Garcia in the middle of the Indian Ocean was enlarged and upgraded to accommodate a more formidable American naval force to offset increased Soviet naval power there. Throughout the first half of the 1980s, the Reagan administration stepped up U.S. military aid to the Afghan *Mujaheddin*, enabling the insurgents to hold their own against the Soviet forces and their collaborators in Kabul.

Peace and War in the Middle East

As the American position in the Red Sea, Persian Gulf, and Indian Ocean was challenged at the end of the 1970s, developments in the Middle East *enhanced* America's political influence in that volatile region. The Kremlin's unwillingness to deliver the requisite military assistance to its Arab clients to tip the balance against Israel, together with Kissinger's assiduous cultivation of Egyptian President Anwar Sadat, brought about a spectacular reversal of Egypt's policy toward the two superpowers. On March 15, 1976, Sadat renounced the 1971 Soviet-Egyptian Friendship Treaty and a month later cancelled Soviet naval privileges in Egyptian ports. President Carter resumed the Kissinger policy of elbowing the Soviets out of the peace negotiations between Israel and Egypt. The prospects for a successful resolution of the remaining differences between the two countries were greatly improved when Sadat made a spectacular trip to Jerusalem on November 19, 1977, in a bold, improvised attempt to break the deadlock in the stalled peace process. This symbolic gesture of goodwill by the charismatic Egyptian leader, together with the appreciative response of an Israeli public weary of the constant threat of war with neighboring Arab states, paved the way for a bilateral accord that the United States had been promoting since the mid-seventies. In September 1978 at Camp David, the American president successfully coaxed Sadat and Prime Minister Menachem Begin of Israel into signing an agreement that mandated the return of the Sinai peninsula to Egypt in two successive stages in 1980 and 1982 in exchange for Egypt's recognition of Israel's right to exist as a sovereign nation. While a vaguely worded understanding left the sensitive issue of Palestinian autonomy in the Gaza strip and on the West Bank of the Jordan River for future negotiation, Egypt and Israel signed a peace treaty on March 26, 1979, exchanged formal diplomatic recognition in February 1980, and resumed their bilateral efforts to restore stability to the Middle East in the face of the unremitting hostility of the Palestinian political organizations and their supporters in the Arab world. Syria, Iraq, Libya, and Algeria took the lead in opposing the Camp David accords and received the strong support of the Soviet Union. But the Israeli-Egyptian rapprochement survived the assassination of President Sadat in October 1981 by Egyptian opponents of Camp David. It also continued in spite of a number of belligerent actions by the Begin government, including the destruction of the Iraqi nuclear reactor near Baghdad in June 1981, the bombardment of PLO offices in Beirut in July, the annexation of the Golan Heights in December, the removal of elected Arab mayors of several West Bank cities in March and April 1982, and the continued construction of permanent Israeli settlements on the West Bank in what many observers viewed as a prelude to de facto annexation. The final Israeli withdrawal from the Sinai took place on April 25, 1982, in accordance with the Camp David timetable, and Sadat's successor, President Hosni Mubarak, reaffirmed his predecessor's policy of peaceful relations with Israel.

But the negotiations concerning the autonomy of the West Bank and Gaza showed no signs of progress amid an atmosphere of deteriorating relations between the Palestinian population of these areas and their Israeli occupiers. The Camp David accord had been based on President Carter's assumption that the removal of the Egyptian threat would make Israel more accommodating on the Palestinian issue. But Israeli Prime Minister Begin, who passionately believed in Israel's right to perpetual control of the West Bank, was emboldened to strengthen his country's military position and deal harshly with the Palestinians. In the meantime, the tense political and military situation in Lebanon set the stage for a Mideast explosion that almost derailed the peace process. As we have seen, the political leadership of the PLO and a large proportion of its military cadres had resettled in Lebanon after having been expelled from Jordan in September 1970. Then, after a bloody clash between left- and right-wing Lebanese factions in the middle of the decade, a large contingent of Syrian troops was deployed in the Bekaa Valley of northeastern Lebanon as part of an Arab peacekeeping force. The Syrians promptly introduced jet fighters and SA-6 ground-to-air missiles in Lebanon and lent support to the Palestinian units that were repeatedly shelling with Soviet-built artillery the Galilee area of northern Israel. In 1978 Israeli forces crossed into southern Lebanon and forced the PLO to fall back behind the Litani River, eighteen miles from the Israeli frontier, while a United Nations peacekeeping force was dispatched to southern Lebanon to separate the belligerents. But once the Palestinians established positions in southern Lebanon outside the UN buffer zone and resumed the shelling of Galilee, the Begin government decided to profit from the instability in Lebanon to establish once and for all a secure northern border.

Apparently believing that he had been given the "green light" by U.S. Secretary of State Alexander Haig, Begin dispatched about 60,000 Israeli

Israel in the Middle East

infantry troops, accompanied by more than 500 tanks and 90 F-15 and F-16 jet fighters, across the Lebanese frontier in early June 1982. The ground forces and tank columns overwhelmed the PLO strongholds in southern Lebanon; the American-built jet fighters used their American-built Shrike and Maverick air-to-surface missiles to knock out all of the Soviet-built Syrian surface-to-air missile sites in the Bekaa Valley; the Israeli planes also used their American-built Sidewinder air-to-air missiles to destroy almost half of Syria's Soviet-built MiG jet fighters. In the meantime, Israeli infantry and tank columns closed in on Beirut as Israeli planes bombed the western part of the city where PLO headquarters were located. By the end of the summer a U.S.-sponsored agreement was worked out whereby the Palestinian political leadership and its military forces were evacuated from Lebanon under the protection of a multinational peacekeeping force consisting of American, French, and Italian marines.

The Israeli invasion of Lebanon in the summer of 1982 achieved its immediate objective: the elimination of the PLO as a military threat along Israel's northern frontier. The Israelis had also demonstrated that with their American-built weaponry they were capable of defeating the Syrians with their arsenal of Soviet-built missiles and fighter planes, thereby tarnishing Moscow's reputation as an effective military patron for the hard-line Arab states. But Israel's military triumph in Lebanon caused a deterioration of relations between the Begin government and the Reagan administration in the United States, which regarded the intervention as a threat to regional stability and expressed its displeasure by announcing an embargo on future sales of F-16 fighter planes to Israel.

A further indication of Washington's irritation with its Israeli client came on September 1, 1982, when President Reagan formally proposed his own comprehensive solution to the Palestinian-Israeli conflict after it had become evident that the autonomy talks mandated by the Camp David accord would lead nowhere. The Reagan plan, which had been formulated without consultation with Israel, contradicted the Begin government's policy of sponsoring Israeli settlements on the West Bank preparatory to the establishment of permanent Israeli authority over the region and its Palestinian majority. The U.S. president rejected both extremes of an independent Palestinian state and the incorporation of the West Bank and Gaza into a greater Israel. Instead, he called for the creation of a Palestinian-Jordanian federation that would administer the Israeli-occupied territories under the authority of King Hussein. Nothing ever came of this proposal, not only because of Israel's lack of enthusiasm but also because Hussein was unable to obtain the assent of the PLO and the major hard-line Arab states for the so-called Jordanian solution.

Two weeks after the unveiling of the abortive Reagan plan for a settlement of the Israeli-Palestinian problem, developments in Lebanon served to dampen U.S. enthusiasm for resuming an active pursuit of peace in that troubled country. On September 15, Israeli military forces occupied the

Moslem section of West Beirut after the assassination of Bashir Gemayel, the newly elected Christian President of Lebanon whom Israel had strongly supported on the expectation that he would agree to a separate peace with the Jewish state along the lines of Camp David. Two days later Gemayel's enraged followers burst into two Palestinian refugee camps in the Israeli-controlled area and massacred about eight hundred civilians while Israeli military authorities looked the other way. Since the United States had pledged to PLO leader Yassir Arafat that the Israelis would protect the Palestinian civilians remaining in Beirut after the evacuation of the PLO fighters, Reagan hastily arranged for the return of the multinational military contingent to provide some semblance of security. But the indefinite presence of American, French, and Italian peacekeeping forces in Lebanon angered the Shi'ite Moslems, who suspected the Westerners of favoring the Christians in the ongoing Lebanese civil war. It also annoyed Syrian President Hafez al-Assad, whose own "peacekeeping" units were deployed in the northeastern part of the country to promote Syrian ambitions. A succession of terrorist attacks on American personnel in Lebanon culminated in the coup de grâce of October 23, 1983, when a suicide mission blew up the headquarters of the U.S. Marines outside Beirut, killing 241 American servicemen as they slept. After a face-saving interval, Reagan pulled all U.S. Marines out of Lebanon and abandoned all hopes of mediating a settlement there.

The only sign of progress toward the reduction of tensions in the Middle East came in the fall of 1984, when the newly established coalition government in Israel headed by the Labor Party leader, Shimon Peres, began the withdrawal of Israeli military units from the southern part of the country. In the meantime, Shi'ite Moslems, Druze, and Palestinians resumed their violent quarrels while the Lebanese government of Amin Gemayel, brother of the slain Christian leader, lapsed into total political impotence. But the Syrian army, lavishly reequipped by the Soviet Union, remained in northeastern Lebanon. Hafez al-Assad, who had come to power in Syria in 1970 just after the death of Egypt's Nasser, had built up his military forces with Soviet aid throughout the seventies as Sadat turned from Moscow to Washington. With Egypt isolated by Camp David and Iraq distracted by its war with Iran, Assad had become (in the eyes of many Arabs) the heir to Nasser as the leader of the Arab struggle against Israel in the eighties.

But the larger aspiration associated with Nasser's name, the quest for Arab unity, had proved as elusive as ever in the years since his death. Despite the common linguistic and religious heritage that linked most of the Arab peoples in the Middle East, the political fragmentation of the region continually prevented the realization of the Pan-Arab ideal. The sharp contrast between secular ideologies (such as that of the Baathist*

---

* The Baath party (otherwise known as the Arab Socialist Renaissance Party), in power in Iraq and Syria since 1963 and influential in many other Arab countries, advocates secularism, socialism, and Arab unity.

ruling elites in Syria and Iraq) and Islamic fundamentalism was one cause of disunity. Another was the divergent positions taken by the various Arab states in the Cold War, with Egypt, Jordan, Saudi Arabia, and Oman maintaining close ties with the United States, while Syria, Iraq, and South Yemen sought and received military and diplomatic support from the Soviet Union. Opposition to the existence of the state of Israel and support for Palestinian nationalism appeared to be the major source of cohesion among the Arab states. But even that consensus was undermined by Egypt's separate peace with the Jewish state—which survived the shock of Begin's invasion of Lebanon as well as Mubarak's recall of the Egyptian ambassador from Tel Aviv in protest—and Jordan's flirtation with the Reagan plan for a Palestinian-Jordanian federation.

The Iraq-Iran war aggravated this disarray in the Arab world. From 1973 to 1979, Iraq's oil revenues had increased from $2 billion to $21 billion, enabling that country to build a formidable military establishment and equip it with weaponry obtainable on the international arms market. After becoming president of Iraq in 1979, Saddam Hussein apparently assumed that he could profit from the internal upheaval and international isolation of Iran by using his Soviet- and French-equipped army for a quick, decisive victory over the tattered remnants of the Shah's military forces. But by 1982 the combination of a spirited Iranian counteroffensive and a sharp decline in Iraqi oil revenues due to oversupply on world markets transformed the conflict into a long war of attrition. If Saddam's ultimate objective was to establish himself as Nasser's heir by mobilizing the Arab world against the two non-Arab states in the Middle East—Israel and Iran—he failed ignominiously. Syria's Assad, who presided over a secular Arab regime faced with an internal threat from Islamic fundamentalists, strongly supported the non-Arab, Islamic regime of Khomeini against the secular, Arab state of Iraq. The explanation of this apparent paradox was simple: Assad regarded his fellow Baathist head of state in Baghdad as his most likely rival in the Arab world. Libya, Algeria, and South Yemen also backed Iran against Iraq for their own reasons, while the rest of the Arab world closed ranks behind Saddam Hussein.

By the mid-1980s, the peace process in the Middle East had badly faltered, as the optimism engendered by the Camp David accords gave way to a bleak pessimism about the prospects of reaching a mutually acceptable resolution of the Israeli-Palestinian problem: Not a single other Arab state joined Egypt in acknowledging Israel's right to exist. On the contrary, Egypt was virtually drummed out of the Arab bloc at the Baghdad summit in 1978 and Sadat, as we have seen, paid with his life in 1981 for becoming the first Arab leader to recognize the Jewish state. Hard-line factions within the increasingly frustrated Palestinian movement resorted to terrorism to publicize its grievances against Israel, such as the murder of an elderly, disabled Jewish man after the highjacking of the Italian cruise ship *Achille Lauro* in 1985. On the other hand, the Israeli government thumbed its nose at the Camp David principle of Palestinian autonomy in the occupied territories by establishing ninety new Jewish settlements on the West Bank between 1977 and 1984 and granting generous tax subsidies and low mortgage interest rates to entice Israeli citizens to relocate there. The negotiations on autonomy for the West Bank and Gaza mandated by the Camp David accords, which had advanced at a snail's pace since August 1979, were effectively killed by the Israeli invasion of Lebanon in 1982.

The goal of peace and stability was just as elusive outside the Israeli-Palestinian imbroglio. Lebanon had ceased to exist as a state in the proper sense of the term, with roving bands of Christian and Moslem gunmen, together with Syrian military forces in the north and Israeli soldiers in the south, providing what passed for law and order. The armed struggle between Iraq and Iran had taken on the appearance of a First World War-type stalemate, with no end in sight as the casualty lists lengthened. In the meantime, the two superpowers continued to arm and support their clients in the region, viewing the complex tangle of rivalries there through the lenses of the Cold War. Despite occasional outbursts of irritation at Israel (as, for example, in response to its invasion of Lebanon in 1982), the Reagan administration maintained intimate relations with the Jewish state. Israel had become, and remained, the world's largest recipient of U.S. foreign economic aid (roughly $2.3 billion annually) and cooperated actively with U.S. intelligence agencies in the Middle East and throughout the world. Egypt was number two on the list of U.S. aid recipients and, in return, accorded the United States a number of favors, including the use of Egyptian ports and air space in emergencies, the conducting of joint military maneuvers, and the sharing of intelligence. Washington also intensified its military ties to Saudi Arabia as part of a mutually advantageous relationship that included Riyadh's willingness to help stabilize world oil prices by increasing production as needed. The Soviet Union, though ejected from its Egyptian bases and frozen out of the Israeli-Palestinian peace process, resupplied the Syrian army after its defeat in Lebanon in 1982, furnished economic and military assistance to Iraq and South Yemen, and diplomatically supported the PLO in various world forums.

PART FOUR

The Developing World:
A Retrospective Comparison

Latin America

CHAPTER 13

Latin America's Quest for Development and Independence

The Cuban missile crisis had dramatically revealed the willingness of the Latin American states to endorse Washington's strategy of excluding Soviet influence from the hemisphere through the unilateral exercise of United States power. Once the option of removing the Castro regime was foreclosed by the Kennedy–Khrushchev agreement of 1962, the United States concentrated on isolating Cuba from its neighbors in order to prevent the spread of its noxious doctrines throughout the region. In response to evidence that Castro was furnishing arms to guerrilla movements in several Latin American countries, the OAS voted in July 1964 to impose economic sanctions on Cuba. All member governments of the inter-American organization except Mexico promptly severed diplomatic relations with Havana. The new pariah in the Caribbean thereafter became increasingly dependent on Moscow for economic and military assistance in exchange for which Castro loyally supported Soviet foreign policy goals throughout the world. By the mid-1970s, as we shall see, Cuba was even serving as a kind of proxy for the Russians in the developing countries, most notably by supplying combat troops to assist Soviet-backed forces in various parts of Africa.

But the Kremlin's new client state in the Caribbean was singularly ineffective in attaining its professed goal of exporting Castro's brand of Marxist revolution to the rest of Latin America. Cuban-supported insurgent groups in half a dozen countries were crushed by state security forces that had been trained and armed by the United States as part of the counterinsurgency program initiated by President Kennedy and expanded by his successor. Even reformist groups with no apparent connection to Havana were suppressed by military or police forces supported directly or indirectly by Washington. The most dramatic instance of overt United States counterinsurgency activity in Latin America took place in the Dominican Republic, a small Caribbean country that, like Cuba, had submitted to various forms of United States domination since the eary part of the century. On April 24, 1965, forces loyal to the reform-minded ex-president,

Juan Bosch, who had been overthrown by a military coup two years earlier, took up arms against the junta in power. Four days later President Lyndon Johnson, without consulting the other member states of the OAS, dispatched a contingent of American marines to Santo Domingo for the announced purpose of protecting the lives of Americans residing in the country. Within a few months the size of the American military force had grown to 25,000, while the president publicly defended its presence on Dominican soil as a necessary precaution against a Cuban-style Communist revolution there. Even if there had been a genuine threat of Communist insurrection, and no evidence was ever marshalled to indicate that there was, the unilateral American military operation represented a patent violation of the nonintervention provision of the OAS charter. For the first time since the advent of Franklin Roosevelt's Good Neighbor Policy in 1934, United States marines were on occupation duty in a sovereign state in Latin America. Nevertheless, a large majority of the other Latin American governments acquiesced in the unilateral military operation of the Johnson administration. Indeed, many of them contributed troops to an inter-American peacekeeping force in the Dominican Republic that supervised nationwide elections in June 1966. Those elections were won by the conservative political party headed by Joaquin Balaguer, a former ally of the dictator Raphael Trujillo who had been assassinated in 1961. In September 1966, the United States marines together with the other contingents of the inter-American peacekeeping force withdrew from the country as Bosch and his leftist supporters receded into political insignificance.

The Dominican intervention in 1965 signified an important shift in priorities for the Latin American policy of the Unied States. The Johnson administration rapidly abandoned the commitment to the goals of social reform and economic development that had been encompassed in the original provisions of the Alliance for Progress. Indeed, the alliance fell far short of its founders' ambitious expectations: Latin American upper classes refused to submit to the tax and land reforms envisioned by the program, government officials pocketed American aid intended for economic development projects, and military regimes that had ousted civilian governments declined to restore democratic liberties. Far from exerting pressure on the social, political, and military elites of Latin America to uphold the progressive principles of the American aid program, the Johnson administration diverted alliance funds from economic development projects to counterinsurgency activities. Washington also accorded prompt diplomatic recognition to autocratic but reliably anti-Communist military regimes that had seized power from democratically elected governments, such as the junta that toppled the left-leaning President João Goulart of Brazil in April 1964.

The shift from the promotion of social reform and economic development to the suppression of Communist or Communist-related activity in Latin America continued under the Nixon administration. During the 1970 presidential election in Chile, the CIA spent lavishly to subsidize the opponents of a self-proclaimed Marxist named Salvadore Allende, who ran on a radical program of social and economic reform that included a pledge to nationalize the holdings of the large American copper companies that dominated the country's economy. When Allende became the first democratically elected Marxist president of a Latin American nation and promptly confiscated the property of the Anaconda and Kennecott copper interests, Washington proceeded to wage a major campaign to destabilize the new regime. This included subsidies for opposition newspapers and labor organizations, pressure on financial institutions to withhold credit, and covert encouragement to Chile's military establishment to rid the country of its Marxist government. With inflation raging, the balance-of-payment deficit widening, and social strife intensifying, the Chilean army moved to oust the Allende regime in 1973. The new military junta headed by General Augusto Pinochet thereupon instituted a pitiless campaign of repression against leftist groups in the country that dashed whatever hopes the supporters of Allende may have entertained of establishing the first Marxist state on the mainland of South America. Military governments in Argentina and Brazil also clamped down hard on domestic dissidents during the 1970s, striking out at communist, socialist, and liberal democratic elements alike.

Thus, in the decade after the Cuban missile crisis, Soviet influence in the Western Hemisphere was confined to Castro's embargoed, isolated outpost of Marxist Leninism in the Caribbean. The United States took the lead in this strategy of containment, but most of the Latin American states proved to be loyal followers. The cause of anti-communism had always had an air of unreality about it during the fifties, when communism itself seemed such a distant peril. It was only through the application of strong pressure, for example, that Dulles had been able to get the Latin American governments worked up about the supposed menace of communism in Central America during Washington's campaign against the Arbenz regime in Guatamala in 1954. But as Cuba unmistakably gravitated toward the Soviet orbit during the early sixties and Castro raised the banner of revolution in Latin America, the entrenched oligarchies in the region had little difficulty perceiving the common interest that they shared with the United States in suppressing indigenous revolutionary activity in the hemisphere and forestalling the projection of Soviet influence there to exploit it.

But this notable increase in hemispheric solidarity as a consequence of the Cuban missile crisis concealed a contradictory trend that turned out to be the most significant feature of Latin America's international position since the early 1970s: This was the gradual, imperceptible loosening of the bonds of economic dependence and political subservience that had long tied that region to the United States. Latin America's gradual emancipation from United States domination was facilitated by two important developments. The first was the novel experience of sustained economic growth in the region, which prompted many of its countries to expand their export trade and diversify their foreign markets at the expense of their traditional customer and supplier to the north. The second was the advent of East–West detente, which eventually moderated Washington's traditional obsession with promoting hemispheric solidarity in anticipation of a Soviet security threat and therefore permitted the Latin American states greater latitude in the assertion of their sovereign rights and the pursuit of a more independent foreign policy.

From 1960 to 1973, the economies of Latin America grew at an average annual rate (after inflation) of almost 6 percent, far surpassing the real growth rates of the rest of the developing world. Several aspects of the economic takeoff of this traditionally backward region are worthy of note. First of all, it was "export driven:" Foreign trade as a percentage of GNP more than doubled between 1970 and 1980 in Brazil, Mexico, Argentina, Chile, Ecuador, and Venezuela, and substantially increased in other Latin American countries. Total Latin American exports increased by almost 11 percent a year from 1965 to 1973, compared to a 3.6 percent annual rate for the previous fifteen years. This expansion of Latin America's trade reflected a historic shift from its traditional reliance on commodity exports— primarily minerals and foodstuffs—to a newly acquired capability to market manufactured goods abroad. The proportion of manufactures in Latin America's total exports increased from 3.6 percent in 1960 to 17.2 percent in 1970. The region's exports of manufactured goods grew at an annual rate of 26.5 percent, compared to a 16.4 percent increase for the entire world during the same period. By 1979, the manufacturing sector in Argentina, Brazil, Uruguay, and Mexico accounted for over a quarter of those countries' GNP. The export-led economic dynamism of these "newly industrializing countries" of Latin America in turn attracted foreign investment on an impressive scale. By the end of the seventies, many experts were predicting a glorious economic future for a region that had for so long languished in poverty and backwardness.

The expansion and intensification of Latin America's involvement in the international economic order inevitably detracted from its special commercial and financial relationship with the United States. By 1979, Latin America was exporting only 25 percent of its manufactured products to the United States, compared to 39 percent to countries within the region and 26 percent to the rest of the industrial world. From 1950 to 1980, Latin America's importance as a market for U.S. exports fell 37 percent, while the region's share of total U.S. imports declined by 66 percent. As the United States gradually disengaged from its dominant commercial position in Latin America, it also began to redirect its foreign investment to other parts of the world: The proportion of total United States foreign investment located in Latin America declined from roughly 25 percent in 1960 to about 12 percent in 1980, while European and Japanese investors increasingly moved in to take up the slack. The era of undisputed U.S. economic supremacy in Latin America was apparently coming to an end.

Latin America's increasing economic independence from the United States contributed to a new political assertiveness that challenged Washington's hegemonic position in the Western Hemisphere. At the height of the Cold War, the Latin American ruling elites tended to accept uncritically United States leadership in hemispheric affairs. We have seen how Washington had successfully mobilized the governments of that region to isolate Cuba after the missile crisis of 1962 and had not hesitated to intervene overtly (as in the case of the Dominican Republic in 1965) or covertly (as in the case of Chile in the early 1970s) to prevent the installation of unfriendly regimes that might be susceptible to Cuban (and therefore Soviet) influence. But by the middle of the 1970s, the emergence of global detente between the superpowers had greatly reduced U.S. anxieties about Soviet penetration of the Western Hemisphere. By that time, most of the Cuban-inspired insurgencies that had erupted in Latin America in the aftermath of Fidel Castro's triumph in Havana had petered out. The capture and execution by Bolivian authorities of the legendary guerrilla leader Ernesto (Ché) Guevara in 1967 foreshadowed the fading of revolutionary hopes. Far from ushering in a period of revolutionary upheaval in Latin America, the Cuban revolution, as we have seen, was followed by a succession of military coups that installed right-wing dictatorships dedicated to the suppression of the left.* The decline of regional insurgency amid Soviet-American detente at the global level afforded Latin American countries much greater freedom to pursue their own national interests without reference to the traditional security concerns of the United States.

In the meantime, the new Carter administration in the United States had begun to deemphasize the counterinsurgency features of United States policy toward Latin America and attempted to resurrect the commitment to political liberalization, social reform, economic development, and hemispheric cooperation that had originally inspired Kennedy's Alliance for Progress. Carter terminated military assistance to many of the right-wing dictatorships as part of a campaign to cultivate the progressive, democratic forces in Latin America and to reestablish the reputation of the United States as a good neighbor in the hemisphere.

The first beneficiary of this new orientation of American policy was the Latin American country whose sovereignty had been most blatantly compromised by its historic relationship with the United States. Since 1965, talks between the United States and Panama concerning the future of the Panama Canal had dragged on inconclusively, as opponents in the United States vigorously denounced any proposal to relinquish U.S. control of the waterway and the five-mile-wide zone surrounding it as an intolerable threat to American security interests in the Caribbean. But in 1977 the Carter

---

* As in Brazil (1964), Chile and Uruguay (1973), and Argentina (1976).

administration finally obtained senatorial consent to a treaty that transferred to Panama (1) immediate legal jurisdiction over the Canal Zone and (2) the sole right to operate and defend the canal by the end of the century. The demise of the most notorious symbol of "Yankee imperialism" in the Western Hemisphere reflected both the decreasing significance of Latin America in the global security concerns of the United States and the increasing willingness of Washington to deal with the region on its own terms rather than as a theater of East–West rivalry.

Two years after the ratification of the Panama Canal Treaty, this new U.S. policy of military disengagement and support for political reform was again put to the test in two other countries in Central America. In a dramatic reversal of previous United States policy in the region, Carter tacitly approved the October 1979 coup against the right-wing Romero dictatorship in El Salvador that brought to power a progressive regime committed to social reform. In the same year the repressive, retrograde regime of Anastasio Somoza Debayle, whose family had ruled Nicaragua like a personal fief for over four decades with solid backing from Washington, was overthrown by a broad-based coalition dominated by an inner directorate of revolutionaries known as the Sandinistas.* Confronted with the first successful leftist insurrection in Latin America in many years, the Carter administration attempted in vain to promote a centrist, pro-American alternative to the Sandinistas. Washington also appealed to the OAS to dispatch a peacekeeping force to Nicaragua to preserve order, but was equally unsuccessful. While the Sandinistas enjoyed the rhetorical support of Fidel Castro, who had recently rekindled the spark of revolution in Latin America after a decade of dormancy, they had also received active encouragement from the neighboring non-Communist governments of Venezuela, Costa Rica, and Panama. These and other Latin American states refused to permit the OAS to become, as it had during the crises in Guatemala (1954), Cuba (1962), and the Dominican Republic (1965), an instrument of United States policy in the region. Gone were the days, or so it seemed, when Washington could single-handedly determine the outcome of political rivalries in Latin America through the application of diplomatic pressure, economic sanctions, or in the extreme case, military force.

As it turned out, however, Latin America's newly acquired independence from the United States proved ephemeral and was sharply curtailed as a result of two important developments in the first half of the 1980s. The first of these was a severe and entirely unanticipated crisis in the international economic order that was to have particularly powerful repercussions in the Western Hemisphere. During the previous decade, the petroleum-exporting countries that had amassed enormous profits from the dramatic increase in

---

* Named after Cesar Augusto Sandino, the rebel leader who led the resistance to American marines stationed in Nicaragua before his assassination by the U.S.-trained national guard in 1934.

oil prices deposited these "petrodollars" in Western (and especially American) banks. As these financial institutions eagerly sought customers for their idle funds, they developed considerable respect for the creditworthiness of the governments of Latin America, whose record of economic growth and political stability stood in sharp contrast to other parts of the developing world. Consequently, while many of the most impoverished states of Africa found it impossible to attract foreign lending on a large scale, the international banking system recycled their huge petrodollar deposits to the treasuries of Latin America. The total foreign debt of the region increased astronomically: From $2.3 billion in 1970, it grew to $75 billion in 1975, $229 billion in 1980, and $340 billion in 1983. In the latter year the total foreign debt burden equaled roughly 47 percent of the region's total GNP, while annual interest payments exceeded a third of the value of its total exports for the year. By the beginning of the 1980s, Latin America accounted for over 60 percent of the entire foreign debt owed to commercial banks in the world. By 1982 this underdeveloped region had paradoxically become a net exporter of capital as its huge annual debt repayments helped to finance the growing budget deficit in the United States.

Indebtedness is no cause for concern (the bankers tell us) so long as sufficient annual income is generated to service the debt. Unhappily for the countries (and banks) involved, the long period of postwar economic growth came to a screeching halt toward the end of the 1970s. The resulting global recession had the effect of reducing demand for Latin American goods at a time when exports were essential to earn the foreign exchange required to cover the mounting foreign debt. As a consequence, Latin America's combined GNP declined in 1982 for the first time since the end of the Second World War and dropped again in 1983.

Mexico furnishes the most dramatic case study of a Latin American country whose exaggerated aspirations for economic development were smothered by the economic downturn of the early 1980s. Between 1960 and 1972, Mexico's annual economic growth rate had average 6.8 percent. Already the most highly developed industrial economy in Latin America, Mexico profited handsomely from the discovery of vast new petroleum reserves in the mid-seventies just as the world price of oil was going through the roof. Mexican oil revenues quadrupled between 1977 and 1979, while the value of proven oil reserves in the country increased from $80 billion in 1976 to $898 billion in 1979. The intoxicating prospect of instant prosperity prompted the Mexican government to launch a massive program of public spending that was to be financed by a combination of expanded oil exports and heavy foreign borrowing against anticipated future oil revenues. Alas, in 1981 the unanticipated glut of petroleum supplies on the world market forced down the price of the product, sharply reducing the export earnings that were necessary to service Mexico's burgeoning foreign debt. In the summer of 1982, Latin America's largest oil exporter and most highly industrialized country ran out of foreign exchange and had to suspend payment to its foreign creditors. By the end of that year, most of the other Latin American governments were in arrears. The imprudent bankers who had abruptly plunged their surplus funds into Latin America during the 1970s just as abruptly withdrew them, thereby aggravating the financial crisis.

In 1983 delegates from eleven major Latin American debtor countries met in Cartagena, Colombia, to explore cooperative means of addressing the debt problem. What Western banking officials feared most of all was the formation of a "debtors' cartel" that might conspire to present the creditors with the choice of a radical reduction of the debt or a joint default that would plunge the international banking system into its greatest crisis since the Great Depression. But the "Cartegena Group" stopped far short of issuing such an ultimatum. Despite provocative trial balloons, such as the announcement a few years later by the newly elected president of Peru, Alan Garcia, that his government would limit foreign debt payments to 10 percent of export earnings, the threat of cooperative, unilateral action by the hard-pressed borrowers vanished. Instead, creditors and debtors met in "clubs" (such as the "Paris club") to discuss ways of rescheduling the loans (which invariably meant extending the maturity dates and reducing the annual interest payments).

Approximately 38 percent of Latin America's foreign debt was held by United States banks. This circumstance, together with the fact that most of these obligations were denominated in dollars and set at variable interest rates, abruptly terminated the region's increasing economic independence from the United States. Latin America's economic development was revealed to be acutely vulnerable to the monetary and commercial policies of United States governmental and private institutions: The slightest increase in American interest rates by the Federal Reserve Board had an immediate and far-reaching effect on the economies of Latin America, as did the tough negotiating position taken by American banks holding the Latin American obligations and by the friendly representative of the American-dominated IMF who invariably attended meetings of the clubs on rescheduling. To make matters worse, the adoption of protectionist measures in the United States to preserve domestic jobs and profits—such as the Generalized System of Preferences scheme that had began operation in January 1976—restricted Latin America's access to the American market and the desperately needed dollars to make the debt payments.*

As the debt crisis of the first half of the 1980s rudely interrupted Latin America's progressive economic emancipation from the United States, the collapse of global detente and the revival of Cold War tensions during the same period reignited Washington's fears of Cuban/Soviet meddling in

* The only exception to this trend toward United States protectionism vis-à-vis Latin America was President Reagan's Caribbean Basin Initiative of 1983, which established a system of nonreciprocal free trade for exports from Central America and the Caribbean islands.

the Central American-Caribbean region and therefore revived the possibility of U.S. political and military intervention there. Signs of this renewed United States anxiety about political developments in Latin America first appeared during the last two years of the Carter administration. As relations between Washington and the new Sandinista regime in Nicaragua deteriorated throughout the year 1979, a pro-American government on the tiny Caribbean island of Grenada was overthrown by a revolutionary movement whose leader, Maurice Bishop, openly advertised his admiration for Fidel Castro and his disdain for the Collosus of the North. On August 31 of the same year, President Carter had startled his countrymen with the announcement that American intelligence sources had detected the presence of a "Soviet combat brigade" in Cuba. Officials in Washington openly worried about a resumption of Communist subversion in the hemisphere facilitated by Moscow's close links with Havana and its increasingly friendly relations with the leftist regimes in Nicaragua and Grenada.

In the meantime, the mild attempts at social reform on the part of the new government of El Salvador had been blocked by the entrenched military and landowning oligarchy, which promptly gained control of the junta that had ousted the Romero dictatorship in 1979. In the following year a number of Salvadoran guerrilla organizations banded together to form a unified military command—the Farabundo Marti National Liberation Front (FMLN)—and a broad coalition of civilian supporters—the Democratic Revolutionary Front (FDR). When it was discovered in the winter of 1980–81 that the Sandinistas in Nicaragua were supplying Cuban arms to the FMLN, Carter resumed deliveries of U.S. military aid—which had earlier been suspended in retaliation for human rights abuses—to the government in San Salvador. He also made plans for the termination of all economic assistance to Nicaragua before leaving the White House.

During his campaign for the presidency, Ronald Reagan had blamed Carter's preoccupation with promoting human rights for hastening the downfall of autocratic but friendly governments such as Somoza's in Nicaragua and Romero's in El Salvador, as well as for alienating the anti-Communist military regimes that governed Brazil and Argentina. Once in office, Reagan moved promptly to curb what he viewed as the spread of Cuban and Soviet influence in the region and to strengthen America's anti-Communist allies there. He lifted all of the major restrictions on United States military assistance to those Latin American governments that had been found by his predecessor to be in violation of human rights. He strongly denounced the arms buildup in Nicaragua and the flow of Cuban military aid to the Sandinista regime. In March 1981 Reagan authorized the CIA to organize and finance a destabilization campaign against Managua to be waged by a motley crew of former supporters of the deposed dictator Somoza and disenchanted rebels operating out of neighboring Honduras and Costa Rica as well as in remote regions within Nicaragua itself. In the spring of 1983 the CIA was found to have mined Nicaragua's harbors and conducted bombing raids on some of its oil storage depots. In order to circumvent a Congressional prohibition in 1984, the Reagan administration used the National Security Council (NSC) to channel military aid, much of it from private and foreign sources, to the 15,000 "Contras" who were attempting to topple the Sandinista regime. By 1985 the United States was enforcing a trade embargo and a credit boycott on Nicaragua and began to increase military aid to Honduras in order to strengthen that country's position as a counterweight to Nicaragua in the region.

To cope with the mounting insurgency in neighboring El Salvador, Reagan increased U.S. aid to that country from $35.5 million at the beginning of his administration to over $1 billion in 1985 and dispatched American military advisers to assist the Salvadoran army. The centrist government of Christian Democrat José Napoleon Duarte, brought to power through relatively free elections in 1984, pursued a cautious program of land reform. But it was hobbled by a congress controlled by representatives of the old landowning and military oligarchy and caught in the crossfire between leftist guerillas associated with the FMLN and right-wing "death squads" that maintained close links to the army and its civilian allies.

On a number of occasions during the early 1980s, Reagan administration officials uttered ominous warnings about the resumption of an interventionist military policy in Central America if a Soviet- and Cuban-backed Nicaragua seriously threatened the stability of the region. Then developments in a nearby location entirely unknown to the average American supplied Washington with the requisite pretext to translate that inflammatory rhetoric into action. We have seen that the government installed on the island of Grenada in 1979 had openly embraced the ideology of Castroism as the most appropriate weapon for combating U.S. interference in Latin America. With the active encouragement of Moscow, the Cuban strongman reciprocated Grenadian President Maurice Bishop's expression of solidarity by delivering small arms for defensive purposes and providing skilled labor for the construction of an airport on the island, ostensibly to promote its tourism industry. These events evoked a predictably hostile response in Washington, which suspended economic aid and attempted to organize opposition to Grenada among neighboring islands in the Eastern Caribbean. When Bishop subsequently toned down his revolutionary rhetoric and hinted at the desire for reconciliation with the United States, he was overthrown and executed by a radical faction of his own movement on October 12, 1983.

Two weeks later the Reagan administration revived the policy of overt U.S. military intervention in the Caribbean that had been shelved since President Johnson's decision to dispatch the marines to the Dominican Republic in 1965. Citing the possibility that the airport runway under construction would be capable of accommodating the military aircraft of unfriendly powers and invoking the immediate threat posed by the increasingly repressive Grenadian regime to 500 American medical students studying on the island, the United States launched an air, land, and sea invasion of Grenada on October 25. After three days of combat with the Grenadian army and the Cuban construction crews, the 1,900 United States troops had toppled the government and rescued the students from whatever it was that threatened them at a financial cost of $75 million and a human cost of 45 dead and 337 wounded. A reliably pro-American regime was subsequently installed, which proceeded to complete the construction of the airport, but without the Cuban crews, to encourage tourism on the little island.

The invasion of Grenada was evidently intended as a warning to Nicaraguan President Daniel Ortega Saavedra that the Sandinistas' delivery of military aid to the rebels in El Salvador ran the risk of provoking a similar response from Washington. As Managua geared up for the anticipated arrival of the Marines, other interested parties proposed the option of a diplomatic solution to the crisis. At the beginning of 1983 the foreign ministers of Colombia, Mexico, Panama, and Venezuela had met on Contadora Island off the coast of Panama to explore means of promoting regional peace negotiations. But the mediation efforts of the so-called Contadora group were hampered during the next several years by the reluctance of the Reagan administration to allow third parties to intervene in its bitter dispute with the Sandinista regime. Another instance of Washington's opposition to outside interference in its showdown with Managua was the Reagan administration's refusal to recognize the jurisdiction of the World Court when it took up a suit filed by the Sandinista government against the United States for the CIA's mining of Nicaraguan harbors in 1983.* What these developments collectively symbolized was the revival of the spirit of unilateralism in United States policy toward the Caribbean basin, a strategically vital region through which two-thirds of America's foreign trade passed. Ronald Reagan took up Teddy Roosevelt's Big Stick, which had been temporarily shelved by his predecessors, and did not hesitate to brandish it at potential adversaries, real or imagined. By the middle of the 1980s, Latin America's prospects for greater independence from the United States faded amid the revival of Cold War tensions in the Caribbean and Central America, just as the hopes for economic development were dashed by the twin curses of foreign indebtedness and industrial stagnation.

* The case was settled in Nicaragua's favor in 1986, but the U.S. refusal to recognize the court's jurisdiction or to participate in the judicial process rendered the verdict moot.

CHAPTER 14

Africa:
From Independence to Dependency

The continent of Africa was the last region of the world to achieve liberation from European colonial domination in the twentieth century. During the late 1950s and the early 1960s—several years after the European powers had withdrawn from most of their imperial outposts in Asia and the Middle East—France, Great Britain, and Belgium relinquished control over their African possessions. The immediate consequence was the abrupt proliferation of independent political units in an area that had been administered from London, Paris, and Brussels since the great age of imperial expansion before the Great War. In 1945 only four African states belonged to the newly established United Nations: Egypt, South Africa, Liberia, and Ethiopia. By the end of 1960, twenty-five new nations on the continent of Africa had joined the world organization, representing a quarter of its membership.

With the notable exceptions of Algeria and the Belgian Congo (subsequently renamed Zaire), the transition to national independence during this first phase of decolonization in Africa was relatively smooth and peaceful. The British and French had been compelled to acknowledge that their continued presence in Africa was untenable when both of the superpowers, not to speak of the newly liberated states throughout the rest of the Third World, opposed colonialism as an anachronism in the postwar era. On the other hand, the retrograde regimes of Salazar's Portugal and Franco's Spain would refuse to abandon the cause of colonial grandeur, clinging tenaciously to their African possessions until the disintegration of the Iberian dictatorships in the mid-1970s hastened the belated demise of these last two remnants of European imperial power on the continent. By 1984, the centenary of the Berlin Conference that had partitioned the continent into European spheres of influence, forty-five African countries operated as sovereign political units in the postcolonial world.

The achievement of national liberation by the former African subjects of

France, Great Britain, and Belgium in the second half of the 1950s and early 1960s generated a euphoric sense of optimism. In May 1963, representatives of the new African countries assembled in Addis Ababa, Ethiopia, to found the Organization of African Unity (OAU). Inspired by the ideology of Pan-Africanism that had been popularized by the defiant, charismatic leader of Ghana, Kwame Nkrume, the OAU's charter enunciated a set of goals that were designed to strengthen the international position and protect the recently won independence of the fledgling member states so that their peoples could thrive and prosper amid their newly acquired freedom.

One of the cardinal principles enshrined in the OAU charter was the recognition of the overriding necessity to prevent territorial conflicts between rival African nations—such as Algeria's ongoing border dispute with Morocco—as well as civil strife between antagonistic groups within each nation—such as the bloody struggle in the former Belgian Congo between the central government and a secessionist movement in the mineral-rich province of Katanga (subsequently renamed Shaba). Such violence had to be averted above all because it threatened to unravel the fragile fabric of African independence by tempting extracontinental powers to exploit for their own benefit the resulting political instability and economic chaos. Accordingly, the member states of the new organization solemnly affirmed the absolute inviolability of the political frontiers that had been inherited from the colonial era, notwithstanding the fact that these borders had been drawn to suit the administrative convenience of the colonizers rather than the economic, strategic, and ethnographic conditions of the colonies.

The second goal of the OAU—as the very name behind that acronym implied—was the eventual political unification of the entire continent under the aegis of a single sovereign authority. How such an ambitious program was to be carried out amid the bewildering diversity of languages, ethnic groups, and religions was not specified. But some African leaders regarded *military* cooperation as the most effective means toward the ultimate end of continentwide political integration. Nkrumah himself had first proposed the establishment of a multinational African army in the early 1960s to restore order during the Congo crisis, and subsequent outbreaks of unrest prompted similar suggestions from various African heads of state. As with the principle of the inviolability of the territorial status quo, the prime motivation behind this enthusiasm for a multinational African military force was the need to remove any pretext for foreign interference in Africa's internal affairs.

The same was true for the third axiom of the OAU's Pan African ideology: the necessity of neutrality in the Cold War. The founders of the new organization were intent on avoiding the fate of other third world peoples, whose independence had been compromised by the extension of superpower rivalry to their regions. Delegates of the new African states had taken an active role in the first international conference of the non-aligned movement at Belgrade in 1961, and the principle of nonalignment was recorded in the OAU charter two years later. Throughout the first decade of independence, the absence of significant Soviet and American interests in Africa spared that continent the trauma of East–West conflict that afflicted Asia during the same period.

But political independence from Europe and military disengagement from the Soviet-American confrontation were insufficient to guarantee postcolonial Africa a bright future. What Africa required above all else was a continentwide program of economic development on a massive scale. Of all the poverty-stricken regions of the non-Western world, Africa indisputably occupied the most precarious position: Though exceptionally well endowed with a variety of raw materials and agricultural products, the continent was sorely deficient in capital, technology, entrepreneurial skills, managerial expertise, and adequate markets for the commodities (mainly foodstuffs and minerals) that continued to represent a predominant proportion of its export trade. It also included the largest number of low-income, resource-poor, and landlocked countries on the face of the earth. A mere recitation of the statistics tells the sad story: In the mid-1980s, only seven of the forty-five African societies had a per capita income of $1,000 or more. Although 10 percent of the world's population lived in Africa, its share of world industrial output was less than 1 percent. Unless this condition of extreme economic backwardness could be remedied, the noble aspirations for Africa's postcolonial future that had been generated in the optimistic era of independence and nonalignment would be dashed.

As they launched their ambitious campaign for economic development during the 1960s, the new states of Africa were confronted with two alternative paths: They could integrate their national economies into the flourishing international economic system dominated by the United States, Western Europe, and Japan. Or they could strive to disengage Africa from the world economic order and pursue a development strategy based on the principles of autarky and self-reliance. In light of Africa's desperate need for foreign investment, loans, aid, trade, technology and technical expertise, it is scarely surprising that the ruling elites of the newly independent African states opted for membership in, rather than withdrawal from, the international economic order that alone could satisfy those requirements.

Consequently, postcolonial Africa promptly established strong links with the international monetary and trading system represented by such organizations as GATT, the IMF, and the World Bank. This involvement in the Western capitalist economic order yielded some notable benefits for the continent during the first decade of independence. The economic boom in the industrial world and the remarkable growth of international trade during the sixties generated ample capital for investment, loans, and development aid to the Third World while stimulating demand in the industrialized countries for the raw material and agricultural exports from Africa. Peace Corps volunteers from the United States flocked to the continent to provide much-needed technical and managerial expertise.* The African countries became frequent customers at the soft loan windows of the IMF and the World Bank. They participated in the rounds of tariff negotiations sponsored by GATT and developed some mutually profitable trading relationships with the developed world on the basis of the exchange of their primary products for its manufactured goods.

But even amid the period of relative prosperity during the 1960s, some ominous trends had already begun to give rise to pessimism about Africa's future prospects for genuine independence and economic development. The first of these warning signs was the stubborn persistence of what has come to be known as "neoimperialism"—the retention by the former imperial powers of indirect control over their erstwhile colonies through the exercise of economic, political and military influence.

The phenomenon of British neoimperialism in Africa developed in a comparatively subtle, covert manner. Originally, London strove to retain a host of military privileges in many of the successor states of its African empire. The Anglo-Nigerian pact of 1960, for instance, reserved for the former colonial power the prerogatives of military intervention, of the retention of British military bases on Nigerian territory, and of the use of Nigerian airspace in times of emergency. But this heavy-handed approach to postcolonial security management represented such a blatant contradiction to the principle of national sovereignty that the Nigerian government summarily abrogated it within a year. Reading the handwriting on the wall, the British substantially reduced their overt security commitments in Africa (though London did not hesitate to send troops during the 1960s to bolster friendly regimes in Uganda, Kenya, and Tanzania). Instead, Great Britain concentrated on preserving its considerable economic influence in the region through the operations of British-based multinational corporations and financial institutions that had retained significant interests there. John Bull was still capable of exercising a residual cultural influence as well through the instrument of the Commonwealth,† a loosely affiliated association of former British dependencies that was dominated by the anglophone African states.

France exercised a much more direct, overt form of neoimperial power on the continent after its departure from the former territories of French West Africa and French Equatorial Africa in 1960. French security interests in tropical Africa were protected through a series of bilateral mutual defense pacts granting the former colonial power the right of military inter-

---

* In countries such as Ghana, Liberia, and Ethiopia during the sixties, roughly 80 percent of the secondary school teaching posts were held by American Peace Corps personnel.
† The adjective "British" was removed from the title in the postcolonial period to emphasize the multilateral nature of the organization.

vention.* To bolster its position as Europe's "gendarme" in the region, Paris obtained the right to maintain garrisons in half-a-dozen West and Central African states. Since the mid-1960s, some 10,000 French military forces have been stationed in Africa and its offshore islands, with six parachute infantry regiments and a parachute artillery regiment retained in the metropole for rapid deployment to the continent. A large French naval force has regularly patrolled the western shores of the Indian Ocean. Paris has utilized the territories of Senegal and Gabon as bases for covert intelligence operations in Africa, while French counterinsurgency experts train the security forces of many of its client states there.

This extensive network of security agreements, combat units, and military installations enabled France to launch a number of military interventions in Africa in support of its own interests or those of its African protégés. In the 1960s French units left their barracks in Cameroon, Gabon, Niger, and Chad to defend client regimes under attack from dissident elements. On other occasions behind-the-scenes French influence was exercised to hasten the downfall of long-time antagonists—such as Modibo Keita of Mali in 1968—or former protégés who had fallen from grace—such as N'garta Tombalbaye of Chad (1975), Moktar Ould Daddah of Mauritania (1978), and Jean-Bedel Bokassa of the Central African Republic (1979). France also intervened in Zaire's Shaba (formerly Katanga) province in March 1977 and May–June 1978, ostensibly to rescue resident European nationals, but also to protect Zairian strongman Mobutu Sese Seko—the Western powers' most reliable client in Africa—against exiled security forces that had returned from their Angolan sanctuary to challenge his authority. Eventually the French contingents in Zaire were replaced by an all-African peacekeeping force, but one that was a far cry from Nkrumah's bold proposal in the early 1960s for the prevention of foreign intervention in African affairs: The brainchild of the Francophile president of Senegal, Léopold Senghor, the multinational army was dominated by contingents from the pro-French states of Morocco, Gabon, and Senegal and depended heavily on French technical and logistical support.

France's privileged security relationship with most of its former African colonies were reinforced by agreements in the economic field. At the time of the establishment of the European Economic Community in 1957, France had insisted on the inclusion in the Treaty of Rome of provisions preserving preferential trade terms for, and special financial relationships with, the overseas dependencies of member states. With Great Britain outside the EEC at the time, this meant that, with the advent of decolonization in the early 1960s, the vast majority of African countries involved were the suc-

---

* At one time or another, France signed security agreements—some of which have since been abrogated—with Benin (formerly Dahomey), Burkina Faso (formerly Upper Volta), Cameroon, Central African Republic, Chad, Congo, Djibouti (formerly French Somaliland), Gabon, Ivory Coast, Madagascar, Mali, Mauritania, Niger, Togo, and Senegal).

cessor states of French West Africa and French Equatorial Africa. The first Yaoundé convention of 1963 (which remained in force from 1964 to 1969) set up a European Development Fund (EDF) of $800 million, subsequently increased to $1 billion in the second Yaoundé accord of 1969 (which operated during the period of 1970–75). The EDF was a foreign aid program (of which France and West Germany each bore roughly a third of the cost) that financed infrastructure and agricultural projects, with most of the appropriations going to sub-Saharan states with close ties to France such as the Ivory Coast, Senegal, and Cameroon. Language ties ensured the preponderence of French technicians and advisers on most EDF-financed projects, while French construction firms received a disproportionate share of the contracts based on EDF funds.

The preferential trade arrangements incorporated into the Yaoundé regime proved exceedingly advantageous to the EEC in general and France in particular. The vast bulk of EDF funds were earmarked for the purchase of manufactured products from Europe, while the Africans had to import grain from EEC countries at prices well above the going rate on world markets. In sum, the preferential commercial nexus codified in the two Yaoundé conventions ensured that France's membership in the EEC would not oblige her to sacrifice protected African markets and traditional sources of strategic raw materials (especially cobalt, uranium, phosphates, and bauxite) and tropical agricultural goods (mainly coffee and cocoa).

To complement this intimate trading relationship, a strong financial connection between France and her former African possessions was forged in the form of the "franc zone," a monetary association that tied the currencies of most sub-Saharan francophone African states (collectively designated as the African Financial Community [CFA] franc) to the French franc. The franc zone in effect established a common monetary system through the mechanism of free convertibility between the CFA and the French franc at fixed parity. This arrangement created an open channel through which French capital could flow in and out of the African countries within the franc zone without encountering the risks of exchange-rate instability or prohibitions against the repatriation of profits; this open invitation to French investors (at the expense of foreign competitors) yielded impressive results in French client states such as Senegal and the Ivory Coast, which became African havens for subsidiaries of multinational (but mainly French) corporations.

Just as France had insisted on the Yaoundé arrangement to preserve its preferential trade ties with francophone Africa after it joined the Common Market, Great Britain demanded similar protection as it belatedly gained admission to the EEC in 1972. A lengthy negotiation between the EEC and the OAU resulted in the first Lomé convention (Lomé I) of 1975, which established the concept of preferential trade between the community and a newly established bloc of former European colonies designated as the Association of African, Caribbean, and Pacific States (ACP).

The patent inequality of the Yaoundé conventions, which had granted the member states of the EEC (notably France) privileged access to African markets but excluded many African products from the European market, had been replaced in the Lomé system by much more favorable terms of trade for the Africans vis-à-vis the Europeans: Whereas all ACP manufactured products and 96 percent of ACP commodity exports were admitted duty free in Common Market Europe, the ACP states were permitted to retain their protectionist restrictions on imports from EEC countries. The agreement also established an aid program for the most impoverished of the African countries. The most advantageous feature of Lomé I from the African perspective was the creation of a commodity stabilization fund (STABEX), which provided financial compensation to African states when the price of their commodity exports dropped below a stipulated level. This latter innovation was hailed as a long-overdue solution to the problem of commodity price fluctuations that had plagued African countries that depended on the world market price of a single commodity for the major portion of their export earnings.

Though the Lomé regime conferred notable nonreciprocal advantages on the African countries, their representatives waged a spirited campaign to rectify some its defects during the renegotiation of the original agreement toward the end of the seventies. They complained bitterly about the inadequacy of the aid program, the rigorous conditions imposed, and the absence of African voices in the decision-making process concerning the disbursement of funds. Despite an increase in the amount of development assistance (which in any case was canceled out by inflation and population increases), the second Lomé Convention of 1980 (Lomé II) encountered widespread opposition in Africa. The Lomé system was denounced by radical critics as an instrument of neoimperialism that perpetuated African dependency in the guise of "Eurafrican" economic cooperation and reinforced the continent's position of inferiority in an international division of labor dominated by high technology and automated manufacturing: By promoting the export of African commodities in exchange for European manufactures as the basis of Africa's foreign trade, the "Eurafrican nexus" inhibited the process of product and market diversification that had paved the way for the economic success of the newly industrializing countries (NICs) of East Asia (see page 458). Instead of exploiting its comparative advantage of abundant, cheap labor to produce low-quality, low-price, manufactured goods and aggressively seek new markets abroad (à la Taiwan and South Korea), Africa remained hopelessly locked in the neocolonial embrace of Western Europe. The third renegotiation of the Lomé convention in 1985 (Lomé III) did not significantly alter this condition of increasing dependency and vulnerability.

Such advantages as Africa did obtain from its participation in the international economic system during the prosperity and expansion of the 1960s vanished as the world slid into deep recession in the 1970s. The two successive "oil shocks" of that decade devastated the economies of all the African nations save the handful with substantial petroleum reserves (such as Algeria, Nigeria, Libya, Gabon, Congo, and Cameroon) or diversified economies (such as Senegal and South Africa) that were able to export and attract foreign investment. On the other end of the developmental scale, those landlocked, resource-poor, or drought-ridden states such as Chad, Niger, Ethiopia, Uganda, and the Sudan were plunged into socio-economic chaos. This striking contrast in economic performance between the fortunate few and the pitiful "basket cases" during the prolonged recession of the seventies and early eighties brought into bold relief the trend of uneven development that had afflicted the continent since independence and represented a formidable roadblock to African unity.

In the meantime, the problem of Africa's lopsided reliance on commodity exports returned to haunt it with a vengeance during the world recession: As prices of commodities other than petroleum sank to their lowest levels in three decades (reflecting the drop in demand in the recession-ridden industrial world), many African producers of primary products were driven to the wall. Unable to pay for essential imports of food and oil, most African nations had to rush hat in hand to the IMF and the commercial banks in the industrialized world. Africa's foreign debt soared, from $14.2 billion in 1973 to $42 billion in 1976 to over $150 billion by 1984, while the ratio of total debt to GNP of all the countries on the continent doubled (from under 20 percent in 1973 to 40 percent in 1984). The fatal combination of unchecked population growth, drought, and decline in food production (due in part to a frantic flight from the countryside to urban areas in search of higher living standards) resulted in widespread famine and disease. The inevitable austerity measures imposed by the banks and the IMF as preconditions for future loans forced the African countries to slash domestic spending and curtail imports. The consequence was negative economic growth for most of the non-oil-exporting states, and the transformation of the postindependence dream of Africa's glorious future into the nightmare of dependency and decline.

The first signs of Africa's economic stagnation during the early 1970s prompted a radical new proposal for relief. At its tenth annual conference in Addis Ababa in 1973 the OAU formally called for the creation of a New International Economic Order (NIEO), an innocuous euphemism for a massive transfer of wealth from the developed countries of the northern hemisphere to the less developed countries (LDCs) of the south. The means to this end would include a drastic increase in development assistance from the industrial world, the cancellation of outstanding foreign debts, the establishment of commodity price stabilization schemes on a global basis, and the reduction of northern protectionism against LDC exports. This project for the reallocation of global economic resources based on need rather than the free-market criteria of supply and demand received the enthusiastic endorsement of the nonaligned movement later in the year, and of the UN General Assembly in 1974. But the proposal for an NIEO ran aground on the shoals of global recession by the end of the 1970s. The soaring rates of inflation and unemployment in the developed world were scarcely conducive to the spirit of altruism required for such a large-scale redistribution of global wealth. Instead, the industrial states responded to the economic downturn by adopting policies that merely aggravated Africa's economic crisis, such as the reduction of foreign aid commitments and the enactment of additional protectionist measures against imports from the Third World.

Confronted with the unwillingness of the wealthy industrial states to endure the reduction in their standard of living that the NIEO scheme for a global redistribution of resources would entail, impoverished Africa was compelled to develop second thoughts about its earlier decision to join the world economic order. Africa's unenviable plight since the mid-1970s was a direct consequence of the tragic asymmetry of its international economic relationships: While the continent has had only marginal importance to the world economic system, the impact of that system on the economic well-being of the African states (which had become highly dependent on the developed world for uninterrupted access to markets, investments, loans, and technical expertise) was devastating. It was entirely understandable that some African leaders, their fragile economies battered by the global recession of the 1970s, began to reconsider the formerly discarded option of continental self-reliance and cooperation. In December 1976 a proposal for the establishment of an African Economic Community, modeled on the EEC, obtained the support of a number of prominent African officials who regarded the political and economic balkanization of the African continent as a major obstacle to its economic development. But the failures of earlier pan-African schemes furnished little hope to those who struggled to keep alive Nkrumah's ambitious project, and the movement petered out.

A middle ground between the bleak reality of balkanization and the utopian aspiration of continental unity was the prospect of regionalism. The emergence of regionalist aspirations in Africa reflected the failure of the economies of the individual African nations to fulfill post-independence expectations. In 1980 the African states endorsed the so-called Lagos Plan of Action (LPA) as an emergency response to the deteriorating economic conditions on the continent. While paying lip service to the ultimate objective of African economic unity by the end of the century, the LPA favored the strengthening of existing regional economic units and the formation of new ones as the most practical means of fostering economic growth in the short term and full continental integration in the long term. The principal regional associations were the Economic Community for West African States (ECOWAS), the Economic Community for Central African States (ECCAS), the Southern African Development Coordination Conference (SADCC), and the Preferential Trade Area (PTA) for East and Southern Africa. Together these organizations covered all of tropical Africa and represented the only existing mechanisms for economic cooperation that might reverse the trend toward degeneration and decay.

The most promising of these regional associations was ECOWAS, founded in May 1975 in Lagos, Nigeria, by the representatives of fifteen West African nations. Based on the principle of collective self-reliance and regional cooperation, ECOWAS rapidly developed into a test case in Africa's campaign to loosen the neocolonial bonds with Europe that had been tightened in the Lomé system. In particular, Nigeria's dominant role in ECOWAS, together with its sponsorship of the LPA, signified a determined bid for regional leadership by that large, populous, resource-rich country as it celebrated the triumph of national unity over the Biafran secessionist challenge of the late sixties and enjoyed the financial windfall from skyrocketing oil prices in the seventies. Nigeria's hegemonic aspirations in West Africa conflicted with France's neoimperial relationship with its clients in the region.* But anglophone Nigeria's cultural and linguistic isolation amid predominantly francophone neighbors who preferred Paris to Lagos as a source of guidance (and financial assistance) hampered Nigeria's ambition to become the dominant regional power in West Africa. The sharp decline in oil prices in the 1980s due to oversupply exposed the error of Nigeria's development strategy of relying on a single export commodity—whose price can go down as well as up—and resulted in a severe drop in that country's foreign exchange reserves. Nigeria's economic problems during the glut in world oil supplies damaged ECOWAS's emerging reputation as an indigenous alternative to the "Eurafrican" nexus in West Africa and as a model for regional integration for other parts of the continent.†

The economic crisis that gripped Africa in the 1970s was accompanied by an epidemic of armed conflict, both within and between a number of African societies, that aggravated the trend toward instability and insecurity on the continent. Two of these confrontations, the civil war in Chad and the rivalry between Morocco and Algeria over the former Spanish Sahara, reduced to shambles the pan-African ideal of the sanctity of frontiers and the sovereignty of postcolonial states. Worse, the new outbreak of violence in the seventies resulted in the very circumstance that the OAU had worked so hard (and so successfully) to prevent: the extension of the Cold War to Africa. Suddenly the Soviet Union appeared on the African scene, inevitably to be followed by the United States, and soon both superpowers were avidly courting clients and employing proxies as their global rivalry was extended to the continent.

The first of these developments occurred in July 1974, when the Kremlin

---

* Nigeria's population alone almost equals the combined population of all the francophone nations of West Africa.
† The cause of West African regional cooperation was boosted in the summer of 1990, when ECOWAS dispatched a five-nation force of 2,500 troops to preserve order in the Liberian civil war.

concluded a pact with the East African state of Somalia, which committed the Soviets to train and equip the Somali army in exchange for access to naval facilities at the port of Berbera on the Gulf of Aden as well as the use of two Soviet-constructed airfields in the country. In the meantime the Russian navy had acquired access to the old British base at Aden on the opposite shore of the gulf through an agreement with the revolutionary regime in South Yemen that had been established in 1967 after the end of British colonial rule.

But the escalating Soviet involvement in the northwest littoral of the Indian Ocean was complicated by a regional rivalry between the new Soviet client state of Somalia and the self-styled "Marxist-Leninist" military regime in Ethiopia that had overthrown the pro-Western Emperor Haile Selassie in 1974 and terminated the country's long standing relationship with the United States in early 1977. When Somali President Mohammed Siad Barre launched a military invasion of Ethiopia with the intention of annexing the Ogaden region with its ethnic Somali inhabitants, he turned from Moscow to Washington for support while the leftist regime in Addis Ababa predictably approached the Kremlin. In November 1977 Siad Barre abrogated the 1974 treaty of friendship, expelled all Soviet military personnel, and revoked Russian access to Somali naval and air facilities. In the meantime, Moscow began supplying Ethiopia with tanks, aircraft, and military advisers and air- and sea-lifted some 18,000 Cuban soldiers and their equipment to Ethiopia to relieve the beleagered forces of the Ethiopian strongman, Mengistu Haile Mariam. By 1978 Ethiopia had defeated Somalia in the Ogaden and proceeded to reward its Soviet benefactor with naval facilities at the port of Massawa to compensate for its loss of the Somali port of Berbera.

Just as the collapse of Haile Selassie's forty-four-year-old monarchy in 1974 resulted in the establishment of a Soviet client state on the Horn of Africa, the breakup of the Portuguese colonial empire after the overthrow in the same year of the forty-two-year-old dictatorship in Lisbon afforded Moscow the opportunity to extend its influence to the southern tip of the continent. In 1975–76 the Soviet Union transported 20,000 Cuban troops together with tanks, armored personnel carriers, and small arms to the former Portuguese colony of Angola on the west coast of Africa to support the Marxist-oriented Popular Movement for the Liberation of Angola (MPLA) in its struggle with an American-backed rival organization. The triumph of the pro-Soviet faction in the Angolan civil war was assured in December 1975 when the United States Congress, as part of a post-Vietnam reaction against overseas military entanglements, voted to cut off American aid to the western-backed faction in Angola. The victorious MPLA proceeded to form a Marxist government in Luanda; its president, Agostinho Neto, concluded a treaty of friendship and cooperation with the Soviet Union in October 1976; and Cuban troops remained in the country to combat rival guerilla groups operating in the south. Moscow appeared, therefore, to have gained a foothold in an African country with substantial oil reserves, vast untapped mineral resources, and a strategic location astride the sea route around the Cape of Good Hope. On the other hand, the Russians failed to obtain naval facilities on the Angolan coast; American multinational corporations such as Gulf Oil, General Tire, and Chase Manhattan Bank retained their large investments in the country; and Angolan President José Eduardo dos Santos (who assumed power after Neto's death in 1979) expressed an interest in reducing his country's dependence on the Soviet Union and in forging closer economic ties to the west.

Nevertheless, the Soviet Union had undeniably advanced its strategic interests in the Horn and southern Africa during the second half of the 1970s. Several hundred Russian military advisers and an estimated 41,000 Cuban troops operated in a dozen countries on a continent that had previously been immune to Communist bloc influence. In addition to the Soviet client states in Ethiopia and Angola, regimes that called themselves Marxist were established with Soviet-bloc assistance in Mozambique, the Congo Republic, and Benin (formerly Dahomey). In North Africa, the radical Arab regime of Colonel Muammar al-Qaddafi in Libya, which had toppled the pro-Western monarchy in 1969, nationalized American oil properties, closed down the American and British air bases in the country, received substantial Soviet economic and military assistance and generally supported Moscow's foreign policy goals. The ambitious Qaddafi also began to intervene in the internal affairs of the neighboring pro-Western regimes of Chad, the Sudan, Somalia, and Liberia in what appeared to be a campaign to establish Libya as the dominant power in its subregion.

As we have seen, Africa had been largely disengaged from the superpower rivalry that had drawn most other parts of the Third World into the Cold War. As Great Britain, France, and Belgium divested themselves of their African possessions the newly independent states that were fashioned out of the former colonial empires succeeded in avoiding having to choose between Moscow and Washington in the East–West struggle. The few instances of superpower engagement in Africa before the mid-1970s—the establishment of American military bases in pre-Qaddafi Libya and Morocco, the unsuccessful Soviet intervention in the Congo—merely prove the rule. Africa played a minor role in United States foreign trade and investment and no role at all in American security concerns. Their former colonial masters in the European Community remained the most important economic partners of the newly independent African states, while France continued to exercise the principal foreign military function in its former domains on the continent. The Soviet Union lacked the capacity and apparently the will to sustain a major campaign to extend its influence to Africa. It was the belated collapse of the Portuguese and Ethiopian empires and the intensification of the struggle for black majority rule in Rhodesia (Zimbabwe) and South-West Africa (Namibia) that permitted Moscow to exploit this African turbulence for its own advantage at a time when the

Kremlin had acquired the logistical capability to project its power to the African continent.

The response of the United States to the escalating Soviet involvement in Africa underwent a gradual transformation in the course of the second half of the 1970s. As noted earlier, the Ford–Kissinger administration was prevented from intervening in the Angolan civil war by a Democratic-controlled Congress traumatized by the Vietnam experience. The Carter administration originally displayed an uncharacteristic sensitivity to African concerns and deemphasized the global context of the regional conflicts that were sweeping the continent. The appointment of the prominent civil rights leader Andrew Young as America's first black ambassador to the United Nations; the repeal of the 1971 Byrd amendment (which authorized the importation of Rhodesian chrome in violation of United Nations sanctions against the renegade white minority regime in Salisbury that had declared its independence from Britain in 1965 rather than submit to black majority rule); the sustained effort to promote a negotiated settlement between South Africa and the South-West Africa People's Organization (SWAPO) with the goal of establishing black majority rule in South-West Africa (Namibia)—all of these actions signaled the determination of the new American president to identify his country with the liberationist aspirations of the African states rather than to see them as mere pawns in the East–West struggle.

But the Soviet-Cuban engagement in Africa gradually produced a shift of Carter administration policy in the direction of greater toughness, as indicated by its refusal to recognize the new Angolan regime unless Cuban troops were withdrawn from the country and its decision to assist French military forces that were dispatched to Zaire in the spring of 1978 to help the pro-Western Mobutu regime repel an invasion of Shaba province by exiles allegedly trained in Angola by Cuban advisers. From 1978 on, President Carter and his anti-Soviet national security adviser, Zbigniew Brzezinski, periodically warned Moscow that its activities in Africa were having an adverse effect on the fragile East–West detente that both Carter and Brezhnev wished to preserve.

The sharp reaction from Washington to the Soviet-Cuban activity in Africa reflected a concern that had been mounting ever since the oil embargo of 1973, namely, apprehension about a possible cutoff of a whole range of strategic minerals that the United States imported from Africa in large quantities: chrome, antimony, cobalt, vanadium, platinum, manganese, and ferromanganese, not to speak of crude oil (of which Nigeria had become America's second largest supplier). The destabilizing activities of the Soviet-backed regime of Qaddafi in Libya, as well as the Soviet-supported challenges to the autocratic American client state in Zaire, threatened to undermine the security of pro-Western regimes on the continent and jeopardize American access to their strategic resources. In a more general sense, the Soviet Union's intervention in Africa, either directly or through its Cuban proxies, confirmed in the minds of American strategic thinkers that country's transformation from a Eurasian land power to a global power with worldwide air and naval capabilities. The rapid deployment of Cuban troops, tanks, and military equipment to Angola and Ethiopia seemed to demonstrate Moscow's ability to leapfrog the ring of containment states that had been forged by the United States during the Cold War era. The Soviet naval squadron that patrolled the Red Sea and the Indian Ocean from bases in Ethiopia and South Yemen was seen in Washington as a potential menace to the Western world's lifeline to the petroleum reserves of the Persian Gulf.

Thus, by the end of the 1970s, the OAU's hallowed maxims of African unity and nonalignment had been dealt a severe blow by the polarization of the continent along ideological lines: The francophone states of West and Central Africa, Zaire, Egypt, Morocco, the Sudan, Kenya, and Somalia had established or intensified security ties with the West. In the meantime Angola, Ethiopia, Guinea-Bissau (formerly Equatorial Guinea), Libya, and Mozambique openly identified with the Socialist bloc, while Algeria, Guinea, and Uganda received Soviet aid. This East–West rivalry in Africa opened deep fissures within the OAU: When the insurgents in Angola invited the covert intervention of South Africa and the government in Luanda welcomed Cuban troops in the mid-1970s, the organization split down the middle on the question of which side to support. Later, when the embattled regimes in Zaire and Chad looked to Paris for military assistance, they received encouragement from other pro-Western, conservative African leaders but aroused the ire of those African states that identified with the East bloc.

But the Soviet-American competition in Africa that had emerged so unexpectedly during the second half of the seventies proved to be short lived because of Moscow's inability to supplement its military aid with much in the way of economic support (such as trade, loans, and investments). In particular, the inconvertibility of East bloc currencies precluded the expansion of African trade with Comecon countries beyond the customary bilateral barter schemes. By the time of Brezhnev's death in 1982, the Kremlin's bid for influence in Africa had failed ignominiously. In rapid succession, African countries that had once welcomed aid and advice from the East bloc—Egypt, Somalia, the Sudan, and Guinea—broke with their former benefactors and dislodged the Soviets from their privileged positions. Even those African states that retained some of the rhetoric of Marxist-Leninism, such as Angola, Mozambique, and Guinea, declined to seek admission to Comecon for the pragmatic economic reasons cited above. When they looked abroad for financial relief, it was not to Moscow, but to New York, London, Tokyo, Paris, or Washington (the IMF and the World Bank). Thus the Western bloc, due to its dominant position in the international economic system from which Africa could not, or would not, shake free, continued to exercise the dominant external influence on the continent throughout the 1980s.

The persistence of Africa's dependence on external powers in the Western world was graphically demonstrated in the civil war in Chad. For fifteen years this resource-poor, landlocked, ethnically divided country languished under the corrupt dictatorship of N'garta Tombalbaye, who displayed undisguised favoritism toward the settled Christian inhabitants of the south at the expense of the nomadic Islamic population in the north. In 1975 the overthrow and execution of Tombalbaye in a military coup plunged Chad into political chaos. In 1977 the northern Moslems, fortified by links with their coreligionists in the Arab world, issued a secessionist demand for the establishment of a separate Islamic republic. In the meantime, the adjacent Islamic state of Libya to the north exploited this civil conflict by dispatching troops to bolster its historic claim to the northern portion of Chad known as the Aouzou strip. French military forces thereupon intervened to counter the Libyans, and Paris eventually threw its support behind a Chadian leader named Hissène Habré, who waged a long campaign throughout the 1980s—interrupted by periodic truces of brief duration—against Qaddafi's army and its indigenous allies in northern Chad. Efforts of the OAU to intervene in the dispute came to naught, and the intrusive French involvement in Habré's campaign to expel Libyan forces from Chad once again revealed the limits to Africa's ability to manage its own affairs.*

Another blow to the cause of African unity and stability was the conflict that erupted during the same period in the territory known as the Spanish Sahara. In 1974 the government of Spain, weakened by the mortal illness of its longtime dictator, Francisco Franco, hastily unveiled plans for a plebiscite to enable the inhabitants of Spain's last remaining colonial possession to determine their political future. The contiguous states of Morocco and Mauritania simultaneously registered strenuous objections to this democratic method of decolonization, asserting their own historic claims to the territory (which coincidentally possessed one of the world's largest deposits of phosphates). The Moroccan monarch, Hassan II, personally led an expedition of 350,000 of his compatriots into the northern portion of the Spanish Sahara to demand its reincorporation into "Greater Morocco," the twentieth-century reincarnation of an ancient Arab Empire that once dominated the region. Faced with the prospect of conflict with African states over a territory it had already decided to evacuate, Madrid prudently shelved the idea of a plebiscite and concluded a secret agreement to hand over the northern two-thirds of the Spanish Sahara to Morocco and the southern one-third to Mauritania. When the last Spanish forces withdrew

---

* After the failure of the Libyan adventure in Chad, Habré was overthrown by a disgruntled former associate in 1990. France declined to intervene on behalf of its former protégé in what it viewed as a quarrel between rival Chadian leaders.

in February 1976, Moroccan and Mauritanian troops promptly occupied the zones alloted to them by their understanding with the departing colonial power, and the former Spanish possession disappeared within the expanding frontiers of its two neighbors.

But this territorial transfer had occurred without the assent of its inhabitants. In 1973 they had founded a national independence movement named Polisario (a Spanish acronym for the Popular Front for the Liberation of the Western Sahara) to hasten the departure of the Spanish. As Spain withdrew, Polisario promptly proclaimed a "Saharawi Republic," obtained diplomatic recognition from most member states of the OAU, and proceeded to wage guerilla warfare against the occupation forces of Morocco and Mauritania. By 1979 the economically depressed, politically unstable Mauritania was compelled to withdraw its troops from, and renounce its territorial claims to, the southern third of the Western Sahara. Morocco thereupon moved its forces southward and proceeded to annex the area evacuated by the Mauritanians. In the meantime Algeria (which had quarreled with Morocco from 1962 to 1972 over their own postcolonial boundary) vigorously opposed Morocco's designs in the Western Sahara and furnished substantial diplomatic and economic support to Polisario. Throughout the 1980s, the Moroccan-Algerian rivalry in the Western Sahara remained another major impediment to the doomed cause of pan-African cooperation, splitting the OAU into pro-Rabat and pro-Algiers (and pro-Polisario) factions.

Another casualty of the struggle over the Western Sahara was the hope for some type of regional cooperation among the peoples inhabiting the area of North Africa commonly known as the Maghreb,* which includes the countries of Algeria, Morocco, Tunisia, Mauritania, and Libya. Linked by a common language (Arabic) and religion (Islam) that set them apart from other African states, the countries of the Maghreb had groped for some type of regional identity and collective purpose ever since their liberation from European colonial control. But these linguistic and religious affinities proved to be inadequate sources of cohesion amid the national rivalries that plagued the region, such as the acrimonious border disputes between Algeria and Morocco and between Libya and Tunisia. These competing territorial ambitions were aggravated by the sharp ideological contrast among the Maghreb's constituent states: Morocco (a conservative, pro-Western monarchy), Algeria and Libya (radical republics with close ties to the East bloc), Tunisia (a conservative, pro-Western republic), and Mauritania (a military dictatorship). Thus, throughout the 1980s the Arab-speaking nations of North Africa were no more successful in forging a strong regional identity—as a less ambitious alternative to the elusive pan-African

---

* The term "Maghreb" means "the Arab West" (literally "where the sun sets"), that is, the Arabic-speaking region of North Africa. It is contrasted with the "Mashreg" ("the Arab East"), which refers to the area known in the Western world as "the Middle East."

ideal—than were the francophone and anglophone countries south of the Sahara. The formation in February 1989 of the Arab Maghreb Union by these five states, though a promising step in that direction, seemed little more than a desperate effort to coordinate regional economic activities in the face of Europe's move toward a single market in 1992.*

If postindependence Africa was being torn apart by the various disruptive tendencies—economic, ethnic, ideological—discussed above, there was one issue on which all of the African states agreed: That was the necessity of removing the last bastion of white supremacy on the continent, the system of racial separation, or apartheid, practiced in the Republic of South Africa† since 1948. As the white ruling elite in the British, French, and Belgian colonial possessions in Africa submitted to black majority rule at the beginning of the sixties, the white minority government of South Africa cracked down on the restive indigenous population that sought to emulate their brethren to the north. The massacre of over a hundred unarmed black demonstrators by the South African police at Sharpeville in March 1960 was Pretoria's defiant response to the growing opposition to apartheid in this mineral-rich country. All attempts by the black majority to obtain the political rights that most other Africans had already acquired met with determined resistance from the ruling National Party, mouthpiece of the Afrikkaner-speaking descendents of Dutch and French emigrants from seventeenth-century Europe. The African National Congress (ANC), originally a moderate organization that had been founded in 1912 to promote the interests of South Africa's disenfranchised, exploited black majority, was brutally suppressed by South African security forces. One of its prominent officials, a Cape Town lawyer named Nelson Mandela, was arrested in 1963 and sentenced to life imprisonment, while the remainder of its leadership fled into exile. Precluded from engaging in legal political activity, the ANC endorsed the only alternative: armed struggle. The first major outbreak of violence came in 1976, when student riots in the black township of Soweto outside Johannesburg resulted in at least 575 deaths. In the meantime, organizations such as the OAU, the Commonwealth, and the UN continually denounced the South African regime and the ruling elites of the newly independent states insistently demanded the end of apartheid and the advent of black majority rule.

Throughout the sixties and well into the seventies, South Africa profited from the presence of a protective shield across its northern border in the form of friendly, white-controlled states that had resisted the trend toward decolonization: the Portuguese possessions of Angola and Mozambique, the white minority regime in Rhodesia, and the former German colony of South-West Africa (which had been administered by South Africa since

---

* See below, p. 483.
† In 1960 the Union of South Africa, a member of the British Commonwealth since 1910, was transformed into an independent republic and severed its ties to the British crown.

the end of World War I under a long-expired mandate from the long-defunct League of Nations).

But the emergence of the two self-professed Marxist-Leninist regimes in Angola and Mozambique in 1975, followed by the belated introduction of black majority rule in Rhodesia (renamed Zimbabwe) in 1980, confronted South Africa with antagonistic northern neighbors that were willing to lend aid and sanctuary to insurgents against the Pretoria regime. Throughout the eighties, South Africa clung tenaciously to South-West Africa (renamed Namibia) as its last remaining buffer against Black Africa. But an insurrection launched by the South-West Africa Peoples' Organization (SWAPO), together with diplomatic pressure from the world community (including gentle prodding from Washington) forced South Africa to enter into negotiations for a transfer of sovereignty in Namibia and to soften the harshness of apartheid at home. As the talks on Namibia's political future bogged down, South African President P. W. Botha took some small steps to broaden the electoral base of his country's rigidly racist political system: A new constitution approved by referendum in November 1983 enfranchised the colored (mixed-race) and Asian minorities, establishing a tricameral parliament with a separate legislative chamber for the white (4.5 million), colored (2.6 million), and Asian (800,000) citizens (but continuing to exclude the 25 million members of the black majority).

The dangling of the carrot, represented by the talks on independence for Namibia and the granting of limited political reform within South Africa, was accompanied by the wielding of the stick against hostile states to the north: In 1980 South Africa began to apply strong pressure against neighboring regimes that had given sanctuary to ANC guerillas. Economic and military assistance flowed from Pretoria to insurgent organizations such as the Mozambique National Resistance Movement (MNR), UNITA in Angola, and the Lesotho Liberation Army in Lesotho. The unrelenting economic warfare and periodic search and destroy raids against Mozambique proved so successful in destabilizing the shaky regime of Samora Michel that it was obliged to sign the Nkomati Agreement* with South Africa in March 1984, whereby South Africa agreed to terminate its support for the MNR in exchange for Mozambique's pledge to control the activities of the ANC guerillas on its territory. A similar pact was foisted on Lesotho, which was totally dependent on South Africa for its economic viability.

But the internal challenge to the South African government continued, resulting in the declaration of a state of emergency in July 1985. With a handful of exceptions—including Hastings Banda of Malawi and Félix Houphouët-Boigny of the Ivory Coast—African leaders pursued a policy of economic sanctions, nonrecognition, and support for the ANC-led armed resistance within South Africa in order to bring down this last bastion of white privilege on the continent. In the meantime the Reagan administration in Washington pursued its policy of "constructive engagement," which

* Named after the river forming the boundary between South Africa and Mozambique.

was aimed at the conclusion of an agreement between South Africa and Angola that would lead to the simultaneous withdrawal of South African and Cuban forces from the latter country, as well as the eventual establishment of black majority rule in Namibia.* But by the mid-1980s, the southern part of the African continent remained mired in violence and instability: insurgencies raged in Angola, Mozambique, Namibia, and South Africa while the two superpowers observed the chaotic situation with interest and concern.

* The imposition of economic sanctions on South Africa by the U.S. Congress in 1986 was also intended to prod the government in Pretoria into adopting political reforms.

CHAPTER 15

The Far East: The Road to the New Co-Prosperity Sphere

The Miracle of Japan

At the end of the summer of 1945, the Japanese empire lay in ruins. This once proud, defiant society had suffered a humiliating defeat in war, the loss of its colonial possessions, and the destruction of a quarter of its infrastructure by American strategic bombing (conventional as well as atomic). During its military occupation of the Japanese islands between 1945 and 1952, the United States had treated its former enemy with a combination of political firmness and economic leniency: By imposing on the defeated power a democratic political system and a constitution that renounced war and the development of the means to wage it, the occupying power banished the threat of Japanese militarism that had plagued East Asia for decades. But by acquiescing in, nay, actively encouraging, the *economic* recovery of Japan, the United States had set in motion the process whereby its former enemy was to become—within a generation of Hiroshima—its major commercial and financial competitor in the world.

We have already noted the important U.S. contribution to the economic recovery of Japan after the Second World War in the context of the emerging Cold War in Asia (see page 377): The provision of almost $2 billion of American aid—mostly in the form of food and raw materials, which were in dangerously short supply—rescued Japanese society from the immediate consequences of its wartime devastation. The abandonment of reparation requirements by the end of the 1940s removed a potentially damaging claim on Japanese production that might well have discouraged domestic savings, investment, and entrepreneurial activity. The revocation of plans to dissolve the industrial conglomerates that had collaborated with the imperial government before and during the war paved the way for the reemergence, in modified form, of old Zaibatsu powerhouses such as Mitsubishi, Mitsui, and Sumitomo. This American willingness to tolerate the cartelization of Japanese industry in the interest of efficiency and economy of scale also facilitated the formation of huge new firms on the Zaibatsu model, such as Hitachi, Toshiba, Toyota, and Nissan. By 1949 Japan had already attained its prewar level of productivity, owing in large part to the benevolent economic policy pursued by the U.S. military occupation authorities. In the following year, the Korean War added a powerful stimulus to Japanese industrial production in the form of American military purchases of war-related goods and equipment. Another notable American contribution to Japan's postwar economic revival was the provision of U.S. military protection under the mutual defense treaty of 1952: Postwar Japan never had to spend more than 1 percent of its GNP on defense, and the resulting financial savings were channeled into industrial reconstruction and development.

But it would be inaccurate to attribute Japan's postwar economic recovery solely, or even primarily, to American encouragement and protection. United States occupation policies between 1945 and 1952 may have laid the foundation for national recuperation, but the subsequent "Japanese miracle" was a product of trends intrinsic to the island nation itself. Foremost among these were such sociocultural factors as the Japanese people's renowned industriousness (which yielded a willingness to work long hours at low pay) and frugality (which resulted in one of the highest savings rates in the world, in some years approaching 25 percent of disposable income). Japanese society's adoption of an ethic of austerity emphasizing production over consumption and deferred over instant gratification was in large part responsible for the low labor costs and high capital formation that afforded the Japanese economy its competitive advantage on the world market.

Another significant factor in Japan's postwar economic revival was the active, interventionist role assumed by the state in the promotion of industrial production and foreign trade. The Japanese government, acting through bureaucratic agencies spearheaded by the powerful Ministry for International Trade and Industry (MITI), skillfully employed monetary incentives such as subsidized interest rates on loans and preferential tax treatment to encourage the diversion of the country's productive factors—labor, capital, and raw materials—to firms engaged in the export trade. The state also looked with favor on the high degree of concentration that characterized Japanese industry in general and the export business in particular. The goals of achieving economies of scale, avoiding duplication, and discouraging destructive competition resulted in the establishment of ten gigantic foreign trade cartels that collectively accounted for more than half of Japan's total exports. This strategy of export-oriented growth reflected Japan's reduced geopolitical situation in the postwar world: Deprived of its colonial empire and the economic resources that it had once provided to Japanese industry, the small island was obliged to ship finished manufactured goods to foreign markets in order to pay for the imports of food, fuel, and raw materials that were sorely lacking at home. The results of this export drive were extraordinary: Japanese exports, which were negligible in 1949, had risen to 3.2 percent of total world exports in 1961 and 10 percent of the total by 1986.

The remarkable expansion of Japan's export trade depended on two characteristics of the postwar international economic order. The first was the relatively free access to foreign markets that had been facilitated by the periodic tariff reduction negotiations undertaken under the auspices of the General Agreement on Tariffs and Trade (GATT). By targeting a handful of potentially lucrative markets and flooding them with manufactured goods priced slightly above or, in some cases, even at the cost of production, Japan succeeded in underselling foreign competitors in their own domains. As a consequence, the United States became Japan's major foreign customer, taking more than a third of Japanese exports by 1984, with Europe occupying a distant second place. By 1986 an astonishing 22 percent of all U.S. imports came from the small island nation across the Pacific. The second sine qua non of Japan's export growth was the assured availability of relatively inexpensive raw materials, food, and, above all, energy. From the end of the Second World War through the early 1970s, commodity prices remained at bargain levels relative to the prices of finished manufactured products. This disparity represented an extremely important advantage to Japan, which was deeply dependent on foreign sources of minerals, agricultural products, and fuel.

But all of the aforementioned domestic and international conditions favorable to Japan's economic development were insufficient in themselves to account for that country's phenomenal postwar recovery. What had also been required was a strategy for exploiting the advantages and compensating for the disadvantages of Japan's economic situation. In retrospect, it is difficult to recall a country with greater economic disabilities than Japan confronted in the years after the Second World War: insufficient arable land, raw materials, and energy; a severe shortage of capital due to the destruction of plant during the war and an epidemic of inflation after it; and the curse of overpopulation, aggravated by the return of six million soldiers and settlers from China, Korea, and the islands that had been conquered and colonized in the years of Japanese imperial expansion.

But what had appeared at first glance to be a severe disadvantage—a population too large for the available land, food, and fuel—came to represent, in the eyes of the economic planners in Tokyo, a veritable bonanza: a large, compliant work force willing to endure working conditions and wage rates that would have been intolerable to organized labor in the Western industrialized countries. Japanese employers, therefore, had the edge on competitors in other industrialized countries, whose higher labor costs led to higher prices for the finished product. In short, Japan compensated for its comparative disadvantage of insufficient raw materials, food, fuel, and capital by successfully exploiting its comparative advantage of low labor costs to produce labor-intensive manufactured goods—mainly in the textile, iron, steel, and shipbuilding industries—which it exported at competitive prices to high-labor-cost markets such as the United States.

By the 1960s, as the profits from foreign sales of these labor-intensive manufactured products accumulated, and as Japanese firms benefited from the continued record-breaking savings rate of Japanese citizens, the second, or capital-intensive, phase of Japan's postwar economic development began. The country's comparative advantage lay no longer in low labor costs—as we shall see, other East Asian nations were beginning to produce labor-intensive goods at lower prices as Japanese workers demanded higher wages—but rather in the accumulation of capital for productive investment. The Japanese government shrewdly responded to this evolution in the country's comparative advantage by shifting resources from the labor-intensive to the capital-intensive sector of the economy. Accordingly, as Japanese exports of textiles, iron and steel goods, and ships declined, they were replaced by new products such as petrochemicals, television sets, transistor radios, motorcycles and, finally, automobiles—of which Japan became the world's leading producer in the year 1980.

By the decade of the seventies, another important evolution in Japan's comparative advantage prompted a further change in the structure of its export trade: Having produced an ample supply of well educated, highly skilled technicians, scientists, and engineers, Japan began to redirect its economic resources from the capital intensive to the technology-intensive sector. At first it concentrated on importing foreign technology and adapting it to Japan's particular requirements, but soon began to promote domestic research and development that would generate homegrown production techniques and technologies. As a result, the label "made in Japan," once associated with cheap manufactured goods of dubious quality, came to designate state-of-the-art products of highly sophisticated design. In the meantime, the old labor-intensive industries that had dominated the first phase of Japan's trade expansion had virtually disappeared: In the mid-1950s, textiles and clothing products had accounted for more than a third of Japanese exports. By 1984, that proportion had declined to 3.6 percent. A similar trend was evident in the old iron, steel, and shipbuilding industries. Instead, world markets were being saturated with technology-intensive products from Japan such as telecommunications equipment, office machines, electrical machinery, computers, and precision instruments. By the early 1980s, this small, resource-poor, overpopulated island off the coast of China had surpassed its gigantic neighbor, the Soviet Union, as the second economic power of the world (as measured by GNP and most other universally recognized indices).

If Japan had surpassed the Soviet Union as the second industrial power of the world by the early 1980s, it was to overtake the United States to become the world's first financial power by the middle of that decade. The collapse of the "Bretton Woods" system of dollar-gold convertibility and fixed exchange rates in the early 1970s had exposed the vulnerability of the American monetary position in the world, which continued to deteriorate throughout the decade. During the 1980s, the combination of drastic tax reduction and increased defense spending under President Reagan during the first half of the 1980s generated an enormous federal budget deficit that was increasingly financed by foreign (and mainly Japanese) loans. As a result of this heavy foreign borrowing, the United States underwent an extraordinary transformation from the world's largest creditor nation—an honor it had retained since the First World War—to the world's largest debtor nation, while Japan replaced it as the premier banker of the world.

As we have seen, Japan's export-driven industrial growth depended to a large extent on the availability of cheap energy supplies and raw materials from abroad as well as the unimpeded access to foreign markets for manufactured products that had been fostered by the postwar international trading system. In the course of the seventies, both of these advantageous conditions were endangered, with serious consequences for Japan. The sharp increase in world oil prices, not to speak of the prospect of petroleum-producer cartels, embargoes, and supply disruptions, represented a grave menace to a country that possessed no oil reserves of its own. Equally as ominous was the mounting threat of protectionism in the industrial world: Japan's enormous annual trade surplus with the European Community (EC), which ballooned from $506 million in 1970 to $12.2 billion in 1975 to $22.5 billion in 1986, generated angry charges of dumping and pleas for protection. By the early 1980s the European Community was erecting selective barriers against Japanese imports while some member states, such as France, were harrassing Japanese firms with cumbersome customs procedures. In the meantime, American manufacturers of automobiles, television sets, video equipment and other products consistently undersold by their Japanese counterparts pressured Washington into insisting that Tokyo agree to "voluntary export restraints." The combined result of the oil price increases and the emergence of protectionism in the developed world was a precipitous drop in Japan's growth rate, from an average of about 10 percent (from the mid-1950s to the mid-1970s) to 5 to 6 percent for the rest of the seventies and 3 to 4 percent in the early 1980s.

In the face of escalating costs of energy imports from the Middle East and protectionist threats to its export trade from the United States and Europe, Japan initiated a compensatory strategy of intensifying its economic links with the developing countries within its own region. Tokyo began to target East Asian countries for massive development assistance as part of a deliberate policy to promote regional economic cooperation. Private Japanese firms followed the government's lead by making substantial direct investments in mining and petroleum facilities in Southeast Asian countries for the purpose of securing reliable supplies of inexpensive raw materials and fossil fuels, while at the same time developing new markets for Japanese manufactured products as a hedge against American and

European protectionism. Meanwhile, Japanese companies that had abandoned labor-intensive production at home invested their retained earnings in light manufacturing concerns operating in low-wage East Asian countries in order to export low-priced goods to markets in the developed world.

The other nations of the region, as we shall see, eagerly welcomed and derived reciprocal benefits from Japan's financial and commercial expansion along the western rim of the Pacific: They received desperately needed capital to finance their own industrial development and obtained access to the Japanese market for their exports. Bitter memories of the wartime occupation combined with current concerns about the influx of Japanese goods occasionally engendered expressions of ill will, such as the anti-Japanese demonstrations during Prime Minister Kakuei Tanaka's tour of Southeast Asia in 1974. But Prime Minister Takeo Fukuda repaired much of the damage during a subsequent visit to the region in 1977 with a combination of tactful diplomacy and generous loan commitments, and this benevolent policy was sustained by subsequent governments.

By the 1980s Japan had largely succeeded in dispelling the residual feelings of distrust in its neighbors and had become not only their premier trading partner, but more significantly, a model for economic development that many of them were successfully emulating. After decades of backwardness and third-class status in the international economic order dominated by the Western industrial powers, the countries of East Asia had made the crucial decision to "look East," to profit from the lesson of the only non-Western country that had reached the highest level of economic performance. So well did they learn that lesson, and so successfully did they apply it to their own particular circumstances, that they became major trading powers in their own right by the 1980s.

The Gang of Four and ASEAN

The earliest Asian imitators of the Japanese example—South Korea, Taiwan, Singapore, and Hong Kong—have acquired, in the lexicon of international economics, two interchangeable sobriquets: "the gang of four"* and "the newly industrializing countries" (NICs). In common with the Japanese prototype, all four of these countries shared a set of characteristics—or what economists refer to as "factor endowment"—that would scarcely be considered conducive to economic development: Like most other developing nations, they suffered from overpopulation and a shortage of capital, but unlike many Third World societies, they were deficient in natural resources such as minerals and fossil fuels as well as arable land. The "Gang of Four" were able to turn these apparent disadvantages into advantages, to make a virtue out of necessity, as they resolutely followed

---

* A sardonic reference to the Chinese radicals Jiang Qing, Zhang Chunqiao, Yal Wenyuan, and Wang Hongwen, who had opposed Deng Xiaoping's economic reforms and his policy of closer ties with the West after Mao's death.

the path of export-driven industrialization that Japan had blazed for them a generation earlier. The shortage of mineral wealth, energy sources, and fertile agricultural land—which precluded nonindustrial alternatives, such as mining and farming, that were available to other developing countries in Africa and Latin America—provided a strong incentive to export finished manufactured products to pay for essential imports of raw materials, fuel, and food. As compensation for the capital shortage, the excess population (as in Japan) yielded an abundant supply of cheap, docile, mobile labor to produce low-cost manufactured goods that did not require large infusions of capital or sophisticated technologies.

Another characteristic that the East Asian NICs all shared—a common cultural heritage based on Confucianism that emphasized the virtues of frugality, industry, self-discipline, and hierarchy—provided a value system that was ideally suited to the type of production that the four industrializing societies had introduced: They all exploited—in both senses of the term— their overabundant, tractable work force by specializing in those labor-intensive sectors of light industry that required a large number of low-skilled workers willing to toil long hours at tedious, low-paying tasks, such as fabricating ready-to-wear garments or assembling discrete components of intricate machines.

The East Asian Gang of Four enjoyed the late-comer's advantage in their relationship with Japan: Once Japan had launched a new product and created a new market for it, South Korea, Taiwan, Hong Kong, and Singapore would move in and undercut the Japanese with their cheaper version of the original item. The NICs launched their earliest export drives in the 1960s with low-cost, low-quality textiles just as Japan was moving beyond the production of such labor-intensive products. In the following decade, as the profits generated by low labor costs enabled them (again, like Japan) to attract foreign capital to supplement domestic savings, they purchased more sophisticated machinery and equipment in a successful adaptation to the shift in comparative advantage from labor-intensive to capital-intensive production. Their export trade advanced up the product scale to radios, televisions, sewing machines, motorcycles, and ships as Japan moved into high technology products. By the 1980s, the advanced educational systems and technical training programs of the Gang of Four had begun to produce such a highly skilled, experienced work force that some of them even began to encroach on the Japanese domain in technology-intensive industries such as computers and biotechnology.

Amid the numerous similarities among the four East Asian NICs, one notable difference between them is to be found in the relative extent of government participation in economic development. At one end of the spectrum, South Korea developed a brand of "state capitalism" in which the government actively intervened in the economy by providing tax incentives and subsidies to encourage production in certain chosen sectors, by protecting favored firms and allowing others to decline, and by maintaining direct state ownership and control of certain basic industries. The ruling elites of Taiwan and Singapore, though less committed to the principle of centralized control of the economy, stressed government planning and made lavish use of public funds to promote private economic development in selected sectors. At the other end of the spectrum was Hong Kong, which introduced an unfettered laissez-faire capitalism characterized by low taxes, minimal government spending (except for the creation of the infrastructure necessary for economic development such as roads, harbors, sanitation, and education), and private ownership of business. But whatever the differences in emphasis between government guidance and private enterprise, they all displayed a preference for letting the invisible hand of world market forces rather than the heavy hand of government planning dictate the allocation of resources within their economies.

The extent of the East Asian economic achievement is revealed in the compartive growth statistics for all non-Western countries. With a combined population of only 3 percent of the total population of the developing world, the Gang of Four accounted for 60 percent of its total manufactured exports in 1976. From 1963 to 1976, their combined growth rate exceeded 6 percent, compared to less than 2 percent for the South Asian countries of India, Bangladesh, Nepal, Sri Lanka, and Burma. In the first decade after the Second World War, the United States and Great Britain had been obliged to supply economic aid to the resource- and food-poor countries of South Korea and Taiwan, and Singapore and Hong Kong, respectively. By the mid-1980s, the Western world could no longer sell manufactured goods to East Asia and faced stiff competition from East Asian manufactured exports in other markets. Canada, Australia, and the United States had settled into a peculiar kind of neocolonial relationship with the region, importing its manufactured products in exchange for food and raw materials while running up huge annual trade deficits with it.

As had been the case with Japan's earlier experience, the NICs' crash program of industrialization had depended on a number of conditions in the international system: In the security sphere, they had all benefited in varying degrees from United States military protection, with South Korea and Taiwan owing their very national existence to the projection of U.S. military and naval power across the Pacific. In the financial realm, all four had received massive infusions of Western capital, originally in the form of U.S. or U.K. government aid, then through commercial loans from American and European banks or direct investments from Western-controlled multinational corporations. But the most significant form of the NICs' dependence on extrinsic economic forces was to be found in the sphere of international trade: Two-thirds of their manufactured exports went to the countries of the industrialized world (primarily the U.S. and the E.C.).

This dependence on the Western-dominated international economic system developed into a potentially serious liability in the early 1980s as a result of three trends that endangered East Asia's continued growth. The first was the international debt crisis, with its flurry of defaults and re-schedulings, which reduced the amount of capital available for foreign lending while inspiring caution in the foreign loan departments of Western banks. The second was the severe recession in the industrialized world that caused a reduction in demand for East Asian exports. The third was the upsurge in protectionist sentiment in the United States and the European Community—already noted in connection with its potentially hazardous effect on Japan's foreign trade.

These three trends in the first half of the 1980s confirmed what had first been brought to light during the oil shocks of the previous decade—that the individual economies of Asia, despite their remarkable record of growth, shared with other developing regions, such as Africa and Latin America, the disadvantage that international economists call an "extra-regional bias." This means that the economic performance of each Asian country depended much more heavily on economic events outside the region than on those within it, leaving it vulnerable to trade disruptions caused by distant forces beyond its control. This preference for trade and financial ties with developed countries *outside* of Asia precluded the formation of an intraregional economic bloc as a buffer against adverse trends in the international economic order.

One of the principal obstacles to the forging of such intraregional economic links was the intense commercial rivalry that had developed among the NICs and between the NICs and Japan. Since these five industrial dynamos of Asia possessed essentially the same factor endowment, produced the same products, and exported to the same markets, competition rather than compementarity characterized their economic relations with one another. But the threat of interruptions in the deliveries of raw materials and energy, followed by the erection of protectionist barriers in the industrialized world, had obliged Japan and the Gang of Four to look for markets and natural resources closer to home. What they found was a new possibility for intensive regional economic cooperation with an organization known as the Association of Southeast Asian Nations (ASEAN).

Formed in August 1967 by the states of Indonesia, Malaysia, Thailand, and the Philippines—later joined by Brunei after its independence from Britain—ASEAN comprised economies that were admirably complementary to those of Japan and the Gang of Four: While deficient in capital and industrially undeveloped, they were richly endowed with many of the natural resources (such as petroleum, natural gas, wood, and foodstuffs) that Japan and the NICs lacked. Responding to this golden opportunity, Japan, South Korea, and Taiwan began to export finished manufactured goods and technology to these Southeast Asian countries in exchange for raw materials and fuel and to invest heavily in the oil, mining, forest, and agricultural sectors of their economies. The result of this intensified exchange of capital, manufactured products, and raw materials was the development of a complementary economic subsystem in Asia that in some respects resembled the neocolonial nexus between the United States and Latin America, or between the European Community and Africa. Or, as some observers recognized, it represented a benevolent version of the old imperial Japanese dream of the Greater East Asia Co-Prosperity Sphere, based on reciprocal economic interchange rather than unilateral military domination.

But by the end of the 1970s, the countries of ASEAN had grown dissatisfied with the role of commodity-producing junior partners of the dynamic industrialized economies to the north. They opted instead for the low-skilled, labor-intensive, low-cost, export-oriented strategy of industrialization that had previously enriched Japan and then the NICs. ASEAN was soon recording annual growth rates of between 6 and 8 percent in a period when most developing countries reeled from the effects of recession and excessive indebtedness. They began to make significant inroads in markets for low-cost manufactures in the industrialized world by edging out the Gang of Four with cheaply made and cheaply priced textile products. Once again, the law of comparative advantage seemed to operate with predictable regularity on the Asian stage as ASEAN made its bid for rapid industrialization.

In contrast to the situation in Japan and the NICs, however, commodities continued to account for the largest proportion of export earnings in Indonesia, Malaysia, Thailand, and the Philippines. Consequently, the members of ASEAN got the worst of both worlds in the seventies and early eighties: They were hit hard both by the sharp decline in commodity prices (with the exception of Indonesian oil) that periodically afflict primary producing countries and by the protectionist policies of the industrialized countries that cut into their earnings from manufactured exports. Then came a substantial increase in foreign indebtedness to finance mounting trade deficits, especially with Japan. In the meantime, the inevitable bill for the social costs of rapid industrialization came due: By attracting impoverished peasants from the countryside to the cities in order to depress wages and enhance their comparative advantage in labor-intensive manufactured exports, the fledgling industrial economies of ASEAN engendered a politically volatile situation. The inflation-induced decline in real wages, the widening gap between the urban wealth of the entrepreneurial few and the rural poverty of the multitude, and the age-old problem of the maldistribution of land resulted in violent rural insurrections in Indonesia, Thailand, and the Philippines that were ruthlessly quelled by their authoritarian governments.

But the most formidable menace to ASEAN's ambitions to follow Japan's and the NICs' path of industrial development while preserving its role as a supplier of raw materials, food, and fuel was the emergence of a new regional rival with similar goals. It also happened to be the world's most populous country and a major military power, whose unexpected plunge into the free-for-all of East Asian economic development confronted its neighbors with a host of new opportunities and risks.

The Deng Revolution in China

In an earlier chapter* we observed that the rapprochement between China and the United States during the first half of the 1970s had been prompted primarily by their common concern about the expansion of Soviet military power, and secondarily by the prospect of mutually profitable economic relations between the two countries. But while the Sino-American entente may have served the purpose of counterbalancing Soviet military power during the second half of the decade, it proved to be a bitter disappointment for American businesspeople eagerly eyeing the untapped China market of 800 million consumers, and even more so for the Chinese officials allied with Premier Zhou Enlai who had anticipated bounteous economic benefits in the form of trade, aid, loans, investments, and technology transfer from the capitalist countries.

China's first foray into the international economic system during the second half of the 1970s proved to be a false start that resulted in a colossal failure. After the death of Mao Zedong in 1976, his heir-apparent Hua Guofeng launched an ill-conceived campaign to modernize the Chinese economy by reverting to the old practice of promoting heavy industry through intrusive government planning while simultaneously soliciting foreign investment and loans from the industrialized world. A combination of excessive foreign borrowing, unsatisfactory contracts concluded with multinational firms, poor planning, and waste resulted in industrial stagnation and low agricultural productivity. The lack of technical, managerial, and entrepreneurial expertise, together with the absence of a sufficient infrastructure, prevented the Chinese economy from successfully employing the capital and applying the technology that was flowing from Japan, the United States, and the European Community. A paradoxical impediment to economic development in the world's most populous country was the absence of a sufficient internal market, owing to the fact that 80 percent of the Chinese population lived and worked on the farm at a bare subsistence level. Indeed, China's rural masses had sunk below that level during 1974–77, when the country's sluggish agricultural performance resulted in widespread famine that necessitated a substantial increase in food imports. China's inability to export manufactured products to pay for these essential food purchases abroad led to a fundamental reassessment of the first post-Mao development strategy and the cancellation or scaling back of most industrial projects in 1978.

The most important lesson learned from the experience of the 1970s was that China's best hope for economic modernization lay in discarding the remnants of the old Maoist plan of autarkic self-reliance and formu-

* See page 395.

lating a development strategy based on full integration in the international financial and trading system. The blueprints for such a scheme were readily at hand: The East Asian NICs and ASEAN countries had overcome their own substantial handicaps to establish impressive records of economic growth while China remained mired in industrial backwardness. The Chinese leader who undertook to implement this new development strategy was Deng Xiaoping, a protégé of Mao's late second-in-command, Zhou Enlai. Between 1978 and 1981 Deng gradually purged those domestic opponents (including his rival for the succession, Hua Guofeng) who bitterly accused him of betraying orthodox Maoist principles by exposing China's economy to the exploitataive forces of the international capitalist order.

Deng's ambitious program for China's modernization required a fundamental restructuring of the country's economic system. From 1950 to 1980 China had constructed a gigantic industrial apparatus by dint of its own efforts. The only foreign assistance it had received was in the form of plant and equipment imports from the Soviet Union during the fifties. In line with the Soviet prototype, resources had been channeled into state-run heavy industries such as defense, metallurgy, chemicals, and petroleum. Goods were allocated by government planning rather than supply and demand, and production was earmarked for the domestic market rather than for export. The path-breaking innovation of Deng, and his protégé Zhao Ziyang who replaced Hua Guofeng as prime minister in 1980, was to shift priorities from heavy to light industry and from import-substitution to export-oriented production. He also introduced into this long-time paragon of Marxist-Leninist orthodoxy a limited free market and private ownership of property. The result was the most spectacular transformation in China since the revolution of 1949. For better or for worse, the 1980s for China will be recalled as the Deng decade.

The Dengist-Zhaoist development strategy for the eighties was unabashedly based on the principle of the "open door," once an epithet associated with Western imperial domination: Through this open door would pass loans, investment, trade, technology, and tourists from abroad, while Chinese college students headed in the other direction in search of educational opportunities in the industrialized world that were unavailable at home. But the door would be open to only a portion of China, which was divided for the purposes of foreign economic relations into two discrete geographical categories: The interior part of the country, backward, rural, and underdeveloped, would remain largely untouched by the outside world; it would be relegated to the subsidiary role of nurturing inland infant industries to produce goods for the domestic market. The coastal region, with a population exceeding 200 million, would be tightly integrated with the international commercial and financial system in the hope that foreign trade and capital would serve as the engines of economic development for the entire country.

The first step in this coastal development strategy was taken in 1979 with the creation of four "special economic zones" comprising the southern cities of Shenzhen, Zuhai, Shantou, and Xiamen. Foreign companies engaged in light manufacturing were encouraged through tax incentives to set up joint ventures with Chinese companies, or to create their own fully owned subsidiaries, for export-oriented production. By the end of 1983, 188 equity joint venture contracts had been concluded with multinational firms, mostly in the tourist, construction, textile, and oil exploration industries. In 1984 the Chinese government designated fourteen additional coastal cities and Hainan island as tax havens for foreign capital. It is ironic that many of the same treaty ports from which Western trading interests had dominated the economy of imperial and republican China became the principal sites of foreign investment and commercial development in the Peoples' Republic. Throughout the 1980s the old imperialist bailiwick of Shanghai accounted for about 15 percent of China's total exports and 70 percent of its light industrial exports (such as clothing, textiles, bicycles, and sewing machines). Its inhabitants enjoyed a per capita income of $1800, placing it on a par with Taiwan and South Korea (the two NICs on whose free export zones the Chinese special economic zones on the southern coast had been modeled). Other success stories included Shenzhen next to Hong Kong and Zuhai opposite Macao. The glaring contrast between the booming treaty port region and the backward hinterland left the impression of two separate countries, the one advancing into the industrialized world, the other languishing in the Third, or what some economists have begun to call the Fourth, World.

It is scarcely surprising, in light of the complementarity of their two economies, that the most important foreign promoter and beneficiary of China's entry into the world economic system was Japan. China possessed the oil, coal, and strategic raw materials that Japan required, while Japan had the capital, technology, and high-level manufactured goods that China needed. With almost 25 percent of the world's population, China customarily received only about 1 percent of the world's total export value. As Japan encountered protectionist pressures from its premier trading partner across the Pacific, the lure of the potentially vast market on the Asian mainland proved irresistible. By 1985, China had replaced oil-exporting Saudi Arabia as Japan's second leading trading partner behind the United States. One-fourth of China's trade is with Japan, which remained China's top trading partner until 1987 when it was edged out by Hong Kong. These important commercial ties were matched by strong financial connections as well: Japan supplied about half the foreign credits that China received from 1979 to 1983. After exhibiting extreme caution in the category of direct investments during the first half of the 1980s (to Beijing's profound disappointment), Japanese direct investment in China soared from $100 million in 1985 to $2.2 billion in 1987.

Behind Japan and Hong Kong, China's other great economic partner throughout the 1980s was the United States. Though the value of Sino-American trade remained half that of Sino-Japanese trade in that decade, the economic links between the two countries came to overshadow their common strategic interest as the Russian threat to both began to subside. Sino-American trade increased from a paltry $375 million in 1977—before the advent of the Deng export strategy—to $2.3 billion in 1979 and 5 billion in 1980. Exploiting its comparative advantage of abundant, cheap labor—Chinese wages averaged $.60 an hour, compared to $12 in Japan and $20 in the United States—China proceeded in the course of the 1980s to replace the East Asian NICs as America's major supplier of low-cost clothing and textile products. But the surge of Chinese exports to the United States provoked a furious response from U.S. textile producers as well as from competitors in Taiwan and South Korea. An arduous round of negotiations produced an agreement in 1987 to restrict annual increases in Chinese textile exports to the United States for the following four years. In exchange for its shipments of light industrial goods to the U.S. market, China imported large quantities of agricultural commodities from the American Midwest.

Apart from food, the three most valuable commodities that the United States supplied to China during the 1980s were capital, technology, and managerial and technical skills, all of which were exceedingly scarce. By 1988, U.S. firms had investment commitments totaling over $3 billion in nearly 400 joint ventures situated in the special economic zones on the southern coast. Unlike the first wave of quick-profit-seeking entrepreneurs of the 1970s, these U.S. businesses had invested for the long haul: A typical example is the set of contracts concluded with U.S. oil companies in the early 1980s to develop China's vast offshore oil reserves. By 1982 oil and oil products already accounted for 21 percent of China's exports. By 1988 China had become, with the help of U.S. and Japanese direct investment, the world's fifth largest petroleum producer. In total, China attracted more than $7 billion of direct foreign investment from 1979 to 1987 at a time when the flow of private foreign capital to other developing countries had virtually dried up.

China's policy of acquiring foreign technology underwent a significant transformation after 1978. During the fifties, as we have seen, China had imported such technology as it received in the form of complete sets of equipment from the Soviet Union, largely in heavy industries such as metallurgy, electric power, and chemicals. The cutoff of Soviet technology deliveries after the Sino-Soviet split during the sixties thrust the country back on its own meager technological resources. Then the new opening to the capitalist world in the early seventies resulted in an expansion of foreign purchases, but the absence of a suitable infrastructure and inadequately trained managerial and technical personnel prevented China from adequately absorbing these technology imports. During the eighties China abandoned the old practice of importing complete plants in favor of a more discriminating strategy of acquiring key technologies and selected equipment through licensing agreements and joint ventures from the United States, Japan, and the European Community. The long-term goal was gradually to reduce dependence on foreign sources and establish a domestic technological base. Though the new policy resulted in a significant flow of technology from the developed world, Beijing remained dissatisfied on two counts. First of all, the old Coordinating Committee (CoCom) regulations dating from the early days of the Cold War imposed restrictions on U.S. technological exports to the People's Republic and these were only gradually removed in the course of the eighties. Second, Japan displayed an irritating reluctance to transfer technology at a sufficiently high level to satisfy those Chinese officials who dreamed of their country's becoming a major power in high tech by the year 2000.

As noted above, one of the principal impediments to the successful application of technology imports in China, in addition to the inadequate infrastructure, was the shortage of managerial and technical expertise. The decadence of the Chinese educational system, aggravated by the outburst of anti-intellectualism during the Cultural Revolution of the sixties, left China with a woefully insufficient supply of scientists, engineers, technicians, and managers to participate in the bold project of economic modernization that Deng had launched. Its only recourse was the acquisition of skills abroad. Between 1978 and 1988, almost 50,000 Chinese students were dispatched to foreign universities (two-thirds of them located in the United States) to learn subjects and techniques that were inadequately taught at home. The return of these educated young people proved to be a mixed blessing for the authorities in Beijing, however. While they had acquired the skills and training that were desperately needed by Chinese industry, they had been exposed to Western cultural influences and political ideas as well. The appearance on the streets of Chinese cities of women with makeup, young men in blue jeans, and teenagers of both genders with a taste for rock music, drugs, premarital sex, and other "Western" practices clashed with the puritanical ethic of Maoism that still prevailed in spite of the revolutionary economic innovations of the eighties. More seriously, the democratic principles that Chinese students had absorbed in the United States and Western Europe undermined the authoritarian, one-party system that continued to operate in China, notwithstanding the new constitution enacted by the National People's Congress in 1982 that ostensibly guaranteed civil liberties.

In addition to seeking bilateral loans and direct investments from the countries of the developed world, Dengist China also sought assistance from the various multinational organizations that ministered to the financial needs of the Third World. In November 1978, China formally requested technical assistance from the United Nations Development Program (UNDP), and within four years had become the largest recipient of UNDP funds (to the consternation of impoverished developing countries that were competing for the same scarce funds). China joined the IMF in 1980 and promptly borrowed funds from that organization to finance its balance of payments deficits in exchange for the customary deflationary pledges to balance the budget, control the growth of the money supply, increase interest rates, and reduce the trade deficit by cutting imports and expanding exports. China also obtained membership in the World Bank in 1980, and within seven years had received over $5.5 billion in funds as well as expert advice on economic policy from its subsidiary, the International Development Agency (IDA). In 1982 Beijing proceeded to acquire observer status in GATT, and in 1986 applied for formal membership (which would bring the advantage of greater access to foreign markets, but also the obligation to disclose domestic economic practices to intrusive officials). China's increasingly intimate relationship with these three Western-dominated international organizations, which had long been denounced by the Maoist leadership as instruments of imperialist hegemony, signified its total acceptance of, nay, avid participation in, the capitalist world order.

It also represented China's abandonment of the other developing nations in the Third World, whose interests it had championed against the superpowers in the Maoist years. By the end of the 1970s China had terminated its own economic assistance program to developing countries and was soon, as we have seen, competing with them for loans, aid, and direct investments from international agencies as well as Western banks and corporations. China's per capita GNP of $280 in the mid-1980s placed it 130th among the world's 169 countries. Yet the post-Mao leadership had decisively rejected the neo-Marxist dependency theory embraced by many intellectual defenders of Third World interests, which promoted national self-reliance and isolation from the world capitalist system. It had also repudiated the radical concept of the global transfer of wealth from north to south associated with the New International Economic Order. Instead, it had unconditionally embraced the familiar Western liberal model of national economic development through global interdependence, the international division of labor, and the pursuit of comparative advantage, which dictated fuller integration with (rather than isolation from or the radical restructuring of) the international trading and financial system.

The record of China's economic achievement during the 1980s was an impressive one: Its foreign trade grew from $38.6 billion in 1980 to almost $80 billion in 1987, with petroleum and petroleum products as well as textiles and clothing representing the major earners of foreign exchange. China's productivity gains catapulted it from equivalency to three times as great as India—an Asian country with which it had been frequently compared—and its growth rates during the eighties approached those of the Gang of Four. Simply put, it has become the latest NIC as its predecessors left behind a huge market for labor-intensive manufactured products on their advance up the scale of comparative advantage. But China also possesses two trump cards that it may be able to play in the future contest for economic primacy in Asia. The first is its lavish endowment of raw materials and energy supplies, which will represent a significant advantage over resource-poor competitors such as Japan and the Gang of Four. The second is the potentially enormous (though currently undeveloped) Chinese domestic market, which could absorb part of the industrial production that might be cut off from markets in the United States and the European Community in the event that current protectionist trends result in a trade war. In any case, the long sleeping giant of Asia has awakened, with incalculable consequences for its neighbors and the world.

Some of the fascinating questions posed by China's entry into the international economic order are worth recording: Will China be capable of developing a mutually beneficial economic partnership with Japan that does not saddle her with a neocolonial form of dependency? If so, will a Beijing–Tokyo axis dominate the rest of Asia, as China's exports of manufactured goods and raw materials (not to speak of its territorial claims against Hong Kong and Taiwan as well as its influence over Chinese minorities in Southeast Asian countries) jeopardize the NICs' and ASEAN's quest for development and generate economic and political tensions in the region. Or will the result be a prosperous economic community on the western rim of the Pacific, characterized by a high degree of regional cooperation—a genuine "*co*-prosperity sphere—that might serve as a useful model for developing countries in other parts of the world? Finally, in light of the bloody suppression of the prodemocracy movement on Beijing's Tiananmen Square in June 1989, will China prove any more capable than the authoritarian regimes that presided over the industrialization of Taiwan, South Korea, Singapore, and the ASEAN countries of discovering a means of making Western-style political liberties compatible with a crash program of economic development in a Third World setting?

As China began its radical *economic* reorientation in the late 1970s, it simultaneously pursued new *diplomatic* and *security* policies that also diverged sharply from past practices. In the diplomatic realm, Deng Xiaoping decisively abandoned Mao's doctrine equating both superpowers as China's adversaries in favor of a full-fledged rapprochement with the United States in the face of what he perceived as the greater threat from Moscow. The arrest in 1976 and the trial and imprisonment in 1980 of the so-called "Gang of Four" (which included Mao's widow Jiang Qing and three associates) signified Deng's triumph over the faction within the Chinese ruling elite that opposed the opening to the West. In the meantime, the evidence of China's increasing diplomatic cooperation with the United States was evident in virtually every region of the world, but was particularly striking in Africa. The Beijing regime that had once promoted and financed Marxist revolutions across the globe sided with the United States and South Africa in support of an anti-Communist insurgency against the Soviet-backed government in Angola in 1975–76. It backed U.S. and French efforts to rescue the pro-Western Mobutu regime in Zaire in 1977–78 from a Soviet-supported insurrection. It denounced Cuba for its military interventions in a number of African states.

At the end of 1978 Deng Xiaoping achieved a long-awaited political breakthrough that confirmed the new direction of Chinese foreign policy. This was the announcement on December 15, 1978, by President Carter that formal diplomatic relations between the United States and China would begin on January 1, 1979, and that the United States–Taiwan Defense Treaty would expire a year beyond that date. Thereafter, the only security link between Washington and Taipei, those two old partners in the war against communism in Asia, would consist of the sale by the United States of defensive weaponry on a restricted basis. While this agreement represented a major compromise on the part of the United States, it also signified a moderation of China's policy toward Taiwan. Though not explicitly renouncing the right to employ force to reacquire its wayward province, Beijing increasingly appealed to Taipei for peaceful reconciliation on the basis of respect for the island's special economic practices.

The alignment of American and Chinese foreign policies in Africa and the establishment of diplomatic relations between Washington and Beijing set the stage for close U.S.-Chinese cooperation in Asia in the face of two developments that appeared to tip the balance of power in the region in favor of the common Soviet adversary. The first was the increasingly antagonistic activities of the recently reunified Communist state of Vietnam.* Throughout the year 1978, China's relations with its erstwhile ally against "American imperialism" in Asia had steadily deteriorated. The ostensible cause of this friction was the plight of the substantial Chinese minority in Vietnam, which was heavily concentrated in urban areas and predominated among the merchant classes. The combination of ethnic antagonism, socioeconomic resentment, and the suspicion that the Chinese nationals constituted a sort of fifth column to promote Beijing's interests in Vietnam, prompted Hanoi to wage a pitiless campaign to relocate many of the Chinese urban dwellers to the countryside after confiscating their property. This policy understandably elicited sharp protests from Deng on behalf of his maltreated compatriots.

But beneath the veneer of humanitarian concern for the plight of ethnic Chinese in Vietnam lay the more deeply felt fear of encirclement by the Soviet Union and what Beijing had increasingly come to regard as Moscow's client state in Hanoi. In spite of China's loyal support and military assistance during the war with the United States, Vietnam had taken several steps throughout 1978 to affirm its allegiance to the Soviet Union. In June, Hanoi obtained membership in the Soviet-controlled economic association Comecon, which prompted the retaliatory termination of all Chinese economic and technical assistance to Vietnam. In November it signed a treaty of friendship with Moscow which provided for the stationing of Soviet air

---

* North and South Vietnam were reunified in April 1976, a year after the defeat of the U.S.-backed regime in Saigon (renamed Ho Chi Minh City).

and naval units in the country. Reassured by these gestures of support from the Kremlin, Vietnam proceeded to launch a military invasion of its newly established Communist neighbor Cambodia (renamed Kampuchea) in December 1978. The purpose of the armed offensive, which was accomplished in short order, was the overthrow of the Chinese-backed regime of the Khmer Rouge dictator Pol Pot and the installation of a Vietnamese puppet government in Phnom Penh. Hanoi's bid for regional hegemony on the Indochinese peninsula confronted Beijing with an aggressive, hostile neighbor to the south allied with adversary number one to the north, with its massive troop buildup and SS-20 missiles targeted on Chinese sites. China retaliated by dispatching its own military forces across the frontier into Vietnam in February 1979 to "teach the Vietnamese a lesson," before withdrawing them a couple of months later with the lesson still unlearned and Vietnamese units still occupying Cambodia.

The Vietnamese invasion of Cambodia reinforced the increasingly cooperative diplomatic relationship between Washington and Beijing. When Pol Pot and his Khmer Rouge followers retreated from Phnom Penh to harass the Vietnamese client government from guerilla bases in the countryside, the United States and China jointly recognized him as the legitimate leader of Cambodia and sent him military supplies through Thailand, even in the face of mounting evidence that his regime had perpetrated grisly acts of genocide against its own population after its accession in 1975.

The second important source of cohesion in the budding partnership between Washington and Beijing was the Soviet invasion of Afghanistan at the end of 1979,* which aggravated Chinese fears of Soviet encirclement as well as American anxieties about the security of oil reserves in the Persian Gulf. The two governments cooperated in supplying the anti-Soviet resistance within Afghanistan via Pakistan and coordinated a tough diplomatic campaign in various world forums—including a boycott of the 1980 Olympic Games in Moscow—to pressure Moscow to withdraw.

The advent of the Reagan administration in 1981 introduced a discordant note in the Sino-American relationship concerning the issue of Taiwan. During his presidential campaign candidate Reagan had denounced Carter for abandoning America's trusted anti-Communist ally, Taipei, and talked of restoring normal diplomatic relations with that government.† In June 1981 President Reagan appeared to reverse the Carter policy of disengagement from Taiwan by authorizing the sale of defensive military equipment to the island, prompting an angry rejoinder from Beijing. But Reagan's anti-Soviet geopolitical objectives eventually overshadowed his sentimental attachment to the old Nationalist Chinese stronghold on Formosa. A com-

* See page 411.
† The Taiwan Relations Act, passed by the U.S. Congress in 1979 as formal diplomatic relations were severed by President Carter, preserved an awkward kind of informal connection with the island by establishing an American Institute on Taiwan staffed by U.S. foreign service officers on temporary leave.

promise arrangement was reached in August 1982 prescribing a gradual reduction of American military aid to Taiwan in exchange for Beijing's pledge to pursue its long-term goal of reunification through peaceful means. In 1986 President Chiang Ching-kuo, Chiang Kai-shek's son and heir, authorized unprecedented visits to the mainland for family reunions, and by the following year Chinese trade with Taiwan (mainly through Hong Kong) had surpassed $1 billion in value.

An intriguing precedent for the peaceful reunification of China and Taiwan was suggested by the agreement concluded between Beijing and London in September 1984 concerning the political future of Hong Kong. The pact specified that the old British crown colony would revert to Chinese sovereignty in 1997, but as a special administrative region enjoying a high degree of autonomy (including its own separate, fully convertible currency) as well as the prerogative of retaining its capitalist economic system for at least fifty years after its absorption.* The People's Republic stood to gain many advantages from a satisfactory resolution of the question of Hong Kong's future. By the end of the 1980s, the thriving little city state had become China's largest trading partner, the entrepôt for over 10 percent of its exports, and a valuable source of foreign exchange in the form of remittances from Hong Kong Chinese to relatives in the People's Republic. It would also afford China entrée to U.S. economic interests, which were heavily engaged there.

China's conciliatory effort to promote a peaceful annexation of the two NICs Hong Kong and Taiwan was paralleled by a marked improvement in its relations with the rest of non-Communist Asia. In an attempt to court the states of ASEAN, Beijing reduced its ties to Communist insurgent groups in Thailand, Malasia, and the Philippines, and (as noted above) cooperated with Thailand in supplying aid to the Cambodian resistance during the Vietnamese occupation. Most importantly, China's expanding trade relationship with Japan during the early eighties was reinforced by a diplomatic entente based on a shared concern about the Soviet military and naval buildup in the Far East and joint support for ASEAN's diplomatic initiative to persuade Vietnam to evacuate Cambodia. The Sino-Japanese rapprochement was not immune to the resurgence of ethnic animosity based on historical memories, however. In 1985 Japanese Prime Minister Yasuhiro Nakasone infuriated Chinese officials with a ceremonial visit to a cemetary for Second World War Japanese soldiers, and a year later Education Minister Fujio Masayuki was forced to resign after some ill-chosen remarks minimizing Japan's wartime atrocities in China.

But these atavistic outbursts did not disturb Sino-Japanese relations for very long. Likewise, though some friction between Washington and Beijing continued throughout the remainder of the 1980s over such issues as the residual CoCom restrictions on technology transfer, U.S. textile protection-

---

* In 1987 an agreement concerning the Portuguese territory of Macao prescribed its annexation by China at the end of 1999.

ism, Beijing's arms sales to various Middle Eastern regimes and its staunch support for the Palestinian cause, and China's human rights abuses, the Sino-American rapprochement appeared firmly established on the basis of mutually beneficial economic ties as well as a modest amount of diplomatic coordination, military cooperation, and sharing of intelligence on Soviet military activities. Even the massacres in Tiananmen Square in 1989 elicited relatively restrained reactions from Washington and Tokyo, both of which recognized the importance of preserving close ties to Beijing.

The End of the Second Cold War (1985-1991): An Interim Assessment

The historian of international relations who approaches the more distant past with a certain degree of confidence hesitates to recount and interpret the event of his or her own time. This reluctance stems from an appreciation of two circumstances that inevitably undermine the scholarly credibility of historical writing about the recent past. The first has to do with the official documents that record the decision-making process in those handful of nations whose governments make such papers available to scholars after a suitable interval. Before the public records and private papers of policymakers are declassified and opened for inspection, the monographic studies on which a general work such as this one necessarily relies are inevitably condemned to be incomplete and speculative. This problem is mitigated to a certain extent by the streams of memoirs that customarily flow from the pens of government officials after their retirement from public life. Though more often than not self-serving, these personal testimonies remain virtually our sole source of firsthand information about foreign policy decision making at the highest level pending the declassification of the public records. For the period since the mid-1980s, this type of primary source material is only just beginning to appear in print and has yet to be digested by scholars.

An even more serious impediment to the study of contemporary international relations than the paucity of primary sources is the difficulty of evaluating such evidence as does exist in the public domain with the degree of discrimination and sensitivity that only the chronological distance from one's subject affords. Without such a perspective, the historian is hard put to separate the ephemeral from the fundamental in an effort to identify those forces that transform the international environment before our very eyes.

Nonetheless, one must hazard what can be no more than a brief provisional assessment of those current trends that appear to be the decisive factors in the shaping of our present world. In this spirit of caution, and with the aforementioned caveats in mind, this historian feels entirely confident in concluding that the second half of the 1980s marked a fundamental turning point in the history of international relations since the end of the Second World War.

The most significant development during this half decade was the extraordinary improvement in the relationship between Washington and Moscow that brought about the definitive and entirely unanticipated end of the Cold War. While it is fashionable in certain scholarly circles to deemphasize the significance of individuals as causal agents of historical change, it would be difficult to deny that the termination of the long-standing rivalry between the two superpowers was a direct consequence of the policies inaugurated by the man who became the General Secretary of the Communist Party of the Soviet Union in 1985. Unlike his predecessors, Mikhail Gorbachev had developed an appreciation of two ineluctable realities about the Union of Soviet Socialist Republics. The first was that the deterioration of its economic system during the Brezhnev years had gravely imperiled that nation's capability of exercising power and influence in the world proportionate to its enormous size and population. The second was that the huge and ever increasing technological advantage enjoyed by the United States vis-à-vis the Soviet Union ensured that the former country would prevail in the bilateral arms race—nuclear and conventional—that had been renewed after the brief period of detente in the 1970s.

Accordingly, the new Soviet leader resorted to the only policy that offered a possible solution to the twin problems of economic decline and military vulnerability: This was the quest for a settlement of all of his country's outstanding political disputes with its adversaries in the Western camp, particularly with the other superpower. The comparatively stable international environment resulting from such a settlement would permit the Soviet Union to redirect its limited internal resources—together with such economic assistance as might be forthcoming from the non-Communist developed world—to his pet project: a set of wide-ranging socioeconomic reforms including decentralization of decision making and self-management in industry, the encouragement of private initiative, and the introduction of a modified market economy in order to boost productivity and eventually satisfy the long-suppressed demands of Soviet consumers. In order to win popular support for this bold program of economic renovation Gorbachev simultaneously pressed for political reforms designed to permit greater public participation in the political life of the nation. This new political openness, or *glasnost*, was to be the accompaniment of economic restructuring, or *perestroika*, in a Soviet Union transformed beyond recognition.

The first dramatic instance of Gorbachev's campaign to improve Soviet-American relations occurred in the most complex and dangerous area of superpower rivalry—the arms race. During the first half of the 1980s, the Reagan administration had undertaken a massive military buildup in virtually every category of weaponry: the deployment of intermediate-range nuclear weapons in Western Europe (Pershing II ballistic missiles and ground-launched cruise missiles), the continued search for a suitable delivery system for the MX ICBM missile, the expansion of research and development on the space-based antimissile defense system designated as the Strategic Defense Initiative (SDI), the application of new technologies to the conventional defense capability of NATO, and the plan to create a 600-ship navy by the end of the eighties. Confronted with the impossible task of matching this stunning military buildup with his country's meager technological assets, Gorbachev desperately sought to negotiate an end to a military competition that could only exacerbate the internal economic crisis of his country. President Reagan, facing a huge budget deficit caused by the U.S. attempt to combine increased military spending with reduced taxation and squeezed by a Congressional resolution requiring budgetary balance, proved receptive to Gorbachev's overtures. Consequently, the stalled arms control negotiations were resumed in 1985 at the behest of the two leaders.

At a summit conference in Reykyavik, Iceland, in October 1986, Reagan and Gorbachev—without any prior consultation with their respective allies—came to the verge of endorsing a remarkable proposal that would have abolished all ballistic missiles and possibly set the stage for total nuclear disarmament. But while this Utopian scheme came to naught, the two sides did make substantial progress on the more circumscribed issue of intermediate-range nuclear forces (INF) in Europe. In February 1987, Gorbachev agreed for the first time to consider the INF matter separately from the rest of the comprehensive arms control package that he had been promoting. Finally, after almost a year of intensive diplomacy, the two leaders signed an historic agreement in Washington on December 8, 1987, which eliminated all intermediate-range nuclear forces (that is, ground-based missiles with ranges from 500 to 5,500 kilometers) from the European theater. This agreement, which resembled Reagan's original proposal for a "zero option" in 1981, represented a significant compromise on the part of the Kremlin in a number of areas. First of all, it had abandoned its demand that the abolition of INF in Europe be accompanied by the termination of the SDI, which Moscow regarded as a potentially devastating threat to its strategy of nuclear deterrence. Second, Gorbachev accepted a drastically asymmetrical reduction of theater nuclear weapons, with the Soviet Union agreeing to destroy 851 launchers and 1,836 missiles by the end of 1991 compared to 283 launchers and 867 missiles by the United States. Third, he agreed to eliminate not only the Soviet SS-20 missiles located in the European part of the country but also those deployed in Asia, thereby allaying the concerns of the country on which those missiles had been targeted: the Peoples' Republic of China. Finally, the Kremlin broke with past practice by accepting an extremely intrusive verification procedure, which prescribed the exchange of extensive information about nuclear forces and the submission to short-notice, onsite inspections by the other signatory for thirteen years after the ratification of the pact.

The INF treaty was the first arms control agreement in a decade. While it removed only about one-fifth of the existing nuclear weapons in the world, it represented a significant departure from the cautious, incremental approach of arms control negotiations in the seventies. Unlike the two previous treaties dealing with strategic nuclear forces (SALT I and SALT II), the INF pact stipulated the elimination of an entire category of nuclear weapons instead of merely limiting the continued growth of existing forces. The Washington summit that produced the INF treaty also drew the broad outline of a strategic arms limitation agreement, which had eluded negotiators ever since the two superpowers resumed the stalled SALT process under the new designation START (Strategic Arms Reduction Talks) in 1982. Considerable progress on this issue was achieved during the first two years of the George Bush presidency, though several stumbling blocks concerning verification procedures and the counting of warheads prevented the completion of a START agreement in time for a Soviet-American summit in the spring of 1991, as originally anticipated. This agreement would place strict quantitative restrictions on ballistic missile warheads and launchers, require deep reductions in the highly accurate land-based ICBMs, and (like the INF treaty) provide for intrusive verification procedures. The effect would be to reduce U.S. and Soviet strategic nuclear forces by about 30 percent. While the exclusion of certain strategic weapons systems from the START agreement—such as ICBMs equipped with Multiple Independently Targetable Reentry Vehicles (MIRV) and Sea-Launched Cruise Missiles (SLCM)—left lots of work for future negotiators, the arms race in strategic nuclear weapons had decelerated significantly by the beginning of the 1990s.

In the meantime both sides had announced a number of unilateral cuts in spending on conventional arms. The budget that President Reagan submitted to the Congress in early 1988 sacrificed the goal of a 600-ship navy that he had once enthusiastically endorsed. In a major speech at the United Nations in December 1988, Gorbachev announced a substantial cut in Soviet military forces to be completed by 1991. Much progress was also recorded in the reduction of conventional forces in Europe. The Mutual and Balanced Force Reduction (MBFR) talks between NATO and the Warsaw Pact had droned on without result in Vienna since 1973, with the Soviets resisting any agreement that would reduce their numerical advantage in conventional military forces in Central Europe. In March 1989, these fruitless exchanges were replaced by a new negotiating forum under the aegis of the thirty-five-state Conference on Security and Cooperation in Europe (CSCE) that was designated as the Conventional Armed Forces in Europe (CFE) talks. After only twenty months of negotiations, the twenty-two members of the two alliance systems signed the CFE Treaty on November 19, 1990. This agreement established a balance of conventional forces in Europe by requiring the Soviet Union to remove a large proportion of its tanks, armored vehicles, aircraft, heliocopters, and artillery from the region west of the Ural Mountains.*

But the achievements in the talks on conventional arms reductions in Europe that transpired in the CFE talks had been overtaken by a spectacular series of political developments on the eastern half of that continent that rapidly rendered obsolete the concept of mutual and balanced conventional arms reductions between the two mutually antagonistic military blocs. As had been the case with Khrushchev's anti-Stalinist campaign in 1956, Gorbachev's denunciation of Brezhnev and his attempts to introduce economic and political reforms in the Soviet Union undermined the position of the hard-line, orthodox Communist bosses in Eastern Europe while inspiring reform-minded citizens to contest their authority. But the difference between 1956 and 1989 lay in the attitude of the Kremlin toward its client states in Eastern Europe. Whereas Khrushchev had regarded them as indispensible allies against NATO, Gorbachev had come to view them as liabilities that received enormous economic benefits from the USSR (in the form of trade subsidies, loans, cheap energy, and raw materials) while giving little in return. In light of the successful arms control negotiations with the West, the strategic value of the satellites to Moscow became less apparent. Consequently, when the populations of Eastern Europe repudiated their Communist leaders in the course of the year 1989, they were able to do so without fear of a repetition of Hungary's experience in 1956 or Czechoslovakia's in 1968. On the contrary, Gorbachev actually appeared to look with favor on, and even to take some credit for, the revolutionary political changes that swept Eastern Europe as the 1980s came to a close.

The pace of change in the East bloc in 1989 was truly breathtaking, as the Soviet satellites cashiered their Communist leadership in rapid succession. Poland, with a popular and powerful labor movement (Solidarity) and an influential religious institution (the Catholic Church) independent of government control, had the easiest time of it. In January 1989 the government of General Wojciech Jaruzelski, which had declared martial law in 1981 and outlawed the Solidarity movement, agreed to enter into negotiations with representatives of the banned labor organization to resolve the country's serious economic and political problems. In the spring, Solidarity's status as an opposition party was legalized, and in the free elections held in June, its candidates won an overwhelming victory. In August, Tadeusz Mazowiecki, a staunch Catholic and Solidarity member, became prime minister of the first coalition government in the East bloc in forty-two years. He promptly introduced a number of free market economic

---

* After the signing of the CFE agreement, U.S. objections concerning the counting of Soviet forces prompted the Bush administration to delay the submission of the treaty to the Senate for ratification pending a satisfactory resolution of the dispute.

reforms aimed at dismantling the Communist system of centralized government control.

In the meantime, the Hungarian parliament had authorized the formation of opposition parties in January 1989. Within a few months a special commission appointed by the Communist party had redefined the 1956 revolution as "a popular uprising against an oligarchic rule that had debased the nation"; Imre Nagy, the prime minister in 1956 who had been overthrown and executed by the Soviets, was publicly praised; and the closed frontier with Austria was thrown open. In January 1990, the Hungarian government asked the Soviet Union to remove all of its military forces from Hungary, which in the following March the Kremlin agreed to do by the summer of 1991. In Czechoslovakia the threat of a nationwide strike in the fall of 1989 forced the hard-line regime of Gustav Husak to tolerate non-Communist participation in a coalition government. On Husak's resignation from the presidency in December, he was replaced by the country's most renowned dissident, the playwright Vaclav Havel. In an act pregnant with historical symbolism, the Czechoslovak parliament elected as its speaker the elderly Alexander Dubcek, whose political and economic reforms during the "Prague Spring" of 1968 had led to the Soviet military intervention in the summer. Like the Hungarians, the Czechs requested and received from Moscow the assurance that all Soviet troops would be withdrawn from their country by the summer of 1991.

The two Soviet satellites whose Communist ruling elites staunchly resisted change were Romania and the German Democratic Republic. The Romanian dictator, Nicolae Ceausescu, refused all compromise, even as his allies in the Warsaw Pact submitted to the sweeping domestic transformation mentioned above. But the revolutionary tide flowing through Eastern Europe could not be stopped, even in Ceausescu's retrograde police state. Facing hostile demonstrations on the streets of Bucharest in December 1989, the Romanian strongman attempted to flee the country and was caught and executed. The new government promptly planned free elections and purged supporters of the Ceausescu regime. As Ceausescu's counterpart in East Germany, Erich Honecker, stubbornly resisted political reform and attempted in vain to organize the forces of repression in that country, tumultuous street demonstrations demanding radical reform broke out in Leipzig and other East German cities. In September 1989, the opening of the Hungarian frontier with Austria afforded East German citizens the opportunity to escape to the West, which they proceeded to do in large numbers. Within a month the ailing Honecker had resigned, and on November 9 his successor lifted all travel restrictions to the West and, in an historic act, opened the Berlin Wall. In free elections held on March 18, 1990, a center-right coalition won almost 49 percent of the votes, against 22 percent for a center-left group, and only 16 percent for the renamed remnant of the old Socialist Unity (Communist) party that had ruled the country with an iron hand for forty years. In April the parliament of the

German Democratic Republic created a democratically elected government in the form of a coalition dominated by the center-right bloc aligned with the ruling Christian Democratic party in West Germany.

But the opening of the Berlin Wall, the collapse of the Communist regime, and the first free elections in East Germany unleashed a new political force that few observers had anticipated. Many of the East German refugees who streamed into the Federal Republic, as well as their compatriots who remained behind to march in the streets against the Communist regime, openly called for the reunification of the two German states. By the time of the East German elections in March 1990, all of the major political groups in both German states had endorsed that long-dormant cause. With the disintegration of the East German political apparatus and the decline of the Socialist Unity (Communist) party, the very *raison d'être* of the German Democratic Republic had been gravely undermined: The state had been created by the Soviet military occupation force and its ruling Communist elite had remained in power at the behest of the Kremlin. Once liberated from the fear of Soviet military intervention and political repression by the Communist apparatus, the populace of East Germany eagerly embraced the cause of reunification in the hope of reaping the economic and political benefits that would presumably flow from citizenship in a single Germany dominated by the capitalist, democratic institutions of the West. Conversely, the citizens of the Federal Republic had harbored the sentimental aspiration to be reunited with their compatriots in the east since 1949, when the goal of German unity had been enshrined in the constitution of the West German state.

The issue of German reunification introduced two complications in the otherwise smooth process of European detente that had unfolded at the end of the eighties. First of all, West German Chancellor Helmut Kohl's hesitation in formally recognizing the Oder–Neisse Line as the eastern frontier of a reunited Germany prompted understandable concern in Poland that its newly acquired independence from the Soviet Union would be threatened by the revival of old territorial disputes with Germany. Second, Bonn's insistence (in concert with its partners in the Atlantic Alliance) that a reunified Germany be permitted to retain membership in NATO rather than (as demanded by the Soviet Union) reverting to neutrality generated serious misgivings in Moscow. But once Kohl accepted the permanence of the eastern frontiers and Gorbachev recognized that a united Germany within NATO would represent less of a menace to Soviet security than a united Germany cut loose from the constraints associated with alliance membership, the anxieties of Germany's neighbors were allayed. Consequently, after a round of negotiations among representatives of the two German states and the four occupying powers that still enjoyed residual occupation rights (the United States, Great Britain, the Soviet Union, and France), the legal basis for German reunification was laid. On October 3,

1990, the frontier markers that had separated the two German states since 1949 were removed, and the most visible symbol of the Cold War had passed into history. With the disappearance of East Germany and the repudiation of communism and Moscow's authority by the remaining East European states, the dissolution of the military structure of the Warsaw Pact* on April 1 and the abolition of the Soviet-led trading system Comecon on June 28, 1991, came as no surprise.

As the Soviet Union's satellite system in Eastern Europe disintegrated at the end of the 1980s, the internal political structure of the country itself began to unravel. Paradoxically, the severe crisis that Gorbachev confronted was exacerbated by the very political reforms that he had initiated: In June 1988 the Nineteenth Party Congress replaced the old rubber stamp Supreme Soviet with a new Congress of People's Deputies, two-thirds of whose members would be selected by democratic means. This body was to elect from its own members a new 450-person Supreme Soviet to function as a democratic parliament in the Western sense. The Supreme Soviet that emerged from the freely elected Congress of People's Deputies in May 1989 provided the Soviet population with their first taste of genuine democracy. Live television broadcasts of its proceedings showed a grim-faced Gorbachev, in his new capacity as president, subjected to harsh criticism from a variety of opposition groups. Grievances that had been ignored or suppressed in the pre-Gorbachev years became the subject of intense nationwide debate, with the whole world watching. The high expectations that had been stimulated by the slogans of *glasnost* and *perestroika* were disappointed as the deteriorating political and economic conditions in the USSR became apparent.

Signs of the economic decline of the Soviet Union were ubiquitous. Agricultural production had fallen far below government targets, oil and coal production declined, GNP dropped 2 percent in 1990 (the worst record since the Second World War), the foreign debt swelled, and trade deficits increased. In the summer of 1989, widespread strikes broke out in a number of cities in protest against severe shortages of basic consumer goods. Despite the government's efforts at fundamental economic reform, the fruits of *perestroika* scarcely represented an improvement over the "period of stagnation" under Brezhnev. In the meantime, long-suppressed nationalist discontent bubbled to the surface throughout 1990 in many of the non-Russian republics: ethnic strife between Christian Armenians and the Muslims of Azerbaijan in the Caucasus; rioting by Muslims in the Central Asian republics of Uzbekistan, Kazakhstan, and Tajikistan; declarations of independence or claims of political sovereignty by parliaments in the Ukraine, Georgia, Armenia and Moldavia. But the most vociferous resistance to Soviet authority came in the three Baltic states of Latvia,

* The last remaining symbol of East bloc unity, the political structure of the Warsaw Pact, was disbanded on July 1, 1991.

Lithuania, and Estonia, which had been annexed by the USSR in 1940. In November 1988, Estonia declared itself a sovereign state within the Soviet Union, with the right to fly its own flag, issue its own passports, and veto legislation passed by the Soviet parliament. In Lithuania, the anti-Soviet government that came to power in March 1990 went a step further, declaring its outright secession from the Soviet Union and instructing its young men to refuse to submit to Soviet military conscription.

After similar developments in Latvia, Gorbachev determined that the trend toward the political disintegration of the Soviet system had gone far enough. In early 1991 Soviet military units intervened in the Baltic states, as Gorbachev, who had assumed the presidency in the previous year and vastly increased his personal powers, appeared to align himself with those forces hostile to further reform (such as the army, the KGB, and the Communist party) that had formed the backbone of the old order he had overthrown. With the angry resignation of Foreign Minister Eduard Shevardnadze in December 1990, the advocates of reform pinned their hopes on another one of Gorbachev's disillusioned collaborators, Boris Yeltsin. After his election as Chairman of the Supreme Soviet of the Russian Republic in May 1990, Yeltsin combined a call for increased democratization and economic liberalization with a sweeping demand for greater autonomy for his own gigantic republic. For the first time, the breakup of the Soviet Union into its constituent ethnic elements became a distinct possibility.

The explosion of ethnic nationalism in the Soviet Union reflected a broad trend throughout the entire region of Eastern Europe amid the recession of Soviet political and military power. Two million maltreated Hungarians in the Transylvanian region of Romania, a million restless Hungarians in the southern part of Czechoslovakia, and Catholic, agrarian Slovaks resentful of Czech dominance, all represented reminders of ancient ethnic antagonisms that had been papered over in the Communist era of proletarian solidarity. The first casualty of this resurgent nationalism was the multinational, multireligious, polyglot state of Yugoslavia. The death in 1980 of Josip Broz Tito, whose thirty-five year rule had successfully kept the lid on the ethnic cauldron of this renegade Communist country on the Balkan peninsula, ushered in a decade of rising tension among the inhabitants of its six federated republics and two autonomous regions.* In the summer of 1991, Slovenia and Croatia, the two most Westernized, anti-Communist, and economically advanced republics, declared their independence. Serbia, the largest, most populous, and most privileged of Yugoslavia's federated republics, vigorously defended the cause of national unity out of concern for the large numbers of Serbs living in other repub-

* The six federated republics include Bosnia and Herzegovina, Croatia, Macedonia, Montenegro, Serbia, and Slovenia. The two autonomous regions are Kosovo and Vojvodina (within Serbia).

lics. The result was widespread violence that threatened to bring about the Balkanization of the country.

The collapse of the Communist satellite system in Eastern Europe, the dissolution of the Warsaw Pact, the unification of Germany and its inclusion in the Atlantic alliance, and the economic crisis and political disarray of the Soviet Union itself rendered irrelevent most of the customary assumptions associated with the Cold War. A surprise conventional attack by East bloc armies against the countries of Western Europe, the nightmare scenario of the "bolt from the blue" that had preoccupied NATO war planners since the early fifties, was inconceivable. Furthermore, the spectacular *disintegration* of the East European bloc coincided with the increasing *integration* of Western Europe. After many years of disappointments, the movement toward West European economic unity inaugurated by the Treaty of Rome in 1957 was relaunched during the second half of the 1980s. The Single European Act of 1985 stipulated that by the end of 1992 full economic integration would be achieved among the twelve member states of the European Community.† In 1989 plans were unveiled for the creation of a European Monetary Union (EMU), which would eventually constitute a European central bank that would issue a common currency. By the beginning of the 1990s, notable progress was made in the coordination of foreign and defense policies among EC members. The expanded European Community responded to the emergence of non-Communist parliamentary regimes in the former Soviet satellites by establishing in December 1989 a European Reconstruction Development Bank to provide economic aid to the eastern half of the continent, as the people of Prague, Budapest, and Warsaw reaffirmed the common cultural heritage that they had long shared with the people of Paris, Rome, and London. Even the Soviet Union sought membership in what Gorbachev wistfully called the "common European home" (recalling de Gaulle's oft-repeated phrase, "Europe from the Atlantic to the Urals").

What seemed to be the definitive demise of the Cold War in Europe facilitated the reduction of East–West tension in all of the other world trouble spots as Gorbachev drastically scaled back Soviet military and political commitments across the globe. He moved first to cut his country's losses in the costly war in Afghanistan, which had dragged on since 1979 with victory nowhere in sight owing to the tenacious resistance of the Moslem *Mujaheddin* armed by the United States and China via Pakistan. In

† Following the expansion of the six-member EEC in 1973 to include Great Britain, Ireland, and Denmark, it admitted Greece in 1981 and Spain and Portugal in 1986. Turkey and Austria applied for membership in 1987 and 1989, respectively. In 1988, the adjective "Economic" was formerly dropped from the community's all-encompassing title to emphasize the renewed aspiration for political integration.

early 1988 the Kremlin announced that all Soviet troops would be withdrawn within ten months, regardless of the fate of the Soviet-installed puppet regime in Kabul, and in February 1989 the last retreating Soviet soldier crossed the frontier. The departure of the foreign invader removed the unifying thread that had kept the loose-knit coalition of antigovernment rebels together. Ethnic and tribal rivalries within the *Mujaheddin* rapidly resurfaced, and by the beginning of the 1990s local military commanders and political leaders began to revert to their old practice of making special deals with the Najibullah government to preserve their own power and restore a measure of stability in the war-ravaged country.

Gorbachev's abandonment of Afghanistan was soon followed by a settlement of the other conflict in Asia that had poisoned relations between Moscow, on the one hand, and Washington and Beijing, on the other, since the late 1970s. In December 1988 the new ruling elite in Hanoi, under persistent prodding from its Soviet patron, announced a major troop withdrawal from Cambodia. By the fall of 1989, most of the Vietnamese units had returned home, leaving the Hanoi-installed government in Phnom Penh to its own devices in its civil war with the rebel coalition dominated by the Khmer Rouge organization. In exchange, the United States terminated military assistance and diplomatic support for the antigovernment group. Here was a remarkable instance of Soviet-American cooperation in disengaging from a bitter regional dispute inherited from the Cold War era. In the meantime the USSR began to withdraw its naval and air forces from Cam Ranh Bay in Vietnam and in 1990 announced a major withdrawal of ground troops and a sharp reduction in economic assistance to its old ally. The leaders in Hanoi followed in Gorbachev's footsteps by renouncing the centralized economic planning learned from the Soviet Union in favor of a market-based economy and began to solicit Western investment.

As East–West rivalries in Asia dissipated, long-standing disputes between U.S. and Soviet surrogates in Africa were terminated by skillful diplomacy. In December 1988 South Africa agreed to a ceasefire with the SWAPO rebel organization in Namibia and consented to a UN-supervised election there in exchange for the phased withdrawal of the 53,000 Cuban troops stationed in neighboring Angola by July 1991. After winning the Namibia elections in November 1989, SWAPO leader Sam Nujoma was installed in March 1990 as its first president after having encouraged white businessmen and farmers to remain in the country. Meanwhile, the termination of South African aid to the UNITA rebel movement and the withdrawal of all South African military forces from Angola in late November 1989, together with the beginning of the withdrawal of Cuban troops that had been protecting the Marxist MPLA government in that country, set the stage for the end of the fifteen-year-old civil war in the former Portuguese colony. On May 31, 1991, UNITA rebel leader Jonas Savimbi and

Angolan President José Eduardo dos Santos signed an historic peace accord that ended the violent confrontation in Angola and prescribed the country's first free elections for the autumn of 1992.

In the meantime, the Soviet-American proxy war on the Horn of Africa petered out as Washington and Moscow left their respective clients in the region, Somalia and Ethiopia, to fend for themselves. Somalia formally renounced its claim to Ethiopia's Ogaden region in April 1988, while Ethiopian strongman Mengistu Haile Mariam turned his attention to separatist agitation in the northern provinces of Eritrea and Tigray. In 1991 both Mengistu and Somali dictator Mohammed Siad Barre, abandoned by the superpowers that had avidly courted them during the Cold War, succumbed to internal insurrections virtually unnoticed by the outside world.

The end of the Soviet-American rivalry in Africa coincided with the emergence of a government in South Africa that had begun to deemphasize military pressure against adjacent African states and internal repression of its black majority in favor of political negotiation as a means of securing that country's future. After the replacement of Prime Minister P. W. Botha by F. W. de Klerk in 1989, the new leader combined the conciliatory foreign-policy initiatives mentioned above with a number of domestic political reforms designed to promote racial reconciliation in the land of apartheid. These included the halting of cross-border raids into Angola and the end of support for the rebel movement in Mozambique. Internally, de Klerk surprised world observers by abolishing the racial segregation of beaches, parks, and libraries; permitting mass demonstrations by dissidents; and in February 1990, legalizing the African National Congress (ANC) and releasing its deputy leader, Nelson Mandela, after twenty-seven years in prison. The ANC, deprived of its sanctuaries in Angola and its military aid from the Soviet Union (following Gorbachev's decision to terminate support for resistance movements in the developing world), was prepared to deemphasize its commitment to revolutionary violence in favor of negotiations with the more enlightened government in Pretoria. During the first half of 1991, de Klerk took bold new steps toward the removal of the remnants of apartheid and opened a dialogue with the ANC concerning political power-sharing with the black majority.

But the disappearance of Cold War tensions in Africa, while reducing the likelihood of external interference in the affairs of the continent, proved a mixed blessing for its inhabitants to the extent that it indirectly resulted in a decrease in foreign aid to that impoverished continent. Just as the Soviet Union sharply curtailed its foreign assistance programs in the Third World, the United States and Western Europe received urgent requests from the newly liberated societies of Eastern Europe for credits, investment, and aid for their struggling economies. In December 1989, the sixty-eight member states of the Association of African, Caribbean, and Pacific (ACP) states and the twelve members of the EC signed the fourth

Lomé Convention, which provided for about $14 billion worth of economic aid over five years, a 25 percent increase in real terms over Lomé III.* But the sluggish agricultural growth, decline in industrial production, and escalating foreign debt increased concerns about Africa's economic future as the Soviet Union turned inward while Europe and the United States looked eastward.

In the Middle East, Moscow and Washington also cooperated to dampen regional rivalries between their clients. The Soviet Union pressured Syria and the Palestine Liberation Organization (PLO) to abandon the cause of armed victory and to seek a negotiated settlement with Israel, while the United States urged the Jewish state to forswear annexation of the occupied territories and halt all settlement activity there. A complicating factor was the unanticipated Palestinian uprising on the West Bank and Gaza in December 1987, widely known as the *Intifada*, which represented a spontaneous popular reaction to the failure of the autonomy talks concerning the occupied territories. It also revealed that the Palestinians there had lost faith in the PLO and the Arab states to bring about an end to the Israeli occupation and were driven to take matters into their own hands. The ceasefire in the Iran-Iraq War in August 1988 refocused Arab and world attention on the Palestinian problem. Facing the threat of a civilian insurrection consisting of rock-throwing and arson, Israel responded with harsh countermeasures that provoked international condemnation, including strong words and renewed pressure for a negotiated settlement from its American patrons.

With Moscow curtailing its support for Syria and the PLO while permitting Soviet Jews to emigrate to Israel in record numbers, the Bush administration grew impatient with the recalcitrance of the government of Yitzak Shamir in Jerusalem, which refused to negotiate with the PLO or to envision any kind of Palestinian political entity on the West Bank. After the PLO formally endorsed UN resolution 242, recognized Israel's right to exist in peace and security, and renounced terrorism, the United States ended its boycott of the Palestinian organization and opened talks with PLO representatives in Tunis.† Egypt was officially readmitted to the Arab League at its Casablanca summit in 1989 without being obliged to renounce its 1979 peace treaty with Israel, an implicit acceptance by the other Arab states of the legitimacy of negotiation with the Jewish state. Syria, isolated in the Arab world and abandoned by its Soviet benefactor, was driven to seek a rapprochement with Egypt and tone down its anti-Israel rhetoric. By the opening of the new decade, the ceasefire in the Iran–Iraq War, the reentry of Egypt into the Arab camp, and the isolation of hard-line Syria made the prospects for peace and stability in the

---

* For background on the previous Lomé conventions, see page 439.
† These unprecedented conversations between the U.S. and the PLO were suspended in June 1990 after PLO leader Yasser Arafat declined to condemn a terrorist attack on Israel's Mediterranean coast.

Middle East seem better than they had been since the Lebanese debacle of 1982–83.

The return of stability to the inflamed region of Central America was also facilitated by Soviet-American cooperation in disengagement, in this case from the civil war in Nicaragua. As Moscow reduced oil deliveries to Managua and urged restraint on the Sandinistas, Washington suspended aid to the Contras in 1987, thereby shifting the burden of peacemaking to the countries of the region. Attempts at a regional settlement had come to naught ever since the advent of the Contadora Group's mediation efforts in 1983. But the peace plan drafted by Costa Rican President Oscar Arias Sanchez and endorsed by five Central American heads of state in August 1987 offered a solution in the form of a ceasefire, the end of all external military aid to the belligerents, and the holding of free democratic elections in Nicaragua. The government of Sandinista President Daniel Ortega Saavedra, weakened by the reduction of Soviet aid, proceeded to institute a unilateral ceasefire in March 1988. In February 1989 it announced its decision to conduct the free elections called for in the Arias Plan on February 25, 1990. The Contras, deprived of their U.S. aid, agreed to demobilize their military forces and participate in the forthcoming electoral process as Washington ended its economic embargo of Nicaragua.

The Sandinista regime's willingness to hold elections appears to have been prompted by two considerations. The first was the deteriorating economic conditions of the country, which included an annual inflation rate of over 3,000 percent in 1989, severe shortages of many essential commodities, a sharp decline in GNP, massive unemployment, and a defense burden that consumed over half of the national budget. The other was the optimistic expectation, reinforced by most opinion polls, that the Sandinista party would win handily against its political opposition. But to the surprise of most observers, the free and fair elections of February 1990 resulted in the triumph of a ragtag coalition of opposition groups ranging from Somoza supporters on the extreme right to democratic socialists on the left that had been formed in June under the name National Opposition Union (UNO). In April 1990 Violeta Barrios de Chamorro, who had served in the Sandinista ruling junta in the first nine months of the revolution before resigning in disillusionment, replaced Ortega as president of Nicaragua in the first democratic, peaceful transfer of power in that country within recent memory. The Sandinistas honored their pledge to preserve the ceasefire in the civil war, while the Contras continued to disband in the expectation of participating in the political system of which their ideological confreres had recently gained control.

The political defeat of the Sandinistas in Nicaragua dealt a crushing blow to their ideological allies in El Salvador, the Democratic Revolutionary Front (FDR) and its military wing, the Farabundo Marti National Liberation Front (FMLN), which had been engaged in an insurgency against the central government throughout the eighties. In March 1989 the right-wing Nationalist Republican Alliance (ARENA) had won the elections in El Salvador and its leader, pro-American businessman Alfredo Cristiani, replaced the ailing Christian Democratic President José Napoleon Duarte (who had attempted in vain to steer a middle course between ARENA on the right and the FMLN on the left). The ARENA government expanded and intensified its predecessor's counterinsurgency campaign against the rebels. But pressure from the United States to seek a negotiated peace and curb its hard-liners in the military forced the Salvadoran government to the conference table, just as the collapse of the Sandinistas and the crisis in the Soviet Union deprived the FMLN of external support. Peace talks in Geneva under the auspices of the United Nations began in April 1990, while the civil war continued at a much lower level of violence. In the meantime, Cuba remained the lone custodian of revolutionary Marxist orthodoxy in the world. As Communist regimes and client states across the globe collapsed or repudiated their ideological heritage and Moscow drastically cut its aid to Havana in 1991, Fidel Castro defiantly reiterated his commitment to the revolutionary cause.

As the final decade of the twentieth century opened, commentators popularized President Bush's reference in September 1990 to a "New World Order" as the successor to the Cold War. The "revolution of 89" in Eastern Europe, together with the economic agony, political instability, military retrenchment, and diplomatic disengagement of the Soviet Union, destroyed the bipolar international system that had operated since the end of the Second World War: Familiar terms such as "the two superpowers" and "the East bloc" that recur throughout this study have lost their meaning. The world of the 1990s seemed to have been left with only one superpower, which had prevailed in the political, economic, and military rivalry with the Soviet Union that had dominated the history of international relations for the last four decades. Its ideology of representative democracy and free market economics discovered eager adherents in the Communist world as the theoretical foundations of Marxist-Leninism crumbled. Though continuously battered by budget, trade, and balance-of-payments deficits and threatened by commercial competition from Japan and a German-dominated, economically integrated Europe, the U.S. economy remained the largest in the world. Finally, America's phenomenal military power, which had increased dramatically during the first term of Ronald Reagan, brought such overwhelming superiority over any potential adversaries as to provide a greater measure of security than the United States and its allies could ever have imagined.

But the achievement of absolute security through victory in the Cold War resulted neither in the revival of American isolationism nor in the dismantling of the formidable military apparatus that had been constructed to cope with a Soviet menace that had ceased to exist. On the contrary, the Bush administration that took office in 1989 proceeded with unexpected vigor to wield American diplomatic influence and military power against other perceived threats to world stability. The first instance of this preoccupation in the post Cold-War era with enforcing the principles of international law and order was the use of American military forces in December 1989 to overthrow and capture General Manuel Noriega, the dictator of Panama who had refused extradition to face drug-trafficking charges in a U.S. court. Unlike earlier U.S. interventions in the Central America–Caribbean region, the Panama operation was entirely unrelated to the fear of either Soviet expansionism or indigenous insurrection. It was justified instead on the grounds that Noriega's unlawful activities, not only in profiting from the international drug trade but in annulling the 1989 elections that had been won by his opposition, required a vigorous response from Washington. Outlaws, regardless of their ideological proclivities or foreign connections, would be brought to justice by the only power willing and able to exercise a sort of international police power.*

A much more striking instance of this new determination on the part of the U.S. government to use its formidable power on behalf of the principles of international law and order was President Bush's forceful response to the invasion and annexation by Iraq of the adjacent, oil-rich emirate of Kuwait in the summer of 1990. The Iraqi seizure of Kuwait had originally been justified by the government in Baghdad not only on the basis of territorial claims dating from the era of the Ottoman Empire, but also by a recent set of grievances: The Iraqi dictator, Saddam Hussein, charged that the emirate's royal family had jeopardized Iraq's economic situation by expanding oil production to depress the world price, illegally diverting oil from Iraqi wells, and refusing to write off Iraq's huge debt incurred during its eight-year war with Iran. But when the Bush administration promptly persuaded the United Nations Security Council to approve extensive economic sanctions against Iraq and later to authorize the use of military force to expel Iraqi forces from Kuwait if they did not withdraw before January 15, 1991, Saddam Hussein tried to redefine the impending confrontation as an Arab-Moslem "Holy War" against the West and its ally in the region, Israel. After securing the diplomatic backing of its former adversary (and Iraq's former patron and supplier) in Moscow, the United States assembled a military force in Saudi Arabia consisting of NATO allies, such as Great Britain and France, together with those Arab states, such as Egypt, Saudi Arabia, and Syria, that feared the consequences of Iraq's hegemony in the region. After the expiration of the UN deadline for the evacuation of Kuwait, the U.S.-led coalition launched a devastating air campaign against Iraqi military targets and then a ground offensive into Kuwait and southern Iraq. The result was a swift military triumph that ejected Iraqi forces from Kuwait and thwarted Saddam Hussein's aspirations for terri-

---

* That the outlaw had previously enjoyed a close association with the policeman— Noriega had allegedly cooperated with the Central Intelligence Agency in various operations during the 1980s—was a source of some embarrassment for the Bush administration, but did not detract from its determination to topple him.

torial expansion in the Persian Gulf and political leadership in the Arab world.

The interventions in Panama and the Persian Gulf represented divergent means of achieving what by the end of the 1980s had become the universally approved goal of global order and stability. The former action, undertaken without the approval of regional allies or the United Nations, seemed a throwback to the era of gunboat diplomacy and the "big stick" when the United States felt entitled unilaterally to employ its military forces to punish wrongdoing and enforce the principles of good government in the Western Hemisphere. The Persian Gulf intervention, executed under the auspices of the United Nations with the military participation or diplomatic support of virtually the entire international community, revived (in the eyes of some observers) the principle of collective security that had proved unworkable during the period of Soviet-American confrontation. Students of international relations who dared to forecast the future of the post-Cold War order in light of "Operation Desert Storm" envisioned three alternative scenarios: Would the decade of the 1990s be characterized by a "unipolar" international system, with the world's only remaining superpower operating as the enforcer of global security with or without the consent of the world community? Would the emergence of "economic superpowers," such as Japan and the European Community, serve as a counterbalance to America's undisputed military superiority and confirm the trend toward a genuinely multipolar world that observers had prematurely announced in the early 1970s? Or would the elusive dream of "one world" without regional poles of attraction become a reality at last through the strengthening of the supranational mechanisms of collective security and peacemaking in the United Nations, or in such untested but potentially useful organizations as the Conference on Security and Cooperation in Europe (CSCE)?

Another more ominous possibility lurked beneath the euphoria generated by the spectacularly successful application of the principle of collective security in the Persian Gulf, as revealed in a number of developments in the realm of international economic relations. These included the breakdown in December 1990 of the Uruguay Round of GATT-sponsored international trade negotiations; the intensification of protectionist sentiment in the European Community as the 1992 deadline for the removal of all internal trade barriers approached; the resumption of Japan's aggressive pursuit of foreign markets for capital investment and high technology exports all along the Pacific rim; a sharp increase in the number of Latin American countries unwilling to service their foreign debt coupled with the refusal of Western banks to incur new lending risks in the region; and the Bush administration's proposal in June 1990 for the establishment of a free trade zone for the Western Hemisphere, interpreted by some observers as a defensive reaction against the formidable economic blocs forming in

Europe and East Asia.* The confluence of these trends in the early 1990s raised the spectre of global commercial warfare and the collapse of the liberal trading and monetary system that had been erected after the end of the Second World War. The possibility of international economic conflict— and the political and military tension that would be likely to result from it—tempered the optimism of those who had heralded the end of the second Cold War as the dawn of a new era of peace, prosperity, and stability in the world.

* The so-called "Enterprise for the Americas" initiative may have also represented an attempt by the U.S. to allay Latin American anxieties about the possibility of a North American Common Market. The U.S. and Canada had signed an agreement in October 1987 to eliminate tariffs and other trade barriers between the two countries by January 1, 1989. Mexican President Carlos Salinas de Gortari, after masterminding a debt settlement with his country's foreign creditors in 1989, joined President Bush in pressing for a free-trade agreement modeled on the U.S.-Canadian pact, and bilateral negotiations on the subject opened in March 1990.

Bibliographical Essay

Since this book is based entirely on secondary sources, the following bibliography makes no reference to available collections of primary sources (such as government records or the papers, diaries, and memoirs of policymakers). Moreover, since the book is addressed principally to students and generalists rather than scholarly specialists, references to journal articles and foreign language studies have been deemphasized in favor of readily accessible general studies in English.

Prologue: The Global Context of International Relations at the Beginning of the Twentieth Century

The Europeanization of the World. Among the dozens of excellent general studies of European imperial expansion before the First World War, the following may be read with profit: Alan Hodgart, *The Economics of European Imperialism* (1977); A. P. Thornton, *Doctrines of Imperialism* (1965), which surveys the impact of imperialism from Roman times to the present; Tom Kemp, *Theories of Imperialism* (1969), which summarizes and evaluates the various contemporary and retrospective interpretations of the phenomenon; and George Lichtheim, *Imperialism* (1971), an elegant essay by a master analyst of twentieth century political behavior. The two most comprehensive and perceptive treatments of British imperial policy are Ronald Robinson, John Gallagher, with Alice Denny, *Africa and the Victorians* (1970), and Clive Dewey and A. G. Hopkins, eds., *The Imperial Impact: Studies in the Economic History of Africa and India* (1978), which stresses the long-term consequences of economic imperialism in the British Empire. The classic study of French imperialism, which deemphasizes its economic motivation, is Henri Brunschwig, *French Colonialism, 1871–1914* (1966).

The Rise of Japanese Power in East Asia. The three best studies of Japanese-American rivalry in the Pacific before the First World War are Edwin O. Reischauer, *The United States and Japan* (1965), which stresses the Japanese perspective; Charles E. Neu, *The Troubled Encounter: The United States and Japan* (1975), which pays attention to the evolution of American governmental policy toward Asia; and Akira Iriye, *Pacific Estrangement: Japanese and American Expansion, 1897–1911* (1972), a penetrating analysis. Two classic studies of the economic underpinnings of Japan's rise to great power status are Lawrence Klein and Kazushi Ohkawa, eds., *Economic Growth: The Japanese Experience since the Meiji Era* (1968), and Henry Rosovsky, *Capital Formation in Japan, 1868–1940* (1961). Valuable monographs on Japanese imperial expansion in particular regions of East Asia include Hilary Conroy, *The Japanese Seizure of Korea, 1868–1910* (1960), which should be checked against C. I. Eugene Kim and Han-kyo Kim, *Korea and the Politics of Imperialism, 1876–1910* (1967). Andrew Molozenoff, *Russian Far Eastern Policy, 1881–1904* (1958), traces the background of Russo-Japanese conflict in East Asia, while Shumpei Okamoto, *The Japanese Oligarchy and Russo-Japanese War* (1970), probes the domestic context of Japanese decision making leading to the war of 1904–5. The most authoritative treatment of anti-Japanese sentiment on the American west coast is Roger Daniels, *The Politics of Prejudice: The Anti-Japanese Movement in California and the Struggle for Japanese Exclusion* (1962).

The Rise of American Power in the Western Hemisphere. The secondary literature on the relations between Latin America and the "Collossus of the North" before the First World War has been enriched by a number of recent studies. A most stimulating interpretive essay on the history of the Latin American region during this period is E. Bradford Burns, *The Poverty of Progress: Latin America in the Nineteenth Century* (1980), which emphasizes the conflict between the elites of the various Latin American states that were intent on pursuing industrial development on the European-American model and the peasant masses that resisted modernization. The two most widely quoted surveys of United States policy toward Latin America approach the subject from different perspectives and reach diametrically opposite conclusions. The classic study by Samuel Flagg Bemis, *The Latin American Policy of the United States* (1943), written by the dean of Latin American historians in the United States amid wartime anxiety about Axis intervention in the Western Hemisphere, stresses the benevolence and protectiveness of the United States toward its southern neighbors. Gordon Connell-Smith's *The United States and Latin America* (1974), an Englishman's caustic indictment of America's economic subjugation of the republics in its hemisphere, reflected the influence of the Vietnam experience and Europe's resentment of American domination. Two less contentious accounts of the United States' replacement of the European states as the preeminent power in the Caribbean are Lester D. Langley, *Struggle for the American Mediterranean: United States–European Rivalry in the Gulf-Caribbean, 1776–1904* (1976), and Dana G. Munro, *Intervention and Dollar Diplomacy in the Caribbean, 1900–1921* (1964). Dexter Perkin's *History of the Monroe Doctrine* (1955) is still regarded by experts as the definitive work on that subject. A valuable collection of essays on American-European economic rivalry in Latin America is Marvin Bernstein, ed., *Foreign Investment in Latin America* (1966). The best comprehensive treatment of British investments in the region during this period is J. Fred Rippy, *British Investments in Latin America, 1822–1949* (1949). For British commercial relations with Latin America before the First World War, see Desmond Platt, *Latin America and British Trade, 1806–1914* (1972). Among a number of excellent monographs on the relations between the United States and individual Latin American nations, the following may be recommended: Karl Schmitt, *Mexico and the United States, 1821–1973* (1973); P. Edward Haley, *Revolution and Intervention: The Diplomacy of Taft and Wilson with Mexico, 1910–1917* (1970); Walter LaFeber, *The Panama Canal: The Crisis in Historical Perspective* (1978); Lester D. Langley, *The Cuban Policy of the United States: A Brief History* (1968), which should be supplemented with David F. Healy, *The United States in Cuba, 1898–1902* (1963), and Allan R. Millit, *The Politics of Intervention: The Military Occupation of Cuba, 1906–1909* (1968); Robert I. Rotberg, *Haiti* (1971); Frederick B. Pike, *Chile and the United States* (1963); Sheldon B. Liss, *Diplomacy and Dependency: Venezuela, the United States, and the Americas* (1978); and Harold F. Peterson, *Argentina and the United States, 1810–1960* (1964).

A Shrinking Earth and the Geopolitical World View. Two of the most useful summaries of the principal theories of geopolitics (or political geography, as the subdiscipline is now called) are Hans W. Weigert et al., *Principles of Political Geography* (1960), and J. R. V. Prescott, *Boundaries and Frontiers* (1978). For brief treatments of the principal individual contributions to geopolitical theory, see Anthony J. Pearce's lucid introduction to Halford J. Mackinder, *Democratic Ideals and Reality* (1962); and Derwent Whittlesley, "Haushofer: The Geopoliticians," and Margaret T. Sprout, "Mahan: Evangelist of Sea Power," both in E. M. Earle, ed., *Makers of Modern Strategy* (1970). For a brilliant analysis of the Mahan school and its role in America's rise to global power, see Richard D. Challener, *Admirals, Generals, and American Foreign Policy, 1898–1914* (1973). Two classic theoretical studies of international relations that emphasize geopolitical considerations are Raymond Aron, *Peace and War: A Theory of International Relations* (1966), and Hans J. Morgenthau, *Politics Among Nations: The Struggle for Power and Peace* (1973).

The Development of an International Economy. The spread of industrialism and the formation of a global network of trade and investment before the First World War is the subject of a number of general works in recent years. See William Woodruff, *The Emergence of an International Economy* (1970), a solid survey that pays attention to the non-Western aspects of the emerging world economic system. The same is true of A. J. H. Latham, *The International Economy and the Undeveloped World, 1865–1914* (1978), which rejects the notion that the international economy was a British and North American phenomenon and emphasizes the contribution of the Souhern Hemisphere, especially Africa and Asia. More Eurocentric, but no less sweeping in their coverage of the subject, are W. W. Rostow, *The World Economy: History and Prospect* (1978), and William Ashworth, *A Short History of the International Economy since 1850* (1975). A lucidly written textbook, still worth reading for its theoretical as well as its historical treatment of international economics, is P. T. Ellsworth, *The International Economy* (1958). Valuable studies of particular aspects of the operation of the world economy before the First World War include J. H. Dunning, *Studies in International Investment* (1970); J. H. Adler, ed., *Capital Movements and International Development* (1967), the first three sections of which are historical in their orientation; A. K. Cairncross, *Home and Foreign Investment, 1870–1913* (1953), a classic study of British capital movements; W. M. Scammell, *The London Discount Market* (1968); and Herbert Feis, *Europe: The World's Banker, 1870–1914* (1965), a still useful summary. The best attempt to relate labor supply to economic development during this period is B. Thomas, *Migration and Economic Growth* (1973). On the role of technology in the growth and spread of industrialization, see B. R. Williams, ed., *Science and Technology in Economic Growth* (1973), and David Landes, *The Unbound Prometheus* (1969). For informative surveys of economic development in the major participants in the global economic system, see Charles Kindleberger, *Economic Growth in France and Britain, 1851–1950* (1964); S. B. Saul, *Studies in British Overseas Trade, 1870–1914* (1960); Maurice Levy-Leboyer, ed., *La Position internationale de la France* (1977); G. Stolper et al., *The German Economy, 1870 to the Present* (1965); L. E. Davis et al., *American Economic History: The Development of a National Economy* (1965); and G. C. Allen, *A Short Economic History of Modern Japan* (1972).

Part One: The Thirty Years' War (1914–1945)

1. Germany's Bid for European Dominance

The best military history of the First World War is B. H. Liddell Hart, *History of the First World War* (1970). An excellent summary of the important tactical and strategic aspects of the war may also be found in Theodore Ropp, *War in the Modern World* (1962). The controversy over the war aims of Imperial Germany sparked by Fritz Fischer's *Germany's Aims in the First World War* (1967), has produced a variety of responses, many of which are summarized in John A. Moses, *The Politics of Illusion: The Fischer Controversy in German Historiography* (1975). See also David Calleo, *The German Problem Reconsidered: Germany and World Order, 1870 to the Present* (1978), which is dominated by the theme that Germany's ambitions constantly outstripped its resources. There have also been a number of incisive studies of the war aims of the other great powers. See, for example, V. H. Rothwell, *British War Aims and Peace Diplomacy, 1914–1918* (1971); Sir Llewellyn Woodward, *Great Britain and the War of 1914–1918* (1967); David F. Trask, *The United States in the Supreme War Council: American War Aims and Inter-Allied Strategy, 1917–18* (1961); David Stevenson, *French War Aims Against Germany, 1914–1918* (1982); Walter McDougall, *France's Rhineland Diplomacy, 1914–1924* (1978), which treats French efforts to detach this strategically and economically valuable region from Germany; Marc Trachtenberg, *Reparation and World Politics* (1980), which absolves France of the vindictive reparation policy traditionally imputed to it; and Carl Parrini, *Heir to Empire: United States Economic Diplomacy, 1916–1923* (1969), which contains a useful analysis of the Paris Economic Conference and the European allies' plans to establish a post-war economic bloc excluding the United States and the Central Powers. America's shift from neutrality to intervention and the impact of that transformation on the international order has been the subject of a number of excellent studies. See Patrick Devlin, *Too Proud to Fight: Woodrow Wilson's*

Neutrality (1975), which complements the earlier work by Ernest R. May, *The World War and American Isolation, 1914–1917* (1959); Ross Gregory, *The Origins of American Intervention in the First World War* (1971); Edward M. Coffmann, *The War to End All Wars* (1968), which focuses on the period of active American participation in the war effort; and N. Gordon Levin, *Woodrow Wilson and World Politics* (1968), which emphasizes the American president's attempt to promote a liberal capitalist alternative to traditional imperialism and bolshevism, a theme also treated in Arno J. Mayer, *Wilson vs. Lenin: Political Origins of the New Diplomacy* (1959). Three recent studies by French scholars have traced the ambivalent relationship between France and the United States during the war: Yves-Henri Nouailhat, *La France et les Etats-Unis, août 1914–avril 1917* (1977); André Kaspi, *La France et le concours américain, février 1917–novembre 1918* (1975); and Denise Artaud, *La Question des dettes interalliés et la reconstruction de l'Europe* (1978), the definitive study of American war loans to the European allies and the resulting debt controversy. On Anglo-American relations during the war, see Parrini, op. cit., for a discussion of the two countries' economic rivalry and cooperation, and Basil Collier, *The Lion and the Eagle: British and Anglo-American Strategy, 1900–1950* (1972), for a treatment of their military relations. The best study of the Russian withdrawal from the war remains John W. Wheeler-Bennett, *Brest–Litovsk: The Forgotten Peace* (1971). The allied intervention in the Russian civil war is covered by George Kennan, *The Decision to Intervene* (1958), and more recently by John Silverlight, *The Victors' Dilemma: Allied Intervention in the Russian Civil War* (1970).

2. The Peace of Paris and the New International Order

There is no comprehensive study of the Paris Peace Conference, but there is a rich literature on particular aspects of the deliberations and decisions of 1919–20 and their impact on the world. Howard Elcock's *Portrait of a Decision: The Council of Four and the Treaty of Versailles* (1972) emphasizes the organizational context of decision making and the clash of national interests. Michael G. Fry, *Illusions of Security: North Atlantic Diplomacy, 1918–22* (1972); Seth P. Tillman, *Anglo-American Relations at the Paris Peace Conference, 1919* (1961); Louis A. R. Yates, *The United States and French Security, 1917–1921* (1957); and Jon Paul Selsam, *The Attempts to Form an Anglo-French Alliance, 1919–1924* (1936), all treat the disintegration of the anti-German coalition and the advent of Anglo-American efforts to mitigate the alleged harshness of the peace treaty with Germany. Preliminary discussions of the related issues of inter-Allied debts and German reparations are exhaustively covered in Artaud, op. cit., and Trachtenberg, op. cit., respectively. The peacemakers' preoccupation with the ideological menace of Russian communism and their attempts to protect Europe from its westward advance is the dominant theme of Arno J. Mayer, *Politics and Diplomacy of Peacemaking: Containment and Counterrevolution at Versailles, 1918–1919* (1967). France's abortive effort to establish a client state in the Rhenish buffer zone is recounted in McDougall, op. cit. The collapse of the inter-Allied wartime economic partnership during the peace conference receives extensive treatment in Parrini, op. cit.; Trachtenberg, op. cit.; and Dan P. Silverman, *Reconstructing Europe After the Great War* (1982). The two best studies of the role of second-rank powers at the peace conference are René Albrecht-Carrié, *Italy at the Paris Peace Conference* (1966), originally published in 1938 but still useful, and Sally Mark's definitive *Belgium at the Paris Peace Conference* (1981).

3. The Western World in the Twenties

The Illusion of Economic Restoration. An ambitious attempt to make sense of the complex developments in international economic relations in the 1920s is Derek H. Aldcroft, *From Versailles to Wall Street: 1918–1929* (1977). America's rise to preeminence in the world economy at Great Britain's expense is treated in Parrini, op. cit., Joan Hoff Wilson, *American Business and Foreign Policy, 1920–1933* (1971); Herbert Feis, *The Diplomacy of the Dollar: First Phase, 1919–1932* (1950); and Mira Wilkins, *The Maturing of Multinational Enterprise: American Business Interests Abroad from 1914 to 1970* (1974). Michael J. Hogan's *Informal Entente: The Private Structure of Cooperation in Anglo-American Economic Diplomacy, 1918–1928* (1977), emphasizes the cooperative spirit in which the two English-speaking powers strove to manage the economic recovery of the postwar world. Several recent studies assess the attempts by the European belligerents to reconstruct their national financial and monetary systems, with or without American assistance: Silverman, op. cit.; Artaud, op. cit.; Charles S. Maier, *Recasting Bourgeois Europe* (1975); Melvyn P. Leffler, *The Elusive Quest: America's Pursuit of European Stability and French Security, 1919–1933* (1979); and Stephen A. Schuker, *The End of French Predominance in Europe: The Financial Crisis of 1924 and the Adoption of the Dawes Plan* (1976). Jacques Bariéty, *Les Relations franco-allemandes après la première guerre mondiale* (1977), is a brilliantly conceived and exhaustively researched assessment of the abortive attempts at Franco-German reconciliation through measures of economic cooperation similar to those successfully implemented a generation later. Trachtenberg's study of reparations, op. cit., should be supplemented by Herman J. Rupieper, *The Cuno Government and Reparations, 1921–1923* (1979), and David Felix, *Walther Rathenau and the Weimar Republic: The Politics of Reparations* (1971). Benjamin M. Rowland, ed., *Balance of Power or Hegemony: The Interwar Monetary System* (1976), is a valuable collection of essays that may be read in conjunction with Stephen V. O. Clarke, *Central Bank Cooperation, 1924–1931* (1967). On Great Britain's postwar struggle to revive its industrial production, foreign trade, and international financial position, see B. W. E. Alford, *Depression and Recovery: British Economic Growth, 1918–1939* (1972), and Ian Drummond, *British Economic Policy and the Empire, 1919–1932* (1972).

The Illusion of Continental Security. The succession of attempts to promote continental stability and security in the 1920s inspired a number of early scholarly analyses that appeared while most of the European diplomatic archives remained inaccessible. Arnold Wolfers, *Britain and France Between the Wars: Conflicting Strategies of Peace* (1940), and W. M. Jordan, *Great Britain, France, and the German Problem* (1943), are two old classics that assess the Western allies' divergent efforts to preserve the postwar settlement. Yates, op.

cit., and Selsam, op. cit., record the failure of successive Fernch governments in the early twenties to revive the defunct security pacts with the two "Anglo-Saxon" powers, while Robert H. Ferrell, *Peace in Their Time: The Origins of the Kellogg-Briand Pact* (1952), demonstrates how the multilateral pledge to "outlaw war" had originated as a French ploy to secure America's unilateral support against a resurgent Germany. The formation of the French alliance system in Eastern Europe and the internal contradictions that already plagued it in the early twenties are carefully examined in Piotr Wandycz, *France and Her Eastern Allies, 1919–1925* (1962). Stresemann's reputation as a sincere advocate of treaty fulfillment is deflated in Hans Gatzke, *Stresemann and the Rearmament of Germany* (1954). The two most useful studies of Soviet foreign policy during this period are George Kennan, *Russia and the West Under Lenin and Stalin* (1960), and Adam Ulam, *Expansion and Coexistence: The History of Soviet Foreign Policy, 1917–1973* (1974). America's relations with the transatlantic world during the "era of isolationism" are shrewdly assessed in L. Ethan Ellis, *Republican Foreign Policy, 1921–1933* (1968); Jean-Baptiste Duroselle, *From Wilson to Roosevelt: The Foreign Policy of the United States, 1913–1935* (1963); and Selig Adler, *The Isolationist Impulse: Its Twentieth Century Reaction* (1951).

Many of these older studies have been superseded by recent works that have benefited from the opening of the European archives in the 1960s and 1970s. The two best general surveys of the period are Sally Marks, *The Illusion of Peace: Europe's International Relations, 1918–1933* (1976), and Arnold A. Offner, *The Origins of the Second World War: American Foreign Policy and World Politics, 1917–1941* (1975). A perceptive assessment of the shifting balance of power on the continent in the course of the twenties may be found in William J. Newman, *The Balance of Power in the Interwar Years* (1969). Though heavily weighted toward economic matters, Bariéty's study of Franco-German relations in twenties, op. cit., also treats the security concerns and policies of the two antagonistic powers on the Rhine. Leffler, op. cit., updates and extends Yates' study of Franco-American relations up to 1933, but is based almost exclusively on American primary sources. Keith L. Nelson, *Victors Divided: America and the Allies in Germany, 1918–1923* (1975), is a carefully researched study of the tensions and policy disputes between the Allied occupation armies in the Rhineland. Judith Hughes, *To the Maginot Line* (1971), and Jacques Néré, *The Foreign Policy of France from 1914 to 1945* (1975), succinctly summarize the security dilemmas of the power whose primary responsibility it was to enforce the Versailles Treaty during this period. Two full-length studies of British foreign policy in the twenties that exploit recently opened government records are Anne Orde, *Great Britain and International Security, 1920–1926* (1978), and Michael Howard, *The Continental Commitment: The Dilemma of British Defence Policy in the Era of the Two World Wars* (1972). On the operation of the League of Nations during its first decade in existence, see Ruth B. Henig, ed., *The League of Nations* (1973), and P. Raffo, *The League of Nations* (1974). The best study of the Locarno conference and its aftermath is Jon Jacobson, *Locarno Diplomacy: Germany and the West, 1925–1929* (1972). For a brilliant reassessment of Soviet-American relations during the period of nonrecognition, see Joan Hoff Wilson, *Ideology and Economics: U.S. Relations with the Soviet Union, 1918–1933* (1974).

4. The Western World in the Thirties

The Collapse of the World Economic Order. The definitive survey of the Great Depression and its global consequences, written by an economist with a flair for lucid historical narrative, is Charles Kindleberger's *The World in Depression, 1929–1939* (1973). The foreign economic policy of the Roosevelt administration in the thirties is evaluated in Lloyd C. Gardner, *Economic Aspects of New Deal Diplomacy* (1964), and found to be motivated by a desire to preserve the open door for American trade. A useful monograph on one important institutional mechanism for the revival of American foreign trade in the depression decade is Frederick C. Adams, *Economic Diplomacy: The Export-Import Bank and American Foreign Policy, 1934–1939* (1976). Wilkins, op. cit., remains the best general account of the expansion and contraction of American direct investment abroad. To the studies by Alford, op. cit., and Drummond, op. cit., of Great Britain's foreign economic policy in the interwar years may be added H. W. Richardson, *Economic Recovery in Britain, 1932–1939* (1967). The two best studies of Nazi Germany's economic recovery and its relation to Hitler's war plans are B. H. Klein, *Germany's Economic Preparations for War* (1959), and Bernice A. Carroll, *Design for Total War: Arms and Economics in the Third Reich* (1968). Tom Kemp, *The French Economy, 1913–1939* (1972), chronicles the decline of French industrial productivity during the very period it was needed to fuel rearmament, while David Kaiser, *Economic Diplomacy and the Origins of the Second World War: Germany, Britain, France, and Eastern Europe, 1930–1939* (1980), demonstrates how the small nations of Eastern Europe became economically dependent on Germany even as they sought to preserve their political and military ties to France during the thirties.

The Collapse of the European Security System. The scholarly literature on the origins of the Second World War in Europe is enormous and has been greatly enriched in recent years by works based on the declassified records of the belligerent states. A. J. P. Taylor's controversial *Origins of the Second World War* (1961), written before all but the captured German documents were accessible, caused a sensation by emphasizing the continuity of German foreign policy throughout the interwar period and depicting Hitler as a traditional German nationalist who implemented the policies of his republican predecessors by exploiting opportunities provided by the mistakes of weak-kneed British and French leaders. Two less tendentious and more recent studies of the subject are Joachim Remak, *The Origins of the Second World War* (1976), and Anthony Adamwaite, *The Making of the Second World War* (1979). Gerhard Weinberg's magisterial two-volume work, *The Foreign Policy of Hitler's Germany* (1970, 1979), is a solid narrative account based on primary sources from half a dozen countries, and it may be supplemented with Klaus Hildebrand, *The Foreign Policy of the Third Reich* (1973). Norman Rich, *Hitler's War Aims* (2 vols., 1973–74), focuses on the objectives of Nazi foreign policy and devotes less attention to the unfolding of events. The three best studies of French foreign policy during the thirties are Anthony T. Komjathy, *The Crises of France's East Central European Diplomacy, 1933–1938* (1977); Anthony Adamthwaite, *France and the Coming of the Second World War* (1977); and Jean-Baptiste Duroselle, *La Decadence* (1980), the latter a poignant account of

French decline amid German renewal. Robert Young's *In Command of France* (1978), assesses the tactical and strategic thinking of the French general staff during the period of German rearmament and European crisis. Britain's shift from appeasement to rearmament is treated in William R. Rock, *British Appeasement in the 1930s* (1977); Keith Middlemas, *Diplomacy of Illusion: The British Government and Germany, 1937–1939* (1971); Maurice Cowling, *The Impact of Hitler: British Politics and British Policy, 1933–1940* (1975); Robert Paul Shay, *British Rearmament in the Thirties* (1977); and Michael Howard, op. cit. The critical turning points in foreign policy between 1933 and 1939 have been analyzed in a number of recent monographs: The Ethiopian affair is treated exhaustively in Frank Hardie, *The Abyssinian Crisis* (1974), and George W. Baer, *Test Case: Italy, Ethiopia, and the League of Nations* (1976). Hugh Thomas, *The Spanish Civil War* (1961), is the best general survey of the subject, and may be read in conjunction with Glen T. Harper, *German Economic Policy in Spain* (1967), and John F. Cloverdale, *Italian Intervention in the Spanish Civil War* (1975). Important studies of Italian foreign policy include Elizabeth Wiskemann, *The Rome-Berlin Axis* (1966); Mario Toscano, *The Origins of the Pact of Steel* (1967); and Denis Mack Smith, *Mussolini's Roman Empire* (1976). The most comprehensive treatment of the German annexation of Austria is Gordon Brooke-Shepard, *Anschluss: The Rape of Austria* (1963). Of the numerous assessments of the Munich crisis, the following may be recommended: Keith Robbins, *Munich* (1968); Roy Douglas, *In the Year of Munich* (1977); Keith Eubank, *Munich* (1963), and Ronald M. Smelser, *The Sudeten Problem, 1933–1938* (1975), for background to the crisis. The best study of the Polish problem at the end of the decade is Anna M. Cienciala, *Poland and the Western Powers, 1938–39* (1968). America's isolationism and its gradual turn toward involvement in the European crisis is covered in Arnold A. Offner, *American Appeasement: United States Foreign Policy and Germany, 1933–1938* (1969); Manfred Jonas, *Isolationism in America, 1935–1941* (1966); Robert A. Divine, *The Illusion of Neutrality* (1962); and Richard P. Traina, *American Diplomacy and the Spanish Civil War* (1968).

5. Germany's Second Bid for European Dominance

The standard military history of the Second World War is B. H. Liddell Hart, *History of the Second World War* (1970). For exhaustive studies of individual campaigns, see General André Beaufre, *1940: The Fall of France* (1968); Telford Taylor, *The Breaking Wave* (1967); and Basil Calber, *The Battle of Britain* (1962), on the failure of Operation Sea-Lion; Paul Carill, *Hitler's War in Russia* (1964); and Trumbull Higgins, *Hiter and Russia: The Third Reich in a Two-Front War, 1937–1943* (1966), on Operation Barbarossa; Correlli Barnett, *The Desert Generals* (1960), on the North African campaign; G. F. Jackson, *The Battle for Italy* (1967); L. R. Ellis, *Victory in the West: The Battle of Normandy* (1963); Sir Charles Webster and Noble Frankland, *The Strategic Air Offensive Against Germany, 1939–1945* (4 vols., 1961); and Captain S. W. Roskill, *The War at Sea, 1939–1945* (3 vols., London, 1954–61). The critical role of Allied intelligence in the winning of the war is highlighted in F. W. Winterbotham, *The Ultra Secret* (1974). Two general surveys of the war that pay attention to the home front as well as the battlefront are worthy of mention: Gordon Wright, *The Ordeal of Total War, 1939–45* (1968), concentrates on the European theater and is more analytical than narrative in its approach, while Peter Calvocoressi and Guy Wint, *Total War: Causes and Courses of the Second World War* (1979), is a comprehensive 900-page narrative treating every important aspect of the world struggle. A stimulating assessment of the European war before the intervention of the two superpowers may be found in John Lukacs, *The Last European War: September 1939–December 1941* (1976). The best study of the economic dimensions of the war is Alan S. Milward, *War, Economy, and Society: 1939–1945* (1977), a worthy successor to his *The German Economy at War* (1965). On America's role in the war and its relations with the European allies, see T. R. Fehrenbach, *FDR's Undeclared War, 1939–1941* (1967); Robert A. Divine, *Roosevelt and World War II* (1969); Philip Goodhart, *Fifty Ships That Saved the World: The Foundations of Anglo-American Alliance* (1965); Warren R. Kimball, *The Most Unsordid Act: Lend-Lease, 1939–1941* (1969); Theodore A. Wilson, *The First Summit: Roosevelt and Churchill at Placentia Bay, 1941* (1969); Robert Beitzell, *The Uneasy Alliance: America, Britain, and Russia, 1941–1943* (1972); and George C. Heering, Jr., *Aid to Russia, 1941–1946* (1973). The diplomatic wrangling at the wartime conferences and the origins of Soviet-American disagreements on postward policy are treated in Anne Armstrong, *Unconditional Surrender: The Impact of the Casablanca Policy Upon World War II* (1961); Diane Shaver Clemens, *Yalta* (1970); and Herbert Feis, *Between War and Peace: The Potsdam Conference* (1960), and his *Churchill, Roosevelt, Stalin* (1957).

6. The Confirmation of United Sates Supremacy in Latin America

The Era of Direct Domination. United States military intervention and economic expansion in Latin America during and after the First World War has been recorded and evaluated in a number of important works. The best general studies of the subject include David Green, *The Containment of Latin America* (1971); C. Neal Ronning, *Intervention in Latin America* (1971); and Dana M. Munro, *The United States and the Caribbean Republics, 1921–1933* (1974). Joseph Tulchin's *Aftermath of War: World War I and United States Policy Toward Latin America* (1971) emphasizes the State Department's role in promoting American export interests in the region at the expense of European competitors. Kenneth J. Greib, *The Latin American Policy of Warren G. Harding* (1976), is a carefully researched study that also devotes considerable attention to America's expanding economic interests south of the border. Joseph Brandes, *Herbert Hoover and Economic Diplomacy: Department of Commerce Policy, 1921–1928* (1962), has much to say about the same subject. Alexander DeConde, *Herbert Hoover's Latin American Policy* (1951), remains a useful account of an important transitional period. Dick Steward, *Trade and Hemisphere* (1975), is a wide-ranging assessment of inter-American commercial relationships that emphasizes the United States' commanding position in hemispheric trade. Wilson, op. cit., and Mira Wilkins, *The Maturing of Multinational Enterprise: American Business Abroad From 1914–1970* (1974), though global in scope, accord extensive treatment to inter-American economic relationships.

Among the numerous monographs on United States military intervention or economic expansion in particular Latin American countries, the following may be recommended: Robert F. Smith, *The United States and Revolutionary Nationalism in Mexico, 1916–1932* (1972), which takes up where Haley, op. cit., leave off; Hans Schmidt, *The United States Occupation of Haiti, 1915–1934* (1971), an exhaustively researched study of the long occupation of Haiti by American marines; Robert F. Smith, *The United States and Cuba: Business and Diplomacy, 1917–1960* (1960); William Kamman, *A Search for Stability: United States Diplomacy toward Nicaragua, 1925–1933* (1968), which should be checked against Neill Macaulay, *The Sandino Affair* (1967). Since few American corporations or banks permit access to their files on foreign operations, there is a paucity of monographs on individual firms doing business in Latin America. The best studies of this type include Stacy May and Galo Plaza, *The United Fruit Company in Latin America* (1958); Thomas L. Karnes, *Tropical Enterprise: The Standard Fruit and Steamship Company in Latin America* (1978); and Theodore Geiger and Liesel Goode, *The General Electric Company in Brazil* (1961). See also the monographs cited for the third section of my Prologue, especially Pike on Chile, Liss on Venezuela, and Peterson on Argentina.

The Era of Indirect Hegemony. U.S.–Latin American relations during the period of Roosevelt's "Good Neighbor Policy" have been comprehensively treated in the following general works: Wilfred H. Callcott, *The Western Hemisphere: Its Influence on United States Foreign Policies to the End of World War II* (1968); Bryce Wood, *The Making of the Good Neighbor Policy* (1961), which deemphasizes Hoover's contribution to the improvement of hemispheric relations and stresses Roosevelt's role; and Donald Dozier, *Are We Good Neighbors?* (1959). A number of works have focused on the alleged threat of Axis intervention in the Western Hemisphere and the United States' efforts to mobilize its Latin American clients to combat it: Alton B. Frye, *Nazi Germany and the Western Hemisphere, 1933–1941* (1967), recounts the expansion of German economic activity and political intrigue in Latin America after Hitler's accession; Stanley E. Hilton, *Hitler's Secret War in South America, 1939–1945* (1981), is a well-documented account of German espionage in Brazil and of Brazilian–U.S. efforts to counteract it. Stanley Hilton, *Brazil and the Great Powers, 1930–1939* (1975), and Frank D. McCann, Jr., *The Brazilian-American Alliance, 1937–1945* (1973), both show how Brazilian President Getúlio Vargas used his country's close relationship with the United States to limit European influence and strengthen Brazil in its regional rivalry with Argentina. Alberto Conil Paz and Gustavo Ferrari, *Argentina's Foreign Policy, 1930–1962* (1962), is a well-documented account of Argentina's challenge to the United States' interests and policies in Latin America. Three superb studies of the inter-American conferences and Washington's quest for a hemispheric security system are Samuel G. Inman, *Inter-American Conferences, 1926–1954* (1965); Tom J. Farer, ed., *The Future of the Inter-American System* (1979); and J. Lloyd Mecham, *The United States and Inter-American Security, 1889–1960* (1961). Bryce Wood, *The United States and the Latin American Wars, 1932–1942* (1966), documents American inaction and indifference in regard to the Chaco, Letitia, and Marañón conflicts in Latin America. In addition to many of the books on U.S.–Latin American economic relations cited in the preceding bibliography section and in the third section of my Prologue, see Frederick C. Adams, *Economic Diplomacy: The Export-Import Bank and American Foreign Policy,*

1934–1939 (1976), and Lloyd Gardner, *Economic Aspects of New Deal Diplomacy* (1964). Green, op. cit., offers the revisionist interpretation that Roosevelt's Good Neighbor Policy rhetoric masked a sustained effort to contain radical social reform and preserve American economic dominance in Latin America.

7. The Confirmation of Japan's Supremacy in East Asia

The Period of Peaceful Penetration. American readers unfamiliar with the history of Japan's foreign relations prior to the expansionist period of the 1930s may consult Ian Nish, *Japanese Foreign Policy, 1869–1942* (1977). The standard account of Japan's relations with the Western imperial powers in the Pacific in the decade after the First World War is Akira Iriye, *After Imperialism: The Search for Order in the Far East, 1921–1931* (1965). Japanese-American conflicts during the First World War and the Paris Peace Conference are judiciously assessed in James W. Morley, *The Japanese Thrust into Siberia, 1918* (1957), and Russell H. Fifield, *Woodrow Wilson and the Far East: The Diplomacy of the Shantung Question* (1952). The background of the Washington Naval Conference is traced in Roger Dingman, *Power in the Pacific: The Origins of Naval Arms Limitation, 1914–1922* (1970). For the conference itself, see Sadao Asada, "Japan's 'Special Interests' and the Washington Conference, 1921–22," *American Historical Review*, 67 (1961), and Thomas H. Buckley, *The United States and the Washington Naval Conference, 1921–1922* (1970).

For Anglo-American reactions to Japan's rise to great-power status in the Pacific, see Gerald E. Wheeler, *Prelude to Pearl Harbor: The United States Navy and the Far East, 1921–1931* (1963); Ian Nish, *Alliance in Decline: A Study of Anglo-Japanese Relations* (1972); and William Roger Louis, *British Strategy in the Far East, 1919–1939* (1971). The role of the British Pacific Dominions in the balance of power during the 1920s is evaluated in William S. Livingston and William Roger Louis, eds., *Australia, New Zealand, and the Pacific Islands since the First World War* (1979). A valuable collection of essays on Sino-Japanese relations during this period is Alvin D. Coox and Hilroy Conroy, eds., *China and Japan: Search for Balance since World War I* (1978). America's involvement in China has been analyzed in exhaustive detail in Roberta A. Dayer, *Bankers and Diplomats in China, 1917–1925* (1980), which concentrates on Anglo-American rivalry; Barbara Tuchman, *Stilwell and the American Experience in China, 1911–1945* (1971); Warren I. Cohen, *America's Response to China: An Interpretive History of Sino-American Relations* (1971); and James L. Larence, *Organized Business and the Myth of the China Market* (1981), a monographic study of the American Asiatic Association and its lobbying efforts on behalf of American economic penetration of China. An authoritative study of the London Naval Conference is Raymond G. O'Connor, *Perilous Equilibrium: The United States and the London Naval Conference of 1930* (1962).

The Period of Military Expansion. Full-length studies of Japan's bid for supremacy in Manchuria and North China during the 1930s include James B. Crowley, *Japan's Quest for Autonomy: National Security and Foreign Policy, 1930–1938* (1966), and David J. Lu, *From the Marco Polo Bridge to Pearl Harbor: Japan's Entry into World War II* (1961). Four excellent analyses of Great Britain's ambivalent response to Japan's aggressive foreign policy in the thirties appeared in the 1970s: Ann Trotter, *Britain and East Asia, 1933–1937* (1975); Stephen L. Endicott, *Diplomacy and Enterprise: British China Policy, 1933–1937* (1975); Bradford A. Lee, *Britain and the Sino-Japanese War, 1937–1939* (1973); and Peter Lowe, *Great Britain and the Origins of the Pacific War* (1977). Among the many monographs on the Manchurian crisis and its global ramifications, Sadaka Ogata, *Defiance in Manchuria: The Making of Japanese Foreign Policy, 1931–1932* (1964), and Takehiko Yoshihashi, *Conspiracy at Mukden: The Rise of the Japanese Military* (1963), emphasize the domestic determinants of the turn toward aggressiveness; Armin Rappaport, *Henry L. Stimson and Japan, 1931–1933* (1963), assesses the tepid American response; while Christopher Thorne, *The Limits of Foreign Policy: The West, the League, and the Far Eastern Crisis of 1931–1933* (1972), is a judicious account of the world community's paralysis in the face of the Japanese action. On Japan's relations with the Axis powers in Europe, see James W. Morley, ed., *Deterrent Diplomacy: Japan, Germany and the USSR, 1935–1940* (1976); E. L. Presseisen, *Germany and Japan: A Study in Totalitarian Diplomacy* (1969); and J. M. Mestill, *The Hollow Alliance: Germany and Japan* (1966). The best studies of the diplomatic and naval decisions preceding the Pearl Harbor attack are Dorothy Borg and Shumpei Okomoto, eds., *Pearl Harbor as History: Japanese-American Relations, 1931–1941* (1973), a valuable collection of essays by Japanese and American scholars; and Paul Schroeder, *The Axis Alliance and Japanese-American Relations, 1941* (1958), a revisionist account of the Japanese-American negotiations that failed to avert war in the Pacific. The Pearl Harbor attack itself has generated a vast literature. Roberta Wohlstetter, *Pearl Harbor: Warning and Decision* (1962), remains the most persuasive explanation of America's lack of preparedness, which the author attributes to an "overload" of conflicting intelligence information rather than to deliberate blindness. The two most notable presentations of the conspiracy theory are Charles C. Tansill, *Back Door to War: The Roosevelt Foreign Policy, 1933–1941* (1952), and Robert A. Theobald, *The Final Secret of Pearl Harbor: The Washington Contribution to the Japanese Attack* (1954). Two more recent tomes, John Toland, *Infamy: Pearl Harbor and Its Aftermath* (1982), and Gordon Prang, *At Dawn We Slept* (1981), supply interesting details but fail to disprove Wohlstetter's convincing assessment. An authoritative account of the military and naval campaigns in the Pacific theater is Basil Collier, *The War in the Far East* (1970). The three best studies of the diplomatic and political context of the war in the Pacific are Christopher Thorne, *Allies of a Kind: The United States, Britain, and War Against Japan, 1941–1945* (1978); John Dower, *War Without Mercy: Race and Power in the Pacific War* (1986); and Akira Iriye, *Power and Culture: The Japanese-American War, 1941–1945* (1981). Several stimulating evaluations of Japan's war aims and its methods of achieving them appear in Joyce C. Lebra, *Japan's Greater East Asia Co-Prosperity Sphere in World War II* (1975), which supersedes F. C. Jones, *Japan's New Order in East Asia, 1937–1945* (1961). The evacuation of Japanese-Americans from the Pacific Coast is treated in Roger Daniels, *Concentration Camps USA: Japanese-Americans and World War II* (1971), and Audrie Girdner and Annie Loftis, *The Great Betrayal: The Evacuation of the Japanese-Americans During World War II* (1969). For two dissimilar accounts of the American decision to drop the atomic bombs on Japan, see Herbert Feis, *The Atomic Bomb and the End of World War II* (1966), and Martin J. Sherwin, *A World Destroyed* (1987).

Part Two: The Thirty Year "Cold War" Between the Superpowers (1945–1975)

8. The Formation of the Bipolar World in the Stalin-Truman Era

The Cold War has generated dozens of polemical studies that strive to explain its origins by attributing primary or even exclusive responsibility to one or the other of the two superpowers. Most of these works concentrate on the period 1941–49 when the Soviet-American relationship was transformed from wartime partnership to global confrontation. But there are also a number of more comprehensive works that cover the entire history of the Cold War. Two of the most useful narrative accounts are André Fontaine, *History of the Cold War* (2 vols., 1968, 1969), and Colin Brown and Peter J. Mooney, *Cold War to Détente, 1945–1980* (1981). Walter LaFeber, *America, Russia, and the Cold War* (1976), is an evenhanded analysis; and Louis Halle, *The Cold War as History* (1967), is an elegant essay by a former State Department official. The roots of the Cold War in Soviet-American disagreements concerning the political future of Europe are laid bare in Robert Beitzell, *The Uneasy Alliance: America, Britain, and Russia, 1941–1943* (1973); Lynn E. Davis, *The Cold War Begins: Soviet-American Conflict over Eastern Europe* (1974); Thomas Paterson, *Soviet-American Confrontation, Postwar Reconstruction, and the Origins of the Cold War* (1973); John Lewis Gaddis, *The United States and the Origins of the Cold War, 1941–47* (1972); Vojtech Mastny, *Russia's Road to the Cold War: Diplomacy, Warfare, and the Politics of Communism, 1941–45* (1979); and Daniel Yergin, *Shattered Peace: The Origins of the Cold War and the National Security State* (1977). For a stimulating assessment of Europe's position in the postwar bipolar system, see A. W. DePorte, *Europe Between the Superpowers* (1979). The role of Germany in the collapse of the Soviet-American wartime partnership has been treated in the following works: Warren F. Kimball, *Swords into Plowshares? The Morgenthau Plan for Defeated Nazi Germany, 1943–46* (1976); Stephen Ambrose, *Eisenhower and Berlin, 1945* (1971); Bruce Kuklick, *American Policy and the Division of Germany* (1972); John H. Backer, *Priming the Germany Economy: American Occupation Policies, 1945–48* (1971); and Jean Smith, *The Defense of Berlin* (1963).

For specific studies of the Marshall Plan, the Truman Doctrine, the containment policy, and the Soviet response, see the following: Joseph Jones, *The Fifteen Weeks* (1955) an insider's account of the decisions leading to the promulgation of the new policies; John Gimbel, *The Origins of the Marshall Plan* (1976); Michael J. Hogan, *The Marshall Plan: America, Britain and the Reconstruction of Western Europe, 1947–1952* (1987); Robert A. Pollard, *Economic Security and the Origins of the Cold War* (1985); Richard Freeland, *The Truman Doctrine and the Origins of McCarthyism* (1971); Richard Barnet, *Intervention and Revolution* (1972); John O. Iatrides, *Revolt in Athens* (1972), which treats the 1944–45 phase of the Greek Civil War; Stephen G. Xydis, *Greece and the Great Powers, 1944–47* (1963); Bruce R. Kuniholm, *The*

Origins of the Cold War in the Near East: Great Power Conflict and Diplomacy in Iran, Turkey, and Greece (1980); and Rouhollah K. Ramazani, *Iran's Foreign Policy, 1941–1973* (1975). The significance of America's atomic monopoly in superpower relations during the second half of the 1940s is treated in Gar Alperowitz, *Atomic Diplomacy* (1965); Sherwin, op. cit.; and Barton J. Bernstein, ed., *The Atomic Bomb* (1975). On Soviet foreign policy toward Europe east and west after the war, see Martin McCauley, ed., *Communist Power in Europe, 1944–1949* (1977); Alvin Z. Rubenstein, *Soviet Foreign Policy since World War II* (1981); Peter J. Mooney, *The Soviet Superpower* (1982); Marshall D. Shulman, *Stalin's Foreign Policy Reappraised* (1963); Ulam, op cit.; and Thomas Wolfe, *Soviet Power and Europe, 1945–1970* (1970). On the origins and early years of the Atlantic Alliance, see Lord Ismay, *NATO: The First Five Years, 1949–1954* (n.d.); Harlan Cleveland, *NATO: The Transatlantic Bargain* (1970); and Alfred Grosser, *The Western Alliance* (1980).

9. Coexistence and Confrontation

Useful general studies of American foreign policy in the Eisenhower years include Robert A. Divine, *Eisenhower and the Cold War* (1980); H. William Brands, Jr., *Cold Warriors: Eisenhower's Generation and American Foreign Policy* (1988); and Charles Alexander, *Holding the Line* (1975). For divergent evaluations of Eisenhower's controversial secretary of state and his diplomacy, see Michael Guhin, *John Foster Dulles: A Statesman and His Times* (1972), and Townsend Hoopes, *The Devil and John Foster Dulles* (1973). Hoopes is unsparingly critical of Dulles, while Guhin see his subject as more pragmatic and less rigidly ideological than he is customarily portrayed. On the post-Stalinist foreign policies of the Khrushchev era, see the titles on Soviet foreign policy cited above, as well as David J. Dallin, *Soviet Foreign Policy after Stalin* (1961), and Edward Crankshaw, *Khrushchev* (1966). For assessments of Russia's relations with the East European satellites during this transition period, see Robin A. Remington, *The Warsaw Pact* (1971); Michael Kaser, *Comecon: Integration Problems of the Planned Economies* (1967); H. G. Skilling, *Communism National and International: Eastern Europe after Stalin* (1964); Kurt London, ed., *Eastern Europe in Transition* (1966); and Alfred Zauberman, *Industrial Progress in Poland, Czechoslovakia, and East Germany, 1937–1962* (1964). The two most dramatic instances of Eastern European resistance to Soviet domination are treated in Stefan Brandt, *The East German Rising* (1957), and Paul E. Zinner, *Revolution in Hungary* (1964).

The challenge of organizing Western Europe's defense and managing the rearmament of West Germany in the fifties is discussed in the following works: Daniel Lerner and Raymond Aron, *France Defeats EDC* (1957); Roger Morgan, *The United States and West Germany* (1974); Richard A. Neustadt, *Alliance Politics* (1970); Robert E. Osgood, *NATO: The Entangling Alliance* (1962); F. Roy Willis, *France, Germany, and the New Europe, 1945–1967* (1968); and Robert McGeehan, *The German Rearmament Question: American Diplomacy and European Defense after World War II* (1971). The best study of the evolution of American defense strategy from "massive retaliation" to "flexible response" during the fifties is Morton Halperin, *Defense Strategies for the Seventies* (1971), which, despite its title, presents an analytical review of changes in strategic doctrine since the Korean War. Edward A. Kolodziej, *The Uncommon Defense and Congress, 1945–1963* (1966), is a massive study of Congressional influences on the adoption of weapons systems and the evolution of strategic policy. For a comprehensive treatment of Warsaw Pact strategy, see Wolfe, op. cit. Attempts to impose limits on the arms race during the second half of the fifties are covered in Robert A. Divine, *Blowing on the Wind: The Nuclear Test Ban Debate, 1954–1960* (1978), and Lincoln Bloomfield, Walter C. Clemens, Jr., and Franklyn Griffiths, *Khrushchev and the Arms Race: Soviet Interests in Arms Control and Disarmament, 1954–1964* (1966).

European decolonization and the Soviet Union's diplomatic offensive in the Third World have been the subject of a number of important studies. See, for example, John D. Hargreaves, *The End of Colonial Rule in West Africa: Essays in Contemporary History* (1979); Thomas J. Noer, *Cold War and Black Liberation: The United States and White Rule in Africa, 1948–1968* (1985); Wynfred Joshua and Stephen P. Gilbert, *Arms for the Third World: Soviet Military Aid Diplomacy* (1969); Marshall I. Goldman, *Soviet Foreign Aid* (1967); Roger Kanet, ed., *The Soviet Union and the Developing Nations* (1974); and Edward Taborsky, *Communist Penetration of the Third World* (1963). On Moscow's relations with particular developing countries or regions during this period, see Helen Desfosses Cohn, *Soviet Policy Toward Black Africa* (1972); Robert H. Donaldson, *Soviet Policy Toward India* (1976); and Geoffrey Jukes, *The Soviet Union in Asia* (1973).

On the Anglo-French withdrawal from the Arab world see Ann Williams, *Britain and France in the Middle East and North Africa, 1914–1967* (1969); Elizabeth Monroe, *Britain's Moment in the Middle East, 1914–1956* (1963); and Howard M. Sachar, *Europe Leaves the Middle East, 1936–1954* (1972). The best studies of the Suez crisis are Hugh Thomas, *The Suez Affair* (1966), and Anthony Nutting, *No End of a Lesson: The Story of Suez* (1967). For studies of France's war in Algeria, see Alistair Horne, *Savage War of Peace* (1978), and John Talbott, *The War Without a Name: The French in Algeria, 1954–1962* (1980). The transformation of Soviet policy toward the Arab-Israeli conflict in the Middle East is discussed in Arnold Krammer, *The Forgotten Friendship: Israel and the Soviet Bloc, 1947–1953* (1974); Aaron S. Kleiman, *Soviet Russia and the Middle East* (1970); and Oles Smolansky, *The Soviet Union and the Arab World Under Khrushchev* (1974). The expanding role of the United States in this region is scrutinized in Kenneth Ray Bain, *The March to Zion: United States Policy and the Founding of Israel* (1979); W. R. Polk, *The United States and the Arab World* (1965); and Robert W. Stookey, *America and the Arab States* (1975). Nadav Safran, *From War to War: The Arab-Israeli Confrontation, 1948–1967* (1969), is the most objective, comprehensive account of Arab-Israeli, inter-Arab, and superpower conflict in this region from the birth of Israel to the Six Day War.

The Berlin problem receives extensive treatment in Jack Schick, *The Berlin Crises, 1958–62* (1974); Robert M. Slusser, *The Berlin Crisis of 1961* (1973); and Honore M. Catudal, Jr., *The Diplomacy of the Quadripartite Agreement on Berlin* (1977). For studies of the Cuban crisis and the advent of Soviet-American rivalry in Latin America, see Trumbull Higgins, *The Perfect Failure: Kennedy, Eisenhower, and the Bay of Pigs* (1987); D. Bruce Jackson, *Castro,*

The Kremlin, and Communism in Latin America (1969); Richard E. Welch, *Response to Revolution: The United States and the Cuban Revolution, 1959–1961* (1985); Herbert S. Dinerstein, *The Making of a Missile Crisis: October 1962* (1976); Graham Allison, *Essence of Decision: Explaining the Cuban Missile Crisis* (1971); David Detzer, *The Brink* (1979); and Richard J. Walton, *Cold War and Counterrevolution: The Foreign Policy of John F. Kennedy* (1972).

10. Detente and Multipolarity

Superpower attempts to reach agreement on arms control from the aftermath of the Cuban missile crisis to the conclusion of the SALT I treaty are recounted in Christer Jonsson, *Soviet Bargaining Behavior: The Nuclear Test Ban Case* (1979); Thomas B. Larson, *Disarmament and Soviet Policy, 1964–1968* (1969); Roman Kolkowicz et al., *The Soviet Union and Arms Control* (1973); John Newhouse, *Cold Dawn: The Story of SALT* (1973); Gerard C. Smith, *Doubletalk: The Story of the First Strategic Arms Limitation Talks* (1980); Mason Willrich and John Rhinelander, eds., *SALT: The Moscow Agreements and Beyond* (1974); Coral Bell, *The Diplomacy of Detente: The Kissinger Era* (1977); and Robert D. Schulzinger, *Henry Kissinger: Doctor of Diplomacy* (1989). The expansion of Soviet strategic and conventional power during the 1960s and the first half of the 1970s is treated in John Erickson, *Soviet Military Power* (1971); William R. Kintner and Harriet F. Scott, eds., *The Nuclear Revolution in Soviet Military Affairs* (1968); Harriet F. Scott and William F. Scott, *The Armed Forces of the USSR* (1979); and C. G. Jacobsen, *Soviet Strategic Initiatives: Challenge and Response* (1979). On the Soviet naval buildup during the same period, see Michael McCgwire and John Donnell, eds., *Soviet Naval Influence: Domestic and Foreign Dimensions* (1977), and Paul Nitze et al., *Securing the Seas: The Soviet Naval Challenge and Western Alliance Options* (1979). For studies of the American response to these developments, see William W. Kaufman, *The McNamara Strategy* (1964); Thomas B. Larson, *Soviet-American Rivalry* (1978); Richard J. Barnet, *The Giants: Russia and America* (1977); and Alexander L. George and Richard Smoke, *Deterrence in American Foreign Policy* (1975).

The breakdown of the bipolar international system during the 1960s and the Gaullist challenge to American leadership of the Western Alliance have been addressed in the following works: Edward Kolodziej, *French International Policy under De Gaulle and Pompidou* (1974); Michael Harrison, *Reluctant Ally: France and Atlantic Security* (1981); Wilfred L. Kohl, *French Nuclear Diplomacy* (1971); and Wolf Mendl, *Deterrence and Persuasion: French Nuclear Armament in the Context of National Policy, 1945–1969* (1970). Great Britain's position between the United States and an increasingly independent-minded continental Europe is discussed in Robert L. Pfaltzgraff, Jr., *Britain Faces Europe* (1969), and Andrew Pierre, *Nuclear Politics: The British Experience with an Independent Strategic Force, 1939–1970* (1972). For the development of European economic integration and its implications for the East–West struggle, see Richard Mayne, *The Recovery of Europe, 1945–1973* (1973); Ernst H. Van der Beugel, *From Marshall Aid to Atlantic Partnership: European Integration as a Concern of American Foreign Policy* (1966); Joseph

Kraft, *The Grand Design: From Common Market to Atlantic Partnership* (1962); Miriam Camps, *European Unification in the Sixties* (1966); and A. E. Walsh and J. Paxton, *Into Europe: The Structure and Development of the Common Market* (1972).

The postwar international monetary system and its stresses and strains during the 1960s is covered in Robert Solomon, *The International Monetary System, 1945–1976* (1977); Robert Triffin, *The World Money Maze* (1966); E. S. Mason and R. E. Asher, *The World Bank since Bretton Woods* (1973); B. Tew, *International Monetary Cooperation, 1945–1970* (1970); and G. Bell, *The Euro-Dollar Market and the International Financial System* (1973).

The transformation of West Germany's foreign policy from the Adenauer to the Brandt era and the response of the Communist bloc is recounted in the following works: Karl Kaiser, *German Foreign Policy in Transition* (1968); Frederick H. Hartmann, *Germany Between East and West: The Reunification Problem* (1965); Zoltan M. Szaz, *Germany's Eastern Frontiers: The Problem of the Oder–Niesse Line* (1960); Gerhard Wettig, *Community and Conflict in the Socialist Camp: The Soviet Union, East Germany, and the German Problem, 1965–1972* (1975); George B. Ginsburgs and Alvin Z. Rubenstein, eds., *Soviet Foreign Policy Toward Western Europe* (1978); Lawrence L. Whetten, *Germany's Ostpolitik: Relations Between the Federal Republic and the Warsaw Pact Countries* (1971); and William E. Griffith, *The Ostpolitik of the Federal Republic of Germany* (1978). Studies of the Soviet Union's relationship with its East European satellites during the era of detente and polycentrism include Adam Bromke and Derry Novak, eds., *The Communist States in the Era of Détente, 1971–1977* (1979); Henry W. Schaefer, *COMECON and the Politics of Integration* (1972); Joseph G. Whelan, *World Communism, 1967–69: Soviet Efforts to Reestablish Control* (1970); and Peter F. Sugar and Ivo J. Lederer, eds., *Nationalism in Eastern Europe* (1969). Ueful studies in English of the causes and consequences of the Soviet intervention in Czechoslovakia include Pavel Tigrid, *Why Dubček Fell* (1971); Z. A. B. Zeman, *Prague Spring* (1969); and Jiri Valenta, *Soviet Intervention in Czechoslovakia, 1968* (1979). The early years of Romania's bid for an independent foreign policy within the Communist bloc are covered in David Floyd, *Rumania: Russia's Dissident Ally* (1965).

The growing engagement of the two superpowers in the Middle East after the Suez crisis is addressed in the following works: J. C. Hurewitz, *Soviet-American Rivalry in the Middle East* (1969); Steven L. Spiegel et al., eds., *The Soviet-American Competition in the Middle East* (1988); M. Confino and S. Shamir, eds., *The USSR and the Middle East* (1973); Ilana Cass, *Soviet Involvement in the Middle East: Policy Formulation, 1966–1973* (1978); Robert O. Freedman, *Soviet Policy Toward the Middle East Since 1970* (1978); Edward F. Sheehan, *The Arabs, Israelis, and Kissinger* (1976); Abdalla M. Battah and Yehuda Lukacs, eds., *The Arab-Israeli Conflict: Two Decades of Change* (1988); and William B. Quant, *Decade of Decision: American Policy Toward the Arab-Israeli Conflict, 1967–1976* (1977). On the internal struggle between Arabs and Israelis in the region, see Nadav Safran, *Israel: The Embattled Ally* (1978); Shaul Mishal, *West Bank/East Bank: The Palestinians in Jordan, 1949–1967* (1978); and Dana A. Schmidt, *Armageddon in the Middle East: Arab vs. Israeli through the October War* (1974). The best study of Lebanon's precarious geopolitical position in the region is Kamal S. Salibi, *Crossroads to Civil War: Lebanon, 1958–1976* (1976).

The position of Latin America in the inter-American system and the expansion of Soviet-American rivalry in the region is treated in the following works: Samuel Baily, *The United States and the Development of Latin America, 1945–1975* (1977); Nicola Miller, *Soviet Relations with Latin America, 1959–1987* (1989); Walter M. Davis, ed., *Latin America and the Cold War* (1978); Lester Langley, *The United States and the Caribbean in the Twentieth Century* (1985); and Herbert Goldhamer, *The Foreign Powers in Latin America* (1972).

11. The Rise of China and the Cold War in Asia

General studies of the birth of the Peoples' Republic of China include John F. Melby, *The Mandate of Heaven* (1968), a lively account of the Chinese Civil War; Suzanne Pepper, *Civil War in China: The Political Struggle, 1945–1949* (1978), a comprehensive, exhaustively researched study; C. P. Fitzgerald, *The Birth of Communist China* (1966); Kenneth E. Shewmaker, *Americans and the Chinese Communists, 1927–1945* (1971); and Tuchman, op. cit., which provides essential background on the Sino-American rift; John R. Beal, *Marshall in China* (1970), which claims that the Marshall mission in 1946 came close to mediating a settlement between the Communists and the Nationalists; John K. Fairbank, *The United States and China* (1971), the standard study of Sino-American relations, which should be supplemented with Michael Schaller, *The United States and China in the Twentieth Century* (1990); and Rang Tsou, *America's Failure in China, 1941–1950* (1963), a reliable narrative account.

For the causes and consequences of the Korean War, see Glenn T. Page, *The Korean Decision* (1968); Robert R. Simmons, *The Strained Alliance* (1975); David Rees, *Korea: The Limited War* (1964); Bruce Cumings, *The Origins of the Korean War* (1981); and Allan Whiting, *China Crosses the Yalu* (1960). The Truman–MacArthur struggle is judiciously assessed in Trumbull Huggins, *Korea and the Fall of MacArthur* (1960), and John W. Spanier, *The Truman–MacArthur Controversy* (1959).

The reengagement of American power in Asia is treated in Robert A. Hart, *The Eccentric Tradition: American Diplomacy in the Far East* (1976); Foster Rhea Dulles, *American Policy Toward Communist China, 1949–1969* (1972); Yonasuke Nagai and Akira Iriye, eds., *The Origins of the Cold War in Asia* (1977); Michael Schaller, *The American Occupation of Japan* (1985); F. S. Dunn, *Peacemaking and the Settlement with Japan* (1963); K. Kawai, *Japan's American Interlude* (1960); Reischauer, op. cit.; and Neu, op. cit. Valuable studies of Sino-Soviet relations before the rift include Robert C. North, *Moscow and the Chinese Communists* (1963); Robert R. Simmons, *The Strained Alliance: Peking, Pyongyang, Moscow, and the Politics of the Korean Civil War* (1975); and Chêng Chu-yuan, *Economic Relations Between Peking and Moscow, 1949–1963* (1964). Russia's relations with Japan after the Second World War are treated in Robert Searingen, *The Soviet Union and Postwar Japan: Escalating Challenge and Response* (1978); Young C. Kim, *Japanese-Soviet Relations* (1974); and Savitri Vishwanathan, *Normalization of Japanese-Soviet Relations, 1945–1970* (1973).

The Sino-Soviet split and its impact on the world Communist movement has prompted a number of important studies. The most comprehensive treatment of the subject is Alfred D. Low, *The Sino-Soviet Dispute* (1978), but the reader should also consult several earlier studies that appeared as the events of the dispute were unfolding: Donald S. Zagoria, *The Sino-Soviet Conflict, 1956–1961* (1962); David Floyd, *Mao Against Khrushchev* (1963); and William E. Griffith, *The Sino-Soviet Rift* (1964). The role of China's long-standing border grievances against the Soviet Union in the deterioration of relations between Moscow and Beijing is assessed in Tai Sung An, *The Sino-Soviet Territorial Dispute* (1973), and George Ginsburgs and Carl F. Pinkele, *The Sino-Soviet Territorial Dispute, 1949–64* (1978). For lucid analyses of the impact of the Sino-Soviet split on Russia's relations with the East European satellites and the West European Communist parties, see William E. Griffith, ed., *Communism in Europe: Continuity, Change, and the Sino-Soviet Dispute* (1966).

The most useful studies of the French phase of the Indochinese War include Ellen Hammer, *The Struggle for Indochina* (1966); F. E. M. Irving, *The First Indochina War: French and American Policy, 1945–1954* (1975); and Bernard Fall, *Hell Is a Very Small Place: The Siege of Dien Bien Phu* (1967). The involvement of foreign powers in the civil war in Laos is covered in Arthur J. Dommen, *Conflict in Laos: The Politics of Neutralization* (1971), and Charles A. Stevenson, *The End of Nowhere: American Policy Toward Laos since 1954* (1972). For the tragic story of America's engagement and disengagement in Indochina, see Frances Fitzgerald, *Fire in the Lake* (1972), Peter Poole, *The United States and Indochina from FDR to Nixon* (1973); George C. Heering, *America's Longest War: The United States and Vietnam, 1950–1975* (1986); Stanley Karnow, *Vietnam: A History* (1983); and *The New York Times*, ed., *Pentagon Papers* (1971), a top secret official history of the American involvement (including classified documents) that was leaked to the newspapers by a disillusioned contributor. For the decision-making process that led to the American escalation in Indochina, see David Halberstam, *The Best and the Brightest* (1972), and Doris Kearns, *Lyndon Johnson and the American Dream* (1976).

The rapprochement between Washington and Beijing during the first half of the 1970s is discussed in Gene T. Hsiao, ed., *The Sino-American Detente and Its Policy Implications* (1974); Alan M. Jones, *U.S. Foreign Policy in a Changing World* (1973); Lloyd Gardner, ed., *The Great Nixon Turnaround* (1973); Harvey W. Nelsen, *Power and Insecurity: Beijing, Moscow, and Washington, 1949–1988* (1989); Bernard and Marvin Kalb, op. cit.; and Donald F. Lach and Edmund S. Wehrle, *International Politics in East Asia Since World War II* (1975).

Part Three: From Detente to Detente. The International Order since 1975

12. The Resurgence of East–West Tension

A number of works address the general issue of the deterioration of superpower relations and the reappearance of global rivalry between the two blocs during this period: Albert L. Weeks, *The Troubled Detente* (1977); Richard

W. Stevenson, *The Rise and Fall of Detente* (1985); Raymond L. Gartoff, *Detente and Confrontation* (1985); Joseph D. Douglass, Jr., *Soviet Military Strategy in Europe* (1980); Paul H. Nitze et al., *Securing the Seas: The Soviet Naval Challenge and Western Alliance Options* (1979); and Coit D. Blacker, *Reluctant Warriors: The United States, the Soviet Union, and Arms Control* (1987). The conflict over theater nuclear weapons in Europe and its corrosive effect on the budding East–West rapprochement is ably treated in Hans-Henrich Holm and Nikolaj Peterson, *The European Missiles Crisis* (1984). Vojtech Mastny summarizes the fading of the hopes for a European political settlement in his *Helsinki, Human Rights, and European Security* (1986). For a fascinating study of the attempts to forge a Paris–Bonn axis as the basis of a powerful European entity between the two superpowers, see Haig Simonian, *The Privileged Partnership: Franco-German Relations in the European Community, 1969–1984* (1985).

International economic relations from 1975 to 1985 are treated in the following works: Bela Belassa, *Change and Challenge in the World Economy* (1985); Theodore Geiger, *The Future of the International System: The United States and the World Political Economy* (1988); Mohammed E. Ahrari, *OPEC: The Failing Giant* (1986); and Omar F. Homouda et al., eds., *The Future of the International Monetary System* (1989). A provocative, sweeping assessment of the economic constraints on great power diplomacy over the past four centuries is to be found in Paul Kennedy, *The Rise and Fall of the Great Powers* (1987).

The continuing tension in the Middle East and South Asia is treated in a number of important works. On the war in the Persian Gulf, see Ralph King, *The Iran–Iraq War: The Political Implications* (1987), and Shahram Chubin, *Iran and Iraq at War* (1988). For analyses of the emergence of Islamic fundamentalism as a destabilizing influence on the politics of the region, see Dilip Hiro, *Holy Wars: The Rise of Islamic Fundamentalism* (1989), and Henry Munson, Jr., *Islam and Revolution in the Middle East* (1988). On the United States debacle in Iran, see Barry Rubin, *Paved with Good Intentions: The American Experience in Iran* (1980). The Soviet intervention in Afghanistan is assessed in Rosanne Klass, ed., *Afghanistan: The Great Game Revisited* (1988), and Mark L. Urban, *War in Afghanistan* (1988). For a broader treatment of the entire subregion of South Asia, see Stanley Wolpert, *Roots of Confrontation in South Asia: Afghanistan, Pakistan, India, and the Superpowers* (1982). On the Arab-Israeli conflict, and the Middle Eastern policies of the two superpowers in the aftermath of the Camp David agreement, see William B. Quandt, *Camp David: Peacemaking and Politics* (1986); Geoffrey Aronson, *Creating Facts: Israel, Palestinians, and the West Bank* (1987); Samuel F. Wells and Mark Bruzonsky, *Security in the Middle East: Regional Change and Great Power Strategies* (1987); William B. Quandt, ed., *The Middle East: Ten Years After Camp David* (1988); and Battah and Lukacs, op. cit. Lebanon's particular trauma in this period is ably recounted in David Gilmour, *Lebanon: The Fractured Country* (1983) and Thomas Friedman, *From Beirut to Jerusalem* (1989).

Part Four: The Developing World: A Retrospective Comparison

13. Latin America's Quest for Development and Independence

For an understanding of Latin American international relations since the mid-1970s, the following works may be consulted with profit: for the Central America–Caribbean subregion—John E. Findling, *Close Neighbors, Distant Friends: United States-Central American Relations* (1987); Walter LeFeber, *Inevitable Revolutions: The United States in Central America* (1983); Robert Pastor, *Condemned to Repetition: The United States and Nicaragua* (1987); Morris Morley, *Imperial State and Revolution: The United States and Cuba, 1952–1986* (1988); and Scott B. McDonald, *The Caribbean After Grenada* (1988); for the entire region of Latin America—Diana Tussie, ed., *Latin America in the World Economy* (1983); Tom J. Farer, *The Grand Strategy of the United States in Latin America* (1988); Esperanza Duran, *European Interests in Latin America* (1985); Nicola Miller, *Soviet Relations with Latin America, 1959–1987* (1989); Robert E. Biles, *Inter-American Relations: The Latin American Perspective* (1988); Kevin Middlebrook and Carlos Rico, eds., *The United States and Latin America* (1986); and Jack Child, *Geopolitics and Conflict in South America: Quarrels Among Neighbors* (1985).

14. Africa

On the extension of Soviet-American rivalry to the continent in Africa and the African response, see Olajide Aluko, *Africa and the Great Powers in the 1980s* (1987); Arthur Gavshon, *Crises in Africa: Battleground of East and West* (1984); Peter Calvocoressi, *Independent Africa and the World* (1985); Tom J. Farer, *Clouds on the Horn of Africa: The Widening Storm* (1979); David Dickson, *United States Foreign Policy Towards Sub-Sahara Africa* (1985); David E. Albright, *The USSR and Sub-Sahara Africa in the 1980s* (1983); and Bala Mohammed, *Africa and Non-Alignment: A Study in the Foreign Relations of New Nations* (1982). For analyses of Africa's changing position in the international· system, see Stephen Wright and Janice N. Brownfoot, *Africa and World Politics* (1987), and Ralph I. Onwuka and Timothy M. Shaw, *Africa and World Politics* (1989).

15. The Far East

The fundamental transformation of the geopolitical situation in East Asia following the collapse of the American position in Indochina in the middle of the 1970s has been treated in Ilpyong J. Kim, *The Strategic Triangle: China, The United States, and the Soviet Union* (1987); Steffan B. Linder, *The Pacific Century: Economic and Political Consequences of Asian-Pacific Dynamism* (1986); W. W. Rostow, *The United States and the Regional Organization of Asia and the Pacific, 1965–1985* (1986); Bruce Dickson and Harry Harding, eds., *Economic Relations in the Asian-Pacific Region* (1987); Jon Woronoff, *Asia's 'Miracle Economies'* (1986); and Wolfgang Klenner, ed., *Trends of Economic Development in East Asia* (1989). On particular countries in the region, see: for China—Hsiang-tse Chiang, *The United States and China* (1988); Robert G. Sutter, *Chinese Foreign Policy: Developments After Mao* (1986); John Wong, *The Political Economy of China's Changing Relations with Southeast Asia* (1984); and Samuel S. Kim, *China and the World* (1989); for Japan—Herbert J. Ellison, *Japan and the Pacific Quadrille: The Major Powers in East Asia* (1987); Robert S. Ozaki and Walter Arnold, eds., *Japan's Foreign Relations: A Global Search for Economic Security* (1985); Karel G. von Wolferen, *The Enigma of Japanese Power* (1989); and Clyde V. Prestowitz, Jr., *Trading Places: How We Allowed Japan to Take the Lead* (1988). For a lucid study of an often-overlooked regional organization in Asia, see Michael Leifer, *ASEAN and the Security of South East Asia* (1988).

Epilogue: The End of the Cold War

The most useful English-language sources for analyses of contemporary international developments are the following periodicals: *Foreign Affairs, Foreign Policy, World Politics, International Security, Survival, International History Review, Diplomatic History*, the occasional papers of the International Institute for Strategic Studies published under the rubric *Adelphi Papers*, and the annual publication of the latter organization entitled *Strategic Survey*.

Glossary of International Economics Terminology

Autarky: Total national economic self-sufficiency, that is, the ability to obtain all essential goods and services from domestic sources.

Balance of Payments: A summary statement of all economic transactions between private citizens or government agencies of one country with all other countries of the world during a particular year. The balance-of-payments statement includes not only exports and imports of merchandise (the balance of trade) but also such activities as foreign tourist expenditures, transportation costs, insurance premiums and indemnities, and investment income.

Balance of Trade: The difference in value between a nation's total merchandise imports and exports during a particular year. The balance of trade is only one part of the balance of total earnings and expenditures of a nation in its transactions with the rest of the world (the balance of payments).

Barter: The exchange of specified quantities of products at a specified ratio without any monetary transactions taking place. Barter arrangements between countries are usually undertaken to circumvent obstacles to foreign exchange.

Capital Intensive Industry: An industry in which the cost of capital represents a relatively large percentage of the total production costs.

Central Bank: A bank (such as the Federal Reserve Board in the United States, the Bank of England, the Bank of France, etc.) that holds the exclusive right to print and distribute the national currency of a nation and coordinates its banking and monetary activities.

Comparative Advantage: The particular ability of a country to produce a product or service relatively more cheaply than other products or services because of the factors of production (land, labor, capital, or technology) with which it is endowed. In international trade theory, the principle of comparative advantage explains why a particular country should concentrate on producing and exporting a product or service for which its cost advantage is greatest while importing from other countries those products or services for which it has a lesser cost advantage.

Debt Service: The payment of interest and principal due on a debt.

Devaluation: A government-engineered reduction in the value of a national currency in relation to other national currencies or gold, usually undertaken to promote exports and reduce imports.

Direct Investment: Investment by citizens of one country in the material assets or the stock of corporations located in another country which establishes ownership and control of the assets or the enterprise by the foreign investor.

Exchange Control: Government regulation of the purchase and sale of foreign currencies, usually undertaken to prevent the flight of capital abroad.

Factor of Production (or Productive Factor): An economic resource that goes into the production of a good. The four major productive factors are land (including natural resources located on or under it), capital, labor, and technology.

Foreign Exchange: The purchase and sale of national currencies; often used to designate the total value of foreign currencies held by citizens of a particular country, as in "Poland's shortage of foreign exchange."

Gross National Product: The market value of all goods and services produced by a particular nation's economy during a particular year.

Import Quota: A government-established restriction on the importation of items into a country. The quota may be specified in terms of either the monetary value or the physical amount of the imported item, and it may apply to all imports of a specific item or to all imports from a specific country.

Labor Intensive Industry: An industry in which the cost of labor represents a relatively large percentage of the total costs of production.

Land Intensive Industry: An industry in which the cost of land represents a relatively large percentage of the total costs of production.

Most Favored Nation Principle: The requirement that all parties to a trade agreement must be granted any tariff reduction that is negotiated between or among any signatories of the agreement.

Portfolio Investment: The purchase by citizens of one country of the financial instruments issued by a foreign government or corporation without the acquisition of ownership or control.

Tariff (or Customs Duty): A tax on the importation of particular goods, levied by a national government and payable to it when the item crosses the nation's customs boundary. Originally a device to raise revenue, tariffs were subsequently employed to discourage imports that might undersell the products of domestic industries that the government wished to protect.

Technology Intensive Industry: An industry in which the cost of technology represents a relatively large percentage of the total costs of production.

Glossary of Nuclear Weapons Terminology

Anti-Ballistic Missile (ABM): A missile designed to intercept and destroy an incoming ballistic missile before it reaches its target.

Atomic Bomb: A bomb whose destructive power results from the immense amount of energy suddenly released when a chain reaction of nuclear fission is set off by neutron bombardment in the atoms of a charge of plutonium or uranium 235. Used by the United States against the Japanese cities of Hiroshima and Nagasaki in August 1945, and first tested by the Soviet Union in July 1949.

B-52 Bomber: The long-range manned bomber employed by the United States Air Force since the mid-1950s.

B-1 Bomber: Successor to the B-52 bomber. First flown in 1974, canceled by the Carter administration in 1977, and revived by the Reagan administration in 1981.

Cruise Missile: An unmanned aircraft with a nuclear warhead and a self-contained guidance system, which can be launched from the ground, from ships at or under the sea, and from manned aircraft. The earliest nonnuclear cruise missile was the German V-1 used against Great Britain toward the end of the Second World War. The most recent version has a range of over 1,500 miles and is very difficult to detect by radar.

Delivery System: The means by which a nuclear weapon is transported to its target. The two superpowers developed three main types of delivery systems for their strategic arsenals: long-range bombers, intercontinental ballistic missiles (ICBMs), and sea-launched ballistic missiles (SLBMs).

Hydrogen (or Thermonuclear) Bomb: A bomb based on nuclear fusion with an explosive force many times stronger than the atomic bombs employed against Japan. The H-bomb was first tested by the United States in November 1952 and by the Soviet Union in August 1953.

Intercontinental Ballistic Missile (ICBM): A missile launched from the United States that is capable of reaching targets in the Soviet Union, and vice versa.

Intermediate-Range Nuclear Forces (INF): The Soviet SS-4, SS-5, and SS-20 ballistic missile systems deployed in the Western part of the Soviet Union, together with the American Pershing II ballistic missiles and ground-launched cruise missiles deployed in various Western European countries. These missile systems were dismantled as a result of the INF treaty of 1987.

Multiple Reentry Vehicles (MRV):   Several warheads attached to a missile; they are aimed at a single target.

Multiple Independently Targetable Reentry Vehicles (MIRV):   Several warheads attached to a single missile; they can be aimed at separate targets.

Mutual Assured Destruction (MAD):   The condition of approximate strategic parity attained by the U.S. and the USSR by the end of the 1960s, whereby each superpower possessed sufficient strategic forces to withstand a first strike and inflict unacceptable damage on the other in retaliation. The resulting inability to "win" a nuclear war was thought to enhance deterrence and therefore minimize the likelihood of either superpower's risking a nuclear exchange.

Missile Experimental (MX):   An American ICBM with ten warheads that was proposed during the Carter administration as a replacement for the vulnerable Minuteman ICBM.

Neutron Bomb: A short-range nuclear missile authorized and then canceled by the Carter administration. Its combination of high radiation and low heat and blast characteristics maximize its lethal effects on humans while minimizing destruction to property.

Pershing II Ballistic Missile: An intermediate-range ballistic missile deployed in Western Europe by NATO after 1983 in response to the deployment of the SS-20 intermediate-range missile by the Soviet Union. Both systems were scrapped as a consequence of the INF Treaty of 1987.

Strategic Nuclear Forces: Nuclear weapons that can hit the Soviet Union from the United States or from American submarines at sea, and vice versa.

Submarine-Launched Ballistic Missile (SLBM):   A ballistic missile launched from submarines, which is less accurate than the land-based missile but much less vulnerable to a first strike.

Surface-to-Air Missile (SAM):   Short-range missile used to shoot down manned aircraft.

Surface-to-Surface-20 (SS-20) Missile: Intermediate-range, land-based ballistic missile with independently targetable warheads that was deployed by the Soviet Union after 1977 and targeted on America's allies in Western Europe. The SS-20 was prohibited by the INF agreement of 1987.

Warhead: The forward section of a missile; it contains the explosive charge.

Index